James Madison

Also by Lynne Cheney

We the People

Blue Skies, No Fences

Our 50 States

A Time for Freedom

When Washington Crossed the Delaware

A Is for Abigail

America: A Patriotic Primer

Telling the Truth

Lynne Cheney

JAMES MADISON

A Life Reconsidered

VIKING

VIKING
Published by the Penguin Group
Penguin Group (USA) LLC
375 Hudson Street
New York, New York 10014

USA | Canada | UK | Ireland | Australia | New Zealand | India | South Africa | China
penguin.com
A Penguin Random House Company

First published by Viking Penguin, a member of Penguin Group (USA) LLC, 2014

Image credits appear on page 564.

LIBRARY OF CONGRESS CATALOGING-IN-PUBLICATION DATA
Cheney, Lynne V.
James Madison : a life reconsidered / Lynne Cheney.
pages cm
Includes bibliographical references and index.
ISBN 978-0-670-02519-0
1. Madison, James, 1751–1836.   2. United States—Politics and government—1809–1817.
3. United States—Politics and government—1789–1815.
4. Presidents—United States—Biography.   5. Statesmen—United States—Biography.
I. Title.
E342.C48 2014
973.5'1092—dc23
[B]
2013047837

Printed in the United States of America
1   3   5   7   9   10   8   6   4   2

Set in Warnock Pro
Designed by Amy Hill

To my grandchildren—
Kate, Elizabeth, Grace,
Philip, Richard, Sam,
and Sarah Lynne

Contents

James Madison

Prologue

PHILADELPHIA, MAY 5, 1787

He hurried along Market Street, his high-crowned hat offering scant protection against the rain. Had he passed this way earlier in the day, shoppers would have slowed his pace, drawn by the covered market that stretched for blocks down the center of the street. Now, with the afternoon wearing on and a thunderstorm over the city, only a few bargain hunters remained. Farmers who had brought produce in from the Pennsylvania countryside were scrambling into their wagons for what promised to be a muddy trek home.[1]

Visitors to Philadelphia found the market a wonder, but the residents of Market Street were not fond of it. They repeatedly—and futilely—tried to halt its expansion, arguing that the crowds did real estate values no good. Better to have the more peaceful setting enjoyed by residents farther west, the direction that the hurrying figure was headed. He crossed Fifth Street, its wet cobblestones glistening underfoot, then with springing step went up the stairs and entered the door of the ample brick building on the corner. It was the comfortable residence of Mary House, an elderly widow who lived there with her son, Samuel, her daughter, Eliza Trist, and Mrs. Trist's son, Hore Browse. It was also one of Philadelphia's most highly regarded boardinghouses, a home away from home for many of America's political notables.[2]

Thirty-six-year-old James Madison, shaking off rain inside the front door, was one of Mrs. House's regulars. He had begun staying with her in 1780, when he first became a member of the Continental Congress, and now, after a day-and-a-half ride by stagecoach from New York, he was at her lodgings again, this time to attend a convention scheduled for the second Monday in May. Over the past seven years, Madison had spent more time at Mrs. House's than at his Virginia home, and he had come to regard her family as his family. He was particularly fond of Mrs. Trist, a woman of spirit and wit. In 1784 she had traveled by flatboat down the Mississippi to Louisiana to be with her husband, Nicholas, a former British officer. She recorded flora and fauna along the way for Thomas Jefferson, another Virginian who stayed at the Market Street lodgings, unaware as she was taking notes that she had become a widow. Between the last letter she received from Nicholas and the beginning of her trip downriver, he had died. Jefferson and Madison, learning of Nicholas's fate, wrote to each other of their concern for Mrs. Trist. With the Spanish having closed the Mississippi to American navigation, how would she get back to Philadelphia? But she found a way, sailing first to Jamaica and from there back home.[3]

At no more than five feet six inches tall, Madison was not physically imposing in the way Jefferson was, or the great Washington, whom Mrs. Trist and her mother were expecting to arrive in little over a week. But he was fit and well proportioned, and as he gazed out at the world from deep-set light blue eyes, he had a presence about him, "a habit of self-possession," Jefferson called it, "which placed at ready command the rich resources of his luminous and discriminating mind."[4]

Madison did not leap forward to meet strangers or try to dominate in conversation. He was naturally reserved and perhaps also influenced by a lesson of his youth. From the *Spectator*, a London periodical that he favored in his early years, he had learned that modesty becomes a man. Famed *Spectator* author Joseph Addison described it as "a guard to virtue" and noted that it "sets off every great talent which a man can be possessed of."[5]

By now Madison also understood that reticence had its political uses. It was wise to avoid strong statements while circumstances were still unfolding. It was often advantageous to put forth proposals anonymously and thus avoid alienating allies who might not agree. If in avoiding center stage Madison missed some of the praise, he also avoided some of the criticism, thus saving his reputation for a future day.

Madison dressed plainly, as befitted a man who did not want to be conspicuous. Eventually, he would wear only black. His public speaking was as unadorned as his dress. His words and ideas came forth with coolness and clarity, unobscured by drama. Although no one thought of him as an orator for the ages, those who paid attention understood that when he spoke he was enormously effective. "If [eloquence] includes persuasion by convincing," his fellow Virginian John Marshall wrote, "Mr. Madison was the most eloquent man I ever heard."[6]

Thomas Jefferson believed that Madison's reserve had held him back when he first began his public career, and another friend, Samuel Stanhope Smith, told him that his early achievements had come "in spite of all your modesty." But the reputation that Madison had acquired by the time he arrived in Philadelphia in May 1787 suggests that his manner had been little hindrance. "Every person seems to acknowledge his greatness," commented William Pierce, who, like Madison, was a delegate to the Philadelphia convention. Indeed, now that Madison's intellect and political skill were so widely recognized, his demeanor seemed to burnish his reputation. Despite all his renown, he remained, in Pierce's words, "a gentleman of great modesty, with a remarkable sweet temper."[7]

ALTHOUGH SHE WAS the same age as Congressman Madison, Eliza Trist sometimes assumed a motherly attitude toward him. She knew from Jefferson that much as he had accomplished, he was likely to achieve still more, and she worried about the "torrent of abuse" he would have to bear as he rose higher. "He has a soul replete with gentleness, humanity, and every social virtue," she wrote to Jefferson, "and yet

I am certain that some wretch or other will write against him. . . . It will hurt his feelings and injure his health, take my word." Mrs. Trist almost certainly knew that in addition to the common ailments of the day— dysentery, fevers, influenza—Madison suffered from "sudden attacks" that he described as "somewhat resembling epilepsy, and suspending the intellectual functions." Historians of a later time would dismiss these attacks. "Epileptoid hysteria," his most influential biographer would call them.[8] But Madison's description fits today's understanding of epilepsy. His sudden attacks might well have been complex partial seizures, which leave the affected person conscious but with his or her comprehension and ability to communicate impaired—the "intellectual functions" suspended, one might reasonably say. In Madison's day such attacks were not generally regarded as epileptic, which may account for the qualifiers in his description. "Epilepsy" was a term reserved for con-vulsive seizures. But Madison saw a relationship between his attacks and those in which people fell to the ground and convulsed, an under-standing that put him in advance of his time.

MADISON DID NOT MAKE a show of himself, but neither did he lack vanity. His jacket and breeches were finely made, his stockings usually silk. He powdered his hair and combed it forward to a point in order to cover a receding hairline.[9] And unassuming though he might seem, he did not hesitate to take on enormous projects. Standing in Mrs. House's parlor, his clothes still damp from the rain, he had a scheme in mind about as grand as could be imagined. He intended to use the upcoming convention to create a nation out of the thirteen individual states that four years before had thrown off the rule of Great Britain—and not just any nation, but one such as never had been seen before.

He envisioned a vast republic where the people were sovereign and their fundamental rights respected as nowhere else on earth. Such a republic had been judged impossible by influential thinkers of the age. Without monarchical power at the center, they believed, a country of great size would come apart, riven by different interests and ambitions.

Only in a small republic, where citizens held views and virtues in common, could there be stability. Madison perceived that this idea was based on a fiction. No society, not even the smallest, was truly homogeneous. Factions, or interest groups, were endemic to the human race, and the challenge was making sure that majority rule, which was at the heart of republican government, did not become an instrument for one faction to suppress others. The way to do this was to make the republic large enough so that no single interest dominated. "Extend the sphere," Madison would soon explain, "and you take in a greater variety of parties and interests; you make it less probable that a majority of the whole will have a common motive to invade the rights of other citizens."[10]

This insight—brilliant and prophetic—not only provided a rationale for the union of states that would be created by the Constitution; it would transform political thought, taking self-government from an impossible realm, in which all citizens virtuously suppressed their self-interest in the name of the common good, and moving it into reality, where interests competed with and checked one another.[11] A republic was no longer a distant ideal but something to which people around the world could aspire. Bringing the idea of the extended republic to bear at a time when a great nation was to be built was Madison's first grand act of creative genius—but by no means his last. Over the next five years, he, more than any other individual, would be responsible for creating the United States of America in the form we know it today.

Madison's time of extraordinary accomplishment came after years of intense focus, deep concentration, and nearly obsessive effort, behavior that describes most lives of genius, from Sir Isaac Newton's to Mozart's to Einstein's.[12] Some who have achieved greatly have had families that encouraged their passions, and Madison was among these fortunate. His father had sent him to fine schools. He had for years freed him from the necessity of earning a living, thus giving him time to study and practice the art of politics. Madison was also lucky to live in an era that demanded the skills he honed while at the same time inspiring the intensity with which he honed them. For a young man drawn to the subject of power and the possibilities of nation building, it is hard to imagine a more thrilling time to come of age than in the years leading up to the American Revolution.

He brought to the cause a fervent commitment to religious freedom, perhaps because he had experienced the misery of being told what he had to believe. In the eighteenth century, people suffering from epilepsy—or sudden attacks resembling it—had a double burden, the disorder itself and the religious view, widely held and fiercely defended, that sufferers were unclean, sinful, even possessed by demons. In his young manhood, when the attacks began, Madison had gone through a period of deep despondency, certain that he would die and worried about his soul. He eventually emerged from the gloom, and when he did, he was on fire with the idea that no one should have to accept ideas that seemed wrong to him. A man's conscience was his own, not the property of church or state.

He acted on this commitment when he was just twenty-two and saw Anglicans in his native Virginia misusing the authority of the state to persecute Baptists. He not only championed the Baptists' cause with a passion that broke through his usual reserve; he also began to explore how society could be organized to protect rights of conscience. More than a year before the Revolutionary War, he was, astonishingly, inquiring into ways "the constitution of [a] country" could foster freedom of belief.[13] Even in his maiden venture into politics, he had a significant contribution to make, insisting that the new state of Virginia not merely tolerate religious differences but view each individual's conviction as a fundamental right.

Madison plunged into politics again and again. While serving in the Continental Congress, he became so immersed that he did not return home for nearly four years. Most recently he had been a member of the Virginia legislature, where he had seen to the passage of a law that Thomas Jefferson had written, the Virginia Statute for Religious Freedom. The enacting clauses of this legislation, he exulted to Jefferson, had "extinguished forever the ambitious hope of making laws for the human mind." He had also been delving deep into history, poring over hundreds of volumes that Jefferson sent him from Paris, a "literary cargo" concerning laws and constitutions.[14] He was determined to find out how past unions of states had fared and, combining history with his own experience, to understand why the United States, under its current governing document, the Articles of Confederation, was failing to live up to its abundant promise.

By the time of the Philadelphia convention, Madison was the political equivalent of Mozart in the late 1770s, who after years of writing music was about to create his greatest works. He was Einstein, who after years of studying with "holy zeal" was on the verge of his *annus mirabilis*, the miracle year of 1905, in which he would establish the basis of the theory of relativity and quantum physics. As Madison climbed the narrow stairs in Mrs. House's boardinghouse and headed for his room, he was more knowledgeable and better practiced in the theories and realities of representative government than anyone in the country or even the world. And he was about to do what geniuses do: change forever the way people think.[15]

AT HIS DESK in the waning light of that rainy afternoon, Madison wrote a hurried letter to William Irvine, a Pennsylvanian who was one of his allies, and then he almost certainly turned his thoughts to the upcoming gathering. He had spent months working to ensure the convention's success: penning legislation to throw Virginia's support behind it, persuading Washington to attend, taking steps to see that the Confederation Congress didn't hinder its proceedings. Now he worked on the convention's agenda, not because anyone had asked him to, but because he understood that the surest path to the governmental framework he envisioned lay in providing the program that would guide discussion. He also knew that having others of influence lined up behind his plan would give it greater force. One of his chief reasons for arriving early in Philadelphia—he was the first out-of-state delegate there—was the chance it gave him to meet with others as they arrived and convince them of the benefits of his proposal.

At the convention, he would be one of the chief participants in debate while at the same time keeping notes that would create a historical record of immeasurable worth. The Constitution that the delegates finally agreed upon would not be everything he had wanted, but he quickly concluded it was more than anyone could have hoped, and with John Jay and Alexander Hamilton he defended it in *The Federalist,* a series of essays that has become a classic of political thought. Madison would be crucial to securing the ratification of the Constitution in Virginia, the biggest and most powerful state, and he would face down Patrick Henry, the most famed orator of the day, in order to do so.

Madison would have a greater hand than anyone at setting the government based on the Constitution in motion, including drafting a bill of rights and getting the necessary amendments through Congress. He would lead in the founding of the first political party, once again upending conventional wisdom. So frowned upon was the idea of partisanship that Jefferson once declared, "If I could not go to heaven but with a party, I would not go there at all." But Madison defended parties as "natural to most political societies."[16] They were a legitimate vehicle for free people to use to advance their views and interests.

Madison's genius would ripen into a wisdom that served him well for the eight years he was Jefferson's secretary of state and for his two terms as president. Through the perilous losses and thrilling victories of the War of 1812, he was as steady a commander in chief as the United States has known. Even after the British burned the nation's capital, he remained calm, resolute, and devoted to founding principles, refusing to heed calls to silence Americans opposed to the war. His contemporaries, while acknowledging that the course of the war with Great Britain was not always smooth, praised his success. "Notwithstand[ing] a thousand faults and blunders," John Adams wrote, Madison's administration had "acquired more glory and established more union than all his three predecessors, Washington, Adams, and Jefferson, put together."[17] Without precedent to guide him, James Madison would demonstrate that a republic could defend its honor and independence—and remain a republic still.

·   ·   ·

PRAISE WOULD FOLLOW MADISON to the grave and beyond. Nine years after his death, Charles Jared Ingersoll would say that "no mind has stamped more of its impressions on American institutions than Madison's." But eventually his fine reputation would suffer, and he is popularly regarded today—when remembered at all—less as a bold thinker and superb politician than as a shy and sickly scholar, someone hardly suited for the demands of daily life, much less the rough-and-tumble world of politicking.[18] The reasons for this transformed image are many, including Henry Adams's late-nineteenth-century history of Madison's administration, in which the fourth president is presented much as his worst enemies liked to describe him. Misunderstandings about Madison's health enter in—as does our twenty-first-century inability to conceive of modesty and reserve as having any compatibility with politics.

IT IS A PROMISING TIME to clear away misconceptions about Madison, brush off cobwebs that have accumulated around his achievements, and seek a deeper understanding of the man who did more than any other to conceive and establish the nation we know. His home at Montpelier, long burdened with massive twentieth-century additions, has now been beautifully restored. One can visit the dramatic red drawing room where the Madisons relaxed with guests; the dining room where they entertained, its walls decorated with historic prints; the library, the center of Madison's intellectual life, where he kept some of his four thousand pamphlets and books.

Pathfinding authors, particularly biographers Irving Brant and Ralph Ketcham, have charted the way for researchers into Madison's life, as Catherine Allgor has done for Mrs. Madison's. J. C. A. Stagg and his team at the University of Virginia—particularly senior associate editor David B. Mattern, as well as Mary Hackett and Angela Kreider—have drawn together thirty-five volumes of Madison's papers in beautifully edited and annotated form and made them available online, providing an ease of access that past researchers could only have dreamed of.[19]

Holly C. Shulman, also at the University of Virginia, has led the project to get Dolley Madison's papers edited and online, together with ground-breaking essays that provide invaluable context.

The thirty-five volumes of James Madison's papers alone run to more than twenty thousand pages, and writing about him requires exploring much more, including the voluminous papers of the leaders with whom his life intersected, figures such as George Washington, John Adams, Thomas Jefferson, and Alexander Hamilton. Reconsidering James Madison's life has been for me a project of many years, but what amazing company I have kept. I particularly treasure the time spent with that determined man in the high-crowned hat, rushing through the rain. He was on his way to creating a nation—and changing the world.

Chapter 1

SUNLIGHT AND SHADOWS

JAMES MADISON, one of the great lawgivers of the world, descended from generations of people who drew their living from the land. His great-great-grandfather John Madison had departed England in the middle of the seventeenth century with the rich soil of Virginia in mind. He sailed between Cape Charles and Cape Henry, entering the Chesapeake Bay with eleven men whose passages he had paid so that he might get "headrights"—grants of fifty acres—for each of them, as well as one for himself. The six hundred acres that the royal governor of Virginia granted him were in Gloucester County along the Mattaponi River, a tributary of the York, which is one of four great rivers flowing into the Chesapeake Bay.[1]

The men whose passages Madison paid had agreed to indenture themselves for four or more years, hoping when they finished their terms to buy land and become tobacco planters themselves. Meanwhile, they labored in Madison's fields, and in decades to come, he would import scores more servants, claiming headrights for each one. By the time of his death, he held grants to several thousand acres, most of them along the north side of the Mattaponi.[2]

John Madison's son, also named John, followed a similar course, first acquiring land near his father's, then moving farther inland, expanding his holdings as tobacco planters had to do if they wanted to survive. Tobacco quickly exhausted the soil, so every three years or so fields had to be abandoned and new land put under cultivation. This second John Madison is listed in a deed book as a "ship carpenter," an occupation he might have taken up to supplement his income. Being a tobacco planter allowed one to live independently, but crops and prices were at the mercy of the weather, the inclinations of Parliament, and the outbreak of foreign wars. Having a sideline, such as building the sloops, shallops, and flatboats that plied the rivers flowing into the Chesapeake, was insurance against contingencies. In 1707, John the ship carpenter also began to assume the responsibilities expected of Virginia's gentry planters, becoming first a justice of the peace, charged with everything from recording cattle brands to deciding criminal cases, then a sheriff, responsible not only for enforcing the law but also for collecting quitrents and levies.[3]

The ship carpenter's son Ambrose Madison married well. His wife, Frances, was the daughter of James Taylor, one of the Knights of the Golden Horseshoe, a group that Governor Alexander Spotswood had led on an expedition into the Shenandoah Valley. Before they crossed the Blue Ridge Mountains, the knights had explored the rolling hills of the Virginia Piedmont, land that glistened green from rain and sun. Spotswood gave each of his fellow explorers a small golden horseshoe to commemorate their trip, but the enduring gift was the knowledge they gathered of uncultivated lands that promised abundant tobacco crops. James Taylor patented vast stretches of the Piedmont, paying a little over a penny an acre, and in 1723, two years after Ambrose Madison had married his daughter, Taylor arranged a transfer of 4,675 acres to him and Thomas Chew, another of his sons-in-law.[4]

Ambrose Madison shipped tobacco to London, ordered goods from there, and supplemented his family's income as a merchant. Like his father, he served as a county official and expanded his landholdings. He and Chew worked on improving their jointly held acreage, but they did not rely on indentured servants to fell the trees or put up buildings. Economic conditions had improved in England, while at the same time Virginia tobacco land had grown so scarce that a man who bound himself into servitude had little hope of becoming a planter. With fewer and fewer willing to indenture themselves, planters turned to another source of labor, the men and women whom they could buy from the slave ships that were an increasingly familiar sight in Chesapeake waters. Ambrose's first known purchase was in July 1721, when he paid the captain of the *Ann and Sarah* fifty pounds for "two Negro women."[5]

In the spring of 1732, Ambrose, in his thirties, took his wife and three young children to the plantation cut from the wilderness by people he had purchased, and not long after the family arrived, Ambrose Madison became very ill. When he died in late summer, three slaves, arrested for "suspicion of poisoning," were put on trial for conspiring to kill him. Pompey, the property of another landowner, was found guilty and hanged. Turk and Dido, Madison slaves, were judged to have been "concerned" in the crime "but not in such a degree as to be punished by death." They were sentenced to twenty-nine lashes each.[6]

Although Ambrose's was the first known instance, it was hardly the last in which slaves in the area were tried for poisoning masters. Another concerned Eve, accused of poisoning Peter Montague. In 1746 she was convicted and condemned to burn at the stake. Her sentence was carried out under the authority of the sheriff of Orange County— Thomas Chew, Ambrose Madison's brother-in-law.[7]

Ambrose's descendants, who almost certainly knew that a slave had been hanged for murdering him, left no record of how he died. A family history told of relatives who had been killed by Indians but mentioned not a word about Ambrose's untimely demise. The silence no doubt reflected a belief that to talk about slave resistance was to encourage it. Any hint that Ambrose was murdered also gave the lie to a benign version of slavery in which his descendants, like many slave owners, tried to believe. In this version, the slave was referred to as a servant or even part of the family. In 1777, James Madison, the future president, would advise his father, "The family have been pretty well since you left us except Anthony," who was an enslaved man with a high fever and a swollen arm.[8]

Frances Madison, widowed with three small children on the Virginia frontier, buried her husband next to their small house and turned to the enormous challenges facing her, not least of which was her husband's will. In his final agony, Ambrose had overlooked a crucial detail—dividing the patent he held jointly with Chew.[9] Thus, upon Ambrose's death, the land on which his wife and children were living passed into Chew's hands and would descend to his heirs.

Unwilling to accept the fate that she had been handed, Frances reached an agreement with Chew. On May 26, 1737, in return for 2,850 acres of the patent, she paid him two hundred pounds, a significant amount, as much as a small planter might accumulate in a lifetime. It was a price per acre above the average of other properties sold in Orange County that month, but Chew doubtless pointed out that the land had been improved, with "houses, buildings, barns, dove houses, yards, orchards, gardens," as the deed specified. He seems to have given little ground to his widowed sister-in-law, but it might well have been that in that time and place neither she nor any of her family expected him to, and in the end the bargain was hers. She gained the acreage and its improvements for her "use and behoof . . . for and during the term of her natural life" and preserved the family estate not only for her son but also for the grandson who would become America's fourth president.[10]

As the person running the plantation, Frances Madison would have been familiar with every step in the growing, harvesting, and marketing of tobacco, a plant that, as one contemporary observed, required "a great deal of skill and trouble in the right management of it." The seeds, so small that ten thousand would fit in a teaspoon, had to be started not long after Christmas, preferably in a wooded site rich with mold. The seedlings were replanted in fields in the spring—but only after a rain shower, or "season," when the ground was wet. Within about a month, the plants had to be "topped" to encourage the growth of large leaves, then repeatedly "suckered," which involved cutting shoots, and "wormed," which meant removing grubs and hornworms. When the leaves began to spot and thicken, the tobacco was cut, and after wilting in the field, it was taken to tobacco houses and hung to cure. About the time that the tobacco was ready to be packed in hogsheads and transported to market, slaves were sowing seed for the next crop.[11]

Frances put her mark ("FM") on hogsheads leaving the Madison plantation and ordered goods from the London merchants to whom the tobacco was shipped, including ten narrow axes, a hydrometer, a quilted coat, and a pair of boots. Frances was a planter, a fact that made her an exception among her sex, but as she did the work of a man on the Virginia frontier, she also upheld the era's standards of womanhood, ordering fabric for dresses and, from John Maynard & Son in London, two "good stays," or corsets, size small. She also added to the modest collection of books that Ambrose had owned at his death. She ordered a Bible commentary, two volumes of the British newspaper the *Guardian,* and, her biggest extravagance, eight volumes of the *Spectator,* a periodical known for its wit and commonsense humanity.[12]

THE MADISONS OWNED thousands of acres and dozens of slaves and worked their land year-round, but income from farming remained unreliable. Frances's son, known to history as James senior, to distinguish him from his famous son, found a multitude of ways to enhance the plantation's earnings. He sold his neighbors everything from gunpowder and silk purses to brandy from his still. He sawed planks, built hogsheads, and rented out his enslaved carpenters, Peter and George, usually for long-term projects, but once to fight a fire. He oversaw the construction of buildings, including a tobacco house for John Norton and a privy for Erasmus Taylor. Eventually, he established an ironworks where he gained a reputation for quality goods and shrewd dealing.[13]

But he also became knowledgeable about the plantation's mainstay and early on would have accompanied his family's hogsheads down rolling roads to the Rappahannock. The few days' journey was a price the Madisons paid for growing tobacco in the Piedmont, which was above navigable waters, but taking the yearly crop to Fredericksburg, a port village where British ships arrived, was also a chance to socialize. After leaving the Madison hogsheads at Royston's warehouse, James senior could ferry across the Rappahannock and ride another day downriver to where one of his best friends, Francis Conway, lived. Their families had long been close. Francis's father had been one of the executors of Ambrose's will and died himself only a year later. Francis had a younger sister named Nelly, and in 1749, when she was seventeen, she and twenty-six-year-old James Madison Sr. were married.[14]

Nelly "was not a beautiful woman," according to Gaillard Hunt, an early Madison biographer, but Hunt was probably relying on a portrait painted by Charles Peale Polk in 1799, when Nelly was sixty-eight. Something in her youth attracted James senior, perhaps her piety, since that was her reputation in old age, but James senior's cousin and close friend, the genial Joseph Chew, suggested the attraction was more than spiritual. Two weeks prior to James and Nelly's wedding, Chew wrote to James, "I hope before this Miss Nelly has made you happy." After their wedding, Chew complained of not hearing from Madison. "Never since I left Virginia have I had one scrape of a pen," he wrote. "I make every allowance in your favor I can. The marrying a young agre[eable] wife will certainly make moments slide away pleasantly, and that you should be happy no one desires or wishes more truly than myself but in that a few hours is due to your friend."[15]

Two years later, while James senior and Nelly were visiting her mother at Port Conway, their first child, a son, was born. The date of his birth according to the Gregorian calendar, adopted the year after his birth, was March 16, 1751. Named James after his father, the baby was called Jemmy by his parents, and they prepared for his homecoming by having a woodworker, William Crittenden, make a cradle. Later the plantation overseer, Robert Martin, made Jemmy two small banyans, or tiny robes open in the front.[16]

When the baby was taken to the Madison family seat in the Piedmont, it was not to the house that dominates the site today but to Mount Pleasant, the simple frame home with a footprint of 416 square feet that Frances, Ambrose, and their three children had moved into nearly twenty years before.[17] Now the house had four occupants: Frances, James senior, Nelly, and the baby. In 1753, when Nelly gave birth to a second son, Francis, there were five in the house, as there had been in Ambrose's time. After a third son, Ambrose, named for his grandfather, arrived in 1755, Mount Pleasant might have seemed crowded, but when Catlett, a fourth son, was born in 1758 and died soon thereafter, the house, like Nelly's heart, must have seemed to have a great and empty space in it.

Life was precarious in colonial Virginia. Newcomers had to survive the "seasoning," the first year of sickness that killed many, and everyone faced a mortality rate much higher than in New England.[18] Although the Piedmont was healthier than the Tidewater, which provided a near-perfect breeding ground for malarial mosquitoes, sickness still abounded, and the death of children was heartbreakingly common. Of the twelve children Nelly would eventually bear, only seven would survive to adulthood.

Learned physicians under the influence of the Enlightenment were struggling to find scientific explanations of illness, but in everyday life the theories of Hippocrates, Aristotle, and Galen still prevailed. They regarded illness as an imbalance among the four humors—air (blood), earth (black bile), fire (yellow bile), and water (phlegm)—and associated the excess of a humor with certain diseases. Black bile, for example, was associated with epilepsy.[19] Bleeding and purging could rid the body, so the theory went, of an excess of one humor or another and bring back a healthful balance. Herbs were prescribed for purging and healing, but the ideas of the medieval physician Paracelsus were also influential. On the theory that sickness was the result of poisons attacking the body from outside, he had recommended counteracting them with internal doses of metals and medicines from the laboratory, such as arsenic, antimony, and mercury.

Almost every plantation had a manual that advanced some mixture of theory and remedy. In the Madison household, it was *Quincy's Dispensatory,* which Frances Madison added to the family library. In 1753, during Jemmy's second year, she ordered medicines "for an epilepsy,"

likely relying on *Quincy's* to do so. She ordered several items—gentian
root, cochineal, saffron, and camphor—that were in *Quincy's* terminology "diaphoretics," believed good for breaking a fever. For epilepsy, as
for most ailments, purging was thought helpful, and on Frances's list
were two laxatives, Anderson's Pills and *pulvis basilicus,* or Royal Powder, a mixture containing antimony and mercury. Frances also ordered
cardamom seeds, which, according to Quincy, eased the irritation
caused by cathartics. Another item was lavender, good for all diseases
of the head, according to Quincy, as was the *sal volatile oleosum* that
Frances ordered. It had a strong ammoniac odor and could be used as
a smelling salt or ingested. She also ordered *sal armoniac,* from which
sal volatile oleosum could be made. Sublimated from sea salt, urine, and
animal excrement, *sal armoniac* could be used in "pocket smelling bot-
tles," Quincy said. In combination with tartar, he recommended it for
"epilepsies, palsies, and all nervous cases, because such fiery irritating
volatiles stimulate and shake the fibers."[20]

Hard as it is for a twenty-first-century mind to contemplate Royal
Powder and *sal armoniac* being administered to a toddler, James
Madison—Jemmy, at this point—was the only member of his family for
whom there is any indication of epilepsy and thus the most likely patient. Assuming that the seizures he suffered were fever related, as the
medicines Frances Madison ordered seem to indicate, doctors today
would likely diagnose febrile seizures, convulsions that can occur
when a small child has a fever. A grandmother in colonial Virginia
might be forgiven, however, for thinking the child had epilepsy. When
Thomas Jefferson's two-year-old grandson, Francis Eppes, suffered
"dreadful fits" in 1804, his aunt wrote, "I cannot help fearing them to
be epileptic."[21]

Although children with febrile seizures are not considered to have
epilepsy today, a history of them in early childhood, especially if they
are prolonged, is common in the syndrome of temporal lobe epilepsy.
The evidence available suggests that this was the pattern of Madison's
ailment: fever-related episodes when he was a toddler, then "sudden
attacks" later in his life.[22]

· · ·

MADISON GREW UP to love the outdoors and probably spent much of his boyhood riding and playing in the fields and forests with his brothers and the slave children on the plantation, but he was also bookish, reading the *Spectator* at an early age. His grandmother Frances likely encouraged him and was surely pleased to have him appreciate the lessons it taught. Early on he would have come across this: "Nothing can atone for the want of modesty, without which beauty is ungraceful and wit detestable." Later he would have read about Prince Eugene of Savoy, who, said the *Spectator* (the eponymous author of the series), exemplified "the highest instance of a noble mind," bearing "great qualities" without displaying "any consciousness that he is superior to the rest of the world." James also encountered immodesty in the person of Simon Honeycomb, who claimed that women had forced him to abandon his modest ways. Because they liked rogues, he had been forced to become one, wenching, drinking, and keeping "company with those who lived most at large." Characters such as Honeycomb were comic touches that would have appealed to a boy, and Madison would long remember the *Spectator* as "peculiarly adapted to inculcate in youthful minds, just sentiments, an appetite for knowledge, and a taste for the improvement of the mind and manners."[23]

In the pages of the *Spectator,* Madison followed friends who gathered at Will's Coffee House, attended the theater in Drury Lane, and in general took advantage of urban pleasures. This world must have seemed wonderfully exotic to a boy in colonial Virginia, where there were no cities. The geography of the colony, with the Chesapeake Bay, the great rivers flowing into it, and the multitude of navigable tributaries flowing into the rivers, undermined the commercial need for cities. "Every person . . . can ship his tobacco at his own door and live independent," wrote one mid-eighteenth-century visitor.[24] Towns developed—Williamsburg, Fredericksburg, Alexandria—but Virginia, the largest and most populous of the colonies, had no Boston or Philadelphia within its borders.

Living on isolated farms and plantations, Virginians compensated by opening their doors and dining rooms to all respectable passersby.

They entertained at oyster suppers and squirrel barbecues, turned court days into occasions for dinners and horse races, and called in dancing masters to teach their children the elaborate steps of the minuet. One popular dancing master, a Mr. Christian, whom James senior paid in 1756 and 1758, started with his pupils after breakfast and kept them dancing until after dark, not hesitating to deliver a sharp rebuke if they failed to show a respectful attitude.[25]

Virginians also looked to Sunday, when going to church was a chance to mend souls and socialize. The Madisons attended the Brick Church, a two- or three-hour ride to the east, where James Madison Sr. was a vestryman and Frances Madison had joined with other good women of the parish to purchase a silver Communion set. The family prayed at the Brick Church, heard official notices, and exchanged news of politics and tobacco prices. As young James wandered among the congregation after services, he would have encountered a plethora of relatives, many of them named Taylor. Frances Taylor Madison's siblings were prolific— her brother George had fourteen sons—and many of Frances's brothers, sisters, nieces, and great-nephews were within easy distance of the Brick Church. Young James would also have seen Chews, Taliaferros, Beales, and Willises, families related to the Madisons and one another by blood, marriage, and sometimes both, forming what historian Bernard Bailyn called the "great tangled cousinry" of Virginia's gentry class.[26] One can imagine a curious young boy on the ride home inquiring which of the Beale cousins were his aunt Elizabeth's children and which belonged to his aunt Frances and asking how the Willises and Hites fit in.

ON A SAD DAY in December 1761, the Madison family gathered at the Brick Church for the funeral of Frances Madison, who had died at sixty-one. The minister, the Reverend James Marye Jr., comforted the mourners with words from Revelations: "Blessed are the dead which die in the Lord . . . that they may rest from their labors; and their works do follow them." That one of Frances's most lasting works was encouraging her grandson's love of learning seems likely from his father's making educational arrangements for him within months of her death. About the time the tulip poplars bloomed in 1762, young James began attending a boarding school on the banks of the Mattaponi, where the Madison family had started in America. There Master Jamie, as he was now known, found an instructor to whom he would be grateful throughout his life, Donald Robertson, an immigrant from Scotland, "a man of extensive learning and a distinguished teacher," in Madison's words. Along with three dozen other boys, many of whom he knew, young James studied arithmetic, geography, algebra, and geometry. He also learned the languages essential for going to college, Latin and Greek, and studied French as well, though, as he later emphasized, he could only read it. He liked to recount how he had once tried to speak to a Frenchman, only to discover that the Scottish burr he had picked up from Robertson rendered him incomprehensible.[27]

At Robertson's school, Madison found a library containing authors of antiquity, such as Thucydides, Virgil, and Cicero, and more recent thinkers, such as Locke and Montesquieu. In Robertson he found a teacher who knew how to make the connection of learning to life, even when teaching theoretical subjects. Notes that young James Madison made in a copybook show that Robertson began one lecture with the definition of a sign: "a thing that gives notice of something different from itself." He next gave examples of natural signs, such as smiling, which indicates joy, and blushing, which speaks of shame. Then, after observing that such signs are universal, Robertson noted this exception: "Politicians and other cunning men of business, [who] by great and refined dissimulation, have in great measure confounded and stifled the natural indications of their inmost thoughts."[28]

Madison's copybook contains drawings that look like assignments in geometry and geography. One, a hexagonal fort surrounded by a twelve-sided moat inside a twenty-four-sided wall, was surely a more interesting exercise for a boy than a rendering of abstract shapes would have been. Another drawing, a standard rendering of planets in circular orbits around the sun, is made personal by the face on the sun, its nose and brows created by a single line and its rays so thickly drawn they appear to be a mane. The result is a solar system that appears to have a mildly friendly lion at its center.[29]

Madison spent part of 1762 studying the English curriculum at Robertson's school, then moved into the Latin curriculum, or the college preparatory course, for four years before departing. He could have stayed longer, but there were now six children in the Madison family, four besides James of school age, and James senior, in whom a strain of frugality ran strong, seems to have decided to economize by hiring a live-in tutor for all of them. He had a candidate for the job, the new minister at the Brick Church, and room for the tutor in the house he had just built, a structure of some twelve rooms, located a third of a mile east of the old family home.[30]

Compared with the great plantations of the Tidewater, the new house was modest, but rising two stories and made of brick, it was the finest dwelling in Orange County. Young James, helping carry furniture from tiny Mount Pleasant to the family's new home, was no doubt impressed by its roominess.[31] The house was also splendidly situated, as the older house had not been, commanding a magnificent view, a thirty-mile vista over fields and forests to a long stretch of the Blue Ridge Mountains.

The tutor living with the Madison family, Thomas Martin, had recently graduated from Nassau Hall of the College of New Jersey, known as Princeton University today. Together with his brother Alexander, another Nassau graduate, Thomas made the case that James should attend the New Jersey college. No doubt the brothers mentioned the school's new president, John Witherspoon, who was, like Donald Robertson, a product of the highly esteemed University of Edinburgh. Perhaps the Martins also talked about students at Princeton opposing British taxes. At the commencement in 1765, the year that Parliament had lit the fires of colonial outrage by imposing the Stamp Act, there had been a rousing oration on liberty, a valedictory address on patriotism, and a determination by the graduating class to wear only clothing made in America.[32] James Madison Sr., a decided foe of British taxation, would have been favorably impressed by such an account.

Nassau Hall was also the least expensive university in the colonies, a fact that would not have escaped James senior's notice. And while the College of William and Mary was the place where aspiring sons of the Virginia gentry traditionally went, there had been troubling reports from Williamsburg of rioting, drinking, and all-night card games. In later years, Madison mentioned another Williamsburg disadvantage: its Tidewater location. He had been sent to Nassau Hall, he wrote, "in preference to William and Mary, the climate of which was unhealthy for persons going from a mountainous region."[33]

IN THE MIDDLE of a parched summer, James, eighteen years old, left the Virginia upcountry for Princeton, accompanied by the Martins and an enslaved man named Sawney, who was also eighteen. The men traveled down dusty tree-lined roads through enervating heat to Fredericksburg, where they crossed the Rappahannock. They next encountered the Potomac, where they used Hooe's ferry to cross into Maryland. Assuming they followed the route of another traveler from about this time, they traveled a road that took them through Upper Marlboro and to the South River, where yet another ferry took them to Annapolis, a town of fewer than two hundred houses that commanded a splendid view of the Chesapeake. "The bay is twelve miles over," one visitor noted, "and beyond it you may discern the eastern shore, so that the scene is diversified with fields, wood, and water."[34]

From Annapolis, they sailed across the Chesapeake in a northeasterly direction, landing on Maryland's Eastern Shore and moving by land northward to New Castle, the colonial capital of Delaware, "a place of very little consideration," according to one visitor, but it was followed by the "pretty village" of Wilmington.[35] Soon the party was on a ferry across the Schuylkill, then a short ride later at Philadelphia, America's largest city and a place full of wonder for a young man from the Virginia frontier. Mariners shouted to one another along crowded Water Street wharves. Splendid gentlemen on fine horses clattered through paved streets that were lit at night. There were coffeehouses, bookstores, a theater—establishments that made Philadelphia a New World version of the London Madison had read about in the *Spectator.* The city's most impressive building, located between Fifth and Sixth streets on Chestnut, was a Georgian structure of red brick surmounted by a bell tower. For now it was known as the Pennsylvania State House, but Americans of a later time would call it Independence Hall.

A ferry across the Delaware and a day's ride brought Madison and his party to their destination, the small village of Princeton, which had a single road and fewer than "eighty houses, all tolerably well built," one observer noted, "but little attention is paid them." Eyes were drawn instead to an immense stone edifice in the center of town, Nassau Hall, where James Madison would spend most of the next three years. The Martins left him there, and as James settled in to study for his entrance exams, he might have been homesick. In a letter to Thomas Martin, he referred to "the prospect before me of three years confinement," hastily adding that the time would be well compensated "by the advantages I hope to derive from it."[36]

In fact, the years at Princeton were some of the happiest of his life. He met young men from every part of the country and formed close friendships with a few: William Bradford, a thoughtful and well-read young man whose father was a printer in Philadelphia; Philip Freneau, the brilliant and perpetually discontented son of a Huguenot wine merchant; Hugh Brackenridge, born in Scotland, a farmer's son, as smart as he was strong. Like the other hundred or so young men of Nassau Hall, Madison and his friends adhered to a rigid schedule. A bell rang at 5:00 a.m., and lest anyone fail to hear it, a servant followed, beating on every door. Students rushed to morning prayers, then returned to their rooms to study until breakfast at 8:00 a.m. Recitation came after breakfast and was followed by a time for study that lasted until a 1:00 p.m. dinner. From 3:00 p.m. to 5:00 p.m. was another study period, followed by evening prayer, supper, and another study period. After 9:00 p.m., students could go to bed, but, as one noted, "to go before is reproachful."[37]

Tight as the schedule was, there was time for the discussions with other students that make college memorable. After his graduation Philip Freneau, who would play an important part in Madison's life, would write to Madison about how he missed "conversation I delight in." Madison remembered chats of "an hour or two" with Bradford that were "recreation and release from business and books."[38]

Philip Fithian, whose time at Princeton overlapped Madison's, fondly remembered the student hijinks of his college days: "Meeting and shoving in the dark entries; knocking at doors and going off without entering; strewing the entries in the night with greasy feathers; freezing the bell; ringing it at late hours of the night." He also recalled "parading bad women, burning Curse-John [the privy], darting sunbeams upon the town-people . . . , and ogling women with the telescope." In the case of Madison and his friends, at least some youthful energy was diverted into the American Whig Society, a debating club that John Witherspoon supported as part of his plan to encourage effective public speaking. No doubt there were many elevated orations as the Whigs took on their rivals in the Cliosophic Society, but what remains from their "paper wars" is spirited doggerel. In one bit of rhyme, Madison urges his fellow Whigs to be of good humor while the Clios manage their own doom:

> Come, noble whigs, disdain these sons
> Of screech owls, monkeys, and baboons
> Keep up you[r] minds to humorous themes
> And verdant meads and flowing streams
> Until this tribe of dunces find
> The baseness of their groveling mind
> And skulk within their dens together
> Where each one's stench will kill his brother.[39]

The paper wars captured a side of James Madison that would be often commented upon but too seldom recorded, a fondness for sharing less-than-elevated wit with his male friends.

THE STUDYING, COMRADESHIP, and raillery of college life did not keep students at Nassau Hall from having a sharp interest in the events of the larger world. The British had repealed the Stamp Act in 1766, but colonists harbored resentment that Parliament, in which they were not represented, had felt authorized to levy a tax on everything from their newspapers to their playing cards. Great Britain had not only tried to use them as a purse but also violated their fundamental rights as Englishmen, taxing them without their consent. In 1767, when Parliament made another attempt to gather revenue with the Townshend duties, which taxed imports such as lead, paper, and tea, new anger toward Britain began to build on old, particularly in Boston, where opposition to what colonists saw as British tyranny was fierce—and grew fiercer as the British reinforced the Boston garrison with additional regiments of red-coated soldiers. Emotions were running high on the evening of March 5, 1770, when a rowdy crowd gathered outside the Custom House and began throwing rocks and snowballs at British soldiers standing sentry. Before the night was over, the outnumbered British fired into the crowd, killing five.

Parliament repealed the Townshend duties (except for the tax on tea) shortly after the bloody confrontation, but the Boston Massacre, as it came to be called, stood as a powerful symbol of British oppression. It also increased the fervor of those determined to pressure Great Britain by refusing to buy British products. In July, when a letter circulated at Nassau Hall that showed New York merchants trying to persuade Philadelphia businessmen to break their boycott of British goods, students donned their black gowns and, as the college bell tolled, marched to the front of the college. There, as one observer described it, they "burnt the letter by the hands of a hangman hired for the purpose, with hearty wishes that the names of all promoters of such a daring breach of faith may be blasted in the eyes of every lover of liberty and their names handed down to posterity as betrayers of their country." Madison wrote to his father about the demonstration, noting that James senior was likely to hear of it in any case: "A distinct account . . . I suppose will be in the *Virginia Gazette* before this arrives."[40] He probably also thought that the letter burning was an extracurricular activity that James senior would approve.

President Witherspoon surely thought the demonstration justified. A bushy-browed, stocky Presbyterian minister, he'd gained a reputation for standing up to authority in his native Scotland—and not minding if controversy ensued. When the church there took what he perceived to be a liberal drift, he published a satire portraying members of the hierarchy as soft-minded relativists who believed there to be "no ill in the universe, nor any such thing as virtue absolutely considered." A student of the Scottish Enlightenment, Witherspoon lectured Princeton students on unalienable rights, on society as a "voluntary compact," and on human beings as creatures "originally and by nature equal and consequently free." These ideas would be important to the graduates of Nassau Hall in the years ahead. One of Witherspoon's students would become president; another, vice president; forty-nine would be members of the House of Representatives; twenty-eight, of the Senate; and three, Supreme Court justices.[41]

Within six years of Witherspoon's 1768 arrival from Scotland, John Adams would judge him to be "an animated Son of Liberty." Within eight years Witherspoon would be the only minister and one of the most colorful delegates in the Continental Congress deciding on American independence. When one delegate hesitated to break ties with Britain, declaring that America was not ripe for independence, Witherspoon responded that "in his judgment it was not only ripe for the measure, but in danger of becoming rotten for the want of it."[42]

In support of the Princeton ideal "of preparing youth for public service in church and state," Witherspoon insisted that students practice public speaking and provided them with an oratorical model that his most distinguished pupil seems to have found inspiring: simple, commonsensical, unadorned with flourishes and gestures. A visitor coming across Witherspoon in his garden observed that he grew only vegetables. "Why, Doctor, I see no flowers in your garden," to which Witherspoon replied, "No, nor in my discourses either."[43]

Witherspoon encouraged study of the classics, as his predecessors had done, but he also brought a modern sensibility to the college, updating the library with hundreds of volumes he had shipped from Scotland and emphasizing "natural philosophy," as science was called. He worked to bring scientific equipment to the college and brought off an early triumph when he persuaded clockmaker and astronomer David Rittenhouse to let Princeton buy his famed orrery, or planetarium, a device of enameled, silvered, and gilded brass that at the turn of a crank showed planets moving around the sun and moons around planets.[44] It was a mechanical demonstration of all the parts of the universe being held in their paths by a delicate gravitational balance. Young James Madison may well have been impressed by how a gain in power in one part, if not countered in another, could throw the planets into disarray. The idea of the stability produced by equipoise would loom large in his thinking in the years to come.

Rittenhouse's hero, Isaac Newton, had demonstrated the laws underlying the planetary orbits, and to exemplify how far man's mind had penetrated the secrets of the heavens, Rittenhouse put a dial at the top of the orrery that allowed observers to predict the position of the planets for the next four thousand years.[45] That man's mind could plumb depths never before understood was another idea that Madison took away from Princeton.

One might think that the man who brought the orrery to Nassau Hall had deist sympathies, so perfectly did the device seem to represent God as a clockmaker who set the universe in motion and then stood back as it proceeded on its course. But Witherspoon regarded the deists as his theological adversaries, calling them "pretended friends to revealed religion, who are worse if possible than infidels." He believed in revelation as well as reason and in the historic truth of the Bible, including the miracles of the Old and New Testaments. And generous of spirit though he was, he did not welcome opposition to these convictions. He made sure that college trustees invested him "with the sole direction as to the methods of education to be pursued" and during his first year as president saw to the removal of a number of tutors who advanced ideas incompatible with his own.[46]

Witherspoon nonetheless wanted his students to know about man's progress in understanding material nature, what he called "the noble and eminent improvements in natural philosophy . . . made since the end of the last century," and he saw the orrery as a way to advance that goal. An appreciation of the new knowledge of science, in his view, offered a further challenge. "Why should [progress] not be the same with moral philosophy," Witherspoon asked his students, "which is indeed nothing else but the knowledge of human nature?"[47]

It was an exhilarating time to be at Nassau Hall, particularly for a young man from the Virginia upcountry who had proved the substantial power of his own mind in a little over a year and a half. Madison had performed well enough in Latin and Greek on his entrance exams to be able to skip his freshman year. Working his way through sophomore studies, he had looked ahead to his junior and senior years and decided he could do both at once, a course that his father, as well as a realization of his own intellectual prowess, might have encouraged. James senior, who had suffered a substantial setback with the drought of 1769, repeatedly warned about the need to cut down on expenses. Student Madison repeatedly explained to his father about how costly things were. "Your caution of frugality on consideration of the dry weather shall be carefully observed; but I am under a necessity of spending much more than I was apprehensive, for the purchasing of every small trifle which I have occasion for consumes a much greater sum than one wou[ld] suppose."[48] In the end, Madison might have decided that not only was he smart enough to shorten his time at Princeton but doing so was a way to save his father money.

After receiving a promise from the faculty that if he did all the work of two years in one, he could graduate early, he began, as he described it, "an indiscreet experiment of the minimum of sleep and the maximum of application which the constitution would bear." He managed to earn his degree, but with devastating effect on his health. A letter carried to Virginia by Dr. Witherspoon that told James senior of the health crisis is missing, but it is reasonable to suppose that it described the first of Madison's "sudden attacks, somewhat resembling epilepsy." The crisis, which came after sleep deprivation, a classic trigger for seizures, seems to have made young Madison wary of participating in his own graduation and convinced him, although he was not bound to a sickbed, that he should wait several months before attempting the long trip home.[49]

During the extra term he stayed at Nassau Hall, Madison did some reading in law and studied Hebrew with Witherspoon. Samuel Stanhope Smith, who was studying under Witherspoon to be a minister, recalled in later years that Madison was drawn to discussions of the topics that occupied philosophers and divines. Prominent among them, thanks to the Scottish philosopher David Hume, were the miracles of the Bible. In *An Enquiry Concerning Human Understanding,* Hume had argued powerfully that miracles could not be assented to because they were incompatible with reason. As Witherspoon and other orthodox defenders saw it, this was an assault on a central tenet of Christianity. Hume had joined the deists in attacking "principal and direct evidences for the truth of the Christian religion," in Witherspoon's words, and there could be no backing off, no giving an inch in this dispute. If the miraculous events described in the Bible seemed different from what a person judged reasonable, it was only because that person failed to understand, in Witherspoon's words, "that revelation immediately from [God] is evidently necessary."[50]

Every member of the Princeton faculty, particularly after Witherspoon's purge, would have said the same, and it is hard to imagine twenty-year-old James Madison registering objection, even in the case of the boy with epilepsy. In the King James translation of Matthew 17:14–18, he is called a lunatic:

And when they were come to the multitude, there came to him a certain man, kneeling down to him, and saying, Lord, have mercy on my son, for he is lunatic, and sore vexed: for ofttimes he falleth into the fire, and oft into the water. And I brought him to thy disciples, and they could not cure him. Then Jesus answered and said, O faithless and perverse generation, how long shall I be with you? How long shall I suffer you? Bring him hither to me. And Jesus rebuked the devil; and he departed out of him; and the child was cured from that very hour.

In Mark 9:17–26, the boy is described as possessed by "a dumb spirit" that "teareth him: and he foameth, and gnasheth with his teeth." Jesus charges the spirit to come out, "and the spirit cried, and rent him sore, and came out of him." In Luke 9:42, as the boy approached Jesus, "The devil threw him down and tare him, and Jesus rebuked the unclean spirit, and healed the child, and delivered him again to his father."

The idea of epilepsy arising from supernatural sources went back to antiquity. Aristotle (or one of his followers) observed that "men who have become outstanding in philosophy, statesmanship, poetry, or the arts are melancholic, and some to such an extent that they are infected by the diseases arising from black bile, as the story of Heracles among the heroes tells." This, says the writer, had led the ancients to call "the disease of epilepsy the 'sacred disease' after him." One of the Hippocratic writings, on the other hand, disputed the idea, declaring the notion that epilepsy came from the gods absurd and suggesting that it had been started by charlatans.[51]

In the Christian era the idea of a supernatural origin arose again, almost entirely because of the story of the epileptic boy. An early church father, Origen, after analyzing the passage in Matthew, concluded that epilepsy "is obviously brought about by an unclean dumb and deaf spirit." The association of epilepsy and possession persisted through the Middle Ages and into the Enlightenment, with theologians declaring madmen, demoniacs, and those with epilepsy ineligible for ordination. Even physicians of the Enlightenment who were trying to move away from supernatural explanations found themselves carving out an exception for epilepsy. In a book published in 1729, the respected physician Jonathan Harle wrote, "That there were some actually *possessed by the devil* is a truth as plain as words can make it: 'Tis true in one place a person is said to *have a devil and be mad,* and another to be a *demoniac,* and yet is called a lunatic, or one troubled with the *falling sickness.* If we take in both texts, we have the full meaning, which is, that the madness and epilepsy these people labored under were caused by the devil."[52]

For someone experiencing "sudden attacks, somewhat resembling epilepsy," such interpretations had to be extraordinarily disheartening. The English poet Samuel Taylor Coleridge, often ill and seeming to suspect that he had epilepsy, wrote in 1802, "If the Evangelists had . . . merely called the demoniacs diseased men or insane men 'whose diseases are believed by the people to proceed from demons' . . . there would have been, I conceive, no physical hypothesis implied, and yet the Gospel . . . confirmed by its authority a belief so wild."[53] It would also have been helpful if eighteenth-century church leaders had admitted such a possibility, but the assault by Enlightenment thinkers seems to have made them wary of giving up any ground.

If, as seems likely, Madison suffered the first of his sudden attacks at Princeton and turned to books, as he did for most of his life, for understanding, he would have found nothing to lift his spirits. In President Witherspoon's personal collection, there were two books the president specifically recommended to students, Dutch philosopher Hugo Grotius's *De veritate religionis Christianae* and French divine Jacques Abbadie's *Traité de la vérité de la religion chrétienne,* both of which firmly asserted the truth of biblical miracles. The president also had the eminent divine Samuel Clarke's paraphrase of the four evangelists, in which Clarke explicitly labeled the possessed boy's ailment "the falling sickness," the popular name for epilepsy. Nor were the misconceptions of classical writers in the Princeton library any more reassuring. Pliny the Elder indicated that epilepsy was contagious. "We spit on epileptics in a fit; that is, we throw back infection," he wrote in *Natural History,* a book in which he also reported on fantastical cures, including elephant liver, crocodile intestine, and "food taken from the flesh of a wild beast killed by the same iron weapon that has killed a human being."[54]

It might have been during the extra time he spent at Princeton that Madison took notes in a commonplace book that survives today. It shows him interested in secrets, which would be natural at a period in his life when he probably wanted as few people as possible to know what had happened to him. Reading the *Memoirs* of Cardinal de Retz, he stopped to copy this passage: "Secrecy is not so rare among persons used to great affairs as is believed." He added his own thought, "Secrets that are discovered make a noise, but these that are kept are silent." De Retz's Machiavellian insights interested him ("To lessen envy is the greatest of all secrets"), as did de Retz's description of a rising churchman who did not reveal much of himself, Cardinal Fabio Chigi, who, wrote de Retz, "was not very communicative, but in the little conversation he had he showed himself more reserved and wise (*savio col silentio*) than any man I ever knew." Reflecting on the sentence, Madison offered his own, more pointed version: "He showed his wisdom by saying nothing."[55]

The most striking entry in the commonplace book paraphrases part of a letter sent to John Locke, the seventeenth-century philosopher, when he was suffering one of his frequent illnesses. Dr. Thomas Moly-neux wrote to Locke deploring "the great losses the intellectual world in all ages has suffered by the strongest and soundest minds possessing the most infirm and sickly bodies." Molyneux went on to speculate that "there must be some very powerful cause for this in nature or else we could not have so many instances where the knife cuts the sheath, as the French materially express it." Scraping his quill across a page, Mad-ison recorded what seemed to him the essence: "The strongest and soundest minds often possess the weakest and most sickly bodies. The knife cuts the sheath as the French express it."[56]

The association of illness and powerful intellect probably brought comfort to a young man recently stricken and impressed Locke's per-sonal story on his memory. Years later Madison likely had Locke in mind when he gave his Piedmont home and the land around it the name of the town in southern France where the great English philosopher repaired for his health. Madison's Montpelier, like Locke's Montpellier (which was actually the spelling Madison preferred), would be a place where one could, when the knife had cut the sheath, breathe deeply, hike green hills, and find renewal.

Chapter 2

SEASON OF DISCONTENT

MADISON RETURNED HOME from Princeton in a state of deep despondency. In 1772, as the oaks and maples shed the last of their leaves, he took up his pen to warn his friend William Bradford not to count on too much from the world: "I hope you are sufficiently guarded against the allurements and vanities that beset us on our first entrance on the theater of life. Yet however nice and cautious we may be in detecting the follies of mankind and framing our economy according to the precepts of wisdom and religion, I fancy there will commonly remain with us some latent expectation of obtaining more than ordinary happiness and prosperity till we feel the convincing argument of actual disappointment." He himself was no longer burdened with optimism, the twenty-one-year-old Madison told his seventeen-year-old friend, because he was convinced that he had no future to be optimistic about. "As to myself I am too dull and infirm now to look out for any extraordinary things in this world for I think my sensations for many months past have intimated to me not to expect a long or healthy life."[1]

Madison had learned from Bradford of the death of Joe Ross, a classmate from Princeton, who had joined him in crowding two years of study into one. He had also been to Berkeley Warm Springs, and the mineral waters had done him little good. In addition, he was reading a book from his father's library that would have contributed to his gloom. William Burkitt's *Expository Notes with Practical Observations on the New Testament* emphasized the literal truth of the Bible, particularly the miracles. In Burkitt's commentary on the story of Christ's curing the boy who "falleth into the fire, and oft into the water," there was no hedging. Satan was the aggravating force of the boy's sickness, as Burkitt explained it, and Christ's casting him out was the cure.[2]

Madison took notes on Burkitt's weighty tome, and from the pages that have survived, we know that he paused over passages about miracles. He noted Burkitt's observation that the miracles wrought by the apostles in curing diseases and casting out devils were so extraordinary that they exceeded Christ's miracles. He took notes on Burkitt's observation that biblical narratives about possession were unique to the New Testament, writing, "Evil spirits none were that we read of in the Old Testament bodily possessed of, and many in the New." The reason for this, Burkitt explained, was so "that the power of Christ might more signally appear in their ejection and casting out."[3]

Madison's interest in how the world works had not been extinguished. He wrote down Burkitt's observation on Acts 18 that "rulers and great men are like looking glasses" in the model they provide for others. Proverbs 11:13 caught his attention with its caution about talking too much: "A talebearer revealeth secrets: but he that is of a faithful spirit concealeth the matter." And he paused over Proverbs 12:23: "A prudent man concealeth knowledge; but the heart of fools proclaimeth foolishness." But he also had a concern about sin and damnation and how easy it was to slide into both. He paraphrased Burkitt on Matthew 3: "Sins of omission as damnable as sins of commission . . . neglects of duty as damnable as acts of sin."[4]

Fall passed into winter with no word coming back from Bradford. After Christmas, slaves spread manure in plant beds, sowed tobacco seed, and covered the beds with branches to protect against frost, while indoors Madison instructed his sisters Nelly and Sarah, twelve and eight, and his brother William, who was ten, in "some of the first rudiments of literature." He read law and looked into other "miscellaneous subjects," perhaps exploring further in his father's small library. Many of the books on James senior's shelves were medical. Some provided practical information on matters from midwifery to dentistry that a Virginia planter, who oversaw the care of his family and slaves, needed.[5] Others must have struck Madison as evidence of how little was really known of the many ailments, including his own, that flesh was heir to.

One of the books in his father's library took up a most curious medical controversy. It began when Mary Toft of Godalming, England, said that after being startled by a rabbit, she had given birth to seventeen bunnies. Some of the most prominent medical men of the day believed her, were even fooled into thinking they had witnessed the births (she had voluminous skirts), causing the physician James Blondel to launch an assault on the underlying idea that allowed them to be so easily gulled: the notion that a mother's prenatal influence was so great it could turn her unborn child into a monster. In *The Power of the Mother's Imagination over the Foetus Examin'd*, a slender book that James senior owned, Blondel called the idea of assigning blame to the mother "mischievous and cruel," and he ridiculed the old anecdotes used to support the notion, such as the story of a mother startled by a cat who produced a baby with a catlike head and the tale of a pregnant woman who gazed too long at a picture of John the Baptist wearing a hair shirt and produced a hairy child. If Madison found these stories diverting—and how could a former member of the Whig Society have not?—there was another to which he would have paid serious attention, one about "a young and lusty woman" who, frightened at seeing someone suffer an epileptic seizure, bore a child with epilepsy.[6]

The idea that epilepsy could be caused by a pregnant woman witnessing a seizure was widespread. Even the famed Herman Boerhaave, perhaps the most eminent European physician of the first half of the eighteenth century, wrote that epilepsy could derive "from the imagination of the mother when she was pregnant being shocked at the sight of a person in an epileptic fit."[7] Blondel's refutation of such a notion would have been of interest to a young man trying to understand his sudden attacks.

While Madison was reading away the winter months in the Piedmont, his friend Bradford was traveling, eventually settling back at Princeton. It was March before he wrote to Madison, apologizing for the delay and taken aback by his friend's gloomy report: "You alarm me by what you tell me about your health. I believe you hurt your constitution while here by too close an application to study; but I hope 'tis not so bad with you as you seem to imagine. Persons of the weakest constitutions *by taking a proper care of themselves* often outlive those of the strongest."[8]

BY THE TIME Madison wrote back in April 1773, his health had improved, "owing I believe to more activity and less study recommended by the phy[si]cians." Perhaps Madison was simply lucky in encountering doctors who subscribed to the idea that patients could be helped by leading measured lives, but he and his family might very well have sought out such physicians, inspired to do so by another of James senior's books, John Wesley's widely popular *Primitive Physic*. Wesley, the founder of Methodism, was unusual in that he left his theology behind when he wrote about health. Prayer was important, he said, but he conveyed no sense of illness being sin. *Primitive Physic* presented exercise as a "grand preventative of pain and sickness of various kinds." Its power "to preserve and restore health is greater than can well be conceived, especially in those who add temperance thereto." Studious persons, Wesley wrote, "ought to have stated times for exercise, at least two or three hours a day."[9]

For good health, a person also needed to be in control of his emotions, Wesley said: "All violent and sudden passion disposes to, or actually throws people into, acute diseases." Blondel, too, wrote about the effects of "violent passions," saying that they "will cause convulsions, shortness of breath, fevers, epilepsy, apoplexy, and even death itself." It was common for physicians who recommended exercise also to recommend emotional control, and the doctors who suggested "more activity" for Madison might also have offered advice about being calm and measured.[10]

Certainly there was a change of mood in his letters to Bradford. The melancholy outpourings ended, and Madison spoke of himself as "sedate and philosophic"—which did not mean being always somber. He joined Bradford in joking about Nassau alumni such as "poor Brian," who after "long intoxicating his brain with idleness and dissipation" acknowledged his marriage to Miss Amelia Horner, who had already borne his child.[11]

Madison was, however, deeply serious when Bradford requested career advice. The younger man wrote that he had rejected the idea of becoming a minister and was thinking of law. Madison supported his decision but urged that there was still an important religious role he could play: "I have sometimes thought there could not be a stronger testimony in favor of religion or against temporal enjoyments even the most rational and manly than for men who occupy the most honorable and gainful departments and are rising in reputation and wealth, publically to declare their unsatisfactoriness by becoming fervent advocates in the cause of Christ, and I wish you may give in your evidence in this way. Such instances have seldom occurred; therefore, they would be more striking and would be instead of a 'cloud of witnesses.[']"[12] The sentiments in this letter are particularly noteworthy because nothing like them would ever come from Madison's pen again.

During the winter of 1773–1774, Madison's thinking underwent a sea change. The young man who embraced traditional views at the beginning became a person who no longer affirmed the religious doctrines with which he had grown up. It has sometimes been suggested that he was swayed from his early acceptance of church orthodoxy by Thomas Jefferson and Thomas Paine, both critics of revealed religion, but the break in Madison's thinking happened before he knew either man. The more likely explanation is that having taken his health in hand by walking and riding over the Virginia hills, he decided now to take his soul in hand, casting aside the notion that his sudden attacks were somehow connected with Satan, demons, or sin.

Virginia's official church, the Church of England, was supported and enforced by the state, and at the same time that Madison was moving away from traditional religious ideas, the government of Virginia was punishing Baptist preachers trying to expand their ministry into the colony. Sheriffs and magistrates, sometimes accompanied by Anglican clergymen, arrested and jailed the Baptists, charging them with disturbing the peace or preaching without a license. When one of the most famous of those jailed, James Ireland, preached to people through the grate in his cell, men on horseback rode through the crowd, driving some of those gathered to the ground, threatening others with clubs, and stripping and lashing the slaves who were listening.[13]

The jailing of five or six Baptists in neighboring Culpeper County brought Madison to a fury early in 1774. Losing all efforts he had been making to control his passions, he lambasted those responsible, including Anglican clergymen. "That diabolical hell-conceived principle of persecution rages among some," he wrote to his friend Bradford, "and to their eternal infamy the clergy can furnish their quota of imps for such business." He had little sympathy for what he later called the Baptists' "enthusiasm, which contributed to render them obnoxious to sober opinion," but he took up their cause with a vehemence, suggesting that he saw in their plight a symbol of his own. They were in jail, which was clearly unjust, but so was any constraint that restricted the intellect to narrow and dispiriting dogma. "Religious bondage shackles and debilitates the mind and unfits it for every noble enterprise, every expanded prospect," Madison told Bradford, writing with the authority of a man who knew firsthand the price of being bound to a received viewpoint—and the liberation of breaking free.

Madison was frustrated in his early efforts to aid the Baptists. He wrote to Bradford, "I have squabbled and scolded, abused and ridiculed so long about it [to so lit]tle purpose that I am without common patience. So I [leave you] to pity me and pray for liberty of conscience [to revive among us]." But this was hardly the end of it. When a basic principle was involved, Madison could be a man of utterly dogged determination—stubbornness, some would call it. He had already decided to study law, not because he intended to be a lawyer, but because, he told Bradford, "the principles and modes of government are too important to be disregarded by an inquisitive mind and I think are well worthy [of] a critical examination by all students that have health and leisure." In eerily prescient language, he asked Bradford for information on "the constitution of your country," meaning Pennsylvania. He wanted to know "its origin and fundamental principles of legislation," and he made particular inquiry about "the extent of your religious toleration." If freedom of conscience couldn't be achieved in Virginia as it was currently organized, then twenty-two-year-old James Madison wanted to think about reorganizing it—and doing away with an official church. "Is an ecclesiastical establishment absolutely necessary to support civil society in a supreme government?" he asked Bradford. "And how far it is hurtful to a dependant state?"[14]

Madison was also developing another idea: that the absence of clashing ideas and competing interests leads to overreaching and corruption. He wrote to Bradford, "If the Church of England had been the established and general religion in all the northern colonies as it has been among us here, and uninterrupted tranquility had prevailed throughout the continent, it is clear to me that slavery and subjection might and would have been gradually insinuated among us. Union of religious sentiments begets a surprising confidence and ecclesiastical establishments tend to great ignorance and corruption, all of which facilitate the execution of mischievous projects."[15] A decade and more hence, when he was contemplating how a republic of vast expanse could succeed, he would call upon the positive side of this idea: that diversity sustains freedom. Upending the conventional wisdom of his time, he would argue that a large republic had a better chance than a small one of succeeding because there are more interests to compete and less chance for any one of them to become tyrannical.

Madison did not make an issue about his departure from the orthodox religious views of his time. To question miracles or the Trinity in one's study or in private conversation was one thing. To do so publicly was more than unacceptable. Heresy, including the denial of the divinity of the Scriptures, could keep a person from holding office and even, technically at least, lead to imprisonment. With his family, Madison was almost certainly discreet. His father was a vestryman at the Brick Church, and his mother a woman of noted piety who was confirmed in the church as an adult. Her son James chose not to be confirmed, but the loving regard he habitually displayed for his parents almost certainly meant that he did not air his differences with church doctrine at home. Bishop William Meade, a friend of the Madison family, wrote, "Whatever may have been the private sentiments of Mr. Madison on the subject of religion, he was never known to declare any hostility to it. He always treated it with respect, attended public worship in his neighborhood, invited ministers of religion to his house, had family prayers on such occasions—though he did not kneel himself at prayers." Nevertheless, he gained a reputation as an unbeliever. As the Reverend Dr. Balmaine, who was well acquainted with him, described it, "His political associations with those of infidel principles, of whom there were many in his day, if they did not actually change his creed, yet subjected him to the general suspicion of it. This was confirmed in the minds of some by the active part he took in opposition to everything like the support of churches by the legislature." Meade reported a private conversation with him that, in Meade's words, "took such a turn—though not designed on my part—as to call forth some expressions and arguments which left the impression on my mind that his creed was not strictly regulated by the Bible."[16]

Madison has often been called a deist, and rejection of supernatural parts of the Bible was common to deist thought, but so, too, was the idea that through reason one could prove the existence of God, and to Madison that smacked of hubris. He posited limits on reason, making him sound very much like David Hume, the Scottish philosopher whom John Witherspoon had classed among "infidel writers," though that is a description Hume would have rejected. Both Madison and Hume agreed that human understanding can take us only so far and beyond is what Madison described as "mystery," arising from "the dimness of the human sight." As Hume put it, "The whole is a riddle, an enigma, an inexplicable mystery."[17]

Hume also argued that a person cannot wrestle with existential problems forever, cannot remain "environed with the deepest darkness." Life summons, inviting participation: "The blood flows with a new tide; the heart is elevated; and the whole man acquires a vigor which he cannot command in his solitary and calm moments." For Madison, the call came from the events of the day, not only the persecution of Baptists in Virginia, but also the dramatic escalation of the conflict with the king and Parliament. After a few years of relative calm, the British had provoked American ire once more, this time with an effort to save the East India Company. Parliament granted the company exclusive rights to the American tea market, a decision that together with the tax on tea imposed by the Townshend Acts infuriated colonists up and down the seaboard. Once more they saw themselves placed in humiliating subservience, used this time by the ministry in Britain not only to fill up royal coffers but to prop up a failing company. In Philadelphia threats of violence persuaded the captain of the *Polly* to turn back to London rather than attempt to enter the harbor with his cargo of tea. In Boston anger and crowds grew until on a cold December night in 1773 thousands of Bostonians swarmed Griffin's Wharf to watch 130 men, many disguised as Indians, board the *Dartmouth*, the *Eleanor*, and the *Beaver* and dump ten thousand pounds of tea into Boston Harbor.[18]

At first Madison preferred Philadelphia's more temperate approach. "I congratulate you on your heroic proceedings . . . with regard to the tea," he wrote to Bradford, whose father's print shop had published a handbill warning the captain of the *Polly* that tar and feathers were in store for him if he landed. "I wish Boston may conduct matters with as much discretion as they seem to do with boldness." Madison understood that Boston had been singled out for "frequent assaults" and that

the conflict was providing colonists with valuable "exercise and practice . . . in the art of defending liberty and property." Still, he admired
the judiciousness of Philadelphians and longed to visit their city. Soon
he had an excuse. His father wanted to enroll his brother William in a
boarding school to the north.[19]

The Madison brothers, accompanied by James's Princeton friend
George Luckey, started their journey in May and were likely in Philadelphia when they heard the stunning news that in retaliation for the
destruction of tea the British Parliament was closing Boston's port and
altering Massachusetts's charter to bring the colony under greater royal
control. Not long after came action and reaction from Virginia. The
House of Burgesses called for prayer and fasting on June 1, 1774, the day
the port of Boston was to be closed, which led the royal governor of
Virginia, Lord Dunmore, to dissolve the assembly. As Madison enrolled
his brother in preparatory school—the family decided on one in
Princeton—events at home were taking on momentous dimensions.
Members of the dismissed House of Burgesses, acting with the aplomb
of men well practiced in governance, reconvened in Williamsburg's
Raleigh Tavern. There, in the long, wainscoted Apollo Room, scene
of many a ball and banquet, George Washington, Thomas Jefferson,
Patrick Henry, and their colleagues reaffirmed their support for Boston, declaring "that an attack made on one of our sister colonies . . . is
an attack made on all *British America*." They called for the colonies
to meet "in general congress . . . to deliberate on those general measures which the united interests of *America* may from time to time
require."[20]

As the crisis grew, Madison's attitude, like that of many colonists,
hardened. In light of the harsh British measures, Pennsylvania's cautious ways seemed inadequate, and when its legislature chose delegates
for the general congress that Virginia had proposed, Madison told Bradford that the instructions they had been given were much too timid.
Instead of waiting to see if the British would make concessions, the
colonies ought to undertake immediate military preparations, he maintained: "Delay on our part emboldens our adversaries and improves

their schemes whilst it abates the ardor of the Americans inspired with recent injuries." From his Piedmont home, Madison also wrote to Bradford that he "heartily repent[ed]" having already made his journey to Philadelphia. The years of his young manhood had been marked by repeated British violations of American rights, from the Stamp Act to the Tea Act to the Intolerable Acts, as Americans were calling the measures taken against Boston. The gathering of the Continental Congress offered hope of concerted action by the American colonies in defense of their rights. Madison yearned to observe the great event, but Bradford assured him that even if he were in Philadelphia, he could not witness the proceedings. They were "a profound secret and the doors open to no one." Bradford had to admit, however, that a city where delegates were convening from such far-flung places as Georgia and Massachusetts provided great spectacle. Philadelphia was "another Cairo," he wrote, swarming not with merchants but "with politicians and statesmen."[21]

Bradford also sent information he knew would fascinate the book-loving Madison: "The Congress sits in the Carpenter's Hall in one room of which the city library is kept and of which the librarian tells me the gentlemen make great and constant use." The delegates were especially interested in works of political theory, Bradford wrote, perhaps inspiring Madison to begin a reading project of his own. He sent to England for Joseph Priestley's *Essay on the First Principles of Government and on the Nature of Political, Civil, and Religious Liberty,* a work advocating natural rights, limited government, and religious freedom. He asked Bradford to send him a copy of Adam Ferguson's *Essay on the History of Civil Society,* which emphasized the need for constitutional checks and balances. Ferguson also asserted liberty to be a right, not a favor granted by the state, a formulation that Madison might have kept in mind as he read pamphlets on religious toleration that he asked another friend to send him.[22] Since freedom of conscience was also a right, why should it be regarded as within the power of the state to grant?

Word leaked out of the Continental Congress that Virginia's delegates were the most aggressive in their proposals for dealing with Great Britain. "*Your* province seems to take the lead at present," Bradford wrote. Madison proudly reported that in Virginia "a spirit of liberty and patriotism animates all degrees and denominations of men. Many publically declare themselves ready to join the Bostonians as soon as violence is offered them or resistance thought expedient." During the winter months of 1774–1775, militias began to train. "There will by the spring, I expect, be some thousands of well-trained high spirited men ready to meet danger whenever it appears," Madison wrote.[23]

Madison was a member of the Orange County Committee of Safety, which his father headed, a group responsible for enforcing the Continental Association, a measure passed by the Continental Congress to boycott British goods. Committee members also encouraged local military preparations for what Madison called "extreme events," efforts that seemed entirely prudent when news arrived that in the dawn hours of April 20, 1775, British marines under the orders of Governor Dunmore had seized gunpowder from the magazine at Williamsburg. Some six hundred armed and mounted men assembled at Fredericksburg "with a view to proceed to Williamsburg [to] recover the powder and revenge the insult," as Madison described it. They were talked out of their plans by a letter from the portly, fifty-three-year-old Peyton Randolph, who had been in the House of Burgesses for nearly thirty years and presided over the Continental Congress, as well as by advice from three of Randolph's colleagues: Edmund Pendleton, Richard Henry Lee, and George Washington. But Patrick Henry, another Virginia delegate, wasn't about to let the event pass. Since the time of the Stamp Act, he had been excoriating the British for their actions. Just the month before, he had stirred his fellow Virginians with a call to arms that would become legendary: "Is life so dear or peace so sweet as to be purchased at the price of chains and slavery? Forbid it, Almighty God! I know not what course others may take, but as for me . . . give me liberty or give me death!"[24]

In Hanover County, Henry called for volunteers, and as they assembled, reports from Massachusetts began arriving. Shots had been fired and Americans killed when a British attempt to seize a cache of arms near Concord, Massachusetts, had provoked a confrontation at North Bridge. Henry told the men gathered in Newcastle on the Pamunkey River that it was hardly a coincidence that the British had also seized Virginia munitions. They had a plan to deprive colonists up and down the land of their means of defense, he said, rousing the assembled volunteers with images of comrades fallen, their blood "gloriously shed in the general cause." He led his motley army toward Williamsburg, and as their march progressed, an alarmed Governor Dunmore sent a message offering reparations. Henry accepted the governor's bill of exchange, wrote a receipt for 330 pounds, and declared himself satisfied.[25]

In Orange County, where indignation was also running high, a group of volunteers, including James Madison, was organizing its own march when its members learned of Henry's success. A letter from the Committee of Safety, probably drafted by Madison, thanked Henry for his "zeal for the honor and interest of your country," and Madison was among those who delivered it as Henry passed triumphantly through Port Royal, Virginia, on his way to Philadelphia and the Second Continental Congress. The twenty-four-year-old from Orange County probably tried hard not to stare at the tall, gaunt, thirty-eight-year-old Henry, a man who would be his adversary in the years ahead but for whom he presently had the highest regard, particularly, he told Bradford, when he compared Henry's upcountry boldness with the "pusillanimity" of the "gentlemen below," meaning the large plantation owners of the Tidewater, "whose property will be exposed . . . should [the government] be provoked to make reprisals."[26]

In mid-June, Madison sent sad news to Bradford. Dysentery, widespread in Orange County, had carried off two of his siblings, "a little sister about seven and a brother about four years of age." Nelly Madison, grieving over the deaths of Elizabeth and Reuben, the fourth and fifth of her children to die, had also fallen ill, but she would later recover.[27]

·   ·   ·

AFTER THE KILLINGS at Lexington and Concord, further armed conflict with Britain seemed inevitable, and Boston, under British occupation, was the most likely place for it. When the Second Continental Congress met in Philadelphia in May 1775, delegates quickly created a Continental army, authorizing militia companies from Virginia, Maryland, and Pennsylvania to march to Boston to reinforce the ragtag assemblage of New Englanders trying to drive the British from the city. Congress then turned to one of its own to lead the army. Colonel George Washington of Virginia, a man of commanding stature, few words, and a reputation for great courage in battling the French and the Indians, accepted the appointment, modestly calling it "a trust too great for my capacity."[28]

Even as Washington was preparing to take up his command, there was further bloodshed. British forces attacked New England militiamen who had taken up fortified positions on Breed's Hill, which overlooked Boston. After fierce fighting, patriot forces retreated to Cambridge over Bunker Hill, from which the battle would take its name, but they had exacted a terrible price from the British, killing or wounding more than a thousand redcoats.[29] As colonists increasingly realized that they were going to have to wage war for their rights, the Battle of Bunker Hill lifted their spirits, encouraging them to think that in a general conflagration their militias would fare quite well.

As happens in great crises, rumors started to fly. In Virginia, Madison heard that Benjamin Franklin, who had been in London for more than ten years, had sold out to the British and that a Virginia delegate had turned traitor and fled from Philadelphia. Neither claim was accurate, but Madison, showing his youth, gave quick credit to both reports. He was also an eager participant in efforts to expose and humiliate those who did not support the American cause. The Committee of Safety on which Madison and his father served required county inhabitants to sign a pledge upholding the Continental Association and demanded that the rector of the Brick Church hand over certain pamphlets in his possession printed by James Rivington of New York, a publisher notorious for his Loyalist sympathies. Declaring the pamphlets full of "the most impudent falsehoods and malicious artifices," the committee ordered them burned. Not long after, mobs in New York destroyed Rivington's press, making the publisher's subsequent career—as a paid spy for George Washington—all the more amazing.[30]

In a letter to Bradford, Madison approvingly described the firing of a parson in Culpeper County who had refused to observe a day of fasting and prayer for the patriot cause: "When called on he pleaded conscience, alleging that it was his duty to pay no regard to any such appointments made by unconstitutional authority. The committee it seems have their consciences, too. They have ordered his church doors to be shut and his salary to be stopped. . . . I question should his insolence not abate if he does not get ducked in a coat of tar and surplice of feathers and then he may go in his new canonicals and act under the lawful authority of General Gage."[31] Full of zeal—and youthful braggadocio—Madison saw no contradiction between championing freedom of thought and endorsing tar and feathers, rationalizing, perhaps, that to create a society in which people could express themselves freely, it was necessary first to make sure British oppression failed. And however humiliating—and painful—a tarring and feathering, Madison probably judged it mild in the context of British actions. General Gage, to whom Madison wanted to send the Culpeper parson, had ordered the fateful raid on the arsenal at Concord and authorized the bloody assault on Breed's Hill.

No British figure ranked lower in Madison's estimation than Governor Dunmore. The fury following his seizure of gunpowder from the Williamsburg magazine had only begun to abate when Dunmore set a shotgun trap on the magazine's doors that subsequently wounded two men. With outrage mounting, Williamsburg began to fill with upcountry riflemen, known as "shirtmen" from the hunting clothes they wore, and, fearing for his safety, Dunmore fled the capital with his family in the early morning hours of June 8, 1775. The last royal governor of Virginia, his pregnant wife, and his eight children took refuge aboard HMS *Fowey*, a British frigate off Yorktown. "We defy his power as much as we detest his villainy," Madison wrote in his report of these events to Bradford.[32]

Madison had worried for months that if a rupture occurred, the British would encourage a slave insurrection as part of their effort to defeat rebellious colonists, and when enslaved people hoping for freedom began making their way to where Dunmore's ship was anchored, he suspected the governor was at work—and cleverly so. "To say the truth," Madison wrote to Bradford, "that is the only part in which this colony is vulnerable; and if we should be subdued, we shall fall like Achilles by the hand of one that knows that secret." A slaveholder himself, Dunmore understood the potential weakness of a colony in which 40 percent of the population was enslaved, and on November 14, 1775, he declared "all *indented servants, Negroes,* or others (appertaining to rebels) *free,* that are able and willing to bear arms, they *joining his majesty's troops* as soon as may be." The emancipation did not encompass the fifty-seven human beings Dunmore owned, or slaves owned by Loyalists, or any women and children, but it sent fear and dread through white Virginia, as did evidence turned up by patriot forces of Dunmore's intent to enlist Indians from the Ohio country in the British cause. In December 1775, George Washington wrote of Dunmore: "[If] that man is not crushed before spring, he will become the most formidable enemy America has; his strength will increase as a snowball, by rolling."[33]

Dunmore was crushed by summer, his strategy of freeing and arming slaves driving even the most cautious Virginia leaders into the patriot cause. He commanded an attack across a causeway at Great Bridge, south of Norfolk, that led to the decimation of British regulars under his command. He bombarded American troops parading in Norfolk and sent landing parties to destroy buildings along the dock area, thereby giving patriot troops, who regarded Norfolk as a Tory stronghold, all the excuse they needed to begin pillaging and burning. Although the destruction of Norfolk had been helped along by the Americans, it became one more item in the litany of British depredations.

Dunmore's troops subsequently sickened with smallpox and hundreds died, including many of the former slaves who had sought freedom with him, but when he abandoned Virginia, others who had seen him as the leader who could bring them liberty sailed aboard his fleet, including a man who had formerly been enslaved by George Washington and another who had been the property of Patrick Henry.[34] There had been no idealism in Dunmore's freeing of slaves owned by patriots, but he nonetheless made it possible for some of them to know freedom.

AMONG THOSE TRAINING to be a Piedmont rifleman was twenty-four-year-old James Madison, likely quite a fit young man by now. It had been two years since he had begun following doctors' recommendations to leave off constant study in order to exercise regularly. He had made at least one long journey and was eager to take more. Judging by his confidence in his marksmanship, he might also have spent time hunting. Although emphasizing that he was "far from being among the best," he reported to Bradford that he counted on hitting "the bigness of a man's face at the distance of 100 yards."[35] That is the rough equivalent of hitting an eight-inch target at one end of a football field when firing from the other—a respectable shot with an eighteenth-century weapon.

But exercise, though seeming to help, turned out not to be a cure, and his military career came to an abrupt end when he was struck by one of his sudden attacks. If he experienced a complex partial seizure, he might have entered a "dreamy state" and engaged in automatic movements, such as plucking at clothes. He might have walked without awareness of where he was going or heard people speak without understanding what they said. Complex partial seizures typically last a minute or two, and the aftermath is brief. "After the seizure," writes Dr. Orrin Devinsky, a foremost expert on epilepsy, "lethargy and confusion are common, but usually last less than fifteen minutes."[36]

But Madison was occasionally affected for days by his sudden attacks. At times they were described as "slight" and at others "severe," suggesting that partial seizures might have sometimes generalized (as they do in more than 30 percent of patients with partial epilepsy). The excessive electrical activity that causes a partial seizure when localized in one area of the brain can spread to both sides, causing the affected person to lose consciousness, fall to the ground, and convulse. If partial seizures did sometimes generalize in Madison's case, it would help explain why he, in advance of his time, understood a connection between attacks "suspending the intellectual functions" and epilepsy. If an experience that sometimes passed quickly also on occasion led to convulsive seizures, a logical mind would posit a relationship.[37]

In the end Madison would decide to avoid the freighted word "epilepsy" altogether, revising his autobiography to refer instead to an "experience" during military training that brought his constitutional weakness home to him. But a congressman whom he knew well would use the term, writing not long after Madison's death that "he was subject to sudden attacks, a mitigated form of epilepsy. And though they attended him through life, this fortunately did not as usual become worse with years and never in the smallest degree dimmed the brightness of his intellect."[38]

It's impossible to know exactly what happened during Madison's sudden attacks, but we can conclude that he was most fortunate, particularly in a time when there was no effective treatment, that they were not more severe. Although the attacks sometimes stopped him in his course, he was able by the time of his military training to cease dwelling upon them and instead focus on the compelling news of the day: the king's troops had fired upon and killed Americans, occupied Boston, and razed Norfolk; the British ministry was intent on spreading further death and destruction by inciting Indians and slaves, an action that even so ardent a foe of slavery as Thomas Paine condemned as "cruelty" with "a double guilt; it is dealing brutally by us and treacherously by them."[39]

Back at his Piedmont home, Madison watched a new year unfold, a fateful year that would be forwarded in its course by Paine, an immigrant from England, who boldly declared what had until recently been unthinkable: that America must not merely resist Britain but break with it. "Everything that is right or natural pleads for separation," he wrote in *Common Sense,* a pamphlet that electrified the colonies in the early months of 1776. "The blood of the slain, the weeping voice of nature cries, 'tis *time to part.*"[40]

Paine pictured what could follow—a freedom unknown on earth, with consequences that would roll down the generations. "'Tis not the concern of a day, a year, or an age, posterity are virtually involved in the contest and will be more or less affected until the end of time," he wrote.[41] Twenty-four-year-old James Madison must have thrilled at these words. It was a time of great change and possibility, and he was a gifted and well-prepared young man.

Chapter 3

GREAT MEN

ALTHOUGH BY FAR THE YOUNGEST member of the Orange County Committee of Safety, Madison, along with his uncle William Moore, another committee member, was elected in 1776 to attend the Virginia Convention, the provisional government of the commonwealth since 1774.[1] That Madison's father was head of the Committee of Safety and a well-regarded planter might have entered into the freeholders' choosing young Madison for what was sure to be a momentous gathering, but in the small, albeit spread-out, community of Orange County they would also have known that he, like most of them, was no longer inclined to temporize with the British. The record of abuse, long and now bloody, seemed proof that if Virginians were to be free men, reconciliation was impossible. The time had come to seek independence.

It had been a wet spring in Virginia, and on the way to Williamsburg, Madison and Moore had to contend with muddy roads, swollen rivers, and creeks overrunning their beds. By the time they arrived, the convention was under way, and they entered the crowded capitol at the end of Duke of Gloucester Street to find that fifty-four-year-old Edmund Pendleton had been elected to preside. He was an impressive figure, six feet tall, "the handsomest man in the colony," some said, with a serene and elegant manner that belied a modest background. His father had died the year he was born, leaving the family impoverished and young Edmund with few choices. Apprenticed at age fourteen to the clerk of the Caroline County Court, he educated himself and succeeded in becoming licensed as a lawyer and earning a handsome income, though never entering the ranks of the wealthy because of substantial sums he spent raising up other members of his family. His long and successful career in politics had begun in 1752, when, at age thirty, he had been elected to the House of Burgesses, and he had served either in that body or in every Virginia Convention since.[2]

Madison was acquainted with Pendleton, whose mother was his grandmother Frances Madison's sister, but aside from him and William Moore he knew few of the delegates. Most were older, and many had been powerful in Virginia while Madison was still a child. He soon fell into conversation, probably on a back bench, with a delegate about his age, Edmund Randolph. Tall and outgoing, with dark eyes and soft features, Edmund carried the highest hopes of the Randolph dynasty. He would become Virginia's first attorney general and its governor, and he would hold high national office, but his life was not without its troubles, and for now his problem was his father. John Randolph, known to history as Randolph the Tory, had chosen to sail to England with Governor Dunmore rather than stay in rebellious Virginia. In part to remove the shadow that his Loyalist father had cast on his reputation, Edmund had successfully sought a position as an aide-de-camp to General George Washington, and after serving with the general for two and a half months in Massachusetts, Randolph no doubt had much to relate about the challenges Washington faced, including scarce supplies, short-term enlistees, and the confounding strangeness of New Englanders. As Randolph remembered it, he also learned much from the delegate from Orange, whose broad knowledge and good judgment were apparent almost as soon as one spoke with him. Wrote Randolph, "He who had once partaken of the rich banquet of [Madison's] remarks did not fail to wish daily to sit within the reach of his conversation."[3]

Madison and Randolph took note as Patrick Henry rose to speak. Henry was neither handsome nor graceful and from his childhood had lacked discipline, preferring to run wild in the Virginia forests and play his fiddle rather than attend to schoolwork. But he had passion, and after failing at farming and shopkeeping, he discovered a gift for inspiring others that had made him, next to George Washington, the most popular man in Virginia. He had enemies, to be sure, people who thought he was lazy and crude, but he won over the crowds with his oratory. "Compared with any of his more refined contemporaries and rivals, he by his imagination . . . painted to the soul [and] eclipsed the sparklings of art," observed Randolph. Madison, too, "thrilled with the ecstasies of Henry's eloquence and extolled his skill in commanding the audience," but he also observed privately that Henry's reasoning was sometimes faulty.[4]

Henry had earlier been among the most forward leaning on the matter of separating from Great Britain, and Pendleton one of the most cautious, but as the moment of decision neared, their positions reversed. Henry, for all his passion, thought independence a decision to be delayed until it could be taken by all the colonies at once in the Continental Congress, while Pendleton proposed that the Virginia Convention immediately declare union with Great Britain at an end. Pendleton crafted a compromise that fulfilled Henry's wish with a resolution "that the delegates appointed to represent this colony in the general congress be instructed to propose to that respectable body to declare the United Colonies free and independent states, absolved from all allegiance to or dependence upon the crown or parliament of Great Britain." An accompanying resolution accomplished what Pendleton wanted by setting Virginia on a new course immediately. A committee would "be appointed to prepare a declaration of rights and such a plan of government as will be most likely to maintain peace and order in this colony and secure substantial and equal liberty to the people."[5]

Now Henry became "a pillar of fire," Randolph reported. He threw the full force of his oratory behind the resolutions, and the delegates voted unanimously in favor of both. Remembering the eloquent case that *Common Sense* had made for American independence, Randolph concluded that "the principles of Paine's pamphlet now stalked in triumph under the sanction of the most extensive, richest, and most commanding colony in America."[6]

The crowd outside the convention thrilled to the new era by pulling down the British flag from atop the capitol and hoisting the red-striped Grand Union flag that George Washington's army was using. As Thomas Nelson, a delegate to both the Virginia Convention and the Continental Congress, set out for Philadelphia with the resolution recommending independence, Williamsburg prepared for celebration. The next day in Waller's Grove, the resolutions passed by the convention were read to the army. Troops paraded and partook of refreshment. Toasts were offered, each followed by cannon salute and the cheers of the crowd. That night, as the *Virginia Gazette* described it, there were "illuminations and other demonstrations of joy."[7]

Several days after the vote, another of Virginia's great men arrived at the convention, George Mason of Gunston Hall, one of the wealthiest planters in the colony. Swarthy, with eyes so dark they looked black, he had been delayed by "a smart fit of the gout," as he put it. This painful ailment plagued him much of his life and might have contributed to his sometimes acerbic tongue, but he was also a man who carried a heavy weight of grief. His beloved wife, Ann, mother of his many offspring, had died in 1773 after bearing twins, who also died. Mason was left with nine children, to whom he was devoted. Pressed to serve in the Continental Congress in 1775, he had refused on account of his children, explaining with great emotion that such service would not be compatible with their needs.[8]

Although Mason had little formal schooling, he was a voracious reader and had acquired a vast knowledge of the letter and philosophy of the law. He was a natural appointment to the committee charged with creating a declaration of rights and a constitution for Virginia. Named its thirty-first member, Mason had no illusions about how it would work. He wrote to Richard Henry Lee, one of Virginia's delegates to the Continental Congress and a man whom Mason desperately wanted to have join him in Williamsburg: "The committee appointed to prepare a plan is, according to custom, overcharged with useless members. . . . We shall in all probability have a thousand ridiculous and impracticable proposals and, of course, a plan formed of heterogeneous, jarring, and unintelligible ingredients. This can be prevented only by a few men of integrity and abilities . . . undertaking this business and defending it ably through every stage of opposition."[9]

Mason, who immediately took charge of the committee, might well have regarded James Madison as part of its deadwood. It would have been hard to expect much from one so young and inexperienced, but when Mason's draft of a declaration of rights emerged, Madison had a key suggestion. The section on religious freedom declared that "religion or the duty which we owe to our Creator and the manner of discharging it can be directed only by reason and conviction, not by force or violence; and therefore . . . all men should enjoy the fullest toleration in the exercise of religion, according to the dictates of conscience, unpunished and unrestrained by the magistrate." These sentiments represented Enlightenment thought, particularly as drawn from John Locke's *A Letter Concerning Toleration*.[10] After centuries in which magistrates had seen it as their duty to burn, behead, drown, and hang people of other religions, Locke's thinking had been a breakthrough, but eighty years and more had passed since his letter, and James Madison thought it was time to push further. Why should religious freedom be regarded as something that the state should tolerate? He had spent much of his young life thinking about the consequences of forcing a person to profess belief he knows is in error and had concluded that to imply that the state had any authority in such a matter was wrong.

Madison, well aware of his junior status, worked through others, including Patrick Henry and Edmund Pendleton, to bring his amendment before the delegates, and he managed to do so with tact sufficient to leave George Mason unperturbed. In the end Madison succeeded in replacing the words "all men should enjoy the fullest toleration in the exercise of religion" with "all men are equally entitled to the free exercise of religion."[11] It was a simple alteration that accomplished a mighty change: legal recognition that freedom of conscience, like life, liberty, and the pursuit of happiness, is a natural right. It was also the first example of the double nature of Madison's genius. He was capable not only of deeply creative thinking but of turning his thoughts into reality.

Madison had studied constitutions, but he took little active part when the convention moved on to create one for governing Virginia, as the Continental Congress, meeting in Philadelphia, had called on states to do, but he learned much as an observer, including a great deal about the temperament of a man he had not yet met and who was not even at the convention. Thirty-three-year-old Thomas Jefferson was the most junior member of the Virginia delegation to the Continental Congress in Philadelphia. Although not much of an orator, he had already proved himself a gifted writer with a pamphlet, *A Summary View of the Rights of British America,* in which he declared that Parliament had no authority over the American colonies and that King George III had acted illegally when he "sent among us large bodies of armed forces."[12] Jefferson had written *A Summary View* for the Virginia Convention of 1774, which he had been unable to attend, and might have learned from this experience how comfortable it was to give instruction from a distance. He did not like personal confrontation and could avoid it by opining without being present.

From Philadelphia, Jefferson sent word to convention delegates in Williamsburg that they had no authority to write a constitution for Virginia. Such a task was not within the purview of an ordinary legislative body and should be put off, he wrote to Edmund Randolph, "until the people should elect deputies for that special purpose." Randolph carried Jefferson's message to other members of the convention, Madison no doubt among them, and probably encountered many a dismayed reaction. As Randolph put it, asking delegates "to postpone formation of a constitution until a commission of greater latitude and one more specific should be given by the people was a task too hardy."[13]

But Jefferson wasn't through. As the convention neared the end of its work on a Virginia constitution, he sent its members another missive—a draft of a Virginia constitution that he had composed, one full of ideas sure to lead to heated debate, such as ending the importation of slaves and allowing women to inherit equally with their brothers. One imagines Edmund Pendleton privately throwing up his hands, but, ever the gentleman in public, he wrote to Jefferson explaining that because the constitution just agreed to in the committee of the whole "had been so long in hand, so disputed inch by inch, and the subject of so much altercation and debate," delegates were reluctant to invite more contention. Moreover, they were worn out "and could not, from mere lassitude," be "induced to open the instrument again." The delegates did, however, adopt the preamble that Jefferson had written for his draft constitution. Since he was dissatisfied with the document that the delegates produced, Jefferson was less than grateful for their adoption of his words. He described the final result as having his preamble "tacked to the work of George Mason."[14] Meanwhile, he found his own use for the preamble, folding it into a writing assignment he had acquired in Philadelphia. With a few alterations, the preamble became part of the Declaration of Independence.

Even before he met him, Madison was learning how maddening Jefferson could be—and how brilliant. In trying to establish popular self-government, Americans were attempting something new under the sun, which required thinking anew, and even though Madison voted in favor of the Virginia constitution that Jefferson thought flawed, within a decade he was arguing Jefferson's point: that the convention wasn't the proper body for creating fundamental law. Elected to run the war and govern the colony, it lacked the status needed to establish a framework for governing. Without what Madison called "due power from people," its actions were legislative, not fundamental, and therefore alterable by the next governing authority.[15]

Jefferson had proposed that Virginia's constitution be ratified by the people "assembled in their respective counties." This suggestion was also ignored, but Madison saw its inherent correctness. This was a further way to distinguish a fundamental document from a legislative act and thereby shelter it from constant change. In later years, when Madison drafted a constitution for the nation, he would provide for "an assembly or assemblies of representatives . . . expressly chosen by the people, to consider and decide thereon."[16]

On June 29, 1776, delegates in Williamsburg adopted the constitution over which they had long labored, and as if to prove the point that they were a legislative body rather than an assembly for creating paramount law, they rolled themselves over into the lower house of Virginia's legislative branch, scheduled to meet in the fall. The constitution also created a governorship, one weak enough so that there was no danger of the incumbent disregarding the legislature, as royal governors had sometimes done, and the delegates elected Patrick Henry to the post.

As the convention in Williamsburg neared adjournment, members of the Continental Congress in Philadelphia approved the proposal that the Virginia Convention had instructed its representatives to offer. On July 2, 1776, they affirmed "that these United Colonies are, and of right ought to be, free and independent states, that they are absolved from all allegiance to the British Crown, and that all political connection between them and the State of Great Britain is, and ought to be, totally dissolved."

On July 4, the Continental Congress approved the Declaration of Independence, giving universal justification to America's course in Jefferson's soaring prose: "We hold these truths to be self-evident, that all men are created equal, that they are endowed by their Creator with certain unalienable rights; that among these are life, liberty, and the pursuit of happiness; that to secure these rights, governments are instituted among men, deriving their just powers from the consent of the governed; that whenever any form of government becomes destructive of these ends, it is the right of the people to alter or to abolish it."

MADISON HAD READ enough history to know that he was at the center of epoch-shaping events, and he had reason to be optimistic about the outcome. While he knew from listening to Edmund Randolph of the many difficulties that General Washington and his army faced, he likely balanced these in his mind against the long string of punishing blows that troops engaged in the American cause had so far delivered: The militia-men of Massachusetts had killed and wounded hundreds of the redcoats who had tried to seize arms at Concord; Ethan Allen and the Green Mountain Boys had captured Fort Ticonderoga; the defenders of Breed's Hill had inflicted punishing casualties on the British. Virginia troops had dealt a devastating blow to Lord Dunmore at the Battle of Great Bridge, near Norfolk, and General George Washington and his army had forced the British from Boston.

Within months, however, the news turned ominous. The British had landed tens of thousands of troops on Long Island and in late August routed the American army, forcing Washington to evacuate across the East River to Manhattan. The British followed, and Washington re-treated north to Harlem Heights, abandoning New York City. In Octo-ber, as Madison traveled the route from Orange County to Williamsburg to serve in the newly formed House of Delegates, Virginians learned from the *Virginia Gazette* that much of New York had burned.[17]

But even the deep concerns of war did not bring a cessation of poli-tics, and Madison found the assembly caught up in a controversy that he had helped create. Pursuing the religious amendment to the Virginia Declaration of Rights to its logical conclusion, petitioners flooded the House of Delegates with calls for ending state support of the Anglican Church. One group, quoting the amendment for which Madison had been responsible, demanded in the pages of the *Virginia Gazette* "that all religious denominations within this dominion be forthwith put in the full possession of equal liberty, without preference or preeminence, which, while it may favor one, can hurt another, and that no religious sect whatever be established in this commonwealth." A group from Prince Edward County wrote that they viewed the religious amendment to the Declaration of Rights "as the rising sun of religious liberty to relieve them from a long night of ecclesiastical bondage" and urged that "without delay, all church establishments might be pulled down and every tax upon conscience and private judgment abolished." The fact that one of Madison's friends from Princeton, Samuel Stanhope Smith, was a Presbyterian leader in Prince Edward County and that Madison had been in recent communication with him suggests that Madison might not have been entirely surprised at the outpouring of response to the amendment he had helped create.[18]

There were zealous Anglicans in the assembly, but delegates such as Madison who wanted to end state sponsorship of the church had gained a powerful leader for their cause. Thomas Jefferson had retired from his seat in the Continental Congress in the late summer of 1776 in order to serve in the Virginia legislature, his aim being to reform "many very vicious points" of legislation that had grown up under British rule, among them the Anglican dominance that he called "spiritual tyranny." Madison and Jefferson, whose Piedmont homes were only thirty miles apart, had not met before, and because of what Madison described as "the disparities between us," they would not yet become fast friends. Eight years older than Madison and a man of national reputation, Jefferson was not a newcomer, expected to watch and learn, but a seasoned politician. He was a force in committee meetings, waging what he called "desperate contests" against the established church. Edmund Pendleton was a particularly adept foe, "the ablest man in debate I have ever met," Jefferson wrote, describing him as "never vanquished": "You never knew when you were clear of him but were harassed by his perseverance until the patience was worn down of all who had less of it than himself."[19] While Jefferson and his allies managed to do away with laws punishing heresy and requiring church attendance, permanently ending state support for religion was, for the moment, beyond their reach. But Jefferson and Madison, no less than Pendleton, knew the meaning of perseverance, and year after year, as friendship between them grew, they held on to this cause, supporting each other, spelling each other, and eventually succeeding.

As the House of Delegates neared adjournment, news of the war caused alarm akin to panic. The British had driven George Washington and his ragtag army out of New York and pursued them across New Jersey. According to the *Virginia Gazette,* thousands of British troops had followed the Americans into Pennsylvania, an account that turned out to be false, but the newspaper's report that the Continental Congress had fled from Philadelphia was accurate. Fearing that Virginia would be attacked, the assembly decided on December 21, 1776, to grant Patrick Henry and his council extraordinary powers.[20] A severely constrained executive was one thing in theory but quite another with the enemy at the door.

As Henry, armed with his new authority, readied a general militia call, an astonishing event unfolded in New Jersey. George Washington led twenty-four hundred men back across the icy Delaware River, surprised Hessian mercenaries quartered at Trenton, and took nearly a thousand of them prisoner. His victories there and at Princeton in early January 1777 raised hopes once more, including, no doubt, those at the Madison home. News was slow to arrive in the Piedmont, but by the end of January, James Madison, home after the adjournment of the House of Delegates, would have heard of Washington's thrilling feats and had reason to think it was a new season for the American cause.

For Madison, however, the early years of the war had even more peaks and valleys than they did for his fellow countrymen. No sooner were there signs that the American effort might succeed than he suffered an ignominious political defeat. "Swilling the planters with bumbo," as providing food and drink for voters was called, was a long-established practice among Virginia politicians. Madison's great-uncle Thomas Chew had gained a measure of fame in 1741, when as a candidate for the House of Burgesses he brought a punch bowl into the courthouse itself. Believing that the spirit of the Revolution demanded a more sober approach, Madison chose not to treat freeholders as they arrived to vote, a decision that caused him to lose the election to Charles Porter, a barkeep who offered an ample supply of spirits.[21]

Porter took Madison's seat in the assembly, but delegates there remembered the impressive young man from Orange, and on November 15, 1777, they elected him to serve as one of the eight members of the Council of State, a body that had to concur with the governor's decisions in order for him to act. Madison thus became, in the words of his biographer Irving Brant, "one-ninth of a governor."[22]

On Madison's first day on the council, he saw the complexities of the war that America was waging. Although American forces under the command of General Horatio Gates had won a crucial victory at Saratoga, General Washington's men were suffering. Together with Governor Henry council members took up a letter from a congressional committee, "representing the alarming accounts of the distresses of the American army" at Valley Forge. Washington had reported that unless provisions were sent, the army would *"starve, dissolve,* or *disperse,"* and the committee wanted Virginia's help. Appalled at the incompetence of the Continental commissary, which should have been supplying the troops, Henry and the council nonetheless sent agents to track down cattle and hogs for Washington's men. "It will indeed be unworthy [of] the character of a zealous American to entrench himself within the strict line of official duty," Henry wrote.[23]

Virginia, meanwhile, had begun to conduct diplomacy and war on its own. On his first day on the council, Madison voted approval of orders to Colonel David Rogers to recruit thirty men at double pay and proceed down the Mississippi, ascertaining British strength along the way. In New Orleans, Rogers was to acquire provisions and, if possible, obtain a loan from the Spanish governor of Louisiana, Bernardo de Gálvez. With the orders to Rogers, Henry enclosed a letter for Gálvez and an explanation that a missive formerly sent was so badly translated into French—the language of diplomacy—that "the meaning . . . was omitted."[24] Madison, with his competent French and, one assumes, great tact, likely helped Henry realize that his previous letter to the Spanish governor had been gibberish.

Madison probably learned within a few days of beginning service on the council of another of Henry's undertakings, this one aimed at protecting Virginia's interest in its western lands, a vast stretch of territory northwest of the Ohio River, which the commonwealth claimed under its royal charters. Henry had agreed to a plan put forward by George Rogers Clark, a charismatic red-haired militia major, for Clark to undertake a campaign aimed at driving the British out of the western lands and subduing their Indian allies. During Madison's time on the Council of State, Clark would accomplish one seemingly impossible feat after another, including capturing both the fort at Vincennes and the lieutenant governor of Detroit, Henry Hamilton. Eventually, Clark's luck would turn, but not before his Virginia-sponsored foray earned him a place in the history books as "the conqueror of the Northwest."[25]

When the council and the governor decided to seek European financial support for the war, Thomas Jefferson, serving in the House of Delegates, suggested his neighbor, Philip Mazzei, as an agent, a cause that Madison took up. Mazzei, who had come to the Piedmont from Tuscany to introduce wine making to Virginia, was commissioned to seek a loan for 900,000 pounds in Europe. Genial and outgoing, Mazzei hoped for the best as he sailed but prepared for the worst. "I have put my papers with a four-pounds ball in a bag to be thrown overboard, if prudence should require it," he told Madison. Mazzei's ship was stopped by a British privateer before he had sailed through the Virginia Capes, and his papers with the four-pound ball went to the bottom of the Chesapeake. The ship was taken to New York, where Mazzei managed to talk the British into letting him sail for Europe. He made it to Paris, where Benjamin Franklin regarded him and other agents acting on behalf of individual states as pests. Franklin apologized to French officials for their behavior.[26]

The failure of this venture into international finance might have been a lesson for both Madison and Jefferson about the hazards of states conducting foreign policy, and for at least the next five years it would have personal consequences as well. In an effort to collect the salary he believed owed to him for his work, the irrepressible Mazzei made the rounds of the powerful in Virginia. In 1784, Madison wrote to Jefferson to warn him that Mazzei was coming to see him. "I tremble at the idea," replied Jefferson, who suffered from migraines. "He will be worse to me than a return of my double quotidian headache."[27]

In later years, Jefferson advanced the idea that Madison had prepared so many of Governor Henry's papers, particularly his foreign correspondence, that he deserved to be recognized as his secretary. The notion is probably exaggerated, but Madison was so skilled at gathering and absorbing information, compiling what was most important from it, and writing quick and cogent responses that Henry, who had a reputation for not liking to take up either book or pen, no doubt found ways to take advantage of his skills. The governor probably relied on Councilor Madison to handle a great deal of routine paperwork and administrative detail, which might account for Madison's sentiment in later years that the council was "a grave of useful talents."[28]

After Henry had served as governor for three years, the maximum allowed, the assembly elected Thomas Jefferson his successor. The tall, loose-limbed Virginian entered office at a time when British strategy had undergone a significant change. The victory of the United States at Saratoga had been a devastating blow to Great Britain, not least because it had persuaded the French to sign a treaty of alliance with the United States. Shaken by the course of the war in the North, the British had shifted focus to the South, which they saw as more vulnerable and where they believed Loyalist sympathies ran particularly strong. By the time Jefferson moved into the governor's palace, the British had taken Savannah, were menacing Charleston, and had sent a flotilla into the Chesapeake, where their troops seized Portsmouth, burned Suffolk, and destroyed ships, armaments, and tobacco. As Jefferson tried to secure the commonwealth and deal with the myriad issues that war brought to his desk, he came to place high value on what he described as Madison's "extensive information" and "the powers and polish of his pen."[29] He no doubt learned, too, that Councilor Madison had a deft political mind, one that instinctively saw contingencies and thought of ways to prepare for them.

An issue that Jefferson and the council had to take up early concerned the treatment of the now-imprisoned lieutenant governor of Detroit, Henry Hamilton. Jefferson's approach to those taken in combat had heretofore been very gentlemanly. He had befriended, even socialized with, captured Hessian and British officers that the Continental Congress had quartered near Monticello. But Hamilton was widely known as "the hair-buyer general" for reportedly encouraging Great Britain's Indian allies to murder and scalp Americans, and the governor and the council decided he deserved to be kept in shackles. Within weeks, General William Phillips, one of the British officers Jefferson had befriended in the Piedmont, protested Hamilton's treatment, writing that since the lieutenant governor of Detroit had surrendered, he could not, according to the rules of war, be put in "close confinement." To Jefferson, this seemed like nonsense, but someone—and it is easy to imagine Madison playing the part—suggested being absolutely sure that George Washington saw things similarly. The general, previously notified of the decision, had not objected, but if there was controversy, perhaps he would. With the council, Jefferson wrote a letter to Washington that took the form of seeking information. Did the general know of any rule prohibiting the confinement of those who agreed to surrender?[30]

As it turned out, once controversy developed, Washington had second thoughts, writing that "this subject, on more mature consideration, appears to be involved in greater difficulty than I apprehended." Hamilton could "be confined to a room" but not shackled, he wrote.[31] The decision rankled Jefferson, but at least he was not in the embarrassing position of having been overruled. Thanks to the council letter, he was instead enlightened by a clarification he had sought.

THE FRIENDSHIP that began to form between Jefferson and Madison as they labored on the council was in some ways unlikely. Although only eight years Jefferson's junior, Madison seemed much younger. He was single, leading a bachelor's life, staying in rooms here and there when he was away from home. While he served on the Council of State, he stayed with his cousin, also named James Madison, an Anglican cleric and the president of the College of William and Mary. Councilor Madison's room in the president's house was better lodging than he would otherwise have had in Williamsburg, but his personal life still had a harum-scarum quality. Someone took his hat, his only hat, forcing him to stay indoors for two days until at last he managed to buy another "from a little Frenchman who sold snuff." His horse either wandered off or was stolen, and he advertised for it in the *Virginia Gazette* of October 30, 1779, offering a hundred-dollar reward, which might have been too

much, particularly if it was the horse his father had sent him the previous June. Madison had described that animal as being in "meager
plight."[32]

Jefferson was a family man with a beautiful wife, Martha Wayles
Skelton, who had brought him a great landed estate, albeit one encum-
bered by debt. The two had lost a daughter before she reached her second birthday and a son in infancy, but Patsy and Polly, much-adored
little girls, survived. Prior to Jefferson's moving into the governor's mansion, he and his family lived for a time in Williamsburg's loveliest home,
the George Wythe house on Palace Green, where Wythe slaves as well
as Jefferson slaves would have attended them. Well cared for as he was,
Jefferson was unlikely to have his hat go missing, and he certainly never
rode a horse in "meager plight." His steeds were magnificent—and spot-
less. "When his saddle horse was led out," wrote Henry Randall, who
interviewed Jefferson family members, "if there was a spot on him that
did not shine as faultlessly as a mirror, he rubbed it with a white pocket
handkerchief, and if this was soiled, the groom was reprimanded."[33]

The men were alike in being reserved. Neither would have dreamed
of keeping a diary full of the personal observations that John Adams
recorded, but among friends both would offer frank, even barbed assessments of others. Madison also liked to poke fun at himself, which
was not a habit of Jefferson's. Madison amused close acquaintances with
a fund of self-deprecating anecdotes, including the story of how he had
managed to lose reelection to the House of Delegates "in consequence
of his refusing to electioneer." In years ahead, he'd also entertain friends
by telling about his stolen hat. He particularly enjoyed describing the
replacement, which was so small in the crown and broad in the brim
that his friends found it an object of endless merriment.[34]

Both men loved chess. Jefferson also loved music and poetry, but
Madison, with no known musical penchant, had decided that life was
too short and the demands of the real world too pressing for him to
spend much time reading poems and plays. Jefferson was the more soaring thinker and would leave behind some of the most uplifting prose
ever written. Madison's genius showed itself in the dismantling of con-

ventional wisdom and the creation of new concepts. Jefferson's ideas sometimes became untethered from reality, but Madison drew him back to the solid earth—and often found himself inspired by the adventure. Thus, they complemented each other, or as historian Merrill Peterson described their relationship, "The account balanced."[35]

They both had disorders that sometimes disrupted their lives. Within months of the time that Madison experienced a sudden attack during military training, Jefferson was incapacitated for weeks with one of the migraines that plagued him. Neither man hesitated to describe the gastrointestinal ailments from which he and almost everyone else in the eighteenth century suffered. Jefferson described being taken ill with dysentery in his autobiography. Madison noted the progress of a bowel complaint in a letter to George Washington.[36] But Jefferson did not talk much about his headaches, and Madison was even more circumspect about his sudden attacks, Jefferson likely being in the small circle of those in whom he confided.

Each was probably the brightest person the other ever knew, and both were well schooled, giving them a vast fund of common learning on which to draw as they talked and planned. Both continued to study throughout life and considered books of mighty importance. Each was known to buy them when they became available whether he had ready cash or not, but Jefferson's acquisitive instincts went beyond Madison's, at times doing violation not only to his finances but to good manners. When Randolph the Tory decided to sail for England rather than support the American rebellion, Jefferson wrote him a heartfelt letter regretting his departure, commenting on the state of human affairs that made it necessary, and asking if he might be interested in selling some of his books.[37]

One of the most important bonds between Madison and Jefferson was Virginia. They knew its seasons, from the redbuds of spring to the orange and gold leaves of sweet gum trees in the fall. They had internalized its pleasant manners and hospitality, and they knew its failings. Neither found much appeal in the gambling and fox hunting to which many a young Virginian devoted his time. The indolence that northerners found disconcerting in the South, particularly in the Tidewater, was no part of their daily existence. When the Virginia Convention adopted the proposal of a committee headed by George Mason to put the Latin words for "God bestowed upon us this leisure" on the seal of the commonwealth, Jefferson erupted. "For god's sake," he wrote, "what is the *Deus nobis haec otia fecit*?" During the time he was governor and Madison on the council, the words were replaced with *Perseverando*.[38]

They both hated slavery, upon which Virginia's culture and commerce were built. They understood the contradiction between the liberty they sought for mankind and the servitude they witnessed daily, yet at the end of long lives they would both die owning slaves.

A traveler noted that Virginians were "haughty and jealous of their liberties, impatient of restraint, and can scarcely bear the thought of being controlled by any superior power." In none of the founders did this spirit burn more brightly than in Madison and Jefferson, and it might have formed their strongest bond, animating them not only to throw off British rule when it became oppressive but to build a new country in which religious freedom—which both saw as part and parcel of intellectual freedom—was assured. Madison's zeal in this cause was likely heightened by the misery he knew as a young man when he realized that Christian orthodoxy insisted on a supernatural explanation for epilepsy. For Jefferson there is no event to pinpoint, "no certain way of knowing," as his biographer Dumas Malone put it, "just when this apostle of freedom first swore eternal hostility against every form of tyranny over the mind of man."[39] It may be telling that they were both men of the Piedmont, the upcountry, where life was more rugged than in the Tidewater and individual pride in overcoming the challenges of isolation and distance more deeply embedded. Jefferson and Madison were from land not long removed from either the frontier or the frontiersman's independent mind.

Beginning June 1, 1779, Governor Jefferson and Councilor Madison met with other council members in daily sessions that began at ten each morning on the second floor of the capitol in Williamsburg. In mid-July, as the malarial season was about to begin, Madison left for Orange

County, not to return until late October, then, on December 16, 1779, he left the council for good when the House of Delegates chose him to serve in the Continental Congress. Thus the two men worked together on the council only thirteen or fourteen weeks, but it was long enough, in Madison's words, that "an intimacy took place."[40] After that, they were often apart, sometimes for years, but their mutual work continued. They encouraged, defended, and had a profound effect on each other— and on the nation they helped build.

Chapter 4

A ROPE OF SAND

WHEN GEORGE WASHINGTON considered how poorly paid, ill-clothed, and ill-fed his army was, he knew exactly where to place the blame—on the Continental Congress. "The great and important concerns of the nation are horribly conducted," he wrote to Benjamin Harrison, Speaker of the Virginia House. It was his "pious wish" that "each state . . . not only choose but absolutely compel their ablest men to attend Congress."[1]

Washington no doubt had in mind luminaries such as Thomas Jefferson and George Mason, but Jefferson was governor of the commonwealth and his wife was often sick, while Mason worried about his motherless children. Philadelphia was many days' travel away, and Congress never recessed, making it extraordinarily difficult for anyone who had a family or needed to earn a living. Madison's friend Edmund Randolph would twice resign from the Continental Congress in order to practice law and support his wife and children.[2]

Madison was thrilled to be asked to be part of the Virginia Assembly's effort to improve its congressional representation. He did not forget to be modest, but his eagerness was apparent as he offered Speaker

Harrison his "assurances that as far as fidelity and zeal can supply the place of abilities, the interests of my country shall be punctually promoted."[3] He had neither wife nor child to support. In fact, his father was willing to support him—albeit sometimes grudgingly. And he might also have had an idea that Congress, much smaller than the Virginia Assembly and with far fewer eminences, was a place where a bright young man who worked very hard could have a large impact.

A winter of unprecedented harshness kept him from leaving for Philadelphia promptly, but he used the time to delve into a problem that lay behind many others bedeviling Congress and the American cause: money. The paper that Congress was issuing to pay for the war had become nearly worthless, and as snow fell on the hills of the Piedmont and rivers froze, Madison pored over books trying to understand the country's troubled finances. Montesquieu and Hume maintained that the value of money decreased as its quantity increased, but Madison decided more was at work, namely, "the credit of the state issuing [the currency] and . . . the time of its redemption." If the military prospects of the United States improved, he sensibly concluded, faith in the country's future would help keep its currency afloat. So, too, would setting a time specific for redemption. Congress had not made such a commitment for several years.[4]

But redeeming currency meant levying taxes, and as Madison traveled to Philadelphia in the company of Billey, one of the family slaves, he no doubt thought about this most basic problem: the Continental Congress had no power to raise money. It was financially dependent on the states, and they were reluctant to use their taxing authority. Unless something changed drastically, Continental currency would continue its decline, a situation made worse by the fact that wartime demand would also continue exerting upward pressure on prices. Sugar already cost ten times as much as at the beginning of the Revolution, and bacon twenty times.[5]

Madison arrived in Philadelphia to find that Congress had grown so desperate about the country's finances that members had decided to give up all authority over money matters. Going forward, the states were to redeem Continental currency and, as that was done, take over the issuance of new money. "An old system of finance" was "discarded as incompetent to our necessities," Madison wrote to Jefferson, and "an untried and precarious one substituted." There was the prospect of "a total stagnation . . . between the end of the former and the operation of the latter." Meanwhile, a widening circle of difficulties was being created by the country's financial woes: "Our army threatened with an immediate alternative of disbanding or living on free quarter; the public treasury empty, public credit exhausted; . . . Congress complaining of the extortion of the people, the people of the improvidence of Congress, and the army of both; our affairs requiring the most mature and systematic measures, and the urgency of occasions admitting only of temporizing expedients and those expedients generating new difficulties." Like Washington before him—indeed, like much of the country by this time—Madison concluded that the Continental Congress, with its "defect of adequate statesmen," was not likely to solve the nation's problems. The mediocrity of its members meant that it was "more likely to fall into wrong measures and [be] of less weight to enforce right ones," he wrote.[6]

THE YEAR AHEAD, the worst of the war, would complicate this assessment. Even the most enlightened delegate, Madison would find, could fall into wrong measures when he lacked adequate information, which members of the Continental Congress usually did. At the end of May 1780, Rivington's *Royal Gazette* put out an extra edition describing the fall of Charleston to the British. Was this to be believed? Or did "the notorious character for lying of the author," as Madison wrote to Jefferson, "leave some hope that it is fictitious"? As it became clear that Charleston had indeed capitulated and nearly the whole of the army in the South had surrendered, the obvious response, or so it seemed to Madison, was to send more troops. As part of a committee, he proposed that Major Henry "Light-Horse Harry" Lee, a Virginian whom he had known at Princeton, "proceed immediately to South Carolina with the

corps under his command," a recommendation forwarded to General
Washington on behalf of Congress. Within weeks, however, delegates
heard from Washington of a battle in New Jersey that was too close to
Philadelphia for comfort. They reversed themselves, endorsing Washington's recommendation that Lee's corps march north.[7]

Madison came to see that the Continental Congress could be a con-
clave of statesmen and still not operate effectively. Not only had the
power of the purse been handed over to the states, so, too, had authority for raising, provisioning, and paying the army. The states were "dilatory" in providing resources, Madison reported to John Page, with
whom he had served on the Virginia Council of State. But there was
nothing Congress could do. Its members could "neither enlist, pay, nor
feed a single soldier," as Madison described it.[8]

All that was left was "to administer public affairs with prudence,
vigor, and economy," and even in that task the delegates' labors were
sometimes counterproductive. When Congress undertook a campaign
to reform abuses in the procurement and transport of goods, Washington's quartermaster and favorite general, Nathanael Greene, was soon
in the crosshairs. The forceful, thin-skinned Greene hadn't wanted to
be quartermaster in the first place. In defiance of his Quaker father, he
had read the works of great military leaders such as Julius Caesar and
Frederick the Great growing up, and it was field command that he found
satisfying. But Washington had prevailed upon him to take the quartermaster's position and had kept him there by releasing him to take
part in battle from time to time. Greene had little patience with congressional suggestions that some of the thousands of agents procuring
supplies for him were corrupt. Indeed, he had little patience with the
"talking gentlemen" of Congress, who, as he saw it, "tired themselves
and everybody else with their long, labored speeching that is calculated
more to display their own talents than promote the public interest."[9]

Because he worked on commission rather than salary, Greene had
made a good deal of money supplying the army, which raised red flags
in Congress, although its members had authorized the arrangement.
Apparently on the theory that he who is abundantly compensated

should be abundantly responsible, delegates began to discuss making Greene personally liable for improper expenditures by his subordinates whether they were fraudulent or merely imprudent. Hearing of this, Greene wrote an eleven-page letter detailing his objections to this "strange, new, and unexpected . . . doctrine." The official resolution in response, written by Congressman Madison, affirmed the principle of Greene's responsibility, adding the caveat that Congress, not wishing "to expose the faithful servants of the public to any unreasonable risks or losses," would "determine on the circumstances as they arise and make such favorable allowances as justice may require." When Greene resigned in fury, Congress threatened to strip him of his rank, at which point Washington entered the fray, backing Congress down on the matter of Greene's commission but having to accept a new quartermaster, Timothy Pickering of Massachusetts, a thin, austere man whom he did not trust.[10]

The results were even worse when Congress concerned itself with one of Washington's least favorite generals, Horatio Gates, widely regarded as the hero of the Battle of Saratoga. During the dark days of Valley Forge, Gates had been put forward by powerful allies as the man who should replace Washington. Although the effort had failed, Washington had not forgotten, and he was dismayed when Congress without notifying him appointed Gates to the southern command. Gates was full of confidence as he arrived in the South to head a newly raised army, but within weeks he made a disastrous decision to lead his men through unfriendly territory to Camden, South Carolina. There he encountered General Charles Cornwallis and his well-trained forces, and on August 16, 1780, they dealt the patriots the war's bloodiest defeat. Gates's army suffered more than two thousand casualties, and Congress, unusually chastened, gave Washington the power to choose Gates's replacement. He put Nathanael Greene in charge.

In the wake of the terrible defeat at Camden came the spectacular and horrifying news that Major General Benedict Arnold had turned traitor. A short, square-jawed man full of energy and ambition, he was one of America's most renowned warriors. Many thought it was he who should be credited for the American victory at Saratoga. He had married a young and wealthy heiress, Peggy Shippen of Philadelphia, but was nonetheless deeply in debt. Convinced that his country did not sufficiently appreciate him, he agreed that in exchange for a handsome payment and a British commission he would surrender West Point. As Madison and other members of the Virginia delegation described Arnold's actions to Governor Jefferson, he "shamefully, treacherously, and ignominiously deserted the important post at West Point, which garrison he commanded, after having concerted measures . . . for delivering it up to the enemy." The plot to hand the fortress over to the British was foiled, but Arnold escaped to a British warship, and American morale suffered a heavy blow.[11]

The discouraging course of the war and the frustrations of Congress helped drive many delegates home, but Madison had no intention of giving up. While others dropped in and out of their duties, he remained in Philadelphia, comfortable in Mary House's lodgings at the corner of Market and Fifth and enjoying the friendship of Eliza Trist. Among the others boarding at Mrs. House's was William Floyd of New York. While Madison's recommendation seems to have persuaded Virginia delegates James Henry, Joseph Jones, and John Walker to join him at Mrs. House's, Floyd might have brought New Yorkers Robert Livingston, John Morin Scott, and James Duane to their table. The last two congressmen were of special service to Mrs. House when she was sued in 1780 by Joseph Bulkley, a man with whom she seems to have had some past close relationship. Scott and Duane defended her, though not successfully enough to prevent a sheriff from seizing furnishings from the house. Shortly after this drama, Mrs. House's establishment, like several other buildings in Philadelphia, was struck by lightning. Although hers was the worst damaged, the harm was less than it might have been because, the *Pennsylvania Packet* reported, a bell wire conducted the lightning through several rooms to the ground. "This incident affords an additional proof of the utility of the electrical rods invented by the ingenious Dr. Franklin," the *Packet* opined.[12]

These domestic crises no doubt reinforced the camaraderie growing out of the great common cause in which Mrs. House's boarders were involved. One imagines the lodgers gathered around the parlor fire, discussing Great Britain's southern campaign, Benedict Arnold's treachery, and, occasionally, the lawsuit and lightning strikes.

Living at Mrs. House's was not cheap. Madison's boarding bill for the first six months was more than twenty-one thousand dollars, an amount that underscored how inflationary the times were, particularly in Philadelphia. Madison's fellow boarder William Floyd declared that "the devil was with all his emissaries let loose in this state to ruin our money." Madison made loans to his congressional classmate Joseph Jones and also helped out Theodorick Bland, elected from Virginia in 1780 and often a thorn in Madison's side. Tall, wavy-haired, and given to making florid speeches, Bland, who was married to the beautiful, utterly frivolous Martha Dangerfield Bland, complained that his money "evaporated like smoke," leaving him "without the means of buying a dinner or . . . a bait of oats for my horses." When Madison ran low on funds himself, he applied to his father, apparently with some success, but Edmund Randolph seems to have been a surer source of financial support, as was Haym Soloman, a moneylender on Front Street, who refused, despite Madison's insistence, to charge him interest.[13]

From Mrs. House's establishment it was an easy walk to the statehouse, where the thirty or so members of Congress attended sessions on the second floor. The boardinghouse was also near the French legation on Chestnut Street, which had been recently and elegantly enlarged. The chevalier de la Luzerne, the French minister, hosted fine parties there, events particularly appreciated by Martha Bland. "Oh, my dear, such a swarm of French beaux, counts, viscounts, barons, and chevaliers," she gushed to her sister-in-law. Mrs. Bland adored what she called the "dissipation" of Philadelphia and did not appreciate the lack of jollity displayed by the Virginia delegation. Madison, "a gloomy, stiff creature," was particularly annoying. "They say [he] is clever in Congress, but out of it he has nothing engaging or even bearable in his manners—the most unsociable creature in existence."[14] One doubts that Madison would have been bothered by her assessment.

. . .

MADISON WAS WELL AWARE of the importance of staying close to the French. Even before the American victory at Saratoga had persuaded them to sign a treaty of alliance with the United States, they had provided essential aid, including money and arms. More was needed, however, if America was to win its war for independence, particularly naval power. American hopes had been raised when the chevalier de Ternay arrived in Newport in July 1780 with seven ships of the line and dozens of transports carrying thousands of French regulars under the command of the illustrious comte de Rochambeau, but summer passed, and both navy and army remained in Newport. For a time in September it seemed as though a large French fleet from the West Indies was off the coast, but Madison had to inform his fellow Virginia congressman Joseph Jones that the ships that had been spotted were actually British ships of the line and frigates.[15]

After the great patriot loss at Camden, South Carolina, frustration with the French reached new levels in Virginia. Joseph Jones wanted to know if Luzerne had explained France's failure to act. "I must confess I am at a loss how fully to satisfy the doubts of some and to silence the insinuations of others who ground their observations upon the transactions of the present year," he wrote. Madison had by now mastered the art of being reassuring, on the one hand, without criticizing the source of the anxiety, on the other. He told Jones that those aware of the reason for French delay understood the consternation it was causing, but "as they give no intimations on the subject it is to be inferred they are unable to give any."[16]

Late October brought good news of a patriot victory at Kings Mountain, South Carolina, but it was followed shortly by word of a British invasion force in the Chesapeake. The British operated mostly around the mouth of the James River and left after a month, but their presence raised ever more urgently for Virginians the question of when France's army and naval forces would engage. It was a measure of the high regard in which Madison was increasingly held that the distinguished Edmund Pendleton had asked to correspond with him, and when the older man

expressed his mystification over French inaction, Madison sympa-
thized—while at the same time praising the French. "The motions of
our allies are no less mysterious here than they appear to you," he wrote.
"We have however experienced so many proofs of [French] wisdom and
goodness towards us that we ought not on slight grounds to abate our
faith in them. For my own part I have as yet great confidence in both."[17]

MADISON REALIZED EARLY in his congressional career that while
he should give due regard to what eminent Virginians had to say, he also
needed to exercise his own judgment. When Arthur Lee, one of the
most contentious men ever to be part of American public life, was recalled from his position as a commissioner in France, he launched an
attack on Benjamin Franklin, who was serving as America's minister
plenipotentiary in Paris. The relentlessly ambitious Lee claimed in a
letter to Congress that "Dr. Franklin is now much advanced in years,
more devoted to pleasure than would become even a young man in his
station, and neglectful of the public business." Madison's fellow Virginia
delegate Theodorick Bland, the chairman of the committee to investigate Franklin, allied himself with Lee, unaware that he, too, had once
been the object of a wicked assessment by a member of the Lee family.
"Never intended for the department of military intelligence," Light-
Horse Harry Lee, Arthur's brother, said of Bland.[18]

As a young man Madison had made brash comments about Franklin's trustworthiness, but he now became his defender, voting against a
proposal to send an envoy to France to do what Franklin was supposedly
failing to do. After the motion passed despite his opposition, Madison
drafted instructions to the envoy that were tailored to support Franklin.
In the end, Franklin saved himself from this particular attack by securing a much-needed loan of ten million livres from the French, but he
and Madison had become firmly allied. When future assaults were
made on the elderly Pennsylvanian, he would find the young Virginian
at his side. For this and other transgressions, Madison drew the cantan-
kerous Lee's ire, but it was perhaps a measure of his political skill that

he managed to avoid the worst of it. Lee wrote of Madison, "Without being a public knave himself, he has always been the supporter of public knaves"—which coming from Lee was practically praise.[19]

At times Madison was bound by instructions from Virginia's legislature, as in the matter of the navigation of the Mississippi. Upon entering the war against Great Britain, Spain had closed the lower part of the river to all but Spanish commerce. This was fine with the French, who hoped that letting Spain have its way would encourage greater Spanish involvement against Britain, but Virginia regarded free use of the Mississippi as crucial to its economy—particularly in the Kentucky part of the commonwealth, which was not yet a separate state. Thus the Virginia Assembly instructed its representatives in Congress to insist on open navigation of the Mississippi, which Madison most willingly did. Elected to chair a committee to explain Congress's position to John Jay, a tall, solemn New Yorker who had recently been president of Congress and was now minister to Spain, Madison drafted a letter setting forth a vision of the "vast extent" of land west of the Alleghenies. "In a very few years, after peace shall take place, this country will certainly be overspread with inhabitants," Madison wrote. He imagined them cultivating fertile soil, raising wheat, corn, beef, tobacco, hemp, and flax—and needing a way to carry on commerce. "The clear indications of nature and providence and the general good of mankind," he wrote to Jay, required that these "citizens of the United States" have "free use of the river."[20]

But rumors of peace began to undercut his position. Neutral powers were said to be supporting a plan that would settle the North American conflict by giving contending parties possession of lands they currently occupied. With crucial parts of Georgia and South Carolina under military occupation, delegates from those states were desperate to do anything that might pull Spain into an alliance and push the British out of their territory before such a settlement occurred—including giving up free use of the Mississippi. Madison argued that free navigation was too important to concede "as long as there is a possibility of retaining it" and contended that Spain was trying "to alarm us into concessions."

But Theodorick Bland decided it was time for the Virginia Assembly to reconsider its instructions to congressional delegates and took the unusual step of writing a personal letter to Governor Jefferson. With many protestations about the "sense of . . . duty" that impelled him to go behind the backs of the rest of the delegation and communicate with the governor directly, Bland argued that free navigation should not stand in the way of "overtures" from Spain that might "relieve our present necessities" and "promise us peace and a firm establishment of our independence."[21]

Bland's view became very convincing to Virginians when, in December 1780, the British sailed into the Chesapeake again, this time with the newly minted British brigadier general Benedict Arnold heading the fleet. Fearful of going the way of Georgia and South Carolina, the Virginia legislature instructed the state's representatives in the Continental Congress to give up free navigation of the Mississippi if that was the price of a Spanish alliance.

The change in Virginia's instructions tilted the balance in Congress, and Madison found himself having to write a letter to Jay altering his orders. The experience was likely a bitter one, since Madison was convinced that cession was a mistake. Jay agreed, believing as Madison did that while Spain wanted America to give over navigation rights, it had no real intention of entering into an alliance. Jay included the concession in a series of offers that he thought Spain would be unlikely to embrace—a judgment that proved correct.[22]

WITH ARNOLD and his fleet at the mouth of the James River, Virginia's assembly fled Richmond, which its members had made the commonwealth's capital some twenty months previously, but just before leaving, they took a crucial vote and agreed to cede the western lands, the territory northwest of the Ohio River that Virginia had long claimed under its royal charter. Other states viewed the lands as belonging to the country as a whole, and Madison agreed that they were properly national—but only if they were used to create free and independent states. It galled him to think of them going to satisfy what he called the "avidity of land mongers," speculators who swarmed Congress, pressing dubious claims. He was furious when he realized that Theodorick Bland and another Virginia delegate, John Walker, were acting on behalf of these interests. He believed the two men were naive rather than corrupt, but he was still so angry that he vowed to make them personally explain the whole matter to the Virginia Assembly. Upon "cooler reflection," however, he decided that the proper course was to get the assembly to put protections against speculators in place—which he did.[23]

Virginia's offer to cede the western lands opened the way for the Articles of Confederation, sent to the states in 1777, finally to go into effect. They created a loose confederacy of the states, with a congress at the center. There was no executive branch, no national judiciary, and each state, no matter its size, had a single vote. Unanimous ratification of the articles was required, and Maryland had refused to sign until there was a Virginia cession. It would be another three years before agreement between Virginia and the United States was complete, but the resolution from the Virginia Assembly was enough for Maryland, and its delegates notified Congress on February 12, 1781, that they had authority to sign the articles.[24]

THE CRISES MADISON dealt with during his first year in Congress did not come in neat sequential order. A starving army, French delays, Arnold's betrayal, Jay's instructions, the western lands—all came rushing at him at a time when the larger cause of which they were part was doubtful. Underscoring the perilous state of the war was a mutiny in the Pennsylvania line that started on New Year's Day 1781. Enlisted men encamped near winter quarters in Morristown, New Jersey, seized weapons, fired on officers, and set off for Philadelphia to demand redress. "The grievances complained of," Madison wrote to Governor Jefferson, "were principally a detention of many in service beyond the term of enlistment and the sufferings of all from a deficient supply of clothing and subsistence and long arrearage of pay." The president of Pennsylvania met with the mutineers and agreed to discharge those who had served more than three years—which amounted to more than thirteen hundred men.[25] Civilian authorities had averted a crisis but set a dangerous precedent. How long before other American soldiers took up arms against their officers?

Meanwhile, Madison learned that Arnold and his men had sailed up the James River and invaded Richmond, burning and pillaging there and in the surrounding countryside. They destroyed records, warehouses, and mills, all the while meeting little resistance. After Arnold had sailed back downriver, Madison wrote to Pendleton, "I am glad to hear that Arnold has been at last fired at."[26]

There was good news from South Carolina, where Virginia general Daniel Morgan and his men celebrated a stunning victory over the legendary Banastre Tarleton at Cowpens, but at nearly the same time word came of a mutiny among New Jersey troops. Not long after, Nathanael Greene and his army began a retreat across the Carolinas, seeking the safety of Virginia. General Cornwallis was at their heels.

As these events piled up, Madison seems to have suffered one or more of his sudden attacks. Between January 13 and 31, he is not mentioned in the congressional journal, and there is a similar absence between February 6 and 12. In March he received a letter from his cousin the Reverend James Madison. "I have heard of a severe attack," the future bishop wrote. He knew Congressman Madison very well and seemed aware that he had once suffered an attack after studying too hard and exercising too little. "How do you relish your business?" he inquired. "Does it interfere with riding and so on?"[27]

As though a conversation were going on among a group close to Madison, Edmund Pendleton wrote to him concerned about the effect of wartime pressures on his "crazy constitution," and James Madison Sr., with whom Pendleton had been visiting, requested that his son get him a copy of William Cullen's *First Lines of the Practice of Physic*. Cullen, who had until recently been president of the Royal College of Physicians in Edinburgh, was a man whose opinions were so valued that *First Lines* was one of the few titles smuggled into the United States during the war with Great Britain.[28] Volume 1 of Cullen's work, edited by Dr. Benjamin Rush, was published in Philadelphia in 1781, and it was probably a copy of this edition that Madison sent to his father.

Volume 2 of *First Lines*, also edited by Rush, was published in Philadelphia in 1783, while Madison was still living there. Madison makes no mention of the second volume in his letters, but since it took up "nervous diseases," it would hardly be surprising if he read it. Cullen wrote that epilepsy was caused by a "debility" arising from "original conformation"—a description very close to the "constitutional liability" to which Madison attributed his attacks. Cullen's description of *"aura eleptica"* would have interested Madison, whose attacks seem to have involved a feeling in his chest. Cullen described "a sensation of something moving in some part of the limbs or trunk of the body and from thence creeping upwards to the head." But most significant was Cullen's description of "particular convulsions which are to be distinguished from epilepsy by their being more partial . . . and are not attended with a loss of sense." Here was authority for Madison's describing his attacks as "somewhat resembling epilepsy."[29]

Cullen mentioned iron, copper, flowers of zinc, mercury, and arsenic as being used to treat epilepsy arising from a "debility" but clearly preferred "a considerable change of climate, diet, and other circumstances in the manner of life." Many sensible thinkers made this recommendation, but in the middle of war taking a leave was no easy matter. Indeed, Theodorick Bland had taken advantage of Madison's absence from Congress in February. Both he and Madison had been working to secure French naval aid for Virginia, but on February 9, 1781, with Madison apparently unwell at Mrs. House's, Bland informed Governor Thomas Jefferson that "my personal application, singly, has been unremitted . . . to have a line of battleship and one or two frigates sent into our bay." He wrote that he had lately "redoubled these applications and enforced them with the strongest arguments I could address," and "the Minister of France has communicated to me and charged me with secrecy to every soul but your excellency" that the French were sending "one or two ships of the line and two frigates into our bay."[30]

As it turned out, claiming credit for getting the French to undertake this particular military action was a bad idea. Washington was furious. He had been working to get not a squadron but the entire French fleet to sail, and he pointed out to Virginia delegate Joseph Jones that because he was circumvented, the moment was lost for sending the commonwealth the full succor it needed. Madison put a copy of the letter from Washington to Jones in his own files, as if to point future historians to Bland's machinations.[31]

The attack that Madison might have suffered in the early months of 1781 did not keep him from vigorously advancing the cause of a stronger Congress. The church bells celebrating the March 1, 1781, ratification of the Articles of Confederation had scarcely ceased to peal when he began to argue that under the new framework a majority of states present and voting should prevail on ordinary matters. If, as some delegates wanted, the votes of seven states (a majority of the thirteen) were required to pass every measure, the result would be that when only seven states were present, one could prevent action desired by six; if eight states were present, two could block action; and so on. Madison saw this as a recipe for weakness, which indeed it was, but in a time when Americans were fighting a revolution to throw off an oppressive government, most states wanted Congress to be weak. The rule that Madison argued for was defeated.

Thomas Rodney of Delaware was one of the delegates on the other side. A new arrival in Congress, he took an instant dislike to Madison, describing him as having "some little reading in the law," being "just from the college," and possessing "all the self-conceit that is common to youth and inexperience in like cases—but . . . unattended with that gracefulness and ease which sometimes makes even the impertinence of youth and inexperience agreeable or at least not offensive." Rodney was a thoroughgoing eccentric who claimed to have personal visits from archangels, but odd though he was, his comment about the thirty-year-old Madison being fresh from college is revealing.[32] A miniature painted by Charles Willson Peale about this time shows how Rodney might have made this mistake. The overall impression is of slender youth—except for Madison's eyes, which seem to be making a very sharp assessment.

Rodney might have been reacting to Madison's undisguised disapproval of Delaware's recent actions. That state refused to go along with an embargo on the export of foodstuffs that was intended to ensure there were adequate provisions for the army. As Madison described it to Jefferson, "Delaware absolutely declined coming into the measure and not only defeated the general object of it, but enriched herself at the expense of those who did their duty." Madison proposed an amendment to the Articles of Confederation authorizing Congress "to employ the force of the United States as well by sea as by land" to force recalcitrant states to fulfill their federal obligations.[33]

Madison had no better luck with this amendment than with his effort to obtain what he believed to be a practical definition of a majority, and while he labored in futility, news of the war seemed increasingly grim. General Nathanael Greene performed brilliantly, escaping into Virginia, obtaining reinforcements, and turning back into North Carolina. He destroyed a quarter of Cornwallis's army at Guilford Courthouse before withdrawing from the field in order to save his own army for future combat. Left with fewer than fifteen hundred men, Cornwallis decided to cross into Virginia, where he united with British forces now under the command of Major General William Phillips, Jefferson's erstwhile friend, whose second-in-command was British brigadier general Benedict Arnold. Washington had sent the marquis de Lafayette with a small force to aid Virginia, but they were well outnumbered by the combined British forces and could do little to stop their rampages. In June, Cornwallis sent an expedition under Banastre Tarleton to Charlottesville, to which the Virginia legislature had retreated from Richmond. The raiders took a number of assemblymen prisoner and nearly captured Thomas Jefferson, who fled Monticello just as British dragoons were approaching.[34]

Madison pinned his hope for relief for Virginia on the French joining General Washington in a siege of New York, a move that, he believed, "will certainly oblige the enemy to withdraw their force from the southern states." In August, however, it became clear that French might was going to be brought to bear on the British in Virginia itself. A huge fleet under the command of Admiral de Grasse was sailing for the Chesapeake from the West Indies and would be met there by the French fleet from Newport. Meanwhile, the American and French armies were on the march to Virginia. Madison watched them pass through Philadelphia, the Americans first, lean and ragged, followed by the French, polished, shining, and exact in their maneuvers. "Nothing can exceed the appearance of this specimen which our ally has sent us of his army," Madison wrote.[35]

French forces at sea and American and French forces on land came together in near-perfect conjunction, trapping General Cornwallis on the Virginia peninsula at Yorktown and forcing him to surrender his entire garrison of some seven thousand British soldiers. When the news reached Philadelphia on the early morning of October 24, there was an outpouring of joy. Citizens thronged into the streets, and that night the city was aglow as Philadelphians lit candles in their windows. An elated Madison wrote to Edmund Pendleton, "If these severe doses of ill fortune do not cool the frenzy and relax the pride of Britain, it would seem as if heaven had in reality abandoned her to her folly and her fate."[36]

A FORMAL PEACE TREATY was nearly two years away, but it was time, Madison believed, for the United States to face up to its enormous debts. Money was owed not only to foreign creditors but to domestic ones, including the men who had fought the war, and there was great unwillingness on the part of several states to provide Congress with the means to settle those debts. Virginia was one of those states, but Madison took the lead nonetheless in trying to establish a funding stream that would allow the nation to meet its obligations, and he gained a valuable ally when twenty-seven-year-old Alexander Hamilton rode into Philadelphia in November 1782.

A seasoned veteran, despite his young age, Hamilton had crossed the Delaware with George Washington, fought at Trenton and Princeton, and served as the commander in chief's aide-de-camp for more than four years. At the climax of the Revolutionary War, he received what he had long coveted, a battlefield command, and he led his men with great bravery at Yorktown. Like Madison, he was small of stature, or "not tall," as one observer described him, but he was the Virginian's opposite in many other ways.[37] Far from being of respectable lineage, he was the child of an illegitimate union. Rather than having roots stretching far back in America, he had spent his childhood in the British West Indies. Instead of being circumspect, Hamilton was high-strung and impatient, a risk taker, who charmed with cosmopolitan ease. But he and Madison shared brilliance and determination, and it seemed obvious to both that Congress needed a source of revenue to pay the nation's debts.

Underscoring the danger of empty federal coffers was a petition carried to Congress by Major General Alexander McDougall of New York reporting the "great distress" under which the officers and soldiers of the army, long unpaid, were laboring. "We complain that shadows have been offered to us while the substance has been gleaned by others," the memorial asserted, continuing, "We have borne all that men can bear— our property is expended—our private resources are at an end—and our friends are wearied out and disgusted with our incessant applications. We therefore most seriously and earnestly beg that a supply of money may be forwarded to the army as soon as possible. The uneasiness of the soldiers for want of pay is great and dangerous. Any further experiments on their patience may have fatal effects." Madison was deeply sympathetic to the officers' cause, but when he met with them as part of a committee, he kept his counsel. "What can a Virginia delegate say to them," he wrote to his friend Edmund Randolph, when his "constituents declare that they are unable to make the necessary contributions and unwilling to establish funds for obtaining them elsewhere?"[38]

Madison and Hamilton both offered motions declaring the need for Congress to collect funds to meet the nation's obligations. Madison's proposal brought the contentious Arthur Lee, now one of Virginia's delegates, to his feet. He declared Madison's motion to be "repugnant to the Articles of Confederation; and by placing the purse in the same hands with the sword was subversive of the fundamental principles of liberty." Moreover, said Lee, the states were averse to a plan of general revenue, and—in case Madison had forgotten—Lee noted that Virginia, in particular, was opposed.[39]

Hamilton entered the debate and managed to inflame it. Since the federal government lacked energy for "pervading and uniting the states," he declared, federal revenue agents should be sent into the states to supply it. Madison tried to appeal to the delegates' better selves. "The idea of erecting our national independence on the ruins of public faith and national honor must be horrid to every mind which retained either honesty or pride," he said. He reminded his colleagues that the debate in which they were engaged had been precipitated by "a very solemn appeal from the army to the justice and gratitude of their country," and he asked, "Is not this request a reasonable one?" He also noted that "the patience of the army has been equal to their bravery, but that patience must have its limits, and the result of despair cannot be foreseen nor ought it to be risked." In addition, he responded to Arthur Lee by setting forth what he believed it meant to represent a constituency: "Although the delegates who compose Congress more immediately represented and were amenable to the states from which they respectively come, yet in another view they owed a fidelity to the collective interests of the whole." Even in the face of express instructions from his state, Madison said, a delegate would find occasions on which clear conviction should lead him to "hazard personal consequences" and ignore the instructions from home. This was such a time.[40]

Madison's speech resulted in a positive vote on the principle of general revenue, but opposing forces tried to walk the decision back. Arthur Lee took the floor proclaiming that he would "rather see Congress a rope of sand than a rod of iron," but his fiery rhetoric had little effect. A committee that included Madison and Hamilton was directed to come up with a plan for general funds.[41] The program they devised, an impost amendment to the Articles of Confederation, had a 5 percent import tax at its heart, as well as a long-term requisition of $1.5 million a year.

The articles required that each state's share of a requisition be determined by the value of each state's land, a plan that was widely recognized as unworkable since states did not trust one another to determine their own real estate values. In private notes, Madison proposed that instead of "apportioning pecuniary burdens according to the value of land," population be substituted. Because much of the wealth of the South came from slave labor, he further proposed including slaves in the count, "reckoning two slaves as equal to one free man." This became a committee report recommending that the financial burden be apportioned according to each state's "number of white inhabitants" and "one half of the number of all other inhabitants." A debate followed, with several northerners recommending that three-fourths of slaves be counted rather than one-half, which would mean southern states paying more in taxes. Madison did the math and came up with a figure that split the difference—three-fifths—which was accepted.[42]

LIKE OTHER FOUNDERS, Madison understood that slavery was a moral issue. When the Virginia Assembly had proposed encouraging enlistments by granting each enlistee a slave, he had objected, "Would it not be as well to liberate and make soldiers at once of the blacks themselves as to make them instruments for enlisting white soldiers? It would certainly be more consonant to the principles of liberty which ought never to be lost sight of in a contest for liberty." When he became convinced that Billey, the enslaved man who had traveled to Philadelphia with him, had become "too thoroughly tainted" by having lived among free blacks to return to Montpelier, he made arrangements that freed him after a time, perhaps after a period of indentured servitude. "I do not expect to get near the worth of him," Madison wrote to his parsimonious father, "but cannot think of punishing him by transportation merely for coveting that liberty for which we have paid the price of so much blood and have proclaimed so often to be the right and worthy the pursuit of every human being."[43]

But Madison, like political leaders in both the North and the South, was completely capable of laying the morality of slavery aside and dealing with it simply as a fact. And thus it was that a dispassionate debate about revenue gave rise to counting three of every five slaves and creating the three-fifths ratio that would rightly appall future generations. In one of history's ironies, the three-fifths ratio, when later used for purposes of deciding how many representatives a state would have in Congress, would result in slave states having fewer representatives and less power than they would have had if slaves had been reckoned equal to free citizens.

HAMILTON WAS NOT SATISFIED with working the revenue issue solely from within Congress. He joined with others in Philadelphia who believed that the most effective way to get Congress to approve a revenue measure was to bring more pressure to bear from the army. Washington, realizing the direction he was heading, warned him: "The army . . . is a dangerous instrument to play with." Meanwhile, at winter quarters in Newburgh, New York, John Armstrong, who had served as an aide to Horatio Gates, posted an anonymous address "To the Officers of the Army," describing "a country that tramples upon your rights, disdains your cries and insults your distresses." He urged officers to carry their appeal "from the justice to the fears of government."[44] So effective was the address that Washington felt obliged to speak before the officers at Newburgh in order to soothe the mutinous impulses it aroused.

AFTER LONG DEBATE Congress passed the impost amendment, "with the dissent of Rhode Island and the division of New York only," Madison wrote to Jefferson. Hamilton, mercurial as ever, had caused the division, voting no, Madison explained, because he had in mind "a plan which he supposed more perfect."[45] Madison, embracing the art of the possible, composed a letter to the states urging the measure's ratification. He wrote anonymously, as there was good reason for him to do. Opposition in Virginia was strong; the state had voted down an earlier impost; and there was no benefit to be gained from making himself the opponents' main target. Moreover, other states were likely to be skeptical of an appeal from a Virginian since his state had proved an unreliable ally in a previous effort. There were advantages to being a modest man, among them that ego didn't get in the way of smart politics.

He began the letter to the states with the simple proposition that having won the war, the United States now had to pay the debts left by the war, and he listed those to whom the debts must be paid, including "that illustrious and patriotic band of fellow citizens, whose blood and whose bravery have defended the liberties of their country." Paying such debts was not only a fiscal responsibility but a matter of acting honorably, which the country had to do or risk betraying the ideals for which the Revolution had been fought:

> Let it be remembered finally that it has ever been the pride and boast of America that the rights for which she contended were the rights of human nature. By the blessings of the Author of these rights on the means exerted for their defense, they have prevailed against all opposition and form the basis of thirteen independent states. No instance has heretofore occurred, nor can any instance be expected hereafter to occur, in which the unadulterated forms of republican government can pretend to so fair an opportunity of justifying themselves by their fruits. In this view the citizens of the United States are responsible for the greatest trust ever confided to a political society. If justice, good faith, honor, gratitude, and all the other qualities which ennoble the character of a nation and fulfill the ends of government be the fruits of our establishments, the cause of liberty will acquire a dignity and luster which it has never yet enjoyed; and an example will be set which cannot but have the most favorable influence on the rights of mankind. If on the other side, our governments should be unfortunately blotted with the reverse of these cardinal and essential virtues, the great cause which we have engaged to vindicate will be dishonored and betrayed; the last and fairest

experiment in favor of the rights of human nature will be turned against them; and their patrons and friends exposed to be insulted and silenced by the votaries of tyranny and usurpation.[46]

Madison's words traveled across the nation, soon to be supplemented and reinforced by a letter from Washington himself urging ratification of the revenue measure.

At age thirty-two, just three years after entering Congress, James Madison was becoming a leader of the new nation. Some who knew him in Virginia suspected that he was the author of the eloquent letter to the states, but even those who did not were aware of how rapidly his star was rising. One ambitious young Virginian, James Monroe, attributed Madison's success to perseverance: "Mr. Madison I think hath acquired more reputat[io]n by a constant and laborious attendance upon Congress than he would have done had he dashed from Philadelphia here as occasion might require." But more than diligence was involved. Madison grew as he worked, learning every day, acquiring wisdom every day, until he was recognized, in the words of French minister Luzerne, as "the man of the soundest judgment in Congress."[47]

It was a happy time in Madison's life. He had managed to persuade his friend Thomas Jefferson to leave the exile into which he had withdrawn at Monticello. The Virginia Assembly had passed a resolution to investigate Jefferson's actions during the British invasion, and although the delegates had finally declared him blameless, their action wounded him deeply. Then his beloved wife, Martha, died, and he seemed for a time to give up on the world altogether. But Madison brought him back, offering a resolution in Congress to make him a peace negotiator in Paris. Jefferson accepted, stopping in Philadelphia on the way to Baltimore, where his ship was to depart, and staying at Madison's boardinghouse. The two men discussed the nation's affairs, drew up a list of books for a library for Congress, and went over the notes Madison had been taking on congressional proceedings.

After Jefferson departed for Baltimore, the two gossiped by letter. Worried about mail being intercepted, they used an agreed-upon code.

Madison commented on correspondence recently received by Congress "from 503.12.13.1" (Mr. Adams) and noted that it had mainly served as a "274.3 of 407.36.845.15," or "display of his vanity." Jefferson commented on Adams's ill temper, noting that he hated "367.4.483.30" (Franklin), "25.427.6" (Jay), "816.27.1006.39" (the French), and "816.27.1004.1" (the English). "To whom will he adhere?"[48]

Peace negotiations with the British advanced so far that Congress suspended Jefferson's mission to Paris, and in late February the Virginian returned to Philadelphia. He stayed at Mrs. House's until after his mission was formally canceled in April and found the group there (he called them family) in a buoyant mood, their hearts lifted by the prospect of peace, by the promise of springtime—and by the observation that one of their own, James Madison, had fallen in love.

Chapter 5

LOVE AND
OTHER RESOURCES OF HAPPINESS

CATHERINE FLOYD—or Kitty, as family and friends called her—was a pretty girl with light brown hair and dark brown eyes. In a miniature painted about the time that Jefferson noticed Madison's interest in her, she wears her hair upswept in a sophisticated style, but her round face, which does not seem fully formed, and her languid expression mark her for the teenager she was, fifteen, soon to be sixteen, an age thought quite appropriate in the eighteenth century for a female to marry.[1]

Kitty had been just nine when the British took Long Island, where she and her family lived. Her father, William, had been in Philadelphia as the redcoats came ashore at Gravesend Bay, and her mother, Hannah, had taken charge. When the Floyd home was threatened, Hannah buried the family silver and fled with Kitty and her other two children across Long Island Sound to Connecticut.[2] The British occupied the estate, and because Floyd had been a member of the Continental Congress and signed the Declaration of Independence, they undoubtedly took pleasure in felling his trees, killing his livestock, and making off with the family's belongings.

Sent back to Congress in 1779, Floyd had his family join him at Mrs. House's. By 1783, Polly, the older Floyd daughter, was being courted by Major Benjamin Tallmadge, and Kitty, the younger, by Congressman Madison.[3]

Thomas Jefferson, realizing that his friend was in love, immediately set out to discover the young woman's feelings for Madison—and even to make Madison's case. In a letter written shortly after he left Philadelphia, he reported, using code, that he had often made the romance "the subject of conversation," even "exhortation" with Floyd and been able to convince himself "that she possessed every sentiment in your favor which you could wish."[4]

Madison wrote back in code, "Before you left us, I had sufficiently ascertained her sentiments. Since your departure the affair has been pursued. Most preliminary arrangements although definitive will be postponed until the end of the year in Congress. At some period of the interval I shall probably make a visit to Virginia. The interest which your friendship takes on this occasion in my happiness is a pleasing proof that the dispositions which I feel are reciprocal." Madison accompanied the Floyds when they left Philadelphia to return to their home on Long Island in late April 1783, riding with them to Brunswick, New Jersey. There he took his leave and returned to Philadelphia, where he waited for a letter from Kitty setting their wedding date.[5] In early June, he was still planning on a trip to Virginia so that he could make arrangements for married life there, but he hadn't heard from Kitty and was probably beginning to worry.

AS JUNE PROGRESSED, reports began to circulate of troops refusing to be discharged until they were paid in full for their service—which Congress, unable to raise funds, had no ability to do. On June 21, several hundred soldiers marched with drums beating and bayonets fixed to the statehouse, where Madison was attending a session. The soldiers circled the building so no one could leave and "remained in their position," Madison noted with considerable sangfroid, "without offering any violence, individuals only occasionally uttering offensive words and wantonly pointing their muskets to the windows of the hall of Congress."[6]

Delegates urgently requested that the executive council of Pennsylvania, meeting in the same building, call out the militia, but the council refused, and the situation grew uglier as "spirituous drink from the tippling houses adjoining began to be liberally served out to the soldiers," Madison wrote. Delegates decided to adjourn, and as they passed through the line of soldiers, they were taunted by some, who put up "a mock obstruction," as Madison described it. When further congressional demands for the Pennsylvania Executive Council to call out the militia were refused, Congress, meeting at night when the soldiers were in their barracks, authorized the president of Congress, Elias Boudinot, to move its meeting place. Over the next few days, as rumors began to fly that mutineers would seize the Bank of North America or kidnap delegates, Boudinot decided on Princeton as the location where Congress might better maintain "the dignity and authority of the United States."[7]

Madison dutifully traveled to Princeton, but he didn't stay long. He, who had been one of the most dependable attendees of Congress, began to miss most meetings. He told Edmund Randolph that he had to be in Philadelphia to prepare for retiring from Congress, which the Articles of Confederation required that he do after serving three consecutive years. To Jefferson he explained he had undertaken a writing project that required him to be near his papers in Philadelphia.[8] And, although he didn't say so, he was surely waiting to hear from Kitty Floyd, who was likely to direct her mail to Mrs. House's.

The letter that finally arrived no longer exists, but from the letter Madison wrote to Jefferson after receiving it, we know that it terminated plans for a marriage at the end of the congressional session. On August 11, Madison explained, "I expected to have had the pleasure by this time of being with you in Virginia. My disappointment has proceeded from several dilatory circumstances on which I had not calculated. One of them was the uncertain state into which the object I was then pursuing had been brought by one of those incidents to which such affairs are liable. The result has rendered the time [of] my return to Virginia less material, as the necessity of my visiting the state of New Jersey no longer exists." Madison, distressed, had not taken time to encode the letter, and in old age he would try to obliterate what he had written. He succeeded in part, but the above can be read, and here and there other words can be discerned beneath the scribblings over, some suggesting that Madison did not yet totally despair: "For myself a delicacy to female character will impose some patience" and "hope for . . . some more propitious turn of fortune."[9]

Jefferson wrote back offering sympathy: "I sincerely lament the misadventure which has happened from whatever cause it may have happened." He seemed to acknowledge Madison's hope that things might still work out but offered suggestions in case they didn't: "Should it be final, however, the world still presents the same and many other resources of happiness, and you possess many within yourself. Firmness of mind and unintermitting occupations will not long leave you in pain. No event has been more contrary to my expectations, and these were founded on what I thought a good knowledge of the ground, but of all machines ours is the most complicated and inexplicable."[10] Jefferson's advice fit with what Madison had learned after his college days, when his sudden attacks had thrown him into despair: the best remedy for gloom was an active and involved life.

One has to wonder when Madison told Kitty Floyd of his disorder. At some point he would have felt honor-bound to do so, and if he used the occasion of the trip with her family to New Jersey, the information might have turned attraction to aversion. According to Floyd family lore, Kitty sealed her final letter to Madison with a bit of rye dough, possibly some calculated message about health, since rye dough was part of a Floyd family remedy. But the gesture might simply have been impetuous, which fits with what we know of Floyd as she grew older. She married William Clarkson, a medical student who became a clergyman, and, according to her father, lived with little forethought. In a will dated 1817, the year Kitty Floyd turned fifty, her father wrote:

As to my daughter Catherine, since she was married to Mr. Clarkson, I have given them considerable sums, money and many things to keep house with, and also a tract of land, which, if they had kept it, would now be worth about seven thousand dollars, but all is spent and gone. I therefore conclude that she is not capable of taking care of property and I think it not prudent to leave any at her disposal, but I do hereby [enjoin] it upon my son Nicoll to give her seventy dollars a year after my decease during her life.

Shortly before he died in 1821, Floyd had a change of heart. In a codicil to his will, he bequeathed to Catherine "a lot of land in Deerfield No. 1" and one thousand dollars.[11]

Disappointed as Madison was at Catherine Floyd's breaking off their romance, both he and posterity likely benefited. Madison had ahead of him the most consequential, history-altering years of his life, and if they were lonelier without Floyd, they were almost certainly more productive. And as grave an error as it usually is to read history backward, perhaps in this instance one might be forgiven for also observing that if he had married Catherine Floyd, there would have been no Dolley Madison.

MADISON LEFT PHILADELPHIA, a former congressman now, but his interest in politics was undiminished. On the way to Montpelier, he stopped at Gunston Hall, George Mason's elegant home on the Potomac, and as he visited with Mason, probably near the fireplace in the gray-painted parlor, he sounded him out on the looming issues of the day. He found Mason to be less opposed to the impost than he had expected and also surprisingly "sound and ripe" on the matter of revising the Virginia Constitution. But when it came to bolstering the national government, Mason was dragging his feet. "His [he]terodoxy," Madison wrote to Jefferson, "lay chiefly in being too little impressed with either the necessity or the proper means of preserving the confederacy."[12]

Madison had a course of study in mind, but his return to Montpelier, where he had not been for nearly four years, inspired an outpouring of Piedmont hospitality that kept him from settling into it. As January snow deepened and drifted, making neighborly visits impossible, he finally had time to read, but now he didn't have the books he needed. The volumes he had shipped from Philadelphia were held up at Fredericksburg, and he could not avail himself of the library at Monticello, which Jefferson had given him permission to use, because the caretaker and the keys were in Richmond. Determined to keep busy, he read Sir Edward Coke's *Commentary upon Littleton,* one of the few law books on Montpelier's shelves. It was an enormously influential exposition of common law but dry and difficult. Madison leavened his law study with an excursion into science, making calculations on the heat of the earth's core. He believed that he was expanding on a theory of the French naturalist the comte de Buffon, but in the absence of books he was depending on what Jefferson had told him about Buffon's theory—and, as Jefferson later confessed, he hadn't gotten it quite right.[13]

Over the next few years, as Madison sought the "unintermitting occupations" that Jefferson had said would provide him solace, he produced detailed descriptions of some of the smaller quadrupeds found at Montpelier, including a woodchuck, a mole, and a weasel, and sent them to Jefferson to help his friend disprove one of Buffon's most irritating theories—that American animals had degenerated so that there were fewer species and smaller specimens than in Europe. He kept records of when rain fell, cherry trees blossomed, and wild geese flew northward. He also had "a little itch to gain a smattering in chemistry," he told Jefferson, asking him to send him two chemistry boxes, as well as a pedometer, a pocket compass that could be carried like a watch, and a telescope that fit into a walking cane.[14]

During these years, Madison would also serve with great distinction in the Virginia Assembly; travel extensively, though never outside the United States; and try to figure out a way to earn a living rather than being dependent on his father. But through all these activities, he would remain intensely focused on the question that his service in Congress had raised time and again: How can a union of states function effectively? A letter to Jefferson, in which he asked his friend to keep an eye out for "rare and valuable books," makes clear that one place he intended to look for answers was in the failures and successes of the past. "You know tolerably well the objects of my curiosity," he wrote. "I will only particularize my wish of whatever may throw light on the general constitution and droit public of the several confederacies which have existed. . . . The operations of our own must render all such lights of consequence."[15]

IN APRIL 1784, with the poplar trees leafing out, Madison left Montpelier in a chaise driven by his brother William and headed for Richmond, where the Virginia Assembly met. As a result of the peace treaty that the United States had concluded with Britain in September 1783, states were more reluctant than ever to provide financial support to the central government. Thus even though Madison knew that participating in the legislature would be "noxious" to his historical study of constitutions, he had agreed to serve, hoping to convince his fellow delegates of the peril the country was in and persuade them to lead the way in rescuing "the Union and the blessings of liberty staked on it."[16]

Montpelier was also short on the intellectual companionship he had grown used to, and he looked forward to seeing old friends such as Edmund Randolph. He must have been gratified upon his arrival in Richmond by the way he was looked to for leadership. "The assembly . . . have formed great hopes of Mr. Madison," wrote Jefferson's protégé William Short. "He is already resorted to as a general of whom much has been preconceived to his advantage," Edmund Randolph observed.[17]

Richmond, the capital of the commonwealth for four years, had foul and muddy streets and fewer than two hundred houses. Many who came to the capital for the assembly stayed in inns such as the one run by Serafino Formicola, who rented beds packed together in two rooms on his tavern's second story. While some legislators, lobbyists, and various hangers-on tried to catch a few hours of sleep in the crowded rooms, others wandered through eating and drinking. There was no possibility of "withdrawing apart . . . from the noisy, disturbing, or curious crowd," a German traveler reported, unless one rented "a private apartment"—which Madison almost surely did, if not at Formicola's, perhaps at City Tavern on Main Street.[18] He had letters to write, legislation to draft, plans to formulate—tasks nearly impossible to accomplish in a dormitory.

Seasoned legislator that he was, Madison knew the importance of getting the lay of the political land. No one's opinion would matter more in the upcoming session than Patrick Henry's, and so Madison met with him in a Richmond coffeehouse. Fulfilling Madison's fondest hope, Henry, likely wearing the scarlet cloak and fully dressed wig for which he was noted about this time, pronounced himself in favor of giving greater power to the federal government. He believed that "a bold example set by Virginia would have influence on the other states" and declared that securing this outcome was his only reason for attending the assembly.[19]

Madison reported Henry's sentiments to Jefferson and told him that he had also tried to sound out Henry on revising the state's constitution. Although Henry had made no commitments, Madison wrote, "the general train of his thoughts seemed to suggest favorable expectations."[20]

Henry did indeed support resolutions to strengthen the powers of Congress—until they required that Virginia tax its citizens. That prospect brought him out in full oratorical opposition. In the wooden frame building that served as Virginia's capitol, he thundered away as though he had utterly forgotten his previous commitments. Madison wrote to his father that the members of the legislature would "make a sharp figure," if after their declarations of support for Congress "we wholly omit the means of fulfilling them."[21] But with Henry leading the way, that is exactly what they did.

When it came to revising the Virginia Constitution, Henry showed "a more violent opposition than we expected," Madison wrote to Jefferson. A resolution proposing a general convention to take up the Virginia Constitution was defeated, causing Jefferson, in Paris now as minister to France, to comment sarcastically that it was probably just as well. Using code, he wrote, "While Mr. Henry lives another bad constitution would be formed and saddled forever on us. What we have to do I think is devo[u]tly to pray for his death." Madison contented himself with a slighting reference to Henry as one of "the forensic members" of the assembly.[22]

With revising the constitution off the agenda, Madison turned to the revision of Virginia's laws, a project that Jefferson, his mentor George Wythe, and the revered Edmund Pendleton had begun half a dozen years earlier. Their goal was to update Virginia's statutes, but few of the bills they proposed had been acted upon, and Madison decided to renew the effort, at first with great success. One of his fellow delegates asked, "Can you suppose it possible that Madison should shine with more than usual splendor this assembly? It is . . . not only possible but a fact. He has astonished mankind and has by means perfectly constitutional become almost a dictator. . . . His influence alone has hitherto overcome the impatience of the House and carried them half through the revised code."[23]

But Madison hit a snag with the bill on crime and punishment. Its main intent was to limit the number of crimes punishable by death to murder and treason, but some of the alternative punishments proposed, based on the idea of *lex talionis,* or "an eye for an eye," met resistance. For rape, for example, the punishment was castration. Jefferson, who had outlined the bill, was embarrassed and agreed the punishment should be changed, offering a weak joke as his reason: that "women would be under [temptation] to make it the instrument of vengeance against an inconstant lover." But after Madison had seen to the removal of the most onerous provisions from the bill, he ran afoul of what he called "the rage against horse stealers." With opposition from those who thought three years of hard labor not nearly enough punishment, the bill was defeated by a single vote. "Our old bloody code is by this event fully restored," Madison wrote to Jefferson.[24]

Code revision was essentially over. Jefferson would later say that it was a wonder that Madison had accomplished as much as he had, given

that he had faced "the endless quibbles, chicaneries, perversions, vexa-
tions, and delays of lawyers and demi-lawyers," but Madison lamented
"that the work may never be systematically perfected." Time and again
he was struck by the way that "important bills prepared at leisure by
skillful hands" were treated to "crudeness and tedious discussion," and
he had seen legislative tricks of the most blatant sort. An effort to make
Virginians liable for their debts to British creditors, which was required
by the peace treaty with Great Britain of 1783, failed when a number of
legislators took a boat across the James River to Manchester and claimed
to be unable to get back.[25]

Madison would not soon forget his frustrations in the Virginia legislature, but it was also the scene of one of his proudest accomplishments.
Patrick Henry championed an assessment to support teachers of the
Christian religion, the rationale being that "the general diffusion of
Christian knowledge hath a natural tendency to correct the morals of
men, restrain their vices, and preserve the peace of society." This was a
proposition widely agreed to, and since the bill allowed taxpayers to
choose the denomination they would support, its sponsors argued that
it could be passed "without counteracting the liberal principle heretofore
adopted."[26]

Madison, who had helped author the "liberal principle" in the Virginia Declaration of Rights, utterly disagreed. The true question, he
wrote in notes to himself, was not whether religion was necessary but
whether state-supported religious establishments were. His answer was
an unequivocal no. Madison's opposition helped postpone consideration of the assessment bill—as did Patrick Henry's election as governor.
When Henry decided to go on a long leave home before assuming the
governorship, it was, Madison noted, "a circumstance very inauspicious
to his offspring."[27]

Assemblyman Wilson Cary Nicholas and his brother George decided to mount a campaign against the assessment bill and sought out
Madison to write a petition. He responded with the "Memorial and
Remonstrance Against Religious Assessments," a document that would
become a landmark in the history of religious freedom. He began by

establishing the remonstrance's origins in the Virginia Declaration of Rights, which he quoted: "Because we hold it for a fundamental and undeniable truth 'that religion or the duty which we owe to our Creator and the manner of discharging it can be directed only by reason and conviction, not by force or violence,' the religion then of every man must be left to the conviction and conscience of every man; and it is the right of every man to exercise it as these may dictate. This right is in its nature an unalienable right." Madison went on to marshal arguments against state support of religion. There must be no overleaping of "the great barrier which defends the rights of the people," he wrote, and while the fact that the bill provided for all Christian religions might make it seem harmless enough, it was "proper to take alarm at the first experiment on our liberties": "We hold this prudent jealousy to be the first duty of citizens and one of the noblest characteristics of the late revolution. . . . Who does not see that the same authority which can establish Christianity in exclusion of all other religions may establish with the same ease any particular sect of Christians, in exclusion of all other sects?" He ended the remonstrance as he had begun it, declaring freedom of religion to be a natural right, a "gift of nature," fully equal to other rights Virginians held dear.[28]

As he had before, Madison wrote anonymously. The idea of a general assessment for Christian churches had not only the support of officials with whom he generally found himself at loggerheads but also the backing of men he admired, such as Edmund Pendleton. Madison saw no reason to alienate friends and didn't believe that adding his name would strengthen his argument. But he was proud of his work, noting after he retired that "the number of copies and signatures" on the petition "displayed such an overwhelming opposition of the people that the plan of a general assessment was crushed under it."[29]

Madison did not let the advantage gained go to waste, but seized the moment to pass the Bill for Establishing Religious Freedom that Jefferson had authored half a dozen years before. Although Jefferson's language was changed slightly as the bill went through the House of Delegates and the Senate, the alterations did not deprive his concepts of their force. "Whereas almighty God hath created the mind free," the statute begins, and "all attempts to influence it by temporal punishments or burthens or by civil incapacitations tend only to beget habits of hypocrisy and meanness and are a departure from the plan of the holy author of our religion, . . . all men shall be free to profess and by argument to maintain their opinions in matters of religion, and that the same shall in no wise diminish, enlarge, or affect their civil capacities."

The Virginia statute also made clear the connection between religious and intellectual freedom. "Truth is great and will prevail if left to herself," Jefferson had written. "She is the proper and sufficient antagonist to error and has nothing to fear from the conflict unless by human interposition disarmed of her natural weapons, free argument and debate." It was this theme that Madison chose to take up when he wrote to Jefferson to tell him of the statute's passage. "I flatter myself [we] have in this country extinguished forever the ambitious hope of making laws for the human mind."[30]

The bill was one of three accomplishments that Jefferson would ask to be memorialized on his tombstone, the other two being his authorship of the Declaration of Independence and his founding of the University of Virginia. The high regard that he and Madison had for the statute has been shared by subsequent generations. Theologian Martin Marty noted that passage of the statute marked "an epochal shift in the Western world's approach to relations between civil and religious spheres of life." The Virginia act, he observes, can rightly be seen "as a hinge between ages."[31]

IN BETWEEN SESSIONS of the Virginia Assembly, Madison spent time at Montpelier, reading and studying. One of his father's cousins, Francis Taylor, who spent a few snowy days in March at Montpelier, noted that Madison, although hospitable, did not, in typical Virginia fashion, devote the majority of his day to socializing. Madison "came to breakfast, of which he eat sparingly," Taylor recorded in his diary, "and then would go to his room till a little before dinner. After dinner play at whist for half bits till bedtime."[32]

Madison also made journeys northward, in part for the exercise and in part to break from the isolation of Montpelier and spend time in Philadelphia and New York. While he was on a "ramble into the eastern states" in 1784, a chance encounter with the marquis de Lafayette led to a wilderness adventure. The two happened to meet in Baltimore, both on their way to Philadelphia, and Lafayette invited Madison to accompany him to Fort Stanwix in New York, where a treaty was to be signed between the United States and the Iroquois Confederacy.[33]

The wealthy and ambitious Lafayette, who had traveled to America when he was just nineteen to fight in the Revolution, had proven himself both skilled and courageous in battle. Tall, with reddish hair, he was, to use a word with which both Benjamin Franklin and James Madison described him, "amiable."[34] He invited friendship, and his offer to include Madison in his frontier journey would have been hard to resist, not only as a chance to see wondrous sights with a good companion, but as an opportunity to converse on a subject Madison thought of great importance—America's right to free navigation of the Mississippi. Spain, hoping to stop the westward expansion of the United States, had recently closed the river to all but Spanish ships, and Madison realized that Lafayette could be most helpful in persuading France to take up America's cause with Spain.

Madison was at Mrs. House's Philadelphia boardinghouse putting into code a letter to Jefferson explaining the efforts he was making to enlist Lafayette's assistance when Lafayette walked into his room. Madison was thus obliged, so he explained to Jefferson, "in order to avoid reserve to let him know that I was writing to you. I said nothing of the subject, but he will probably infer from our conversation that the Mississippi is most in my thoughts." Particularly at Mrs. House's, it could not have been otherwise. Eliza Trist, Mrs. House's daughter, who was on her way down the Mississippi River to be with her husband, would soon learn of his death, and then what would she do? "When and how she will be able to get back since the Spaniards have shut all their ports against the U.S. is uncertain and gives much anxiety to her friends," Madison wrote to Jefferson.[35]

Madison and Lafayette traveled to New York, where the marquis received "a continuation of those marks of cordial esteem and affection" that Madison had observed since the two had first joined forces in Baltimore. From the city they set off in a barge up the Hudson to Albany, a journey that took them past lovely country homes and the commanding sites where Forts Washington and Lee and Stony Point had once stood. Their barge wound through highlands that curved and narrowed at West Point, where during the Revolution a great chain had been stretched across the Hudson to prevent British ships from sailing farther north. Slowed for six days by heavy wind and rain, the party finally sailed past family seats of the Rensselaers and Schuylers, over dangerous sandbars, and into Albany on September 22.[36] As they were making arrangements for traveling overland to Fort Stanwix, François de Barbé-Marbois, the witty French chargé d'affaires whom Madison knew well from Philadelphia, arrived at the dock, and soon he had joined their party.

After stopping at a Shaker community and observing the sect's "convulsive dances," the party rode on to Fort Stanwix, a journey of several days. "Mr. Madison directed the march," Barbé-Marbois reported, "and I was cook for the troop." It was often cold and rainy, but Lafayette seemed impervious to the weather, protected as he was by "a cloak of gummed taffeta, which had been sent him from France, wrapped up in newspapers. The papers had stuck to the gum, and there had not been time to get them off, so that the curious could read on his chest or his back the *Journal de Paris,* the *Courier de l'Europe,* or news from other places."[37]

At Fort Stanwix, Lafayette made a speech to the assembled Iroquois that was enthusiastically received. Lafayette so commanded the stage at Fort Stanwix that the official commissioners to the event were miffed, a fact that Lafayette understood, Madison wrote, using code, but he "consoled himself with the service which he thought the Indian speeches . . . had rendered to the United States." Madison also thought that Lafayette was looking forward to reading about his performance. "It will form a bright column in the gazettes of Europe," Madison wrote, continuing to use code, hinting that Lafayette would make sure of that. "He will be impatient for its appearance there without seeing any mode in which it can happen, of course." As it turned out, Madison underestimated Lafayette, who managed to get copies of his remarks in American papers even before the commissioners had officially reported the treaty signing to Congress.

Lafayette was often praised for his modesty, but Madison thought that a bit off the mark. Continuing in code, he described the young Frenchman as combining "great natural frankness of temper" with "very considerable talents" and "a strong thirst of praise and popularity . . . In a word, I take him to be as amiable a man as his vanity will admit." But Lafayette was a steadfast ally. He took on the task of encouraging the French to support America's right to freely navigate the Mississippi. "I am every day pestering government with my prophetics respecting the Mississippi," he wrote from Paris in March 1785. And he took up this cause, so dear to Madison, despite George Washington's being cool to it. He wanted to see the Potomac become the commercial route into the interior. One of Lafayette's tactics was to take advantage of the well-known penchant of Spanish officials to read other people's mail. "I have written letters by post to Madrid and Cadiz to be intercepted and read," he told Madison. It was impossible not to be charmed by such an open-hearted soul. Madison's assessment of Lafayette grew noticeably softer: "His disposition is naturally warm and affectionate and his attachment to the United States unquestionable."[38]

MADISON'S THOUSAND-MILE journey from Montpelier to Philadelphia to New York, then through the Mohawk valley and back, makes the point that when he wasn't ill, he was vigorous. The stereotype of him as forever weak and frail does not stand up well to the trips he took, including the relatively routine ones between Montpelier and Philadelphia—or Montpelier and Washington, after the capital was moved. They were always over roads that would not be thought to deserve the name today and seemed often to occur in downpours. Once Madison was forced to dismantle his carriage, make three trips with it "in something like a boat" over a swollen pond, and swim his horses across to get home.[39]

Madison's predisposition to sudden attacks did lead him to take certain precautions, such as avoiding "deep waters," as one manual advised patients with epilepsy. Madison refused several opportunities for government service in Europe and in 1785 declined an invitation from Jefferson to visit Paris. "I have some reason . . . to suspect that crossing the sea would be unfriendly to a singular disease of my constitution," he wrote.[40]

An ocean voyage was an entirely different matter from a trip over a pond or up the Hudson. A journey of many weeks increased many times the odds he would suffer a sudden attack, fall overboard, and drown. Jefferson also invited Madison to move closer to Monticello. He had persuaded James Monroe to do so, he reported, as well as William Short, who was in Paris with him, serving as his secretary. "Would you but make it a 'partie quarrée,'" Jefferson wrote, "I should believe that life had still some happiness in store for me. Agreeable society is the first essential in constituting the happiness and, of course, the value of our existence."[41]

Ever so politely, Madison put Jefferson off. "Your invitation has the strongest bias of my mind on its side," he wrote, "but my situation is as yet too dependent on circumstances to permit my embracing it absolutely." Much as he valued his friendship with Jefferson, Madison might well have perceived that a little distance was healthy, and even if he had wanted to be part of the philosophical neighborhood that Jefferson proposed, he had no way to do it. At thirty-four he was still relying on his father and the enterprise at Montpelier for a living.[42] He could hardly expect his family to finance his setting up a household somewhere else.

Jefferson's proposal underscored for Madison a situation he wanted to change. "My wish," he wrote to his friend Edmund Randolph in the summer of 1785, "is if possible to provide a decent and independent subsistence." He wanted to be on his own—and he wanted a life, he told

Randolph, that would "depend as little as possible on the labor of slaves." Recognizing the contradiction involved in working to advance the cause of freedom while relying on income produced by slave labor, he was looking for a way out, and he had some ideas in mind, "several projects from which advantage seemed attainable. I have in concert with a friend here, one at present on the anvil which we think cannot fail to yield a decent reward for our trouble."[43]

The deal "on the anvil" probably had to do with buying land, then selling it at a profit. One area that he thought particularly ripe for speculation was the Mohawk valley, which he remembered as a place of rich soil near navigable water. His enthusiasm only grew after he discussed the valley with George Washington, an experienced land speculator, who intimated "that if he had money to spare and was disposed to deal in land, this [was] the very spot which his fancy had selected out of all the U.S."[44]

Madison found a willing partner in James Monroe, twenty-eight, a newlywed and now serving in Congress. Although Monroe, like Madison, was part of Jefferson's circle, he was less given to intellectual pursuits than the other two men. Over his life, he would amass a substantial library, but his letters give almost no indication that he took pleasure in it. One contemporary observed of Monroe that "nature has given him a mind neither rapid nor rich" but that he made up for it through "a habit of application which no difficulties can shake, no labors can tire." Washington admired the bravery with which Monroe, as an awkward and rawboned teenager, had fought in the Revolution. Jefferson admired Monroe's honest character and had recommended him to Madison. "The scrupulousness of his honor will make you safe in the most confidential communications," Jefferson had written. "A better man [there] cannot be."[45]

Together, Madison and Monroe bought nine hundred acres of Mohawk land for $1,350 and wanted to purchase more, but neither had the cash. It was a measure of Madison's eagerness to invest further that he wrote to Jefferson describing the land and the bargain it represented in glowing terms and suggesting that Jefferson borrow the money in

France for them to make a larger purchase. Jefferson explained that the French government borrowed more money than was lent in France, regularly and reliably paying attractive interest and making it unlikely that a foreign borrower would succeed. After buying out Monroe's interest in the nine hundred acres, Madison sold the land in 1796, ten years after he had purchased it, for $5,250, leaving him a profit but hardly providing an independent subsistence.[46]

Madison would never accumulate the resources to live independently. If he had devoted full and extended attention to the endeavor, perhaps he could have done so, but 1786, the year of his investment efforts, was also a time of national crises, and he increasingly turned his mind toward them. His absorption in politics, which would continue for decades to come, was fateful for the nation—and it would leave him linked forever to Montpelier and the enslaved people who lived there.

One of the first crises came in April, when New York State refused to accept the impost in the form in which Congress proposed it. Twelve states had approved the measure about which Madison had written so eloquently three years before, but New York's obstinacy effectively ended hope for the national government as it existed under the Articles of Confederation being able to raise revenue.[47]

By late summer, "the general rage for paper money" headed Madison's concerns. With Congress having no authority to prohibit states from printing money, various state legislatures were producing it willy-nilly. Rather than accept it, farmers were withholding their crops from market and shopkeepers were shutting their doors. Paper money was also producing "warfare and retaliation among the states," Madison wrote, as were the taxes that states with "convenient ports for foreign commerce" were levying on neighboring states that had no such ports. New Jersey, located between Philadelphia and New York, was being taxed from two sides, like "a cask tapped at both ends," as Madison described it. North Carolina, situated between Virginia and South Carolina, was "a patient bleeding at both arms."[48] And Congress had no ability to do anything about it.

The Union's increasingly dire straits gave special meaning to the study project Madison had embarked upon. In the library at Montpelier, he took notes on the books that Jefferson had sent him in a "literary cargo," noting the strengths and weaknesses of ancient confederacies such as the Amphictyonic Council and the Achaean League and more modern ones such as the Belgic Confederacy. His reading revealed that lack of strength at the center made confederacies unable to act as a whole and predisposed them to falling apart.[49] This history confirmed what his experience had shown him: if the United States was going to survive as a union, a strong central government was required.

But he did not see clearly the vehicle for establishing such a government. His efforts to strengthen Congress had largely come to naught. He had doubts about states gathering in small groups to work out issues that were troubling them, thinking that was likely to excite "pernicious jealousies."[50] This may explain his failure to take offense when Governor Patrick Henry neglected to notify him of the time and place at which Virginia and Maryland commissioners were to gather to discuss commerce on the Potomac River. Madison had been appointed one of the representatives, but by the time he learned of the details, the meeting had already occurred.

He did not miss the follow-on, however, a gathering in Annapolis to which Virginia invited all the other states "to take into consideration the trade of the United States." Madison's reputation by now was such that at least one of his contemporaries saw the Annapolis Convention as his handiwork, but he was, in fact, not at all sure that it would succeed. He described it to James Monroe as an effort that "will probably miscarry," though it was "better than nothing," he allowed, and "may possibly lead to better consequences than at first occur." On the chance that something would come of it, he arrived early for the convention, taking up lodging on September 4, 1786, at Mann's Tavern, an elegant hostelry at Church and Conduit streets that had formerly been the grand home of a Tory, Lloyd Dulany. The next evening he had dinner there, complete with wine, probably in the company of two other delegates.[51]

Eventually, nine more delegates attended, but only five states were represented, which meant that the convention was, formally speaking, a failure. There might have been plans for meetings in the Senate chamber of the Maryland State House, just up the hill from Mann's, but with only a dozen attendees it was more suitable to gather in a room at the tavern.[52] There and at other Annapolis taverns and coffeehouses, the delegates, no doubt with Madison nudging them along, began to discuss the need for more than commercial agreements if the young country was to save itself.

Alexander Hamilton, attending from New York, was also doing a fair amount of nudging. He had been critical of the Articles of Confederation since before the end of the war, finding them "neither fit for war nor peace." In 1780, far in advance of anyone else, he had recommended a convention to remedy the articles. His time come round at last, he wrote a proposal to Congress and the states that was dire in its description of problems and dramatic in setting forth the need for change. So passionately did Hamilton make his argument that Edmund Randolph balked. Hamilton resisted changing the tone of his proposal until Madison took him aside: "You had better yield to this man, for otherwise all Virginia will be against you." Hamilton listened, toning down his words so that the proposal calmly and respectfully suggested "the appointment of commissioners to meet at Philadelphia on the second Monday in May next, to take into consideration the situation of the United States [and] to devise such further provisions as shall appear to them necessary to render the constitution of the federal government adequate to the exigencies of the Union."[53]

NOW MADISON SEEMED to be everywhere and all at once. Not long after departing Annapolis, he was in Richmond, penning the legislation that would throw Virginia's weight behind the proposed convention. "The crisis is arrived," he wrote, "at which the good people of America are to decide the solemn question, whether they will by wise and magnanimous efforts reap the just fruits of that independence which they have so gloriously acquired" or whether "they will renounce the auspicious blessings prepared for them by the revolution." Virginia's path was clear. It would work to make the United States "as happy in peace as they have been glorious in war" by appointing commissioners "to meet such deputies as may be appointed and authorized by other states to assemble in convention at Philadelphia."[54]

Even before the bill passed the House of Delegates, Madison was trying to persuade George Washington to attend. Virginia's endorsement would come in "very solemn dress," he wrote to the general, and it would carry "all the weight which could be derived from a single state. This idea will also be pursued in the selection of characters to represent Virginia in the federal convention. You will infer our earnestness on this point from the liberty which will be used of placing your name at the head of them. How far this liberty may correspond with the ideas by which you ought to be governed will be best decided where it must ultimately be decided. In every event it will assist powerfully in marking the zeal of our legislature and its opinion of the magnitude of the occasion." Washington could not have been terribly surprised by the nomination. In a recent letter to Madison, he had lamented America's decline. "No morn ever dawned more favorable than ours did—and no day was ever more clouded than the present!" he wrote. He was particularly troubled by a report from Massachusetts of the tax revolt that would become known as Shays's Rebellion. Farmers who could not pay what they owed were taking up pitchforks and marching on county courthouses to protest seizure of their land. The country appeared "fast verging to anarchy and confusion," Washington wrote to Madison. "What stronger evidence can be given of the want of energy in our governments than these disorders?" he asked. "Will not the wise and good strive hard to avert this evil?"[55]

No one in the country was regarded as wiser or more virtuous than Washington, as he himself well knew. He seemed to be inviting a nomination to serve at the Philadelphia convention, but when Madison presented it to him, he demurred, explaining that the convention was to meet in Philadelphia at about the same time as the Society of the Cincinnati, whose invitation he had already declined. Washington was president of the society, an organization of officers who had served in the Revolution, and he had at first been pleased to lead the group, but because membership in it passed down to oldest sons, the organization was soon perceived as planting the seeds of a hereditary aristocracy. The Massachusetts legislature denounced it. Pamphleteers railed against it. And Washington, ever careful of his reputation, had decided to put some distance between himself and the Cincinnati by sending regrets for their Philadelphia meeting. This meant, he wrote to Madison, "that I could not appear at the same time and place on any other occasion."[56]

Madison persisted, stressing the importance of the convention and pointing out that Washington's name at the head of the Virginia delegation would help ensure that other states sent their most respected men. It was for these reasons that he had put Washington's name forward, he explained, and he hoped that the general would seriously consider "whether the difficulties which you enumerate ought not to give way to them." Perhaps aware of Washington's concern that he might find himself at a gathering of delegates so unimpressive that their efforts would surely fail, Madison sent him the names of worthies who would be attending, men such as John Rutledge of South Carolina, a distinguished lawyer; Elbridge Gerry of Massachusetts, a signer of both the Declaration of Independence and the Articles of Confederation; and Alexander Hamilton, Washington's brilliant and sometimes difficult protégé.[57] Finally, a little more than a month before the convention was to begin, Washington yielded and said he would attend.

IN THE MIDDLE of organizing the gathering in Philadelphia, Madison agreed to serve in Congress again. Although it would consume time he could scarcely spare, he saw the assignment as crucial to the convention's success. Congress had still not acted on the report of the Annapolis Convention and had it in its power to create mischief. There was also the matter of John Jay, whom Congress had appointed its secretary of foreign affairs. Convinced now that war would ensue if the United States did not complete a treaty with Spain, Jay had managed to get Pennsylvania and six other states to the north to vote him authority to negotiate away U.S. rights to free navigation of the Mississippi for twenty years. Madison not only still opposed the idea of giving up navigation rights on principle but understood the trouble that even proposing to do so could cause. It had already made Patrick Henry into "a cold advocate" of a stronger federal government, and others would follow if doubts grew about the central government's dealing evenhandedly with all parts of the Republic.[58] To southerners the offer to cede Mississippi navigation was an argument for a weaker rather than a stronger government.

Determined "to bring about, if possible, the cancelling of the project of Mr. Jay for shutting the Mississippi," Madison set out in late January on a journey that took him across ice-clogged rivers and through a blizzard. "From Princeton to Paulus Hook we had a Northeast snowstorm incessantly in our teeth," he wrote to Eliza Trist. In New York he found delegates to Congress much "divided and embarrassed" about the Philadelphia gathering. On February 21, New York, having received instructions from its legislature, moved to recommend a convention, but, as Madison recorded in his notes, "there was reason to believe" that New York's "object was to obtain a new convention under the sanction of Congress rather than accede to the one on foot, or perhaps by dividing the plans of the states in their appointments to frustrate all of them." Madison voted for the motion, nonetheless, noting that he had considered it "susceptible of amendment." But with suspicions running high, it went down. A proposal from Massachusetts was next, and while it was subject to the same objections as New York's, this time Madison's idea of amending took hold, and the proposal was folded into plans for the Philadelphia convention. The resolution as it finally passed read, "That on the second Monday in May next a convention of delegates who shall have been appointed by the several states be held at Philadelphia for the sole and express purpose of revising the Articles of Confederation." The resolution was more focused on the articles than the Annapolis Convention's proposal had been, but if that troubled Madison, he gave no sign of it. In a letter to Edmund Pendleton, he expressed relief that it now looked as though the meeting would occur "and that it will be a pretty full one." There was at least some hope for a situation that was growing increasingly dire.

"No money is paid into the public treasury," he told Pendleton. "No respect is paid to the federal authority. Not a single state complies with the requisitions."[59]

When it came to determining how far John Jay had progressed in his dealings with Spain, Madison found himself stymied by the veil of secrecy that Congress allowed Jay to draw around his negotiations. Thinking that even Spain's minister to the United States might be more open, Madison arranged a meeting with Don Diego de Gardoqui on March 13. He found the Spanish diplomat inflexible, but in between threats about the consequences to America if it did not sign a treaty ceding its rights to navigation, Gardoqui let slip a crucial piece of information. He had not seen Jay for months, had no plans to meet with him, and would soon be returning to Spain. This meant no treaty agreement for the time being, and indeed other intelligence Madison picked up made it seem unlikely that there would ever be one based on forgoing navigation rights. The coalition that had voted to give Jay such authority was breaking up. New Jersey and Pennsylvania had reversed course and now saw open navigation on the river as in their interest. Even Rhode Island was showing signs of breaking with "the New England Standard."[60]

But by now Patrick Henry had firmly announced he would not be a delegate to the Philadelphia convention, and lest the possibility of a treaty move others in a similar direction, Madison decided to nail up the treaty's coffin. He did so by fiercely attacking the vote of the seven states as illegitimate. Treaties required nine votes under the Articles of Confederation, and it was quite obvious that instructions for negotiating a treaty ought to require the same. He also launched an assault on a rule forbidding the losing party to readdress the matter once decided. That amounted to trying to fetter the minority, Madison said, which in the case of the Mississippi, he pointedly reminded the assembled delegates, had been five states with another nearly voting with them. By the time he was through, Madison had called the legitimacy of Jay's instructions into such doubt that it is easy to imagine Jay's appetite for proceeding with negotiations declining rapidly, particularly since Madison had also made clear that even if a treaty ceding Mississippi navigation were agreed to, it was never going to get the nine votes necessary in Congress

for approval. Several months later, one of Madison's congressional colleagues reported that the matter of the Mississippi was in "a state of
absolute dormification."[61]

MADISON WAS LIVING in the boardinghouse of Vandine Elsworth
on Maiden Lane, not far from New York's city hall, where Congress met.
The company was "agreeable," he wrote to Eliza Trist, "but I almost
hesitate in deciding that to be an advantage, as it may expose the unso-
cial plan I have formed to the greater reproach." He wanted time "to
revolve the subject which is to undergo the discussion of the convention," and despite the temptations of pleasant company and the work he
had to do in Congress, he found it. The product of hours spent in his
room was "Vices of the Political System of the United States," a document that neatly bookended his earlier survey of the flaws in other con-
federations and showed a different aspect of his genius. He was not only
a scholar, as "Notes on Ancient and Modern Confederacies" had shown.
He was also a man of experience who had seen the flaws he set forth—
and most of them originated with the states. They failed to comply with
congressional requisitions, they encroached on federal authority, and
they trespassed on one another's rights. No doubt remembering the
Virginia legislature's insistence on shielding Virginians from British
creditors, he noted that states had violated international treaties, including the treaty of peace.[62]

In addition to vices that affected the states collectively, there were
those found within them individually: the multiplicity, mutability, and
injustices of their laws—which he had seen firsthand in the House of
Delegates. The injustices of state laws, as Madison saw it, sometimes
resulted from honest representatives falling under the sway of a "favorite
leader" (and surely he was thinking of Patrick Henry) who varnished "his
sophistical arguments with the glowing colors of popular eloquence."
Legislators themselves too often acted out of self-interest instead of for
the public good. And, of course, those who elected them shared in the
blame. They were given to uniting in majorities that violated the rights
and interests of minorities. In his youth, Madison had seen the religious

majority in Virginia persecute members of a religious minority. More recently, he had watched states take actions that relieved debtors at the expense of a minority holding debt. Madison pointed to Rhode Island, which had not only issued fast-depreciating paper money but also passed laws forcing creditors to take it.[63]

Madison had thought long and deeply about majority rule. "There is no maxim in my opinion which is more liable to be misapplied and which therefore more needs elucidation than the current one that the interest of the majority is the political standard of right and wrong," he had told Monroe.[64] The matter of the Mississippi, in which he was involved at the same time he was writing "Vices of the Political System," showed majority rule could result in an unfair decision in a federal as well as a state council. As Madison had carefully recorded, however, in the end the majority of seven states imposing a misguided policy came apart. Pennsylvania and states to its north covered such vast and varied territory that in the end their interests were too diverse for them to hold together.

The larger the arena for a decision, the example suggested, the safer is liberty—though such a notion was "contrary to the prevailing theory," as Madison noted in "Vices of the Political System." Since 1748, when Montesquieu had written *The Spirit of the Laws,* conventional wisdom had held that republics needed to be small or else they fell apart. But there was another way to look at it, as Madison was doing now: in an expansive republic, the rule of the majority was less likely to be oppressive, meliorated as it was by a greater diversity of interests.[65]

Madison had likely encountered the seed of this idea in David Hume's "Idea of a Perfect Commonwealth," published in 1752, but it might have been that when he saw the concept illustrated by the breakup of the northern coalition, he realized its power—and understood it could be more powerful still if instead of thirteen state legislatures clashing, the interests of millions of citizens could compete. He took this idea with him, like a pearl in his pocket, when he left New York on May 3 for the convention in Philadelphia.[66] It was a theory on which a great nation could be built—a vast republic such as the world had never seen.

Chapter 6

THE GREAT WORK BEGINS

MADISON HAD BEEN IN PHILADELPHIA more than a week when Washington made his dramatic entry. The general's carriage was accompanied by Philadelphia's City Troop, splendid in white breeches, high boots, and round black hats edged with silver. Church bells welcomed the hero of the Revolution, as did cheerful crowds along the way. Washington alighted from his carriage in front of Mrs. House's, and although he did not stay there as he had planned—Robert Morris persuaded him to move into his grand house down the street—Madison knew that what truly mattered was Washington's presence at the statehouse on the morrow.[1] His shining reputation would cast a favorable light on the convention as nothing else could.

But the next day, May 14, when the convention was supposed to begin, Madison, Washington, and other members of the Virginia delegation arrived at the statehouse to find that Pennsylvania was so far the only other state represented. Travel was always uncertain in the eighteenth century, and it had been a wet spring, which meant that overflowing creeks and washed-out roads were causing delays for even the most intrepid travelers.

When after a week the convention had still not assembled a quorum, Washington grew impatient, but Madison was putting the time to good use, having the delegates from Virginia meet in daily conferences, where they formed what George Mason called "a proper correspondence of sentiments." What Mason described in letters on May 20 and 21 as the intentions of "the principal states"—meaning Virginia and Pennsylvania—matched proposals that Madison had set forth in letters during previous months: "a total change of the federal system and instituting a great national council or parliament upon the principles of . . . proportionate representation"; a legislature of two branches empowered with "a negative upon all such [state] laws as they judge contrary to the principles and interest of the Union"; an executive, as well as a judiciary system, "with cognizance of all such matters as depend upon the law of nations."[2]

By Friday, May 25, a majority of states had mustered a sufficient number of delegates, and the convention finally got under way. Twenty-nine of the fifty-five men who would eventually attend made their way through a spring downpour to the east chamber of the Pennsylvania State House. It was a handsome room, forty feet square and twenty feet high with tall, stately windows on two sides, and it resonated with history. Every delegate knew that within these walls the Declaration of Independence had been signed. Indeed, four men who had signed the declaration were present at the first meeting of the convention, and eventually four more would attend.

The delegates likely arranged themselves by state, with those from the North sitting in clusters on the north side of the room, those from the South on the south, and the others in between. When all the states sending delegates were represented, there would be only twelve such groupings, because Rhode Island declined to participate. The governor of the state later said that the legislature was fearful of breaking "the compact" established by the Articles of Confederation, lest "we must all be lost in a common ruin." A less elevated explanation was the one Madison offered to his father: "Being conscious of the wickedness of the measures they are pursuing, they are afraid of everything that may become a control on them."[3]

The first order of business was to elect a presiding officer. Washington was chosen unanimously, and as he moved, tall and commanding, to the low dais on the east wall of the chamber, it is hard to imagine the delegate who was not struck by the high importance of the work about to begin. The convention was an event charged with destiny, one that would "decide forever the fate of republican government," Madison said, and he was determined to preserve the proceedings for future generations. From a seat front and center, he would write down "in terms legible and in abbreviations and marks intelligible to myself what was read from the chair or spoken by the members," and at night he transcribed his notes, a project that was voluntary and arduous. He later said the work "almost killed him," but his labors produced one of the most treasured records of American history.[4]

On the following Monday, the number of delegates increased to thirty-eight. Among those newly in attendance was Benjamin Franklin, "the greatest philosopher of the present age," William Pierce, a delegate from Georgia, called him. Eighty-one now, white-haired, and "trunched," according to one observer, he arrived in an enclosed sedan chair that he had brought home with him from Paris. Mounted on long, pliant poles and carried by four men, the chair provided a smoother ride than a carriage over Philadelphia's cobblestoned streets, which was important to a man suffering from stones and gout. Franklin had missed the first day of the convention, possibly because of the rainy weather, but he might have chosen to be absent because his grandson William Temple Franklin was vying to be the convention's secretary, in charge of keeping an official journal of proceedings. As much as his grandfather loved him, Temple, a self-absorbed dandy in his late twenties, was hard to like, and when the delegates voted on opening day, he lost badly to William Jackson of South Carolina.[5] Perhaps Franklin, foreseeing the loss, wished to embarrass neither Temple nor himself nor his fellow delegates by being present.

The delegates adopted rules, including two that were to make give-and-take much easier than it would have been otherwise. The first reflected the fact that the delegates could not know at the outset the details of their final plan. Proposals adopted early might need to be altered in the light of others accepted later. They needed to be able to go back and make changes, and so they voted that even though a decision on a matter had been made by a majority, it was possible to bring the issue up again. The second rule required secrecy, which meant that when a delegate changed his mind or decided to compromise, the world would not be able to accuse him of inconsistency. Jefferson, off in Paris, called the secrecy rule "abominable," but Madison's assessment from later years was probably correct. "No constitution would ever have been adopted by the convention if the debates had been public," he said.[6]

WITH THE RULES established, Washington recognized Edmund Randolph, the thirty-three-year-old governor of Virginia, who made clear in his pleasant voice that the plan he was proposing was not his but his state's. In fact, it was mostly Madison's. "Resolved," Randolph said, as Madison began taking careful notes of his own proposals, "that the Articles of Confederation ought to be so corrected and enlarged as to accomplish the objects proposed by their institution; namely, 'common defense, security of liberty, and general welfare.'"[7]

Randolph was a proponent of revising rather than replacing the articles, so this first resolution would have caused no surprise, but there must have been glances exchanged as he read on. Item two of Virginia's plan, which provided for states to be represented in the legislative branch in proportion to either wealth or population, totally upended the articles, which gave each state an equal vote. Madison had likely added the first resolution to bring Randolph on board. Much as he liked him, Madison probably also suspected that Randolph would be untroubled by the inconsistency between article 1 and the rest of the plan and would confidently present both, although they pointed in opposite directions.[8]

But Gouverneur Morris of Pennsylvania, who supported a strong central government, was impatient with the ambiguity. Thirty-five years old and of commanding bearing despite the loss of a leg in a carriage accident, Morris was a fiercely charming man. Women were said to melt at his glance, and the list of his amours was so long that John Jay, a man serious to the point of stuffiness, was moved to humor. "I am almost tempted to wish he had lost *something* else," he quipped. On May 30, after the delegates had resolved themselves into the committee of the whole so that they could proceed less formally, Morris turned the force of his personality on Randolph and persuaded him to offer a substitute for the first resolution in order to make the Virginia Plan all of a piece. Randolph then proposed "that a national government ought to be established consisting of a supreme legislature, judiciary, and executive."[9]

A stunned silence followed as delegates took in the implications of Randolph's words. George Wythe of Virginia broke the spell to ask if "gentlemen are prepared to pass on the resolution." Delegates jumped to their feet, one declaring that the resolution carried the convention beyond what Congress had mandated, another that it could abolish state governments and annihilate the confederation. Gouverneur Morris hammered home its necessity. Every community needed "one supreme power and one only," and self-government would eventually fail if a central authority were not instituted. "We had better take a supreme government now," he said, "than a despot twenty years hence—for come he must." The delegates passed Randolph's resolution and entered wholly new territory.[10] They were no longer considering a revision of the Articles of Confederation; they were planning an entirely different form of government.

The monumental difficulty of that task was apparent as soon as delegates began to debate the Virginia Plan's second item, the one providing for proportional representation in the national legislature. George Read of Delaware, one of the signers of the Declaration of Independence, rose to say that should the convention move away from the formula that gave each state an equal vote, his state's delegates might find it "their duty to retire from the convention." Madison pushed back, arguing that while equal representation for each state made sense in a confederacy, "it must cease when a national government was put into the place." But so firmly did Read dig in his heels that delegates finally agreed to postpone consideration of the second article. Even as Madison recorded the postponement, however, he remained confident that "the proposed change of representation would certainly be agreed to."[11] How could it be otherwise? It was both unjust and unreasonable for Delaware to have the same power in the general government as Virginia—which had nearly ten times the population.

There was quick agreement to article 3, which provided that the legislature would have two branches, but when delegates came to article 4, which provided for the first branch to be elected "by the people," a major dispute broke out. Roger Sherman of Connecticut, an ungainly, square-jawed man with little education but a canny mind, declared that the people "should have as little to do as may be about the government. They want information and are constantly liable to be misled." Elbridge Gerry of Massachusetts wholeheartedly agreed. A thin man of forty-two with pointed, birdlike features, Gerry had served in the Massachusetts legislature during the uprising of Daniel Shays and his rebels, and that experience had informed his opinion of popular rule. "The evils we experience flow from the excess of democracy," he declared. "The people do not want virtue, but are the dupes of pretended patriots." George Mason, on the other hand, his hair turned white now, believed popular election would be one of the glories of the new-modeled government. It would make the first branch of the legislature "the grand depository of the democratic principle." Madison offered the image of a majestic edifice, declaring, "The great fabric to be raised would be more stable and durable if it should rest on the solid foundation of the people themselves."[12]

The debate gave Madison the opportunity to advance the theory he had mulled over in New York. In jurisdictions as small as states, majorities had trampled on minority rights. "Debtors have defrauded their creditors," he said. "The holders of one species of property have thrown a disproportion of taxes on the holders of another species." The way to secure private rights and steady justice, he said, was to "enlarge the sphere and thereby divide the community into so great a number of interests and parties that in the first place a majority will not be likely at the same moment to have a common interest separate from that of the whole or of the minority; and in the second place, that in the case they should have such an interest, they may not be apt to unite in the pursuit of it." Having the people vote rather than the states would create a scale sufficient to counteract the injustices that "had more perhaps than anything else produced this convention."[13] When the question was called, delegates affirmed popular election of the first branch, but they stumbled over the method of electing the second. Delegates rejected the idea proposed in article 5 of the Virginia Plan for having the first branch choose the second out of persons nominated by individual legislatures and moved on without approving an alternative.

Article 6 contained a clause particularly important to Madison. It gave the national legislature the right "to negative all laws passed by the several states, contravening in the opinion of the national legislature the articles of union." This wasn't quite the "negative *in all cases whatsoever*" that he had advocated in letters written in March and April, but Madison must have run into resistance in preconvention meetings and so had placed some limits on the legislative veto over the states set forth in the Virginia Plan. Still, even modified, the negative amounted to a sweeping power, one Madison thought essential to controlling state governments. And so—for the moment—did the delegates. The measure passed "without debate or dissent."[14]

The framework Madison had conceived for a new government was making fine progress—until June 7, when Delaware reentered the fray. Fifty-four-year-old John Dickinson, the delegation's frail, scholarly leader, pressed the idea of having the second branch of the national legislature, now being called the Senate, appointed by state legislatures. This would ensure that even Delaware, the least populous state, would have a place. "Let our government be like that of the solar system," Dickinson said. "Let the general government be the sun and the states the planets, repelled yet attracted, and the whole moving regularly and harmoniously in their respective orbits."[15] After no less a personage than George Mason expressed sympathy for Dickinson's view, the proposal passed in the committee of the whole by a vote of 11 to 0. Madison failed to carry his own delegation, nor could the shrewd, bespectacled James Wilson, who had become Madison's close ally, carry Pennsylvania.

The next day Madison circled back to the legislative veto. He had made alliance with Charles Pinckney, a handsome twenty-nine-year-old from South Carolina, who stood on June 8 to urge that the veto be absolute, as Madison had originally wanted. Without it, the states would intrude on national powers, "however extensive they might be on paper," said Pinckney. Madison seconded Pinckney's motion and used his own Newtonian metaphor, calling the absolute veto essential for keeping the proper balance between the center and the satellites: "This prerogative of the general government is the great pervading principle that must control the centrifugal tendency of the states; which, without it, will continually fly out of their proper orbits and destroy the order and harmony of the political system."[16]

John Dickinson, having beaten Madison soundly the day before, now took the floor to agree that without proper control the states posed a threat to the general government. His declaration brought Gunning Bedford Jr., the firebrand of the Delaware delegation, out of his chair. He was "very corpulent," according to William Pierce of Georgia, and smart as well. But, to use Pierce's words, he was also "warm and impetuous in his temper, and precipitate in his judgment." The large states, empowered by proportional representation, would use the absolute veto to "crush the small ones whenever they stand in the way of their ambitions or interested views," Bedford insisted. He charged Pennsylvania and Virginia with wishing "to provide a system in which they would have an enormous and monstrous influence."[17]

Madison, who had known Bedford at Princeton, responded with a temperate tone but a sharply pointed question. "What would be the consequence to the small states of a dissolution of the Union?" he asked. That would happen, he was suggesting, if the small states did not yield. But as Madison watched, the universal veto went down by 7 to 3, with one state divided. Virginia voted for the absolute veto, but as Madison noted, both Mr. Randolph and Mr. Mason voted no.[18] His plans for bringing state governments under control were encountering stiff resistance even within his own delegation.

On June 9, a fair and warm Saturday, another small state made its opposition known. William Paterson of New Jersey, a short, unassuming man, asked that the act authorizing delegates from Massachusetts to the convention be read. Like the commissions from several states, it echoed the congressional resolution that the convention meet "for the sole and express purpose of revising the Articles of Confederation," and Paterson used the authorization to make the case that delegates were exceeding their authority. "We ought to keep within [the congressional resolution's] limits or we should be charged by our constituents with usurpation," he said, and he went on to rail against the idea of proportional representation. "New Jersey will never confederate on the plan before the committee," he said. "She would be swallowed up." He would "rather submit to a monarch, to a despot, than to such a fate."[19]

On the following Monday, June 11, as a hot spell settled in, Roger Sherman of Connecticut formally proposed that representation be according to population in the first branch and that equality of states be the rule in the second. But Madison and his allies were not interested in compromise, and they had the votes to prevail. Sherman's motion failed 6 to 5. A subsequent motion by James Wilson and Alexander Hamilton for proportional representation in the Senate passed 6 to 5.

The small states, getting organized now, found the narrow margins heartening, as was the support they were receiving from states not so small. The newly arrived Luther Martin of Maryland, a confirmed antinationalist, took up their cause. Robert Yates and John Lansing Jr. of New York, who did not want their state under any sort of national control, supported the small states. These delegates joined in producing what history has come to call the New Jersey Plan, and Paterson presented it to the convention on June 15. Hewing closely to the words of the congressional charter, Paterson proposed a series of amendments to the Articles of Confederation that enhanced the powers of Congress and left the one-state-one-vote provision unaltered.[20]

Now there was an alternative to the Virginia Plan, and John Dickinson of Delaware told Madison that his stubborn refusal to compromise was to blame. Some might have taken Madison's generally low-key behavior as a sign that he was naturally conciliatory, but Dickinson had witnessed how firmly fixed he could become. He told him he was at risk of losing small-state support for a strong national government by refusing to meet the small states halfway: "We would sooner submit to a foreign power than submit to be deprived of an equality of suffrage in both branches of the legislature and thereby be thrown under the domination of the large states."[21]

The next day, Saturday, Madison was silent, taking notes, while James Wilson challenged the idea that the Virginia Plan violated the congressional mandate. "With regard to the power of the convention," Wilson said, "he conceived himself authorized to *conclude nothing*, but to be at liberty to *propose anything*." Edmund Randolph agreed, saying that "when the salvation of the Republic was at stake, it would be treason to our trust not to propose what we found necessary." Randolph also reminded the delegates of the perilous state of the nation. "He painted in strong colors," Madison recorded, "the imbecility of the existing confederacy and the danger of delaying a substantial reform."[22]

Madison probably spent Sunday preparing his own critique of New Jersey's proposal, but the following Monday, Alexander Hamilton dominated the proceedings with a six-hour speech. New Jersey's proposal would lead to a government "weak and distracted," said Hamilton, and Randolph's proposals were not much better. "What even is the Virginia Plan but *pork still, with a little change of the sauce*?" he famously asked. The mistake of both plans was their reliance on democracy: "The people are turbulent and changing; they seldom judge or determine right." What was needed was a government similar to Britain's, with an executive and a senate that served for life. Giving permanent place to "the rich and well-born" would protect the public good from the "uncontrolling disposition" of the masses.[23]

Hamilton made a few practical suggestions, such as providing for executive succession. Should a vacancy occur, the president of the Senate would step in until a new "governor" was determined. But his plan was in general so far from what the convention was likely to accept—and the weather so miserably hot and muggy—that delegates did not bother to refute him. In later years, when he became very powerful, his opponents would recall his speech, however, and hold it up as effective evidence of his monarchical leanings.[24]

On June 19, Madison made his case. While the New Jersey Plan aimed at strengthening the Congress of the Confederation, Madison said, there were a multitude of ways in which it left the central government too weak. The states would still encroach on the general government and "bring confusion and ruin on the whole." The states would still trespass on one another, threatening "the tranquility of the Union." Nor could the small states be sure of their "internal tranquility," he said. Paterson's plan would do nothing to help them deal with insurrections, such as the recent uprising in Massachusetts. Madison warned the small states "to consider the situation in which they would remain in case their pertinacious adherence to an inadmissible plan should prevent the adoption of any plan." If the Union dissolved, they would be far less secure than "under a general government pervading with equal energy every part of the empire and having an equal interest in protecting every part against every other part."[25]

When Madison finished, Rufus King of Massachusetts posed a choice for the delegates: "whether Mr. Randolph's [propositions] should be adhered to as preferable to those of Mr. Paterson." The Virginia Plan won the day, 7 to 3, with one state divided, ending any hope the small states had of the New Jersey Plan being accepted—or of a future government resembling the one created by the Articles of Confederation.[26]

But the small states hadn't given up on having an equal voice for each state in the Senate. Their chance came in late June, when rules for representation came up for formal consideration by the convention. On June 27, Luther Martin of Maryland took the floor. He offered a theoretical basis for the small-state view, arguing that since states, like individuals, enjoyed natural equality, equal voting for states "was founded in justice and freedom, not merely in policy." But any summary of his speech misses the effect it had, because it went on for two days, exhausting him and everyone who listened. Some historians have suspected he was drinking, and he did have a reputation for consuming large amounts of alcohol, but either he didn't drink when it counted or what he did drink didn't generally affect his performance. He had a thriving law practice and would achieve historic acquittals, an unlikely outcome if he were given to drunken ramblings in the courtroom.[27]

Martin's speech, which Madison said "was delivered with much diffuseness," was probably a filibuster, a rhetorical form given to wandering diversions. He could well have been trying to hold off a vote on representation until a time advantageous to the small states. He had been a good friend of William Paterson since they had attended Princeton together in the mid-1760s, and Paterson might well have alerted him to absences in the New Jersey delegation that would keep that state from being able to vote.[28] The small states were also hoping that delegates from New Hampshire would appear and strengthen their numbers.

If Martin's purpose was to delay, he succeeded magnificently. He inspired Madison to give a long speech using reason and history to refute his ideas, and he so angered other delegates that they began quarreling. James Wilson rose to compare the small states to England's rotten boroughs. Roger Sherman countered by describing the Virginia Plan as giving four states the power to govern nine. "As they will have the purse," he declared, "they may raise troops and can also make a king when they please."[29]

The wrangling, in turn, led Benjamin Franklin to address the delegates. Heretofore he had asked others to read his speeches, but now he delivered his words himself. Speaking directly to Washington, who was seated in the president's chair, Franklin noted the "small progress" the delegates had made despite their "continual reasonings" with one another:

> In this situation of this assembly, groping as it were in the dark to find political truth and scarce able to distinguish it when presented to us, how has it happened, sir, that we have not hitherto once thought of humbly applying to the Father of lights to illuminate our understandings? . . . I have lived, sir, a long time, and the longer I live, the more convincing proofs I see of this truth—*that God governs in*

the affairs of men. And if a sparrow cannot fall to the ground without his notice, is it probable that an empire can rise without his aid?

Franklin wanted the delegates to step back from their quarrels, consider their larger purpose, and adopt an accommodating spirit. But the next morning, when Connecticut's William Johnson renewed the idea that there be proportional representation in the first branch of the legislature and equality in the second, Madison made clear that he had no interest in compromise. He urged the small states "to renounce a principle which was confessedly unjust, which could never be admitted, and if admitted must infuse mortality into a constitution which we wished to last forever."[30]

But the small states would not give up. On the next day, Saturday, Oliver Ellsworth, a tall, distinguished-looking delegate from Connecticut, said that equal representation in the Senate was necessary in order to protect the small states from large ones, and he appealed to the commitment states had made under the Articles of Confederation to give each an equal right of suffrage. Madison, clearly exasperated, fired back by holding Connecticut up as an example of what was wrong. It was the last state that ought to be calling for "an adherence to a common engagement," he said. That state's legislature "had by a pretty recent vote *positively refused* to pass a law" complying with federal requisitions and followed up by cheekily sending notice of the vote to Congress. And if the issue was protecting the interests of a group of states, what about those that arose from climate and from "having or not having slaves"? In his frustration Madison told a truth that the convention generally avoided. "The great division of interests in the United States . . . did not lie between the large and small states," he said. "It lay between the northern and southern." Therefore, he proposed sarcastically, in one branch of the legislature, representation would be determined by the number of free inhabitants plus the number of slaves. In the other, only free inhabitants would be counted. Thus, "the southern scale would have the advantage in one house and the northern in the other."[31]

Franklin, alarmed at the hostile turn, again urged compromise, this time by evoking an artisan who, finding that two planks do not fit, "takes a little from both and makes a good joint." But his words were followed shortly by the most inflammatory speech of the convention. The volatile Gunning Bedford proclaimed that for all their high-flown words, the big states were seeking dominion over the small ones. *"I do not, gentlemen, trust you,"* he declared. "Sooner than be ruined, there are foreign powers who will take us by the hand." Rufus King of Massachusetts shot back: "Whatever may be my distress, I never will court a foreign power to assist in relieving myself from it."[32] And on that harsh note, the Saturday session ended.

Sunday was a day of respite from the quarreling but not from worry about the convention's fate. George Washington and Robert Morris were "much dejected," a visitor to the Morris home reported. "Debates had run high, conflicting opinions were obstinately adhered to, animosities were kindling, some of the members were threatening to go home, and, at this alarming crisis, a dissolution of the convention was hourly to be apprehended."[33]

Sunday was also a time when members from the small-state coalition might have finalized a scheme for pushing the convention toward a middle ground. It is impossible to prove that they met and planned, but the events of Monday, July 2, suggest that small-state supporters identified two men who, although inclined to the large-state view, were sufficiently concerned about the convention's failing that they were willing to help achieve a compromise.

The first was a Maryland delegate, the wealthy Daniel of St. Thomas Jenifer, a jovial man who owed his unusual name to a Jenifer family tradition of naming all males Daniel. "Of St. Thomas" had been added to distinguish him from his brother. One of the convention's elders, Jenifer had a record of steady attendance—and of canceling Luther Martin's vote— but when the convention met on Monday, he was absent. Oliver Ellsworth of Connecticut renewed the call to have equality of voting in the Senate, and when the roll call reached Maryland, Luther Martin cast a yes vote, moving Maryland, usually divided, into the small-state column. After the vote, Daniel of St. Thomas Jenifer reappeared in the East Room.[34]

Madison, taking notes, probably still counted on a victory. Even with Maryland added to Connecticut, New York, New Jersey, and Delaware, the small states would get only five votes. The large states had six they could count on: Massachusetts, Pennsylvania, Virginia, North Carolina, South Carolina, and Georgia. But when the roll call reached Georgia, the last state to vote, thirty-two-year-old delegate Abraham Baldwin had a public change of heart. He had been born and educated in Connecticut and had spent more of his adult life there than in Georgia. He had apparently become convinced that the delegation of his native state was right to seek compromise, because he voted for Ellsworth's motion, moving Georgia from support of the large states to a divided position. The result was a tie vote: five ayes, five nays, and one state divided.[35]

Delegates jumped to their feet, urging that the matter be sent to a committee. Madison and Wilson were the only voices against, and when the vote came, it was 9 to 2, with even Virginia voting yes. The states then balloted on delegates to serve on the Grand Committee, as it became known, and the news was even worse for Madison. Committed opponents of proportional voting were elected—Luther Martin, William Paterson, Gunning Bedford—and there were ardent advocates of compromise, such as Oliver Ellsworth and Benjamin Franklin. But determined supporters of proportional representation, such as Madison and James Wilson, were notably absent.

WEDNESDAY, JULY 4, a day on which the convention was in adjournment, was a festive time in Philadelphia. The anniversary of the Declaration of Independence was marked by bell ringing, gun salutes, and fireworks. Sermons were preached, orations declaimed, and many a toast was drunk. A group of militia officers at Mr. Preston's Tavern raised their glasses and offered thirteen toasts, including one for the state that had refused to attend the convention: "May Rhode Island be excluded [from] the Union until they elect *honest* men to rule them."[36]

Madison could not have been in a celebratory mood, knowing as he did that the Grand Committee was almost certain to endorse a compromise that he believed fundamentally unfair. On July 5, just as he feared, the committee report proposed a first chamber in which the representation would be proportional and a senate in which each state would have an equal voice. An enticement was included for the large states, namely, that all money bills would originate in the lower chamber, where they were more powerful, but Madison declared that to be no real concession. The matter remained the same, he said. Delegates faced a choice "of either departing from justice in order to conciliate the smaller states and the minority of the people of the U.S. or of displeasing these by justly gratifying the larger states and the majority of the people."[37]

Gouverneur Morris joined Madison in condemning the report of the Grand Committee. The large states could not go along with it, and "civil commotion" was likely to be the result. Then, his temper seeming to rise to meet the temperature (there hadn't been a break in the heat for nearly a week), he declared, "This country must be united. If persuasion does not unite it the sword will." So rancorous was the debate and so recalcitrant the delegates that George Washington began to think that his attendance had been a mistake. "I almost despair of seeing a favorable issue to the proceedings of the convention," he wrote to Hamilton, "and do therefore repent having had any agency in the business."[38]

The issue was still hanging fire on July 13, when Madison took a night off from transcribing his notes to dine at the Indian Queen, an elegant pile of buildings where many delegates stayed. A genial out-of-town visitor, the Reverend Manasseh Cutler, joined the dinner group and proposed a visit to the famed naturalist William Bartram, who lived two miles beyond the Schuylkill River. Cutler, a lobbyist as well as a clergyman, understood that politicians yearned for occasional breaks from their labor, and his suggestion proved popular. The next morning at 5:00, two carriages full of delegates headed out of the city, Madison among them. He knew as well as any the importance of leaving off work and getting into the countryside.

Madison and the other delegates startled William Bartram, who was hoeing barefoot when they arrived, but he soon made them welcome, and they wandered the alleys of his very old garden for nearly two hours. On the way back to Philadelphia, they stopped at Gray's Tavern, where graveled walkways had been laid out. One imagines Madison first following the path that led to a "shady valley, in the midst of which was a purling stream of water," then wandering along another that brought a view of "one of the finest cascades in America."[39] Gray's was a place where one might gather spiritual sustenance to meet the defeat that seemed certain to come.

ON THE FOLLOWING MONDAY, July 16, delegates took up the report of the Grand Committee and by a vote of 5 to 4, with Massachusetts divided, voted for proportional representation in the first house of the legislature and equality of votes in the second. Predictably, Connecticut, New Jersey, Delaware, and Maryland voted for the proposal, as did North Carolina. Voting with Virginia against the compromise were Pennsylvania, South Carolina, and Georgia, which voted last. Abraham Baldwin, apparently seeing that his vote was not needed for the compromise to succeed, returned to the fold.

Edmund Randolph took some time before he spoke, likely pondering the inflammatory suggestion he was about to make. "He wished the convention might adjourn," Madison recorded, "that the large states might consider the steps proper to be taken in the present solemn crisis of the business." Paterson understood the threat: the large states might abandon the convention. Fresh from victory, he dared Randolph to go through with it. If a permanent adjournment was what Randolph had in mind, Paterson declared that "he would second it with all his heart."[40]

Randolph responded calmly but let the idea of a threat linger. As Madison wrote in his notes, "He had in view merely an adjournment till tomorrow in order that some conciliatory experiment might if possible be devised, and that in case the smaller states should continue to hold back, the larger might then take such measures, he would not say what, as might be necessary."[41]

When the large states gathered the next morning before the convention started, it quickly became apparent to Madison that many of the delegates had lost heart for the fight. They "seemed inclined to yield to the smaller states," Madison wrote. How little he was of a mind to do so is clear from his description of the compromise as "imperfect and exceptionable . . . decided by a bare majority of states and by a minority of the people of the United States."[42] But he couldn't fight on without allies.

After the convention was called to order, Madison was dealt a second major setback. The limited legislative veto came up, the check on state laws proposed in the Virginia Plan and previously approved in the committee of the whole. Now, however, delegate after delegate spoke against it. One declared it "likely to be terrible to the states," another said it was "unnecessary," a third that it was "improper." Madison defended it as essential in order to control "the propensity of the states to pursue their particular interests in opposition to the general interest." He said he understood there was sentiment in the convention for the idea that courts could accomplish this task, but they were too slow. The states "can pass laws which will accomplish their injurious objects before they can be . . . set aside by the national tribunals," he said. But the measure received only three aye votes, while seven states voted no. Luther Martin immediately moved "that the legislative acts of the United States made by virtue and in pursuance of the articles of Union and all treaties made and ratified under the authority of the United States shall be the supreme law of the respective states," a proposal that was unanimously adopted.[43] The supremacy clause, as it became known, would be modified and strengthened during the course of the convention, making it clear that the Constitution was also "the supreme law of the land," but even then Madison would not think the delegates had found an effective substitute for a congressional veto.

THE CONVENTION MOVED ON to consider the executive branch. After delegates had agreed to have the executive chosen by the national legislature, one of Madison's Virginia colleagues, Dr. James McClurg, proposed that the executive serve "during good behavior"—which would amount to a lifetime appointment unless the executive was impeached. Madison, astonishingly, took the floor in support. "If it be essential to the preservation of liberty that the legislative, executive, and judiciary powers be separate, it is essential to a maintenance of the separation that they should be independent of each other," he said, and an executive who looked to the legislature to be reappointed would not be independent. The idea of lifetime tenure deserved "a fair hearing and discussion, until a less objectionable expedient should be applied."[44]

In later years, Madison would say that he had merely "meant to aid in parrying the animadversions likely to fall on the motion of Dr. McClurg," for whom he "had a particular regard," but the course of events surely helped prompt his comment. Having the executive chosen by the national legislature, as the convention had just voted, had been proposed in the Virginia Plan, but when Madison had devised that plan, he had not contemplated the states being represented as states in the Senate. Now nothing was as it should be. When George Mason took the floor to predict that tenure during good behavior for the executive would lead to hereditary monarchy, Madison gave a sharp reply. He "was not apprehensive of being thought to favor any step towards monarchy," he said. "The real object with him was to prevent its introduction." State legislatures were "omnipotent," he said. "If no effectual check be devised for restraining the instability and encroachments of the latter, a revolution of some kind or other would be inevitable."[45]

Madison soon reined in his frustration and adjusted his plans. At the convention's beginning, he had expressed concern about enumerating exactly what the powers of Congress were, but once the states gained equality of voting in the Senate, he supported enumeration—and thereby the limitation—of congressional powers.[46] At the beginning of the convention, he had seen the national legislature as the body that would subordinate the states, but with the states to be represented in the Senate and the legislature to have no veto over state actions, he decided that strength was needed outside the legislative branch to provide a check. The executive could fulfill that function, but not if it were chosen by the national legislature as the Virginia Plan proposed.

From the convention's earliest days, Madison's ally James Wilson of Pennsylvania had been proposing election of the executive by the people in order to make that office "as independent as possible." There were practical problems with this idea. The nation had voters in so many far-flung places it was hard to imagine how a single candidate could emerge with a majority or anything approaching it. Wilson's solution was to divide the states into districts and have the people of each district vote for electors, who would then gather and cast their votes for the executive. On July 19, delegates approved the idea of electors but wanted them chosen by state legislatures, a plan that could not have made Madison happy, since those were the very bodies he wanted to disempower. Five days later, the delegates put the selection back in the hands of the national legislature. The to-and-fro prompted Wilson to suggest mockingly that a lottery be tried. Legislators would pick from a bowl of balls, and those who chose gilded ones would become electors.[47]

On July 25, Madison took the floor to note that "there are objections against every mode that has been or perhaps can be proposed" for electing the executive, and he reviewed them. Appointment by the national legislature would not only undermine the independence of the executive, he said; it would also give rise to intrigues between candidates and factions within the legislature. It could even invite foreign meddling. Appointment by state legislatures was objectionable for many reasons, including the "strong propensity" of those legislatures "to a variety of pernicious measures." In the end, there were only two acceptable choices: "appointment by electors chosen by the people" or "an immediate appointment by the people." The former had much to recommend it, he said, but "had been rejected so recently and by so great a majority that it probably would not be proposed anew." That left "election by the people." He said that "with all its imperfections he liked this best." He noted that such a selection was of advantage to northern states, which were likely to have a greater number of qualified voters than southern states, but he, "as an individual from the southern states . . . was willing to make the sacrifice."[48]

Oliver Ellsworth of Connecticut thought Madison's profession of selflessness was a diversion, meant to keep the convention from seeing that the real issue was once again whether the big states would dominate. Since there was no method for narrowing down the number of people from which a voter might select, he was likely to choose a person from his own state, and thus, in Ellsworth's words, "the largest states would invariably have the man." Suggestions followed to fix this problem, such as having citizens cast two votes, only one of which could be for someone from their state. It was an imaginative remedy but did not satisfy Elbridge Gerry of Massachusetts, who had another concern: that the Society of the Cincinnati, being well organized, would take over. "They will in fact elect the chief magistrate in every instance, if the election be referred to the people," he said.[49] The next day, delegates returned to their default position: election by the national legislature.

Madison was finding it uphill work to secure an independent executive, nor was it easy to make that office stronger. He had tried and failed to move the power to appoint judges from the Senate, where he had early in the convention thought it should be, to the executive. He had also tried and failed—and would try and fail again—to establish a council of revision that would bolster the executive with judicial power when it came to vetoes.[50]

Quick action did bring Madison a success in August that would have profound consequences down the years. The convention was considering a list of legislative powers, among them "to make war." He moved successfully to insert "declare" in the place of "make," "leaving to the executive the power to repel sudden attacks."[51] His experience in Congress during the Revolution, when congressmen, including himself, had ordered troops here and there, probably also influenced his thinking. Once war had begun, the executive—now being called the president—had to be the commander in chief.

By August 31, the matter of how to select the president was still sufficiently unsettled that delegates voted to refer it to the memorably named Committee on Postponed Parts. Madison was a member of the committee, as were Rufus King of Massachusetts and Gouverneur Morris of Pennsylvania, both opposed as Madison was to having the national legislature choose the president. But there were strong advocates of that method as well, including the committee's chairman, David

Brearley of New Jersey, and Roger Sherman of Connecticut, and they seem to have brought enough of their fellow committee members around to their view to prevail. They were in the statehouse library, preparing to move to the East Room and make their recommendation—which delegates would have been likely to follow. Selection of the president by the national legislature was the original proposal, it had been positively voted on several times, and it was in many ways the simplest solution.

It is hard to be sure what the United States would look like today if members of Congress selected the president, but certainly the list of White House occupants would be different. There would have been fewer congressional outsiders, such as Ronald Reagan and Bill Clinton. Instead of only one Speaker of the House, James K. Polk, being elected president, there would surely have been several. But the possibility of congressional selection was foreclosed when John Dickinson of Delaware walked through the library door. He was a member of the committee but had been ill, and committee members paused so that the minutes of their deliberations could be read to him. When he heard the recommendation for having the president be elected by the national legislature, he objected: "I observed that the powers which we had agreed to vest in the president were so many and so great that I did not think the people would be willing to deposit them with him unless they themselves would be more immediately concerned in his election." As Dickinson described what happened next, "Gouverneur Morris immediately said, 'Come, gentlemen, let us sit down again and converse further on this subject.' We then all sat down, and after some conference, James Madison took a pen and paper and sketched out a mode for electing the president agreeable to the present provision." Madison pulled together ideas that had previously been discussed in the convention and refined them into a compromise that with a few changes established today's Electoral College system. At one point delegates had passed a proposal to have state legislatures choose electors. Madison put the legislatures in charge of deciding how electors would be chosen, a plan that opened the way for voters to choose electors, as they do today. Each state was to have a number of electors equal to its number of representatives in the House and Senate, which was of advantage to large states. To bring small states along, Madison returned to a version of a plan discussed earlier, proposing that each elector cast two votes, one of which had to be for someone outside his state. Virginia's electors, in other words, would have to cast as many votes for non-Virginians as for Virginians. When the subject had come up previously, Madison had worried aloud about second votes being thrown away in order that a voter might "ensure the object of his first choice," but now he had the solution: make the second vote count. And thus the vice presidency came into being. The person with the second-greatest number of electoral votes would fill that office. He would be first in line of succession, serve as president of the Senate, and have the ability to cast tie-breaking votes in that body.[52]

The committee's report put the matter of choosing the president in the hands of the Senate should no single candidate gain a majority of electoral votes. When there was objection in the convention, Madison explained that giving tie-breaking power to the Senate was the surest way of keeping the matter out of legislative hands. "Whereas if the Senate in which the small states predominate should have the final choice, the concerted effort of the large states would be to make the appointment in the first instance conclusive," he said. Still, there was a slew of objections to giving the Senate, which many delegates viewed as aristocratic, the de facto power of determining the president, and delegates finally agreed to put the responsibility in the House, with each state casting a single vote.[53]

The vice presidency came in for a good deal of criticism. Some objected to having the vice president serve as president of the Senate, as Madison's plan proposed. Elbridge Gerry declared, "The close intimacy that must subsist between the president and vice president makes it absolutely improper," which inspired Gouverneur Morris to counter, "The vice president then will be the first heir apparent that ever loved his father." Roger Sherman observed that "if the vice president were not to be president of the Senate, he would be without employment," an argument that Hugh Williamson of North Carolina, who had been on the Committee on Postponed Parts, did not find convincing. He believed that "such an officer as vice president was not wanted. He was introduced only for the sake of a valuable mode of election which required two to be chosen at the same time."[54] In the end, however, delegates approved having the vice president serve as ex officio president of the Senate.

Another change proposed by the Committee on Postponed Parts— and one Madison had previously put forward—removed from the Senate the power to appoint judges, ambassadors, and other public ministers. Instead, the president would appoint them, by and with the "advice and consent of the Senate." This remarkable enhancement of presidential power passed the convention without dissent. By a vote of 9 to 2, the convention also gave the president the right to appoint "all other officers of the United States whose appointments are not otherwise herein provided for."[55]

IN THE MOST impassioned debates of the convention, the ones concerning slavery, Madison was not a forceful participant. Delegates had adopted the three-fifths rule, which provided that three of every five slaves would be counted to determine a state's population and thus the number of representatives it would have. Gouverneur Morris, unable to abide the benefit that this rule gave to slaveholding states, unleashed a tirade in which he declared slavery to be "the curse of heaven on the states where it prevailed."[56] Madison was silent. He seems to have concluded that the convention could not both grapple with slavery and build a nation—and most delegates seem to have agreed. Morris's proposal to overturn the three-fifths rule went down 10 to 1.

Madison did comment briefly on a proposal concerning the slave trade. A compromise had been reached between states that wanted Congress to have no authority over it (South Carolina, North Carolina, and Georgia) and other states, including Virginia, that wanted Congress to end it. The agreement was that Congress would have no authority until after 1800, but when that proposal was taken up, General Charles

Cotesworth Pinckney of South Carolina, an older cousin of the other Pinckney at the convention, immediately moved to extend the date to 1808. Madison objected, declaring that "so long a term will be more dishonorable to the national character than to say nothing about it in the Constitution."[57] But with votes not only from the Deep South but also from Connecticut, New Hampshire, Massachusetts, and Maryland, General Pinckney's amendment passed.

Gouverneur Morris wanted to be very clear about what had happened. Instead of "such persons as the several states now existing shall think proper to admit," he wanted the word "slaves" to be used. Madison objected, saying that he "thought it wrong to admit in the Constitution the idea that there could be property in men," and his view prevailed. Euphemisms were a way of avoiding the terrible truth that slavery existed, but they also allowed the delegates to create a document suitable for a time when it would not. As political scientist Robert Goldwin observed, they created a constitution for a society that would offer more justice than their own.[58]

BY THE TIME the delegates were ready to send their work to the Committee of Style, which would give the Constitution its words and arrangement, they had, following Madison's lead, created an executive much stronger and more independent than Madison had originally set forth in the Virginia Plan. Although Madison was still not certain that the president would be strong enough to resist the "legislative vortex," the office that had been created appeared too formidable to some. Edmund Randolph had objected in the convention's early days to a single executive as "the fetus of monarchy." He did not see "why the great requisites for the executive department, vigor, dispatch, and responsibility, could not be found in three men, as well as in one man." He was also troubled, he said, by certain "ambiguities of expression."[59] He repeatedly tried to persuade his fellow delegates to deal with these and other matters in a second convention, and when that idea was not accepted, he refused to sign the Constitution.

Elbridge Gerry, who also refused to put his signature to the finished document, listed numerous reasons, including "the vice president being made head of the Senate," a situation he regarded as "dangerous." George Mason, whom Madison reported "in an exceeding ill humor," refused to sign because the Constitution contained no bill of rights—an idea he did not broach until late in the convention. He also objected to the vice president, "that unnecessary (and dangerous) officer . . . , who for want of other employment is made president of the Senate, thereby dangerously blending the executive and legislative powers."[60]

Madison was a member of the Committee of Style, but he emphasized that Gouverneur Morris should be credited "for the *finish given* to the *style* and *arrangement* of the Constitution."[61] Thus we know it is to Morris that we owe the elegant preamble:

> We the people of the United States, in order to form a more perfect union, establish justice, insure domestic tranquility, provide for the common defense, promote the general welfare, and secure the blessings of liberty to ourselves and our posterity, do ordain and establish this Constitution for the United States of America.

The power of the preamble comes in large measure from Morris's having anticipated the Constitution going into effect, which would occur, according to article 7, after state conventions, chosen "by the people," had ratified the document. Then it would be no longer the creation of delegates in Philadelphia but the decree of "We the people."

ON SEPTEMBER 17, 1787, a clear, cool day, delegates gathered for the last time. After the Constitution was read aloud, Benjamin Franklin proposed that they subscribe their names to the document in witness to "the unanimous consent of the states present." This "ambiguous form," Madison explained in his notes, "had been drawn up . . . to gain the dissenting members."[62] A delegate's signature on the document, in other words, indicated not personal approval but rather recognition that a majority of the delegates present from each state had voted aye. Franklin's proposal, which Madison observed in his notes had originated with Gouverneur Morris, did not induce Randolph, Gerry, or Mason to sign, but it did allow the convention to cloak the result of its efforts in the fine cloth of unanimity—despite the presence of delegates who did not approve.

As the last of the delegates was signing, Madison, still taking notes, recorded remarks that Benjamin Franklin made to those sitting near him about the half sun carved on the back of George Washington's chair: "I have, said he, often and often in the course of the session and in the vicissitudes of my hopes and fears as to its issue, looked at that behind the president without being able to tell whether it was rising or setting. But now at length I have the happiness to know that it is a rising and not a setting sun." Madison finished his note taking with this image of optimism, but it did not reflect what he felt. With the states represented as states in the Senate and with no national veto over their actions, he was concerned, as he wrote to Jefferson, "that the plan should it be adopted will neither effectually answer its national object nor prevent the local mischiefs which everywhere excite disgusts against the state governments."[63] After all the effort of weeks and months, he had little confidence that the framework for government that the convention had created would work.

Chapter 7

IF MEN WERE ANGELS

WHEN JOHN QUINCY ADAMS called Madison "the father of the Constitution," he was not only paying tribute to what Madison accomplished in Philadelphia but also recognizing his achievements in the months afterward.[1] Crucial as Madison was to the creation of the Constitution, he was at least equally important to seeing that it went into effect.

But before he could begin his efforts on behalf of ratification, he had to reconcile himself to what he thought of as the Constitution's great flaw: it failed to do enough to control what he called "the unwise and wicked proceedings" of the states.[2] The Constitution did place some restrictions—states could not coin money, for example, pass ex post facto laws, or engage in war—but Madison did not think this was enough. He had seen states pass laws that made it impossible for creditors to collect what was owed to them and that violated international treaties. He had seen them try to legislate religious belief and refuse to pay requisitions even when it meant that soldiers in the field went hungry. He had also seen that respect neither for the general good, nor for reputation, nor for religion had the power to prevent the actions of self-interested majorities in the states. Thus his conviction that a national veto was necessary—and his doubt that a constitution without it would work.

Madison stayed in Philadelphia for several days after the convention, finishing up his notes and trying to figure out his way forward. His delay in getting to New York, where Congress was meeting, prompted one of his fellow Virginians to write to hurry him along. In case Madison was taking his time in getting back to New York because he supposed that the Virginia delegation was doing fine without him, Edward Carrington wrote, he should be aware that all was not well, particularly in the case of Richard Henry Lee, who had pretty clearly been in touch with convention dissenters. Having made history for proposing in Congress in 1776 that the colonies "are, and of right ought to be, free and independent states," Lee was a powerful politician whose opposition to the Constitution could not be discounted. Tall and thin, he possessed noted oratorical powers, which he enhanced with sweeping gestures made all the more dramatic by a black silk handkerchief he kept over his left hand. It covered the results of a long-ago hunting accident in which he had lost four fingers.[3]

The realization that the Constitution could be in trouble might have helped Madison put his doubts aside. Perhaps during the postconvention days in Philadelphia, he also visited with Benjamin Franklin, who had been eloquent about his own misgivings. On the last day of the convention, Franklin had said that despite what seemed to him the Constitution's faults, he supported it: "For when you assemble a number of men to have the advantage of their joint wisdom, you inevitably assemble with those men, all their prejudices, their passions, their errors of opinion, their local interests, and their selfish views. From such an assembly can a perfect production be expected? It therefore astonishes me, Sir, to find this system approaching so near to perfection as it does. . . . Thus I consent, Sir, to this Constitution because I expect no better, and because I am not sure, that it is not the best." Madison came around to a similar view. While not glossing over his disappointment, he told Jefferson that given "the natural diversity of human opinions on all new and complicated subjects, it is impossible to consider the degree of concord which ultimately prevailed as less than a miracle." He advised another friend that it was a mistake to compare the document produced by the convention with an ideal theory, "which each individual may frame in his own mind." The proper comparison was "with the system which it is meant to take the place of." Whatever its failings, the Constitution was superior to the Articles of Confederation. It would provide "some anchor for the fluctuations which threaten shipwreck to our liberty."[4]

Madison arrived in New York, moved into Mrs. Elsworth's boardinghouse, and soon found himself countering efforts by Richard Henry Lee to amend the document created in Philadelphia. Some of the changes Lee proposed were structural, including a senate in which representation was according to population. Madison had fought for proportional representation in the Senate but realized that any amendment would throw the ratification process into chaos. "There will be two plans," he said. Some states would likely consider the document proposed by the convention, others the Constitution as amended by Congress, and nine states had to ratify exactly the same document in order for the Constitution to go into effect.[5]

Lee also proposed a declaration of rights to include freedom of the press and freedom of religion, a suggestion that seemed almost a surprise to Madison. Such a declaration was not necessary, he explained. The proposed constitution based all power in the people, who then granted certain enumerated powers to the government. They had not given over their rights in those enumerated powers and thus did not need the Constitution to guarantee them. The delegates to the Philadelphia convention, who had been part of creating the Constitution, seem for the most part to have grasped this. Only in the last days of the convention did George Mason, growing increasingly hostile, bring the subject up.[6] During the ratification process, it would become very clear, however, that this theoretical understanding was not widely shared. Suggestions in ratifying conventions for amending the Constitution to include various rights would present to Madison one of his greatest challenges, particularly since opponents to the Constitution figured out early the chaos that amendments could cause.

Lee did not have the votes to pass his amendments, but Madison and his allies viewed their very existence as a threat. Word of them would spread, and delegates from various state conventions might well pick and choose, resulting in the confusion that pro-Constitution forces dreaded. Thus proponents of the document agreed that in exchange for expunging Lee's proposed amendments from the congressional journal, they would send the document to the states without making a recommendation that they ratify it.

The Federalists, as pro-Constitution forces were beginning to call themselves, did take advantage of the agreement of all states present and voting to the compromise by inserting the word "unanimously" in the resolution. Lee understood what they were doing—hoping that the population at large would think that "unanimously" applied not merely to the sending of the Constitution but to "unanimous approbation" for the document itself. When George Washington learned from Madison what the Federalists had done, he pronounced himself "pleased": "This apparent unanimity will have its effect. Not everyone has opportunities to peep behind the curtain; and as the multitude often judge from externals, the appearance of unanimity in that body, on this occasion, will be of great importance."[7] Washington was not so much of a statesman that he failed to appreciate a skillful political maneuver. He had, after all, presided over a similar one at the Constitutional Convention.

ON OCTOBER 11, 1787, Madison, writing from New York, told his brother Ambrose that the Constitution was being favorably received in the middle and northern states, but a week later his assessment changed. "Newspapers here begin to teem with vehement and virulent calumniations of the proposed government," he wrote to Washington. He worried about the effect on the public—and he was not alone. On October 27 a concerned citizen calling himself Publius struck back by defending the Constitution in the New York *Independent Journal.* The ratification of the Constitution, he wrote, would decide "whether societies of men are really capable or not of establishing good government from ref[l]ection and choice, or whether they are forever destined to depend for their political constitutions on accident and force." Publius, in reality Alexander Hamilton, promised a series of articles that would demonstrate to his fellow New Yorkers that the very survival of the Union depended on ratification.[8]

Hamilton's doubts about the Constitution ran even deeper than Madison's, but he had concluded that a failure to ratify it would bring chaos, and he invited Madison to join him in persuading New Yorkers in its favor. He had already drawn his friend William Duer into the project, as well as John Jay, whose experience in foreign affairs Hamilton probably thought would be useful. Madison might have had some doubts about that, given the mischief that Jay's efforts to negotiate away the Mississippi had caused; nonetheless, he agreed to become part of the writing team. New Yorkers were not the only ones for whom the case for the Constitution needed to be made. Support in Virginia was waning. "All my informations from Richmond concur in representing the enthusiasm in favor of the new Constitution as subsiding and giving place to a spirit of criticism," Madison wrote to Washington.[9]

Hamilton was fortunate that Madison signed on. While Duer's writing was "intelligent and sprightly," as Madison described it, he was not asked, after submitting a few essays, to write others, and what he did produce was never made a part of what became known as *The Federalist*. As for Jay, he soon became too ill to write and would author only five of the eighty-five essays. Madison wrote knowledgeably. He had, after all, attended every day of the Philadelphia convention, while Hamilton, after his fiery speech, had been absent for more than a month. Madison also wrote quickly, which the publication schedule demanded. "Whilst the printer was putting into type parts of a number," Madison later recalled, "the following parts were under the pen."[10]

Madison and Jay assumed the Publius pseudonym (for Publius Valerius Publicola, one of the founders of the Roman Republic), which meant that Madison's finest work would again appear before the public anonymously. But it was customary for writers who had a political point to make to use classical names, and there was additional reason in this case to keep the identities of the authors secret. The people of New York, to whom the essays were addressed, were unlikely to yield to the arguments of a Virginian, nor were Virginians going to find a New Yorker's opinions persuasive.

As Madison set to work on *The Federalist,* he did tell a few people, in confidence, of his participation, including George Washington, who he hoped would help him get the essays printed in Virginia, and Governor Edmund Randolph, whom Madison was gently trying to bring around to the Federalist side. Randolph needed a lot of tending. He had come up with a scheme for the Virginia Assembly to propose amendments to the Constitution and then get them approved or rejected by other state legislatures before Virginia's ratifying convention met. Randolph thought this was a way to avoid having different states ratify the Constitution with different amendments. When Madison failed to comment on his proposal, the Virginia governor was hurt—even though by now he had abandoned the project. "Why would you not give me your opinion as to the scheme I proposed[?]," he asked Madison. "I am now convinced of the impropriety of the idea, but I wish to open to you without reserve the innermost thoughts of my soul and was desirous of hearing something from you on this head." Madison patiently explained that many legislatures would have already provided for their state's ratifying convention and adjourned before Virginia could send out possible amendments. In his next letter to Randolph he enclosed two of the *Federalist* essays and in a gesture of openness let him in on the secret: "I am in myself for a few numbers."[11]

One person whom Madison conspicuously did not tell about his essays was Thomas Jefferson. For years he had written frankly to Jefferson about his political views, and he had shared personal details about the failure of his romance with Kitty Floyd, but during the time he was immersed in writing *The Federalist* and for six months afterward, Madison wrote not a word to his friend about the task he had taken on. After four of his *Federalist* essays had been published, he sent Jefferson fifty trees as well as other plants, including rhododendrons, and promised he would try to find opossums and Virginia redbirds to ship to him. He also described at length the progress of ratification across the country (every state but Rhode Island had agreed to a ratifying convention) and in Virginia ("Mr. Henry is the great adversary who will render the event precarious"). But he told Jefferson nothing about *The Federalist*.[12]

Jefferson had a habit of opining from a distance that might have caused Madison to think twice about involving him. Early in 1787, at the height of concern about Shays's Rebellion and amid worries that insurrection would spread, Jefferson had airily written from Paris, "I hold it that a little rebellion now and then is a good thing and as necessary in the political world as storms in the physical." It was a statement that must have struck Madison, who thought that stability in government was paramount, as singularly imprudent. More recently, Jefferson had pronounced on the national veto, writing, "*Prima facie* I do not like it." Madison, who had thought long and deeply about the veto, had explained to Jefferson that he thought it necessary not only to ensure national unity but also to guard private rights. Nonetheless, Jefferson denounced it: "It fails in an essential character that the hole and the patch should be commensurate. But this proposes to mend a small hole by covering the whole garment."[13] To Madison, who didn't view the vices of the states as a small matter, Jefferson's words must have carried a sting, particularly since he received them when his disappointment at having failed to secure the veto was fresh.

On October 24, after the convention was over, Madison sent Jefferson a letter describing the new plan of government and defending at length the negative on state laws that he had advocated but failed to secure. When Jefferson wrote back, however, he seemed oblivious to Madison's explanation. His primary complaint now was about something the Constitution lacked. "A bill of rights is what the people are entitled to against every government on earth, general or particular," Jefferson proclaimed, "and what no just government should refuse or rest on inference."[14] Madison was extremely good at separating the wheat from the chaff in Jefferson's thinking, and his friend's conviction might have spurred his thinking about the importance of a bill of rights for gaining popular support for the Constitution. But even as he took Jefferson's observation on board, Madison must have been irritated at the implication that he was not concerned with protecting rights. It was in order to defend them in the states that he had fought for a national veto—the instrument that Jefferson had so summarily dismissed.

Jefferson also seemed to ignore his friend's description of the agreement reached at the Philadelphia convention as nothing "less than a miracle." Although he had participated in neither the work of putting the convention together nor any of the nerve-racking months of give-and-take that had produced the Constitution, Jefferson put forward the possibility of a second convention as though agreement could easily be reached again. Find out what parts of the Constitution people like or dislike, Jefferson advised Madison, then say to them, "We see now what you wish."[15] As Jefferson viewed things from Paris, a second convention could then perfect the Constitution, but in Madison's world amendments and a second convention were weapons being wielded by foes in order to destroy the Constitution. The two Virginians on opposite sides of the Atlantic had vastly different perceptions of what was happening on Madison's side, and if Madison deemed it unfruitful to take up his work on *The Federalist* with Jefferson, he certainly had cause.

THE *FEDERALIST* ESSAY that would eventually become most famous was the first one Madison wrote. In *Federalist* 10, published November 22, 1787, he set forth the failures of "our governments" (rather than "our states," where, after all, the Constitution would be ratified), noting the instability and injustices that had caused good citizens across the country to increasingly distrust those governments and feel "alarm for private rights." The cause of government failures was "faction," which he explained as people "united and actuated by some common impulse of passion or of interest adverse to the rights of other citizens or to the permanent and aggregate interests of the community." There was no cure for faction. Its causes were "sown in the nature of man." But an extended republic such as the Constitution proposed could control its effects:

> The influence of factious leaders may kindle a flame within their particular states but will be unable to spread a general conflagration through the other states. A religious sect may degenerate into a political faction in a part of the confederacy, but the variety of sects dispersed over the entire face of it must secure the national councils against any danger from that source. A rage for paper money, for an abolition of debts, for an equal division of property, or for any other improper or wicked project will be less apt to pervade the whole body of the Union than a particular member of it.

Madison had not forgotten the convulsions charismatic leaders could cause or the injustice that could spring from "a zeal for different opinions concerning religion," but in *Federalist* 10 he emphasized the owning or not owning of property as a source of faction. A stable and just society required that property owners and creditors, though they be a minority, have governmental arrangements that protected their rights—as he believed the extended republic created by the Constitution would do.

Madison also wrote in *Federalist* 10 that a large republic would have the advantage of more "fit characters" for people to choose from for public office and suggested that since a greater number of voters would choose each official in a large republic, the representatives who emerged would be more likely to rise above faction and focus on the greater good.[16] This theory, for all its appeal, would not survive the 1790s, when it would become clear to Madison that ideas about the greater good were also subject to fierce and factious controversy. The principles to which he was devoted would not prevail unless he fought for them.

The government Madison described in *The Federalist* was new under the sun, a point that Antifederalists, as those opposed to the Constitution were being called, advanced as a critique. In his second contribution to *The Federalist*, no. 14, Madison asserted that novelty was not to be shunned: "But why is the experiment of an extended republic to be rejected merely because it may comprise what is new? Is it not the glory of the people of America that, whilst they have paid a decent regard to the opinions of former times and other nations, they have not suffered a blind veneration for antiquity, for custom, or for names to overrule the suggestions of their own good sense, the knowledge of their own situation, and the lessons of their own experience?" America's leaders had "accomplished a revolution which has no parallel in the annals of human society," he concluded, and it should be no surprise that "they reared the fabrics of governments which have no model on the face of the globe."[17]

Madison's goal was a stable republic where citizens were free and private rights respected. His method was that of the Enlightenment: to look to the ages for the lessons of history. And when he did, as in *Federalist* 18 and 19, what he saw time and again was that confederacies failed without a strong central government. The trick was to be sure that government did not become tyrannical—and here again the extended republic came into play. So many people of so many diverse opinions, living across such vast territory, made it difficult for "an interested and over-bearing majority" to gain "superior force."[18]

A second protection was the partition of power that Madison explained in *Federalist* 51. Authority was to be divided between states and the general government, among the branches of the government, and within the legislative branch. The structure was devised, he wrote, so "that its several constituent parts may, by their mutual relations, be the means of keeping each other in their proper places." Separated powers and countervailing forces could make swift and decisive action difficult, but the point of this plan was not efficiency. We are familiar with Madison's words "if men were angels, no government would be necessary," but his next sentence is equally important: "If angels were to govern men, neither external nor internal controls on government would be necessary."[19]

Countering critics in his own time who believed that the Constitution made the central government too strong, Madison wrote that the powers given to it were "few and defined." Critics called particular attention to the first provision of article 1, section 8, which grants Congress the power "to lay and collect taxes, duties, imposts and excises, to pay the debts, and provide for the common defense and general welfare of the United States." They argued that the last phrase granted unlimited power, an objection that Madison called "extraordinary." It was, he said, simply a general expression of the enumerated powers that followed, such as the powers to declare war and provide post offices. Moreover, he pointed out in *Federalist* 41, the language had come straight from the Articles of Confederation, where it had certainly never been used to exercise unlimited power.[20]

The last provision of article 1, section 8, brought objections even more strenuous from Antifederalists. It granted Congress the power "to make all laws which shall be necessary and proper for carrying into execution the foregoing powers and all other powers vested by this Constitution in the government of the United States." Answering those who saw this as opening the way for Congress to "exercise powers not warranted by [the Constitution's] true meaning," Madison declared, "No axiom is more clearly established in law, or in reason, than that wherever the end is required, the means are authorized; wherever a general power to do a thing is given, every particular power necessary for doing it is included."[21] Madison had argued for general and implied powers before, but it was the case he made in *Federalist* 44 that would come back to haunt him.

The *Federalist* essays did more than answer the Constitution's critics. In them, Publius set forth the reasons that a new form of government was necessary and explained in great detail how government under the Constitution would work. And he did so in an overwhelming torrent of words. "Publius has already written twenty-six numbers, as much as would jade the brains of any poor sinner," wrote one wag, when the series was less than a third complete. "In decency, he should now rest on his arms and let the people draw their breath for a little." Twenty-seven subscribers to the *New York Journal*, sounding very much like Antifederalists, instructed the newspaper to stop "cramming us with the voluminous Publius."[22]

Hamilton was practicing law as he wrote *The Federalist*, and Madison, a member of Congress, was also collecting and disseminating intelligence on the progress of ratification with a network of correspondents. Madison, later remarking on "the haste with which many of the papers were penned," observed how vital to the effort were the "historical and other notes which had been used in the convention."[23] The reading he had done on the structure, strengths, and weaknesses of ancient and modern confederacies was still serving him well, as were his reflections on vices of the political system of the United States.

Madison and Hamilton quickly learned to save time by dispensing with the process of reviewing each other's essays, which makes their achievement all the more remarkable. Writing at breakneck speed, thirty-six-year-old James Madison and thirty-three-year-old Alexander Hamilton created a classic of Western political thought, a document that stands alongside the Declaration of Independence and the Constitution as a fundamental text of American history.[24]

Although he had not told Jefferson of his work on *The Federalist*, Madison seems to have kept his friend in mind as he wrote. Jefferson did not understand how difficult the creation of the Constitution was, which might have prompted Madison, in *Federalist* 37, to set forth the obstacles that delegates had faced. They had to balance not only "the interfering pretensions of the larger and smaller states" but also "energy in government" with stability, as well as the authority of the general government with that of the states. The diversity of interests in the United States that would be of such advantage when the country was formed had been, in the forming of it, a great challenge: "The real wonder is that so many difficulties should have been surmounted, and surmounted with an unanimity almost as unprecedented as it must have been unexpected. It is impossible for any man of candor to reflect on this circumstance without partaking of the astonishment. It is impossible for the man of pious reflection not to perceive in it a finger of that Almighty Hand which has been so frequently and signally extended to our relief in the critical stages of the revolution." In *Federalist* 49, published some three weeks later, Madison specifically cited what seemed to him Jefferson's misplaced faith in conventions. After praising his friend's creativity and enlightenment, Madison brought up a proposal that Jefferson had made in his draft of a constitution for the state of Virginia. Jefferson's idea had been for successive conventions, which would provide ways to change periodically the framework of government. But, Madison noted, it would inevitably lead to instability. "A nation of philoso phers" might have no need for the steadiness of venerable institutions, Madison observed, "but a nation of philosophers is as little to be expected as the philosophical race of kings wished for by Plato."[25]

WHEN HAMILTON was called away from New York City on legal business early in 1788, Madison took over the writing of *The Federalist.* In an amazing burst of creative energy, he wrote nos. 37 through 58— twenty-two essays—in forty days, a record that not even the frenetic Hamilton matched. After Hamilton returned to the project, Madison wrote nos. 62 and 63. Then he had to leave New York, and the task, except for a single essay by Jay, fell to Hamilton. When *The Federalist* was finished, Hamilton would have contributed 60 percent of the essays— and later he would claim even more. Shortly before his duel with Aaron Burr, Hamilton tucked a memorandum into a book in the law office of his friend Egbert Benson claiming authorship of sixty-three of the essays, or nearly 75 percent of *The Federalist,* attributing fourteen essays to Madison, five to Jay, and three to a joint effort by him and Madison. After he retired from public office, Madison offered a correction: Hamilton had written fifty-one of the essays; he himself, twenty-nine; and Jay, five—an accounting that, after years of controversy, scholars have generally accepted.[26]

Madison attributed Hamilton's erroneous list "to the hurry in which the memorandum was made out," but Hamilton's claim clearly irritated him. It wasn't surprising that Hamilton's memory should have failed him on the occasion of attributing authorship of the *Federalist* essays, Madison wrote many years later, since there was an even more startling example of his forgetfulness. Hamilton had claimed that during the convention he had favored a three-year term for the president, "when in fact . . . he desired a president 'during good behavior'"—a ruler for life, unless impeached.[27] It was risky to remember wrongly what happened at the Constitutional Convention since Madison had his notes.

MADISON HAD TO BREAK OFF his work on *The Federalist* to return to Virginia. He had agreed in November 1787 to let his name be put forward in the contest for delegates to the ratifying convention. In light of the fact that in the previous month he had been overwhelmingly re-elected to Congress without returning home, he apparently assumed he would not need to travel back to Orange in order to be chosen for the convention. But then he began to get word of growing resistance to the Constitution. His father wrote that "the Baptists are now generally opposed" to the Constitution. "I think you had better come in as early in March as you can." Governor Edmund Randolph urged, "You must come in." By this time, Randolph had buried his reasons for not signing the Constitution so deeply in strong arguments for it that he was seen as more helpful than not to the ratification effort. Madison was sympathetic to what he called Randolph's "particular way of thinking on the subject" and in years to come would continue to be tolerant of his friend's inclination to bend with what he thought were prevailing winds.[28]

When George Washington wrote to Madison to say that it was "of indispensible necessity" that he be in the Virginia Convention, Madison confessed that a March journey from New York to Orange County was not an attractive prospect, nor was he looking forward to the convention, where he was going to end up contending with men whose friendship he valued.[29] Nevertheless, he was coming. Six states had ratified the Constitution so far, and none had turned it down—although Rhode Island had refused to call a convention. Madison was worried about New Hampshire, where the ratifying convention had adjourned without taking action, but hopeful for Maryland and South Carolina. Their conventions would precede Virginia's, and their ratifications would bring the total to eight. The Old Dominion could make it nine—the number required to bring the new government into being.

TO BREAK UP the long trip home, Madison stopped in Philadelphia for several days, and then on Tuesday, March 18, 1788, he arrived at Mount Vernon. The weather was cool, and Washington had been out riding all day, tending to his plantation as slaves repaired fences, prepared some fields for planting, and sowed peas, beans, and oats in others. Madison was in time for dinner—and in time to escape the hard downpour that started toward night. The next day, Washington took a rare break from riding over his fields, and he and Madison discussed the upcoming convention. Washington was feeling optimistic. Just two days before, he had been present when Fairfax County had elected two supporters of the Constitution as delegates. Madison was likely more cautious. He knew from his correspondence how divided opinion was in Orange County.[30]

The next morning Washington lent Madison his carriage to take him to Colchester. There he caught the stage to Fredericksburg, where he found a letter awaiting him. It contained another warning about the Baptists. "Fearing religious liberty is not sufficiently secured," Joseph Spencer wrote, leaders of that community were opposing ratification. Spencer recommended that Madison spend a few hours with John Leland, one of the most influential of Virginia's Baptist preachers, who happened to live between Fredericksburg and Orange. It was a suggestion that Madison found appealing. There were many Baptists in Orange County; he needed to do something about their opposition, and John Leland was a very good place to start. Just a few years younger than Madison, Leland, a tall, thin man who radiated warmth, was at the height of his powers. He had mastered the use of reasoned argument in his preaching and in 1788 alone had baptized three hundred people in Virginia's waters. Second only to his dedication to saving souls was Leland's determination to see religious liberty prevail. "Should not government protect all kinds of people, of every species of religion, without showing the least partiality?" he asked. "Has not the world had enough proofs of the impolicy and cruelty of favoring a Jew more than a Pagan, Turk, or Christian; or a Christian more than either of them?"[31]

There is no firsthand account of Madison's meeting with Leland, but one story has it that the two men sat for many hours on a grassy hill underneath a shade tree, and by the time they took leave of each other, Madison had won Leland's support for the upcoming election—an outcome for which there is a good deal of circumstantial evidence. Leland would have known going into the meeting that Madison, like himself, was a champion of religious freedom and that he had stood by the Baptists in a time of great need. Perhaps Madison told him of things he would not have known—such as Madison's anonymous authorship of the "Memorial and Remonstrance Against Religious Assessments," written to prevent a religious tax that Baptists had opposed. Perhaps he shared with him the difficulties that would be created if the Constitution were to be amended before it was fully ratified. At some point, Leland concluded that "the plan [for the Constitution] must be good, for it has the signature of a tried, trusty friend." Leland also drew comfort from knowing that the new government would almost certainly be presided over by George Washington, whom he greatly admired.[32]

When Madison finally reached home on March 23, he found "the county filled with the most absurd and groundless prejudices against the federal constitution," as he described it to Eliza Trist. Although he had managed to be elected repeatedly to the Virginia legislature and the Continental Congress without ever giving a campaign speech, now one was required. On the day following his arrival, he reported, "I was . . . obliged . . . to mount for the first time in my life the rostrum before a large body of the people and to launch into a harangue of some length in the open air and on a very windy day." When the balloting at the Orange County courthouse was over, he had finished first in a field of four, winning support from some 80 percent of the voters. Leland later attested he was one of those who had backed Madison, and judging from Madison's success in becoming a delegate to the Virginia ratifying convention, he brought more than a few Baptists into Madison's camp with him.[33]

· · ·

AT THE URGING of George Nicholas, a veteran of the Revolutionary War and a supporter of the Constitution, Madison worked to get copies of *The Federalist* (now being printed in two volumes) for convention delegates, "the greater part" of whom, Nicholas wrote, "will go to the meeting without information on the subject." Nicholas also wanted Madison to lay out for him arguments to counter the fear that the government being proposed would cede navigation rights on the Mississippi. Madison obliged in a lengthy letter, pointing out that the stronger, more competent government outlined in the Constitution would be more likely to have its way in a face-off with Spain. It was an idea that he would hear echoed back to him when Nicholas spoke on the subject of the Mississippi at the ratifying convention.[34]

Madison's skill at planting ideas in other people's minds was also evident with Governor Edmund Randolph. Still bringing him along, Madison wrote to him that the only acceptable kind of amendment to the Constitution was "recommendatory"—the kind that Massachusetts had passed with its ratification. If Virginia's amendments were added as a condition of ratification, there was no certainty that states that had already ratified wouldn't reconsider, and the result might be, as Madison ever so tactfully put it, "something much more remote from your ideas and those of others who wish a salutary government than the plan now before the public." Moreover, those who didn't want a new government would use conditional amendments "to carry on their schemes." Soon Randolph was writing back that he had always had two doubts about previous amendments: that they would be frustrated if too many other states had already ratified and that "under their cover, a higher game might be played." But he wasn't ready to make a final determination, he said, "until I hear something from Maryland at least."[35] After that state overwhelmingly ratified the Constitution at the end of April, Madison apparently felt secure enough about Randolph that he did not write to him on the subject again.

George Mason, on the other hand, seemed to become more hostile by the day. Shortly after he had returned to Virginia from the Philadelphia convention, he had declared that despite his objections he would rather have the Constitution than not, but by spring he was dead against it. George Nicholas reported that Patrick Henry had also become unyielding: "Mr. Henry is now almost avowedly an enemy to the Union and therefore will oppose every plan that would cement it."[36]

On top of all this, Jefferson was meddling. Less than a week before the ratification convention was to convene, Madison received word that a letter from Jefferson had been circulated at the Maryland convention in Annapolis. It was, in fact, an excerpt from the long missive that Jefferson had sent to Madison on December 20, 1787, describing his dissatisfaction with the Constitution. Marylander Daniel Carroll was appalled at the letter, calling it "not consistent with that delicacy of friendship I thought he possessed," and Madison was unhappy as well. But within a few months, he received a typically generous letter from Jefferson, reporting that he had sent the pedometer Madison had requested and offering instructions: "Cut a little hole in the bottom of your left watch pocket. Pass the hook and tape through it and down between the breeches and drawers, and fix the hook on the edge of your knee band, an inch from the knee buckle. Then hook the instrument itself by its swivel hook on the upper edge of the watch pocket. . . . When you choose it should cease to count, unhook it from the top of the watch pocket and let it fall down to the bottom of the pocket."[37] What could one do with a friend who was at once so aggravating and so amiable? Madison ignored the letter circulated in Annapolis—for the time being.

RICHMOND WAS PACKED when Madison arrived. The people of Virginia wanted to see and hear the giants of the commonwealth debate their future, and they flooded into the capital in unprecedented numbers. Madison took a room at the Swan, an unpretentious tavern known for good food, good wine, and its beckoning sign, a gilded and graceful swan painted on a board high above the street. The tavern was only a few blocks from the theater on Shockoe Hill where the ratifying convention was meeting, and on June 3, 1788, Madison probably walked to the gathering. The day was given over to rule making, and he listened as George Mason insisted that the Constitution be debated clause by clause before any vote was taken on it. Since the Pennsylvania and Maryland conventions had ratified quickly, Mason's goal was to have Virginia move slowly. He apparently expected some objection to his proposal, but Madison quickly took the floor to concur in it.[38] Mason's motion played to Madison's strength. No one in the country was better able to explicate the Constitution in detail than he.

On the next day, June 4, Antifederalists suffered a number of setbacks. Almost as soon as the convention dissolved into the committee of the whole, the chief Antifederalist spokesman, Patrick Henry, made a motion intended to show that the Constitutional Convention had exceeded its mandate. Edmund Pendleton, the sixty-six-year-old chairman of the convention, objected. On crutches since falling from a horse and dislocating his hip in 1777, he probably had to struggle to his feet, but there was no doubt about his authority, and in the face of Pendleton's opposition Henry withdrew his motion. He was soon back, however, with another attack. By what right had the delegates at the Philadelphia convention used the words "We, the People"? he wanted to know: "My political curiosity, exclusive of my anxious solicitude for the public welfare, leads me to ask, who authorized them to speak the language of *We, the People,* instead of *We, the States?*" Before the delegates to the Philadelphia convention had worked their mischief, "a general peace and an universal tranquility prevailed in this country," Henry said. Their proposal to change the government might well result in liberty being lost and tyranny arising. "Instead of securing your rights you may lose them forever," he thundered.[39]

Edmund Randolph, taking the floor immediately after Henry, noted that politics is "too often nourished by passion at the expense of the understanding" and asked to be forgiven for having thought the convention would be "one exception to this tendency of mankind." Then he took up Henry's question of "why we assumed the language of 'We, the People'": "What harm is there in consulting the people on the construction of a government by which they are to be bound? Is it unfair? Is it unjust? If the government is to be binding on the people, are not the people the proper persons to examine its merits or defects?" But the most important part of Randolph's speech was a dramatic announcement. He would support the ratification of the Constitution without previous amendments. Although he had been in favor of them before, he said, he now realized that it was too late in the day. They would result in "ruin to the Union," and he said, raising his arm, "I will assent to the lopping of this limb . . . before I assent to the dissolution of the Union."[40]

The governor's stand was a blow to the Antifederalists, as was news arriving that day of South Carolina's ratifying the Constitution. George Mason seemed unsettled when he spoke after Randolph. He had a potent point to make: that the general government should not have taxing power. But he made his argument in a weak and wandering way, and by the time of the day's adjournment Federalists were elated. Madison wrote a short note to George Washington, telling him that Governor Randolph had "thrown himself fully into the Federal scale." He also observed that "Henry and Mason made a lame figure and appeared to take different and awkward ground." But positive as he was feeling, Madison sounded a note of caution. "I dare not . . . speak with certainty as to the decision," he wrote.[41]

Henry continued his attacks the next day. The new plan of government was "radical," he said. It represented a "relinquishment of rights." It "squints toward monarchy." At one point, the convention's note taker became so overwhelmed by Henry's barrage that he resorted to summary: "Here Mr. Henry strongly and pathetically expatiated on the probability of the President's enslaving America and the horrid consequences that must result." Why, Henry demanded, would America want to abandon the "strong and vigorous" government currently in place and expose itself to such dangers?[42]

On the following day Madison struck back, declaring that the question of primary concern was whether the Constitution would "promote the public happiness": "We ought not to address our arguments to the feelings and passions, but to those understandings and judgments which were selected by the people of this country to decide this great question by a calm and rational investigation. I hope that gentlemen in displaying their abilities on this occasion, instead of giving opinions and making assertions, will condescend to prove and demonstrate by a fair and regular discussion." He addressed Henry's claim that the Constitution endangered liberty. "Let the dangers which this system is supposed to be replete with be clearly pointed out," he said. He also noted the foolishness of Henry's assertion that "the people of this country are at perfect repose": "I wish sincerely, Sir, this were true. If this be their happy situation, why has every state acknowledged the contrary? Why were deputies from all the states sent to the general convention[?] . . . Wherefore have laws been made to authorize a change, and wherefore are we now assembled here?" Madison went on to defend the Constitution "with such force of reasoning and a display of such irresistible truths that opposition seemed to have quitted the field," in the words of Bushrod Washington, George Washington's nephew. Or at least opponents should have. In truth, Washington confessed to his uncle, for all the good Madison had done, the outcome of the convention was still uncertain.[43]

Madison spoke again the next day, Saturday, but in the middle of his remarks he suddenly stopped and took his leave. "I shall no longer fatigue the committee at this time," he said, "but will resume the subject as early as I can." He hurried to his room at the Swan and for the next few days was incapacitated with what he told Alexander Hamilton and Rufus King was "a bilious attack." If this was one of his "sudden attacks, somewhat resembling epilepsy," the description would have been accurate without giving away too much, since epileptic seizures had long been thought to be the result of an excess of black bile. Later in his life he would, perhaps revealingly, call what happened to him on that Saturday in June "a fit of illness."[44] This particular event also suggests that Madison had learned to recognize certain premonitory symptoms—depression, perhaps, irritability, or a headache—that hours or even days before warned him of a seizure and allowed him to remove himself from public view.

On Wednesday, June 11, though still not feeling well, Madison took the convention floor to defend the taxing power of the general government. It was a necessity in order for that government to be regarded as strong by the country's enemies. With foresight, he pointed out that Britain and France might well go to war and Britain had a history of seizing neutral ships. That posed a danger to the United States, particularly if it was perceived as weak. "Weakness will invite insults," he noted the next day. "The best way to avoid danger is to be in a capacity to withstand it."[45]

Madison also expressed hope that the convention would finally begin the regular discussion of the Constitution previously agreed to, but Patrick Henry soon took the floor with another volley of attacks, including one for which Jefferson had provided ammunition. In a letter to a friend, Alexander Donald, Jefferson had expressed the wish that nine states would ratify the Constitution but four hold out until amendments were agreed to. An extract of that letter had made its way to the Virginia Convention, and Patrick Henry made the most of it: "This illustrious citizen advises you to reject this government till it be amended. His sentiments coincide exactly with ours." Madison felt obliged to take the floor and point out that as long as illustrious citizens were being cited, "could we not adduce a character equally great [that is, George Washington] on our side?" Was the convention "now to submit to the opinion of a citizen beyond the Atlantic"? Besides, he assured the delegates, as only Jefferson's closest correspondent could do, "were that gentleman now on this floor he would be *for* the adoption of this Constitution."[46]

Another of Henry's attacks played on the old fear that northern states would support closure of the Mississippi to American commerce. This was an assault for which Madison was thoroughly prepared. He declared that he had not only had personal knowledge of the situation but "documents and papers"—no doubt the notes he had taken while serving in Congress in 1787—to back it up. Later in the debate, he offered further assurance. "Were I at liberty, I could develop some circumstances which would convince this house that this project will never be revived in Congress," he said, "and that therefore no danger is to be apprehended." Patrick Henry, who had not been a member of Congress for more than a dozen years, was reduced to bluster. It didn't matter what Madison knew, Henry said. Madison couldn't foretell the future. But apparently he thought that he himself could. "This nefarious abominable project will be again introduced [at] the first favorable opportunity," he proclaimed.[47]

On June 14, the delegates finally began the point-by-point debate of the Constitution that George Mason had proposed eleven days before. Soon a pattern developed. Henry, George Mason, or James Monroe, who also opposed the Constitution, would claim there were reasons for grave concern in this clause or that one, and Madison would rise to explain briefly and cogently why their worry was unfounded. To Madison it often seemed a Sisyphean effort. He later told Edward Coles, his secretary, that Patrick Henry could undo an hour's work with a single gesture. It didn't help that on June 16, Madison had what he called a "relapse." He wrote to Hamilton, "My health is not good, and the business is wearisome beyond expression." Three times that day, the convention note taker recorded that his voice was so low that he could not be heard. Two days later, Madison wrote to Washington, "I find myself not yet restored and extremely feeble." He was, nevertheless, putting in a magnificent performance. One observer reported that although "the division" in the Virginia Convention was very close, a narrow win could be expected for the Federalists—"notwithstanding Mr. Henry's declamatory powers, they being vastly overpowered by the deep reasoning of our glorious little Madison." One of the delegates, Archibald Stuart, wrote to a friend on June 19, 1788, "Madison came boldly forward and supported the Constitution with the soundest reason and most manly eloquence I ever heard. He understands his subject well and his whole soul is engaged in its success and it appeared to me he would have flas[h]ed co[n]viction into every mind." But Stuart, a supporter of the Constitution, was still worried about its fate. While most states that had ratified the Constitution had done so overwhelmingly, that was not going to be the case in Virginia. "The fate of Virginia is thus suspended upon a single hair," he wrote.[48]

On June 24, George Wythe, a man widely venerated for his integrity, stood to propose ratification of the Constitution, with "whatsoever amendments might be deemed necessary" to be recommended to the First Congress under the Constitution. Henry objected at length. Surely Wythe was joking, he said: "Evils admitted in order to be removed subsequently and tyranny submitted to in order to be excluded by a subsequent alteration are things totally new to me. But I am sure he meant nothing but to amuse the committee. I know his candor. His proposal is an idea dreadful to me. I ask—does experience warrant such a thing from the beginning of the world to this day?"[49]

After other speakers took the floor, Madison made his last extended speech of the convention. He began by noting how wondrous it was that Americans had been able in the middle of their revolution to establish free governments. "How much more astonishment and admiration will be excited," he asked, "should they be able, peaceably, freely, and satisfactorily, to establish one general government when there is such a diversity of opinions and interests, when not cemented or stimulated by any common danger?" It filled him with dread, he said, to think that the Constitution might not be ratified: "I cannot, therefore, without the most excruciating apprehensions, see a possibility of losing its blessings—It gives me infinite pain to reflect that all the earnest endeavors of the warmest friends of their country to introduce a system promotive of our happiness may be blasted by a rejection, for which . . . [the] previous amendments are but another name." Those of Henry's amendments "not objectionable or unsafe . . . may be subsequently recommended," he said, "not because they are necessary, but because they can produce no possible danger and may gratify some gentlemen's wishes." But he could not consent to conditional amendments "because they are pregnant with dreadful dangers."[50]

Henry took the floor with a passionate refutation: "He tells you of the important blessings which he imagines will result to us and mankind in general from the adoption of this system. I see the awful immensity of the dangers with which it is pregnant. I see it—I feel it. I see *beings* of a higher order, anxious concerning our decision." Archibald Stuart described what happened next: "A storm suddenly rose. It grew dark. The doors came to with a rebound like a peal of musketry. The windows rattled; the huge wooden structure rocked; the rain fell from the eaves in torrents, which were dashed against the glass; the thunder roared." Henry kept on speaking. As Stuart reported it, "Rising on the wings of the tempest, he seized upon the artillery of heaven and directed its fiercest thunders against the heads of his adversaries." Spencer Roane, Henry's son-in-law, later described the storm as making it seem as if Henry "had indeed the faculty of calling up spirits from the vasty deep."[51]

But delegates were not so transfixed that they stayed in their seats. They fled into the center of the building and, when the storm passed, convened briefly before adjourning. Madison seemed to think he had given too much away when it came to Henry's amendments and offered a clarification. The only amendments he would oppose after ratification were those that were dangerous, he repeated, but that category, he emphasized, included a "declaration of our essential rights." Such a declaration implied that the general government had been given the power to violate rights—which it had not. The implication that the government had that power, however, meant that any right left off the list was vulnerable. "An enumeration which is not complete," he said, "is not safe."[52]

The first vote on the next day, June 25, was the crucial one. Antifederalists proposed that before the Constitution was ratified, their amendments be submitted to other states for consideration. The motion was defeated by 88 to 80, ensuring that there would be a positive vote for ratification. In the afternoon delegates voted 89 to 79 to ratify the Constitution and to recommend "whatsoever amendments may be deemed necessary" to the consideration of Congress.[53]

It was a victory for the Union and, although Madison would never have said so, for him. Even Monroe, who looked with jealousy on Madison's accomplishments, acknowledged in a letter to Jefferson, "Madison took the principal share in the debate." A French diplomat reported home: "Mr. Madison is the one who, among all the delegates, carried the votes of the two parties. He was always clear, precise, and consistent in his reasoning and always methodical and pure in his language."

Madison's leadership was not simply in the clarity and intellectual force of what he said but in the fact that his thinking informed most of the Federalist speeches at the convention.[54] In a sense, the theater on Shockoe Hill was an echo chamber, with Madison's ideas bouncing off every wall.

MADISON INTENDED to go straight back to Congress in New York after the ratification was read and signed, but George Washington wrote with an invitation and some advice: "I hear with real concern of your indisposition. . . . Relaxation must have become indispensably necessary for your health, and for that reason, I presume to advise you to take a little respite from business and to express a wish that part of the time might be spent under this roof. . . . Moderate exercise and books occasionally, with the mind unbent, will be your best restoratives."[55] Madison made it to Mount Vernon in time to salute the Fourth of July with Washington. If the happiness of the two men over the Virginia ratification was weighed down somewhat by the enormity of what lay ahead, news from New Hampshire would have buoyed them. That state had ratified the Constitution four days before Virginia, meaning that there were now ten states committed to the new government. Although New Hampshire's ratification meant that the Constitution could have gone into effect without Virginia, both Madison and Washington understood that it did not undercut the significance of what had happened in Richmond. If Virginia's vote had been negative, New York's, still upcoming, would almost certainly be as well, and no union could long endure without these two states.

For two days, Washington took time off from riding over his plantation. Although the plan had been for Madison to enjoy a respite from politics, the two men could not have avoided the subject of the new nation that they would soon play central roles in forming. It was probably during this time that Washington talked to Madison about his reluctance to do what everyone expected—and that was to become president. With the men in his family dying young, Washington, age fifty-

six, was concerned that he didn't have many more years to live, which
made time at Mount Vernon, which he loved, all the more precious.
Moreover, his countrymen lauded him as Cincinnatus, the Roman who
surrendered power after victory and returned home to his fields. Washington worried that posterity would regard him as a hypocrite if, having
taken leave of power, he now assumed it again. Madison advised that
Washington's friends knew his real situation, that serving was a "severe
sacrifice . . . of his inclinations as a man to his obligations as a citizen."
The best public proof of this, he suggested, would be "a voluntary return
to private life as soon as the state of the government would permit."[56] A
few years might be enough.

It is an indication of the sense Washington had of his own mortality
that Madison also told him that "if any premature casualty should un-
happily cut off the possibility of this proof, the evidence known to his
friends would in some way or other be saved from oblivion and do justice to his character." A few months later, Washington was writing to
Hamilton that should he become president, he hoped "that at a convenient and an early period my services might be dispensed with and that
I might be permitted once more to retire."[57]

IT WAS MORE THAN two weeks before Madison sent news of the
ratification to Jefferson, suggesting that he had indeed been feeling some
estrangement from his friend. In the letter he finally wrote from New
York on July 24, 1788, he let Jefferson know, politely of course, that extracts from letters of his had been handed about at the Maryland and
Virginia conventions with a "view of impeding the ratification." Not
until August 10, 1788, did he mention to Jefferson that he had been one
of the authors of *The Federalist.*[58]

Meanwhile, between August 5 and November 18, 1788, Jefferson did
not write to Madison. "The first part of this long silence in me was occasioned by a knowledge that you were absent from New York," he explained. "The latter part, by a want of opportunity, which has been
longer than usual." But one wonders if Jefferson didn't feel a certain

embarrassment at having his attempts to influence the ratification process come to light—particularly since they had failed. In the November 18 letter ending his long silence, however, he was all grace and courtesy, saying he had read *The Federalist* with "care, pleasure, and improvement. . . . I confess it has rectified me in several points."[59]

Jefferson reiterated how much he favored a bill of rights, not knowing that he would soon receive a letter from Madison indicating that he did as well. Although their reasons were different, the two greatest minds of the eighteenth century were now in accord on the importance of amending the Constitution.

Chapter 8

SETTING THE MACHINE IN MOTION

IN THE SUMMER OF 1788, after Madison had returned to New York City from the Virginia ratifying convention, he asked a French visitor to attend a dinner with him. J.-P. Brissot de Warville was clearly thrilled at being invited by the "celebrated" Madison: "Though still young, he has rendered the greatest services to Virginia, to the American confederation, and to liberty and humanity in general. He contributed much . . . in reforming the civil and criminal codes of his country. He distinguished himself particularly in the conventions for the acceptation of the new federal system. Virginia balanced a long time in adhering to it. Mr. Madison determined to it the members of the convention by his eloquence and his logic." Madison was not the kind of fellow who attempted to ingratiate himself on first meeting, Brissot de Warville observed: "His look announces a censor." But his bearing was appropriate for a serious person about serious business: "His reserve was that of a man conscious of his talents and of his duties."[1]

The dinner was at the home of Alexander Hamilton, who had triumphed at the New York ratifying convention. Brissot de Warville called Hamilton "the worthy fellow laborer of Mr. Madison" but also observed some tension between the two. The price that New York Federalists, including Hamilton, had paid for ratification had Madison concerned. To appease Antifederalists, they had sent a circular letter to the states recommending a second convention to revise parts of the Constitution. "If an early general convention cannot be parried," Madison wrote, "it is seriously to be feared that the system which has resisted so many direct attacks may be at last successfully undermined."[2]

The talk at dinner turned to North Carolina's recent and surprising refusal to ratify the Constitution. Madison assured the group that the effects would be minimal, but North Carolina's rejection was not good news. It proved the power of the bill of rights issue, since one of the arguments against ratification had been the absence of rights guarantees. The defeat also energized Antifederalists. In Virginia, Patrick Henry was rallying support for a second convention, and one of those joining him was Edmund Randolph. The Virginia governor had not finished with his "doublings and turnings."[3]

Henry was also agitating the matter of the Mississippi, and Madison made yet one more attempt to reassure his fellow Virginians, arranging for Congress to affirm again "that the free navigation of the River Mississippi is a clear and essential right of the United States and ought to be considered and supported as such." Madison heard from Edmund Pendleton that the message had the soothing effect for which Madison had hoped, but as if to emphasize the long road ahead, Pendleton also reported that outrage had greeted news that the capital of the newly formed nation would be temporarily located in New York. The decision was seen as evidence of the North's intention to dominate the South under the new government.[4]

THE DATE FOR appointing presidential electors was set for January. Washington would become president. Everyone was sure of that, but who would be in the second spot? For balance, it should be someone from the North, but Madison was dissatisfied with the names being put forward. John Hancock, he wrote to Jefferson in cipher, "is weak, ambitious, a courtier of popularity given to low intrigue." As for John Adams, his vanity continued to annoy Madison. He overflowed with self-importance, and that, Madison thought, would be his undoing. People would realize that he could not be "a very cordial second to the general."[5]

As Madison turned in his letter to the subject of amendments to the Constitution, he said that a declaration of rights would probably be added and noted that was fine with him. "My own opinion has always been in favor of a bill of rights," he wrote, a statement that would surely have surprised those who had heard him declare at the Virginia ratifying convention that a declaration of rights was "dangerous because an enumeration which is not complete is not safe" and "unnecessary because it was evident that the general government had no power but what was given it." But his shift on this issue was nuanced by the caveat he added. He favored a bill of rights "provided it be so framed as not to imply powers not meant to be included in the enumeration."[6] And that was bound to be the case, since he would be doing the framing.

As for a declaration's being unnecessary, Madison confessed that he had "not viewed [a bill of rights] in an important light," in part because of his experience in Virginia. There he had seen the "parchment barriers" of that state's declaration of rights "violated in every instance where it has been opposed to a popular current." In a republic that was where the danger lay—with oppressive majorities. "This is a truth of great importance, but not yet sufficiently attended to," he wrote to Jefferson, who had spent the last four years observing the court of Louis XVI. In a monarchy, where the possibility of abusing power rested with the government, a bill of rights was useful, Madison wrote. It set forth standards for the king and could serve to rally the people against him. But in a popular government, where power was vested "in a majority of the people," there was no greater force to rally in opposition. Still, there were noble purposes for a bill of rights. In the first place, it could help citizens internalize the axioms underlying a republic: "Political truths declared in that solemn manner acquire by degrees the character of fundamental maxims of free government, and as they become incorporated with the national sentiment, counteract the impulses of interest and passion." The second argument he offered would hold up equally well over the years. It was possible, he said, that the government in a republic could usurp power. In that case, "a bill of rights will be a good ground for an appeal to the sense of the community."[7]

Madison's comments to Jefferson were philosophical, not political, but in the months ahead politics would be very much on his mind. He hoped to be chosen for federal office, and Virginia friends urged him to consider the Senate. As he thought about his prospects, he decided that Patrick Henry's control of the Virginia legislature, which would make the choice, ruled the Senate out, but his name was nonetheless submitted. He didn't lose badly, running a strong third behind Federalist candidates Richard Henry Lee and William Grayson, but he nonetheless lost—and had to endure a verbal assault by Patrick Henry in the process. On the floor of the House of Delegates, Henry declared Madison "unworthy of the confidence of the people" and warned that his election "would terminate in producing rivulets of blood throughout the land."[8]

Madison was in Philadelphia when he learned of his defeat and of Henry's intention to keep him out of the House of Representatives as well as the Senate. At Henry's direction, the House of Delegates passed an election law that put Orange County into a district with counties in which there was strong Antifederalist feeling. The law also required a year's residence in the district, eliminating any possibility of Madison's seeking another place to represent. Henry no doubt also had a hand in finding an attractive candidate to run against Madison for Congress— James Monroe. Madison's friends were appalled. One called Monroe "the beau," suggesting that vanity was at work. Others thought that personal hostility was involved. "You are upon no occasion of a public nature to expect favors from this gentleman," Edward Carrington wrote. So troubled were Madison's supporters at the effort to keep him out of elective office that when one of them, James Gordon Jr., "lost his reason" and had to be confined, the cause was said to be Gordon's utter disappointment with the conduct of the House of Delegates toward Madison and the Constitution.[9]

Madison set out for Virginia, stopping on the way at Mount Vernon, where he spent the better part of a week visiting with George Washington. While Madison's election was no doubt one of the subjects the men talked about, the larger part of their conversation probably concerned Washington's becoming president, which was increasingly likely, and the strength and stability of the new government, which seemed less likely by the day. Under Patrick Henry's guidance, the Virginia Assembly was petitioning the outgoing Congress for a second convention, writing to Governor George Clinton of New York about cooperating in such an effort, and sending a circular letter to all the states seeking support. Both men were worried about Henry's power. "He has only to say let this be law—and it is law," Washington wrote. As Madison saw it, Henry's aim was nothing less than "the destruction of the whole system."[10]

Madison arrived in Orange County to find his opponents whispering that he was "dogmatically attached to the Constitution in every clause, syllable, and letter" and would not therefore countenance amendments on any subject, including fundamental rights. He launched a letter-writing campaign to dispel that notion, particularly among his Baptist supporters, who were being told that he was no longer "a friend to the rights of conscience." He explained to Baptist minister George Eve that before the Constitution was ratified, he had "opposed all previous alterations as calculated to throw the states into dangerous contentions and to furnish the secret enemies of the Union with an opportunity of promoting its dissolution." But now that ratification had occurred, he believed Congress "ought to prepare and recommend to the states for ratification the most satisfactory provisions for all essential rights, particularly the rights of conscience." A letter in which he made the same points to a Spotsylvania County resident ended up, surely not by accident, in the *Virginia Herald*.[11]

Madison even took to the road, making campaign stops not just in Orange but also in Louisa and Culpeper counties. Soon he and Monroe were making joint appearances, one of which followed a Lutheran church service. After "music with two fiddles," as Madison later remembered it, "we addressed these people and kept them standing in the snow listening to the discussion of constitutional subjects. They stood it out very patiently—seemed to consider it a sort of fight of which they were required to be spectators." Afterward Madison rode twelve miles through the night to his home, acquiring a touch of frostbite on his nose along the way. In later years he would point to the scar with pride.[12]

For all his insistence that he didn't like campaigning, Madison proved effective at it. In a district where the deck had been stacked against him, he garnered 1,308 votes to 972 for Monroe. Among the congratulatory letters he received was one from his old friend Baptist minister John Leland, who modestly wrote that if his effort in the late campaign accomplished nothing else, "it certainly gave *Mr. Madison* one vote."[13]

Madison received a letter from George Washington that suggested how extensive a role he was likely to play in the new government. Washington wanted Madison's help with his inaugural address. He had a draft—a seventy-three-page creation produced by an aide—but he was doubtful about it and hoped that as Madison traveled to New York to assume his seat in Congress, he would stop at Mount Vernon and offer his advice. When Madison reached the president-elect's home on February 22, 1789, he found that Washington was right to have concerns. The seventy-three-page draft was, he later observed, a "strange production." He stayed with Washington for a week, writing a much shorter speech for him.[14]

Seven of the ten representatives to Congress elected in Virginia were Federalists, and Madison left Mount Vernon with one of them, John Page, and met another, Richard Bland Lee, in Alexandria. The three men slogged toward New York through wintry weather, but reports of Federalists sweeping other states no doubt took some of the edge off the chill. Outside Baltimore, they fell in with "the bearer of the electoral votes of Georgia," and Madison was able to write to Washington that "they are unanimous as to the president."[15]

LIKE MANY eighteenth-century events, the First Congress was late in convening—four weeks late, in fact—but after a quorum was finally formed in both houses, what everyone knew became official: Washington would be the first president. Every elector in every state had voted for him. John Adams, although he received less than half the number of votes that Washington did, still had the second-highest number and would be vice president.

On April 30, Madison took his place in the inaugural procession, his carriage behind Washington's grand equipage—a bright yellow carriage drawn by white horses. The train of troops and dignitaries made its way through Dock and Broad streets to the splendidly remodeled Federal Hall, where Madison, as part of the official five-man inaugural committee from the House, likely accompanied the president-elect as he walked up the stairs and stepped out on the colonnaded balcony. At Washington's appearance a great roar went up from the multitudes assembled below. The president-elect, dressed for the occasion in a suit of brown American broadcloth, white silk stockings, and silver-buckled shoes, put his right hand on a Bible lent for the occasion by a New York Masonic lodge and took the oath of office prescribed by the Constitution. At the end of the oath, according to well-established tradition, he added "So help me God." Then he bent to kiss the Bible.[16]

In the second-floor Senate chamber of Federal Hall, a splendid room with a high arched ceiling, tall windows, and crimson curtains, Washington, uncharacteristically nervous, read the address Madison had drafted at Mount Vernon. They had doubtless consulted about it as Madison wrote, because it suited Washington well, capturing his modesty, his belief in the providential agency that guided the nation, and his love for his country. But one moment in the address was quintessentially Madisonian. It occurred when the president declared that "the sacred fire of liberty and the destiny of the Republican model of government are justly considered as *deeply,* perhaps as *finally* staked, on the experiment entrusted to the hands of the American people." Madison often used the word "sacred" to convey the ultimate nature of such civic concepts as rights, responsibilities, and liberty. He used the word "staked" to indicate crucial dependencies, once describing the Constitution as a document "on which would be staked the happiness of a people."[17] He had used the metaphor of government as an experiment in more than a dozen numbers of *The Federalist,* conveying the notion that human arrangements, particularly those aimed at establishing self-government, are fragile and might fail. Their preservation required vigilance.

Madison's hand was also evident in the sole legislative measure the president mentioned, amendments to the Constitution, which had now become a priority for Madison. Washington spoke of amendments in a way that fit with Madison's thinking, expressing confidence that Congress would "carefully avoid every alteration which might endanger the benefits of an united and effective government" and at the same time have "reverence for the characteristic rights of freemen and a regard for the public harmony."

After the inauguration, Madison wrote the House of Representatives' formal response to Washington's speech, and he soon heard from the president, who wanted him to take yet another step. "Notwithstanding the conviction I am under of the labor which is imposed upon you by *public* individuals as well as public bodies," Washington wrote, tacitly admitting that he owed his inaugural address to Madison, "yet as you have began, so I would wish you to finish the good work in a short reply to the address of the House of Representatives." Madison wrote Washington's reply to the House address (which he had written in response to the president's address, which he had ghostwritten), and twelve days later, again at the president's request, he wrote Washington's response to the Senate as well.[18] Never again in the history of the United States would any politician's voice reverberate as Madison's did in the early days of the Republic.

BY THE TIME OF Washington's inaugural, the House of Representatives had been in operation nearly a month. It had been the new government during that time and would continue to be until the executive branch could be filled out and the judiciary branch created. The members met in the airy, first-floor, octagonal chamber of Federal Hall, and it was there, under a coved ceiling that stretched upward forty feet and more, that they elected Frederick Muhlenberg, a Lutheran pastor from

Pennsylvania, to be their Speaker. From the beginning, however, they recognized Madison as their leader, "our first man," as one of his colleagues wrote.[19]

Madison introduced the first piece of business: raising revenue. He suggested that the basis be the Impost of 1783, which he had written, and proposed duties to be placed on imported items such as spirituous liquors and sugar. Now that the United States had "recovered from the state of imbecility" that had made it unable to pay its debts, he said, the country needed "to revive those principles of honor and honesty that have too long lain dormant."[20]

But as is inevitably the case in representative government, the high purpose of the legislation quickly devolved into a debate over details as congressmen fought for the interests of their constituents. The battle over molasses was particularly fierce, with Fisher Ames of Massachusetts, an intense and brilliant man, pointing out that a duty would hurt not only his state's distilleries, which used molasses to manufacture rum, but its fisheries, which traded fish for rum. It would even harm the poor, he said, who used molasses as a sweetener. This last claim was too much for Madison, who responded by pointing out that Virginia's imports were three times those of Massachusetts. Many of those imports were necessary for the poor and would be subject to tariffs—which meant that Virginians had even more reason than citizens of Massachusetts to lament their lot. His point was that partial interests had to be put aside in order to support the general government, which had been "instituted for the protection of all."[21] The House passed the tariff bill—but not until the duty on molasses had been reduced.

Fisher Ames seemed to be fascinated with Madison and described him in several letters he sent back home. In one he wrote:

He derives from nature an excellent understanding . . . , but I think he excels in the quality of judgment. He is possessed of a sound judgment, which perceives truth with great clearness and can trace it through the mazes of debate without losing it. He is admirable for this inestimable talent. As a reasoner, he is remarkably perspicuous and methodical. He is a studious man, devoted to public business and a thorough master of almost every public question that can arise or he will spare no pains to become so, if he happens to be in want of information.

Ames knew whereof he spoke. Madison had compared the laws of all the states in preparation for the debate on revenue and collected information on what the various states imported and exported. But for all Madison's hard work, Ames, a man not easy to content, found him wanting. "He is probably deficient in that fervor and vigor of character which you will expect in a great man," he wrote. Ames thought him "too much of a book politician" and "too much attached to his theories."[22]

Ames, who favored an emotional oratorical style, might have been reacting to Madison's plain way of speaking. Madison made no attempt to practice oratory, which, given how often he spoke—124 times in the first session of the new Congress alone, more than twice any other member—was probably a mercy for all involved. His unadorned rhetoric had served him quite well thus far, including in the battle with Patrick Henry at the Virginia ratifying convention. His lack of artifice conveyed sincerity and underscored the importance of the ideas he was presenting rather than distracting from them.[23]

AFTER THE TARIFF BILL was passed, Madison began the work of building out the executive branch. He proposed the formation of the Departments of State, Treasury, and War. The heads of these departments were to be "appointed by the president by and with the advice and consent of the Senate"—and, according to Madison's motion, "to be removable by the president." This last provision, which was not in the Constitution, led to the first debate in Congress about the meaning of that document, and Madison was at the center of it. "I think it absolutely necessary that the president should have the power of removing from office," he said, and his view prevailed.[24]

Despite Ames's observation that Madison was too fixed on his theories, Madison listened to the congressional debate and learned from it. He found a point made by Egbert Benson of New York particularly telling. Since the power of removal was not in the Constitution, said Benson, Madison's proposal looked as though it were a grant of power from Congress. Benson suggested that the motion be worded so as to assume the president had the power of removal—and Madison agreed. It was an approach he would remember when he sat down to compose a bill of rights.

A matter on which Madison was less flexible was whether tariff and tonnage fees ought to be different for nations such as France, with which the United States had commercial treaty agreements, than they were for nations such as Great Britain, with which the United States did not. Madison was fixed on the notion that there should be a distinction, in part because France had been America's crucial ally in the war against the British, but more because he wanted Britain to change what he called "her monopolizing regulations." Since the Revolution, American ships had not been allowed to trade in the British West Indies, nor could they carry anything except American goods to England. Madison argued that such policies "bound us in commercial manacles and very nearly defeated the object of our independence."[25]

Madison was of the view that America could achieve an alteration in British navigation laws because Britain needed the food and raw materials that the United States exported more than the United States needed the manufactured products of Britain. Madison's language, as he made this case in a letter to Jefferson, was revealing in the way that it cast the agricultural products that America produced as "essential" and the products of English factories as "superfluities or poisons." Madison, like Jefferson, had long had a vision of America as a young, vigorous, and virtuous land where independent farmers reaped the bounty of the soil, producing necessities rather than manufacturing luxuries. It was an image fitting for a country in which the vast majority of people drew their living from the land, and it would play an important role in debates about the direction of the new government. In 1789, Congress was not persuaded, however, and in the end passed tariff and tonnage measures giving American goods and ships an advantage but making no distinction among other nations.[26]

IN THE FIRST SESSION of the First Congress, the Senate took the lead in establishing a federal court system. The Judiciary Act of 1789 provided for district courts, circuit courts of appeal, and a chief justice and five associate justices for the Supreme Court. But the pace of the Senate scarcely matched that of the House. William Maclay, an exceedingly slender Pennsylvania senator with deep worry lines between his brows, noted in the journal he kept, "We used to stay in the Senate chamber till about 2 o'clock, whether we did anything or not, by way of keeping up the appearance of business. But even this we seem to be got over."[27]

Perhaps because of the light press of business, the Senate spent weeks debating the question of titles. Senators, and particularly the president of the Senate, John Adams, were eager to have Washington called "Excellency," "Elective Highness," or even *"His Highness the President of the United States of America and Protector of the Rights of the Same,"* and they continued to press the matter even after the House rejected elevated titles. Madison soothed his thoroughly irritated colleagues by praising them for their republican instincts and even persuaded them to treat the other body courteously, appointing still another committee to decline Senate suggestions. After the Senate had finally given up, Madison reported to Jefferson that "J. Adams espoused the cause of titles with great earnestness." Jefferson responded, "The president's title as proposed by the Senate was the most superlatively ridiculous thing I ever heard of." He was reminded, he wrote, of what Benjamin Franklin had once said of Adams, that he was "always an honest man, often a great one, but sometimes absolutely mad."[28]

Washington was said to favor a majestic title, just as he favored a stately presentation of himself at his Tuesday receptions, or levees. Wearing black velvet, a long sword in a white polished-leather scabbard, and—the latest in fashion—yellow gloves, he bowed to visitors one by one as they approached him. Madison noted, however, that the president did have his limits when it came to grand behavior. At one levee, as folding doors were thrown open to admit him into the room, Washington's assistant, David Humphreys, announced, "The President of the United States," in what Madison called "a loud and pompous voice." Reported Madison, "The effect was the more ludicrous as not more than five or six gentlemen had assembled." Washington threw Humphreys a look, which, Madison said in later years, "he could more easily remember than describe."[29]

SHORTLY BEFORE the House adjourned for the day on Monday, May 4, 1789, Madison gave notice that in three weeks he "intended to bring on the subject of amendments to the Constitution."[30] His most immediate purpose was to undercut a proposal that he knew was coming from Theodorick Bland, his old nemesis, once handsome, but grown corpulent now. The next day, Bland presented Virginia's call for a convention of all the states to consider amendments to the Constitution. After Madison pointed out that the Constitution required applications from two-thirds of the states before Congress could act, Virginia's application was tabled. The next day, a New York congressman presented that state's application for a second convention, and it too was tabled.

Madison hoped that by introducing amendments in Congress—the second way that the Constitution provided for change—he could take away the rationale for a second convention while at the same time making a conciliatory gesture to those whom he called "well-meaning opponents."[31] He also had a campaign promise to keep. He had told Virginia voters that the First Congress should recommend amendments to the states for ratification, and he had to make sure that happened. Thus it was that over the next weeks as he was debating tariffs, titles, and offices in the executive branch, he was also sifting through the more than two hundred amendments that had been proposed by various state ratifying conventions. He put aside those that would change the governmental framework the Constitution provided and concentrated on those aimed at securing rights.

While Madison was sorting out amendments, he was also worrying about his mother. He told Eliza Trist that he sent to the post office for his mail "with the most serious apprehensions." He also told her that Theodorick Bland had received "a melancholy memento of mortality": "After experiencing for several weeks occasional sensations very disagreeable, he was suddenly attacked with either an apoplectic, epileptic, or paralytic stroke under which he would have expired if the lancet had not been instantly applied. He remained senseless for some time. After a few hours, however, his mind became right, and he is at present in a manner well, but not without the disquietude incident to the nature of such attacks and the bare possibility of relapses."[32] Madison's description seems to come from someone who knew well how unsettling it was to experience such an attack—and to be aware that another could follow.

Few of Madison's fellow congressmen shared his urgency to proceed with amendments, and he agreed to two delays in order to finish the revenue measure. Finally, on June 8, saying that he felt "bound in honor and in duty," he moved that the House go into the committee of the whole so that he could present his proposals. He was met by a hail of objections, not only from Antifederalists, but from Federalist congressmen, who said there were more important matters and that the Constitution hadn't been in effect long enough to consider changes to it. Madison pressed ahead, arguing that he wanted only to introduce the amendments and did not expect an immediate decision. Roger Sherman grumpily observed that Connecticut had ratified the Constitution by a large majority, wanted the government it set forth, and had no desire for amendments. Why, then, interrupt crucial work to discuss them? he asked.[33]

Late in the day, when he was finally able to begin, Madison emphasized that he wanted to make the Constitution "as acceptable to the whole people of the United States as it has been found acceptable to a majority of them." Moreover, he said, the amendments he had in mind, by satisfying objections being made in Rhode Island and North Carolina, would ease the way for those two states to come into the Union.[34]

Most of those who had opposed the Constitution, Madison asserted, disliked it not because of its structure but "because it did not contain effectual provisions against encroachments on particular rights." One can imagine the dozen or so Antifederalists in the hall shaking their heads, since structural change was exactly what they had in mind. They wanted to alter the government that the Constitution had framed, particularly to limit the federal government's powers. But Madison plunged ahead as if there were no doubt about his premise. There were ways "to satisfy the public mind that their liberties will be perpetual, and this without endangering any part of the Constitution," he said, thus bringing to Congress the case he had made during his Virginia campaign.[35]

Madison did not inflate the value of the amendments beyond what he believed it to be. He described a bill of rights as "neither improper nor altogether useless." Indeed, should the states as well as the federal government adopt such bills, "upon the whole, they will have a salutary tendency." Rights amendments, he said, could have a positive effect on the way in which people thought of the rights themselves: "As they have a tendency to impress some degree of respect for them, to establish the public opinion in their favor, and rouse the attention of the whole community, it may be one means to control the majority from those acts to which they might be otherwise inclined."[36]

Madison's proposals did not call for the government to grant rights, but rather enjoined interference with them. "The civil rights of none shall be abridged on account of religious belief" was a formulation that avoided even a hint that people had ever for a moment given over their right to worship freely. Other amendments followed the same pattern: "The people shall not be deprived or abridged of their right to speak, to write, or to publish their sentiments"; "The right of the people to keep and bear arms shall not be infringed"; "The rights of the people to be secured in their persons, their houses, their papers, and their other property from all unreasonable searches and seizures shall not be violated by warrants issued without probable cause." Lest there be any confusion that forbidding interference with these rights somehow made others fair game, Madison had an amendment specifically addressing the issue: "Exceptions here or elsewhere in the Constitution made in favor of particular rights shall not be so construed as to diminish the just importance of other rights retained by the people."[37]

In a nod to one of the amendments most commonly suggested in ratifying conventions, Madison also proposed that powers not delegated by the Constitution to Congress be reserved to the states. In addition, he used the occasion to propose a remedy for a problem that continued to concern him: the ability of the states to deny rights to their citizens. "No state," he proposed, "shall violate the equal rights of conscience, or the freedom of the press, or the trial by jury in criminal cases."[38]

As Madison's proposals became public, he was criticized both by those who thought what he was doing was unnecessary and by those who accused him of creating a diversion—throwing "a tub to the whale," they called it. Richard Peters, the Speaker of the Pennsylvania General Assembly, offered a good-humored critique: "I see you have been offering amendments to the machine before it is known whether it wants any." Peters joked that the only people who should throw out tubs were those "who were afraid of the whale," which caused Madison to counter that far from being fearful, he had the whale in his sights. A bill of rights, by bringing the public around to support of the Constitution, would, Madison wrote, "kill the opposition everywhere."[39]

But progress was slow. Not until August 13 was there a motion to consider amendments, and as soon as it was made, one annoyed congressman after another took the floor to argue for postponement. Thirty-year-old John Vining, a leading citizen of Delaware, used the occasion to needle Madison, saying that he was only going along with the motion because he was "impressed by the anxiety which the honorable gentleman from Virginia had discovered for having the subject of amendments considered."[40]

As soon as the House had resolved itself into the committee of the whole, Roger Sherman of Connecticut rose to object. Madison's proposal interwove amendments into the Constitution rather than adding them at the end, and Sherman argued that so doing would create an entirely new document. The debate that ensued took up the rest of the day. Gentlemen who had argued that the amendments would consume too much time took the floor to speak at length, which, in turn, encouraged others. Said one congressman, "As so much has been said, I wish to give my opinion."[41] Sherman's motion was defeated, but he would bring it up again and prevail. Thanks to his persistence, amendments would be appended to the Constitution, which served Madison's purposes better than interweaving would have. If one wants to encourage respect for rights, how wise to have them in a form that can be displayed on classroom walls across the land.

The House finally took up the first amendment—though not the one we call the First Amendment today. This one capped the size of the House of Representatives and seems an odd place to have begun after all the time that Madison had spent talking about rights. But five of the six states recommending amendments had taken up this subject, leading Madison to propose that the Congress be authorized to alter the formula for representation set forth in the Constitution—one representative for every thirty thousand constituents—so that the number of House members would never exceed 175. Fisher Ames took to the floor to argue against allowing the number of House members—59, as he spoke—to increase at all. The House would degenerate as its numbers grew, he said, attracting men of lesser abilities as increased membership made the job of representative less consequential. Elbridge Gerry accused Ames of snobbery, and other congressmen jumped in, a few actually speaking to the motion on the floor. In the end, the members voted to cap the size of the House at two hundred and, having exhausted themselves with the first amendment proposed, quickly approved the next proposition—that any pay raise they passed for themselves could not take effect until after an intervening election.[42] Then they adjourned.

On the next day's agenda were propositions that would form most of the First Amendment, the one so revered today that many Americans think that Congress must have considered it first in recognition of its primacy. That was not the case, nor did the debate, which began August 15, reveal an abundance of veneration on the part of the delegates. A discussion about prohibiting state-sponsored religion descended briefly into name-calling before the House approved the proposition that "Congress shall make no laws touching religion or infringing the rights of conscience."[43]

Many Federalists were still irritated at what appeared to them a waste of time. When delegates took up "freedom of speech and of the press and the right of the people peaceably to assemble and consult for their common good and to apply to the government for redress of grievances," Theodore Sedgwick of Massachusetts tried to show what trivialities the House was concerning itself with by moving to strike out "assemble." Said he, "They might [as well] have declared that a man should have a right to wear his hat if he pleased, that he might get up when he pleased, and go to bed when he thought proper." Antifederalists, angry and bitter at being forced to debate Madison's amendments instead of ones they preferred, sidetracked the debate onto other matters, such as whether the people had the right "to instruct their representatives."[44]

Aedanus Burke, an Antifederalist from South Carolina, accused the Federalists of deceit. They pretended to be amending the Constitution in order to conciliate people, but the amendments they were offering were "little better than whip-syllabub, frothy and full of wind, formed only to please the palate." He took the floor to demonstrate the kind of "solid and substantial amendments" he had in mind, holding up what states such as South Carolina had approved: propositions to constrain the power of Congress by requiring term limits and sharply restricting the authority to tax; to restrain the president's war powers and deny him removal power; and nearly to eliminate the federal judiciary. But Madison had the votes to render Burke's show ineffective, and members passed the proposition forbidding Congress to interfere with speech, publication, or assembly. They had discussed a possible deletion to the clause (the right to assemble) and a possible insertion (the right to instruct), but they had not debated the intricacies of free speech or free press that have concerned Americans since. Are there occasions when free speech may be properly abridged? Is it possible for a free press to go too far?[45]

· · ·

FISHER AMES, although not averse to trying to hijack the debate himself, had apparently grown tired of his colleagues' multiple pronouncements on everything besides the matter under consideration, and he moved to cut off debate. Following many objections, he withdrew his motion, but not before thoroughly infuriating a southern member, probably Aedanus Burke of South Carolina, who "hinted an intention" to challenge Ames to a duel. If he followed through, it was the first known instance of one congressman challenging another, and what was likely the second quickly followed. Elbridge Gerry reported that he was approached by someone who said that as long as there was talk "of calling out, he had reason to be offended at something I had said and should use the same freedom with me." Congressman George Leonard of Massachusetts observed that the bill of rights debate was driving "the political thermometer high each day."[46]

The House was off on Sunday, and the debate on Monday improved to the extent that no member is recorded as having threatened another's life. But Antifederalists continued to make motion after motion that they had no hope of winning. Madison let other Federalists answer them—until Thomas Tudor Tucker of South Carolina tried to strike out the proposition that prevented states from infringing upon personal rights. Madison took the floor immediately, saying this was "the most valuable amendment in the whole list," and it was retained.[47]

Antifederalists were intent on getting a vote on all the amendments states had proposed, including those that would substantially change the government. They got their chance—and their comeuppance—on August 18, when members without debate and on a voice vote turned them down.[48]

As the direction of the House became clear, Madison turned to his correspondence. Richard Peters had sent him a rhymed fable about eleven cooks (that is, states) who make a delicious soup, only to have a rude group of guests (Antifederalists) insist on altering the recipe before they even take a taste. Madison, amused, wrote back, "May I hope that 'The Wise Cooks and Foolish Guests' is but a sample of the treat you meditate for your friends." He went on to report to Peters on "the nauseous project of amendments," a phrase that has been taken to mean that the father of the Bill of Rights was sickened by the undertaking that would bring him such renown. Certainly he was tired. "The work has been extremely difficult and fatiguing," he told Edmund Pendleton a few days before House passage of seventeen amendments.[49] But in the context of the fable, the word "nauseous" is probably a reference to the gut-wrenching mess that the rude guests intended to make of the soup. Madison had managed to prevent their mischief and in his success must have found satisfaction.

But when the amendments came back to the House from the Senate, there was a disappointment. The number had been reduced to twelve, in some cases by combining and in others by eliminating, and gone was the amendment Madison had valued most, the one prohibiting the states from infringing on individual rights. It had been part of a campaign he had started at the Constitutional Convention, and he would not see victory in his lifetime. The Fourteenth Amendment, ratified in 1868, would, however, prohibit states from abridging "the privileges or immunities of citizens," depriving them "of life, liberty, or property, without due process of law," and denying them "the equal protection of the laws." Eventually, this amendment would be construed to mean that most provisions of the first ten amendments apply to the states, thus affirming the importance of Madison's goal.

The twelve amendments passed by the Senate were passed by the House and sent to the states, where early on the first two (one about capping the size of the House, the other about congressional pay) ran into trouble.[50] The other ten went into effect on December 15, 1791, when they were ratified by the eleventh state out of the fourteen now in the Union— Virginia. It hadn't happened easily in the Old Dominion. Indeed, nothing seemed to. Among those who raised objections was Edmund Randolph.

Madison had, almost single-handedly, formulated the amendments, insisted on their introduction, and pushed their passage through the apathy of his friends and the obstructionism of his opponents. By doing so, he not only gave us the Bill of Rights, which, as he predicted, we hold in great solemn regard, but also secured the Constitution against the threat of a second convention. By reaching out to opponents, he undermined the anti-constitutional cause to such a degree that it soon ceased to have any importance. By reaffirming rights, he reassured Rhode Islanders and North Carolinians, and by the following summer both states would be part of the Union.[51] Taken all in all, it was a magnificent performance, one unmatched by any congressional leader since.

CONTENTIOUS AS THE DEBATE over amendments was, the next one before the House was even more so. It concerned the location of the nation's capital and all the prestige and economic advantage that went with it. Thomas Scott of Pennsylvania moved "that a permanent residence ought to be fixed for the general government," and Benjamin Goodhue of Massachusetts proposed that the site be on the banks of the Susquehanna. As Goodhue explained it, the Pennsylvania location was part of a deal. He said that "the eastern members," by which he meant the members from New England, "with the members from New York have agreed to fix a place upon national principles without a regard to their own convenience, and have turned their minds to the banks of the Susquehanna."[52]

Madison sarcastically thanked Goodhue for candidly admitting that an agreement had been reached behind closed doors and "that more than half the territory of the United States and nearly half its inhabitants have been disposed of, not only without their consent, but without their knowledge." Harking back to the Virginia ratifying convention, he made as sharp a comment as he ever would on the floor, declaring, "If a prophet had risen in that body and brought the declarations and proceedings of this day into view . . . [I] firmly believe Virginia might not have been a part of the Union at this moment."[53]

Two days later, when Madison repeated the charge that eastern states and New York had "disposed" of the South in deciding where to locate the capital, Jeremiah Wadsworth of Connecticut felt obliged to correct the record: "It is a notorious fact to the members within these walls that the New England members to a man were opposed to a decision at present. . . .

They refused all bargaining till they were assured there was a bargaining set on foot to carry them to the Potomac." Wadsworth was right about the "bargaining set on foot." Members from Pennsylvania had approached southern states and offered a Potomac location for the capital—if the South would agree to move the temporary capital to Philadelphia. Hearing of this, New Englanders and New Yorkers approached Pennsylvania and offered to locate the capital there in exchange for temporary residence in New York. Madison, who seems to have had good intelligence, had actually interrupted their negotiations and, he thought, their plans. But financier and Pennsylvania senator Robert Morris had continued to maneuver, cutting a deal with states to the north.[54]

Madison spoke at length on the floor of the House about the advantages of a Potomac location, giving special attention to the access it would provide to people in the western country, but the House approved the proposal for the Susquehanna and sent it to the Senate. There, under pressure from Morris, who wanted the capital adjacent to Philadelphia, the location was changed to Germantown. As the other Pennsylvania senator, William Maclay, recorded in his journal, an agreement was reached with New York and New England members in the House to concur in the Germantown site. In exchange Congress would stay three years in New York.[55]

When the bill with the Germantown location arrived in the House, Madison protested but finally gave in to the inevitable—or pretended to. Pennsylvania, New York, and New England had the votes needed to prevail, but there was one detail, Madison said, a small provision that was needed to make sure that Pennsylvania laws would operate in the district chosen for the capital until Congress took over. That provision was added, meaning the bill had to go back to the Senate, where no action was taken on it before the first session of the First Congress adjourned.[56]

Madison had promised Pendleton that he would "parry any decision" on a bill setting the location of the capital anywhere besides the Potomac, and he had done exactly that. But he was exhausted. He stayed several days in New York, hoping that the ship bringing Jefferson home on leave from Paris would arrive. On October 9, 1789, he departed from

New York, leaving behind a letter for Jefferson telling him that he would stay several days in Philadelphia, where he hoped that Jefferson would catch up with him. "I need not tell you how much pleasure I should feel in making my journey to Virginia coincide with yours," he wrote.[57] Besides, there was a public matter he wanted to discuss. Madison couldn't be specific in a letter, but he was now doing personnel work for Washington. The president wanted Jefferson to be secretary of state and had given Madison the task of persuading him.

Jefferson's trip from Paris to Monticello did not bring him through Philadelphia, and the meeting Madison had hoped for did not occur. Madison did manage to get a little political work done, however. Senator Morris approached him about wanting to keep the possibility of an arrangement with the South alive. Having been badly dealt with by Pennsylvania once, Madison warned him that if any future arrangements were made, Pennsylvania must stand by its word. Madison learned in the conversation that Morris considered the bill in the Senate postponed, ready to be acted upon as soon as the next session of Congress should start. He reported this intelligence to Washington and likely used it to complicate life for Morris. It is hard to imagine that Madison did not have some role to play in a rule that would be adopted early in the second session requiring that all legislation begin from scratch.[58]

Madison left Philadelphia at the end of October, and on November 2, a pleasant day, he reached Montpelier. His mother was still very sick, which might have relieved him of some of the social obligations of the season—the visitors, the dinners that occasioned much slaughtering of hogs, the eggnog and hunting on Christmas Day. Thus, he might have had time to take notice of the trees being planted, a pecan near the slave quarter, another near the horse shed, and a buckeye in the southwest corner of the yard. The aurora borealis streaked the sky red while he was home, and one imagines him standing on the front steps of the brick house his father had built, admiring the dazzle and dance of the northern lights.[59]

But not even nature's spectacle could keep politics long from his mind. Shortly after Christmas he rode to Monticello to recruit a secretary of state.

Chapter 9

THE EARTH BELONGS TO THE LIVING

MADISON ARRIVED AT A MONTICELLO very different from the architectural wonder we know today. Jefferson had yet to tear off the second story, with which he was dissatisfied, extend the northeast front, and add a dome, and even on the lower floor the interior was far from complete.[1] The walls were probably unplastered, making them inadequate to the winter chill, but Madison would have been made welcome by a blazing fire in the fireplace and warm greetings from the friend he had not seen in five years.

Madison found Jefferson reluctant to become secretary of state. If the president insisted, he would, but Jefferson really wanted to sail back to France. Revolution was under way, brought on in no small part by the millions that Louis XVI had sent to the colonies to support the American struggle for independence. The debt France had run up had brought financial calamity, which together with the spirit of freedom emanating from the American Revolution had led to uprisings against the king. Jefferson was well familiar with the French Revolution's violence. Less than two weeks after the fall of the Bastille, he had joked with his paramour, Maria Cosway, that cutting off heads was becoming so fashionable "one is apt to feel of a morning whether their own is on their shoulders." But he believed that violence would pass and liberty advance. Rather than be secretary of state, a position he thought would enmesh him in domestic affairs, he wanted to return to France, where he had not only witnessed events that he knew would be "forever memorable in history" but been sought out for his advice, most notably on the Declaration of the Rights of Man.[2]

Madison tried to correct Jefferson's view of the secretary of state's responsibilities, but Jefferson wasn't ready to commit, and the two moved on to other topics. Jefferson had an idea that had occurred to him in France that he wanted Madison to ponder. It was that "the earth belongs always to the living generation," and he followed up their discussion at Montpelier with a letter laying out the principle that no obligation of any sort, whether it had to do with laws and constitutions or with debt, should be passed on to future generations. If that were to happen, when the time of those generations came around, they would not own the earth. "The lands would belong to the dead and not to the living," in Jefferson's words. "Turn this subject in your mind, my dear sir," Jefferson wrote, "and particularly as to the power of contracting debts; and develop it with that perspicuity and cogent logic so peculiarly yours."[3] Madison did exactly what Jefferson asked and more, producing a response that is a masterpiece in itself and an enduring example of the nature of his mind. He did not roll up ideas into grand syntheses without testing them. He held them up and turned them this way and that, seeing how they fared by the lights of reason and practicality.

Madison began his response with utter politeness, calling Jefferson's idea "a great one," but then he allowed that he did not see it "in *all* respects compatible with the course of human affairs." When it came to constitutions, he asked, "Would not a government so often revised become too mutable to retain those prejudices in its favor which antiquity inspires?" Laws that frequently changed would lead to such uncertainty as to "discourage the steady exertions of industry produced by permanent laws." As for passing on debt to future generations, he pointed out instances in which it was justified, such as "debts for repelling a conquest, the evils of which descend through many generations."

Using demographic data, Jefferson had argued that nineteen years was the length of time that any generation was at the height of its power and that nineteen years, therefore, was the limit for extending debt and allowing laws and constitutions to be in effect. But how could that work? Madison wanted to know, probing at an embarrassingly weak point in Jefferson's argument. Generations didn't come of age all at once. Individuals were continuously entering "ripe age," as Madison put it, and it was necessary, if one held strictly to the concept that "the earth belongs to the living," either to revise all the laws with each new entrant or to obtain that individual's consent to the laws in force. Both schemes were unworkable. For civil society to function, Madison wrote, one had to assume the "tacit assent" of persons entering society to the constitutions and laws then in force.

Jefferson had asked Madison to use his "station in the councils of our country" to bring his idea forward and force it into discussion: "It would furnish matter for a fine preamble to our first law for appropriating the public revenue." Madison agreed that the theory had cautionary value: "It would give me singular pleasure to see it first announced in the proceedings of the United States and always kept in . . . view as a salutary curb on the living generation from imposing unjust or unnecessary burdens on their successors." But, he told Jefferson, he wasn't sure the country was ready for it. "The spirit of philosophical legislation has never reached some parts of the Union, and is by no means the fashion here, either within or without Congress."[4]

Jefferson seemed to take Madison's critique in stride and even be impressed by it. It was less than a month later that he called Madison "the greatest man in the world." Jefferson did not give up on his idea, but he did modify it. In a letter written in the last years of his life, he declared that "our creator made the earth for the use of the living and not of the dead." This time, however, he added Madison's caveat that "the laws of our predecessors" ought "to stand on our implied assent . . . until the existing majority positively repeals them."[5]

Madison, for his part, came around in his view of Jefferson's idea as a touchstone. In the contentious years ahead, he would use the idea that the living generation ought not to unduly burden successive ones to try to shape public opinion. The interaction of Madison's and Jefferson's thoughts on this subject was an example of what John Quincy Adams called "the mutual influence of these two mighty minds upon each other." It was "a phenomenon," Adams observed, "like the invisible and mysterious movements of the magnet in the physical world, and in which the sagacity of the future historian may discover the solution of much of our national history not otherwise easily accountable."[6]

Determined that Jefferson would become secretary of state, Madison wrote to him several weeks after leaving Monticello: "Such an event will be more conducive to the general good and perhaps to the very objects you have in view in Europe than your return to your former station."[7] Jefferson finally accepted, joining Alexander Hamilton, who was secretary of the Treasury; Henry Knox, the secretary of war; and Attorney General Edmund Randolph in Washington's cabinet. But it took him many weeks to get to New York, and by the time he arrived, Madison was locked in a fateful battle with Hamilton. Theirs was an epic struggle that would divide the administration and result in a new political configuration for the young country.

MADISON AND HAMILTON had never been close friends, but they were friendly colleagues, working together on *The Federalist,* sharing books and meals, and enjoying each other's company. An old lady remembered observing how the two of them "would talk together in the summer and then turn and laugh and play with a monkey that was climbing in a neighbor's yard." Hamilton had expected to have Madison's support for his plan to deal with the debt incurred during the Revolutionary War, some fifty-four million dollars on the part of the Congress (twelve million foreign and forty-two million domestic) and another twenty-five million on the part of the states. But on February 11, 1790, the fourth day of debate on Hamilton's plan, Madison took the floor, and after an eloquent acknowledgment of the nation's obligation to pay its creditors, objected on moral grounds to the way Hamilton proposed to do it. In his *Report on Public Credit,* Hamilton maintained that the United States should not differentiate between those who had received government securities for goods and services provided during the Revolution and subsequent holders, who, during troubled and doubtful times, had bought the securities at deep discounts from the original owners. Madison declared it unjust that those who had purchased the securities would now receive something close to their full face value, while the original holders, soldiers in particular, were shut out of any benefit. "The sufferings of the military part of the creditors can never be forgotten while sympathy is an American virtue," he declared. Madison proposed a plan that would allow present holders of the securities "the highest price which has prevailed in the market" (about half the face value), with the balance going "to the original sufferers."[8]

Madison's proposal was not popular in the House, and for several days his colleagues railed at it. Theodore Sedgwick of Massachusetts declared that discriminating between original and current holders would be economically destructive: "Little dependence will be placed on the plighted faith of a government which, under the pretence of doing equity, has exercised a power of dispensing with its contracts and has thereby formed for itself a precedent of future violations." Fisher Ames of Massachusetts demanded to know, "If government has this right, what right of private property is safe?" Madison pointed out that Hamilton's proposal had already fundamentally changed the terms of the original bargain by lowering the interest rate to be paid. Moreover, he simply could not agree "that America ought to erect the monuments of her gratitude, not to those who saved her liberties, but to those who had enriched themselves in her funds." He spoke not just of soldiers but of farmers whose property was "taken at the point of the bayonet, and a certificate presented in the same manner." He had had something to do with that, having made the motion in Congress in May 1781 that Washington be allowed to impress supplies, and now it was his duty to see that those who had fed and clothed the army were treated justly.[9]

To opponents who argued that his plan was impractical—that tracking down original stockholders and figuring out what they had paid was simply too hard—Madison admitted that "it would be attended with difficulties and that perfect justice would not be done," but that was not the point: "It was sufficient that a grievous injustice would be lessened and that the difficulties might be surmounted."[10]

Madison did not often let his emotions rule his political judgment, but in this case he seemed to, taking on a political battle that from the outset he looked likely to lose. Even when the inevitable was about to happen, he seemed unable to reconcile himself to defeat, as though his personal investment in his proposal was so great that he could not bear to watch it go down. He was uncharacteristically brusque with Senator William Maclay of Pennsylvania, also an opponent of Hamilton's plan, who came to Madison's boardinghouse with what he believed was an alternative proposal that could win. "His pride seems of that kind which repels all communication," Maclay wrote in his diary. A few hours later, when Madison's proposal lost by a vote of 36 to 13, the Reverend Manasseh Cutler, watching the debate, observed that the loss was clearly painful for Madison. "On taking the question," Cutler wrote, "Mr. Madison had the mortification, which he appeared sensibly to feel, to be in a minority." Senator Maclay, a dour man, ever the pessimist, concluded that Madison had destroyed any possibility of defeating Hamilton's plan: "The obstinacy of this man has ruined the opposition."[11]

Madison had been moved before by what seemed an ungrateful nation's response to those who had sacrificed in the Revolution. Soldiers unpaid at the end of the Revolution had caused him deep chagrin. His stubbornness now also came from a deep aversion to speculators, whom he had regarded as a species of northern vulture since at least the time they had hovered around the Confederation Congress, hoping to benefit from Virginia's cession of western lands. With Hamilton's report they were swarming again, this time around Federal Hall, where they hoped to pick up profitable information—and too often succeeded. Senator Maclay observed that all of New York was caught up in the frenzy: "I call not at a single house or go into any company but traces of speculation in certificates appear." Even members of Congress were playing the game, according to Maclay: "Henceforth we may consider speculation as a congressional employment." Some of Hamilton's strongest supporters held securities and stood to benefit if his plan succeeded. For Madison it would be a lifelong point of pride that he "laid down strict rules for himself in pecuniary matters," the first one being "never to deal in public property, lands, debts or money whilst a member of the body whose proceedings might influence these transactions."[12]

Madison heard that northern speculators were sending vast sums of money to the South to buy up securities before those holding them became aware of the profits they stood to gain from Hamilton's plan. Such activities disgusted Madison and symbolized a future for the country that he thought appalling. He had not dedicated himself to building a nation where people traded in ephemera and were encouraged in greed and dishonesty. He had imagined a country where wealth grew as citizens cultivated the land and where national character was elevated by the steadiness and self-reliance that rural life encouraged. Jefferson had made this point in *Notes on the State of Virginia,* writing that "those who labor in the earth are the chosen people of God . . . whose breasts He has made his peculiar deposit for substantial and genuine virtue."[13]

Madison's response to Hamilton's report wasn't caused by ignorance of how to build a commercial nation. He had read Adam Smith and David Hume. He knew the model Hamilton had in mind, and that was part of the problem. Hamilton hoped to emulate the British system of political economy, which, as Madison and many others saw it, was at the mercy of a moneyed aristocracy that consigned lower classes to such a debilitating condition of dependence that they lost their capacity for citizenship. Britain itself, as Madison viewed it, was mired in the social decay that occurred when the pressures of population pushed people off the land and into factories. All societies progressed in this direction, but there was no need to hurry the process in an America where the West beckoned, holding out the promise of independent lives lived on the land.[14]

• • •

SLAVERY CAST a great shadow over this agrarian vision, and there was a sharp reminder of it when antislavery petitions interrupted the congressional debate on the nation's finances. On February 11, 1790, two groups of Quakers petitioned for "a sincere and impartial inquiry" into whether Congress should in the name of "justice and mercy" abolish the slave trade. On the next day, February 12, came another petition, this one from the Pennsylvania Abolition Society. It earnestly entreated Congress to give "serious attention to the subject of slavery . . . promote mercy and justice," and "step to the very verge of the power vested in you for discouraging every species of traffic in the persons of our fellow men." Benjamin Franklin, in one of his last acts, had signed the society's petition.[15]

Madison wanted to treat the petitions in a regular manner, sending them to a committee that would report on the powers of Congress under the Constitution. Perhaps there were ways that Congress could regulate the slave trade and "countenance" its abolition, he suggested. But South Carolinian Aedanus Burke declared that merely sending the petitions to committee "would sound an alarm and blow the trumpet of sedition in the southern states."[16]

Madison won out, with almost all of Virginia's delegates joining with the North to commit the petitions, but the report that came from committee a few weeks later caused more contention. The Georgia and South Carolina delegations believed the report went beyond the agreement reached at the Constitutional Convention by implying that when Congress gained power to act on the slave trade eighteen years hence, that body would also then have power over domestic slavery. This was an interpretation that those opposing the Constitution had advanced in the South. Reassurances had been offered to obtain ratification support, but now it looked as though they had meant nothing, and the men of Georgia and South Carolina were in a fury. They delivered what had never before been presented in a great national forum: a defense of slavery itself. It was not a necessary evil, they said, but a humane institution, one sanctioned by history and the Bible. James Jackson of Georgia, a hot-tempered war veteran with a cleft in his chin, argued "the situation of slaves here" to be "immensely preferable" to their lot in Africa and predicted race war would follow on the freeing of slaves. William Loughton Smith of South Carolina, wealthy and European educated, read extracts from Jefferson's *Notes on the State of Virginia,* which maintained the inherent inferiority of the black race. A disgusted Madison called the debates "shamefully indecent."[17]

Not content with defending slavery, Georgians and North Carolinians attacked the petitioners. Jackson said that Franklin would never have signed such a document "unless his age had weakened his faculties." Burke likened the Quakers watching from a gallery to "Satan sitting like a cormorant." Madison wrote to Benjamin Rush, "The gentlemen from South Carolina and Georgia are intemperate beyond all example and even all decorum."[18]

John Pemberton, one of the Quakers observing the debate, was shocked at the "abuse and malevolence" of Burke and his colleagues. On the other hand, Pemberton noted, "Madison from Virginia spoke well on our cause." A member of a wealthy Philadelphia family, Pemberton was intent on shutting down the slave trade worldwide, and to that end he wanted to keep Americans from participating in the trade between Africa and other countries. Madison helped him toward that goal by ensuring that in the report finally put forward, Congress declared its authority "to restrain the citizens of the United States from carrying on the African trade." The report also declared in Madison's words that Congress could regulate "for the humane treatment during their passage of slaves imported by the said citizens into the states admitting such importation." William Loughton Smith objected—unsuccessfully—to specifying humane treatment on the grounds that doing so could end the slave trade. John Pemberton wrote to his brother, "Some of their hearts seem hard."[19]

Madison also quieted the explosive debate in Congress by making the final report reflect what he—and most congressmen—believed the Constitution had established: Congress had no authority over the emancipation or treatment of slaves, "it remaining with the several states alone," in Madison's words, "to provide any regulations therein which humanity and true policy may require." The report passed, establishing what has been called the "federal consensus." In the years ahead, this decision would be cited repeatedly by those who maintained that slavery was a matter exclusively under the jurisdiction of the states.[20]

One of Madison's motives in quieting the debate over congressional jurisdiction, it has been suggested, was that the discussion exposed the contradiction in his own position: that slavery was wrong—"the most oppressive dominion ever exercised by man over man," he had called it—but that an immediate end to it was impossible. Indeed, there was one point in the debate that must have made Madison inwardly cringe, and that was when William Loughton Smith addressed what he called "fanciful schemes" that would relocate former slaves to "a remote country." Privately, Madison advocated exactly that, and Smith struck at one of the major vulnerabilities of such colonization plans. "How could [former slaves] be called freemen if they were against their consent to be expelled?" Smith asked.[21]

But for all his legislative skills, Madison could not have accomplished the federal consensus without the backing of northern congressmen. His colleagues from Georgia and South Carolina opposed him at every step, but he had the crucial, albeit often tacit, support of the men of New England and the middle Atlantic states. Quaker John Pemberton noted that congressmen "who heretofore had professed highly respecting freedom and being united with us" left the House rather than speaking up in debate, and he believed he knew the reason. Congress was a body where the philosophy of "scratch me and I will scratch thee" prevailed, he wrote, and "the funding system is so much their darling" that northerners were willing to keep silent in order to gain southern support. It was an astute observation. The delegates from Massachusetts, for example, were exquisitely aware that on upcoming votes concerning the assumption of state debts by the United States, South Carolina would be their most reliable ally. But something else was also at work: a belief that while the new nation was getting started, it made no sense to discuss an issue more divisive than any other. Congressman Theodore Sedgwick, who had pressed the lawsuit that made slavery illegal in Massachusetts, called the consideration of the Quaker petitions "a very foolish thing and very indifferently managed." Vice President John Adams, who considered slavery a "foul contagion in the human character," presented the slavery memorials to the Senate "rather with a sneer," according to William Maclay, and in private correspondence referred to "the silly petition of Franklin and his Quakers." Wrote Fisher Ames, "I am ashamed that we have spent so many days in a kind of forensic dispute—a matter of moonshine."[22]

A month later, when news of Benjamin Franklin's death reached New York, Madison had the sad task of memorializing him and moving that House members wear "the customary badge of mourning for one month." The motion carried, but in the Senate a similar motion had to be withdrawn. The South Carolina senators hated Franklin, and other members of the Senate, wanting South Carolina's votes on financial matters, were unwilling to wear crepe lest the South Carolinians be offended. Madison no doubt found the incivility reprehensible, but he would also have been aware of the pleasure his old friend Franklin would have taken from stirring up such trouble. One of Franklin's last acts had been to lampoon James Jackson of Georgia, noting in a newspaper article the wondrous similarity of Jackson's speech justifying African slavery to a speech given by one Sidi Mehemet Ibrahim, a fictional Algerian pirate who was intent on justifying the enslavement of Christians.[23]

ALEXANDER HAMILTON'S PLAN to restore the nation's credit included having the federal government assume the debts that states owed for wartime expenditures, a proposition that was pleasing to Massachusetts and South Carolina, which carried large debts, but displeasing to states such as Virginia and North Carolina, which had paid off large portions of their wartime obligations. Theoretically, no state would lose from assumption because a settlement of accounts was under way, and if a state's wartime expenditures turned out to be greater than the debt assumed by the government, that state would be owed the difference. But Virginians worried that a final settlement could take a long time to happen, or might in fact never happen, in which case the Old Dominion would end up paying for liabilities incurred by other states. Moreover, to Virginians, Hamilton's attitude toward debt itself seemed cavalier. He said that after state liabilities were rolled up with national ones, the federal government would pay down the consolidated debt, but it was hard to trust him on this point since he also called the debt a "national blessing." By that he meant that once Congress had the ability to collect taxes and pay the interest on the debt, it would become a vehicle for restoring the nation's credit. Madison agreed that the nation's financial house had to be put in order and was willing to take necessary steps to that end, but he wanted to be clear, he told Harry Lee, "that a public debt is a public curse."[24]

Pro-assumption forces managed a victory on March 9 by pulling out all the stops, even having two pro-assumptionist congressmen carried to the floor. One was Daniel Huger of South Carolina, who was lame. The other was Theodorick Bland of Virginia, who was too ill to walk. Before summer Madison would be writing to Virginia of his death.[25]

But on April 12, after three North Carolinians had taken their seats, assumption was defeated 31 to 29. Senator Maclay, who had been watching the debate, noted the reaction of the Massachusetts men, who could feel their state's creditors breathing down their necks. Sedgwick left the chamber and, when he returned, appeared to have been weeping. Fisher Ames "sat torpid, as if his faculties had been benumbed." Soon, Madison wrote to Monroe, the pro-assumptionists were speaking "a strange language on the subject," intimating "danger to the Union from a refusal to assume." Full of his victory, Madison bragged, "We shall risk their prophetic menaces." It cannot have been long, however, before he realized that he needed to take them seriously. They were under increasing pressure to pay their debts, but the Constitution forbade the usual means, such as issuing paper money. States could levy taxes, but the memory of Shays's Rebellion took that off the table. For the deeply indebted states, walking away from the prohibitions imposed by the Constitution—and thus walking away from the Union—had its attractions. Meanwhile, there was also talk coming from the South of breaking off from the newly formed Union. Madison's friend Harry Lee, concerned that the central government was establishing "a system calculated only for commercial society," was beginning to think that only in "disunion" would Virginia find relief.[26]

Madison was sick for a few days at the end of April and probably worried through the course of the flu that laid him low about the stability of the nation. Then President Washington became dangerously ill with what Madison reported to be "a peripneumony united probably with the influenza," and concern about the future of the country seized nearly everyone. Abigail Adams expressed the dread many felt when she wrote to her sister, "It appears to me that the union of the states and consequently the permanency of the government depend under providence upon [Washington's] life."[27] The president began to recover in mid-May, but his illness underscored the fragility of the new-modeled nation, no doubt especially for Madison, who would, until the end of his days, see the Republic as tentative and provisional—an experiment, the result of which was not known.

THE QUESTION of where to locate the nation's capital was still riling Congress in the spring of 1790, and it soon became caught up in the dispute over assumption. As Thomas Jefferson recorded it, one June day, about eight weeks after he arrived in New York, he ran into Hamilton in front of the president's house. The Treasury secretary looked as if he had been sleeping in his clothes—if he had been sleeping at all. "Somber, haggard, and dejected beyond description," as Jefferson described him, Hamilton lamented that his entire financial program was at risk. He bemoaned the fact that the dispute over assumption had put the Union in danger. Jefferson was sufficiently struck by the distraught Treasury secretary that he agreed to host a dinner at his new quarters in Maiden Lane to find "some temperament for the present fever." The main guests were Madison and Hamilton, and as Jefferson reported on the results of the evening:

It ended in Mr. Madison's acquiescence in a proposition that the question [of assumption] should be again brought before the House by way of amendment from the Senate, that though he would not vote for it, nor entirely withdraw his opposition, yet he should not be strenuous, but leave it to its fate. It was observed, I forget by which of them, that as the pill would be a bitter one to the southern states, something should be done to soothe them; that the removal of the seat of government to the Potomac was a just measure and would probably be a popular one with them and would be a proper one to follow the assumption.

As good storytellers often do, Jefferson oversimplified his narrative, ignoring the feverish dealing that had been going on behind the scenes for months. He was not the first person Hamilton had waylaid. The Treasury secretary had approached Senator Robert Morris on the Battery and offered Pennsylvania the permanent capital in exchange for votes on assumption. When Morris, wanting a bird in the hand, insisted on Philadelphia as the temporary capital, Hamilton had dropped out of that bargaining. There was also likely a negotiation at the dinner that Jefferson didn't describe: some consideration for Virginia in the assumption measure, such as an increase in the amount of its debt to be assumed.[28] As events would show, Madison might also have insisted that the residence question be settled before he delivered the votes needed on assumption.

Executing the bargain required staring down New Yorkers who were desperate to extract something—the temporary capital for five years, say, or failing that for two. The Senate didn't admit visitors, but after that body passed the residence bill, as it was called, New Yorkers packed the House gallery for the debates that began on Tuesday, July 6. On the following Friday, they watched in anger and dismay as the House passed the residence bill by the narrow margin of 32 to 29. To finish the bargain, Hamilton's bill for funding the debt, complete with assumption, passed the Senate on July 16. In the House, as William Loughton Smith recorded it, four congressmen had been persuaded to change their votes: "Lee and White of Virginia and Gale and Carroll of Maryland."[29] All four voted for the funding bill including assumption on July 26, and it passed 34 to 28. Madison, as he had told Hamilton he would do, voted against assumption. Also true to his word, he did so silently.

Hamilton no doubt concluded that he got the best of the bargain. By giving up something on which he placed a lesser value (the capital), he got something supremely important to him (assumption). But Madison probably had a different view. Threats of secession and Washington's illness might well have convinced him by the time of the dinner at Jefferson's that assumption, although he did not like it, would keep the Union knit together. By giving up active opposition and thus doing right by the nation, he did very well for Virginia, not least by ensuring his home state proximity to the new capital. He also managed, by making his no vote a part of the bargain, to shield himself from the anger of Virginians who, no matter what the concessions, despised assumption.

Madison and Jefferson set out for Virginia in early September, accompanied by an ingratiating young Princeton graduate, Thomas Lee Shippen, who provided a rare picture of the two men at leisure. When they had to wait all day for a vessel to take them across the Chesapeake Bay, Shippen reported, "We talked and dined and strolled and rowed ourselves in boats and feasted upon delicious crabs." In Annapolis they went to "the top of the State House" to enjoy what Shippen called "the finest prospect in the world, if interest, variety, wood, and water in all their happiest forms can make one so." A friend of Shippens who accompanied them proved skilled at "opening the roofs of the houses and telling us the history of each family who lived in them."

A few days later, after staying overnight in Georgetown, Madison, Jefferson, and Shippen set off on a daylong excursion to view the "fine prospects" of the area where the new capital would soon rise. In the early evening, they took a boat six miles upriver to the Little Falls of the Potomac, where they enjoyed what Shippen called a "romantic view."[30] Surveying the river and its unspoiled tree-lined shores, Madison must have enjoyed a moment of deep fulfillment. The new capital would grow far from cities in this bucolic place.

· · ·

A BITTER NOVEMBER cold had settled in by the time Madison, in the company of Jefferson, arrived in Philadelphia, the new, albeit temporary seat of government. Madison moved into Mrs. House's, as did Jefferson for a short time, while remodeling and expansion were being completed on a house he had rented several blocks west on Market Street. Once in his new quarters, Jefferson invited Madison "to come and take a bed and plate with me," declaring that "it will be a relief from a solitude of which I have too much; and it may lessen your repugnance to be assured it will not increase my expenses an atom." Madison, probably enjoying the familiar boardinghouse surroundings, politely declined.[31]

Congress met in Congress Hall, a Georgian structure of red brick next to the statehouse, and as the third session of the First Congress got under way, there was a period of unusual amity. Madison supported Secretary Hamilton's proposal for a new source of revenue: an excise tax on domestic spirits. It had long seemed to Madison a sensible source of supplemental funds, and he defended it now because it would not only provide necessary revenue but also "tend to increase sobriety and thereby prevent disease and untimely deaths."[32] It would also, as he later found out, make farmers in the Pennsylvania backcountry furious.

But then came Hamilton's report advocating a national bank, and Madison went into full revolt. He had long acknowledged the usefulness of banks. In the last days of the Constitutional Convention, he had tried to gain for Congress the power "to grant charters of incorporation," which would have permitted the chartering of banks, but the effort had failed, and that was Madison's point now. Hamilton's proposal assumed authority that had not been designated. Madison did not believe, as bank proponents argued, that article 1, section 8, of the Constitution, which gave Congress the power to provide for the "general welfare of the United States," justified establishing a bank. Such a stance would give Congress "unlimited power" and make pointless the list of specified powers set forth in that section. Nor did he think that "the power to pass all laws necessary and proper to execute the specified powers," which article 1, section 8, delegated to Congress, provided justification. "Whatever meaning this clause may have," he said, "none can be admitted that would give an unlimited discretion to Congress."[33]

During the course of debate, Congressman Elias Boudinot of New Jersey used *Federalist* 44 (which he believed had been written by Hamilton) to support the assertion that the government had the constitutional power to establish a bank. This particular number of *The Federalist* had, in fact, been written by Madison, who had declared, "No axiom is more clearly established in law or in reason than that wherever the end is required, the means are authorized; wherever a general power to do a thing is given, every particular power necessary for doing it is included."[34] In Madison's mind there was no contradiction between what he had written then and his stance now. He believed there was no power granted by the Constitution that a bank was necessary to carry out—unless one used a long and tortured chain of reasoning.

His emphasis had nonetheless changed from what the federal government could do to what it couldn't. A supporter of a strong central government in the 1780s, Madison was now increasingly bent on limiting its power, in large part because of the value he placed on "the exact balance or equipoise contemplated by the Constitution," a phrase he used during the bank debate. In the 1780s it was "the centrifugal tendency of the states" that jeopardized that balance and made creating a strong force at the center crucial. Without it, the states would fly out of their orbits and the United States join the long list of republics that had fallen apart and failed. Now, however, the expansive views of Hamilton and his supporters threatened to make the gravitational pull of the center so strong that the states would be pulled into its vortex and all counterpoise to central power annihilated. In later years, when charged with having deserted Hamilton, Madison would say, "Colonel Hamilton deserted me; in a word the divergence between us took place from his wishing . . . to administer the government . . . into what he thought it ought to be, while on my part I endeavored to make it conform to the Constitution as understood by the convention that produced and recommended it and particularly by the state conventions that *adopted* it."[35] There was more than one way to destroy a republic, and Madison's strategy changed as his perception of the danger changed.

The bill to establish a national bank passed the House 39 to 20, but Madison still hoped that it would not become law. During several conversations with the president, he found Washington "greatly perplexed" over the issue of the constitutionality of the bank. He was getting conflicting advice from his cabinet, with Hamilton urging him to sign the bill and Jefferson nearly as opposed to it as Madison. Madison believed that the president was inclined toward a veto, the first in American history, and his opinion was reinforced when Washington asked him to draft a document justifying such an action. But at the last moment, Washington signed the bill.[36] Madison, who had once been the president's closest adviser, found himself on the losing end of a debate over an issue that had vast implications. If the federal government could establish a national bank, he worried, were there any limits on federal power?

MADISON'S RESPONSE to Hamilton's financial program and the bank bill, in particular, would lead to the establishment of the first opposition party in the United States, to the demise of the Federalists, and to the presidencies of Jefferson, Madison, and Monroe. Madison could not have had all these consequences mapped out, but when it came to building an opposing party, he seemed from the outset to have a sense for the necessary steps along the way.

The first was to bring balance to the debate over the country's direction, which in Madison's view was skewed because Congress was in Philadelphia. Merchant and moneyed interests prevailed there as they had in New York. "It is no reflection on Congress," Madison wrote to Benjamin Rush, "to admit for one the united voice of the place where they may happen to deliberate." Madison took up with Jefferson ways of expanding the number of opinions heard, and three days after Washington signed the bank bill, Jefferson wrote to Madison's Princeton friend Philip Freneau offering him a position as a translator at the Department of State. Moody and brilliant, Freneau had never quite found his place in life. Since his teaching days, he had been a poet and a privateer and had recently become a newspaper editor. Jefferson admitted in offering Freneau the translator's job that the pay was modest, just $250 a year, but, he told him, the position "gives so little to do as not to interfere with any other calling the person may choose."[37] In other words, Freneau would have plenty of private time in which he could start a newspaper in Philadelphia, one that would counter the pro-Hamilton bias of both the city and John Fenno's *Gazette of the United States*. Freneau at first declined, but Madison thought he could be persuaded and visited with him in New York as soon as Congress adjourned. He thought Freneau was coming around, but again his old friend demurred. As others had found, however, Madison did not give up easily, and he kept up the pressure on Freneau throughout the spring and into the summer.

The second step was a four-week excursion to the North with Jefferson, the aim of which, Madison said, was "health, recreation, and curiosity." Political foes saw a political object, however, particularly after Madison and Jefferson visited with Chancellor Robert R. Livingston, the chief judicial officer of New York and a member of a powerful New York family, and with Aaron Burr, a sleek and ambitious new senator. Livingston, whom Madison had known since his days in the Continental Congress, had been frustrated in his quest for high office in the Washington administration and blamed his failure to receive an appointment on Hamilton. Burr had wrested his Senate seat from Hamilton's wealthy father-in-law, Philip Schuyler. Thus Robert Troup, one of Hamilton's friends, wrote to the Treasury secretary, "There was every appearance of a passionate courtship between the Chancellor, Burr, Jefferson and Madison when the two latter were in town. *Delenda est Carthago* [Carthage must be destroyed] I suppose is the maxim adopted with respect to you." As Hamilton's son later told the story, Madison and Jefferson subsequently traveled to Albany "under the pretext of a botanical excursion" to meet with another of Hamilton's enemies, New York's governor, George Clinton, "thence extended their journey to Vermont; and having sown a few tares in Connecticut, returned to the seat of government."[38]

Hamilton advocates overstated the case, but they likely had hold of an essential truth. The contextual evidence is strong that Madison in particular was working a political agenda. The trip occurred during a time when he was consumed with countering Hamilton, and the journey with Jefferson was not his only planned excursion. His schedule also included a trip to Boston with John Beckley, who with Madison's help had become clerk of the House of Representatives. No "botanical" label was put on that planned journey, perhaps because Beckley's relentlessly political approach to the world would have rendered it incredible.

Both Madison and Jefferson were interested in getting some idea of northern opposition to the plans Hamilton was so effectively putting in place. In Vermont, they met with the newly elected senator Moses Robinson, who in the years ahead would be an ally. On Long Island they visited with William Floyd, Kitty's father, who was remarried now, with two small daughters. During his term in the First Congress, Floyd had usually been on the other side of issues from Madison, but the complicated politics of assumption had sometimes brought them together.[39]

Whether Jefferson, who prided himself on being above partisanship, had any notion of establishing a political party is doubtful, but Madison likely did. He had equated parties with factions, meaning that although they were to be looked upon with suspicion for the "instability, injustice, and confusion" they caused, they were a fact of human nature and could not be wished away. They could be opposed, however, and needed to be when they had the power and inclination to move the country in the wrong direction. "Ambition must be made to counteract ambition," he had written in *Federalist* 51 to explain the Constitution. His subject then had been the branches of government, but now, as he and Jefferson sounded out opinion and looked for allies, he almost certainly perceived the usefulness of the concept in the larger society.[40]

The trip north was not all politics. Madison and Jefferson toured historic sites such as Saratoga and Bennington, where America had triumphed during the Revolution. They took a sail on Lake George ("the most beautiful water I ever saw," wrote Jefferson), and the fishing was good ("an abundance of speckled trout, salmon trout, bass, and other fish"). Near Fort George, Madison noted a flourishing farm owned by "a free Negro" who possessed "about 250 acres." The man's industry and good management would not have surprised Madison, who by this time was relying on Sawney, the slave who had accompanied him to Princeton, to oversee a 560-acre tract his father had deeded to him in 1784. Billey, the slave he had sold into indenture, was now a free man and would soon be acting as Madison's agent in business transactions. But Madison found it noteworthy that the black farmer had "six white hirelings."[41] Madison was doubtful that a racially mixed society could work, in large part because, he believed, whites would never consider blacks their equals—but here was an example that turned that thesis upside down.

Both men hoped that the trip would improve their health, and at the end of it Jefferson reported that during the excursion he had been "entirely clear" of the headache with which he had "been persecuted through the whole winter and spring." Madison, he said, was "in better health than I have seen him." Soon, however, Madison was writing to Jefferson of both "a fever attended with pretty decided symptoms of bile" and "a nausea and irritation in the stomach which were the more disagreeable as they threatened a more serious attack." Madison also mentioned "different shapes" of bile, indicating, perhaps, that he was suffering from more than one malady. A letter he received from Edmund Randolph after he had recovered contains a similar hint. Wrote Randolph, "I learn with sincere satisfaction that you have emerged from your late attack, but I wish that you would prevent a return in the fall by an abstinence from study." On the one hand, Randolph is worried about a recurrence in the autumn months, high malarial season; on the other, he draws a line back to Princeton and too many hours spent studying. When Madison was an old man, his doctor would say that he had three diseases that might carry him off.[42] Perhaps by 1791 he was already suffering from two, and they were interacting, with high malarial fevers triggering sudden attacks.

His health concerns were soon dwarfed by his outrage at the wild speculative frenzy he witnessed in New York for subscriptions for shares in the Bank of the United States: "It seems admitted on all hands now that the plan of the institution gives a moral certainty of gain to the subscribers with scarce a physical possibility of loss. The subscriptions are consequently a mere scramble for so much public plunder which will be engrossed by those already loaded with the spoils of indi[vi]duals." Hamilton, who took no part in the scramble, saw it merely as an unpleasant side effect of his financial plan, but to Madison it was galling, particularly since public officials were caught up in it: "Of all the shameful circumstances of this business, it is among the greatest to see the members of the legislature who were most active in pushing this job openly grasping its emoluments."[43] It would not have escaped Madison's notice that also among the profiteers was the flashy William Duer, Hamilton's close friend. After serving for a time as assistant secretary of the Treasury, Duer had resigned and set about making himself very rich.

The mania spread to Philadelphia, and Harry Lee reported it even south of there. Describing a journey from Philadelphia to Alexandria, Virginia, Lee wrote, "My whole route presented to me one continued scene of stock gambling; agriculture, commerce, and even the fair sex relinquished to make way for unremitted exertion in this favorite pursuit—thousands even at this late hour entering into a line of life which they abhor, in order to participate in legal spoil and preserve in some degree their relative station and rank with their neighbors." Most confounding, Lee observed, the rapid appreciation of bank stock was reckoned "a positive proof of wisdom and integrity in government."[44] Not only was the new government further off course than Madison had ever imagined possible; there was popular support for its direction. Battling Hamilton in the councils of government was no longer enough, but Madison would soon have in place an instrument for conducting the fight in a larger arena. Freneau had finally agreed to come to Philadelphia, and before the next Congress convened, there would be a newspaper at the seat of government to provide an alternative view. No longer would Alexander Hamilton's be the only voice that the public heard.

Chapter 10

THE SPIRIT OF PARTY

MADISON HAD BEEN CONSULTED about the speech Washington was to give at the opening of the Second Congress, but as he listened to the president deliver the final version in the Senate chamber of Congress Hall, he could not have been happy. Washington, citing "the rapid subscriptions to the Bank of the United States" as a sign of the nation's progress, sounded much like the misguided citizens Harry Lee had encountered on his trip south.[1] What could be more wrongheaded than regarding a speculative frenzy as a positive sign?

As head of the committee charged with writing the House response to the president, Madison tried to damp down the idea that Hamilton's financial plans had made the country better off. The representatives expressed "gratitude to Heaven" that the nation's economic prospects had improved. They also credited "the Constitution and laws of the United States"—which was too much for Harry Lee, who had recently become governor of Virginia. He wrote to Madison, "Tell me how you could impute the prosperity of the United States in any degree, much more in the degree you did, to the laws of Congress. . . . We owe our prosperity, such as it is, for it is nothing extraordinary, to our own native vigor as a people and to a continuation of peace, not to the wisdom or care of government."[2]

Madison replied rather sharply that it was an error to think that government had no role in improving the nation's prospects. The Constitution and the laws enacted in accordance with it had provided the stability that America needed to flourish. Madison's point was one that twenty-first-century scholars have begun to linger over: namely, that a country's fundamental arrangements are critical to determining its long-term economic growth, even more critical than economic policies. Security in property rights, which Madison explained in *Federalist* 10 as one of the purposes of the Constitution, is an essential underpinning of a sound economy. So too is security in contracts, which the Constitution addresses by forbidding states to impair them. So too are the uniform commercial regulations and the checks and balances on power that the Constitution provides.[3] Alexander Hamilton's *Report on Public Credit* has been widely praised for moving the nation into the modern financial world, but the opportunity and prosperity that Americans have enjoyed owe at least as much to Madison's work on the Constitution.

MADISON'S FINAL BREAK with Hamilton came when he perceived that the secretary's plans threatened to turn the limited government proposed by the Constitution into one with unlimited power. "This change," he wrote to Harry Lee, "will take place in defiance of the . . . sense in which the instrument is known to have been proposed, advocated and ratified." The question, as he saw it, was "whether the people of this country will submit to a constitution not established by themselves but imposed on them by their rulers. . . . It must unquestionably be the wish of all who are friendly to their rights that their situation should be understood by them and that they should have as fair an opportunity as possible of judging for themselves."[4] For the next year and a half Madison worked not only to enlighten the public but to put forward the idea that an awareness of what was wrong wasn't enough. Oppositional thought had to be organized in order to put ideas into practice, which is what a party did. This was breakthrough thinking in a society where revolution was still a living memory. Americans had thrown off a king to become an independent people, and now, it was almost universally believed, citizens should work for unity and harmony, pulling together for the greater good. Partisanship was divisive, selfish, and even subversive, a threat to the order that had been won at such cost. No one had a kind word to say about parties until Madison concluded that the established order was itself undoing the Revolution and that the greater good required effective opposition.

Madison conducted his campaign to enlighten the public in Philip Freneau's *National Gazette,* the newspaper he had made possible. Writing anonymously, he set the stage by describing a vision of the country in which people worked the land, were nourished by its harvests, and encouraged in "*health, virtue, intelligence,* and *competency.*" Manufacturing and mechanical industry, he wrote, ought not to be "forced or fostered by public authority," but rather viewed as regrettable "as long as occupations more friendly to human happiness lie vacant." He offered up the story of Great Britain's shoe buckle industry to illustrate the instability fostered by the manufacture of superfluities. Twenty thousand people had been thrown out of work when shoestrings and slippers came into fashion: "What a contrast is here to the independent situation and manly sentiments of American citizens, who live on their own soil or whose labor is necessary to its cultivation, or who were occupied in supplying wants . . . founded in solid utility."[5]

Hamilton, meanwhile, was heading rapidly in the opposite direction. In his *Report on Manufactures* for Congress, he recommended having the government pay cash bounties for factory start-ups. "Incitement and patronage" on the part of government would hurry the country along to a state in which labor could be constant rather than seasonal, as on a farm; indeed, people could work around the clock. This new and prosperous world would see "the employment of persons who would otherwise be idle (and in many cases a burden on the community)." It was a measure of the relentlessness of Hamilton's vision that he found it "worthy of particular remark that, in general, women and children are rendered more useful and the latter more early useful by manufacturing estab-lishments than they would otherwise be." He helpfully pointed out that "of the number of persons employed in the cotton manufactories of Great Britain, it is computed that four-sevenths nearly are women and children, of whom the greatest proportion are children and many of them of a very tender age."[6]

Hamilton advanced an argument for the constitutionality of his pro-posal that Madison had contended with before—that the general wel-fare clause of article 1, section 8, permitted Congress a wide range of activities that were not specifically authorized. As Madison viewed it, the general welfare clause was simply a general expression of the enu-merated powers that followed in section 8 of the Constitution, such as the powers to coin money and provide post offices. To interpret the clause as Hamilton did was to abolish the idea of limited government. "If Congress can apply money indefinitely to the general welfare and are the sole and supreme judges of the general welfare," Madison said on the floor of the House, "they may take the care of religion into their own hands; they may establish teachers in every state, county, and parish, and pay them out of the public treasury; they may take into their own hands the education of children, establishing in like manner schools throughout the Union, they may undertake the regulation of all roads, other than post roads. In short everything from the highest object of state legislation down to the most minute object of police would be thrown under the power of Congress." Hamilton was driving the nation toward the Leviathan state that Thomas Hobbes had described, some-thing never assented to in Philadelphia or the ratifying conventions. To a friend Madison wrote that if such an interpretation of the Constitu-tion were to prevail, "the parchment had better be thrown into the fire at once."[7]

Madison's opposition to the *Report on Manufactures* gained force from financial panic in 1792. Bank and government securities suddenly plummeted, and among those whose fortunes followed was former as-sistant Treasury secretary William Duer. Hamilton's friend had bor-rowed vast amounts in all corners of the city to place large bets that securities would continue to rise. When they fell instead, he ended up in debtors' prison, and hundreds to whom he owed money were ruined as well. "The prince of the tribe of speculators has just become a victim to his enterprises," Madison wrote to Edmund Pendleton. "Every description and gradation of persons from the church to the stews are among the dupes of his dexterity and the partners of his distress." Among the swindled was the Society for Establishing Useful Manufactures, another brainchild of Hamilton's, which with private funds and a charter from William Paterson, now governor of New Jersey, intended to build factories and a factory town (named Paterson) along the banks of the Passaic River. Hamilton had picked Duer to head the society, and it soon became evident that he had looted the society's funds.[8] With government involvement in private industry suddenly having little appeal, Congress shelved Hamilton's report.

Madison's *National Gazette* essays now became more pointed. In "The Union: Who Are Its Real Friends?," Madison did not mention Hamilton's name, but he noted that real friends were "not those who favor measures, which by pampering the spirit of speculation within and without the government, disgust the best friends of the Union." Nor did real friends "promote unnecessary accumulations of the debt of the Union instead of the best means of discharging it as fast as possible."[9] Madison did not mention parties, but nevertheless took a crucial step in changing their image by putting Hamilton and his supporters on a level with those who opposed them. The public tended to view the Treasury secretary and his allies in Congress not as a faction but as the government. By setting their behavior against that of real friends of the Union—who dampened speculation and eschewed debt—Madison showed, though did not yet say, that the Hamiltonians weren't above party, they *were* a party, one to which there was a vastly superior alternative.

In another of his *National Gazette* essays, Madison used Jefferson's notion that each generation should bear its own burdens in order to attack the idea of accumulating debt. A friend of his from the Virginia House of Delegates, John Mercer, now a representative from Maryland, subsequently took up the idea on the floor of the House: "The God of nature has given the earth to the living. That He will make our children and our children's children as free as He made us is what no parent, I trust, will deny. Under the divine impression, the voice of United America has declared that we cannot deprive posterity of their natural rights, which, from generation to generation must continue the same as we came into the world with; we have a right to the fruits of our own industry—they to theirs." Mercer had studied law with Jefferson, who might also have tutored him in the philosophy of his speech, but it was Madison who caught Hamilton's attention by letting it be known that he favored Mercer's sentiments.[10] Madison's attacks on his policies vastly irritated Hamilton, but this assault on his legacy was more than he could endure.

Hamilton decided to "unbosom" himself. In a six-thousand-word letter full of furious underlinings to Edward Carrington of Virginia, he wrote that he would never have taken the post of secretary of the Treasury had he not expected to have "the firm support of Mr. Madison." He had counted on it because the two of them had been in such agreement, but now instead of backing a strong central government, Madison was "disposed to narrow the federal authority." Madison's differences with him came from personal animosity, he believed. They had sprung "from a spirit of rivalship," perhaps. Whatever the reason behind Madison's opposition, Hamilton wrote, it had certainly caused him to change his mind about the man: "The opinion I once entertained of the candor and simplicity and fairness of Mr. Madison's character has, I acknowledge, given way to a decided opinion that *it is one of a peculiarly artificial and complicated kind.*"

Time and again, Madison, in cooperation with Jefferson, had opposed him, not only on fiscal issues but also on foreign policy, Hamilton went on. "*They have a womanish attachment to France and a womanish resentment against Great Britain,*" he wrote. But the best example of their opposition was the *National Gazette*. Jefferson and Madison had brought Freneau to Philadelphia, where he had been given a State Department position and started a newspaper. Hamilton's concern wasn't about the ethics of putting Freneau on the public payroll while he undertook other activities. It was not uncommon for even high officials to have second jobs, including ones that might take them away from the capital for extended periods. Rather, the issue was that Madison and Jefferson were behind "a paper devoted to the subversion of me and the measures in which I have had an agency." An impartial man would also conclude, Hamilton wrote, "that it is a paper of a tendency *generally unfriendly* to the government of the United States."[11]

Hamilton's grandiosity seems to leap off the page. The idea that opposition to him and his policies was subversive to the Republic smacks of the kingly *l'état, c'est moi,* but to be fair to the Treasury secretary, he was representing—in an extreme way, to be sure—the widely held view that party spirit was evil and quite naturally exempting himself from it. Madison agreed that parties could have evil effects, but the difference was that he didn't regard himself as above the fray. "Parties are unavoidable," he wrote in one of his *National Gazette* essays, and the task was to make "one party a check on the other."[12]

WITH THE ELECTION of 1792 on the horizon, George Washington was contemplating retirement. He sent a note to Madison requesting him to call and confided his reasons: he felt unfit to make many of the judgments required of him, particularly those of a constitutional nature. "He found himself also in the decline of life, his health becoming sensibly more infirm and perhaps his faculties also." Moreover, he was miserable in his job, in part because of the "spirit of party" that had arisen. Madison summoned all his tact. Instead of confronting the president's assumption that party spirit was ever and always a threat, he tacitly acknowledged that unchecked it could be. The president ought to remain rather than retire, Madison argued, because by the end of another term the government would have "a tone and firmness" that would protect against any of the dangers that party represented, such as "disaffection" for the government among a few on one side and an ambition on the other for "mixed monarchy." A few days after meeting with

Washington, Madison agreed to suggest what the president might say in a farewell address, but he did so, he carefully noted, in a way that did not indicate even the slightest agreement to such a plan.[13]

If Washington was aware of Madison's involvement with the *National Gazette*, he betrayed no hint of it. Madison had never told him and might have felt some uneasiness about not doing so. A critique of Hamilton's policies was inevitably a critique of the president who approved them, and after his meeting with Washington, in which the president had consulted him in such a personal way, Madison did not write for the *National Gazette* for more than five months. He would take up his pen again only after a severe escalation of the paper wars.

Washington himself helped in that escalation. He held off on making up his mind about a second term until the fall and thereby inflamed the party spirit he so despised. As Hamilton thought about a contest for the presidency, he became ever more convinced that the attacks on him had been orchestrated by Jefferson to get rid of him as a rival. He inundated John Fenno, editor of the *Gazette of the United States*, with letters written under a variety of pseudonyms that attacked Jefferson by name and told the story of Freneau's being recruited to come to Philadelphia, work in Jefferson's State Department, and begin a newspaper. This made Freneau, Hamilton wrote, "the faithful and devoted servant of the head of a party." When Freneau responded that the modest pay he received for translating had nothing to do with the views he expressed in the *National Gazette*, Hamilton snipped his words into a seeming admission of guilt, then asked this pointed question: How could Jefferson continue to serve in an administration that he was attacking?[14]

Driving the knife in deeper, Hamilton cited the meddlesome letter that Jefferson had written prior to the Virginia ratifying convention, in which he had expressed the hope that nine states would ratify the Constitution but four hold out until amendments were agreed to. As Hamilton presented it, this meant that "Jefferson was in the origin opposed to the present Constitution." Thus it made perfect sense that he should have established a paper to express views "virulently hostile both to the government and to its measures."[15] By conflating opposition to government measures with opposition to the Constitution, Hamilton was at once reflecting the widely held view that government was above party and calling Jefferson disloyal.

Madison was at Montpelier when he learned of Hamilton's attacks on Jefferson, and he immediately rode to Albemarle to confer with Jefferson and Monroe. Madison and Monroe took on the task of fighting back in *Dunlap's American Daily Advertiser.* They accused Hamilton (though not by name) of wanting to silence anyone who pointed out "the mischievous tendency of some of the measures of government." They also published extracts of a number of letters that Jefferson had sent "to a particular friend" in order to show his support for the Constitution. Madison also defended Freneau, pointing out his Princeton friend's education, his worthy character, and his suffering during the war, when he had been held in a British prison ship.[16]

Freneau needed some boosting. Skilled polemicist though he was, the assault on his journalistic integrity pained him. Nearly a decade later he would still be denying that he had been Jefferson's "pensioner" or "confidential agent." In the months ahead, as if to show his independence, Freneau would launch harsher attacks than either Jefferson or Madison thought wise on the president himself. A cartoon in the *National Gazette* that showed a kingly Washington paying for his misdeeds on the guillotine would cause the president to bring a cabinet meeting to a full stop while he raged about "that *rascal Freneau.*"[17]

While defending Jefferson and Freneau, Madison also continued his effort to shift public thinking about parties. In a *National Gazette* essay, he made their inevitability clear by placing them in historical context. They had been present when some argued for independence while others remained loyal to Britain. They had existed when some supported the Constitution and others opposed it. Now there was "a third division, which being natural to most political societies, is likely to be of some duration in ours." Madison described one of the current parties as "more partial to the opulent than to the other classes of society; and having debauched themselves into a persuasion that mankind are incapable of governing themselves, it follows with them of course that government can be carried only by the pageantry of rank, the influence of money and emoluments, and the terror of military force." The other party, clearly needed as a check, believed "in the doctrine that mankind are capable of governing themselves." This second party, he wrote, was "the Republican party, as it may be termed."[18] It was a designation that would cause confusion for generations of students because Madison's Republican Party is unrelated to today's, which came into being during the decade before the Civil War. The name was cleverly chosen, however, to indicate that Republicans adhered to the idea of the Republic as set forth in the Constitution. The opposing party, Madison suggested, should be known as Antirepublicans, but the Federalists, not surprisingly, preferred the name they'd had since the battle over the Constitution.

The fledgling Republicans tried out their wings in 1792. Once it was evident that George Washington was a candidate for the presidency, all idea of a contest for the top office was abandoned, but Republicans thought they saw a ripe target in Vice President John Adams. He had not only made himself ludicrous with his emphasis on high-sounding titles but actually written a series of essays in which he had praised the idea of hereditary succession. In the search for an alternative to Adams, Madison's name was mentioned—presumably by Republicans who failed to understand that Virginia's electors could not vote for both him and George Washington. The early favorite, however, was longtime New York governor George Clinton. Not only was he firmly opposed to everything Alexander Hamilton stood for, but with his flyaway hair and bulbous nose he looked the populist part. But in October, Republicans from New York and Pennsylvania wrote to Madison and Monroe to tell them that Aaron Burr had mounted a campaign. Where did they stand now that there was a choice? They remained with Clinton, as did Republicans who caucused in Philadelphia. John Beckley, clerk of the House and a reliable source of party intelligence, wrote to Madison that the caucus had dropped "all thoughts of Mr. Burr." Beckley, who had been in New York, also warned Madison about Hamilton. "It would be wise to be watchful; there is no inferior degree of sagacity in the combinations of this *extraordinary* man, with a comprehensive eye, a subtle and contriving mind, and a soul devoted to his object."[19]

In an age when it was difficult even to get out the news that Adams had an opponent, Madison knew that a Clinton victory was unlikely. But the Republicans hoped to make a good enough showing to provide Adams with some useful enlightenment. "As the opposition to him is leveled entirely against his political principles and is made under very great disadvantages," Madison wrote, "the extent of it, whether successful or not, will satisfy him that the people at large are not yet ripe for his system."[20] In the end Clinton received fifty electoral votes to John Adams's seventy-seven, which was impressive. Washington remained as popular as ever. For the second and last time in American history, the vote of the Electoral College for a presidential candidate was unanimous.

AMONG HAMILTON'S FOES it was widely believed that he had used his office to enrich himself. John Beckley told Madison that he thought he had "a clue to something far beyond mere suspicion on this ground," and at the end of 1792 a scandal seemed about to break.[21] Three members of Congress received information that Hamilton had been providing money to James Reynolds, a shady character who had been jailed for fraud, and that the payments had to do with speculation. Since one of the members apprised of this was Senator James Monroe, it is likely that Jefferson and Madison were aware of the charges almost immediately— and were as stunned as Monroe when Hamilton confessed that yes, he had been paying Reynolds, but it had nothing to do with speculation. Rather, for more than a year, Hamilton, husband of the lovely Elizabeth Schuyler, who had recently borne him his fifth child, had been involved in an affair with Reynolds's wife. He had been buying Reynolds's silence.

Hamilton's affair was not the kind of thing that gentlemen brought up in public. Indeed, the members who confronted Hamilton apologized for "the trouble and embarrassment" they had caused him, and it would be five years before the matter reached the press. Thus, even though Madison, Jefferson, and Monroe were now confirmed in their belief that Hamilton was hardly the paragon of virtue he liked to claim, they were constrained from making that evident. When the new Congress convened, William

Branch Giles of Virginia, who was Theodorick Bland's successor, tried an attack along financial lines. A Princeton graduate with a sloping forehead and pugnacious manner, Giles proposed a series of resolutions intended, he said, "to obtain necessary information." They suggested that Hamilton was playing fast and loose with Treasury funds, including putting money borrowed for one purpose to another use. Hamilton provided the information Giles requested—indeed, gave fulsome responses, indicating that if he had on occasion violated "the strict letter of the law," it was for good reason and with presidential authority. And then, as if to drive his critics mad, he claimed that such administrative discretion was a necessary part of his office. Only "pusillanimous caution" would demand a "strict regularity."[22]

The Second Congress was near adjournment, and Madison, aware that the questions raised and Hamilton's answers needed a lengthy discussion, wanted to wait until a new Congress met to continue the dispute. But Jefferson wanted resolutions of censure against Hamilton introduced immediately and went so far as to draft them himself. Giles was his willing handmaiden, and Madison's role seems simply to have been in softening Jefferson's language before Giles brought the resolutions to the floor.[23]

The resolutions lost—and lost badly. Jefferson blamed the outcome on the number of "stockjobbers," "bank directors," and "holders of bank stock" in Congress and believed that the rejection would show the public "the desperate and abandoned dispositions with which their affairs were conducted." But Madison viewed it as "very unfortunate" that the resolutions were offered.[24] He was trying to build a party, and the last thing he needed was to force votes that drove members to the other side.

Not long after the Second Congress ended, Madison set out for Virginia with James Monroe, who just four years before had been his rival for a seat in Congress. Madison's move away from an emphasis on strong central government and his opposition to Hamilton had strained some relationships, including with the president, but he found himself more in harmony than he had been for years with Virginians who were suspicious of federal power. George Mason, before he died, had made a point of sending his respects to Madison and letting him know he was held in high regard. In a time that in many ways was disappointing, there was comfort to be found in being embraced at home.[25]

There was also pleasure in being recognized for the role he had played in advancing liberty. After arriving in Orange, he received notice that the French National Assembly had made him an honorary citizen. Like Jefferson, Madison saw the French Revolution as a continuation of the work America had begun in "reclaiming the lost rights of mankind," and in that spirit he accepted.[26] But the French Revolution was devolving into something very different from an uprising against tyranny. Savage mobs had stormed the Tuileries and slaughtered hundreds of the king's Swiss Guards. Lafayette, who had been at the center of events in the Revolution's hopeful early days, had been forced to flee France, had been arrested, and would endure a cruel imprisonment. Rampaging crowds had broken into Paris prisons and killed indiscriminately, piling the corpses of political prisoners, clergymen, common criminals, and children into bloody heaps. The royal family had been placed under arrest, and just a few months before Madison accepted honorary French citizenship, the National Assembly had passed a death sentence on Louis XVI (or Louis Capet, as the revolutionaries insisted, refusing to acknowledge him as a monarch). The sentence was carried out by guillotine.

From our perspective in the twenty-first century, we know that matters would only grow worse. The guillotine in Paris would soon be chopping off more than one head a minute. In outlying areas such as Pont-de-Cé and Avrillé thousands were shot. At Nantes, thousands were drowned in the Loire in what were called "republican baptisms." But Madison did not know what lay ahead, and like many before and since who have watched the overthrow of tyrants with great hope, he convinced himself that the French Revolution would turn out for the best. Concern that failure of the Revolution would be seen as evidence that people could not govern themselves also influenced his thinking and made it easier in a time of uncertain communications, most filtered through a hostile British press, to dismiss reports of blood running in the streets of Paris. As for Louis XVI, Madison could not quite bring himself to say that he had gotten what he deserved, but instead reported that plain men had repeatedly expressed to him a statement that seemed fair: "If he was a traitor, he ought to be punished as well as another man." Madison's old college friend Hugh Brackenridge was less respectful. He headlined a piece he wrote for the *National Gazette* on the king's demise "Louis Capet Lost His Caput."[27]

Madison's hope in the French Revolution was widely shared—as became evident in the reception that Americans accorded to Edmond-Charles Genêt, or Citizen Genêt, as he was known in revolutionary France. Named minister to the United States, the thirty-year-old Genêt, a florid-faced, bright, and bustling redhead, arrived aboard the French frigate *Embuscade* in Charleston, South Carolina, on April 8, 1793. He was greeted by jubilant crowds and enthusiastic officials, who seemed not the least taken aback when he began to fit out privateers to sail in the French cause—and man them with Americans. He also began to recruit American citizens to invade Spanish possessions in the Southwest. As he made his way north, Genêt received one enthusiastic reception after another, all climaxed by a grand dinner in Philadelphia, where the company joined in singing "La Marseillaise" and took turns donning a *bonnet rouge,* the red cap symbolizing liberty. At Montpelier, Madison took heart when he heard of Genêt's reception. He hoped it would "testify what I believe to be the real affections of the people," he told Jefferson.[28]

ABOUT THE TIME that Genêt arrived in America, so did news that revolutionary France had declared war on Great Britain. President Washington issued a proclamation that the United States would "pursue a conduct friendly and impartial toward the belligerent powers," a policy with which Madison generally agreed, but he fretted about the word "impartial." It seemed "stronger than was necessary," he wrote to Jefferson, and perhaps stronger than was proper, given the treaty that the United States had signed with France in 1778. It might have been worse, Jefferson explained. He had at least managed to keep the word "neutrality" out of the proclamation.[29]

The president was soon under attack, particularly in the pages of the *National Gazette*. Someone, perhaps Freneau himself, writing under the pen name Veritas, accused Washington of "double-dealing" in the proclamation, effectively nullifying the United States' treaty with France, although not saying so. Had the president consulted his fellow citizens, instead of relying on "the aristocratic few and their contemptible minions of speculators, Tories, and British emissaries," he would have realized, wrote Veritas, that the people had no inclination to treat on equal terms those "who so lately deluged our country with the blood of thousands and the men who generously flew to her rescue and became her deliverers." Madison wrote to Jefferson that the proclamation seemed "to violate the forms and spirit of the Constitution," but he nonetheless regretted "the position into which the president has been thrown." Jefferson began to think the attacks in the *National Gazette* were somehow a Federalist trick to further alienate Washington from Republicans and drive him into Federalist arms.[30]

Hamilton, with perfect timing, weighed in to defend Washington in a series of energetic essays in John Fenno's *Gazette of the United States*. Writing under the pseudonym Pacificus, he brought forward the word that Jefferson had avoided and labeled the president's statement a "Proclamation of Neutrality"—a name that would stick. He insisted that the treaty of 1788 put the United States under no obligation to assist France in its war on Great Britain. Moreover, he wrote, the president had the perfect right under the Constitution to make that judgment, and those who disagreed were angling for war with the British.[31]

A frantic Jefferson urged Madison to respond: "For god's sake, my dear sir, take up your pen, select the most striking heresies, and cut him to pieces in the face of the public." Jefferson was rattled in part because at the same time Hamilton was attacking the Republican, pro-French position in the pages of the *Gazette of the United States*, Genêt was undermining it by his conduct in Philadelphia. Warned by the president to cease fitting out privateers, Genêt had continued to do so right under the president's nose, using the port of Philadelphia to arm a British vessel captured by the French. When told the vessel should not sail, he responded by threatening to go over the president's head to Congress and, if necessary, to the people. Jefferson, who had once had high hopes for Genêt, wrote to Madison, "Never, in my opinion, was so calamitous an appointment made, as that of the present minister of France." He described Genêt as "hotheaded, all imagination, no judgment, passionate, disrespectful, and even indecent towards the president." So destructive was Genêt's behavior to the relationship between France and the United States that Madison was tempted to think him an agent of the anti-French Hamiltonians.[32] It was not the last time that he would find the French to be difficult allies.

Madison was not eager to enter the fray. He was at Montpelier, far from the scene of the crisis, and deprived, as he put it, "of some material facts and many important lights." He was no longer even sure what the president's position was. He forced himself to take up the task but called it "the most grating one I ever experienced." The pseudonym under which he wrote, Helvidius, for Helvidius Priscus, who had died resisting imperial rule, might have been an indication of his misery—as well as a biting comment on Washington's administration. Madison's task was complicated by the ground shifting under his feet. Even as he wrote, he learned that Jefferson was joining Hamilton and the rest of the president's cabinet in demanding Genêt's recall. As he was arguing the nuances of legislative versus executive power to make proclamations concerning war and peace (and favoring the legislative), he heard from Jefferson that the president's proclamation was now so popular that "it would place the Republicans in a very unfavorable point of view with the people to be caviling about small points of propriety." Madison threw up his hands. Citing social obligations and "the new posture of things," he stopped writing.[33]

FALL WAS COMING ON, a reflective, melancholy time, and as Madison looked back, he saw a Second Congress that had begun badly and ended worse. Hamilton's *Report on Manufactures* had been shelved, but that was the result of speculation and panic as much as a triumph of republican principles. His best effort had been the essays he had written to help enlighten public opinion. His pride in them would be apparent when in his old age he initialed them so there would be no question of authorship. He had written anonymously, but his role as opposition leader was widely acknowledged. The Republican Party was now often called Madison's party.[34]

Jefferson was retiring, and while it might be a relief not to have his friend constantly urging him to the barricades, he would miss his companionship in Philadelphia. When he returned for the Third Congress, Madison would also be without his familiar household. Mrs. House had died in June, and Mrs. Trist was closing up the boardinghouse. Madison might have begun to think that the time was growing near when he, like Jefferson, could enjoy more permanently the pleasures of rural life. After his brother Ambrose died on October 3, necessity began to enter into his thinking. Ambrose had helped James Madison Sr. run Montpelier, and someone needed to take up his responsibilities.

But the pull of political life was strong, and he was making plans. He had worked with Jefferson on a report to be submitted to the Third Congress showing that Great Britain imposed more onerous duties on American products than any other nation and detailing the restrictions that it placed on American shipping. A recent British decree—called an Order in Council—authorizing the Royal Navy to stop and detain American vessels carrying grain to France would help him make his point that British policies should be resisted.[35] Madison was convinced that the United States had the commercial power to change Great Britain's ways, and he wanted to see the U.S. Congress use it.

As fall advanced, it became unclear when Congress would meet again. Yellow fever had struck Philadelphia and was taking a devastating toll. There was a report of 150 buried on a Wednesday, which a few days later was revised upward to 200. Jefferson described the course of the disease: "It comes on with a pain in the head, sick stomach, then a little chill, fever, black vomiting and stools and death from the second to the eighth day." So many succumbed that the ringing of church bells for the dead was forbidden. As many as twenty thousand fled, and even after spells of cool weather in early October the funerals continued.[36]

In mid-October, Madison received what was now very rare: an inquiry from the president. Washington wanted to know if he had power under the Constitution to call for Congress to meet in another place. He did not, Madison replied, but a late October frost rendered the question moot. No one understood that the freezing weather brought an end to the fever by killing the mosquitoes transmitting it, but Philadelphians knew that the terrible plague was over.[37]

The freeze did not come in time for John Todd, a young Quaker lawyer in Philadelphia. He had moved his wife, their toddler, and a newborn outside the city to lodgings on the west bank of the Schuylkill, where he hoped they would be safe, and then returned to Philadelphia to care for his parents. They died, and on October 14, 1793, Todd died, like his parents a victim of the fever. On the same day, the Todd baby, named William, died. Little John Payne Todd survived, and so did his twenty-five-year-old mother. Her name was Dolley.

Serving in the Continental Congress, James Madison, although in his early thirties, looked much younger. One member thought he was a recent college graduate.

Madison's 1783 romance with Kitty Floyd ended badly, and she changed her mind about marrying him.

George Washington presides as a delegate signs the Constitution in September 1787. Madison, holding a quill, is to the right of Washington.

The FEDERALIST. No. X.

To the People of the State of New-York.

AMONG the numerous advantages promised by a well constructed Union, none deserves to be more accurately developed than its tendency to break and control the violence of faction. The friend of popular governments never finds himself so much alarmed for their character and fate, as when he contemplates their propensity to this dangerous vice. He will not fail therefore to set a due value on any plan which, without violating the principles to which he is attached, provides a proper cure for it. The instability, injustice and confusion introduced into the public councils, have in truth been the mortal diseases under which popular governments have every where perished; as they continue to be the favorite and fruitful topics from which the adversaries to liberty derive their most specious declamations. The valuable improvements made by the American Constitutions on the popular models, both ancient and modern, cannot certainly be too much admired; but it would be an unwarrantable partiality, to contend that they have as effectually obviated the danger on this side as was wished and expected. Complaints are every where heard from our most considerate and virtuous citizens, equally the friends of public and private faith, and of public and personal liberty, that our governments are too unstable; that the public good is disregarded in the conflicts of rival parties; and that measures are too often decided, not according to the rules of justice, and the rights of the minor party; but by the superior force of an interested and over-bearing majority. However anxiously we may wish that these complaints had no foundation, the evidence of known facts will not permit us to deny that they are in some degree true. It will be found indeed, on a candid review of our situation, that some of the distresses under which we labor, have been erroneously charged on the

Alexander Hamilton worked with Madison to produce *The Federalist,* but they later became fierce opponents.

Madison's first contribution to *The Federalist* is his most famous. In *Federalist* 10, defying conventional wisdom, he argued that a large republic would better protect minority rights than a small one.

Madison wrote Washington's first inaugural address and was his most influential adviser as the new government began.

By this time of this portrait in 1792, Madison was the powerful leader of the House of Representatives. Always simpler in his dress than his fellow Virginians, he would eventually wear only black.

In 1794, Madison, one of the nation's most prominent politicians, wooed and won the glamorous widow Dolley Payne Todd. Ten years later, after Madison had become secretary of state, Gilbert Stuart painted their portraits.

Madison's father built the original
brick home at Montpelier.

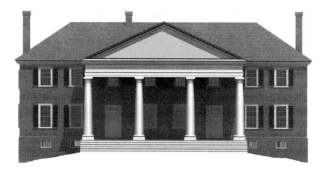

After his marriage, Madison built an
addition to the left with a separate entrance
for him and his family. His parents lived in
the original part of the house to the right.

As president, Madison added a central
doorway, which together with the portico
unified the structure. He also added wings.

Thomas Jefferson won the presidential election of 1800 with Madison's help, but it was close. Jefferson's intended vice president, Aaron Burr, received an equal number of electoral votes.

The refusal of Burr, shown here, to give way to Jefferson threw the election into the House of Representatives, destroyed Burr's political career, and made Madison, whom Jefferson had named secretary of state, the likely successor to the presidency.

Washington City became the capital of the United States in 1800, and to the secretary of state-designate and Mrs. Madison, arriving by carriage in late April 1801, it might have looked something like this.

When James and Dolley Madison arrived in Washington City
in 1801, they found just one wing of the Capitol finished.

One of the early diplomatic
challenges for Secretary of State
Madison occurred when
President Jefferson, who had his
own ideas of etiquette, escorted
Dolley Madison rather than
Elizabeth Merry, wife of the
British minister, shown here, into
a dinner at the president's house.

The Spanish minister, the marquis de Yrujo, who was married to the former Sally McKean, a childhood friend of Dolley Madison, took up the Merrys' cause. Secretary of State Madison helped control the diplomatic damage.

Marquis de Casa Yrujo and *Marchioness de Casa Yrujo*, Gilbert Charles Stuart. Collection of Thomas R. and Susan McKean; photographs courtesy of the Philadelphia Museum of Art.

John Randolph of Roanoke was Madison's bitter enemy. Eccentric to the point of instability, Congressman Randolph railed with such vitriol on the floor of the House while Madison was secretary of state and president that his speeches became largely ineffective.

Anna Payne, Dolley Madison's younger sister, who was virtually raised by the Madisons, had her portrait done by Gilbert Stuart. The painter entertained himself by shaping the curtain in the background into his own profile.

In 1804, Anna Payne married Congressman Richard Cutts at the Washington Navy Yard. His later financial insolvency would be expensive for James Madison.

John Payne Todd, Dolley Madison's son from her first marriage, was a toddler when the Madisons married. He grew up to be a handsome, hard-drinking gambler.

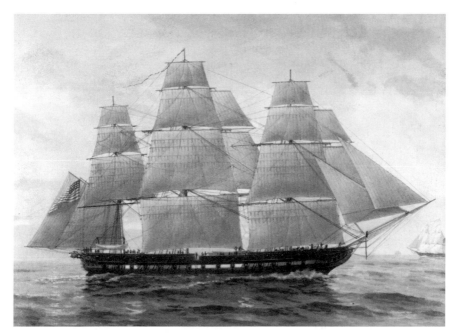

The USS *Chesapeake* as she might have appeared before the British frigate *Leopard* launched a surprise attack on her in June 1807. Madison called the action, which helped provoke the War of 1812, "lawless and bloody."

President Madison welcomed news of the stunning victory of the USS *Constitution* over the British frigate *Guerriere*. The message arrived in Washington as the presidential election of 1812 approached.

Convinced that the British would never attack Washington, John Armstrong, President Madison's secretary of war, dragged his feet when it came to the capital's defense.

Madison's concern that the British would attack the capital city proved well founded. British troops burned the Capitol, the White House, and other public buildings on August 24, 1814.

After the British attack, Madison named his former rival James Monroe to head the War Department.

This enormous flag, which flew over Fort McHenry on the morning of September 14, 1814, inspired "The Star-Spangled Banner." Each star is two feet wide.

Finding the White House uninhabitable when they returned to Washington, President and Mrs. Madison moved into the Octagon House. It was there that Madison signed the Treaty of Ghent, ending the war.

This 1816 portrait of President Madison emphasizes the steady resolve with which he brought the nation through its first war under the Constitution.

This pair of portraits painted in 1817, after Madison had retired from office, shows Dolley still beautiful at forty-nine, but James showing his years at sixty-six. The painting of the former president also hints at the kindness that Madison's friends consistently attributed to him.

Montpelier has recently been restored so that visitors can see it as James and Dolley Madison knew it. Twentieth-century additions have been stripped away. Pink stucco that had been applied over the brick has been removed. Interiors are being recreated so that it is once again possible to imagine James Madison playing chess in the drawing room or reading and studying maps and globes in his library.

Chapter 11

DOLLEY

AS THE FEVER ABATED, Philadelphians whitewashed the walls of their homes, scrubbed the floors with vinegar, and burned gunpowder to cleanse the air. Finally, in mid-November 1793, the city was declared safe for the government to gather. Madison arrived, moved in with James Monroe on North Eighth Street, and reentered the political fray, putting forward measures to place the same restrictions on British shipping that Great Britain applied to the United States. "The commerce of the United States is not at this day on that respectable footing to which from its nature and importance it is entitled," he declared on the House floor. The evidence was there for all to see, and he proposed tariffs and tonnage fees to bring the British around.[1]

Madison had tried before to institute commercial policies that he believed would change British behavior, and he had failed before. But now his proposals seemed to come at a particularly apt moment. Not only were the British treating grain as contraband; they had also brokered a truce between Portugal and Algiers that had resulted in freeing Algerine pirates to prey on American vessels in the Atlantic. Nevertheless, Madison ran into a firestorm of opposition from merchants and shipowners who did not want to offend their biggest customer. Hamilton, who as recently as *Federalist* 11 had been a proponent of using trade policy to influence other nations, was now fearful that Madison's proposals, by leading to a decrease in trade, would bring a decrease in tariff revenues. He began passing talking points to Madison's opponents, and both they and the Federalist press attacked him, alleging that his proposals would lead to war.

Provocations on the part of Britain soon muted that charge. News came of a speech by Lord Dorchester, the governor-general of Canada, confirming suspicions that the British were urging Indian attacks on Americans in the Northwest, where Great Britain still had not left military garrisons that it had agreed to give up in the peace treaty of 1783. The British also issued an even harsher Order in Council, one that put at risk not just foodstuffs but any cargo—and the vessels carrying it—to or from the French West Indies. Then, bringing the crisis to a head, the British began seizing American ships. Soon they had captured some 250 vessels in the West Indies and declared most of them prizes of war. They stripped crew members of papers and possessions, including the clothes they were wearing, and threw the naked seamen into rusting prison hulks.[2]

Retaliatory trade policies suddenly seemed beside the point, and leading Federalists began advocating a military buildup. In response to the threat posed by the Algerine corsairs, Congress passed and the president signed a bill authorizing the construction of six American warships. Madison voted against the measure, arguing that the ships could not be ready in time to deal with the crisis. Moreover, he said, since the Algerine pirates "were known to be in the habit of selling a peace," the United States might find it could "be purchased for less money than the armament would cost."[3] In fact, the nation would bribe the Algerines—but also build the six frigates, a project for which Madison would one day be very grateful.

Federalist Theodore Sedgwick of Massachusetts followed up by proposing fifteen regiments of a thousand men each and authority for the president to declare an embargo. Madison regarded armies, like navies, as potentially ruinous expenses. He also worried that a standing army would dangerously enhance governmental power. The Republic would be better off if the United States worked its will on the world through trade restrictions rather than military establishments, he believed. The embargo thus struck him as a wise move, and although New England members at first resisted, on March 25 the House unanimously passed a bill halting trade between America and all other countries for thirty days.[4]

Members clamored to do more, and partly in hopes of blocking further anti-British measures, President Washington, spurred on by Hamilton, decided to send an envoy to London. His choice, to Madison's way of thinking, was not the worst he could have made. That would have been Hamilton himself. But Washington's pick was nearly as bad: the chief justice of the Supreme Court, John Jay. As Madison saw it, the tall, thin New Yorker simply wasn't a dependable protector of America's interests. It was he who had proposed that the United States forgo navigation on the Mississippi for thirty years in exchange for a trade deal with Spain. Moreover, Jay was decidedly pro-British and anti-French in his thinking, a bias that Madison attributed in part to anti-Catholicism.[5]

IN THE HIGH COUNCILS of the executive branch, there was now no strong voice representing the Republican view, a situation that Madison could have remedied. President Washington had brought up the subject of his replacing Jefferson as secretary of state, but Madison had seen Jefferson's frustration in a cabinet in which he was an outsider and wanted no part of it. Edmund Randolph had replaced Jefferson, and although ostensibly Republican, he vacillated so often that Jefferson called him a chameleon, "having no color of his own and reflecting that nearest him." William Bradford, who had been Madison's friend at Princeton, had become attorney general when Randolph moved up, but he and Madison were no longer close, and Bradford was a committed Federalist. The president was increasingly under the Federalist spell, as Madison saw it, and that, combined with his enormous popularity, was "an overmatch for all the efforts Republicanism can make." Allegiances were shifting in Congress so that the party of republican sentiment in the Senate was "completely wrecked," he told Jefferson, and the House was headed in the same direction.[6]

IN THE MIDST of what was not a good time for him politically, Madison experienced a most happy turn in his personal life. Out walking one spring day, he caught sight of the recently widowed Dolley Payne Todd. Nearly five feet eight inches tall and of shapely figure, she turned many a head. Her friends teased her about the men who lingered in the streets for a glimpse of her. "Really, Dolley," they would say, "thou must hide thy face."[7]

She had black hair, blue eyes, and a startlingly fair complexion that she had learned as a child growing up in Virginia to shelter from the sun. When she was fifteen, her Quaker father, John Payne, decided as a matter of conscience to free his slaves, and he moved his family to Philadelphia, where they joined the Northern District Meeting. Many years later, female Friends remembered that young Dolley was "inclined . . . for the gaieties of this world" and often gave offense with the way she wore her caps, "the cut of her gowns, and the shape of her shoes." One Quaker matron recalled that during an effort to convince her of the seriousness of life, the young girl "at first smiled and afterwards fell fast asleep."[8]

John Payne tried to support his family by manufacturing laundry starch, but the business went under, and overwhelmed by failure, he took to his bed. Dolley Payne, age twenty-one, fulfilled her dying father's wish by becoming the wife of a promising young Quaker lawyer, twenty-seven-year-old John Todd, who had been kind to John Payne through his trials. The newlyweds, together with Dolley's sister Anna, moved into an imposing brick house at Fourth and Walnut streets. Dolley's mother, Mary, began to take in boarders, one of whom was Aaron Burr.[9]

Madison had known Burr since they had both been students at Princeton, so it was natural for the congressman to turn to him when he wanted an introduction to the lovely widow Todd. "Thou must come to me," Dolley wrote to a friend. "Aaron Burr says that the great little Madison has asked him to bring him to see me this evening." Dolley wore mulberry satin and yellow glass beads to greet James in her parlor, and he was thoroughly smitten. Soon he was letting Dolley know how he felt through her friend Catharine Coles. "Now for Madison," wrote Catharine to Dolley on the first day of June 1794: "He told me I might say what I pleased to you about him. To begin, he thinks so much of you in the day that he has lost his tongue; at night he dreams of you and starts in his sleep a calling on you to relieve his flame, for he burns to such an excess that he will be shortly consumed and he hopes that your heart will be callous to every other swain but himself." Lest Dolley think this breathless prose didn't sound like Madison, Catharine assured her, "He has consented to everything that I have wrote about him with sparkling eyes." She also noted that James Monroe had been appointed minister to France and that Madison had taken over his house. "Do you like it?" she inquired.[10]

Madison was not Dolley's only suitor. Another, Philadelphia lawyer William Wilkins, pursued her with such intensity that he felt obliged to apologize for the "violence of attachment which made me appear so unamiable in thy eyes."[11] That was not Madison's style—except when Catharine Coles served as his amanuensis—and he had many other marks in his favor. A great man who would possibly be greater, he had achieved a level of fame and respect matched by few in the nation. He would be a powerful protector, which a struggle to extract her rightful inheritance from John Todd's estate likely convinced Dolley she needed, and he would treat her with kindness and thoughtfulness. Dolley, like many a woman before and since, might have found that the most essential point.

They discussed finances and agreed to settle Dolley's real property "with a considerable addition of money" upon two-year-old John Payne Todd.[12] Dolley was aware that she would be expelled from meeting for marrying out of the Quaker faith, and they might have discussed that as well. It is entirely possible that Dolley, who felt hemmed in by Quaker strictures, looked forward to the event with relief.

By mid-August, Dolley had written James an affectionate letter accepting his offer of marriage. "I cannot express but hope you will conceive the joy it gave me," he wrote back. The wedding took place in the
parlor of the stone house at Harewood, the estate in Virginia where
Dolley's sister Lucy and her husband, George Steptoe Washington, the
nephew of the president, lived. There is no record of Dolley's dress, but
we know that James's shirt was trimmed with a Flemish lace that the
exuberant young women who attended Dolley cut up for souvenirs.[13]

On the morning of her wedding, Dolley wrote a letter to her friend
Eliza Collins Lee describing her husband-to-be as "the man whom of all
others I most admire." She wrote that "in this union, I have everything
that is soothing and grateful in prospect—and my little Payne will have
a generous and tender protector." She signed the letter "Dolley Payne
Todd," but that evening, after the wedding, she signed it again, this time
"Dolley Madison," and she added, "Alass! Alass!" The marriage would
endure until Madison's death forty-two years later and be a happy one,
but at that moment Dolley was distressed. Did the age difference suddenly hit home with her? James was seventeen years her senior and, as
she was surely aware by this time, given to "sudden attacks, somewhat
resembling epilepsy."[14] Perhaps she was simply responding to all she had
been through in the last ten months—losing a husband and a baby and
marrying again.

She was not a woman to be dispirited for long, and one imagines her
smiling happily as she set out with James on their honeymoon, accompanied by Anna, her fourteen-year-old sister, whom she regarded as a
daughter.[15] Anna would live with James and Dolley until she married,
providing company in which both Madisons delighted.

WHILE MADISON was traveling in northern Virginia with his new
family, George Washington, spurred on by Hamilton, sent thirteen
thousand militia into western Pennsylvania, where citizens were in
open rebellion over the excise tax on domestic spirits that the First
Congress had passed. Nearly every farm had a still, and the whiskey

produced wasn't just for local consumption; it was transported for sale. Angry farmers tarred and feathered tax collectors and burned down the house of one. Some six thousand rebels gathered in an armed show of strength in a field a few miles outside Pittsburgh.[16]

In the face of the overpowering force with which the president responded, the Whiskey Rebellion, as it came to be called, quickly dissipated, but its effects lingered. For one thing, it made Hamilton an ever more menacing figure in Republican eyes. He had been in effective charge of the army in western Pennsylvania, the man on horseback using force to govern men. The Whiskey Rebellion also increased Washington's suspicions of several dozen political societies that had formed across the country. They called themselves "democratic," a word that had come to be interchangeable with "republican," and they quickly adopted the agenda of the emerging Republican Party. Federalists regarded them as a threat, and Washington blamed them for the Whiskey Rebellion. Sitting in the audience in Congress Hall for the first presidential address since his marriage, Madison heard Washington denounce "associations of men" for threatening lawful agents of the government. "Certain self-created societies," said the president, had incited riots and violence until the government had been forced to act.[17]

Madison was shocked. Although one of the democratic societies had named its branch after him, both he and Jefferson steered clear of the clubs, whose members did not make a practice of tact or subtlety. But their right to meet and make pronouncements seemed nonetheless clear. In a letter to Jefferson, Madison called Washington's condemnation an "attack on the most sacred principle of our Constitution and of republicanism," and to Monroe, now in Paris, he wrote that Washington's "denunciation of the 'self-created societies' . . . was perhaps the greatest error of his political life."[18]

Still, Madison's instinct was to let the matter pass, and the House of Representatives' reply to the president did not at first mention it, but Thomas FitzSimons of Pennsylvania insisted on the floor of the House that the reply condemn "the self-created societies . . . which by deceiving and inflaming the ignorant and the weak may naturally be supposed to have stimulated and urged the insurrection." In the ensuing debate Madison declared that "opinions are not the objects of legislation," and he worried aloud, "How far will this go? It may extend to the liberty of speech and of the press." Finally, a compromise was reached in which members expressed concern that "any misrepresentations whatever of the government and its proceedings, either by individuals or combinations of men, should have been made and so far credited as to foment the flagrant outrage which has been committed on the laws." Madison wrote to Jefferson that Republicans considered the compromise language something of a victory while Federalists claimed "a final triumph on their side," because Washington in his response made veiled reference to the democratic societies, urging that every effort be made "to discountenance what has contributed to foment" the rebellion.[19]

As Madison saw it, an assault on fundamental rights had been undertaken for political reasons. He wrote to Jefferson, "The insurrection was universally and deservedly odious. The democratic societies were presented as in league with it. The Republican part of Congress were to be drawn into an ostensible patronage of those societies and into an ostensible opposition to the president." He worried—rightly, as it would turn out—that this deeply troubling tendency would become ever more threatening to what he regarded as first principles of the Republic.[20]

JEFFERSON, HEARING RUMORS that Madison would not be a candidate for Congress again, urged him to stay in office. "Hold on then, my dear friend," he wrote, reporting that people with whom he talked had no "greater affliction than the fear of your retirement; but this must not be, unless to a more splendid and a more efficacious post." Madison's newly married state might have caused some to think that he would be settling into home life at Montpelier, and, as Madison told his father, there were "perhaps . . . many considerations to do so," among them James senior's need for assistance in the wake of Ambrose's death. But Madison had unfinished business in Philadelphia, including the treaty that John Jay had been sent to negotiate with Great Britain. Madison was hearing that it had been concluded on grounds disadvantageous to the United States. "I suspect that Jay has been betrayed by his anxiety to couple us with England and to avoid returning with his finger in his mouth," he wrote to Jefferson. Dolley Madison might also have subtly encouraged him to serve another term. Their marriage meant that she and Anna, fifteen now, were included in all the festivities of the social season, including the splendid ball held by the City Dancing Assembly to celebrate Washington's birthday.[21] If James served until 1797, they could enjoy two more winters of the social whirl.

Madison asked his father to contradict the rumors of his retirement and began advising him by letter about crops and caretakers, a task that became easier once the mail route was extended to Orange Court House. It wasn't a perfect solution. James senior was not always prompt about answering mail and seemed to ignore his son's suggestions for a rotation of red clover in the fields, but the makeshift arrangement, Madison decided, would get him through another congressional term.[22]

WITH THE EUROPEAN WAR expected to result in an influx of immigrants to the United States, the short session of the Third Congress passed a naturalization bill that extended the time of residence required from two years to five and mandated three years' notice of intent to become a citizen. Madison supported the extension but objected to efforts to make the waiting period longer. He also supported a proposal from his colleague William Branch Giles that anyone wishing to become a citizen must renounce noble titles and took a certain pleasure in watching the Federalists, who had tried to devise such titles for Washington, squirm. But when Samuel Dexter of Massachusetts declared that "priestcraft had done more mischief than aristocracy" and mocked Catholicism, Madison was all business. He would have Catholics derided no more than he would have Baptists scorned. He said that he did not "approve the ridicule attempted to be thrown out on the Roman Catholics," and added that there was nothing in Catholicism "inconsistent with the purest republicanism."[23]

. . .

THE TREATY that John Jay had negotiated did not arrive in Philadelphia until early March, and it was immediately cloaked in "impenetrable
secrecy," as Madison described it. Details had still not been made public
in April, when Madison left Philadelphia with his wife, his sister-in-law
Anna, and his stepson, Payne, to spend the interval between the Third
and the Fourth Congresses in the Piedmont. The secrecy continued
through May and into June, when a special Senate session began debating the treaty in secret. Shortly thereafter, Madison, at Montpelier,
began to receive a leaked copy of the treaty, page by page. "Convinced
that this—as they term it—most important secret is much safer with you
than in the hands of many to whom it is confided," South Carolina senator Pierce Butler wrote, "I shall by every post send you a sheet of it."[24]

The treaty was worse than Madison had expected. The United States
gained certain items: a British commitment to withdraw from posts in
the territory northwest of the Ohio River, which was supposed to have
happened earlier; the creation of commissions to which Americans
could appeal for losses they had suffered at the hands of the Royal Navy;
and the opening of some trade to the West Indies, though on terms so
harsh the Senate would reject this provision. But there was no mention
of impressment, the increasingly troublesome British practice of forcing
seamen who were deemed British but were often American, into British
service. And there was abandonment of the U.S. principle that the cargo
of neutral vessels should not be subject to search and seizure by warring
nations. Perhaps worst of all, the treaty barred the United States for ten
years from imposing the kinds of restrictions on British trade that Madison had repeatedly proposed. Jay had guaranteed the British that no
matter the circumstances they would pay no higher duties than any
other nation, thus, in Madison's view, making any effective retaliation
short of war impossible. The treaty was, Madison wrote, "so full of
shameful concessions, of mock reciprocities, and of party artifices that
no other circumstances than the peculiar ones which mark our present
political situation could screen it from universal execration."[25]

The Federalist Senate approved the treaty, the article about West

Indian trade excepted, on June 24, 1795, by a vote that was exactly the two-thirds necessary: twenty senators in favor and ten opposed. The Senate voted not to release the treaty, but Virginia senator Stevens Thomson Mason decided the public deserved a look and sent a copy to Benjamin Franklin Bache's Philadelphia newspaper, the *Aurora*. As Madison described it, from there "it flew with an electric velocity to every part of the Union." Fourth of July crowds up and down the nation would probably not have reacted well to any treaty with Britain, but the taint of unfairness attaching to this one made them furious. On Bastille Day in Charleston, protesters dragged a Union Jack through the streets and set it afire. In Philadelphia, according to Vice President Adams, "an innumerable multitude" gathered at Washington's house, "huzzaing, demanding war against England, cursing Washington, and crying success to the French patriots and virtuous Republicans." In New York, when Hamilton tried a public defense of the treaty, someone threw a rock that struck him in the forehead. So many stuffed figures of Jay were set to the torch that it was said a person could travel from one end of the nation to the other by the light of his burning effigies.[26]

Madison noted that "addresses to the president against his ratification swarmed from all quarters," but events behind the scenes were pushing Washington in the other direction. Not long after Senate passage of the treaty came news that the British had begun once more to seize American ships carrying grain to France, something they had not done while negotiations with Jay had been ongoing. Secretary of State Randolph recommended that the president hold off on ratification until the situation was better understood—and remedied. Washington agreed, and Randolph told the British minister George Hammond of the president's intent. Perhaps Randolph, once described as "*too Machiavellian* and *not Machiavellian enough*," exaggerated his role in delaying the treaty, because he soon became a British target. Hammond turned over a French dispatch that the British had intercepted at sea. Known as Number 10, it indicated that Randolph was conveying a decidedly Republican view of the administration to the French, portraying it as so bent on power that the Whiskey Rebellion had been exaggerated in order to justify raising an army. The dispatch also reported Randolph making an "overture," which was not fully described, apparently having been detailed in another dispatch. It was possible, however, to draw the worst possible conclusion about it: namely, that Randolph had demanded a bribe.[27]

The members of Washington's inner circle were prepared to believe the worst. Secretary of War Timothy Pickering, stern-faced and humorless, declared to the president at first opportunity that Randolph was a "traitor." Whether the president believed that accusation isn't clear, but certainly Randolph's having advanced the views reported in Number 10 would have infuriated him. In order, so he said, to give Randolph a chance to explain, he surprised the secretary by springing the dispatch on him in front of the cabinet and observing his reaction. Randolph, confused, hurt, and insulted, resigned—which might have been exactly what Washington wanted his far too talkative secretary of state to do.[28]

In the middle of these events, Washington put his signature to the ratification document. The intercepted dispatch had nothing to do with the treaty, as Madison wrote to Monroe, and should have had no influence. But the president's angry response to betrayal by the person who had been urging him to delay seemed to have been to stop delaying. As Bache's *Aurora* described it, the ratification came "in a fit of bad humor occasioned by an enigmatical intercepted letter," an assessment that does not seem far off the mark when one remembers that Washington's approval of ratification came while the British were still seizing American ships.[29]

Randolph, having departed the cabinet, tried proving his innocence in a pamphlet he called *Vindication*. He obtained other dispatches that Number 10 had referred to and printed them. He got an affidavit from the former French minister to the United States exonerating him. But he buried important information in so much extraneous detail that his main point was lost. He was far too expansive in his *Vindication*, as he apparently had been with the French—not betraying state secrets, but spilling forth too much. After reading Randolph's pamphlet, Madison

wrote to Monroe, using code, "His greatest enemies will not easily persuade themselves that he was under a corrupt influence of France, and
his best friend can't save him from the self-condemnation of his political career as explained by himself."[30]

Jefferson described the Jay Treaty as a political coup engineered by
the executive and the Federalist Senate to circumvent the House, where
the Republicans were strong. "A bolder party stroke was never struck,"
he wrote to Madison. Hamilton was behind the whole thing, Jefferson
believed, but neither he nor Madison had any idea of the extent of the
New Yorker's involvement. Hamilton had recommended that Washington send an envoy to London and, realizing that he himself was too
much of a lightning rod for the assignment, suggested Jay. Hamilton had
laid out the framework of Jay's instructions in a letter to Washington
and made private recommendations to Jay as well. Hamilton had even
briefed the British minister to the United States and given him a clear
indication of where Great Britain could hold fast in negotiations.[31] One
wonders: Could Washington possibly have known of this? Hamilton's
coaching the British was an indiscretion many times worse than Randolph's loose talk with the French.

Hamilton, wanting to repair his family's finances, had resigned from
Treasury, but months later he remained influential. Watching him
swing into action to defend the treaty, Jefferson could not help but be
impressed. "Hamilton is really a colossus to the Antirepublican party,"
he wrote. "Without numbers he is an host within himself." Jefferson
wanted Madison to answer the essays that Hamilton was publishing
under the pseudonym Camillus, urging him as he had before: "For god's
sake take up your pen." But Madison had had enough of warring with
Hamilton from the isolation of Montpelier. Instead, he worked to involve the Virginia Assembly in efforts against the treaty and pondered
what action he might take in Congress.[32]

BY THE TIME Madison returned with his family to Philadelphia in
late November 1795, it was clear that a majority of House members

disapproved of the treaty, thus opening an avenue for undoing it. While the president had the right to make treaties with the advice and consent of the Senate, the House had to approve funding for them. But, Madison was asking himself, if the House refused to approve funds, thus killing the treaty, did that mean it was assuming treaty powers—which the Constitution had not authorized?[33]

Sooner than he had expected, Madison found himself having to take a stand on this question. A new and impatient member from New York, Edward Livingston, called upon the president to turn over Jay's instructions and all other documents relating to the treaty to the House of Representatives so that members could ponder "important constitutional questions." The result was to inject into the great controversy over the treaty an issue that lent itself to easy demagoguery. Republicans were soon defending themselves against charges that they were traitors, intent on "*rebellion* against the constituted authorities."[34]

Madison tried to defuse the confrontational mood with analysis, presenting a number of ways that the House might interpret its powers. None was perfect, he admitted, but the most "rational, consistent, and satisfactory" was to recognize that the president and the Senate had the authority to make treaties and the legislature the authority to make laws. It was not usurpation for the House to carry through on its legislative authority. Indeed, if members accepted the principle that they could not, what checks would there then be on the Senate and the president acting in concert? What if they decided to conclude "a treaty of alliance with a nation at war," thus making the United States a party to that war?[35]

The House passed the resolution demanding that the president turn over papers. Washington, with encouragement from Hamilton, refused and threw the entire weight of his reputation behind the rejection, saying in his message that the only constitutional reason for the House to request the documents was if members intended to impeach him. Both the substance and the combative tone of the president's response came as a surprise to Madison but did not slow his response. In a caucus of Republican members—the first on record—Madison called for a stand on the principle that if a treaty required enabling legislation from Congress, "it is the constitutional right and duty of the House of Representatives, in all such cases, to deliberate on the expediency or inexpediency of carrying such a treaty into effect."[36] He won his point, 57 to 35.

Madison turned from his victory on the prerogatives of the House to the Jay Treaty itself, taking the floor on April 15 to note the treaty's "want of real reciprocity." The British gained commercial advantage from Jay's negotiation, but the United States did not. He also took up the idea that war would follow if the treaty were not put into effect. Such a notion, advanced by treaty advocates, was "too visionary and incredible to be admitted into the question," he said. There was no cause of war in a sovereign nation's declining a treaty that was not in its self-interest, nor was Great Britain, "with all the dangers and embarrassments which are thickening upon her," likely to seek war.[37]

Meanwhile, another treaty was complicating Madison's life. President Washington had sent the U.S. minister to Britain, Thomas Pinckney, to Spain as an envoy, and he had negotiated an agreement that guaranteed the United States navigation of the Mississippi. Knowing how dear this goal was to western hearts, Madison's opponents in the House had tried to combine appropriations for several treaties, including Pinckney's and Jay's, into a single resolution, thus forcing members who wanted any of the treaties to vote for all. Madison fended off that effort but was soon facing a similar move in the Senate.

"Vast exertions are on foot" not only within the House but outside it, Madison told Monroe, to get a positive vote on funds for the treaty. Commercial interests were organizing mass meetings and petition drives. "The banks, the British merchants, [and] insurance companies," Madison wrote, were "sounding the tocsin of foreign war and domestic convulsions." Opponents were also building support for the treaty in unexpected places, including Pennsylvania. Madison's Princeton friend Hugh Brackenridge, now a judge in Pittsburgh, had become seized with the idea that without the Jay Treaty, which required the British to leave their western posts, the Pinckney Treaty opening up the Mississippi would be ineffective. Through a petition campaign and newspaper editorials based on this message, he whipped up western support.[38]

Toward the end of April, Madison watched with dismay as a bright young Philadelphia congressman presented pro-treaty petitions to the House. Albert Gallatin, born in Switzerland, had been firm in his defense of the right of the House to ask Washington for Jay documents, but like other Republicans he was under pressure from his constituents. Madison told Jefferson that the Republican strength that the Jay Treaty had helped create was dissipating fast. "The majority has melted by changes and absence to eight or nine votes," he wrote. Three days later, Gallatin rose on the floor of the House to announce he would vote to fund the treaty. Two days after that, Edward Livingston, who had submitted the resolution demanding treaty papers, indicated that he, too, would be voting in support.[39]

Then a gaunt Fisher Ames rose to speak. Directly addressing families on the frontier, he predicted that they would be slaughtered by Indians unless the British left the western garrisons, as the Jay Treaty provided, and American troops moved in: "Your cruel dangers, your more cruel apprehensions are soon to be renewed; the wounds yet unhealed are to be torn open again; in the daytime your path through the woods will be ambushed; the darkness of midnight will glitter with the blaze of your dwellings. You are a father—the blood of your sons shall fatten your cornfield; you are a mother—the war whoop shall wake the sleep of the cradle." As Ames pictured it, Congress stood with "one hand . . . held up to reject this treaty," while "the other grasps a tomahawk."[40]

Ames's fearmongering would have been less effective had not he and everyone else thought he was dying. A debilitating illness had taken hold of him, and he used it for all it was worth. If the treaty were not ratified, he said at the end of his speech, "Even I, slender and almost broken as my hold upon life is, may outlive the government and Constitution of my country." John Adams reported to Abigail that Ames's speech left "not a dry eye" in the House, and it seems to have been particularly effective with Pennsylvania congressmen.[41] Already worried that the treaty's defeat would inhibit opening of the Mississippi, they were now being told that voting against the treaty would make them complicit in their constituents' brutal deaths.

The portly, round-faced Frederick Muhlenberg of Pennsylvania chaired the committee of the whole when the House voted on appropriating funds for the treaty. He usually voted with the Republicans, who had elevated him to the speakership in the Third Congress, but when the vote on the Jay Treaty tied 49 to 49 in the committee of the whole, Muhlenberg joined the Federalists, saying that he did so in order that the treaty "go to the House and there be modified." When it came before the House unmodified, however, he voted for it again. Another Pennsylvania congressman was conveniently absent. William Findley, a weathered farmer and usually dependable Republican, later claimed that he had been mailing a trunk at the time of the vote. Muhlenberg's switch and Findley's absence converted what would have been a tie to a victory for pro-treaty forces.[42] Fifty-one members voted to fund the treaty, and forty-eight opposed.

Muhlenberg might not have read his constituents as well as he thought he had. He would never be elected to Congress again—and that wasn't the worst of his troubles. His stand so enraged his Republican brother-in-law that a few days afterward, he stabbed Muhlenberg, nearly killing him. Findley's disappearing tactic, on the other hand, worked. There was some caustic commentary at his expense; the *Pittsburgh Gazette* wished that the trunk had been Findley's coffin. But he would have such a long career in Congress that he would become known as "the venerable Findley" for his length of service.[43]

THE RATIFICATION and implementation of the Jay Treaty, the most controversial in the nation's history, have been praised by many, who argue as the Federalists did that although it was unpalatable, it was necessary for peace. But there is reason to doubt that war with Britain would have followed on the heels of the treaty's failure. Madison made a crucial point in his April 15 speech when he noted that it would be "madness" for the British, in the middle of war with France, to take on the United States as well. It had its navy fully employed in the fight against the French. It needed the resources gained from trade with the United States, its biggest customer, to underwrite that navy and subsidize allies on the Continent. Matters were soon to grow even worse as a twenty-six-year-old general named Napoleon Bonaparte began to roll up one military triumph after another. Meanwhile, Britain had domestic troubles. A series of bad harvests had spiked the price of wheat and threatened mass starvation. Bread riots had already broken out across England.[44] The argument that the treaty was necessary for peace is a weak one, made weaker still by the indisputable fact that it would soon lead the United States into an undeclared war with France.

Madison took the treaty loss hard, telling Jefferson that "the progress of this business throughout has to me been the most worrying and vexatious that I ever encountered, and the more so as the causes lay in the unsteadiness, the follies, the perverseness, and the defections among our friends more than in the strength or dexterity or malice of our opponents." The Republican cause was now "in a very crippled condition," he wrote, citing elections in New York and Massachusetts, "where the prospects were favorable, [but] have taken a wrong turn under the impressions of the moment."[45] Republican strength mattered for many reasons, including the presidential election of 1796, which Madison and Jefferson had been discussing since before debate on the Jay Treaty had begun.

Jefferson had broached the topic by hinting in the spring of 1795 that he wanted Madison to be Washington's successor, a suggestion that prompted a strong response. "Reasons of *every* kind," Madison wrote, "and some of them of the most *insuperable* as well as *obvious* kind, shut my mind against the admission of any idea such as you seem to glance at." Madison might have been thinking of his need to spend more time at Montpelier, but his emphasis on the reasons being "insuperable" suggests that he might also have had his sudden attacks in mind. To anyone who knew about them, as Jefferson surely did, they were an "obvious" impediment.[46]

It was clear to Madison that for all Jefferson's talk about how much he loved retirement—he had said he would not trade it "for the empire of the universe"—he was the one who should carry the Republican standard. "You ought to be preparing yourself . . . to hear truths, which no inflexibility will be able to withstand," he wrote. Madison likely delivered these truths during visits to Monticello in the summer and fall of 1795, but Jefferson continued to resist. Early in 1796, Madison wrote to Monroe that Republicans, realizing that Jefferson was their only hope for success, were pushing his candidacy forward. There was no formal process for choosing a nominee at this early stage of party politics. Party leaders, with Madison first among them, simply reached a consensus, and they had decided Jefferson was their man. Madison was concerned, however, that Jefferson might "mar the project and ensure the adverse election by a peremptory and *public* protest."[47] A presidential candidate in the early republic did not have to say yes, but he could derail his candidacy by saying no.

Even after Washington published his Farewell Address in September 1796 and the campaign took off in earnest, Jefferson remained ensconced at Monticello, experimenting with "a threshing machine made on the Scotch model" and trying to get new walls up at the main house, where he had demolished the upper story, before winter set in. Madison was now avoiding him, explaining to Monroe that he "thought it best to present him no opportunity of protesting to his friend against being embarked in the contest." For vice president, there was some Republican support for Aaron Burr, but there were also recommendations that Republican electors cast one vote for Jefferson and the other for anyone except the top Federalist candidates. In the end Burr would gain just a single electoral vote from Jefferson's supporters in Virginia, an outcome the New Yorker would not soon forget.[48]

Vice President John Adams was the candidate Federalists were coalescing behind, and Thomas Pinckney, who had successfully negotiated the popular treaty with Spain, had strong support for the second slot—though Pinckney, in a ship crossing the Atlantic on his way back to America, had no idea he was being pushed forward. Alexander Hamilton, not a fan of John Adams's, was even advancing Pinckney for the top position.[49] With parties still in their formative stages, it was next to impossible to reach nationwide agreement on a ticket, and since electors, according to the Constitution, cast two votes of equal weight, it was impossible to be certain exactly who would end up where when the votes were counted.

Political operative John Beckley brought what seems a decidedly modern spirit to a campaign in which candidates didn't acknowledge they were running—or sometimes even know it. Beckley, who had come to America as an indentured servant and with Madison's backing become the clerk of the House of Representatives in the First Congress, had an aptitude for politics—and no embarrassment about deploying it. He organized Pennsylvania, a state in which Federalists were strong, to achieve a victory for Jefferson in 1796. His first bit of shrewdness was to encourage a slate of Republican electors with high name identification, men such as former senator William Maclay. Then he kept the list of electors under close hold until after the Federalists had made known their much less distinguished slate. Beckley accurately assessed the areas of Republican strength in Pennsylvania and gave them extra attention, making sure, for example, that handbills were sent across the Alleghenies into areas supportive of Jefferson. As the election approached, he dispatched teams throughout the state to distribute thousands of ballots containing names of Republican electors. Since voters could not submit printed ballots on Election Day, Beckley, his agents, and activists across Pennsylvania handwrote thousands of them. Anyone who didn't want to write out the slate himself—or perhaps couldn't write—could submit the ballot at voting time.[50]

So clever was Beckley that historians generally agree that he was responsible for a diplomatic note published in the *Aurora* shortly before Election Day. In it the French minister set out his country's decidedly hostile attitude toward the United States. As Republican operatives were happy to point out, this was the result of the Jay Treaty, and if it led to war, Federalists were to blame. Madison was not pleased with the note's publication. He thought it would drive a further wedge between the United States and France. But the threat of war might well have influenced Quakers to vote Republican and thus been responsi-

ble for the narrow victory Jefferson eked out in Pennsylvania. Because the state's overconfident Federalists had voted a winner-take-all
system, Jefferson's slim margin nevertheless gave him all but one of the
state's cache of electoral votes.[51] In the end it wouldn't be quite enough.
When electoral votes were finally counted, Adams would have seventy-
one to Jefferson's sixty-eight. But the fact that Jefferson had fallen just
three votes short sent a strong signal. Despite the Federalist win on
the Jay Treaty and what was likely to be a Federalist Congress, the Republicans had demonstrated they were far more than a passing phenomenon.

Results were trickling in when Madison arrived back in Philadelphia
with Mrs. Madison and his twenty-two-year-old sister, Frances Madison, on November 22. By the time the second session of the Fourth
Congress convened on December 5, the outcome was still uncertain,
but Madison felt obliged to send a warning to Jefferson: "You *must* reconcile yourself to the secondary as well as the primary station."[52]

As it became clear that Jefferson would indeed be John Adams's vice
president, Jefferson wrote Adams a letter. Such a communication was
not a bad idea, particularly since the election had made the candidate
of the party opposed to Adams his vice president, but the letter dramatically claimed that Jefferson had never wanted to be president: "I leave
to others the sublime delights of riding in the storm, better pleased with
sound sleep and a warm berth below." It seemed at once haughty and
harsh, referring to Hamilton a little too cleverly as Adams's "archfriend."
Jefferson might have had an inkling that the letter wasn't quite right,
because he sent it by way of Madison and asked his friend to review it.
Madison did and tactfully suggested that Jefferson consider whether the
letter might not change his relationship with Adams, which was cordial,
for the worse, particularly since Adams was of a "ticklish" temper. The
letter went unsent.[53]

Madison had announced his retirement from Congress. He was
"wearied with public life," he would later write, "and longed for a return
to a state in which he could indulge his relish for the intellectual pleasures
of the closet and the pursuits of rural life." He also noted that his farm,

as he liked to call Montpelier, was "the only resource of his future support." William Wirt, a Virginia lawyer, would later write that Madison's health, "in a visible and alarming decline," was another reason for his retirement. Wirt explained that "his constitution had received a serious shock," so he might have experienced another sudden attack of some severity.[54]

Madison and his family were still in Philadelphia when Jefferson arrived to be sworn in, and the vice president elect stayed with them overnight before moving to a hotel. It was spring before the Madisons had packed up their furniture, including purchases that Monroe had made for them in Paris, and were ready to leave the city. They took a roundabout way to their Virginia home, traveling through Harpers Ferry and visiting relatives along the way, and it was the end of April when they neared Montpelier.[55] In the woods along the road, dogwoods were flowering, and sweet spire blossomed where the ground was damp.

As they approached the house, Madison might have noticed pale yellow flowers on the buckeye tree that had been planted in the southwest corner of the yard some seven years before. Who could have imagined all that would happen in the meantime, Hamilton's ascendancy and the threat his policies posed, the Jay Treaty, which had completed Madison's break with President Washington? He would never visit Mount Vernon again. Seven years earlier, he had just begun to suspect that the threat to the Republic would come not from the states, as he had originally thought, but from a too strong central government. Now he was certain of it—and alarmed that opposition to government policies, which he viewed as utterly necessary, was taken as subversive. Even in his Farewell Address, Washington had continued to advance that notion.

Madison's personal life had also undergone remarkable change. Seven years earlier he had been a bachelor, and who would have supposed that those days would end with the lovely woman in the carriage beside him?

· · ·

JOHN ADAMS took note of Madison's retirement. "It is marvelous how political plants grow in the shade," he wrote to Abigail.[56] Madison had no formal plans to reenter politics himself, but he was certainly ambitious for his friend Jefferson, and should he achieve the presidency, it was as certain as day following night that he would call on Madison to assist him. In the event that happened, Madison would, as Adams observed, benefit from time spent out of the glare.

Chapter 12

REIGN OF WITCHES

ABOUT THE TIME THAT JOHN ADAMS was sworn in as president, William Martin, captain of the *Cincinnatus,* a ship out of Baltimore, was being tortured with thumbscrews. The officers of the French brig that had captured Martin's ship wanted him to say that his cargo was English property and therefore liable to French seizure. Martin resisted and got away with his cargo intact when more attractive prey, a British ship, sailed by, but his story and others in a similar vein made it clear that the French, furious about the Jay Treaty, had reached a determination: if British ships were no longer going to give neutral vessels a pass, neither would they.[1]

The French also broke off diplomatic relations, and one of the people Adams asked to be part of a negotiating team to go to Paris and repair them was James Madison. The former congressman refused, probably in part because of his aversion to deep water, but he might have also found the experience of his neighbor James Monroe instructive. As minister to France, Monroe, rather than following the Washington administration's policy and defending the Jay Treaty, had urged that it be renegotiated. Diplomats weren't supposed to give free rein to their own opinions but to represent those who appointed them, which in the case of the Adams administration Madison had no desire to do. Better to continue the path he was on, gradually becoming the patriarch of Montpelier and paying serious attention to farming. The war in Europe had sent grain prices skyrocketing, and by carefully cultivating his wheat fields, Madison hoped to put the estate's finances on a firmer footing.[2]

He also wanted to enlarge the house at Montpelier so that it suited two families, and he came up with an ingenious and lovely plan for building a thirty-foot addition on the north and shifting the axis of the house in that direction. A two-story Tuscan portico across the front of the extended house unified the whole, although the house was in fact a duplex now, with separate spaces for the older Madisons on one side and for James, Dolley, and their family on the other. In later years, a central doorway with fanlight and sidelights would be added, and the illusion of a single, gracious dwelling would be complete.[3]

Madison was his own architect, and while he probably relied on books in his library, including one showing Palladio's designs, he was not a stickler for rules. His portico combined Tuscan columns with an Ionic entablature, and his practicality showed itself when it came to the fanlight over the front door. It was originally designed as a semicircle, probably to harmonize with a semicircular window intended for the portico, but when Madison learned that the first-floor ceiling would have to be raised to accommodate the fanlight, he decided instead on a semi-oval window that would fit the existing structure.[4]

Madison was also his own general contractor, ordering materials, hiring workmen, and supervising construction. On Christmas Day 1797, he wrote to Jefferson to place an order with the nailery at Monticello for nearly 150,000 nails. Madison also asked the vice president to purchase window glass, brass locks, and brass hinges for him. Jefferson not only tended to his friend's request but also advised him on a better hinge for his doors.[5]

The Madisons visited friends in the neighborhood and traveled farther afield to see relatives. After their furniture from Philadelphia arrived, they acquired a few more things from Monroe, who had brought extra goods back from Paris. An eighteen-foot tablecloth was one of the items purchased, which suggests that the Madisons were entertaining despite renovations under way. Dolley, unconstrained now by Quaker demands for simplicity, no doubt carried out her duties as hostess dressed as fashionably as was possible far from a city. One of her letters hints at the difficulty. She had asked her friend Eliza Collins Lee to buy and send her hose, but unfortunately the ones that arrived were too small. "The hose will not fit even my darling little husband," Dolley wrote.[6]

Missing from this new life were offspring. "Madison still childless," wrote Aaron Burr to James Monroe, "and I fear like to continue so." Why James and Dolley had no children will never be known, and although he no doubt regretted not being a father, it might also have been a relief, given the widespread belief that epilepsy was hereditary. A highly influential treatise that Madison could have easily found in Jefferson's library went so far as to declare it a duty for those with epilepsy to remain celibate. In any case, the Madisons' childlessness did not equate with loneliness. James and Dolley were surrounded by young people: her son, Payne, and her sister Anna; his youngest sister, Fannie; and dozens of nieces and nephews.[7]

Since his arrival back home coincided with his father's failing health, Madison's new role seemed to satisfy them both, though one wonders how the frugal James senior regarded the great expansion of the family home. And James junior must surely have been conscious of how far he had come from the aspiration of his younger years "to depend as little as possible on the labor of slaves." There were a hundred human beings enslaved at Montpelier, some of whose names we know from Madison's letters. When he had learned that Billey Gardner, whom he had helped become a free man, had died in an accident at sea, Madison had asked his father to "let old Anthony and Betty know that their son Billey is no more." When his parents traveled to take healing waters, Madison kept them apprised of the whereabouts and health of Jacob, Sam, Simon, Ralph, and Joseph. The house slaves at Montpelier were an ever-present part of the Madisons' lives, serving them meals, helping them dress, and taking care of the multitude of tasks that made the household function. The quarters in which the domestic slaves lived were very close to the house. Smoke from the fires and the smells of cooking would have drifted into Madison's library while he read. He would have heard the sounds of slave children playing.[8]

MADISON FOUND HIMSELF a counselor of sorts to James Monroe. Still shaken by his recall, Monroe, back in Albemarle now, sought Madison's advice about preventing new blows to his reputation. Monroe's first worry had to do with the payments that Alexander Hamilton had made to James Reynolds some five years before. They had become public, thanks to a brilliant, twisted, and starving immigrant from Scotland, James Callender, who was on his way to becoming the greatest scandalmonger in American history. Sarcastically dismissing the idea that the payments had been made to keep Reynolds quiet about the affair that Hamilton was having with his wife, Callender insinuated that Hamilton had been using Reynolds to purchase speculative certificates for him. The charge drove Hamilton into a frenzy. He blamed Monroe for leaking information to Callender, and the two nearly came to a duel. Hamilton even published a pamphlet aimed at proving definitively that he was an adulterer, not a speculator, and it was an angry exchange of letters reproduced in that pamphlet that had Monroe concerned. He asked Madison, was he obliged to pursue Hamilton further? Madison assured him that he was not, perhaps smiling to himself as he did so, realizing that the sensational details that Hamilton had revealed about his affair with Mrs. Reynolds made it highly unlikely that anyone was going to focus on Monroe.[9]

Several months later, when Monroe became concerned about insults that President Adams was directing his way, Madison again urged caution, noting that "the present paroxysm may pass off with as great a rapidity as it has been brought on." When the younger man became agitated over Adams's military buildup and the taxes he was proposing to pay for it, Madison sounded like a soothsayer on a mountaintop, responding that it was all part of a steady movement away from revolutionary principles that would soon reverse itself. "The tide of evil is nearly at its flood," he wrote, and "will ebb back to the true mark which it has overpassed."[10]

Madison seems to have managed a psychological separation from events in the world below, but it soon came to an end. President Adams reported that his diplomatic attempt to reach out to the French had failed and, when Congress demanded to know the details, sent it dispatches showing that three agents of the French foreign minister, dubbed X, Y, and Z, had demanded a bribe and a loan for the French war effort before the government would even receive the diplomats. Madison, hearing of the news at Montpelier, was amazed, though not about the French foreign minister, Charles-Maurice de Talleyrand-Périgord, being corrupt—that was widely acknowledged. But Talleyrand had spent time in America, understood how hard it was to keep secrets in the United States, and should have known better than to think his attempt to secure a bribe would work. "Its unparalleled stupidity is what fills one with astonishment," Madison wrote.[11]

As citizens pictured America's upright and honest envoys being pestered by decadent Frenchmen with their hands out, the XYZ Affair, as it became known, led to a great surge of patriotism. President Adams was lionized. The newspapers were full of addresses declaring affection for him and expressing confidence in his wisdom. At Jim Cameron's Philadelphia tavern, he was toasted repeatedly as the crowd "roared like a hundred bulls." More than a thousand supportive young men wearing black cockades (ribbons pinched to look like flowers) marched to his house, two by two, to pay respects.[12]

The anti-French rallying cry became "Millions for defense, but not a cent for tribute," and Republican congressmen who would once have been hesitant enthusiastically joined the Federalists in expanding the army and the navy. Congress declared all treaties with France null and void and authorized the president to order his commanders to seize armed French vessels anywhere on the high seas.[13] The nation was at war—although war had not been declared.

· · ·

CONGRESS ALSO PASSED and the president signed measures to deal
with what many considered the enemy within. The first target was immigrants, who, as Federalists saw it, were likely to have foreign allegiances. They were a political nuisance besides, since they tended to
align themselves with Republicans. One piece of legislation gave the
president power to expel aliens of any nation during either peace or war
simply on the grounds that he suspected them of being dangerous.
Madison, writing to Jefferson, declared the bill "a monster that must
forever disgrace its parents."[14]

A sedition bill that would throttle the Republican press was clearly
on the way, but in the case of Benjamin Franklin Bache, the twenty-
eight-year-old grandson of Benjamin Franklin and publisher of the *Aurora*, the administration could not bring itself to wait. On June 26, 1798,
even as a sedition bill was being introduced into the Senate, Bache was
arrested under common law for "libeling the president and the executive government in a manner tending to excite sedition and opposition
to the laws." It was also on that day that Vice President Jefferson requested leave from the Senate for the rest of the term and left the city.
He probably did not know but likely suspected the efforts the administration was making to unearth information about him and worried that
he, too, would be arrested.[15]

On his way to Monticello, Jefferson stopped to see Madison at Montpelier, and as candles were lit, the two men could hear the sound of
evening thunder.[16] The distant rumblings provided a fittingly ominous
background for their discussion of how to confront the dangers to liberty that the nation faced.

Both Madison and Jefferson had been counseling a watchful waiting,
Madison on the grounds that the Federalists' oppressive acts would
awaken the citizenry. Jefferson had believed that with patience "we shall
see the reign of witches pass over." But now something had to be done.
There were many reasons to have formed a union of states under the
Constitution, but none higher than the liberty to think and speak freely,
which was now in jeopardy. As the two men explored remedies, they re-

alized that there was no recourse to be had in Congress, where the legislation they so abhorred was in favor. Nor did they see the courts as an option. They were also controlled by the Federalists, as had been demonstrated the previous year, when Richmond jurors had charged Virginia congressman Samuel J. Cabell for daring to criticize the Adams administration in circular letters to his constituents.[17] Madison and Jefferson finally concurred in a plan to persuade state legislatures to oppose the Alien and Sedition Acts, and they agreed that they would act secretly, not writing under their own names, but working through others.

BY MID-JULY a sedition bill was passed and signed into law by President Adams, making it illegal to write, print, utter, or publish "any false, scandalous, and malicious writing or writings against the government of the United States or either house of the Congress of the United States or the president of the United States with intent to defame the said government, or either house of the said Congress, or the said president, or to bring them or either of them . . . the hatred of the good people of the United States."[18] Anyone reading the law would have been hard put to miss the fact that one prominent federal officer was not on the list of the protected: John Adams's chief political rival, the vice president of the United States. It was a clear sign of the political intent of the bill, though Federalists, still operating out of an older way of thinking, no doubt saw the omission of the vice president as insuring against Jefferson's traitorously attacking the government.

Violators of the Sedition Act were soon being thrown in jail. One was Vermont congressman Matthew Lyon, who had the temerity to accuse the Adams administration of overlooking the people's welfare "in a continual grasp for power, in an unbounded thirst for ridiculous pomp, foolish adulation, and selfish avarice." Editors and journalists with Republican leanings were indicted, including William Duane, who had succeeded Bache at the *Aurora;* Thomas Cooper of the *Gazette* in Northumberland, Pennsylvania; and Thomas Adams of Boston's *Independent Chronicle.*

David Brown, an impoverished, semiliterate man who wandered the Massachusetts countryside preaching Republican doctrine, was tried and convicted. The Federalist Fisher Ames viewed him as one of the "runners" sent "to blow the trumpet of sedition" and was particularly perturbed that he had inspired Dedham citizens to set up a liberty pole, an "insult on the law," Ames deemed it. New Jersey's Luther Baldwin was also caught up in the frenzy, fined, and jailed after he informed a barkeep that he did not care if cannon fire hit John Adams in the arse.[19]

After their meeting at Montpelier, Madison and Jefferson did not communicate by mail, largely for fear that Federalists, who controlled the post offices, would use their words against them, but they worked at their agreed-upon plan. Jefferson ghostwrote resolutions that would be introduced in the Kentucky legislature by John C. Breckinridge. "Whensoever the general government assumes undelegated powers," Jefferson wrote, "its acts are unauthoritative, void, and of no force." He went on to declare that "a nullification of the act is the rightful remedy" and that "every state has a natural right . . . to nullify of their own authority all assumptions of power by others within their limits." When the resolutions reached Kentucky, someone's editorial pen cut the passage about nullification, but enough was left to convey the idea that each state had a right to decide on such matters as the Alien and Sedition Acts. The Kentucky legislature, using Jefferson's words, urged others to join in the effort to oppose such laws, lest the acts "drive these states into revolution and blood."[20]

Likely because of concern about the mail, Madison did not see Jefferson's resolutions until after they were on their way to Kentucky, but he did read them before he completed his own. They arrived at Montpelier in November 1798 with a cover letter from the vice president urging that "we should distinctly affirm all the important principles they contain, so as to hold to that ground in future." Madison set his own course, however, anonymously drafting resolutions for Virginia that began by affirming that state's intention "to maintain and defend the Constitution of the United States" and declaring its "warm attachment to the Union of the states." The resolutions protested the federal government's unjustified enlargement of its powers, particularly in the Alien and Sedition Acts. They were "infractions of the Constitution" for their assertion that the federal government could punish speech and writing, "a power which more than any other ought to produce universal alarm," Madison wrote, "because it is leveled against that right of freely examining public characters and measures, and of free communication among the people thereon, which has ever been justly deemed the only effectual guardian of every other right." There was no talk of nullification in Madison's resolutions. He instead spoke of the states having a duty to "interpose" when the federal government asserted powers not granted to it, a word general enough to cover the appeal made at the end of the resolutions for other states to join with the commonwealth in declaring the Alien and Sedition Acts unconstitutional.[21]

When Jefferson saw Madison's draft of the Virginia Resolutions, he thought it insufficiently strong and managed to get inserted into it an invitation for other states to join in declaring the Alien and Sedition Acts "null, void, and of no force, or effect." Someone, perhaps Madison, saw to it that these words were stricken, but the careful distinctions that Madison drew and Jefferson did not were quickly lost sight of. After Virginia, like Kentucky, had passed the resolutions, seven states responded, all of them negatively, their objections when they were given seeming to respond to Jefferson's assertion that a state could nullify a federal law, rather than to Madison's more subtle point about the right to "interpose." But gaining approval of the resolutions was not the sole purpose for sending them around. They were also a way of enlightening public opinion by setting forth arguments that might not otherwise be heard. There were people all across the country who felt uneasy about the Alien and Sedition Acts but had not formulated their objections. Madison and Jefferson provided arguments, less efficiently than modern politicians might when they make the case for their viewpoints through mass media, but about as efficiently as the eighteenth century would allow. Every state in the Union received the resolves, and two years before the next presidential election, citizens inclined to the Republican way of thinking gained a great cause to rally around. The idea of Jefferson's running against Adams in 1800 had probably been on both Jefferson's and Madison's minds since he had come so close to winning in 1796. The Federalist attempt to suppress free expression not only threatened fundamental rights; it gave Jefferson a key part of his platform.[22]

In early December, Madison read in the Fredericksburg paper that Napoleon Bonaparte had suffered a stunning naval defeat in Aboukir Bay, near Alexandria, Egypt, an event that sharply decreased the likelihood of France going to war with the United States. He also heard from Jefferson that the French might be actively seeking reconciliation. In addition, Jefferson reported, the Republican cause—helped in no small part by the direct taxes that military preparations required—was gaining in states from Massachusetts to South Carolina. The defense buildup was nonetheless continuing, with plans being made for a new armed force of thirty thousand men and a volunteer force besides.[23]

Military expansion had now gone so far that John Adams himself was unhappy with it. Congress was gathering a force to counter a French invasion, which Adams had never thought likely. Even before news came of the destruction of the French fleet in Egypt, the president had protested to his secretary of war, James McHenry, that there was "no more prospect of seeing a French army here than there is in heaven." Adams was also bitter about Hamilton, who he increasingly realized was manipulating the military buildup from New York. Adams had come into the presidency with little fondness for Hamilton, who had supported Thomas Pinckney in the 1796 presidential election, and when the question of who would be in charge of the new army had come up, Adams had been determined to deny Hamilton a major role. But Hamilton had elbowed his way in by helping George Washington see how, despite his age and declining energies, he could manage to be formally in command. He promised the sixty-six-year-old former president that he would support him as his number two, relieving him from burdens Washington felt he could not take on. Thus, when Adams nominated Washington to command the new army, the deed was done. Washington insisted on Hamilton as his second-in-command, and Adams was forced to swallow hard and take him.[24]

As Hamilton began to assemble the new army, Virginians became concerned that it was to be aimed not at France but at them—and they had reason to worry. Hamilton, labeling the Virginia and Kentucky Resolutions "a regular conspiracy to overturn the government," urged the new Speaker of the House, Theodore Sedgwick, to strengthen the Alien and Sedition Acts and speed up troop recruitment. "When a clever force has been collected, let them be drawn towards Virginia," he wrote, "then let measures be taken to act upon the laws and put Virginia to the test of resistance."[25] Hamilton was not the only Federalist to think that Republicans were conspirators and must be brought to heel, but he was the only one putting together a military force to do it.

Meanwhile, John Adams was hearing that Talleyrand was ready to negotiate seriously and yearning for it to be true. The adulation he had known in the early days of the XYZ Affair had turned to complaint. Both he and Congress were receiving petitions protesting taxes, objecting to the army, and condemning the Alien and Sedition Acts. In addition, Adams had come to suspect that Hamilton intended a military coup. He told a confidant that the New Yorker and his party "were endeavoring to get an army on foot to give Hamilton the command of it . . . and thus to proclaim a regal government and place Hamilton at the head of it." Peace with France, Adams's goal in the beginning, would remove all rationale for the new army and put an end to Hamilton's military ambitions—which were at least a match for what his worst enemies imagined. He had begun to talk about seizing Florida and Louisiana from the Spanish and even liberating South America. In later years, Adams would recall his reaction to Hamilton's grandiose plans: "This man is stark mad or I am."[26]

Adams knew that by renewing negotiations with the French, he would infuriate high Federalists, but he would also distance himself from the advocates of armies, taxes, and oppressive laws, and unless he did that, there was no way he could prevail in the upcoming election. He sent a message to the Senate on February 18, 1799, nominating William Vans Murray, then at The Hague, to be minister to France. Jefferson, who read the president's message aloud in the Senate chamber, reported that the Federalists had evidently not been consulted before the announcement, "as appeared by their dismay." They were "graveled and divided," he told Madison. The Federalists in the cabinet, as Timothy Pickering described it, "were all thunderstruck." A Senate committee met with the president, but the only concession he would make was to appoint two additional envoys to join Murray. The Senate confirmed his nominees, but Hamilton's influence was still strong, particularly in Adams's cabinet, and it would be eight months before the envoys set sail.[27]

IN VIRGINIA, Republicans were worried about their prospects in upcoming legislative contests. John Taylor of Caroline, who had been Madison's schoolmate at Donald Robertson's, wrote to tell him that Washington had prevailed on Patrick Henry to run for the Virginia Assembly. Washington had persuaded Henry "to step forward and save his country," a request that Taylor found more than passing strange since Henry would be saving it from opponents of a too powerful government—of which he, Henry, had once been one. Personal animosity toward Jefferson and Madison was driving Henry, Taylor thought, bringing him back into public office just as a presidential election neared. "I believe you are co-extensively involved in the danger with Mr. Jefferson," Taylor wrote, "but if it be otherwise and you can discern a conspiracy against your friend, will you not step forward and save him?" Six members of the Virginia congressional delegation also wrote to say that Madison was desperately needed to oppose "the executive party" and advance Republican principles. Madison agreed to have his name be advanced. On a partly cloudy day in late April 1799, just as the corn-planting season was coming to an end, voters gathered at the courthouse in Orange and elected him to the House of Delegates.[28]

Patrick Henry died before the Virginia General Assembly convened, but making sure that Henry did not sabotage Jefferson's presidential prospects was not the only task Madison had set for himself. One of the first orders of business was to get James Monroe elected Virginia's gov-

ernor, thus ensuring that pro-Jefferson forces had their hands firmly on
the tiller of the commonwealth. Madison nominated him on December
5, 1799, speaking "highly of his private character as pure and of his
public character as unimpeachable."[29] Monroe was elected handily.

News of Monroe's ascension troubled one prominent Virginian.
George Washington remained angry about a lengthy vindication that
Monroe had written of his service in France. Since Washington had
removed him from the post in Paris, Monroe's defense, not surprisingly,
was less than kind to the Washington administration. At Mount Vernon, the former president, suffering from a sore throat, listened on a
wintry evening as Tobias Lear, his former aide, read reports from the
Virginia Assembly. His irritation mounted, and then, "on hearing Mr.
Madison's observations respecting Mr. Monroe," Lear reported, the former president was "much affected and spoke with some degree of asper-
ity." Lear tried to calm him, and Washington went to bed, but overnight
the sore throat worsened. In the early hours of the next day, December
14, 1799, after hours of struggling for breath, Washington died.[30]

During the period of national mourning that followed, Jefferson
made no public comment. Madison delivered a brief eulogy on the floor
of the House of Delegates: "Death has robbed our country of its most
distinguished ornament and the world of one of its greatest benefactors.
George Washington, the hero of liberty, the father of his country, and
the friend of man is no more. The General Assembly of his native state
were ever the first to render him, living, the honors due to his virtues.
They will not be the second to pay to his memory the tribute of their
tears." It was left to Harry Lee, Madison's friend from Princeton, to
deliver the most memorable eulogy. Washington, he said, was "first in
war, first in peace, and first in the hearts of his countrymen."[31]

After Madison had reflected many years on the nation's first president, he would list among his attributes "remarkable prudence," "love
of justice," "fortitude," and "the advantage of a stature and figure, which
however insignificant when separated from greatness of character, do
not fail when combined with it to aid the attraction." Many things set
Washington apart from the rest of mankind, but most worthy of note,

in Madison's estimation, was that he had in full measure a trait that Madison had long admired, *"a modest dignity,"* he termed it, which in Washington's case *"at once commanded the highest respect and inspired the purest attachment."*[32]

ANOTHER TASK MADISON HAD SET for himself upon deciding to enter the House of Delegates was to answer critics of the Virginia Resolutions, and he worked on a response in the rooms he rented at Watson's, a tavern and oyster house on Shockoe Hill. Watson's was in a prime location, near the elegant capitol that Jefferson had designed, but Madison realized immediately that little else good could be said for it. Experienced now in the ways of marriage, he wrote to warn his wife. The rooms were "in a style much inferior to what I had hoped," he advised. "You must consequently lower your expectations on this subject as much as possible before you join me." About the time he wrote the letter, he came down with a severe case of dysentery, leading the modern reader to suspect that Watson's was unhygienic as well as unstylish. Madison did not make that connection, however, nor would it have occurred to his peers. Well into the nineteenth century, dysentery was thought to be caused by "exhalations from the soil."[33]

Madison was in bed for one week, then "in a state of debility" for two more, but he worked through the illness to produce what would become known as the *Report of 1800,* a document of nearly twenty thousand words defending the 1798 resolutions of the Virginia General Assembly. Other states had refused to go along with them on the grounds that it was the responsibility of the Supreme Court to declare a law unconstitutional, not of the states. Madison argued that since it was possible to conceive of the judiciary concurring with other branches in usurping power, final authority had to rest with the "parties to the constitutional compact," or the states. He was careful to emphasize that this authority should seldom be called upon but that in "great and extraordinary cases" the states (which most broadly defined meant "the people composing those political societies in their highest sovereign capacity") were justified "in interposing even so far as to arrest the progress of the evil."[34]

Some state legislatures, in responding to the 1798 resolutions, had gone so far as to embrace the Sedition Act. New Hampshire, for example, had opined that it was "constitutional and in the present critical situation of our country highly expedient." Madison emphasized that it violated freedom of the press, an action explicitly forbidden by an amendment to the Constitution. Some were trying to construe that amendment to mean that while Congress could not prevent publication, it could pass laws punishing opinions once printed. Such a distinction made "a mockery" of press freedom, Madison wrote, which in a country where the government was elective had to be most strenuously defended. The Sedition Act would keep the people from knowing when public officials failed to discharge their trusts properly. It would keep them from being able to hold those officials accountable. And it would do so, Madison noted pointedly, in the upcoming presidential election. Those in power "will be covered by the 'Sedition Act' from animadversions exposing them to disrepute among the people," while challengers "may be exposed to the contempt and hatred of the people."[35]

Madison took the opportunity to put the Sedition Act in context, pointing out that it was part of a "*design*" in which the federal government accumulated power "*by forced constructions of the constitutional charter.*" This was a dangerous tendency, he observed. Interpreting the general welfare clause of article 1, section 8, of the Constitution to give the federal government sovereignty in "*all cases whatsoever*" would ultimately transform "the republican system of the United States into a monarchy," and "whether it would be into a mixed or an absolute monarchy might depend on too many contingencies to admit of any certain foresight."[36]

In Madison's old age, the *Report of 1800,* like the Virginia and Kentucky Resolutions, would be used in the great battle over whether states could nullify federal laws and secede from the Union. As he wrote, however, he focused on fundamental rights and the preservation of a republic in which the people were sovereign. With the presidential election of 1800 growing ever closer, he was also surely aware that the report was a reminder to voters of the threat that Federalist government represented. Five thousand copies of the report were distributed throughout Virginia, and Jefferson, in Philadelphia, made sure that members of Congress had copies to take home with them.[37]

Madison spent some of his time in the House of Delegates on election mechanics. When Virginia had voted by district in 1796, Jefferson had received only twenty of the state's twenty-one electoral votes. Since there was a difference between Jefferson and Adams of only three electoral votes nationwide in 1796, the single electoral vote in Virginia plus a single vote that had been cast for Adams in North Carolina could have made Jefferson president. In order to ensure all the Virginia electoral votes for Jefferson in 1800, Madison prepared a bill that would provide for a general ballot to be presented to voters. Since Republicans were thought to dominate, their ticket would win statewide, and the victorious electors, Republicans all, would vote for Jefferson. Madison reported that the "general ticket was so novel that a great number who wished it shrunk from the vote, and others apprehending that their constituents would be still more startled at it voted against it." But it passed by five votes, and on January 21, 1800, ninety-three Republicans, including Madison, gathered in Richmond to put the electoral slate together. As John Beckley had done in Pennsylvania, the gathered Republicans made their slate as prestigious as possible. Edmund Pendleton was on it, as were George Wythe and James Madison. A central committee was established as well as committees in each county to make sure not a single electoral vote went astray. The gathering even agreed upon an election program for easing the public into acceptance of the new voting method: speakers in favor of it would appear in each district to laud not only the candidate for elector from that district but also the "prominent characters" from other districts who would finish out the ticket.[38]

Sometime before he left Richmond in January 1800, Madison encountered George Tucker, a young writer and law student, who left a memorable portrait of him:

He was then nearly fifty years of age, dressed in silk stockings and black breeches and wore powder according to the practice that still prevailed in full dress. The first [impression] made on me was that of sternness rather than of the mildness and suavity which I found afterward to characterize [him]. I saw him at the home of Mr. Monroe, then recently appointed governor of Virginia, on whom I called to deliver a letter of introduction, and I know not whether it was that they were engaged in some matter of grave conference which left its impression on his features when I saw him, or such was the ordinary effect first produced on a stranger, but I never perceived it afterwards.[39]

Madison had plenty to be looking grave about, but Tucker identified something others also observed: Madison gave nothing away to strangers, but once a person gained his trust, he became agreeableness itself.

MADISON WAS BACK at Montpelier when he learned that Napoleon had overthrown the French Republic, replacing the Directory with a consulate and installing himself as first consul. Madison knew that Federalists would use the event to point out the importance of ensuring order with alien and sedition laws and a large army. Too much liberty, they would argue, brought about chaos, which in turn led to monarchy. Madison hoped that the people would see that this was not the American situation and "ultimately rescue the republican principle." "Such a demonstration," he wrote to Jefferson, "will be the more precious as the late defection of France has left America the only theater on which true liberty can have a fair trial."[40]

Jefferson, in Philadelphia, waited to write to Madison until he had someone whom he could trust completely to carry the letter. He found that courier in Hore Browse Trist, son of Eliza Trist, grown now and living in Charlottesville, as was his mother. He would carry messages between Madison and Jefferson several times during the year.

Jefferson's letter contained a rundown on the upcoming presidential

election. New York would provide an early sign of prospects, with legislative elections to be held in late April. The legislature appointed electors in that state, and if the Republicans gained control, New York's
electors, which in 1796 had gone to Adams, would go to Jefferson. New
York City, which dominated the legislature, was the place to watch. A
Republican victory there would almost certainly mean that Jefferson
would take all of the state's electoral votes in the fall.

The upcoming New York City election was not the only thing Madison had on his mind. The peace delegation to Paris seemed to have
dropped off the face of the earth. It had been more than a year since
President Adams had nominated William Vans Murray as minister to
France and added Chief Justice Oliver Ellsworth and Governor William
Davie of North Carolina to the mission, but as the spring of 1800 approached, they still had not arrived in France. From Senator Stevens
Thomson Mason of Virginia, Madison learned that Ellsworth and Davie
had landed in Portugal and were proceeding from there to Paris by land.
"Why they should have landed at so remote a place seems hard to be
accounted for," Mason wrote, "unless it is to be considered as a part of
that system of procrastination which detained them in this country
above eight month[s] after their appointment."[41]

There was also the matter of dressing the columns of the portico at
Montpelier. Madison asked the vice president to oblige him "by enquir-
ing whether there be known in Philadelphia any composition for en-
crusting brick that will . . . stand the weather, and particularly what is
thought of common plaster thickly painted with white lead overspread
with sand."[42]

Before Madison got an answer, he received momentous news from
Virginia congressman John Dawson. "The Republic is safe," Dawson
exulted. "Our ticket has succeeded in the city of New York." In a letter
written a week later—and apparently sent through the mail—Jefferson
said not a word about the victory, but he did advise on Madison's columns. "In Lord Burlington's edition of Palladio," he wrote, "he tells us
that most of the columns of those fine buildings erected by Palladio are
of brick covered with stucco and stand perfectly." And he added "that

three fourths of the houses in Paris are covered with plaster and never saw any decay in it."[43]

Good news continued to come in. In Virginia the Republicans did well in legislative races, and in Philadelphia the Federalist caucus in Congress seemed to be tying itself in knots. Caucus members named John Adams and Charles Cotesworth Pinckney as their candidates but refused to give priority to Adams, a move some hoped would put Pinckney in the White House. The idea of Hamilton and others was that states in New England would support Pinckney as part of a ticket with Adams while South Carolina, his home state, would choose electors committed to him and Jefferson, thereby giving Pinckney the greatest number of electoral votes. Following the caucus, a furious John Adams fired his secretary of state, Timothy Pickering, and his secretary of war, James McHenry, both of whom he suspected—rightly—of being loyal to Hamilton rather than to him.[44] Adams, who knew by now that the American envoys to France would be cordially received in Paris, also ordered the disbandment of the new army. There would be no military adventurism on Hamilton's part on his watch.

The Republicans in Congress held their caucus, and the results were straightforward: Jefferson for president and Aaron Burr for vice president. It was true that the darkly handsome Burr had irritated many of his fellow Republicans, including Thomas Jefferson, with his ill-concealed ambition, but he had earned a place on the ticket by crucial work he had done in New York to put that state in the Republican column.

MEANWHILE, IN RICHMOND the associate justice of the Supreme Court Samuel Chase, a high Federalist, was dealing his own party a severe setback. Someone had given him a booklet written by the scandalmonger James Callender that called President Adams a "hoary headed incendiary" and asserted that his "reign" was "one continued tempest of malignant passions." Furious that these calumnies were going unpunished, Chase had seen to it that Callender, who was living in Virginia, was indicted under the Sedition Act—and was in the process

of ensuring his conviction. Chase instructed the marshal at the Richmond trial to disqualify Republicans from being on the jury and refused
to reject a juror who announced he had already made up his mind that
Callender was guilty. He browbeat defense witnesses and interrupted
defense counsel so often that they could not present a case. When the
inevitable guilty verdict came in, Chase, seemingly determined to destroy whatever Federalist support was left in the Old Dominion, declared the verdict "pleasing to him, because it shewed that the laws of
the United States could be enforced in Virginia, the principal object of
this prosecution." Madison took a certain pleasure in watching "the
party which has done the mischief . . . so industriously cooperating in
its own destruction."[45]

Madison received a letter from Jefferson in mid-June inviting him
and Mrs. Madison to Monticello so that the two men could discuss
topics they could not take up in the mail. The Madisons arrived on
Jefferson's mountaintop during a lovely stretch of July weather and
probably stayed in an octagonal room on the first floor that is known
today as the Madison Room.[46] Madison would visit Monticello again in
August to discuss the upcoming election with Jefferson in person. Few
letters passed between them, and those that did were less about politics
than they were about nails. Should outsiders have read the interchange,
they might have concluded the correspondence was between two carpenters.

IN OCTOBER, Federalists suffered another self-inflicted wound, this
one courtesy of Alexander Hamilton. His disdain for President Adams
had ripened into hatred after Adams had sent a peace mission to Paris,
fired Hamiltonian cabinet members, and disbanded the army, and his
plans to have Federalists elevate Pinckney over Adams in their voting
were not going well. In frustration, Hamilton laid out the case against
Adams in a pamphlet. He depicted a paranoid and suspicious man, subject to "eccentric tendencies" and "paroxysms of anger." He detailed the
personal affronts he had suffered, and after declaring Adams "unfit . . .

for the office of chief magistrate," he did a strange reversal and urged Federalists *not* to withhold a single vote from the president.[47]

Hamilton had intended to have his pamphlet privately distributed, but no sooner had it reached the printer than a copy was leaked to political operative John Beckley and passages soon appeared in the *Aurora*. Hamilton's descriptions of Adams created a sensation, and the endorsement that followed on them made Hamilton appear at least as deranged as the man he was writing about. In Madison's judgment, the pamphlet damaged Hamilton more than Adams, but the injury to the president was nonetheless significant. "The pamphlet of H," Madison wrote to Jefferson, "which, though its recoil has perhaps more deeply wounded the author than the object it was discharged at, has contributed not a little to overthrow the latter, staggering as he before was in the public esteem."[48]

In the end the election came down to South Carolina, and in late November, as Vice President Jefferson stopped at Montpelier on his way to Washington City, the new capital, Madison handed him a letter that must have buoyed them both. It was from Senator Charles Pinckney of South Carolina, whom Madison had known since the Constitutional Convention. The cousin of Thomas and General Charles Cotesworth Pinckney, Senator Pinckney was now referred to as Blackguard Charlie for having strayed from the Federalist fold. He had been working hard in the Republican cause and reported he was convinced that "we shall have a *decided majority* in our legislature." That meant that Republican candidates for elector would prevail. There was still a possibility that some Republican electors would cast their second votes for General Pinckney, the favorite son, rather than Aaron Burr, and that those electoral votes added to Federalist electoral votes for Pinckney could elevate him above other candidates, but Republican Party discipline was strong and General Pinckney was a gentleman, refusing to back any candidate for elector who was not faithful to John Adams. On December 2, Senator Pinckney was able to report to Jefferson, "The election is just finished, and we have (thanks to heaven's goodness) carried it."[49]

In the months before the election, Madison had served as a liaison to vice presidential candidate Aaron Burr's campaign. Still smarting from Burr's having received only one electoral vote from Virginia in 1796, Burr's forces wanted assurances that all the Virginia electors would vote for Burr as well as Jefferson. Madison provided them and was in turn assured that all of New York's electors would vote for Jefferson as well as Burr. Burr's agent also reported that in two or three states electors voting for Jefferson would not vote for Burr, thus assuring that Jefferson would come out first in the electoral count and be elected president.[50]

Madison had managed to overcome the extreme reluctance of Virginia elector George Wythe to keep his part of the bargain, but as December advanced, he began to worry that he had been dealt with falsely. No Jefferson electors in other states had thrown away their second vote to assure Jefferson precedence. Thus, Jefferson and Burr were tied with seventy-three electoral votes apiece.[51]

THIS STUNNING RESULT meant that the contest for the presidency would be decided in the House of Representatives, where the Federalists had a majority of members but Republicans controlled more state delegations: eight to the Federalists' six, with two states divided. Since voting would be by state, with each casting a single vote, the Republicans had an advantage, but they did not have the majority of nine votes (out of sixteen) necessary to put Jefferson into the presidency.

Federalists decided in a caucus to support Burr. This was not an endorsement of his character, as Speaker of the House Theodore Sedgwick made clear. In a letter to Hamilton, he wrote of Burr, "His ambition is of the worst kind. It is a mere love of power, regardless of fame but as its instrument. His selfishness excludes all social affections and his profligacy unrestrained by any moral sentiment and defying all decency." But however unworthy Burr was, Federalists were willing to use him to keep Jefferson, whom they considered more unworthy, from becoming president. One scheme was to keep blocking Jefferson until the term of the Adams administration expired so that on Inauguration Day 1801, the presidency and the vice presidency would be empty. Since

Congress had the constitutional power to provide for succession in "the case of removal, death, resignation, or inability both of the president and vice president," Federalists could then, with only "a stretch of the Constitution," pass a bill naming a federal officer such as Secretary of State John Marshall to the vacancy.[52]

Jefferson reported this scheme to Madison, who responded that he could hardly believe it—and surely he did not want to, realizing that by persuading Wythe he had contributed to the electoral nightmare. He shot off a furious letter to Virginia Republican John Dawson that he clearly intended for distribution among Federalists. If the current House was unable to choose a president, the next House, which would be controlled by Republicans, would gain the right, he said. Jefferson and Burr should call that House into session early in order for the decision to be made, he wrote, adding that the attempt to elect Burr was degrading the country. Madison's plan got Federalist attention but had a fatal flaw. It depended on Burr's cooperation, and he was giving no hint that would be forthcoming. Jefferson, even more outraged than Madison, informed the Federalists that if they should "pass a law for putting the government into the hands of an officer, . . . the middle states would arm and that no such usurpation even for a single day should be submitted to."[53]

On Wednesday, February 11, 1801, as a snowstorm whipped around the unfinished buildings of the Capitol, the House met and the states cast their ballots. The result was what everyone expected: eight votes for Jefferson, six for Burr, and two states divided. The voting continued around the clock until midday Thursday, by which time there had been twenty-eight votes, each with the same result. The deadlock continued through Friday, Saturday, Monday, and a vote at 1:00 p.m. on Tuesday. Finally, on a second Tuesday vote, there was a break. Ten states voted for Jefferson, and on the thirty-sixth ballot he became president-elect of the United States.[54]

Why did the Federalists give way? The fact that the Republicans had the upper hand and kept it throughout the balloting might have helped, and Jefferson's threats likely did as well. Jefferson might also have been lobbying. James Bayard, Delaware's sole delegate and thereby in control of its vote, was first to change his mind, and he later testified that he had received assurances about Jefferson's intentions regarding the public debt, the navy, and certain Federalist officials—an assertion that Jefferson vehemently denied. Another factor was Alexander Hamilton. Convinced that Burr would be a disastrous president, he undertook a letter-writing campaign in which he accused Burr of being an American Catiline, ready to overthrow the Republic as Lucius Sergius Catilina had tried to do in Rome, in order to gain permanent power and wealth. One of Hamilton's most powerful letters went to Congressman Bayard. "This man has no principle, public or private," Hamilton wrote of Burr. "As a politician his sole spring of action is an inordinate ambition; as an individual he is believed by friends as well as foes to be without *probity*, and a voluptuary by system." He added that there was no one of either party in New York "who does not think Mr. Burr the most unfit man in the U.S. for the office of president." What might have made the letter particularly convincing was Hamilton's confession that there was nothing he would rather do than "contribute to the disappointment and mortification of Mr. Jefferson," but he thought Burr would bring such calamity that he would rather see Jefferson as president.[55]

IN JANUARY, before the election was decided, Madison had been ailing with "several complaints." One was rheumatic, and he practiced "temperance and flannel" for relief, the flannel being wrapped around painful joints to keep them warm. What his other complaints were, he did not say, but in telling Jefferson about them, he struck a note of pessimism: "I am much afraid that any changes that may take place [in my health] are not likely to be for the better." He was also concerned about his father, who was in a "very declining state," and although Jefferson wanted Madison in Washington before the change in government on March 4, he had to decline. He made clear, however, that he did not mean by his delay "to retract what has passed in conversation between us." Jefferson had asked him and he had agreed to serve as secretary of state.[56]

He had thought he could get to Washington not long after the inauguration, but his father died. "Yesterday morning rather suddenly
though very gently the flame of life went out," he wrote to Jefferson.
Now Madison was truly his family's patriarch, and he must have thought
with gratitude of the man he was replacing, the father he had addressed
in so many letters as "Honored sir." James senior had come to Montpelier when it was newly cut from the wilderness. He had been just nine
years old when his own father, Ambrose, died. He had helped his mother,
Frances, come through those days and over the years had expanded
Madison holdings. He had managed Montpelier into his seventies, and
if he had not rotated his crops as often as he should have, he had been
frugal, eschewing the extravagance typical of many plantations, which
might have meant that Montpelier, though likely dependent on credit,
was less so than other great estates. His greatest indulgence had been
his eldest son. He didn't provide lavish support, probably a good thing
then as now, but it was enough to enable James junior to become architect, builder, and leader of a great nation.[57]

Madison was the executor of his father's estate, and settling it was
a complicated matter, he explained to the new president, because there
were many heirs, and apportionment would be not by fiat but "by amicable negotiations, concessions, and adjustments." Jefferson responded
graciously, but he was feeling overwhelmed, "harassed with interruptions and worn down with fatigue," he told his son-in-law Thomas
Mann Randolph. It wasn't just Madison who was missing from the new
government. Secretary of the Treasury Albert Gallatin was settling his
affairs in Pennsylvania. Jefferson had also been turned down repeatedly
in his effort to find a secretary of the navy. His response, finally, was to
take a break himself. Less than four weeks after he was inaugurated,
he departed the capital city to spend three weeks at Monticello. He
wrote to Montpelier that he hoped Madison would return to Washington with him, but Madison reported "an attack on my health, which
kept me in bed three or four days." Settling his father's will was also
turning out to be more complicated and contentious than he had
thought. In his hurry to get to Washington, he left much undone, which

meant that his brother William was left to advise on many details.[58] William's role in settling James senior's will would have repercussions decades hence.

Finally, in late April, James and Dolley Madison, Payne Todd, and Anna Payne set out from Montpelier. The roads were muddy in places and Madison was still feeling unwell, but there were also long firm stretches, and as the carriage rolled along, the travelers could admire the redbuds in bloom. Spring had come round again.[59]

Chapter 13

THE REVOLUTION OF 1800

REPUBLICANS CLAIMED that Jefferson's victory signified a revolution, by which they meant that the Federalists had been turned out and their policies rejected, but Margaret Bayard Smith, wife of the publisher of the *National Intelligencer,* caught a deeper meaning when she described Jefferson's inaugural to her daughter: "I have this morning witnessed one of the most interesting scenes a free people can ever witness. The changes of administration, which in every government and in every age have most generally been epochs of confusion, villainy, and bloodshed, in this our happy country take place without any species of distraction or disorder."[1] The peaceful transfer of power from a party of one philosophy to that of another made Jefferson's election and inauguration a turning point not just for the United States but for the world.

When James Madison arrived with his wife in the new capital in late April, he surely saw that it reflected the new direction of the country. Here there were no kingly gardens, no grand buildings lining palatial avenues—indeed, no avenues save the one named after Pennsylvania, and it was unpaved. The president's house was an imposing building, but it stood on a barren plain, its grounds seeming "never to have been touched by spade or pick-axe," a British visitor observed. As for the Capitol, rising on Jenkins Hill a mile and a half away, it consisted of two wings unconnected by a central structure, and only one of the wings was finished.[2]

Washington City wasn't a city at all, which was fitting enough for a new administration that held up rural life as the American ideal. The new capital had "several points of natural beauty to recommend it," a visitor observed, "the ground being elevated on both sides of the Potomac, and the views varied as well as in many parts romantic, particularly just above the city where the river is obstructed by rocks and at the Eastern Branch where there are fine woods and some delightful rides." Cows grazed where the city's planner, Pierre L'Enfant, envisioned grand plazas. Fields of corn grew not far from the president's house. Such was Washington's undeveloped state that the clusters of buildings here and there were mostly known not by street numbers but by how many buildings were in the group. Ask people where they lived and they might respond "Seven Buildings" or "Twenty Buildings."[3]

As the Madisons rode up to the president's house in their carriage, they would have seen that Jefferson was already remodeling, changing the entrance from the north side to the south. He was also having the wooden privy that had stood alongside the house torn down and installing water closets inside. He probably showed the new arrivals how he was changing around the way the rooms were used, pointed out the cornices he was upgrading and the location he had chosen for a wine cellar. The Madisons, used to his "putting up and pulling down" at Monticello, would not have been surprised at any of this.[4] Jefferson had once advocated that governments be newly formed every nineteen years. His buildings were fortunate to get nineteen months.

James and Dolley Madison stayed with Jefferson for three weeks, time during which he had another houseguest as well. Twenty-six-year-old Meriwether Lewis was living behind hastily constructed partitions at one end of what is today the East Room. Jefferson might have intended to use him for a secretary, but he seemed to be more a youthful companion, running errands for the president and spending time with him in long discussions about the American West, where Lewis had served in the army. In the mornings, Lewis could often be found hunting just off Pennsylvania Avenue, where snipe and partridge abounded.[5]

When the Madisons moved from the president's house, it was to "Six Buildings," a row of brick houses on Pennsylvania Avenue where the State Department was temporarily located. Madison was still not feeling well, which probably made living where he worked, at least for a few months, appealing. He arrived at his temporary office to find a nearly overwhelming backlog of work. He apologized to a friend for not answering his letter sooner by explaining that he had found it "absolutely necessary to devote the whole of my time and pen to my public duties and consequently to suspend my private correspondences altogether."[6]

It was not diplomatic dispatches that were so much the problem. If anything, there was a temporary lull on that front. The Convention of Mortefontaine, negotiated by John Adams's emissaries, had ended hostilities between France and the United States, and France was being unusually (if suspiciously) conciliatory. Great Britain, meanwhile, was focusing on the war in Europe. The great burden for Madison was answering letters from job seekers. A Rhode Island lawyer with whom he had served in the Continental Congress wrote to be sure that an aging acquaintance would be allowed to stay in his Newport customs post for life. The former congressman also wanted his son to be considered for "office of surveyor or any higher office" of port customs. A Pennsylvania Republican wrote to advocate the firing of all the Federalist excise officers in his state and to urge that he himself be considered for a post. Charles Peale Polk, who had painted portraits of Madison's parents, solicited Madison's help "obtaining *any situation, here or elsewhere.*"[7]

By far the most troublesome job seeker was James Callender. The Sedition Act under which he had been convicted in Samuel Chase's court had expired with the Adams presidency, and Jefferson had restored Callender's rights—as well as those of others so convicted—with a presidential pardon. But Callender had paid a fine in addition to serving time in jail, and although he was entitled to his money back, the U.S. marshal in Virginia, an enemy of Jefferson's, would not repay him. The unhappy Callender wrote a letter to Madison threatening to ruin Jefferson's reputation unless he got his two hundred dollars—and the job of postmaster in Richmond. "Surely, sir," Callender wrote, "many syllogisms cannot be necessary to convince Mr. Jefferson that, putting feelings and principles out of the question, it is not proper for him to create a quarrel with me." In May, Callender appeared at the Six Buildings in Washington. When he was shown into Madison's small office, what he got was "plain dealing," which likely meant an explanation that although every effort was being made to get his two hundred dollars returned, he wasn't getting the Richmond job. Jefferson, hearing that Callender was in town, sent Meriwether Lewis to offer assurances and give Callender fifty dollars to tide him over. Callender took the money, "not as a charity," he said, but as "hush money" and "intimated that he was in possession of things which he could and would make use of" should he not get the post in Richmond.[8]

Jefferson once said that he had "no secrets" from Madison, and Madison probably knew what Callender was hinting at: Jefferson's intimate relationship with Sally Hemings, an enslaved woman at Monticello. Hemings had borne Jefferson four children by this time, two of whom were living. The relationship had now been ongoing for over a decade, more than long enough for rumors to circulate and hints to appear in newspapers.[9] At the least, Madison would have had suspicions—and been very relieved to learn in mid-June that Callender's fine had been refunded. Callender took the money and went silent—for a time.

THE CONSTITUTION provided that although the president was commander in chief, only Congress could declare war. But what if another nation put the United States into a state of war? Could the president then act without Congress? That was the question discussed at the first cabinet meeting that Madison attended, which probably occurred in Jefferson's office in the president's house, located where the State Dining

Room is today. Maps and charts were pinned on the walls, and globes were scattered around the edges of the room. A mockingbird that Jefferson sometimes let fly around his office sang in a cage hanging in a window recess, where pots of roses and geraniums bloomed. A long, baize-covered table was in the center, and it was probably here that cabinet members sat to discuss the pasha of Tripoli. The tribute that the United States had been paying him for several years to protect its shipping was overdue, and he was demanding $225,000 immediately and $25,000 a year after that. He was already fitting out corsairs to attack American ships in case the money wasn't handed over promptly. Although Congress, which would not be in session for another six months, could not be consulted, Madison and the rest of the cabinet endorsed the idea of the president's ordering American ships to the Mediterranean. Madison, who had seen to it at the Constitutional Convention that the president had "the power to repel sudden attacks," also endorsed the idea that if American commanders found a state of war to exist when they reached the Mediterranean, they were authorized "to search for and destroy the enemy's vessels wherever they can find them." Before the American frigates could leave the harbor at Norfolk, the pasha cut down the American flagpole at the consulate in Tripoli—his way of formally declaring war.[10]

Madison's long-standing principle was that the United States should stay out of war, thus avoiding the debt, taxes, and executive aggrandizement that were sure consequences, but in this instance he believed that it would cost little more for ships to sail than it did to maintain them in harbor. It was a point on which he would turn out to be spectacularly wrong. The United States would lose a frigate in the harbor at Tripoli, more than three hundred Americans would be captured, and expenses would skyrocket as reinforcements had to be sent. Finally—and with Madison's blessing—the United States would launch a land and sea assault on Tripoli aimed at replacing the pasha with his equally corrupt brother, thus inspiring the pasha to agree to a truce that involved no tribute. The United States would, however, pay him sixty thousand dollars to ransom its prisoners.[11]

Madison also thought that the mission to Tripoli would provide U.S. mariners with valuable experience, and in this case he was spectacularly right. Veterans of the Barbary War, among them William Bainbridge, Isaac Hull, Stephen Decatur, and Oliver Hazard Perry, would be naval heroes in a later war that Madison would oversee as commander in chief. The Barbary War of 1801–1805 would also be memorable because eight U.S. marines marched with the force of Greek mercenaries, Arabs, and Bedouins that intended to overthrow the pasha. While they participated in a land assault on the fortress at Derna, their fellow marines attacked from the bay. Success in that battle gave the United States its first victory on foreign soil and the Marine Corps hymn its beginning lines: "From the halls of Montezuma to the shores of Tripoli / We will fight our country's battles on the land as on the sea."[12]

BY THE SUMMER of 1801, Madison's health had improved "in a moderate degree," but July brought a setback. The language he used to describe it—a "slight attack of bile to which my constitution is peculiarly prone"—suggests that this was another example of his "constitutional liability to sudden attacks, somewhat resembling epilepsy," though a mild one. Jefferson hoped that Madison could get off to Montpelier by the middle of July, which seemed like a fine idea to Madison. "If I can get into the pure air which I breathe at home," he wrote, "without a return of the attack, I shall have a more flattering prospect than I have had for nearly two years past."[13] It was the end of the month, however, before he got away. The next day, Jefferson also departed the federal city and headed home.

Spending the high malarial season of August and September away from Washington and in the Piedmont became a pattern for Madison and Jefferson. They continued to work during the summer, sending messages back and forth between Monticello and Montpelier by special courier. The Madisons typically visited Monticello in early September, and Jefferson often returned the visit later in the month.

Jefferson relied on Madison's judgment to an extraordinary degree, as the two men's letters from the summer of 1801 on the subject of "prizes" reveal. The British chargé d'affaires, Edward Thornton, had made the case that because of the Jay Treaty, British ships captured by France and brought to American ports should not be turned over to a prize court to have their disposition determined, but should be ordered away. The president thought Thornton's argument was sound, but knowing that Madison objected, he wrote to his secretary of state, "Still, wishing you to revise this opinion of mine, I refer it back to yourself to give the order for departure or any other answer you think best." Madison found a precedent for sending the ships away that did not involve the Jay Treaty, which he despised, and passed the decision to the British minister. When Madison communicated decisions, he routinely framed them as the president's, and he did so in this case—even though he was, in fact, with the president's permission, effectively reversing the president.[14]

Jefferson and Madison offered differing views on the right policy for the United States toward the ambitious and charismatic Toussaint Louverture, who had helped lead a slave rebellion in Saint Domingue (the Dominican Republic and Haiti today) and now ruled the island. Because Saint Domingue was one of France's most valuable possessions, the French chargé d'affaires, Louis Pichon, tried early in the administration to determine whether the United States would be of assistance if France tried to regain control. He got studied neutrality from Madison, who said that the United States was not ready to become involved. But from the president Pichon got quite a different message. "Nothing would be easier," he said, "than to supply everything for your army and navy and to starve out Toussaint."[15]

Rumors abounded in 1801 that Saint Domingue was not France's only interest in the Western Hemisphere. Napoleon was said to be trying to get Spain to agree to give back the Louisiana Territory, which France had ceded to it in 1762. This "retrocession," as it was called, had, in fact, already occurred, though France was not admitting to it, and for France to be in control of Louisiana was clearly not in the interests of the United States. It was one thing to have a weak and feckless government such as

Spain's in control of New Orleans and the vast territory to the west of the Mississippi. It was quite another to have Napoleon on one's doorstep. In this light, Madison's message to Pichon seems much more sensible than Jefferson's. Why help Napoleon get a foothold?

Jefferson's response likely had to do with the worry most Virginians had about slave revolt, particularly after a planned insurrection had come to light in 1800. An enslaved man named Gabriel and hundreds of others had planned to march on Richmond under the banner "Death or Liberty" and to kill anyone who got in their way. The rebels were betrayed, caught, and tried. Thirty-five men, including Gabriel, were hanged.[16] They had been inspired by many things, including Toussaint Louverture, and Jefferson wanted him gone. The president had a moment of too much candor—and a secretary of state on whom he could depend to convey the proper message, even though Madison no doubt shared Jefferson's concerns about slave uprisings.

Madison was not the only cabinet member whom Jefferson had wisely chosen. The sharp-witted Treasury secretary, Albert Gallatin, had a blunt manner that was refreshing in the evasive world of politics—though one wonders if his wife, Hannah, always appreciated it. He once described her as "neither handsome nor rich, but sensible." Gallatin had come to the United States in 1780, served in the Pennsylvania ratifying convention and state legislature, and was chosen for the U.S. Senate in 1793. He served only a short time, being removed from his seat for not having been a citizen long enough. He had made himself a nuisance by asking pointed questions of Secretary of the Treasury Alexander Hamilton, and the vote against him, which turned on what Gallatin called "a nice and difficult" legal point, was along party lines. He did not help his case, however, when he matter-of-factly expressed his own doubts about whether he had actually been a citizen for the requisite nine years.[17]

As Treasury secretary, Gallatin helped the president craft the "frugal government" he had promised in his inaugural address. When the Seventh Congress convened in 1801, Jefferson recommended cutting government expenditures, getting rid of the internal taxes that Federalists had imposed to support the conflict with France, and gradually paying off the nation's debt—all proposals that met with congressional approval. In the interest of smaller government, Jefferson also suggested that Congress take a close look at the Judiciary Act of 1801, which had been passed in the closing days of the previous administration. The Republican Congress turned to that eagerly, not least because Federalists had used the act to provide themselves with sinecures.[18] On his last day in office, John Adams had spent part of his time signing commissions for judgeships that the act had created.

Repealing the Judiciary Act of 1801 and replacing it with the Judiciary Act of 1802 meant that some judges lost their jobs, which brought heated Federalist objections because the Constitution provided for service during good behavior. The new act also provided for one rather than two Supreme Court sessions each year, which meant the court would not meet until February 1803, and that caused more angry outbursts from Federalists. But they raged in vain. The Revolution of 1800 proceeded on its way, leading some Federalists to fear that anarchy lay ahead. Fisher Ames believed there would be plunder and bloodshed. The only hope, as he saw it, was that states might provide a shelter for "the wise and good and rich."[19]

In point of fact, Jefferson proceeded cautiously in replacing Federalists with Republicans. As he saw it, anyone Adams had appointed after he had lost the election was inherently disqualified, as was anyone guilty of official misconduct. Early on, he expanded this policy to include removing men from office in order to obtain a better political balance, pointing out that under the late Federalist administration Republicans had been excluded. Federalists naturally objected, but so did Republicans who thought the president wasn't moving fast enough. Jefferson found the matter of appointments extremely vexing, but two of them must have given him particular satisfaction. He appointed Hore Browse Trist, son of Eliza, to be a customs collector, and after his old political ally John Beckley, who had been fired by the Federalists, was reinstated as clerk of the House, Jefferson saw to it that he also became the first librarian of Congress.[20]

·   ·   ·

BRITAIN AND FRANCE signed a preliminary peace agreement in October 1801, enabling Napoleon to send a fleet and an army to Saint Domingue, where his men, using lies and deception, captured Toussaint Louverture. Napoleon had him transported to a prison high in the Jura Mountains on the border of Switzerland, where he died. Soon, however, Napoleon's troops began to sicken with yellow fever, and after he issued orders to reenslave the blacks of Saint Domingue, his men faced a fierce insurrection. Napoleon's commander on the island, Charles Leclerc, reported that of the twenty-eight thousand men sent to Saint Domingue, four thousand remained able to serve, and then Leclerc, who was Napoleon's brother-in-law, died. Napoleon had been bested by yellow fever and what Henry Adams described as "the desperate courage of 500,000 Haitian Negroes who would not be enslaved."[21]

Meanwhile, Madison had been speaking in strong terms to the French chargé d'affaires about Louisiana. Given the pressure of the burgeoning American population, the secretary said, France was unlikely to hold the territory long. Moreover, its possession of it was likely to drive the Americans into an alliance with the British. The president himself, going through back channels, delivered the same message.[22] Both Jefferson and Madison hoped that France could still be talked out of taking possession of Louisiana and that the United States might purchase New Orleans, thereby ensuring access by way of the Mississippi to the Gulf of Mexico. The president and the secretary also looked longingly on West Florida, land that is today contained in Louisiana, southernmost Mississippi and Alabama, and a portion of the Florida Panhandle. The watershed of several rivers, West Florida, like New Orleans, promised access to the gulf.

How tenuous U.S. navigation rights were on the Mississippi became apparent at the end of 1802 when the Spanish intendant of New Orleans closed the port to American commerce. Madison, who had by now been working the issue of the Mississippi for more than twenty years, urged Charles Pinckney, whom Jefferson had appointed America's minister to Spain, to be sure that the Spanish government understood the importance that America's western citizens attached to commerce on the river: "The Mississippi is to them everything. It is the Hudson, the Delaware, the Potomac and all the navigable rivers of the Atlantic states formed into one stream." He hinted to the French chargé d'affaires that the thousands of Americans floating their cargoes down the Mississippi might be moved to take up arms when they found the port of New Orleans closed to them. He sent bellicose talking points to Robert Livingston, the U.S. minister to France: "There are now or in two years will be not less than 200,000 militia on the waters of the Mississippi, every man of whom would march at a minute's warning to remove obstructions from that outlet to the sea, every man of whom regards the free use of that river as a natural and indefeasible right and is conscious of the physical force that can at any time give effect to it."[23]

Madison was not exaggerating western anger, which was being aided and abetted by accusations from eastern Federalists that the administration had gone soft when it came to defending America's interests. To quiet the agitation, the president took the step of nominating James Monroe as envoy extraordinary to France and Spain. Monroe had holdings in Kentucky and had long been involved in matters concerning the territory beyond the Appalachians, with the result that he was well regarded in the West. The president also managed to get a two-million-dollar appropriation from Congress. Its purpose, discussed in secret session, was to allow Monroe, acting with Livingston and Pinckney, to begin negotiations to buy New Orleans and the Floridas.[24]

Monroe, who heard of his nomination after it had been made, was initially reluctant, in part because he was strapped for cash. He had just finished two terms as Virginia's governor and was hoping to make some money practicing law in Richmond, where he had just leased a house. Moreover, he knew that the salary that Congress paid diplomats was not enough to cover their expenses. Madison helped out by agreeing, in exchange for some china and silver, to pay off loans that Monroe took out. It was a deal that Monroe was no doubt glad to make because he could replace the china and silver in Paris for less than Madison was paying. For Madison, on the other hand, the arrangement might have been something of a strain. He had explained to a visitor the previous summer that after he had covered expenses for farming the land around Montpelier, his profit was about equal to the amount he paid his caretaker. He did have a two-thousand-acre tract farther away, but the income from it, the secretary of state said, was "very fluctuating."[25]

At the same time that Madison was acquiring table settings from Monroe, he was also buying a dark green silver-monogrammed carriage fitted out with venetian blinds and candleholders. The Madisons probably justified these purchases as investments in their expanding social life, which in Washington, they were discovering, was usually indistinguishable from political life. Now living in a three-story brickhouse on F Street, the Madisons had begun to entertain, and in a way quite different from Jefferson's. The president had small dinner parties of a dozen or so, usually stag affairs, but when women were to be in attendance, he often invited Mrs. Madison and her sister Anna Payne to act as hostesses. At first Jefferson's dinners were bipartisan, but he didn't like debate at his dinner table and was soon hosting gatherings where the dinner guests were of the same party. Even then, he let it be known, he did not want politics discussed. The Madisons, on the other hand, mixed men and women, as well as Federalists and Republicans, and they had no objections to crowds or political discussions. John Quincy Adams, a Federalist, wrote in his diary of a February party at the Madisons' where "there was a company of about seventy persons of both sexes." Adams reported that he "had considerable conversation with Mr. Madison on the subjects now most important to the public."[26]

People enjoyed coming to the Madisons' in large part because of Dolley's seemingly artless charm. "Very amiable and exceedingly pleasant and sensible in conversation," the Reverend Manasseh Cutler pronounced her. At dinners she served southern comfort food, such as ham surrounded by mashed cabbage. After tea, she might have card tables set up. A favorite game was loo, and ladies failing to take a necessary trick would daintily announce, "I've been loo'd."[27] In his home and among people he knew, the secretary of state dropped his public reserve and was warm and witty. Republicans grew closer to him in such a setting, and Federalists, having accepted his hospitality, might have found it a little harder to demonize him.

AS MONROE was sailing to France, the peace accord between the British and the French was falling apart. Napoleon added the financial requirements of war resuming with Britain to two other circumstances: the French catastrophe in Saint Domingue and the clear message he was getting from the United States that his plans for an empire in the Western Hemisphere would meet staunch resistance. He heard this not only from his diplomats, who reported on their Washington conversations, but from the press. One recent story told of a congressional effort to authorize the president to seize New Orleans. On Monday, April 11, 1803, Napoleon called in one of his ministers, Barbé-Marbois, who had been Madison's companion on the Mohawk valley excursion some two decades before. "I renounce Louisiana," the first consul told Barbé-Marbois. "It is not only New Orleans that I cede; it is the whole colony without reserve." In a letter to Madison, Livingston reported a meeting with Talleyrand in which the foreign minister inquired whether the United States wanted to buy all of Louisiana. Livingston told him no, he reported to Madison. His instructions didn't encompass such a purchase. But Livingston soon came to his senses, and after Monroe's arrival a deal was struck. In documents dated April 30, 1803 (though actually signed some days later), the United States purchased the 828,000 square miles of French Louisiana for fifteen million dollars.[28]

Word of the purchase began to arrive in the United States at the end of June, and official news of it followed not long after, enclosed in a letter to Madison. The public announcement was made on July 3, 1803, and there was widespread acknowledgment that this was, as Madison described it, "a truly noble acquisition." After years of struggle, the United States had gained control of the mouth of the Mississippi and nearly doubled its territory in the process. "This mighty event forms an era in our history and of itself must render the administration of Jefferson immortal," wrote the newspaper editor Samuel Harrison Smith. The Fourth of July began in Washington City with an eighteen-gun salute. The anniversary of independence was one of two days each year when Jefferson opened the executive mansion to the public, and in 1803 citizens flocked to see their president. As they celebrated one of the most momentous events in the nation's history, Meriwether Lewis was finishing up preparations to set out from Washington City to begin his fabled expedition with William Clark. The trip, months in the planning, was more compelling now than ever. The Corps of Discovery would be exploring lands that were now part of the United States.[29]

WHILE THOMAS JEFFERSON was overseeing the historic acquisition of Louisiana, James Callender was making every effort to destroy him. On September 1, 1802, a Callender essay on the president in the *Richmond Recorder* had declared, "It is well known that the man, *whom it delighteth the people to honor,* keeps and for many years has kept as his concubine one of his slaves. Her name is Sally." Callender's article, picked up by the Federalist press, led to an outpouring of bawdy verse, including one ditty to be sung to the tune of "Yankee Doodle":

Of all the damsels on the green,
On mountain, or in valley,
A lass so luscious ne'er was seen,
As Monticellian Sally.

Jefferson's daughters gathered around him, coming to Washington in late November, but the salacious rhymes and vicious commentary did not stop and even gained new energy when Thomas Paine, *"the greatest infidel on earth,"* as one newspaper called him, took up a two-week residence at the president's house. Jefferson's enemies lumped them together as blasphemers and atheists, and one balladeer suggested that Paine, too, was sleeping with Sally.[30]

Jefferson refused to address Callender's charge about Hemings but found it necessary to take action when Callender enthusiastically promoted another theme: that Jefferson had made unwanted advances to a married woman, Betsey Walker, many years before. Mrs. Walker's embarrassed husband, John, decided that the situation was an affair of honor, and Madison helped with damage control. Jefferson and Walker met at Montpelier to sort things out, and Madison was able to report to Monroe on April 20, 1803, that a duel had been averted. Putting many of his words into cipher, he wrote, "The affair between the president and J. Walker has had a happy éclaircissement."[31]

The enormous significance of the acquisition of Louisiana helped the administration move beyond James Callender and his stories about Jefferson's intimate life, as did Callender's death just a few weeks after word of the purchase reached Washington. Callender drowned in three feet of water in the James River in what the coroner's jury ruled was an accident caused by his being intoxicated. One of Jefferson's friends thought it was suicide, an explanation that fits what must have been Callender's psychological situation.[32] He had tried to bring down a powerful man he had hated beyond measure and no doubt thought that he had the information to do it. How it must have stung to see Jefferson move onward and upward, to ever greater glory.

During a visit to Monticello a year or so after the scandal, Dolley Madison, so the story is told, promised Sally Hemings a gift if she could name Hemings's newborn child. Hemings consented, and Dolley, according to Sally's son, "dubbed me by the name I now acknowledge"— which was Madison. Sally's children had been named after people important to Jefferson. Was Dolley slyly acknowledging the naming pattern with her suggestion and perhaps as well indicating an understanding of the reason behind it? Southern white women typically wore blinders when it came to masters sleeping with slaves, but one wonders if Dolley grew momentarily weary of the pretense. Of course, something simpler might have been at work, but Dolley was not a simple person. Whatever the explanation, Madison Hemings later wrote that his mother never received the gift Mrs. Madison had promised: "Like many promises of white folks to the slaves she never gave my mother anything."[33]

LIKE MOST GREAT EVENTS, the acquisition of Louisiana was not over when it was announced. There was contention about who should get the credit, and Madison had to soothe Monroe, who was aggrieved by what he perceived as Livingston's self-promotion. There was also concern that the Floridas had not been part of the bargain and still belonged to Spain. It was generally agreed at a July 16 cabinet meeting, however, that after the purchase of Louisiana, "they cannot fail to fall into our hands." Indeed, Robert Livingston had already advised that by reading past treaties, it was possible to make a case that West Florida was part of the purchase. Madison would hold fast to this interpretation in the years ahead.[34]

For the moment the biggest stumbling block was Jefferson's worry that in the absence of a specific provision in the Constitution about acquiring territory, the purchase might not be strictly constitutional. To Madison it was obvious that the United States, like any nation, had the right to acquire territory. He agreed with Gallatin, who pointed out to the president that the Constitution provided for the admission of new states and gave the power to make treaties (such as the one executing the purchase of Louisiana) to the president and Congress. But Jefferson continued to worry, indeed over-worry, the matter. If the United States could acquire Louisiana, what was next? the president wanted to know. Ireland? Holland? He wanted to amend the Constitution to take the matter of Louisiana into account, and even though Madison did not think it was necessary, he dutifully offered advice: namely, that the amendment should not preclude the United States from acquiring further territory, such as the Floridas.[35]

On August 17, Jefferson received a letter at Monticello from Robert Livingston. Much of it was in a cipher that he did not have the key to decode, but what he could read worried him, and he sent the letter on to Madison the next day. Were the French threatening to retract their offer if there was a delay in ratification? Madison did not think that was the intent, and Jefferson continued to work on a constitutional amendment, but he was convinced now that it would be best to keep his concerns about constitutional complications "sub silentio." If the French were even the least uneasy, they should not be further alarmed. It was not until the Madisons visited Monticello in September, however, that the president dropped his plan for amending the Constitution.[36]

When Jefferson addressed the matter of the treaty with Congress in October 1803, he indicated that once ratified, the treaty would be "constitutionally confirmed." Not everyone agreed. Timothy Pickering of Massachusetts, now a Federalist senator, declared the president and the Senate were not "competent to such an act of incorporation." Senator Uriah Tracy of Connecticut agreed. Representative Roger Griswold of Connecticut let slip that it was not just the constitutionality of the purchase that troubled New England Federalists but "the destruction of that balance . . . between the eastern and western states" which, he said, "threatens at no very distant day the subversion of our Union." William Plumer of New Hampshire raised the stakes even higher. "Admit this western world into the Union," he said, "and you destroy at once the weight and importance of the eastern states and compel them to establish a separate, independent empire." Jefferson dismissed such talk, but this was not the last time there would be discussion among New Englanders about creating a northern confederacy.[37]

The Senate voted in favor of the treaty by 24 to 7, and the historic deed was done. It was, Henry Adams later observed, "an event so portentous as to defy measurement; it . . . ranked in historical importance next to the Declaration of Independence and the adoption of the Constitution—events of which it was the logical outcome."[38]

PARTICULARLY IN CONTRAST with the annexation of Louisiana, the decision handed down by the Supreme Court in *Marbury v. Madison* seemed at the time of little significance. William Marbury, a self-made man and Adams loyalist, was one of the "midnight" justices whom

John Adams appointed during his last days in office. The Federalist Senate confirmed his appointment on Adams's last day as president, but after Jefferson assumed office and found that Marbury's commission had still not been delivered, he ordered that it be withheld. Marbury subsequently sought from the Supreme Court a writ of mandamus that would compel Secretary of State Madison to deliver his commission. In 1803, the court issued its opinion, saying that Marbury was entitled to the commission but that the Supreme Court could not issue the writ because the section of the Judiciary Act of 1789 that would have permitted the court to do so was unconstitutional. On the surface, the outcome seemed positive for the Jefferson administration. Madison did not have to deliver the commission. But Marshall's decision also allowed the chief justice to avoid direct confrontation with the administration, which was riding high, even while pointing out that the president, whom he despised as only one Virginian cousin could another, had broken the law.[39]

Most important, in the decision Marshall declared, "It is emphatically the province and duty of the judicial department to say what the law is," thus establishing a platform on which the giant superstructure of judicial review would be built. Madison did not believe that the Constitution sanctioned such a power. The Council of Revision that he had proposed in the Constitutional Convention, by giving the executive and the judiciary together final sign-off on legislation, would have precluded the possibility of the courts acting alone to decide constitutionality, but the council had been turned down, leaving "no provision . . . for the case of a disagreement in expounding [the laws]." In the absence of a provision, Madison saw that a pattern would develop: Congress would pass a law, the president sign it (thereby offering his opinion that it was constitutional), and the courts take the last word, thereby stamping the law "with its final character." Observed Madison in 1788, "This makes the judiciary department paramount in fact to the legislature, which was never intended and can never be proper."[40]

By the time of *Marbury,* Madison was becoming somewhat reconciled to the arrangement, largely because there was no reasonable alternative, but he was hardly so satisfied with it that he felt obliged to acknowledge Marshall's authority to make the decision he had.[41] Thus the defendant in what would become the most celebrated case in American judicial history left no recorded reaction to it, thereby lending support to the notion abroad at the time that there was nothing earthshaking about it.

LATE IN 1803, a full-blown minister arrived in Washington to represent Great Britain. Anthony Merry and his wife had a difficult journey, encountering rough weather in the last stages, and once they arrived in Washington City, matters seemed only to grow worse. There were the challenges of the raw capital, which many a newcomer considered unfit for habitation. Not a single house was deemed suitable for the Merrys, and they finally combined two residences into one for their quarters. And then there was the president, given to wearing two vests, one red and threadbare and the other described as "grey-colored" and "hairy," with an old brown coat over the top of both. His favorite stockings were yarn and his favorite shoes a pair of slip-ons. He was known to cross his legs and dangle a shoe off his toes while he was seated. Both his breeches and his linen were on different occasions described as soiled, and he seems to have placed little importance upon combing his hair.[42] One can well imagine the shock of Minister Merry, dressed in full diplomatic uniform, encountering the carelessly clad Jefferson when he presented his credentials.

Merry's secretary, Augustus John Foster, was sure that Jefferson, who had attended the most sophisticated salons of Paris, knew better but was chasing popularity by dressing like the masses, and there was probably truth in his assessment, though as far as the soiled shirts and uncombed hair are concerned, Jefferson might simply have been suffering from having no wife.[43] But when it came to his clothing generally, he probably had an idea of trying to appear as befitted a citizen of the Republic, particularly one living in what was essentially a rural setting—and he wasn't about to make an exception to his dress, especially not for a minister from Britain.

Jefferson was similarly relaxed when it came to the dinners he gave. Instead of worrying about rank and precedence when it was time to move to the table, he turned to the woman who was serving as hostess for him and led her into dinner. Minister Merry and his wife arrived at the president's house to dine unaware of this habit and were shocked when Jefferson escorted Dolley Madison to the table rather than Elizabeth Merry. A few days later, dining at the Madisons', the Merrys suffered another blow. The Madisons were no doubt dressed properly—James, as was now his custom, in a black coat and breeches buckled at the knee, black silk stockings, and lace-up shoes, and Dolley in something low cut and elegant. But when it came time to move from the drawing room to the dining room, Secretary Madison turned to Hannah Gallatin and escorted her to dinner, rather than Elizabeth Merry. This was one insult too many for the minister, who decided that he and Mrs. Merry would attend no more official events unless his government instructed him otherwise.[44]

Madison tried to control the damage, writing to Rufus King, who had just recently returned from representing the United States at the Court of St. James's. Could he spell out what the rules were there? King replied that foreign ministers were seldom invited to royal entertainments, but when the king had his annual levee, the rule, with some exceptions, was pell-mell—which basically meant there was no rule. At dinners in "higher English circles," King reported, the ladies left the drawing room for the dining room first, followed by the gentlemen. With this information, Madison went to the president, who agreed that in the future, when crowds were involved, he would adhere to pell-mell practice. He even worked with Madison to sketch out rules of etiquette. At dinners, the rule would be "gentlemen in mass giving precedence to the ladies in mass, in passing from one apartment where they are assembled into another."[45]

Madison sat Merry down for a long talk, probably in his small office in the brick building next to the president's house, where the Department of Foreign Affairs was now headquartered, and the minister spilled out all his complaints, but what he regarded as the insult to his wife loomed largest. All questions of rank aside, she was a newcomer and for that reason alone deserved special courtesy, Merry said. Madison expressed his personal sympathy: "At my own house in private life, it is probable that Mrs. Merry as a stranger would have received the first attention." He explained that he was not a private citizen, however, but secretary of state in the Jefferson administration. "I had thought it most proper not to deviate from the established course," that is, the one set by the president.[46]

Madison told Merry that he and his wife had been treated no differently from others who had attended the president's dinners over the last three years and that the practice of pell-mell, to which the administration would henceforth adhere at crowded events, was also used in England. Merry refused to be placated, saying only that "he should conform to our ideas if so instructed." Not long after his meeting with Madison, the minister was thrown into another tizzy when he heard about a party at the president's house attended by Napoleon's brother Jérôme Bonaparte and his new wife, the former Elizabeth Patterson of Baltimore. The president, rather than escorting a cabinet wife into dinner, had offered his arm to Mrs. Bonaparte, thereby, as the Merrys saw it, according the wife of a French visitor the treatment that he had not accorded Mrs. Merry. In the middle of the battle over precedence, escorting Mrs. Bonaparte into dinner was not the most tactful thing Jefferson could have done. It suggests that he took some delight at sending the Merrys into a tizzy, but he might simply have been delighting in Mrs. Bonaparte. She was gorgeous and given to wearing dresses so transparent that she nearly launched another front in the etiquette war. Several high-ranking Washington women threatened to quit attending parties where she would be present unless she wore more clothing.[47]

Madison wrote a letter of great length to James Monroe, who had replaced Rufus King as the U.S. minister to Great Britain, explaining the contretemps in great detail. "I blush at having put so much trash on paper," he wrote. But foolish as the affair was, the diplomatic fire had to be extinguished, and Madison was giving Monroe information he needed to work the problem from the British side. Madison continued to meet frequently with Merry, refusing to let the social contretemps lead to a break in communications. He might have rounded out his work on what became known as the Merry Affair by dropping a tactful hint or two to the president about his apparel. By the end of the year, Jefferson was looking "well dressed," Senator William Plumer of New Hampshire reported. He was wearing "a new suit of black, silk hose, shoes, clean linen, and his hair highly powdered."[48] In other words, he was dressed much as Madison habitually was.

AARON BURR had become Jefferson's vice president despite Jefferson's suspicions about him. His ambition was entirely too obvious for Jefferson's taste, but Burr's work to put New York in the Republican column had earned him his place on the ticket. After the tied election, which Jefferson suspected Burr of trying to manipulate to his advantage, Jefferson made clear his lack of faith in his vice president by not appointing Burr's right-hand man and faithful friend, Matthew Livingston Davis, to a high post that Burr sought for him. Albert Gallatin worried about the consequences of this "declaration of war." If this was a signal that Burr was not to be the Republican candidate for vice president at the next election, then whom was the party going to nominate? Madison was the obvious choice, but he was from Virginia, and electors from that state could not vote for two Virginians. "Mr. Madison cannot on that occasion be supported with you," Gallatin wrote to the president. The party could stick with Burr, but if that was the intent, why make him furious, stir up the Federalists, and incite a plot that might make Burr, with both Republican and Federalist votes, president in the next election?[49]

By 1804, there was no longer any possibility of Burr's being on the ticket. A widower, he had been under steady attack as a libertine who seduced and corrupted both men and women. Burr ignored these charges, which he blamed on political rivals in New York, but he felt obliged to deny accusations that he had "crouched and fawned and surrendered himself" to Federalists in 1800 in an attempt to wrest the presidency from Jefferson. Burr went to see the president and told him that his main reason for agreeing to the vice presidential nomination had been a desire to promote Jefferson's "fame and advancement, and from a desire to be with [Jefferson], whose company and conversation had always been fascinating to him." Jefferson was having none of it, Burr saw the writing on the wall, and on February 18, 1804, his friends announced his candidacy for governor of New York. A week later, the Republican congressional caucus unanimously nominated Jefferson for president and by a two-thirds vote chose George Clinton of New York as the vice presidential nominee. Burr received not a single vote.[50]

Jefferson might well have urged the choice of Clinton not only because he brought regional balance to the ticket but because he was unlikely to stand in Madison's way when it came time for the presidential election of 1808. The New York governor would be sixty-nine that year, and while he had once been a man of powerful physique, age had diminished him. Indeed, he had explained to Jefferson that his reason for not seeking reelection in New York was so that the governorship might be filled "with some suitable character not so far advanced in years and enjoying a better share of health."[51]

Madison's health, meanwhile, had markedly improved. After reporting a "pretty severe interruption" due to an "attack" in early 1802, he gives no indication in his letters of sudden attacks for the rest of that year or for 1803 and 1804. What he had once seemed to view as an "*insuperable*" obstacle to the presidency might no longer have appeared that way.[52] He had seen the presidency up close and knew he could do justice to it. Indeed, he'd had his differences with the presidents he had known, Jefferson included, and probably thought he could do better. It was not the custom of the time to make announcements or even drop hints, but by the time Clinton became the vice presidential nominee, every indication is that Madison as well as Jefferson viewed Madison as the heir apparent.

THE SUMMER OF 1804 was a good time to be a Republican. "Our affairs continue on a prosperous train," Madison reported to Monroe. "The tide of opinion is more and more favorable to the administration."

Even in New England the Republicans were making advances. New Hampshire had a newly Republican legislature and had recently provided the vote necessary to complete ratification of the Twelfth Amendment, which would require electors to vote separately for president and vice president. There had been Federalist objections—that the quality of vice presidential candidates would diminish if they were on a separate ballot, that the office itself would become "the subject of barter"—but Republicans prevailed, ensuring that there would be no opportunity for the Federalist mischief that had caused such turmoil with the election of 1800.[53]

It was a sad time to be a Federalist, a member of a party that was, in Henry Adams's words, "prostrate, broken, and torn by dying convulsions." Since Jefferson's election, Alexander Hamilton, once high and powerful, had come to feel like a stranger in a strange land. He wrote to Gouverneur Morris, "Mine is an odd destiny. Perhaps no man in the United States has sacrificed or done more for the present Constitution than myself—and contrary to all my anticipations of its fate, as you know from the very beginning I am still laboring to prop the frail and worthless fabric. Yet I have the murmurs of its friends no less than the curses of its foes for my rewards. What can I do better than withdraw from the scene? Every day proves to me more and more that this American world was not made for me." But when Aaron Burr announced his candidacy for the governorship of New York, Hamilton could not stay out of the political fray. Although some Federalists hoped that a win for Burr would place him in a position to lead northern states in an effective opposition to Virginia, Hamilton thought he was dangerous and didn't hesitate to say so. His comments made it into print, and after Burr lost the election for governor, he sought Hamilton's disavowal of his harsh words, which Hamilton would not provide. And so it was that on a cool July morning, Burr and Hamilton met on the dueling ground at Weehawken. Both men fired, Hamilton fell, and the next day he was dead.[54]

At the end of the year, when electoral votes were counted, Thomas Jefferson was reelected president of the United States by 162 to 14. It was a time of nearly complete victory that Madison as well as Jefferson must have found thrilling, but like most heady moments this one contained hints of trouble ahead. Some were coming from abroad, where Great Britain, at war once more with France, was in need of naval manpower. With increasing frequency its ships were stopping American vessels and demanding that all on board muster for inspection by a British officer, who would decide which of the sailors would be impressed for service in the Royal Navy. In truth, there were many British deserters serving aboard American ships, where both conditions and pay were better, but the British, not recognizing the right of a citizen to expatriate and adopt another nationality, also seized many who had been born in Britain and become naturalized Americans. In the sweep to man the British fleet, many who had been born in the United States were impressed as well. A man's fate could depend on how he pronounced the word "peas." If he said "pase," odds were he would be seized.[55]

Closer to home, fissures in the Republican Party were becoming evident. Southern conservatives, particularly in Virginia, were increasingly convinced that the Jefferson administration was too accommodating. It was not carrying on the fight to minimize federal power with sufficient vigor. When the most influential conservatives assigned blame for this drift away from principle, James Madison's was the name they mentioned first, and by the time Jefferson was sworn in for his second term, they were searching for someone who could keep the secretary of state from becoming his successor.[56]

Chapter 14

PORTRAITS

"STUART IS ALL THE RAGE," one woman reported. "He is almost worked to death, and everybody afraid that they will be the last to be finished." In 1804 and 1805, a steady stream of carriages brought Washington dignitaries and their wives to a two-room studio just off Pennsylvania Avenue where the famed Gilbert Stuart was painting furiously. Among those sitting for him were the secretary of state and Mrs. Madison, he fifty-three and she thirty-five, but in their portraits the age difference is not apparent. Stuart, known for flattering his subjects, overlooked the web of fine wrinkles that was beginning to give Madison's face a parchment-like quality and perhaps a few other signs of middle age as well. "Quite pretty he has made us," Dolley Madison declared.[1]

Stuart's portrait of Madison captures the "self-possession" that Jefferson, who knew Madison so well, described, but one can also see why people first meeting Madison found him daunting. The man in the black suit, white shirt, and white cravat looking out from the canvas is the man of whom Brissot de Warville wrote after a 1788 introduction, "His look announces a censor." This is, one imagines, the face Madison presented to young George Tucker, who was disconcerted by his "sternness" when he met Madison at Monroe's home sometime around 1800. Madison's expression was probably occasioned in no small part by Stuart himself, who tried to relax his subjects with a steady stream of chatter—a tactic that would probably have made Madison more standoffish. In this 1804 portrait, Stuart caught the public man, who was, his friends agreed, quite different from the private person. Friends saw twinkling eyes and a smile that lit up his face. They heard him joke and laugh and provoke laughter in others. After Tucker had known him for a long time, he wrote, "He had an unfailing good humor and a lively relish for the ludicrous which imprinted everything comic on his memory and thus enabled him to vary and enliven his conversation with an exhaustless fund of anecdote."[2]

For her portrait, Dolley wore a cream-colored gown with an extremely low neckline, as was the latest French fashion. This portrait, later displayed in the White House, would be, at least until the time of this book, unmatched among paintings of first ladies for the amount of flesh displayed and the apparent absence of underpinnings. Dolley looks out from the painting unfazed by the exposure, although very self-aware. Looking at the portrait, one understands why her niece Mary Cutts noted that her mouth "was beautiful in shape and expression." Her upper lip is a perfect Cupid's bow, and her slight smile wonderfully enigmatic.[3]

Dolley's younger sister Anna also went to Stuart's studio. Both she and her new husband, Congressman Richard Cutts of Massachusetts, a stolid fellow, had their portraits done. In hers, Anna wears a gown cut as low as Dolley's, though she appears less comfortable in it. By the time he painted Anna Cutts, Stuart might, despite all the décolletage, have grown a little weary of painting women seated in his studio armchair, their hands folded in their laps. The billowing drapery behind Mrs. Cutts forms a profile, one with a prominent nose. Stuart later admitted that the profile was his own, thus acknowledging that he had entertained himself by putting himself into the Cutts portrait.[4]

The British minister and Mrs. Anthony Merry also visited Stuart. Dolley Madison had called Mrs. Merry, who was widely blamed for being at the bottom of the imbroglio over precedence, a "strange lass," but her portrait shows a handsome, confident woman. In contrast to the French fashion worn by Dolley Madison and her sister, Elizabeth Merry wears a white chemisette tucked into her bodice so that it rises up to cover her bosom and frame her face.[5] Stuart also painted Spanish minister Don Carlos Martínez de Yrujo y Tacón and his wife, the former Sally McKean. The marquis, possibly displaying more arrogance than anyone else Stuart ever painted, has his hand tucked in his jacket in the fashion Napoleon made famous. His wife, who had grown up with Dolley Madison in Philadelphia and remained her good friend, wears a gown in the French style.

The Merry and Yrujo portraits, particularly in the contrasting dress of the wives, could be seen as symbolizing the breach between Britain, which was at war with France, and Spain, which was essentially a French satellite. But on one point the British and Spanish ministers were in accord. They were furious with the United States. Yrujo had taken Merry's side in the dispute over protocol and even poured oil on the fire with suggestions of events they might boycott. A volatile man, Yrujo was enraged by U.S. claims that West Florida had been part of the Louisiana Purchase, so much so that at one point he stormed into Madison's State Department office and loudly upbraided the secretary. To protest American policy, he pulled up stakes in Washington and moved to Philadelphia—but only after he and his wife had finished their sittings with Stuart.[6]

Yrujo was a minor problem for Madison compared with another of Stuart's subjects: John Randolph of Roanoke, a Virginian who hailed from a plantation called Bizarre. In Stuart's painting, Randolph looks like a dark-eyed schoolboy, though he is thirty-one. A youthful illness had arrested his sexual development, leaving him beardless and with a high-pitched voice. He was apparently impotent, but woe be it to anyone who tried to embarrass him about it. When one enemy taunted him for being sexually incapable, Randolph responded, "Does the honorable gentleman mean to boast *here in this place* a superiority over me in those parts of our nature which we partake in common with the brutes?

I readily yield it to him. I doubt not his animal propensities or endow-
ments."[7] A brilliant man, Randolph developed a scathing oratorical
style, and he used it—and threats of duels—to intimidate, which made
him an effective if unloved leader in Congress. As chairman of the Ways
and Means Committee, he had at first served the Jefferson administration well and faithfully, but then he turned his vitriol on Secretary of
State James Madison.

Madison's original sin was to serve, together with Albert Gallatin
and Levi Lincoln, the attorney general, on a commission to sort out the
great Yazoo landgrab. The scandal had begun when the Georgia legislature sold its "western lands"—most of what is today Mississippi and
Alabama—for pennies an acre to speculative groups called the Yazoo
companies. Georgia voters, realizing they had been swindled, elected a
new legislature that repealed the contract, even though in the meantime
lands had been sold to third parties who stood to lose from the over-
turned sale even if they had no part in the corruption. Madison and the
other two federal commissioners agreed to a compromise whereby
Georgia, in return for ceding all the lands between its western border
and the Mississippi River to the federal government, would receive $1.25
million. The commissioners thoroughly documented the corruption
involved in the original transaction—every member of the legislature
who had supported the sale, save one, had been bribed—but recommended nonetheless that five million of the thirty-five million acres
deeded to the United States be set aside and used to settle claims arising
out of that sale. Some of those settlements would go to Yazoo companies, and although they would get only a small portion of their claims,
the commissioners were likely aware that even that would excite controversy. But the Yazoo companies, shady though they might be, had to
be reckoned with. They had contracts—which the Constitution forbade
states to overturn.[8]

In Randolph's eyes, the commissioners' compromise was an "act of
stupendous villainy," which attempted "under the forms and semblance
of law to rob unborn millions of their birthright and inheritance." With
his unerring gift for spotting anything that even vaguely smacked of

hypocrisy, he denied that there were innocents involved. Those who had bought land in secondary sales had been gambling, he said. They had been speculators, many of them northern ones, no less, intent on taking advantage of the South.[9]

Randolph laced his accusations, in the words of Senator Plumer, who watched the House debate, with "allusions to brothel-houses and pig sties," the kind of language no member wanted directed toward him. With his intimidating tactics, Randolph kept the Yazoo matter from being settled for years. Agreement would be reached only after the Supreme Court ruled in 1810 that the Georgia Repeal Act was unconstitutional. But in the meantime Randolph gained an epithet to hurl at Madison. "Yazoo man," he called him, ignoring the fact that Secretary of the Treasury Albert Gallatin probably had more to do with the compromise recommendations than did the secretary of state. Randolph's focus on Madison, the biographer Irving Brant suggested, lies "in the realm of psychiatry." Jefferson's biographer Dumas Malone offered a general concurrence: "It would be impossible to give a wholly rational interpretation of the conduct of as neurotic a person as the Majority Leader."[10]

But there were ideological differences that Randolph would enthusiastically point out in the years ahead and personality differences as well. Randolph, a most immoderate man, hated what he called Madison's "cold and insidious moderation." The impeachment trial of Justice Samuel Chase was a case in point, with Randolph making a deep emotional investment in the outcome while Madison stood safely aloof. Jefferson, having heard of Chase's delivering a political harangue to a grand jury in Baltimore, privately suggested that Congress do something about the associate justice. A willing Randolph led the way to a House vote of 73 to 32 to impeach Chase, who had a long record of highly partisan and deeply intemperate behavior, and in February 1805, after Jefferson had been reelected but before he was sworn in, Randolph presented the case against Chase at an impeachment trial in the Senate. Vice President Aaron Burr, under indictment in two states for killing Hamilton, presided, and senators seated themselves to his right and left on crimson-covered benches. When Justice Chase appeared, white-haired, red-faced, and suffering from gout, he was directed to a box in front of and to the left of the vice president. Randolph, from a box opposite, set forth articles that related, among other things, to Chase's "highly indecent" charge to the Baltimore grand jury and the "spirit of persecution and injustice" he had exhibited in the trial of Jefferson's nemesis James Callender.[11]

Randolph was a gifted orator, but he was no lawyer, and he was up against some very good ones, including Luther Martin, the famously bibulous and passionate Marylander who had filibustered at the Constitutional Convention. Randolph's speeches in favor of impeachment reached moments of eloquence, but they failed to refute Martin's arguments. Indeed, Randolph had an almost impossible case to make. Chase might have been unfit to be a judge, but that did not mean he was guilty of "treason, bribery, or other high crimes and misdemeanors," the standards set forth for impeachment in the Constitution. At the end, realizing he had lost, Randolph broke down, with "much distortion of face and contortion of body, tears, groans, and sobs," as Senator John Quincy Adams described it.[12] The prosecution managed to get a majority vote in the Senate on three of the eight articles of impeachment, but on no article was there the necessary two-thirds vote to convict.

Chagrined, Randolph rushed over to the House of Representatives, where he denounced Chase and the Senate and proposed an amendment to the Constitution that would allow the president to remove a judge upon a majority vote requesting him to do so by both houses of Congress. Another of the impeachment trial managers proposed an amendment that would allow state legislatures to recall senators and declare their seats vacant. Neither motion had the slightest chance of passing, and later that evening Senator Adams, encountering Secretary of State Madison at a social event, noted that the secretary "appeared much diverted at the petulance of the managers on their disappointment." Whether word of Madison's amusement reached Randolph is uncertain, but it would have been crystal clear to him that neither Madison nor the president intended to defend him. When a group sympathetic to the impeachment wrote to Madison to protest that he had not condemned Chase's acquittal, he replied that it would be improper for cabinet officers "to pronounce for public use their opinion of the issue, however little disposed they may be to reserve."[13] It was a perfectly valid point, but Randolph must have felt, to use modern political parlance, that he had been hung out to dry.

One might have expected Jefferson to be the object of Randolph's anger. He, after all, had suggested that something be done about Chase, only to cut Randolph loose when the impeachment trial failed to convict. But the president had just overwhelmingly won a second term, and his popularity made him an uninviting target. It was Madison, who had remained invisible as far as the impeachment proceedings were concerned, whom Randolph blamed.[14]

Particularly after Jefferson let it be known that he had no intention of running for a third term, Randolph and his allies turned their fire on the secretary of state. Was the central government growing too strong at the expense of the states? Blame Madison. Was our foreign policy wrongheaded? Again Madison was to blame. Randolph and his allies cast Madison, as biographer Ralph Ketcham described it, "in the role of the evil genius who debauched the president from his principles."[15] The secretary of state was, without doubt, influential, but even at this early stage in the nation's history, politicians understood the advantages of blaming what they perceived to be an administration's shortcomings on someone other than the president. Such an approach managed two things at once: making the person blamed seem threatening while simultaneously making the president look weak.

IN THE SPRING OF 1805, Dolley Madison developed a painful abscess on her knee that would not heal. She was confined to bed, doctors were called in, and they applied a caustic paste to the abscess to cauterize it. A month later, however, she was still writing to her sister Anna Payne Cutts from bed. The growth had advanced to "a dangerous state," she told Anna. But then it seemed to improve, and the Madisons hoped to travel to Montpelier in mid-July.[16]

Instead, they found themselves on the road to Philadelphia so that Dolley's knee, grown worse again, could be treated by one of the most famous doctors of the day, Philip Syng Physick. Because riding in a carriage was one of the few activities Mrs. Madison could undertake, she enjoyed the journey—until James was stricken. As Dolley described the awful event to her sister Anna, "On our way one night he [was] taken very ill with his old bilious complaint. I thought all was over with me. I could not fly to him and aid him as I used to do—but heaven in its mercy restored him next morning." Although James had apparently not had a sudden attack in three years, he pretty clearly had one on this trip. Dolley's language indicates her urgency, even panic, as well as something of his symptoms, with the phrase "restored him" suggesting that he was temporarily not himself—as he would not have been had his "intellectual functions" been suspended. The word "bilious" ties this event to others in the past, including the "bilious attack" at the Virginia ratifying convention in 1788, Madison's concern about "a bilious attack to which I am become very subject" in 1790, his worries about "symptoms of bile" in 1791, and a "slight attack of bile to which my constitution is peculiarly prone" in 1801.[17] Referring to bile, as people had done since ancient times in connection with epilepsy, seems to have become a way of talking about his sudden attacks. Friends would know what he meant, and those not well acquainted with him would not be given too much information.

Madison seems to have recovered quickly, and he and Mrs. Madison continued on their way, but once she was settled in Dr. Physick's care, she started worrying. Three years since his last attack was long enough to have grown complacent, and the shock of what was apparently another filled her with sudden dread. She told a friend that she was "often miserable with fears" for her husband's health. Both James and their friends in Philadelphia tried to laugh her anxieties away and convince her they were both safe, and after a time she seemed to grow more confident.[18]

Dr. Physick splinted Mrs. Madison's leg so that she had to lie flat in bed and applied caustic three times, "a sad thing to feel," Dolley wrote, "but it does everything that the knife could do." In the end, although she resisted it, Physick performed minor surgery, and both Madisons settled in, waiting for her to heal.[19] Committed as he was to his work, Madison stayed in Philadelphia for three months.

MADISON HEARD FROM MONROE, who had been delegated to affirm U.S. claims to Florida. Spain would not act without French approval, Monroe had found, and the French foreign minister, Talleyrand, was contradicting the American position that West Florida was part of the territory purchased by the United States. Closer to home, there were also signs that Napoleon, who had declared himself emperor, was intent on a new and tougher approach. He had appointed a new French minister to the United States, General Louis-Marie Turreau, who arrived in America with a reputation for being cruel as a soldier and profligate in his private life. His beefy face inspired Senator Plumer to attribute "a ferocious disposition" to him, and his domestic life seemed to prove the point. Dolley Madison wrote to her sister that Turreau "whipped his wife and abused her before all his servants." Senator Plumer recorded an incident in which Turreau's wife hit him with an iron and he beat her with a cane. In a vain effort to cover the shouting and shrieking that ensued, the legation secretary opened a window and played frantically on his French horn.[20]

Jefferson worried that the collapse of negotiations over who owned West Florida meant war, either with Spain or with its sponsor, France. The United States ought to seek a treaty of alliance with England, he wrote to Madison. He pressed the matter for a second time on August 7, 1805, then again in ten days with even greater urgency: "Should negotiations with England be advisable, they should not be postponed a day unnecessarily." When Madison responded that U.S. "conduct towards Great Britain is delicate as it is important" and warned that an alliance with Britain would draw the United States into war against France, Jefferson protested that he had meant a provisional alliance, one that would go into effect only if the United States became engaged in a war with France or Spain. Madison continued to demur, pointing out that there was no advantage to England in such an agreement, and although Madison's recalcitrance might have annoyed another man, Jefferson listened. When Mrs. Madison's knee would still not permit her to return to Washington in early October and Madison had to miss a scheduled cabinet meeting, Jefferson assured him that no decision would be reached in his absence. The subject of seeking alliance with Britain was "too important and too difficult to be decided but on the fullest consideration," he wrote, "in which your aid and counsel should be waited for."[21]

Madison turned to books, as he had so often done. Using volumes he had brought with him to Philadelphia as well as others he borrowed, he worked furiously on a treatise intended to show the illegality of British navigation policy. His target was the Rule of 1756, which forbade neutrals such as the United States to engage in shipping that was not open to them in peacetime, most importantly between the West Indies and Europe. The British had been allowing American ships to evade this rule by stopping in the United States with their cargoes and reexporting them from there, but in 1805 an Admiralty court ruled such "broken voyages" a violation. American vessels carrying goods between France and Spain and their Caribbean colonies were now subject to seizure, even if they off-loaded and reloaded their cargoes in an American port. While Madison waited with Dolley for her knee to heal, he produced a document of seventy thousand words demonstrating the lack of basis in international law for the Rule of 1756. When Jefferson saw the result, he declared the British rule "pulverized."[22]

The Royal Navy, unimpressed by Madison's logic, stepped up ship seizures. Britain also continued to impress sailors from American merchant ships. As these actions doomed the possibility of a British alliance, President Jefferson's thoughts turned again to France and Spain. Perhaps remembering 1803, when Napoleon, under war pressure, ceded Louisiana, Jefferson and his cabinet decided to try to resume negotiations about Louisiana's boundaries, this time with money on the table. Since Spain was indebted to France, Napoleon might encourage Spain to accept an American offer for the Floridas—five million dollars, say—which it could then use to pay off its debts to France. But if the administration saw this new effort as based on what had worked in the case of Louisiana, John Randolph saw it as a repeat of the XYZ Affair, only this time the United States was volunteering to bribe the French. When he was shown a plan that proposed a partial payment of two million dollars, he peremptorily declared that he would not vote a single shilling for it.[23]

DOLLEY'S KNEE had healed sufficiently for Madison to leave Philadelphia for Washington toward the end of October, expecting that she would be able to follow soon. James had scarcely departed before Dolley began a letter to him. "A few hours only have passed since you left me my beloved," she wrote, "and I find nothing can relieve the oppression of my mind but speaking to you in this *only* way." His departure had stirred up her worries about him, but "three or four drops of laudanum" helped her calm down. She passed along Dr. Physick's compliments ("He says he regards you more than any man he ever knew and nothing could please him so much as passing his life near you") and closed her letter, "Adieu, my beloved, our hearts understand each other."[24]

In his letters, James tried to keep Dolley's spirits up, pretending to flirt with her friend Betsy Pemberton, who was staying with her. He sent her letters from her mother and her son, John Payne Todd, now thirteen, whom they both called Payne, and signed one of his letters "with unalterable love." She wrote to him, "To find you love me, have my child safe and that my mother is well seems to comprise all my happiness."[25]

He made considerable effort to secure a place for Payne at a Catholic school in Baltimore and asked his wife's permission to let his niece Nelly and her husband, John Willis, transport furniture in a wagon the Madisons were sending back to Montpelier. He located a pair of earrings someone had sent her as a gift and reminded her to insure the buildings she was renting out in Philadelphia. For the most part their communications are from one equal to another, but there is a change in Dolley's tone when she brings up politics. "I wish you would indulge me with some information respecting the war with Spain and disagreement with England," she wrote. "I am extremely anxious to hear (as far as you may think proper) what is going forward in the cabinet." Her way of assuring him that she had no intention of becoming an "active partisan" was to stress "her want of talents" and her "diffidence in expressing her opinions [on matters] always imperfectly understood by her sex."[26]

James did not reveal cabinet deliberations, but he paid respect to her inquiry by offering a prescient assessment: "If a general war takes place in Europe, Spain will probably be less disposed to insult us and England less sparing of her insults." He also reminded her that "the power . . . of deciding questions of war and providing measures that will make or meet it lies with Congress and," he added, "that is always our answer to newsmongers." If his tone was a trifle condescending, it is easy to understand the need he felt to caution her. Despite her ailing knee, Dolley had an active social life in Philadelphia. Among her callers were the Spanish minister the marquis de Yrujo and the French minister General Turreau. Finally, in late November, Dolley's knee had healed enough for her to travel. Accompanied by her sister Anna and Anna's husband, Richard Cutts, she returned to Washington and the husband she called her darling, her dearest, and her best friend.[27]

AS THE YEAR 1805 was coming to an end, word arrived that Lord Nelson had utterly defeated the French and Spanish fleets off Cape Trafalgar on the southwest coast of Spain. Jefferson, determined to find good news in the report, reflected that Napoleon still dominated on land: "Our wish ought to be that he who has armies may not have the dominion of the sea and that he who has dominion of the sea may be one who has no armies. In this way we may be quiet, at home at least." In his heart of hearts, Jefferson had to know this was wishful thinking. As long as Napoleon held sway on the Continent, the British were going to continue their crackdown on U.S. ships carrying goods to Europe, and that meant discontent at home. James Monroe reported from London that the seizure of American ships was not happening willy-nilly, but had become British policy. He also said that there was no indication of any desire on the part of the British government to end impressment. He speculated that these insults were at least in part a result of an opinion held by many "that the United States are by the nature of their government being popular incapable of any great, vigorous, or persevering exertion," and he recommended that the United States defend its interests "in a decisive manner."[28]

Jefferson forwarded this letter to Congress without recommending any course of action, much less a decisive one, perhaps because he did not want to be accused of violating the separation of powers. Whatever his motive, he created a situation ripe for Randolph to launch an attack on Madison. When Representative Andrew Gregg of Pennsylvania put forward a bill forbidding the import of British goods, Randolph demanded to know if this was a secret project of the administration and particularly of one secretive high official: "Is this a measure of the cabinet? Not of an open declared cabinet, but of an invisible, inscrutable, unconstitutional cabinet without responsibility, unknown to the Constitution. I speak of backstairs influence." Randolph claimed that when he had inquired about the opinion of the cabinet, he was told, "*There is no longer any cabinet,*" the meaning being that Madison was now so totally dominant that no one else mattered.[29]

In a rant that extended for two days, Randolph attacked the president and the secretary of state, using invective that one observer called "the most severe that the English language can furnish." Madison's treatise on the illegality of British navigation policy was a particular target. Calling it "a tangled cobweb of contradictions," Randolph read from it disdainfully, then tossed it to the floor. Observed Senator Plumer, "Mr. Randolph has passed the Rubicon. Neither the president or the secretary of state can after this be on terms with him."[30]

The multimillion-dollar plan to settle the matter of the Floridas with Spain, using France as an intermediary, was also on Randolph's mind. The House had passed it over his objections, and the defeat rankled. Because the deliberations on the plan were secret, he had to be content

with insulting them metaphorically, comparing them to patent medicine advertisements: "Here you have 'the worm-destroying lozenges,'
there 'Church's cough drops,' and to crown the whole, 'Sloan's vegetable
specific'—an infallible remedy for all nervous disorders and vertigoes of
brainsick politicians." Brilliant and devious as Randolph was, one has
to wonder if with the last comparison he was aiming at Madison, who
earlier in the year had an accident that newspapers reported on for
weeks. As Kentucky senator John Breckinridge described it to his wife,
"Mr. Madison fell out of his door . . . and put his knee out of place."
There is no indication that the accident had anything to do with a nervous disorder, vertigo, or being "brainsick," but Randolph, likely aware
that Madison had been subject to sudden attacks, might have been hinting at the connection. In the same speech he referred to the "mercantile
megrims," or migraines, afflicting the nation, a phrase that probably
called to mind for many on the floor the sick headaches that periodically
incapacitated Jefferson.[31]

Ironically, the administration also had difficulties with the measure
that Congressman Gregg had introduced and that Randolph had used
as a starting point for his fulminations. Cutting off British imports
would mean a drastic decline of import duties to the Treasury and cause
discontent among the merchant class. The president and his cabinet
preferred a milder resolution offered by Congressman Joseph Nicholson
of Maryland that listed specific goods that could no longer be imported
from Great Britain. To Randolph, who had viewed the Gregg proposal
as too strong, the Nicholson resolution was too weak, particularly since
it wasn't scheduled to take effect until November 1806. Randolph ridiculed it as "a milk and water bill, a dose of chicken broth to be taken
nine months hence."[32]

In a humiliating defeat for Randolph, Nicholson's resolution passed
the House by 87 to 35, and the Non-importation Act based upon it enjoyed an even wider margin: 93 to 32. Randolph was one of the most
eloquent speakers ever to rise in the House of Representatives. Senators
regularly came to the House to hear his speeches. But he had pushed
too hard and gone too far. As Senator Samuel Smith of Maryland de-

scribed one of his performances, "He astonished all his hearers by the boldness of his animadversions on executive conduct, the elegance of his language, and the pointed and fine strokes of oratory. But he has left stings in the breasts of many that never can be extracted." As Randolph's tactics were becoming less and less effective, the president started reaching out to members of Congress, including a senator who had opposed the Non-importation Act and the Speaker, whom he invited to the president's house for the evening. Jefferson also wrote to James Monroe in London. He knew that Randolph hoped that Monroe would challenge Madison for the presidency in 1808 and had already warned the minister to Britain that "some of your new friends are attacking your old ones out of friendship to you, but in a way to render you great injury." The day after the Nicholson vote, on March 18, he emphasized how soundly Randolph had been defeated, writing to Monroe that he had "never seen a House of Representatives more solidly united in doing what they believe to be the best for the public interest. There can be no better proof than the fact that so eminent a leader should at once and almost unanimously be abandoned." But neither of these letters reached Monroe, leaving him uninformed for months about Jefferson's thinking on the political situation among Republicans.[33]

Monroe did hear from John Beckley, who described Randolph's downfall but also told Monroe that he should be the one to succeed Jefferson. Apparently in the market for a new patron, Beckley turned on his old one, criticizing Madison as "too timid and indecisive as a statesman." Randolph wrote to describe an administration plot intended to embarrass Monroe and elevate Madison. Monroe responded cautiously, writing to Randolph that there were "older men whom I have long been accustomed to consider as having higher pretentions to the trust than myself." He didn't quite close the door, however, saying that there would be other opportunities to discuss the matter.[34]

IN THE AUTUMN of 1806, Jefferson received word that Meriwether Lewis and his party had arrived safely from their journey of exploration.

The news brought him "unspeakable joy," he wrote, probably all the more so since most of the reports he received that fall and winter were discouraging. Both he and Madison had heard from credible sources that the former vice president Aaron Burr, who had taken a seven-month, three-thousand-mile excursion in the West, was up to no good. The chief suspicion was that he was involved in a conspiracy to separate western states and territories from the Union and create a separate empire. One of those whom he had repeatedly consulted about his plans was General James Wilkinson, who, despite his reputation for fast dealing, commanded the U.S. Army and was governor of the Louisiana Territory. In October, after a rush of rumors linking Wilkinson with Burr, the general decided that the better part of valor was to betray the former vice president. He wrote to Jefferson about a plan to converge an army in New Orleans and from thence, with naval assistance, to invade Mexico. He did not identify Burr as the leader of this enterprise, and neither did the president, when on November 27, 1806, he proclaimed a conspiracy and urged authorities to bring to punishment those involved. But whether he was named or not, by now everyone knew that this was about Burr. Wrote Senator Plumer on November 28, "Reports have for some time circulated from one end of the United States to the other that Aaron Burr, late vice president, with others in the western states are preparing gun boats, provisions, money, men and so forth to make war upon the Spaniards in South America; that his intention is to establish a new empire in the western world and that he contemplates forming this empire from South America and the western states of North America."[35]

When John Randolph of Roanoke demanded more information, Jefferson sent a message to Congress that described the evidence for a Burr conspiracy as "a mixture of rumors, conjectures, and suspicions"; nevertheless, in an ill-considered statement, he also declared Burr's guilt "beyond question." Senator Plumer was not so sure. Much of the case against Burr was based on a ciphered letter that he had supposedly sent to Wilkinson and that the general had helpfully deciphered. Plumer thought the letter sounded more like Wilkinson than Burr, and in fact

Wilkinson had altered it. He was on the payroll of the Spanish and by no means the honorable soldier and good citizen that Jefferson credited him with being. But Wilkinson's treachery did not mean that Burr was without guilt. As early as 1804, Burr had approached British minister Anthony Merry with a request for the British to assist in a scheme to liberate the inhabitants of Louisiana from the United States. To accomplish this purpose, Merry reported to his government, Burr wanted a half-million-dollar loan and a British squadron. When the British failed to come through, Burr sent one of his associates, former senator Jonathan Dayton of New Jersey, to sketch out for the Spanish minister, the marquis de Yrujo, a plan for a coup d'état. Jefferson would be seized, along with the vice president, public money would be taken from Washington banks, and ships from the naval yard would be used in a plan to liberate the West. Burr himself began an effort to draw discontented military officers into the conspiracy.[36]

Captured in February 1807, Burr appeared in court in Richmond on April 1. Presiding was Chief Justice John Marshall, Jefferson's longtime adversary. Marshall allowed a misdemeanor charge against Burr to go forward but refused to commit him on a charge of treason, saying that there was insufficient evidence. "The hand of malignity" could not "capriciously seize" and charge an individual, Marshall said, a comment that was widely assumed to be directed at the president. Jefferson, thoroughly enraged, assigned Madison to the task of gathering information for the trial. One of Madison's contacts sent him a number of affidavits concerning Burr's recruiting men and ordering arms and ammunition. Madison forwarded them to the lead prosecutor in the Burr case, George Hay. The president also asked Madison to arrange to get witnesses from distant places to the trial in Richmond and sent him a warrant for five thousand dollars to cover expenses.[37]

In June a grand jury that had assembled in Richmond handed down an indictment against Burr for treason. In August, the jury formed for his trial heard testimony centering on Blennerhassett Island in the Ohio River, where the prosecution alleged that Burr, by directing the assemblage of armed troops and boats, had levied war against the United

States. The phrase "levying war" was one of the constitutional definitions of treason.

Burr had left the island by the time the conspirators assembled, but the prosecution was confident in its approach because in a Supreme Court decision less than six months earlier, Chief Justice Marshall had written with regard to a case of treason that "all those who perform any part, however minute or however remote from the scene of action . . . are to be considered as traitors." But after the prosecution had presented witnesses who told of the activities on Blennerhassett Island, the defense moved to have all further testimony declared irrelevant. Whatever further witnesses might reveal about Burr's motives, intentions, and connections to the assemblage on the island, it wouldn't show him actually levying war—because he wasn't there when the forces came together, Burr's lawyers argued. As for the Supreme Court's recent statement that one did not have to be present to be a traitor, that should be regarded as *obiter dictum,* said the defense, something said merely in passing. The prosecution was startled, to say the least, at such a claim. A bright young attorney for the prosecution, William Wirt, responded, "A plain man would imagine that, when the Supreme Court had taken up and decided the case, its decision would form a precedent on the subject."[38]

Marshall sided with the defense, writing in a long and, some have thought, labored opinion that "no testimony relative to the conduct or declarations of the prisoner elsewhere and subsequent to the transaction on Blennerhassett's Island can be admitted." With more than a hundred prosecution witnesses waiting in the wings, including some, no doubt, whom Madison had helped bring to Richmond, Marshall sent the case to the jury, which returned the predictable verdict but seemed irritated at not having heard the full prosecution case. Declared the members, "We of the jury say that Aaron Burr is not proved to be guilty under this indictment by any evidence submitted to us. We therefore find him not guilty."[39]

Jefferson made no comment on the legal niceties of the trial, but the verdict was surely galling, as was the public pummeling the president had taken. Not only had Marshall subpoenaed him (Jefferson provided papers but did not appear), but Luther Martin, the erstwhile defender of Justice Samuel Chase, had taken him to task for declaring Burr guilty before his trial had even begun: "The president . . . has assumed to himself the knowledge of the Supreme Being himself and pretended to search the heart of my highly respected friend. He has proclaimed him a traitor in the face of that country which has rewarded him. He has let slip the dogs of war, the hellhounds of persecution, to hunt down my friend." Showing a side of himself that had no corollary in his friend Madison's personality, Jefferson suggested that Martin also be tried for treason.[40]

THE BURR TRIAL was not the only thing going wrong for the Jefferson administration. Not long after Jefferson and Madison had become truly alarmed at the former vice president's activities, Madison had received a letter from John Armstrong, American minister to France, whom Jefferson had commissioned to reopen negotiations about the Floridas. Armstrong reported that efforts to get the French to help the United States persuade Spain in America's favor had hit a wall. Napoleon had personally intervened, dressing down Talleyrand for even contemplating such an intervention.[41]

Some three months later came bad news about negotiations that James Monroe and William Pinkney had conducted with the British. Jefferson and Madison had initially been hopeful about them, partly because England had a new foreign secretary, Charles James Fox, thought to be friendly to the United States. One of his first acts had been to recall Anthony Merry, the "diplomatic pettifogger," as Madison referred to him, whose relationship with the president and the secretary of state had been so strained. But the rotund Fox would die after only seven months in office, and when the new British minister to the United States, young David Erskine, came hurrying to Madison with a copy of the treaty that Monroe and Pinkney had negotiated, Madison suspected that all was not well. His first question was, "What [has] been determined on the point of impressment?" When Erskine told him the treaty

did not address the matter, Madison "expressed the greatest astonishment and disappointment," Erskine wrote to his government. Madison
was further dismayed when Erskine handed him a note supplementary
to the treaty relating to a recent edict Napoleon had issued from Berlin.
The emperor, having decided to use his control of Europe to impose a
naval blockade on Britain, had decreed that British ships would no longer be received in continental ports, nor would any ship that had traded
with Britain. The British wanted the United States to promise that it
would defy the edict, which would inevitably have pushed it into war
with France. Madison told Erskine that the note itself was sufficient to
keep the treaty from being ratified.[42]

Jefferson was ill, suffering from a migraine that would plague him
for most of March. As Dolley Madison described the situation, "The
president has a sick headache every day so that he is obliged to retire to
a dark room at 9:00 in the morning." Thus it might have been Madison
who made the decision not to try to keep Congress, which was about to
adjourn, in session to deal with the treaty. If he did so, it was in the
knowledge that the president thought that no treaty would be better
than one that did not address impressment. Late that night Jefferson,
who got relief from his migraines when the sun went down, made clear
to a group of senators bringing bills for him to sign that the treaty would
never be submitted.[43]

When Monroe, in London, learned of the treaty's fate, he was
shocked and angry. He believed that he had negotiated the best treaty
possible and had fully expected the president to approve of it. Monroe's
disappointment was not likely to have been assuaged by Jefferson's letter
of March 21, 1807. Even though the president went to some effort to
deny rumors in the Federalist press that the treaty was rejected in order
to damage Monroe and advance Madison, he also emphasized how
much he objected to the agreement Monroe had negotiated: "The British commissioners appear to have screwed every article as far as it
would bear, to have taken everything and yielded nothing." Nor would
Monroe have responded well to the businesslike tone in which Madison
wrote to him about "the particular difficulties" that had restrained the

president "from closing the bargain with Great Britain." The spring of
1807 saw a deteriorating relationship not only between the United
States and Britain but also between James Monroe and the administration he represented, particularly as it was embodied by James Madison.
In a letter that he wrote to the president but never sent, Monroe declared his disappointment with the months he had spent negotiating
with the British. "At no period of my life," he wrote, "was I ever subjected to more inquietude."[44]

IN JUNE 1807, about the time of Aaron Burr's indictment, word came
of a disaster at sea. It involved the USS *Chesapeake,* one of the six frigates originally authorized in 1794. Although the *Chesapeake* was less
gracefully shaped than its sister ships, it was nonetheless a beauty.[45] A
painting of the *Chesapeake* in the art collection of the U.S. Navy shows
how it might have looked just before disaster struck, its sails full and the
Stars and Stripes flying aft.

On June 22, the *Chesapeake* passed Cape Henry, headed for the
Mediterranean. Its commodore, James Barron, noticed the maneuver-
ings of a British frigate, HMS *Leopard,* but made little of them until late
afternoon, when there came a message from the *Leopard* requesting
permission to send an officer on board. When he arrived, he demanded
that the crew of the *Chesapeake* be mustered so that he could look for
a British deserter. Commodore Barron refused. The *Chesapeake* was not
a private merchant ship but an American ship of war. He could not
submit it to being boarded and searched.[46]

Barron ordered his men to prepare for battle, but before they were
ready, the *Leopard* fired a warning shot, then another, and then, as
Henry Adams described it, "poured [its] whole broadside of solid shot
and canister, at the distance of one hundred and fifty or two hundred
feet, point-blank into the helpless American frigate." After taking another broadside, the *Chesapeake* struck its colors. As the flag was being
lowered, a third broadside came, and then the British boarded. They left
with four sailors they claimed were deserters, three of whom, it would

turn out, were American citizens. The *Chesapeake*, three of its crew
dead and eighteen wounded, made its way back to Norfolk.[47]

As news spread of the attack, so did the public's indignation. The
Chesapeake incident seemed to encapsulate all the insults that Britain
had dealt the United States since the beginning of the European wars,
and Republicans and Federalists alike shook their fists and demanded
vengeance. "This country has never been in such a state of excitement
since the Battle of Lexington," Jefferson wrote, a comment that conjured
up a time when the nation had been a colony. Britain seemed to be
treating the United States as though the American Revolution had never
occurred, and resentment of that attitude fueled American anger. Madison, normally the coolest member of the cabinet, caught the fever. In
the draft he prepared for the proclamation to be issued by the president
on July 2, he wrote of British "insults as gross as language could offer"
and described British actions as "lawless and bloody." In a turning of the
usual tables, it was Jefferson who toned down Madison's rhetoric in the
proclamation as it finally appeared.[48]

Meeting almost every day, the cabinet agreed on defensive measures,
such as recalling warships from the Mediterranean, and approved Madison's draft of a diplomatic dispatch to be sent to England aboard an
aptly named schooner, the *Revenge*. The president decided to call Congress to meet on October 26, 1807, some three months hence, calculat-
ing that by that time there might be an answer to American demands
for return of the *Chesapeake* seamen, reparations, and the ending of
impressments. In an indication of the nature and pace of early-nine-
teenth-century diplomacy, the president then left for Monticello and
Madison for Montpelier.[49]

By the time they returned and Congress had gathered, there was still
no response to the dispatch. The actions of Admiral George Berkeley,
who commanded British ships assigned to North America, made it hard
to be optimistic. After a trial in Halifax, he ordered one of the men
seized from the *Chesapeake*, who had been judged to be British, summarily hanged.[50]

The *Revenge* arrived in New York on December 12, and suddenly there was a rush of news, none of it good. The king had declared that the practice of impressment, even from warships, would be accelerated. In a decree issued from Milan, Napoleon had made clear that his determination to blockade Britain included seizing American ships, not only those that had entered British ports but also ships that allowed themselves to be searched by the British. There was also word of a new British edict intended to counter Napoleon's Berlin Decree. The British Order in Council declared that ships found in commerce with France, its allies, or its colonies would be seized.[51] If American ships went to England, in other words, France threatened them. If they went to almost any other destination, they risked seizure by England.

The Non-importation Act that had been passed some twenty months previously was finally allowed to go into effect on December 14, 1807, but more was clearly needed. Jefferson recommended an embargo, which Congress quickly passed, and Madison explained the action in a series of unsigned editorials in the *National Intelligencer*. The embargo was a protective measure, he wrote, one that would keep American ships safe in harbor, and it would "have the collateral effect of making it the interest of all nations to change the system which has driven our commerce from the ocean." It was an energetic measure, to be sure, but it would not lead to war, "being universal and therefore impartial."[52]

Madison acknowledged the economic disruption the embargo would cause and tried, not very successfully, to put it in the best possible light. Yes, there would be privation among the citizenry, he wrote, but that, in turn, would encourage "frugality" and hard work, the virtues of the yeoman farmer. It would spur "household manufactures which are particularly adapted to the present stage of our society." And, yes, there would be "much inconvenience" produced in the mercantile world, but that, in turn, would "separate the wheat from the chaff," the responsible merchants from the irresponsible, speculative ones. It is hard to imagine either citizens or merchants drawing much comfort from these arguments. More persuasive, perhaps, was the case he made that an embargo was a step short of war that could allow the United States to achieve its ends.[53] That argument, part of Madison's long-held belief that U.S. commercial power was sufficient to change the policies of other nations, would turn out to be wildly optimistic.

MEANWHILE, THE PRESIDENTIAL CONTEST of 1808 was under way, and it was almost certain to be won by the Republican nominee. For all the policy shifts and political attacks of the last seven years, Thomas Jefferson and his administration were still hugely popular. Jefferson had reduced taxes, he had paid down the public debt, and although war seemed constantly in the offing, he had kept the nation at peace. A senator from Vermont, who was dismayed by the clout that Jefferson's popularity gave him, told Senator Plumer that "Mr. Jefferson's influence in Congress was irresistible, that it was alarming, that if he should recommend to us to repeal the gospels of the evangelist, a majority of Congress would do it."[54]

Madison had another advantage, which was that the congressional caucus would decide the Republican candidate and Dolley Madison was enormously skilled at winning over members of Congress. She repeatedly invited them to the Madison home, where for several hours they could forget their personal misery. Most of them lived in boardinghouses on Capitol Hill, rooming and taking meals with other members. One senator compared it to living "like bears, brutalized and stupefied . . . from hearing nothing but politics from morning to night." There were no clubs or theaters they could escape to, except for one establishment that specialized in ropedancers.[55] How pleasant, then, was an evening on F Street with the secretary of state and his wife.

One member described the edge that Dolley's entertainments gave Madison over Vice President George Clinton, who, though long regarded as too feeble to run, was harboring presidential ambitions in his sixty-nine-year-old heart. Wrote Senator Samuel Mitchill to his wife, "The former gives dinners and makes generous displays to the members. The latter lives snug at his lodgings and keeps aloof from such captivating exhibitions. The secretary of state has a wife to aid his pretensions. The vice president has nothing of female succor on his side. And in these two respects Mr. M. is going greatly ahead of him." When James Monroe began to be talked about as a Republican contestant, Madison managed to keep quiet, even as he was experiencing a cash strain from paying off the last of the bank loans that had helped finance Monroe's diplomatic venture. But Dolley Madison found it hard to bite her tongue. About the time that James Madison was arranging to borrow money in order to pay rent on the F Street house, Dolley, so John Quincy Adams reported, "spoke very slightingly of Mr. Monroe."[56] One can hardly blame her. Monroe was supposed to be her husband's friend, but it was looking very much as though he were, for the second time, being seduced into running against him. As she must have seen it, he had succumbed to Patrick Henry's blandishments in 1788 and now was letting John Randolph of Roanoke lead him astray.

Dolley paid for her visibility by often being the subject of ugly rumors. In the period before the 1804 election, both she and her husband had shown great shrewdness in dealing with one gossipy incident. A story passed around that a Federalist congressman had impugned Mrs. Madison's morals and those of her sister Anna Cutts. Postmaster General Gideon Granger rushed to defend the Madison women, whereupon the congressman, Samuel Hunt of New Hampshire, challenged him to a duel. When Granger declined, thereby making himself look foolish, the Madisons did something quite unexpected. The secretary himself carried Mrs. Madison's compliments and a dinner invitation to Congressman Hunt, courtesies that made clear they did not believe he had gossiped about her—and further implied that there was nothing to gossip about.[57]

But not all stories were easy to combat. At about the same time, James's supposed friend Richard Peters had also weighed in on Dolley's morals. In a letter to his fellow Federalist Timothy Pickering, who had talked about the sexual insatiability of democratic (that is, Republican) men, Peters wrote, "You should not have forgot to give precedence to the insatiability of democratic [that is, Republican] women. The leader of the ceremonious flock you mention carries with her, if not the thing itself, at least the appetites of the second of the four insatiable things mentioned in the thirtieth chapter of Proverbs, verse 16."[58] The second of the things never satisfied in Proverbs is "the barren womb." Peters's implication, which he, no doubt, thought wittily made, was that Dolley Madison was sexually insatiable because her husband had failed to impregnate her.

As the election of 1808 approached, the rumors picked up again. Senator Mitchill wrote to his wife, "Your friend Mrs. Madison is shockingly and unfeelingly traduced in the Virginia papers." One of those encouraging the rumors was John Randolph of Roanoke. Writing to Monroe about opposition that was supposedly building against Madison, he cited a list of the secretary's shortcomings, adding at the end, "There is another consideration which I know not how to touch. You, my dear sir, cannot be ignorant, although of all mankind you, perhaps, have the least cause to know it, how deeply the respectability of any character may be impaired by an unfortunate matrimonial connection. I can pursue this subject no further. It is at once too delicate and too mortifying." The rumors were probably particularly painful for Dolley Madison because she was going through a very difficult time. Her mother died in October 1807 while nursing her sister Mary, who had tuberculosis and had lost two of her three daughters the previous year. Then Mary died in early 1808, about the time that the stories about Dolley were, to use Richard Peters's delicate words, running "on all fours."[59]

WHEN JAMES MONROE returned home from England, he settled on a strategy of not promoting himself to be the Republican candidate in 1808 but not closing the door either. He would serve if elected, he said, and he stuck with this approach even as friend after friend, convinced he could not win, dropped away. He got only three votes in the Republican caucus to Madison's eighty-three, a lopsided result that would have been a little better for him—though not much—if a number of Old Republicans hadn't chosen to absent themselves. Many of the dissident Republicans were by now trying to avoid all association with Randolph, but it was nonetheless he who took up the cudgels, leading a group to protest Madison's nomination. Besides the accusation that Madison was a Yazoo man, members of the group claimed that he suffered from "want of energy," which might have been a coded way of talking about his health. And they charged him with writing *The Federalist* with John Jay and Alexander Hamilton, "in which the most extravagant of their doctrines are maintained and propagated."[60] Madison was not a true Republican, in other words.

Madison was fiercely defended by attorney William Wirt, who had been part of the prosecution team in the trial of Aaron Burr. Writing as "One of the People" in the pages of the Richmond *Enquirer*, he demanded to know just when Madison had lacked energy. Was it when he acted as one of "the first and most effective agents" in the creation of the Constitution? Was it when he triumphed over Patrick Henry in the Virginia ratifying convention? Or when "he watched the first movements of the federal Constitution" and resisted with boldness "what he deemed infractions of its spirit"? And what about the way he fought back when advocates of "the Alien and Sedition Laws waved their baleful scepters over the continent"? Those protesting Madison's nomination had no evidence for their assertions, Wirt declared, regarding either Madison's supposed want of energy or his association with *The Federalist*. "We know that it is a defense of the Constitution, which we are all sworn to support, and where is the crime of Mr. Madison's having participated?"[61]

The "want of energy" charge also received a strong check after Federalist senator Timothy Pickering of Massachusetts accused the administration of catering to the French and trying to provoke war with the British. In answer, Jefferson released some 100,000 words of diplomatic correspondence, much of it in Madison's hand. Over several days it was read aloud in the House and Senate. Newspapers of both parties published the documents, and not even a hostile editor could find evidence of the bias that Pickering alleged. The documents showed how hard Madison had worked as secretary of state—and how well. An early Madison biographer, George Tucker, thought that it was by the labors of his pen that Madison's "merits were most conspicuous and that he most recommended himself to the nation." The diplomatic correspondence, wrote Tucker, "always showed a masterly acquaintance with the subject never expressed in harsh or uncourteous manner and exhibited in a form to carry conviction to every unprejudiced mind." Tucker added an observation that will ring true with anyone acquainted with Madison's State Department writings. It would be impossible, he wrote, to identify any part of them "in which he has omitted anything it was material to say."[62]

Samuel Harrison Smith, the editor of the *National Intelligencer,* noted Madison's "irreproachable morals."[63] This was a point often made by Madison advocates but usually without much elaboration. To be too specific or go on too long might have invited unwelcome comparisons with President Jefferson.

GEORGE CLINTON, planning to run for president, had been chosen as the vice presidential candidate by the Republican caucus. When he received word of his vice presidential nomination, he decided to hedge his bets. Protesting loudly that no one had told him his name would be put forward, he claimed that he had certainly not approved it, but he didn't withdraw, thus managing the neat—and never repeated—trick of running for vice president on a ticket with a man whom he was running against for president. Clinton was showing his years. As Senator Plumer described him, "He is old, feeble, and altogether incapable of the duty of presiding in the Senate. He has no mind—no intellect—no memory. He forgets the question—mistakes it—and not infrequently declares a vote before it's taken—and often forgets to do it after it is taken." Perhaps because of Clinton's feebleness, his advocates tried at least once to make Madison's health an issue. They might also have been inspired by Madison's being ill for weeks earlier in the year. For a time he had been too sick to meet with a British emissary, too sick even to write a note. A Clinton advocate, whose work appeared in the Troy, New York, *Farmers' Register,* noted that Madison was "a little younger than George

Clinton—but unfortunately for his country, he is sickly, valetudinarian, and subject to spasmodic affections, which operate unfavorably on his nervous fluid, considered by philosophers as one of the most powerful agents of our intellectual faculties." The phrase "spasmodic affections" was a clever choice, calling to the nineteenth-century reader's mind not only epilepsy, with its dreaded associations, but hysteria, which, being regarded as a womanly affliction, suggested that Madison was not only weak but effeminate.[64]

Clinton's advocates do not seem to have followed up on this line of attack, and one has to wonder why. Perhaps they worried it would underscore Clinton's own bad health. Perhaps illness was so ever present in the nation's beginnings that it was hard to make it into a political liability. Officeholders, just like those they represented, were expected to get sick. The great Washington, after all, had nearly died of pneumonia during his first term in office. John Adams was known to collapse and once lay in a coma for five days. Jefferson's headaches could put him out of commission for weeks. Sickness was also the shadow of death, and few were the families that had not lost a spouse or child. Martha Washington had been a widow when she married George Washington, and her children, who became his beloved stepchildren, Patsy and Jack, both died before he took office. Adams had lost a little girl, Susanna, of whom he could barely speak. Jefferson had lost his wife, three daughters, and a son by the time he assumed office, and his adult daughter, Maria, died during his first term. In an era when everyone had death as a constant and tragic companion, even the most zealous politician might have had qualms about using illness as a political weapon.

THE MOST substantive issue of the campaign was the embargo, which had a serious economic impact at home, driving exports, which had been $108 million in 1807, down to $22 million in 1808. Believing they finally had an issue, the Federalists, who had been nearly moribund, became animated, once more nominating Charles Cotesworth Pinckney as their presidential candidate and launching an anti-embargo campaign that eventually had a mascot: a snapping turtle named Ograbme ("embargo" spelled backward), shown in one cartoon taking a chunk out of a merchant's backside. The Federalist press never tired of attacking, and Madison grew bitter about the criticism, which he viewed as undercutting the effectiveness of the embargo by making it seem likely the United States wouldn't stick to it. He wrote to Jefferson that only "some striking proof of the success of the embargo can arrest the successful perversion of it by its enemies, or rather the enemies of their country."[65]

There would be no striking proof. Napoleon ridiculed the embargo by offering to help the United States enforce it. He would capture any American ship on the high seas, he said, on the grounds that it must be there illegally. As for the British, occasional news articles indicated that the embargo was causing pain, but they were cold comfort to citizens in the northeast part of the United States, where both financial losses and unemployment were mounting rapidly. Gallatin had warned Jefferson that "governmental prohibitions do always more mischief than had been calculated; and it is not without much hesitation that a statesman should hazard to regulate the concerns of individuals as if he could do it better than themselves."[66] Neither the president nor the secretary of state, both committed to restraining government, heeded this advice, perhaps because they could not allow themselves to. As they perceived it, the only alternatives to economic sanctions were even greater threats to the Republic: a return to being under the British thumb—or war.

MADISON WON HANDILY in 1808, receiving 122 electoral votes to Pinckney's 47 and Clinton's 6. Monroe received no votes at all. The embargo had taken a toll—Madison had lost most of New England—but he prevailed in other parts of the country to chalk up a substantial victory.

There was little time to savor it. To Madison's heavy official correspondence were now added pleas from job seekers, but perhaps that made thoughtful notes of congratulation all the more appreciated. "Blackguard" Charles Pinckney, the Republican in the Pinckney family, wrote, "I . . . congratulate you on your election to the most honorable station in your country's gift." Madison also heard from his cousin the Reverend James Madison, who had become a bishop of the Episcopal Church in 1790. "You will indeed, I fear, have a stormy time to encounter," the clergyman wrote, "but that is the season in which the pilot discovers his superior skill."[67]

The embargo, which New Englanders continued to violate, was the most pressing problem, particularly when President Jefferson decided after Election Day to let matters drift until his successor was inaugurated. He said that he wanted "to leave to those who are to act on them the decisions they prefer." With Madison's blessing, Gallatin wrote to the president, urging him to decide between "enforcing the embargo or war . . . so that we may point out a decisive course either way to our friends." Jefferson decided on enforcement, signing a bill on January 9, 1809, that would become known as the Force Bill by those who despised its strict measures.[68]

There was concern that New Englanders might themselves resort to force, so furious were they about the new law. The Massachusetts legislature resolved that enforcing the embargo should be a state crime. Connecticut's governor refused to assign militia officers to assist in enforcement, and its legislature, echoing the language of the Virginia Resolutions of 1798, declared it to be the duty of states "to interpose their protecting shield between the rights and liberties of the people and the assumed power of the general government." In petitions and memorials, irate citizens poured out their anger and offered more than a few threats to secede. "I felt the foundations of the government shaken under my feet by the New England townships," Jefferson later recalled.[69]

And so did Congress. As New England Republicans reacted to their constituents' rage, party discipline began to crumble—and then collapsed. By early February, President-elect Madison, apparently deciding that he could no longer stand aside, began to work with Virginia congressman Wilson Cary Nicholas on a plan that would allow the United States to maintain at least some commercial pressure on France and Great Britain. The plan he recommended was to lift the embargo except for those two countries and further provide that should either of them withdraw its hostile edicts, the president had authority to open trade with that country.[70]

Congress passed such legislation, calling it the Non-intercourse Act, and Jefferson signed it on March 1, 1809. Three days later, with his party splintered, the nation divided, and both of the world's great powers threatening, James Madison was sworn in as the fourth president of the United States.

Chapter 15

MR. PRESIDENT

JAMES MADISON TOOK THE OATH of office in the new chamber of the House of Representatives, a large, gracefully shaped room with fluted columns, crimson curtains, and a painted ceiling. He was pale and trembling with emotion as he contemplated the great honor and vast responsibility that were about to be his, and when he delivered his inaugural address, he could not at first be heard. But his voice strengthened as he spoke about peace, which, he said, had "been the true glory of the United States to cultivate." Following the path of right and justice had not protected the United States from "belligerent powers," which "in their rage against each other" had issued the "arbitrary edicts" responsible for the nation's present troubles, and the new president said he could not predict how long the country would be caught up in this conflict. He could be sure, however, of the principles he would follow in leading the nation through difficult times. He would always prefer peaceful accommodations to war, he would support the Constitution, and he would be strengthened in these tasks by "the well-tried intelligence and virtue of my fellow citizens." In them he would place his confidence, "next to that which we have all been encouraged to feel in the guardianship and guidance of that Almighty Being whose power regulates the destiny of nations."[1]

After passing by troops in review, Madison rode back to F Street in a coach and four. Jefferson had still not moved out of the president's house, and the Madisons invited guests into the home they had lived in for more than six years, receiving their company just outside the drawing room. Margaret Bayard Smith, wife of the publisher of the *National Intelligencer,* observed that Mrs. Madison "looked extremely beautiful . . . dressed in a plain cambric dress with a very long train, plain round the neck without any handkerchief [covering her bosom], and beautiful bonnet of purple velvet and white satin, with white plumes." So striking was Mrs. Madison's outfit, the latest in French fashion, that Mrs. Smith seems not to have noticed the president's suit, which was not only made in the United States but cut from cloth woven from the wool of American-raised merino sheep.[2]

A ball was held that evening at Long's Hotel on Capitol Hill. Thomas Jefferson, a former president now, was among the first to arrive. Relaxed, even ebullient with the weight of office lifted from his shoulders, he jokingly noted that he was unprepared for the social life of the new administration. "You must tell me how to behave," he said to a friend, "for it is more than forty years since I have been to a ball."[3]

After the diplomatic corps had arrived, the musicians struck up "Madison's March," and the president and Mrs. Madison entered the ballroom. She looked gorgeous, wearing a light buff-colored velvet dress and matching turban decorated with two superb bird-of-paradise plumes. Margaret Bayard Smith reported this and also observed the absolute propriety of her behavior. Asked to take the floor for the first dance, Mrs. Madison declined, saying she did not dance. Asked to choose someone else for the honor, she declined again, lest her choice looked like "partiality." Having recounted this story of Mrs. Madison's "unassuming dignity, sweetness, grace," Mrs. Smith, in a letter to her daughter, asked a curious question: "Ah, why does she not in all things act with the same propriety?" Mrs. Smith was one of Mrs. Madison's most ardent admirers, and one can only guess at what was bothering her. Perhaps the low-cut dresses, perhaps Mrs. Madison's taking snuff, a habit she had been unable to break, or perhaps it was that Mrs. Madison was open and uninhibited with men as well as women. Not long before her husband became president, Mrs. Madison had kissed an old bachelor full on the lips to prove she was not a prude.[4]

By most, Dolley was admired uncritically. "She loved life and people and her world loved her," an early biographer wrote. At the inaugural ball, guests crowded toward her, "those behind pressing on those before and peeping over their shoulders to have a peep of her," Mrs. Smith reported. The president managed to escape the crush by standing on a bench with Mrs. Smith. When the managers of the ball came to ask him to stay for supper, he agreed, but as soon as they were out of earshot, he turned to Mrs. Smith and said, "But I would much rather be in bed."[5]

One can hardly blame him. The ballroom was not only crowded but hot. The upper windows had to be broken out for ventilation. Moreover, from his bench, Madison could survey the hall and see the characters who were already making his political life difficult. Representative John Randolph of Roanoke was there, less powerful than he had once been, but with a tongue sharp as ever. George Clinton was in attendance, not only Madison's vice president but his recent rival for the presidency and thereby thoroughly untrustworthy. Secretary of the Navy Robert Smith was at the ball and probably quite a cheerful presence. He would soon become secretary of state, though that was not how Madison had wanted it. His plan had been to elevate Albert Gallatin to that office, but William Branch Giles of Virginia, now a senator and apparently miffed that he hadn't been offered the position, had formed an alliance with Senator Samuel Smith of Maryland, Secretary Robert Smith's brother. The two had enough votes to sink Gallatin's nomination and to make life very unpleasant should Robert Smith be kicked out of the cabinet. Madison knew he needed the wise and straight-talking Gallatin, and his first thought had been to get Senator Smith behind Gallatin's nomination by putting Robert Smith in at Treasury. But Gallatin knew that Smith, whose joviality was his greatest asset, wasn't up to the Treasury job. Realizing that he was going to end up doing all the work of Treasury in addition to the work of the State Department, Gallatin refused to go along. He would stay at Treasury, and Smith was moving to State—which meant that Madison was going to be doing not only the work of the presidency but the work of the secretary of state.[6] Small wonder that he wanted to go home and go to bed.

In his first weeks in office, Madison used the foreign policy weapon that Congress had provided him to try to deal with hostile edicts and actions from both England and France. He wrote instructions, which Secretary Smith signed, to American ministers in those countries, not only emphasizing the willingness of the United States to begin trade with whichever government withdrew its hostile orders, but also stating the likelihood of Congress's authorizing "acts of hostility" against the other country unless it too should respect American rights. Hardly was the ink dry on the instructions when David Erskine, Great Britain's minister to the United States, came forward with an amazing offer: the king would withdraw the vexatious Orders in Council in exchange for repeal of the Non-intercourse Act as it pertained to Great Britain. At Erskine's suggestion, Madison agreed on June 10, 1809, as the day that the Orders in Council would be vacated and U.S. trade with Britain resumed, and on April 19, Madison issued a statement to the nation to that effect: "Whereas the honorable David Montague Erskine, His Britannic Majesty's Envoy Extraordinary and Minister Plenipotentiary, has by the order and in the name of his sovereign declared to this government that the British orders in council of January and November 1807 will have been withdrawn as respects the United States on the 10th day of June next, now therefore I, James Madison, president of the United States, do hereby proclaim that . . . after [that] day the trade of the United States with Great Britain . . . may be renewed."[7]

The satisfaction that this proclamation gave Madison must have been immense. It was ratification of his long-held belief that commercial sanctions worked, that the American republic did not have to go to war with Great Britain in order to assert its rights as an independent nation. The *National Intelligencer* put out an extra edition to announce "the happy result" of negotiations, and as news of the agreement spread, Madison had the heady experience of being the object of almost universal praise. Even a normally hostile newspaper like the *Philadelphia Gazette* had good words for him: "Never statesman did an act more popular or more conducive to the true and permanent interest of his country." John Randolph of Roanoke congratulated him, offering a resolution in Congress approving "the promptitude and frankness" with which he had acted.[8]

The happy mood of the country likely pervaded the president's house, where Mrs. Madison, working with the architect Benjamin Latrobe, was renovating and decorating. Operating with an appropriation from Congress of twenty-six thousand dollars, they were turning Jefferson's office into the State Dining Room, which it remains today. The smaller room next to it, today's Red Room, was being made into Mrs. Madison's parlor. Yards and yards of sunflower-yellow satin were being cut to cover sofas and chairs and to festoon the windows and make cornices. Mrs. Madison wanted music in her parlor, and so Latrobe went shopping for a pianoforte and a guitar. He had trouble finding fabric for the draperies for the oval room next to the parlor, which was to serve as the drawing room, but by late March he had found enough crimson velvet not only for the windows but for chair cushions. This room, known as the Blue Room today, was regally decked out, with cream-colored walls setting off the crimson velvet. A new fireplace mantel was installed, and above it was hung a large looking glass, one of several Latrobe purchased. They all sparkled brilliantly in candlelight, but the mirror over the mantel in the drawing room was especially festive, with gilded balls trimming a cloth valance over the top.[9]

As spring approached, the Madisons were ready to entertain, and Mrs. Madison began her "Wednesday drawing rooms," events that anyone acquainted with the Madisons—or anyone recommended by someone who was—could attend. In summer the windows might be thrown open in the elegant rooms; in winter large blazes were set in the fireplaces. A military band played as guests promenaded, the men dressed in dark coats and breeches, the women in elegant dresses that followed

French fashion. Mrs. Madison's outfits seemed to grow increasingly fanciful. At one of the Wednesday drawing rooms, a guest reported, she wore "a robe of pink satin trimmed elaborately with ermine, a white velvet and satin turban with nodding ostrich plumes and a crescent in front, gold chains and clasps around the waist and wrists." After guests had greeted the president and his wife, they moved to the dining room, where the table was piled high, mostly with sweets, including Mrs. Madison's favorite, ice cream inside a baked pastry shell. Coffee and wine were passed, and for the guest who wanted something stronger, there was a bracing whiskey punch.[10]

A European visitor to the first levee, held on May 31, was impressed by Mrs. Madison, describing her as "plump, tall, well-looking, and very pleasant and affable," but the president, he wrote in his diary, "is a very small, thin, pale-visaged man of rather a sour, reserved, and forbidding countenance."[11] Smiling at strangers still wasn't in Madison's social repertoire—as it was never in George Washington's—even when things seemed to be going very well. In little more than a week, the United States would resume trade with Britain, and that, in turn, might bring the French around.

But on June 10, with hundreds of American ships having already departed from port, Madison received word of new British Orders in Council. These had been issued before the British government would have received news of the Erskine agreement, but it was odd that there should be fresh edicts in light of the terms that Erskine had offered. Erskine, a genial young man with an American wife and genuinely friendly feelings toward the United States, gave many reassurances. Madison wrote to Jefferson that he expected the British government to "fulfill what its minister has stipulated." Still, he said, he was prepared for the possibility that the British would be "trickish."[12]

Dolley's sister Anna, her husband, Congressman Richard Cutts, and their three small boys had moved into the White House, and they accompanied the Madisons when they set out for Montpelier in mid-July. Although construction would soon begin on the first of two wings to be added to the Piedmont house, James Dinsmore, the Irish joiner in charge of construction, would have moved bricks and lumber out of sight before the president's party drove up the road to the mansion. Remodeling had already started inside, but Dinsmore had made sure that the house would be usable during the Madisons' summer stay.[13]

Samuel Smith, the editor of the *National Intelligencer,* and his wife, Margaret, arrived at Montpelier in early August. The president greeted them at the door, as "plain, friendly, communicative, and unceremonious as any Virginia planter could be," said Mrs. Smith. Mrs. Madison, "kindness personified," wrote Mrs. Smith, asked her why she hadn't brought her little girls. To Mrs. Smith's answer that she didn't want to inconvenience friends, Mrs. Madison said with a laugh, "I should not have known they were here among all the rest, for at this moment we have only three and twenty in the house." Mrs. Madison led Mrs. Smith to her bedroom, where she helped her loosen her riding habit and take off her bonnet. She then joined her in lying on the bed, where the two of them were served wine, punch, and pineapple. Mrs. Smith was overwhelmed by Mrs. Madison's "simplicity, frankness, warmth, and friendliness." The Madisons' life, she noted, "was characterized by that abundance, that hospitality, and that freedom we are taught to look for on a Virginian plantation."[14]

This summer idyll was interrupted by news that the British had indeed been "trickish." They had repudiated the agreement Madison had negotiated with David Erskine and recalled Erskine, in disgrace, to London for having violated his instructions. That amiable young man had presented certain conditions set forth in his instructions not as requirements, as the British Foreign Office had told him to do, but rather as negotiating points. He had been overeager, to be sure, but some of the conditions must have struck him as too harsh to be anything other than points to be negotiated away. One, for example, was that the Royal Navy be at liberty to capture American vessels that were trading with France and its allies in violation of American law. What nation would let another enforce its laws? Erskine had let the matter drop, but foreign secretary George Canning was now releasing dispatches demonstrating that he had instructed Erskine to make this obvious violation of American sovereignty mandatory. Madison, upon learning of all this, observed that Canning had been as determined to prevent a good outcome to the negotiations as Erskine had been to bring one about.[15]

Madison made the trip to Washington City in two and a half days and, after arriving, quickly settled a cabinet dispute. Secretary of State Smith was arguing that since Madison had received authority from Congress to lift nonintercourse with Britain, he needed congressional authority to reinstate it, but Congress was not in session, and Madison could hardly leave matters as they were. He did what the moment demanded, signing a new proclamation suspending trade with Great Britain. With matters back to where they had been when he entered office, he returned to Montpelier.[16]

BACK IN WASHINGTON in the fall, Madison found a new British minister in place, Francis James Jackson, whom the British Foreign Office clearly believed would present a stout defense of British policy. Jackson was notorious for having been chosen in 1807 to deliver an ultimatum to the court of Denmark: either surrender the Danish fleet to the British or see Copenhagen destroyed. The prince regent had refused, and shelling began that ultimately killed some two thousand civilians. Caesar Rodney, Madison's attorney general, recommended that the president not receive a minister whose conduct had made him "personally obnoxious to our country," but after learning of Napoleon's decisive defeat of the Austrian army at Wagram, Madison no doubt thought it was worth giving Jackson a chance.[17] Perhaps Napoleon's dramatic success would render the British willing to reach a real accommodation with the United States.

The thirty-eight-year-old Jackson, a round-faced man whose sideburns verged on muttonchops, found much to admire about the new capital to which he had been assigned. "I am surprised no one should before have mentioned the great beauty of the neighborhood," he wrote. He shot partridge near the Capitol and took long rides with his wife,

Elizabeth, a Prussian baroness. But he could barely conceal his contempt for the president and his wife. He described Madison as not only "plain" but also "mean-looking," by which he probably meant lacking in dignity and importance. As for Mrs. Madison, she was, he said, "fat and forty, but not fair." He also passed along to his mother back in England Federalist gossip that the president's wife had once been a comely barmaid.[18]

Madison quickly discerned that Jackson's only purpose in the United States was to try to intimidate the government, but he also perceived the usefulness to be found in such an attitude. At his instructions, all official communications between the secretary of state, Robert Smith, and Jackson were to be in writing. This served a twofold purpose: first, putting Madison, who wrote all of Smith's significant correspondence, in charge of negotiating with Jackson, and second, creating a record. Jackson fell into the trap right away, sending a letter to Smith in which he insinuated that the Americans had connived with Erskine, that the president himself had fully understood that the conditions set forth by the British were mandatory but chose to act as if they were not.[19]

On the surface Madison was all graciousness, hosting the Jacksons at a dinner party. "I do not know that I had ever more civility and attention shown me," Jackson wrote. Madison even took Mrs. Jackson into dinner, thus settling what Jackson called the "foolish question of precedence" that had arisen when Anthony Merry was the British minister in Washington. Meanwhile, however, Madison was also demanding in a letter sent over Smith's name "a formal and satisfactory explanation" for why the British government had disavowed an agreement made "by its acknowledged and competent agent." The letter brushed lightly past the accusation of connivance, expressing surprise at "the stress you have laid on what you have been pleased to state as the substitution of the terms finally agreed on for the terms first proposed." Some of the terms were "palpably inadmissible," the letter noted. Did the British government really expect that the United States would give over the enforcement of its laws? When Erskine, the acknowledged agent of the king, saw that these proposals would not be successful, Madison-writing-as-Smith explained, he did what negotiators do and went instead with the reasonable terms.[20]

Jackson foolishly responded by repeating his charge that the Americans had ratified the agreement in bad conscience, which brought a response from Madison, again writing as Smith, that "such insinuations are inadmissible." When Jackson stood by the accusation, he received a letter signed by Secretary Smith informing him "that no further communications will be received from you."[21]

Within a week, Jackson read an account in the *National Intelligencer* of his correspondence with the secretary of state. It portrayed the American government, in the face of repeated insults by the British, acting in a fashion both strong and reasonable. Jackson realized what had happened. The Americans had told the "story in their own way and at the time they [thought] best," and he was indignant about it. He wrote to his brother that he had come "prepared to treat with a regular government and have had to do with a mob and mob leaders." He demanded his passport and prepared to leave Washington. Just as he was departing, the *Intelligencer* struck again, editorializing that he was the "fit tool of a treacherous and abandoned government" and suggesting that a man of his ilk could succeed at diplomacy only when accompanied, as he had been in Copenhagen, by dozens of frigates and ships of the line, as well as thirty thousand troops.[22]

Jackson found some sympathy as he traveled north to New York and Massachusetts. In Boston, he was honored by a banquet at which Senator Timothy Pickering, the most extreme of the Federalist leaders, raised his glass to "the world's last hope—Britain's fast-anchored isle." But Jackson's reputation made him a difficult man to defend. Moreover, because the Federalists had been enthusiastic about the deal with Erskine, they looked foolish when they tried to reverse course and blame the administration for duping him. Madison had turned what could have been a political disaster into a benefit. Observed Representative Ezekiel Bacon, a New England Republican, "I think that James Madison's administration is now as strongly entrenched in the public confidence as Thomas Jefferson's ever was at its fullest tide, and I do think that it will be quite as likely not to *ebb* as much as that did towards its close."[23]

Just two days after Bacon's positive assessment, Isaac Coles, Mrs. Madison's cousin and the president's secretary, caused a scandal by slapping Maryland congressman Roger Nelson in the face. Coles apologized to the House of Representatives, saying that he was "the last who would willfully manifest a deficiency of that reverence which is due to the representatives of my country," and managed to get off with a reprimand for breaching House privileges, but he felt obliged to resign from his job and was replaced by his brother Edward.[24]

Coles's assault on Representative Nelson, who was not only a member of the president's party but a seemingly sensible fellow, was a personal matter. Coles thought Nelson had slandered him. But a more serious incident five days later had politics behind it. Virginia congressman John G. Jackson, Mrs. Madison's fiery brother-in-law (the widower of her sister Mary), suffered a serious hip wound in a duel with a North Carolina congressman who had insulted Jefferson and Madison. Jackson, one of the president's firmest allies, returned to the House the following spring but after an "unfortunate fall," perhaps caused by the unsteady gait with which the gunshot wound left him, finally had to resign.[25]

Congress seemed disjointed, veering this way and that in an effort to find an alternative to either submission or war. In his message of January 3, 1810, Madison tried to provide direction, recommending that Congress reauthorize a statute that would allow him to raise 100,000 militiamen, provide for a standby volunteer force of 20,000, and fill out the regular army, which had been enlarged in the wake of the *Chesapeake* crisis. He also directed congressional attention to the navy, where, according to Secretary of the Navy Paul Hamilton, decommissioned frigates needed to be repaired and the cost would be $775,000. In addition, Madison noted "the solid state of the public credit," indicating that a loan to finance these measures was appropriate.[26]

John Randolph of Roanoke, who had been ill, returned to Congress in time to object. "Is there a man who hears me who feels one atom of additional security to his person or property from the army of the

United States?" Randolph asked on the floor of the House. "Has it ever been employed to protect the rights of person and property? Has it ever been employed but in violation of personal rights and property—in the violation of the writ of *habeas corpus* and as a new modern instrument of ejectment?"

Randolph proposed "that the military and naval establishments ought to be reduced"—a proposition that was, as it turned out, not the most extreme to be offered. Other congressmen called for doing away with the army and navy entirely.[27]

Representative Roger Nelson of Maryland, several months earlier the recipient of Isaac Coles's slap, pointed out how inane these proposals were in light of previous steps Congress had taken: "It is a perfect child's game. At one session we pass a law for raising an army and go to expense. In another year, instead of raising money to pay the expense by the means in our power, we are to disband the army we have been at so much pains to raise. We shall well deserve the name of children instead of men if we pursue a policy of this kind." On April 17, the House approved general proposals to reduce both the army and the navy, but when members began to discuss where to cut, consensus vanished, and Congress, proceeding in what Madison called its "unhinged state," failed to resolve the issue.[28]

Members did pass a new trade measure, a mirror of the one expiring. Macon's Bill Number 2, as it was known, lifted all trade restrictions but gave the president power to reimpose them on France should Britain withdraw its Orders in Council, or on Britain should Napoleon back off his edicts. It was widely regarded as an embarrassingly weak measure, a virtual surrender to both nations, but Madison saw possibilities in it. The French would have little interest in maintaining a situation in which all trade restrictions were lifted because it gave a clear advantage to the British, who dominated ocean commerce and thus benefited most when it was freed up. France might, therefore, by backing off, use the act "to turn the tables on Great Britain by compelling her either to revoke her orders or to lose the commerce of this country," Madison wrote to William Pinkney, U.S. minister to Great Britain.[29]

Madison might have been looking into a crystal ball. Scarcely two months later Napoleon responded, dictating a letter to his foreign minister, the duc de Cadore. Addressed to John Armstrong, the American minister in Paris, the Cadore letter offered to lift the Berlin and Milan decrees, which were the French justification for seizing American ships. This revocation, proposed to go into effect after November 1, was conditioned upon the British renouncing their blockades—or the United States causing "their rights to be respected by the English." In a highly controversial decision, the president accepted. On November 2, 1810, he issued a proclamation declaring that France had lifted the edicts violating the commerce of the United States and noting that according to Macon's Bill Number 2, Great Britain had three months to either lift its decrees or find American commerce with it interdicted.[30]

Critics of Madison, both at the time and since, have pointed to this episode as evidence of his gullibility. How could he possibly have thought he could take Napoleon's word? But Madison had been around too long not to have realized how untrustworthy Napoleon could be. Madison was a chess player, and his proclamation was not an end in itself but an opening move. While it was unlikely that the reimposition of trade restrictions would result in the British lifting their orders, it might; and if it did not, it clarified who the enemy was. No longer would the nation have to choose between "a mortifying peace or a war with both the great belligerents," Madison wrote to Attorney General Caesar Rodney. A few weeks later, he wrote to Jefferson, "We hope from the step the advantage at least of having but one contest on our hands at a time." And it was the right contest in Madison's mind. As a neutral power in a warring world, the United States had suffered at the hands of both Britain and France, but, as Madison put it, "The original sin against neutrals lies with Great Britain." The more potentially harmful offense did as well. For the United States, a former British colony, to submit to further injuries and insults from Great Britain would be to return to the subservient role Americans had cast off with the War of Independence.[31]

· · ·

FOR MORE THAN twenty years, since the convening of the first session of the First Congress, Madison had been trying to defend U.S. sovereignty with economic weapons, from discriminatory tariffs and tonnage fees, through embargoes, to the Non-intercourse Act and its reverse image, Macon's Bill Number 2. He deeply believed that for a republican government, the peaceful way was the better way: "Of all the enemies to public liberty war is, perhaps, the most to be dreaded, because it comprises and develops the germ of every other. War is the parent of armies; from these proceed debts and taxes; and armies and debts and taxes are the known instruments for bringing the many under the domination of the few."[32] But the peaceful way simply hadn't worked. Economic measures, even when they caused the British some pain, had not been enough to convince them, locked as they were in a death struggle with Napoleon, to ease off on Orders in Council. Nor were those measures enough to stop Britain from obtaining manpower for its fleet by impressing Americans. In accepting the offer in the Cadore letter, Madison, although still technically relying on economic measures, was clearing the path toward war.

Madison buttressed his acceptance of the Cadore letter with legislative sanction. Jefferson's son-in-law John Eppes introduced a bill in the House imposing trade restrictions on Britain on the grounds that the French had lifted the Berlin and Milan decrees. The legislation emphasized that it was the president's prerogative, not the courts', to make the determination that the French decrees had been lifted. The last thing the president needed at this point was to have Federalists on the bench overturning his decision.

The bill was debated in the last days of the Eleventh Congress, and a handful of Federalists joined by John Randolph of Roanoke tried to defeat it by delaying it. When Eppes, speaking the truth, accused Randolph of dilatory tactics, Randolph called him a liar, reason aplenty according to the *code duello* for Eppes to issue a challenge, which he promptly did. In the confusion that followed, the Republican majority strong-armed the legislation through. Some weeks later Dolley Madison intervened to achieve an accommodation between Randolph and Eppes, who wrote to his father-in-law, "So detestable a minority never existed in any country."[33]

THE GENIAL MANNER Madison assumed with most members of Congress seems to have kept them on occasion from realizing the audacity of his decisions. That phenomenon might have been at work as he took a very aggressive approach to West Florida, where the population was overwhelmingly American and since 1808, the year Napoleon invaded Spain, increasingly restive. With Spanish authority weakening, discontented citizens in West Florida held a convention, organized forces to capture Spain's fort at Baton Rouge, and requested that the United States make them a part of the Union. Madison decided on a proclamation asserting that West Florida was a part of U.S. territory, a position he had maintained since the Louisiana Purchase. The United States had long expected to gain authority over West Florida through negotiations, the proclamation said, but now that a crisis had arisen, he, as president of the United States, had "deemed it right and requisite that possession should be taken of the said territory in the name and behalf of the United States."[34]

To Jefferson, Madison admitted there were "questions as to the authority of the executive" concerning West Florida, but, he wrote, there was "great weight" in the argument that the United States could legally take possession of it, "above all if there be danger of its passing into the hands of a third and dangerous party."[35] The British had been losing no time in trying to take advantage of Spanish weakness in the New World, and a British threat to West Florida, as Madison saw it, trumped any doubts he had. If he did not act, the United States could find West Florida—and its invaluable outlets to the gulf—under British occupation.

Congress was between sessions, and so Madison, taking advantage of the long delays that occurred between making a decision and implementing it some distance away, sent copies of his proclamation south but made no public announcement until he delivered his message to Congress—which was about the same time that West Floridians began to learn that the United States had taken possession. There was surprisingly little grumbling about the president's having kept the proclamation secret for more than a month, and a Senate effort to prove the unconstitutionality of his actions came to a bad end. Timothy Pickering of Massachusetts tried to show that the United States had no right to occupy West Florida since it had not been part of the Louisiana grant. He read from a letter written by Talleyrand to make his point, but it turned out that document had never been made public. Pickering became the first person in the history of the Senate to be censured by that body. By a vote of 20 to 7, he was found to have violated the injunction of secrecy.[36]

MADISON HAD fiercely opposed a national bank in 1791, but now, twenty years later, it had become a central part of the country's financial system. Madison had become convinced of the necessity of renewing its charter, particularly as the country drew nearer to war and would likely need loans. But Secretary of the Treasury Gallatin, who worked on the renewal, found himself facing the same Republican senators who had objected to his presence in the Madison cabinet in the first place. On the crucial vote in the Senate, both Giles and Smith opposed the bank, with the result that the vote was tied. Vice President Clinton, who wanted to be president rather than Madison's number two, cast the deciding vote—against the administration's position and against the bill.[37]

Madison's efforts to mollify Republican opponents in the Senate had not worked and had left him with a secretary of state who was not merely incompetent but untrustworthy. Time and again, the president heard reports of Secretary Smith undercutting his policies. His worst sin had been letting the British know that he, Smith, did not believe the French decrees had been lifted. Smith was also divisive, lining up with his brother and his senatorial allies, particularly in opposition to Gallatin. They used the Philadelphia *Aurora*, a newspaper with which they were aligned, to accuse Gallatin of everything from financial irregularities to being the real power behind Madison's policies. Gallatin wrote to the president pointing out the damage that a cabinet divided against itself was causing and submitting his resignation. Madison refused it. Gallatin was not the cabinet member he needed to get rid of. He called in Robert Smith, read him chapter and verse on his failings, and asked for his resignation.[38]

Getting rid of Smith was an essential step as the nation approached war, and so was appointing a qualified replacement. Good cabinet members have always been hard to find, but that was especially true in the early republic, when cabinet departments were very small, some composed of fewer than a dozen clerks. This meant there was no training ground to produce a cadre of former deputy and assistant secretaries from which a future president might choose. Thus it is not surprising, given his limited choices, that Madison thought of James Monroe, even though Monroe, despite their many personal connections, had twice challenged him for office. Madison had been truly irritated with Monroe for letting his name be put in competition for the presidency. In the months leading up to the 1808 election, he had pointedly skipped a summer visit to Monroe's Albemarle County farm, a snub for which Dolley Madison tried to compensate by sending Mrs. Monroe some snuff wrapped in paper. But Jefferson had since been giving the president reports that Monroe had separated himself "from those who led him astray," and while he was distinctly interested in "his own honor and grade," he was "not unready to serve the public." After ensuring that Monroe would accept the State Department position if asked and soothing Monroe's feelings, still hurt over the treaty he had negotiated with the British in 1806 not being sent to the Senate, Madison offered him the position of secretary of state.[39]

Smith did not go quietly. He published a pamphlet in which he accused the president of being weak and endeavored to show himself as a strong defender of U.S. interests—his evidence of the latter being documents that Madison had written for him. Even the president's opponents thought Smith's pamphlet hurt him rather than the president. One of them called it a singular example "of a man's giving the finishing stroke to his own character in his eagerness to ruin his enemy."[40]

• • •

MADISON WAS NOW on a track from which he would not waver, although the French frequently made a steady course difficult. While they left some American ships unmolested, they took hostile action against others, undercutting the president's claim that the French decrees had been lifted. In July 1811 came reports that Napoleon had opened French ports to American commerce and released American ships that had been held there for having traded with Britain before they arrived in France. This news put the president in a triumphant mood— until he found out that the French were keeping American ships they had captured at sea.[41]

The British, by contrast, consistently justified the stance Madison had taken against them. Their frigates once more blockaded New York's harbor, stopped American ships, and sailed away with impressed American sailors. To counter these activities, the forty-four-gun USS *President* was sent from Annapolis to New York, but before the ship rounded Cape Charles, the *President*'s commodore, John Rodgers, saw a British ship, apparently the *Guerriere,* a man-of-war. The *President* gave chase and late in the evening drew within hailing distance. As Rodgers explained what happened next, he called to the ship twice, and it answered with cannon fire. The *President* responded in kind, and after a few more exchanges the other ship grew silent in the ocean darkness. The next morning Rodgers discovered that instead of a frigate, he had been in combat with a much smaller twenty-gun ship, the *Little Belt.* Nine of its crew were dead, twenty-three wounded, and the British, who claimed that the Americans had fired first, were furious. The president supported Rodgers's actions and so did most members of the public, who regarded the attack on the *Little Belt* as just retaliation for the British assault on the USS *Chesapeake.* Some measure of national feeling was evident in a toast offered at a Fourth of July party held on the banks of the Potomac. After high-ranking officials had departed, General John Mason raised his glass to Rodgers. "*Suaviter in modo, fortiter in re,*" he said, offering a loose translation: "Speak when you are spoken to, or God damn you, I'll sink you."[42]

The British government sent a new minister to the United States, Augustus John Foster, who upon arrival questioned Madison's assertion that the French decrees had been lifted, protested the trade restrictions that the United States had imposed on his country, and threatened retaliation. Most important in the president's eyes, Foster revealed that even if Britain were convinced that France had lifted the Berlin and Milan decrees insofar as the United States was concerned, the British would not rescind their Orders in Council. For that to happen, Foster said, the French would have to repeal the decrees with respect to Great Britain as well. This was an impossible condition, and if the British stuck to it, as they were likely to do, war, in Madison's mind, was inevitable.[43]

Like most presidents before and since, Madison showed the weight of office. The lines in his face were frequently commented upon now, perhaps most unkindly by writer Washington Irving, who called him "a withered little apple-John." Still, his health was generally good during the first two and a half years of his presidency. He had a fever in the summer of 1810 and apparently some anxiety that a sudden attack was in the offing, but the concern passed. He put the highest priority on keeping himself well, which meant that in 1811, even with war likely impending, he made plans to be out of Washington during the late summer months. After calling upon the Twelfth Congress to convene on November 4, a month early, to consider "great and weighty matters," he departed for what Mrs. Madison called "two months on our mountain in health and peace."[44]

THE TWELFTH CONGRESS opened in November under new leadership. A young and charismatic Kentuckian, Henry Clay, was elected Speaker of the House, and his ascendancy was no accident. Clay had served briefly in the Senate, a body of too much "solemn stillness," he said, but while he was there, he made his view on war with Great Britain unmistakable. In a memorable speech, he had declared, "I prefer the troubled ocean of war demanded by the honor and independence of the country . . . to the tranquil, putrescent pool of ignominious peace."[45]

His election to the speakership had been driven by men of similar views, who were, like him, young and relatively new to the House. Coming from the South and the West, they brought a fiery frontier pride to Washington that made them regard British insults and injuries as intolerable. These war hawks, as they soon were called, hated the attack on the *Chesapeake,* deeply resented the ship seizures the British were guilty of, and viewed impressment as a dreadful affront to national honor.

Many of them had also lost close relatives in Indian raids. John C. Calhoun, an intense, square-jawed newcomer from South Carolina, had lost a grandmother, an uncle, and two cousins. His fellow South Carolinian the eloquent Langdon Cheves remembered an aunt who had been scalped near Bulltown Fort, where he had been born. Felix Grundy, a rotund Tennessean, had lost three brothers in the Indian wars, and among his indelible memories was the sight of his oldest brother dying from tomahawk wounds.[46] It was an article of belief with these congressmen that the British were inciting Indians to murder settlers, and that conviction increased their determination for war.

Madison had a new and different audience to address in the Twelfth Congress, and the message he wrote for its opening was strong—too strong in Gallatin's view. Madison softened some of his words in deference to the Treasury secretary, but the point of his address remained unmistakable. Despite all the efforts the United States had made, the British persisted in treating American commerce as though it were that of a colony: "With this evidence of hostile inflexibility in trampling on rights which no independent nation can relinquish, Congress will feel the duty of putting the United States into an armor and an attitude demanded by the crisis and corresponding with the national spirit and expectations." Specifically, the president wanted the ranks of the regular army filled out and enlistments extended. He recommended both an auxiliary force and a volunteer force and noted that the militia should be readied. Aware of the resistance that remained in Congress to an expanded navy, he did not press hard on that point, simply asking members to consider "provisions on the subject of our naval force." He was also anticipating that the war would primarily be a land campaign, one that would attempt to coerce Britain by invading Canada.[47]

Madison's address was sent to the Committee on Foreign Relations, to which Clay had assigned both Calhoun and Grundy. To head the committee, Clay had chosen Peter Porter, a second termer from the northern borderlands of New York. Reporting out proposals to strengthen military forces, Porter cited the need to respond to Britain's "progressive encroachments on our rights" and noted as well the advantages to seizing parts of Canada. That evening Secretary of State Monroe met with Porter and his fellow committee members and offered "the strongest assurances that the president will cooperate zealously with Congress in declaring war if our complaints are not redressed by May next."[48]

Felix Grundy spoke for the proposals, pointing to Britain's long history of laying waste to U.S. commerce and to its impressment of seamen, which he called an "unjust and lawless invasion of personal liberty." He also cited a battle in Indiana Territory that had recently seized the attention of the nation. It had come about because a Shawnee warrior named Tecumseh was determined to resist the further advance of white settlers. He had created a confederation of Indian tribes and together with his brother, known as the Prophet, established a village at Great Clearing, where the Tippecanoe River flows into the Wabash. Indian raids and Tecumseh's activities greatly alarmed Indiana settlers, causing the ambitious governor of the Indiana Territory, William Henry Harrison, to march on Great Clearing. The Indians attacked Harrison's army, killing and wounding some two hundred of his men. When Harrison's forces subsequently destroyed the Indian village, Harrison declared a victory, although Tecumseh, who had been in the South working to strengthen his confederation at the time of the battle, remained a potent force.[49]

A contingent of Kentucky volunteers had marched with Harrison, and Felix Grundy knew some of the fallen. The Indians were not solely responsible for the murders, he said. The British had supported them, incited them. "War is not to commence by sea or land," he thundered on the floor of the House, "it is already begun; and some of the richest blood of our country has already been shed." Grundy maintained that the United States should "drive the British from our continent" and thus keep them from inciting "the ruthless savage to tomahawk our women and children." Like Peter Porter of New York, he saw Canada as more than a bargaining chip; it would make a fine addition to the United States. "I am willing to receive the Canadians as adopted brethren," Grundy said.[50]

UPON ASSUMING the speakership, Henry Clay had been determined to bring order to the House, and that meant getting John Randolph of Roanoke under control. So volatile was Randolph that no one had previously dared to deal with the hunting dogs he habitually brought onto the House floor, but early on, when he showed up with one of his pointers, Clay ordered the dog out and Randolph acceded. This did not, however, signal any diminution in the ferocity with which he went after opponents. Randolph demanded proof that the British had incited the Indians at Tippecanoe and accused his fellow Republicans of pushing a "war of conquest and dominion." One theme was repeated throughout their remarks, he said, "one eternal monotonous tone—Canada! Canada! Canada!"[51]

Randolph's eloquence had lost its power to persuade, but it nevertheless took more than two weeks for the House to approve measures to strengthen the military. In the Senate, William Branch Giles complicated matters by giving the president more men than he wanted: instead of enlarging the army by ten thousand for three years, he pushed through a proposal calling for twenty-five thousand for five years. That number would require a large tax levy and was a number impossible to raise in any case, given the length of enlistment, but the House went along with those numbers in January. The Senate also played havoc with the volunteer force by putting the states in charge of it. An exasperated Madison observed that while there was support for war, Congress seemed intent on making it as hard as possible to wage. He wrote to Jefferson, "With a view to enable the executive to step at once into Canada, they have provided . . . for a regular force requiring twelve [months] to raise it and . . . a volunteer force on terms not likely to raise it at all for that object." Responded Jefferson, "That a body containing one hundred lawyers in it should direct the measures of a war is, I fear, impossible."[52]

Langdon Cheves, whom Clay had made chairman of the Naval Committee, brought forth a proposal to build ten new frigates, but it was voted down at the end of January. The House did give its support to measures that allowed merchant vessels to arm and capture enemy ships as prizes. Peter Porter called this use of privateers "war . . . by individual enterprise," and it would be enormously successful.[53]

It took until early March, but Congress also took steps to pay for the war, passing a series of tax resolutions. Even though they were made contingent on the event of war, Madison was grateful that the members of Congress "have got down the dose of taxes," as he described it to Jefferson. "It is the strongest proof they could give that they do not mean to flinch from the contest to which the mad conduct of Great Britain drives them."[54]

Intent on maintaining the momentum toward war, the president sent documents to Congress that James Monroe had acquired from a handsome Irish immigrant named John Henry. The governor-general of Canada, Sir James Craig, had dispatched Henry to Boston as a secret agent during the unpopular embargo of the Jefferson administration, and the documents sent to Congress included Craig's instructions to Henry to determine the sentiment among New Englanders for separating from the Union rather than suffering "a continuance of the difficulties and distress to which they are now subject" and to identify individuals interested in such an effort. U.S. officials had long suspected Great Britain of making efforts to sever New England from the rest of the nation, but here was proof. "Who would now assert that Great Britain was friendly disposed towards us," Richard Johnson of Kentucky demanded to know, or "that she was fighting our battles or the battles of freedom, [or] that she stood between us and universal domination." Like other war hawks, Johnson drew a connection between British attempts to subvert Bostonians and their efforts to incite Indians along the frontier. The Henry letters, he

said, accounted "for the news we are daily receiving of the hostile intentions of the savages upon our borders."[55]

Federalists energetically objected that the administration was trying
to smear them. In the letters, Henry had written about New Englanders
"of talents and property who now prefer . . . open resistance and a final
separation to an alliance with France and a war with England." But who
exactly were these citizens? Federalists demanded, pointing out that
Henry had named no names. They also denounced the administration
for paying an exorbitant amount—fifty thousand dollars—for the papers. Soon it was revealed that the comte de Crillon, who had introduced Henry to official Washington, had credentials that were entirely
bogus, and the administration suffered further embarrassment when it
became public that the United States had sent an American agent,
George Mathews, into East Florida (Florida today). Mathews had been
sent in case citizens there decided to break from Spain as they had in
West Florida, but, apparently impatient, he had decided to hurry things
along by organizing a rebellion. Mathews had far exceeded his brief, but
his actions nevertheless made the Madison administration look guilty
of worse violations of another nation's sovereignty than the British were
in the Henry affair. Henry's letters should have served as a warning
about New England discontent and British willingness to take advantage of it, but events that had nothing to do with the substance of the
letters largely obscured those messages.[56]

The administration suffered an undeniable setback when a squadron
of French warships captured and burned two American merchant ships
carrying flour to Spain. The incident provided the British opportunity
to demand evidence that Napoleon had lifted the decrees of Berlin and
Milan and provided an opening for domestic opponents of war. The
administration took a step back. Monroe and Clay had previously
agreed that Congress would vote a thirty-day embargo that would be
followed by war. Such a move would allow American ships to seek safe
harbor and serve as a notice to the nation and the world that war was
on the horizon. Now it seemed prudent to lengthen the embargo to sixty
days. Some of Madison's opponents believed this request represented

wavering on the president's part, but in an April 3, 1812, letter to Jefferson the president seemed to be on his steady course. The British "prefer war with us to a repeal of their orders in council," he wrote. "We have nothing left, therefore, but to make ready for it."[57]

On April 20, Vice President George Clinton, long in poor health, died, setting off a scramble for a successor. The Republican caucus chose Elbridge Gerry, who as governor of Massachusetts had signed into law a bill reshaping the state's election districts to give Republicans an advantage. One of the reconfigured districts looked distinctly like a salamander, giving rise to the term "gerrymander," still recalled today when politicians redraw district lines to give their party an edge. Gerry's fierce opposition to antiwar Federalists made him an attractive vice presidential choice—as did his age. He was sixty-seven, and Madison might well have pushed for his choice as a way of preserving the presidency for his erstwhile rival Secretary of State James Monroe.[58] It is a measure of Madison's ability to rise above personal animosity that by this time he was almost surely thinking of Monroe, who had twice challenged him for office, as his successor.

At about the same time as the Republican caucus, the House sent out an official call for its members to be present by June 1, 1812, and as representatives were gathering, Madison met with Clay and his war hawks. As Madison's foes liked to tell it, the Speaker used the occasion to stiffen the president's spine, but there is no indication that the president lacked fervor for confronting Britain. His only hesitation had to do with readiness for war. Congress had already passed legislation allowing the president to enlist fifteen thousand men for eighteen months of service and would soon agree to measures that would bring numbers of regular forces more in line with his thinking, but troops had to be organized for war, and Congress had indefinitely postponed action on his request for two assistant secretaries of war to assist the secretary, William Eustis. In the end, the president concluded that the country was as ready as it was ever likely to be—until war was upon it. "It was certain," he would write, "that effective preparations would not take place whilst the question of war was undecided."[59]

He had also concluded that opposition to war was not going to go away, particularly while opponents felt they might force a change in course. And so the president decided, as he would say many years later, "to throw forward the flag of the country, sure that the people would press onward and defend it." This was thinking not that different from the war hawks'. Felix Grundy had declared on the floor of the House, "Whenever war is declared, the people will put forth their strength to support their rights."[60]

Clay almost certainly told the president in their meeting that he had a sufficient number of votes, and the two men undoubtedly discussed how to take the nation to war under the Constitution. Doing something that had never been done, they apparently agreed on the steps that followed. On June 1 the president sent a message to Congress setting forth British offenses, from impressment to Orders in Council to inflaming tribes along the frontier. These acts, declared the president, were "hostile to the United States as an independent and neutral nation," and he recommended that Congress take up the "solemn question" of whether the country should "continue passive under these progressive usurpations" or take up "defense of their national rights."[61]

On June 4 the House voted a declaration of war, and two weeks later the Senate followed. Madison signed the measure, and on July 18, 1812, the nation was at war.

Chapter 16

A FRIEND OF TRUE LIBERTY

THEIR "VOLUNTARY AND HEARTY COOPERATION" was not to be expected, the citizens of Charlemont, Massachusetts, told the president. They could not, they wrote, support a war that put the United States on the same side as Napoleon, "who holds beneath his iron sway the distressed nations of continental Europe." The citizens of Lyman, Maine, put it more dramatically: "We should prefer the lot . . . of Daniel in the lions' den rather than fall a sacrifice to that despot."[1]

Napoleon wasn't the only reason that New England Federalists opposed the war. They had suffered four years of maritime restrictions at the hands of a national government controlled by the Republicans, and war with Britain would continue the disastrous decline they had witnessed in shipbuilding and commerce. It would also pit them against a nation that they looked fondly upon. David Osgood, pastor of the church at Medford, Massachusetts, described Great Britain as "a nation of more religion, virtue, good faith, generosity, and beneficence than any that now is or ever has been upon the face of the earth," while the French, in Pastor Osgood's words, were "a race of demons."[2] Federalist New England remembered the mob violence of the French Revolution and worried that Madison and his fellow Republicans, with all their emphasis on government by the people, were taking the United States down the same path.

In July 1812 a riot in Baltimore underscored their concerns. At the center of it was a Federalist newspaper editor, Alexander Hanson, and Madison's old friend from Princeton Harry Lee, who had been through difficult times since leaving public office. The father of ten children, including Robert E. Lee, who would command the Army of Northern Virginia in the Civil War, Harry Lee had tried to make his fortune in land speculation but managed instead to ruin his reputation as an honest man and spend a year in debtors' prison. It is hard to be sure what brought him together with Alexander Hanson, but both of them opposed the war and hated mobs. Lee had even supported the Alien and Sedition Acts because he saw them as a way of preventing those ambitious for power from fomenting the masses.[3]

Hanson had attacked the declaration of war in his Baltimore newspaper, the *Federal Republican,* claiming it to be the result "of undisguised foreign influence." After a dissenting mob tore down his office on Gay Street, Hanson moved to a brick house on Charles Street, and on July 27 he and a number of Federalist colleagues defiantly issued a paper from there. Harry Lee and another veteran of the Revolution, James Lingan, were on hand to provide security, which everyone suspected would be needed. Not only was Baltimore a Republican hotbed, but its nickname was "mob town," and that evening a crowd gathered and began to pelt the house with rocks. The group inside the house fired their weapons, aiming over the heads of the crowd but inciting them nonetheless. The attackers broke into the house; several of them were wounded and one was killed, provoking further fury from the mob. Lee convinced his colleagues that protective custody was their best option, but the next night a crowd overran the jail in which the men were being held, killed James Lingan, and seriously wounded several others, including Harry Lee, who would never fully recover. He would wander through the West Indies, trying to restore his health, and die on Cumberland Island, Georgia, at age sixty-two.[4]

Federalists could see the Reign of Terror approaching, and they began, in Samuel Eliot Morison's words, "to look on the national administration as a far more dangerous enemy than the nation against which war had been declared." Some Federalists went so far as to accuse Madison of having set the mobs on the *Federal Republican,* a charge that must have been particularly galling to a man who had spent his adult life defending free expression. An early investigation indicating the falsity of the charge cheered the president by lifting the cloud of reproach from those whom he called "the friends of true liberty." He modestly refrained from including himself among the "friends," but in the war against Great Britain he would show himself to be their steady leader.[5]

THE AMERICAN PLAN was to begin by attacking the British at their point of greatest vulnerability—Canada, which was thinly settled and, given the extent of its border with the United States, lightly defended. Brigadier General William Hull, who had served with distinction in the Revolution, moved an army of two thousand from Ohio to Fort Detroit and from there crossed into the British territory of Upper Canada (southern Ontario today). After learning of the fall of a small American post on Mackinac Island, however, Hull became exceedingly fearful of being overrun by Indians and ordered a withdrawal to Detroit. Once there, terrified now about what Indian allies of the British would do in a battle for the fort, he surrendered his army without a shot being fired.[6]

A court-martial would find Hull guilty of cowardice, but two subsequent battles in the West made clear that U.S. forces had reason to fear Britain's Indian allies. Responding to Hull's orders to evacuate Fort Dearborn on the Chicago River, Captain Nathan Heald arranged to turn it over to the Potawatomi. When he marched his party of fewer than a hundred out of the fort, it was set upon by the Indians, and most of the Americans were killed. The Indians beheaded one of the officers, cut out his heart, and ate it. After a battle at the Raisin River in Michigan Territory, dozens of Kentucky volunteers who had been taken prisoner were tomahawked and burned alive. "Remember the Raisin" became a powerful cry for rallying war spirit along the frontier.[7]

Stephen Van Rensselaer, a militia major general, opened a second front along the Canadian frontier by ordering troops across the Niagara River, where they captured Queenston Heights, but when Rensselaer ordered militia to reinforce the position, they refused to leave American territory. The result was the subsequent loss of the heights and the killing, wounding, and capture of more than a thousand Americans, including Lieutenant Colonel Winfield Scott, who would one day become commanding general of the U.S. Army.[8]

Meanwhile, to the northeast, Major General Henry Dearborn was supposed to push forward on a third front by attacking Montreal, but after the Federalist governors of Massachusetts, Connecticut, and Rhode Island refused to send their allotments of militia, he wouldn't leave Boston, despite repeated orders from the secretary of war that he raise what volunteers he could and move on to northern New York, where he would find troops awaiting him. Dearborn saw it as his duty to protest the Federalist governors' refusals to send militia and was thoroughly alarmed by the vitriolic tone of war opponents. Convinced that Massachusetts was about to see a "Tory revolt," he became caught up in the efforts of Massachusetts Republicans to counter it, and autumn was well advanced before he began his move toward the Canadian border.[9]

President Madison was also concerned about Federalist opposition in New England. "The seditious opposition in Massachusetts and Connecticut with the intrigues elsewhere insidiously cooperating with it have so clogged the wheels of the war that I fear the campaign will not accomplish the object of it," he wrote to Jefferson. But he didn't see any advantage in confronting opponents head-on, as Dearborn seemed determined to do, nor, even though he called their opposition "seditious," did he have any intention of trying to suppress them, which was Jefferson's inclination. "Hemp and confiscation" would take care of them, the former president said, joking, probably, about hanging northern dissenters and taking their property, but Justice Joseph Story, whom Madison had appointed to the Supreme Court, quite seriously advocated "an internal police or organization" as "necessary to protect the government." He urged Attorney General William Pinkney to seek a congressional remedy to counter "the violence of party spirit in some of the New England states," and Pinkney passed the advice along to Madison. Philadelphia publisher Mathew Carey also urged the president to seek a law that would make "any attempt to dissolve the Union a high crime and misdemeanor." But these ideas were utterly incompatible with the defense of free speech that the president had been offering since he was a young man. He thanked Carey for his concern but turned away his proposal with the soothing hope "that the wicked project of destroying the Union of the states is defeating itself."[10]

THE REPEATED HUMILIATIONS of U.S. land forces in 1812 contrasted sharply with stirring triumphs at sea. They began on August 19 when Captain Isaac Hull of the USS *Constitution* found what he had been looking for some 750 miles off Boston: a British man-of-war. Hull, a sturdy thirty-nine-year-old, had been a naval officer for fourteen years—as long as there had been a Department of the Navy. He had fought in the Barbary War and was eager to fight again, as he had shown by taking hurried leave from Boston Harbor just a few weeks before. He had lifted anchor in a rush so that he could avoid receiving orders that might give command of his ship to a more senior officer, and now his hasty departure paid off. As his ship drew closer to the British frigate, Hull could see—no mistake this time, as there had been in the USS *President*'s attack on the *Little Belt*—this was HMS *Guerriere*.[11]

For an hour or so, the *Constitution* and the *Guerriere* tried to maneuver into advantageous positions. Finally, at 6:00 p.m., the *Constitution* closed alongside, and Hull gave the order to fire. The British ship fired back, but its eighteen-pound balls seemed to bounce off the *Constitution*'s heavy oak frame, a phenomenon that would lead to the ship's nickname, Old Ironsides. Within thirty minutes the *Guerriere* surrendered, its prisoners were transferred to the *Constitution,* and ten days later Hull sailed triumphantly into Boston Harbor. Massachusetts might have been Federalist territory, but well-wishers rowed out to greet the *Constitution,* bells rang, and cannon boomed. Spirits lifted across the nation as news of the victory spread, and there was good reason for the elation. The tiny American navy had 16 ships, including 9 frigates; the British, 183 frigates plus 152 heavier ships of the line. For the United States to prevail in a confrontation with the Royal Navy was nearly unthinkable. "However small the affair might appear on the general scale of the world's battles," Henry Adams observed, the American victory over the *Guerriere* "raised the United States in one-half hour to the rank of a first-class power in the world."[12]

The victory was welcome news for Madison as the 1812 presidential election approached. His chief opponent was actually another Republican, George Clinton's nephew DeWitt Clinton of New York, called Magnus Apollo in tribute to his fine looks and vanity. Clinton was playing the war card for all it was worth, successfully winning Federalists to his side by promising peace while seeking Republican support by promising to be a more effective commander in chief. Unprincipled as such a campaign was, in an age of slow communications no one could be sure that it wouldn't work. Federalists were doing well in state legislative contests and were likely to be more successful in the presidential election of 1812 than they had been in 1808. But Madison could still win if he solidified most of his Republican base—and the *Constitution*'s triumph would help with that.[13]

In early November, as electors were being chosen, Madison sent a message to the second session of the Twelfth Congress. In it he mentioned the success not only of "our public ships" but also of "private cruisers," which had already captured hundreds of British ships and brought them into American ports as prizes. The president asked for increased pay for the regular army (which he would get), a revision of militia laws (which he would not), and an enlargement of the navy (which would require only the slightest persuasion). The president also sent to Congress diplomatic correspondence showing that Great Britain had, unbeknownst to the United States, repealed the hated Orders in

Council before the United States had declared war. The governor of Canada, Lieutenant General George Prevost, had subsequently proposed an armistice, but the United States was unwilling to suspend hostilities, the British were told, because Britain reserved the right to reinstate the orders and was unwilling to stop impressing sailors.[14] Madison was also probably thinking about how hard it had been to put the country on a war footing and how difficult it would be to maintain that status during an armistice.

ON NOVEMBER 26, 1812, Captain Charles Stewart of the USS *Constellation* demonstrated the political savvy for which the navy would become legendary, hosting a party aboard ship for Washington dignitaries, including members of Congress who were soon to vote on a substantial expansion of the navy. Guests were ferried to the ship, lying in the Eastern Branch of the Potomac, and treated to an "elegant cold collation of the choicest viands and liquors." There was "concord and hilarity," the *National Intelligencer* noted, as well as "sprightly dance." Captain Isaac Hull was in attendance, and the president and Mrs. Madison made a grand entry, stepping on board as salutes were fired.[15]

The president's appearance was especially thrilling because everyone aboard the *Constellation* was aware that he had almost certainly been elected to a second term. The Electoral College count was not yet complete, but on the same day that the *National Intelligencer* reported the party aboard the *Constellation,* the paper also printed the news that Madison, who needed 109 electoral votes to win, had already gathered 107. The states outstanding, South Carolina, Tennessee, and Louisiana, were certain to put him well over the top. By December 8, when the citizens of Washington gave a reciprocal ball to thank Captain Stewart for his hospitality, Madison's reelection was certain, but he did not attend the affair, which was held at Tomlinson's Hotel. Mrs. Madison represented him and, when she returned home, had an unforgettable evening to report. In the middle of the ball had come word of yet another stunning naval triumph. Between the Azores and the Canary Islands, Captain Stephen Decatur, in command of the USS *United States,* had pounded the British frigate *Macedonian* into surrender, then brought it home as a prize. The ship's flag, rushed to Washington, was carried triumphantly into Tomlinson's. The crowd cheered, "Yankee Doodle" was played, and after being carried around the ballroom, the *Macedonian*'s colors were laid in front of Mrs. Madison. The evening was so exciting that Congressman Samuel Mitchill of New York confessed to his wife that he had a hard time getting to sleep that night: "I believe I was in the very condition of Themistocles after viewing the trophies won by the Athenians from the Persians at the Battle of Marathon."[16]

THE PRESIDENT was keenly aware that U.S. victories at sea, exhilarating though they were, did not make up for the dreadful performances on land. Brigadier General Hull had not only failed to invade Canada successfully but also left the British in control of U.S. territory. Dearborn, who like Hull had compiled a fine record in the Revolution, had finally made it to the Canadian border with an army of six thousand but after a single skirmish had fallen back to northern New York. Neither Hull nor Dearborn should have been leading forces in 1812. They were fifty-nine and sixty-one, respectively, Hull was not well, and Dearborn was physically unfit. Their selection to lead military action revealed the failure of the United States to train new leaders. West Point, established in 1802, was small, its programs had not been formalized, and as Madison had noted in his 1810 message to Congress, its buildings were in decay. In that message as well as in the one sent to Congress in 1811, he had recommended additional "seminaries, where the elementary principles of the art of war can be taught without actual war and without the expense of extensive and standing armies." Two months before war was declared, Congress had finally provided additional professors and expanded the corps of cadets at West Point, but the early war effort was at the mercy of generals whose time had passed. Madison's secretary of war, William Eustis, though not responsible for the generals' failings, was widely perceived to be, and he knew it. On December 3, 1812, he resigned.[17]

The other change in the Madison cabinet was a different matter. Naval secretary Paul Hamilton's department had overseen glorious successes, but his drunkenness had become notorious. He had been embarrassingly inebriated at the celebrations aboard the *Constellation* and at Tomlinson's Hotel and was seldom able to work past noon. The French minister to the United States, Louis Sérurier, reported home that "Mr. Madison and his friends tried by every means to cure him. It was useless."[18] At the end of December, Hamilton resigned, and Madison replaced him with William Jones, a sea captain and former member of Congress, who would serve with distinction.

Finding a new secretary of war was much harder. Madison had at least two refusals (including Secretary of State James Monroe's) before John Armstrong, who had recently served as U.S. minister to France, accepted. Armstrong's résumé was impressive. He was a Republican from New York with military experience, had served in the Senate, and came with outstanding recommendations. But even after appointing him, Madison remained troubled by questions about how loyal he would be. It was widely known that he had authored the address posted at Newburgh at the end of the Revolution, which had urged army officers to threaten Congress if that was what was necessary to get their back pay. And Armstrong was a man of curious personality, haughty, disputatious, and ambitious, while at the same time being indolent.[19] He left enemies wherever he served and quickly set about making more of them in Madison's cabinet. Tensions grew particularly high between Armstrong and Secretary of State Monroe, both of whom saw themselves as potential presidents.

In the midst of making cabinet changes, Madison attended the launching of the rebuilt frigate *Adams* at Washington's naval yard. As a newspaper reported it, "An opposition member of Congress, who was standing next the president when the frigate glided off the stocks, abruptly said to him, 'What a pity, sir, that the vessel of *state* won't glide as smoothly in her course as *this* vessel does.' 'It would, sir,' replied the president, 'if the *crew* would do their duty as well.'" Madison's sense of humor had taken on an edge. Although he had gotten much of what he wanted from the Twelfth Congress, he had endured unrelenting abuse from the Federalist minority. Boston's Josiah Quincy, who said that the country had been led since 1801 by "two Virginians and a foreigner," meaning Jefferson, Madison, and Gallatin, distinguished himself with castigations so foul that he had to edit his words before they were printed. Fortunately, the president had Henry Clay on his side. Clay had worried to a friend that Madison was too kind "for the storms of war," writing that "nature has cast him in too benevolent a mold," but in two days of remarks on the floor of the House he put his much-lauded eloquence to use showing that virtue in the executive had its advantage. "The Rising Star of the West," as the Speaker was called, reminded Josiah Quincy that Federalists had violated "freedom of the person" and "freedom of the press" with the Alien and Sedition Acts. There was a great difference, Clay said, between Madison's administration and its opponents—and "it is in a sacred regard for personal liberty."[20]

WHEN THE THIRTEENTH CONGRESS gathered in May 1813, Madison had another naval victory to report. The American sloop of war *Hornet* had defeated the *Peacock,* a British sloop, near British Guiana. He had to work harder to make the case for good news on land. "The attack and capture of York [Toronto today] is . . . a presage of future and greater victories," he told Congress. But American losses had been substantial at York, not in battle, but as the result of a powder magazine exploding. Among those killed was Brigadier General Zebulon Pike, famed for his expedition to the American Southwest. The victory would turn out to be costly in another way. The Parliament buildings of York, which was the capital of Upper Canada, had been set afire, and the British, convinced that the United States was responsible, would find occasion for revenge.[21]

In his address the president assured Congress that a loan arranged by the Treasury would suffice for the rest of the year. He did not mention, though was surely aware, that no thanks was due to a new member of the House. Federalist Timothy Pickering of Massachusetts, defeated in his reelection bid for the Senate and now returned to Washington as a freshman representative, had conducted a vigorous campaign in the pages of the *Salem Gazette* to discourage Federalist moneymen from subscribing to the loan. The strategy of starving the government in order to stop the war would be increasingly taken up by Federalist newspapers such as the *Boston Gazette* and even employed from the pulpit. Declared the Reverend Elijah Parish of Byfield, Massachusetts, "If the rich men continue to furnish money, war will continue till the mountains are melted with blood—till every field in America is white with the bones of the people."[22]

Taxes would have to be laid going forward in order to ensure the nation's credit, the president told Congress in his message, which was not news that was happily received. A new Republican member noted that "Congress was to impose the burden of taxes on a divided people" after years of hearing from party leaders "to look upon a tax gatherer as a thief, if not to shoot him as a burglar."[23]

But perhaps the most newsworthy part of Madison's message concerned his acceptance of an offer by Czar Alexander of Russia to mediate a peace settlement between the United States and Britain. The Russian offer had reached the United States at a crucial time. Napoleon, who had invaded Russia with some half million men, had been forced to retreat from Moscow and had fled to Paris, leaving behind the remnants of the Grande Armée. Such a huge defeat did not bode well for the United States. The weaker Napoleon became, the greater the likelihood of the British focusing more attention on their foe across the Atlantic. Great Britain had already announced a blockade of the coast, New England excepted, and a British flotilla had sailed into the Chesapeake, where it was burning and pillaging coastal areas, usually unhindered, though there were examples of citizen soldiers effectively fighting back. Militia and sailors on Craney Island turned back the British to save Norfolk from ruin. On St. Michaels on the Eastern Shore, a few hardy militiamen gave as good as they got from British artillery and managed to save their town's shipyards. The citizens of Washington feared that the British would march on the capital and, as Dolley Madison reported the rumor, "set fire to the offices and president's house." "I do not tremble at this," she wrote, but she was insulted when the British rear admiral George Cockburn managed to get a message to her saying he would soon "make his bow" in her drawing room.[24]

Madison had not waited for Congress to assemble to name a delegation to the Russian peace talks. John Quincy Adams, already in St. Petersburg, was to be joined by Federalist senator James Bayard and Secretary of the Treasury Gallatin. By the time of the president's message to Congress, Bayard and Gallatin had already sailed, Gallatin taking Dolley's son, Payne, with him. Despite her efforts and those of the president, Payne had found no respectable occupation that interested him. The Madisons no doubt hoped that time spent in Gallatin's sensible company would be of benefit.

Madison might have hoped that the Senate would regard the Treasury secretary's posting as a fait accompli, but as anything concerning Gallatin had long done, his nomination as envoy sent some senators, Republicans as well as Federalists, into a rage. Senate committees demanded a meeting with the president, but before one could take place, Madison became extremely ill. James Monroe wrote to Thomas Jefferson that he suffered from a fever "of that kind called the remittent." Because such fevers were thought to be caused by miasma, or bad air coming from marshes, they were also called *mal'aria,* or malaria. Chills and vomiting were followed by high temperatures, then sweating and remission before the cycle began again, usually in two or three days. Remittent fever was one of the few ailments for which there was an effective treatment in Madison's time: Peruvian bark, or the bark of the cinchona tree. It worked because it contained quinine, which attacked the parasites transmitted to humans by infected mosquitoes. These mechanisms were not understood in Madison's day, which meant that bark was also taken for other ailments. Jefferson took it for his headaches. William Cullen, author of *First Lines of the Practice of Physic,* recommended it for epilepsy.[25]

The bark in the president's house was probably kept in a small maple medicine chest that is displayed today in the White House Map Room. Madison had three doctors in attendance, one of whom probably ground the bark and stirred it into a liquid, possibly wine, but Madison was so sick that for more than two weeks it was difficult for him to drink the bitter infusion.[26] One imagines Dolley Madison, at his bedside around the clock, trying time and again to get him to take a sip.

Many well-wishers wrote to the president, but his political enemies were relentless. The *Federal Republican* predicted his demise, reporting that he was in "a state of debility, so exhausted, as to render his chance of even a few more months at least precarious." The illness had affected his mind, the newspaper reported: "It is weakened and disordered, now utterly sinking beneath his high duties and *now* bursting forth in paroxysms of rage. . . . Not a few who have recently visited him have left his chamber under a full conviction of the derangement of his mind."[27]

John Randolph of Roanoke was no longer a member of Congress, having been defeated by Jefferson's son-in-law John Eppes, but there were new representatives with considerable skill at vituperation and little inclination to cut the president any slack. One was Representative Daniel Webster, a brash young lawyer from New Hampshire. From the moment he was sworn in, he was determined to prove that the president had duped the nation into war by misrepresenting French intentions. He went so far as to elbow his way into the president's sickroom to present resolutions to that effect. "The president was in his bed," he reported, "sick of a fever, his night cap on his head, his wife attending him." Added Webster with satisfaction, "I think he will find *no relief* from my prescription."[28]

Finally, on July 2, Mrs. Madison was able to tell the president's secretary, Edward Coles, who was ill himself, "Mr. Madison recovers. For the last three days, his fever has been so slight as to permit him to take bark every hour and with good effect. It has been three weeks since I have nursed him night and day—sometimes in despair! But now that I see he will get well I feel as if I should die myself, with fatigue." While Madison had been ill, details had come in of defeats on the Niagara front at Stoney Creek and Beaver Dams. The president was probably still in his sickbed on July 6, 1813, when he ordered Secretary Armstrong to relieve General Dearborn of his command. He was still returning to health in mid-July when word came that British warships were headed up the Potomac. Secretary of War Armstrong rode with a troop of regulars to man Fort Warburton, which overlooked the Potomac. Secretary of State Monroe, not to be outdone, led volunteer cavalry all the way to Blackiston Island on the Chesapeake Bay and suggested attacking the British forces he found there. Madison told him no, tactfully emphasizing that if anything went wrong, it "would be peculiarly distressing not only to your friends but to the public." After setting pulses racing in the summer of 1813, the British squadron moved away from the coast but continued to keep nerves frayed by leaving some ships to linger in the Chesapeake for months.[29]

Senators pushed again for a meeting about peace commissioners, and Madison received them but refused to discuss their objection that Gallatin should not serve as both Treasury secretary and envoy. Because he would go no further than acknowledging an executive-senatorial disagreement, the senators' meeting with the president was brief—as was the interval before they voted down the Gallatin nomination.[30] Madison's stubborn defense of presidential prerogative had come at a cost.

His recovery continued despite the Senate, and on August 2, 1813, Richard Rush, the comptroller of the Treasury, was able to report to John Adams that "Mr. Madison rides out and attends to business again." This was news the former president was glad to hear. He believed the war "both just and necessary" and was thrilled with U.S. victories at sea. He was gratified that Madison was in favor of expanding the navy, which he, Adams, had led the way in creating. "I rejoice that Mr. Madison['s] health continues to improve," he wrote. "His life is of great importance."[31]

Madison had not had his two months on the mountain in 1812, but in the summer of 1813, war or not, he was determined to spend time at Montpelier. He and Mrs. Madison made the journey in four days, but even as he breathed the fresh air of the Piedmont, he could not keep his thoughts from the war and the northern theater in particular. He had concluded that command of Lakes Erie and Ontario was crucial to obtaining security along the border with Canada, and to that end Master Commandant Oliver Hazard Perry, twenty-seven years old, had been sent to oversee the building of a naval squadron to seize control of Lake Erie. Madison received positive reports of Perry's progress, and then came the news of victory in late September. Perry, aboard his flagship, *Lawrence,* had defeated the British in a bloody fight. When it was over, he had written a short message on the back of an old letter to General William Henry Harrison, who was anxiously awaiting word of the outcome: "We have met the enemy and they are ours."[32]

The British, their Lake Erie supply line cut, withdrew from Detroit into Canada, and Harrison, reinforced by Kentucky volunteers, pursued. Crying "Remember the Raisin," he and his troops defeated the British and their Indian allies near the Thames River. Among those killed was the Indian leader Tecumseh, and as if to show that no one in this war had a corner on brutality, American forces cut souvenir slices of skin from his corpse.[33]

News of the Battles of Lake Erie and the Thames reached Madison before he left Montpelier. Perry's triumph alone, John Adams opined, should be "enough to revive Mr. Madison if he was in the last stage of a consumption."[34] The land victory was also sweet. The United States had recovered the territory it had lost when Hull had surrendered and, by breaking up the Indian confederacy, as Tecumseh's death had done, was a step nearer a goal Madison had been pursuing since his time on the Virginia Council of State: control of the lands northwest of the Ohio River.

But by the time the Thirteenth Congress met in its second session in December 1813, the president also had a most disappointing failure to report. American troops attempting to advance on Montreal had not managed even to get in sight of the city. One failed invasion force had been led by Aaron Burr's erstwhile ally General James Wilkinson, who had revealed yet once more his capacity for startlingly bad judgment. Suffering from dysentery, he had tried to command his troops while heavily dosed with laudanum.[35] Soon would come word of a major reversal along the Niagara frontier, with American forces abandoning Fort George, which just six months before they had captured in a combined action led by Winfield Scott and Oliver Hazard Perry.

Madison was also faced with conflict in his cabinet. Secretary Armstrong had spent most of the last half of 1813 in New York, trying futilely to buttress planning for the attack on Montreal. Monroe, probably thinking that a success would improve Armstrong's presidential prospects (a thought that had certainly occurred to Armstrong), tried to turn Armstrong's absence to his advantage. He removed all the correspondence concerning the war effort of 1813 from Armstrong's department to his, thus putting himself in a position to control information about the war. When the president found out, he was furious. He summoned Monroe and, upon learning that he had left town, personally went to the State Department and had the papers transferred back to the War Department. Later in the year when Armstrong, concerned about a lack of recruits in the regular army, began to float the idea of conscription, Monroe demanded the president fire him: "This man, if continued in office, will ruin not you and the administration only, but the whole Republican party and cause."[36] Madison was not the first president to experience cabinet rivalries, nor would he be the last. He chose the course that many chief executives have taken—and a few have found successful—of trying to stay above the fray.

Madison followed up on his message to Congress with a secret recommendation for a complete embargo on American exports and a ban on importing British products. He knew that such a move would further anger New England, which, possessing the only coastline not under British blockade, had a virtual monopoly on American exports, but he was angered that goods from the United States were supplying not only "British armies at a distance," as he told Congress, "but the armies in our neighborhood with which our own are contending." Just months before, Congress had rejected an embargo, but it now swiftly passed a measure imposing one, no doubt a sign that members were growing increasingly concerned about the war. The weeks ahead gave them more reasons to worry. News came that the British had captured Fort Niagara; moved down the Niagara River, wreaking havoc along the way; and destroyed the village of Buffalo. Daniel Tompkins, the Republican governor of New York, wrote to Madison describing "the massacre and scalping of a number of inhabitants of Lewiston and Niagara, many of whose bodies have been found mangled in a most shocking manner." Citizens were panicking, Tompkins reported. "They are abandoning their possessions and retiring into the interior."[37]

A ship called the *Bramble* arrived in the harbor at Annapolis bringing news of Napoleon. He had managed to raise another army and drive the Prussians over the Elbe and the Oder, but at Leipzig, where he also faced the Austrians, Russians, and Swedes, he had been dealt a stunning defeat, which renewed worries about Great Britain's stepping up its war effort against the United States.[38] The *Bramble* also brought news offering some hope of peace. Although the British had turned down the Russian offer of mediation, they now proposed direct negotiations. Madison quickly nominated John Quincy Adams, James Bayard, and Albert Gallatin, all in Europe, to the negotiations and added Speaker of the House Henry Clay and diplomat Jonathan Russell. They were soon confirmed by the Senate, whose members were in part pacified by Gallatin's formal exit from the Treasury. Republicans who had been recalcitrant before could also imagine Britain fast turning its attention to its former colonies.

The news of Leipzig heartened Federalists, whose opposition to the war had been growing steadily more threatening. Some suspected that they were actually aiding the enemy. In December 1813, the British had extended their blockade to include New England, an action that trapped naval hero Stephen Decatur's squadron in a Connecticut river. When a stormy night offered the chance for him to sail out of the harbor at New London, blue lights suddenly appeared onshore. He believed—and reported to the secretary of the navy—that they were signals to the British of his movements. Decatur's story, fitting as it did into the pattern of extreme Federalist opposition to the war, was instantly picked up by Republicans, who began to use the phrase "Blue Light Federalists" to describe seditious opposition.[39]

Madison managed to keep in mind that while Federalists might be aiding the enemy, they weren't the enemy. When Governor Martin Chittenden of Vermont ordered his state's militia, who were in New York under federal authority, to return home to protect Vermont, Congressman Solomon Sharp of Kentucky claimed the governor had thus enticed "soldiers in the service of the United States to desert" and demanded a federal prosecution. Apparently, with the encouragement of the president, the House tabled his motion.[40]

But it was not possible to ignore events in Europe, particularly after the coalition allied against Napoleon entered France. The embargo that the United States had instituted in December 1813 could no longer be thought of as having any impact on Great Britain, since it could now trade with the entire European continent with the exception of France. Its main effect now was to drive down badly needed Treasury revenues and alienate New England. Swallowing his indignation about Americans provisioning British armies, President Madison asked Congress to repeal the embargo, which the two houses voted to do. Some Republicans were stunned by the change in policy, but Congressman John Calhoun, although no supporter of the embargo, pushed back against the charge of inconsistency. "Men cannot always go straightforward, but must regard the obstacles which impede their course," he said. "Inconsistency consists in a change of conduct when there is no change of circumstances which justify it." Federalists, on the other hand, were in a jubilant mood. Observed Representative Nathaniel Macon of North Carolina, one of the Old Republicans, "They have all a smile on their countenances and look at each other as if they were the men which had brought this great and good work about."[41]

Madison, as though aware that the summer months would exceed in difficulty anything he had experienced as president thus far, decided to spend most of May in Montpelier. His crops there showed no effect from the previous summer's drought, but Hessian fly was in evidence. The insect that Jefferson had studied during their 1791 tour of New York was now ravaging Virginia crops, but the damage to his wheat was hardly Madison's biggest concern. He worried about what kind of military campaign the United States should wage given the changed circumstances of the world. And he worried about the man he had placed in charge of America's military, John Armstrong. He was furious when he read in the *National Intelligencer* that Armstrong had, in the process of consolidating regiments, taken it upon himself to decide which general officers would stay and which go. That was a presidential prerogative. Wrote Madison to Armstrong in an icy tone, "You must have inferred more from my conversations than I could have meant to convey by anything in them on the subject."[42]

The thin-faced, haughty Armstrong had brought much-needed change to the army, moving younger men into general ranks, but he alienated nearly everyone with whom he worked, and the president was fast joining their numbers. Both men agreed that forty-seven-year-old Andrew Jackson, who had won notable victories in the South over a militant band of Creeks, should become a major general, but there was no opening. Thus the president decided to promote him to brigadier with a brevet (or promise) of major general when an opening occurred. When Madison received news from Armstrong that William Henry Harrison had resigned, creating such an opening, he responded that now Jackson could be moved directly into a major generalship but very specifically told Armstrong to wait until he, Madison, had returned to Washington: "I suspend a final decision, however, till I see you, *which will be in two or three days after the arrival of this.*" But the president arrived back in the capital to find that Armstrong, despite being told to wait, had already notified Jackson of his promotion to major general. Madison suspected that two factors were at work: Armstrong wanted to get the credit from Jackson for the promotion, and he wanted to eliminate any possibility of the president's persuading Harrison, whom Armstrong did not like, to withdraw his resignation. Realizing that he needed to rein in his secretary of war, Madison began a detailed examination of Armstrong's conduct of the war thus far, and he began sending him instructive memos on how he could improve his performance.[43]

The news from Europe grew ever more unsettling. Napoleon had been deposed, and, reported Albert Gallatin in his clear-eyed way, "the numerous English forces in France, Italy, Holland, and Portugal, ready for immediate service and for which there is no further employment in Europe, afford to [the British] government the means of sending both to Canada and to the United States a very formidable army." The British were also ready to "turn against us as much of their superabundant naval forces as they may think adequate to any object they have in view." An expanded war effort against America would be well received by the British public, Gallatin noted. "In the intoxication of an unexpected success, which they ascribe to themselves, the English people eagerly wish that their pride may be fully gratified by what they call the 'punishment of America.'" Gallatin and Bayard, writing together, reported that the British ministry was being petitioned to demand concessions from the United States, including restrictions on American commerce and fisheries and control of the great inland lakes. It was hardly the time, they observed, for the United States to be making demands about impressment, particularly since it could well become an abstract issue. With the defeat of France, the British would no longer be desperate to build up naval manpower. On June 27 the cabinet met and agreed to change instructions to the negotiators, authorizing them to conclude a treaty silent on the matter. On hearing the news, the French minister commented to his government, "The cabinet is frightened."[44] They had good reason to be concerned.

The British were almost certain to launch a major attack; the only question was where. On the Niagara front, at the Battles of Chippawa and Lundy's Lane, a new generation of military leaders, including Jacob Brown and Winfield Scott, were demonstrating that American regulars and even militia, well drilled and well commanded, were the equal of British regulars, but how would they fare as more British troops poured in? The entire eastern coastline was vulnerable, and in June the president began to think that Washington might be a prime target. His cabinet members were not convinced. The false alarm of the previous summer might have influenced their thinking, and they also believed that the British would attack locations of more strategic significance. Washington was, in the words of one of them, "a meager village," its inhabitants numbering little more than eight thousand. The prosperous port of Baltimore was more inviting, and as the secretary of war, the most skeptical member of the cabinet, noted, it could be attacked with some rapidity, whereas Washington had to be approached by either the Potomac ("long and sinuous") or the Patuxent, which would require an overland march of some twenty miles.[45]

But the president, understanding "the éclat" that the British would gain by a successful attack on the capital, summoned his cabinet to a July 1 meeting from which emerged specific recommendations: create a tenth military district that would include Washington, Annapolis, and Baltimore; immediately establish a force of more than three thousand to defend the new district; hold in readiness in their jurisdictions ten thousand militiamen from the District of Columbia and neighboring states; and create caches of military equipment and arms to be readily available in an emergency. There was no dissent, which likely gave the president confidence the plan would be executed—a false confidence, it would turn out.[46]

One important failure occurred as a result of Brigadier General William Winder's having less effective connections than had been thought. Winder was assigned to command the newly created military district in large part because his uncle was the Federalist governor of Maryland and Winder was believed likely to be able to gain his cooperation. Winder traveled to Annapolis, where Levin Winder, the governor, offered reassurances about fielding the initial force of three thousand but ultimately delivered fewer than three hundred.[47]

Other failures came about because of the lack of urgency that the secretary of war attached to the situation. On July 17 he wrote to Winder authorizing him to notify Pennsylvania to ready five thousand militiamen and Virginia to ready two thousand for the Tenth Military District. By this time Armstrong had received word of a new British squadron in the Chesapeake and suggested that it might be a "precursor of the main fleet," but he did nothing to ensure that his letter reached Winder, who was traveling around the Tenth District. It would be more than three weeks before Winder got the notice, far too late for action upon it to aid in the defense of Washington.[48]

Armstrong's apathy might have been a result of his conviction that the British would not attack Washington, but it is also the case that few people have risen as high as he with as low a level of industriousness. His biographer, C. Edward Skeen, noted that Armstrong freely admitted to lacking diligence and loving ease. He might also have been encouraged in his naturally indolent ways by Madison's continuing examination of his department. On August 13 the president sent him a memorandum in which he made clear that he was tired of reading in the newspaper about actions on which he should have been consulted. Henceforth, Armstrong was to check first on matters involving the "responsibility of the president," such as making notifications of commissions or issuing directives to the commanders of military districts, corps, or stations concerning military movements.[49] To a person who found it difficult to gear himself up for action in any case, this might have seemed like an invitation not to bother. Armstrong was also both proud and petulant, and being told that he had to get certain of his ideas approved might have determined him to cease making suggestions altogether.

Both the president and the secretary of war did have things to worry about besides the British invading Washington. An August 16 letter from Madison to Armstrong conveyed presidential concern for the Niagara front, where American forces in Fort Erie were under siege, and stressed the importance the president placed on a combined land and naval operation to gain control of Lake Ontario. But to the citizens of Washington, the capital was what mattered, and by the end of July 1814 they had worked themselves into what Dolley Madison called "a state of perturbation." She wrote to her friend Hannah Gallatin that she'd rather she and James were in Philadelphia. "The people here do not deserve that *I* should prefer [this place]. Among other exclamations and threats they say if Mr. Madison attempts to move from *this house* in case of an attack, they will *stop him* and that he shall *fall with it.*" She claimed not to be alarmed, but she also expressed frustration that probably echoed her husband's: "Our preparations for defense by some means or other is constantly retarded." News that a large British force

had arrived in the Chesapeake and was beginning to ascend the Patuxent River sent Major General John P. Van Ness of the District of Columbia militia rushing to the secretary of war to complain of inadequate
preparations. Armstrong told him not to worry: "Baltimore is the place,
sir. That is of so much more consequence."[50]

With the president's approval, James Monroe, accompanied by a
troop of cavalry, undertook a scouting mission to Benedict, Maryland,
where British troops were landing, and the secretary watched from a
distance as they debarked. The next morning, he reported to Madison
that he had seen some two dozen square-rigged vessels, a number that
the president found surprisingly modest, given how far the British were
from their transports. He warned Monroe that the enemy "may however
count on the effect of boldness and celerity on his side, and the want of
precaution on ours," which would turn out to be astute analysis.[51]

Brigadier General Winder, meanwhile, had issued a mass militia call.
A motley army from Washington and Georgetown, joined by 120 marines, marched to the Woodyard in Maryland, about twelve miles from
Washington, where some 300 regular troops had already assembled. On
the morning of August 22, Winder marched the combined forces, some
1,800 strong, toward Nottingham, where the British had camped. Re-
connoitering with Monroe, who had joined the march, Winder got a
glimpse of the battle-hardened British troops. They seemed to be headed
straight toward the Americans, and thinking their numbers to be from
5,000 to 7,000, Winder ordered his forces to fall back.[52]

As they withdrew, they heard a series of loud explosions. It was the
sound of Commodore Joshua Barney's flotilla being blown up. Barney
and his men had thoroughly irritated the British with guerrilla-like attacks on their ships in the Chesapeake, and one of the British missions
up the Patuxent, where Barney had retreated, had been to get rid of him
and his squadron. Realizing that capture was inevitable, Barney had
ordered the flotilla destroyed. He and some four hundred sailors and
marines fell in with Winder's troops, and the men spent the night at
Battalion Old Fields, some eight miles southeast of Washington.[53]

Late on August 22 the president, accompanied by members of his cabinet, joined the troops. He had been concerned about leaving Mrs. Madison in the chaotic capital, where panicked citizens were fleeing, but she had assured him, she reported to her sister Lucy, "that I had no fear but for him and the success of our army." Determined to do what he could to lift the spirits of the men in the field, he had departed, urging his wife as he left to take care of herself and of "the cabinet papers, public and private." The papers of the State Department—including the Declaration of Independence—were already being put into coarse linen bags and loaded into wagons. A clerk named Stephen Pleasanton would hide them first in a gristmill on the Virginia side of the Potomac and then in a locked farmhouse near Leesburg, Virginia.[54]

On the morning of August 23, the president reviewed the troops. He reported to Mrs. Madison that they were "in high spirits and make a good appearance." He was probably putting the best face on things for her as the troops no doubt had done for him. In fact, they were not well prepared, being, as their militia commander put it, "not three days from their homes, without organization or any practical knowledge of service on the part of their officers." Nor were they well equipped. Two companies were carrying muskets, which fired less far and less accurately than the rifles that their captain had requested from the War Department. He had been told by General Armstrong that it was muskets or nothing; the rifles were for the troops in the North. The riflemen had also been issued an inadequate number of flints, a request for one thousand yielding only two hundred.[55]

The president wrote to Mrs. Madison that the British had neither cavalry nor artillery, and he was surely glad to observe as he passed by the troops in review that American forces had both. But skilled horseman that he was, he no doubt noted that many of the cavalry horses were "raw." They had been purchased just two weeks before.[56]

During the day the president became increasingly concerned. A sentinel named Thomas McKenney rode into camp with two deserters and reported to the president and Armstrong his belief that the British were readying an attack on the American position. According to McKenney, Armstrong responded, "They can have no such intention. . . . If an attack is *meditated by them upon anyplace,* it is Annapolis." It was not an unreasonable assessment. From where the British had encamped at Upper Marlboro, the route to Annapolis was a natural one and the town itself a pleasant place to wait if the British were expecting reinforcements. Winder later testified that he, too, thought at this point that the British target was Annapolis:

> Having, therefore, already accomplished one great object of the expedition—the destruction of Commodore Barney's flotilla—if [the enemy] was not in a condition to proceed further into the country, Annapolis offered him a place in all respects such as he would desire. It brought him to a fine port, where his ships could lie in safety; it afforded abundant and comfortable quarters for his men; magazines and storehouses for all his stores and munitions of every description; was capable with very little labor of being rendered impregnable by land and he commanded the water.[57]

Indeed, it wasn't until the early hours of August 23 that the British themselves had decided on Washington as their target. Rear Admiral George Cockburn, leading the British naval forces, and Major General Robert Ross, leading the land forces, had received orders to retreat to their ships. They had done enough, their high command told them. But in a predawn conversation, the headstrong admiral persuaded the more cautious general to disregard the orders and make a strike on the American capital.[58] An event that would be long remembered in American history was thus the result of a spur-of-the-moment decision.

If the British weren't sure of their target until dawn on August 23, it is hard to blame Armstrong for being in error about it that afternoon, but his general attitude was inexcusable. When Brigadier General Walter Smith, commander of the Washington and Georgetown militias, approached him with a note seeking permission for a Colonel George Minor to head for Washington with seven hundred Fairfax County militiamen, Armstrong, so Smith later reported, "treated the matter with great indifference and in a very unsatisfactory way declined to give any order." Armstrong was no doubt reluctant because of Madison's telling him on August 13 to check with him before giving instructions "relative to military movements or operations." But the commander in chief was right there, and Armstrong could have consulted rather than being dismissive. Smith went to the president, who issued the order for Minor to proceed.[59]

Before he left Old Fields, Madison concluded that Armstrong was likely in error and that he, the president, had been right in the first place about the British targeting Washington. He penciled a note to Mrs. Madison sounding alarms. "The enemy seemed stronger than had been reported," he told her, and "it might happen that they would reach the city with intention to destroy it." She "should be ready at a moment's warning to . . . leave."[60]

Chapter 17

TRIAL BY FIRE

ON AUGUST 23, the last day that the Madisons would spend in the White House, the bell at the north entrance clanged repeatedly. One visitor after another desperately wanted to see the president. At twilight, it was Colonel George Minor of Fairfax County reporting that he had brought seven hundred men to fight the British—but they had no weapons. The president sent him on to John Armstrong, trusting that the secretary would understand the urgency of arming Minor's men, but when the colonel arrived at Armstrong's lodgings by "early candle light," the secretary told him that nothing could be done that night. He did bestir himself to pass on the name of Colonel Henry Carbery, whom, he said, Minor could contact in the morning.[1]

One of the next callers was General William Winder, whom Madison was surely surprised to see. Concerned that his troops at Old Fields would be attacked at night, when their artillery would be of no advantage, the commander of the Tenth Military District had led his men, about twenty-five hundred now, in a fast retreat toward Washington. They were encamped, exhausted, near the Eastern Branch Bridge over the Potomac, which Winder intended to secure. He believed it the most likely entry point into Washington for the British. Meanwhile, another part of Winder's army was gathering to the north. Responding to his urgent militia calls, more than two thousand Maryland troops had gathered at Bladensburg, Maryland, where there was another bridge over the Eastern Branch and a turnpike leading directly to Washington. The Marylanders thought the British would choose that route to the capital.[2]

At midnight a messenger pulled the bell at the White House door, bringing a note to the president from Secretary Monroe. "The enemy are in full march for Washington," it read. "Have the materials prepared to destroy the bridges." And then in a postscript, "You had better remove the records."[3]

Early the next morning a note from General Winder arrived. It was intended for Secretary Armstrong, but the president opened it and found that the general was urgently requesting advice. After sending the note on to Armstrong, Madison headed for Winder's quarters near the Eastern Branch Bridge, where he was soon joined by Secretary of State Monroe, Secretary of the Navy William Jones, and Attorney General Richard Rush. The group learned that the British course was now certain. They were marching on the capital by way of Bladensburg. The president dispatched Monroe to the Maryland village, and Winder readied his troops to march. Cavalry had just found hay for their horses, and it was no easy task to persuade them to mount the hungry animals rather than feed them.[4]

Secretary Armstrong was as slow to join the rest of the cabinet as he had been to recognize the danger to Washington. When he finally arrived, the president asked him if he had any advice to offer. Armstrong said he did not, Madison wrote in notes he was keeping, but the secretary did venture a singularly unhelpful assessment—that American troops, being militia, would be defeated by the British regulars.[5]

As the group mounted their horses outside Winder's quarters, Secretary of the Treasury George Campbell, who stayed in the same boardinghouse as Armstrong, expressed concern to the president about the secretary of war's "great reserve." Campbell thought that Armstrong's behavior was due to his believing that General Winder was in charge, but in the present emergency, Campbell said, he shouldn't hold back, particularly given his military experience: "No considerations of delicacy ought to jeopard the public safety." The president agreed and had a conversation with Armstrong. He certainly hoped, he told the secretary of war, that he wasn't holding back because of the August 13 instructions. According to Madison's notes, he told Armstrong that "he should proceed to Bladensburg and give any aid to General Winder that he could." Should there be "any difficulty on the score of authority," Madison said, he would be "near at hand to remove it."[6]

Armstrong's diffidence might not have been the only reason Madison wanted to be at Bladensburg. He could also have had in mind the blow that Jefferson's reputation had suffered when he had fled the British. There is no record that he gave thought to what would happen if he were killed or captured, although he must have considered it, and, indeed, at the end of the five-mile ride to the scene of the impending battle he made a miscalculation that could have been costly. Thinking that American forces were defending the town itself, the president and Attorney General Rush, who was accompanying him, passed by American artillery and riflemen and headed toward the bridge leading to Bladensburg. Fortunately, a scout warned them off. The British had entered the town, and the Americans whom Madison had passed were preparing to defend the near bank. Had the president proceeded on his course, he would have found himself in the middle of a British advance party.[7]

American troops were still arriving as the enemy came in sight, and they were hastily deployed into three lines. The president and Rush, in the company now of Monroe and Armstrong, held a quick meeting behind the first of the lines. "I asked General Armstrong whether he had seen occasion to suggest any improvement in any part of the arrangements," the president reported. "He said that he had not; that from his view of them they appeared to be as good as circumstances admitted." Congreve rockets, inaccurate but terrifying weapons, began to fly overhead, the British pushed forward to the bridge, and the president took himself and his cabinet to the rear, "leaving the military movement to the military men."[8] If the rear was a less heroic place to be, it was also more sensible, not just for Madison, but for the country.

American artillery fire created carnage among the enemy troops advancing on the bridge, and the British briefly fell back. They, like the Americans, were fatigued from marching in the August sun, but they came again, faster this time, and were soon across. The American lines began a quick collapse, and at about 2:00 p.m., "when it became manifest that the battle was lost," the president wrote, "I fell down into the road leading to the city and returned to it."[9]

Riding the dusty turnpike back to Washington, militia and civilians fleeing past, perhaps he heard that one part of the American force had demonstrated true heroism. It would have raised his spirits to learn that Commodore Joshua Barney and the marines and flotilla men under his command had stayed their ground and fought the British with great bravery until they were out of ammunition and Barney was severely wounded. One of the last things Madison had done before leaving Washington was countermand orders that would have left Barney and his men defending the Eastern Branch Bridge instead of fighting at Bladensburg.[10]

DOLLEY MADISON waited nervously at the White House. She had stuffed as many cabinet papers as she could into trunks and sent them off in a carriage. She had watched her friends flee the city and the hundred-man security guard around the president's house leave. She had discouraged Jean-Pierre Sioussat, the White House doorkeeper as well as chef, from spiking the cannon at the gate and sprinkling a trail of powder into the president's house, which he planned to light at the approach of the British. And all the while, she looked for James. Since sunrise she had been directing a spyglass out various windows, hoping to see him approach, but, she wrote, "Alas, I can descry only groups of military wandering in all directions, as if there was a lack of arms or of spirit to fight for their own firesides."[11]

At three o'clock, a rider came galloping toward the president's house.

James Smith, a free black who had been with the president at Bladensburg, was waving his hat in the air and shouting, "Clear out! Clear out!"
Wrote Mrs. Madison to her sister, "I must leave this house or the re-
treating army will make me a prisoner in it by filling up the road I am
directed to take." Charles Carroll, a wealthy friend from Maryland,
stopped by to urge her onward, but she had a few last things to take care
of. Determined that the full-length portrait of George Washington,
proudly displayed in the dining room, would not become a British souvenir, she ordered "the frame to be broken and the canvas taken out."
When it, most of the silver, and her beloved crimson draperies had been
sent away, she consented to leave.[12]

The president arrived not long after she departed, and soon he, too,
left. As the French minister, who stayed in Washington, described it,
Madison "coolly mounted his horse, accompanied by some friends, and
slowly gained the bridge that separates Washington from Virginia."[13]

Riding along the Virginia side of the Potomac, the president and his
party could see the fires as the British burned Washington. Richard
Rush, accompanying the president, described "columns of flame and
smoke ascending throughout the night . . . from the Capitol, president's
house, and other public edifices, as the whole were on fire, some burning slowly, others with bursts of flame and sparks mounting high up in
the dark horizon." Occasionally, the road dipped down, and "the dismal
sight was lost to our view," but "we got it again from some hilltop or
eminence, where we paused to look at it."[14]

Mrs. Madison could also see the flames of the burning city. Her
plans to meet her husband had gone awry, but she had found lodging at
Rokeby, the Virginia estate of her pretty friend Matilda Lee Love, the
niece of Light-Horse Harry Lee. Rokeby was just above the Little Falls
of the Potomac. A mile and a half farther up the road was Salona, the
handsome redbrick home of the Reverend William Maffitt, where, tradition has it, the president spent the night of August 24. Close by as the
president and Mrs. Madison might have been, neither knew where the
other was, and their anxiety must have been considerable. The next day,
as he took shelter from a fierce summer storm, Madison learned that

she had gone on to Wiley's Tavern, near Great Falls, and he headed there, accompanied now by Mordecai Booth, a navy yard clerk, who had made it across the Potomac with several wagons full of gunpowder and was eager to get instructions about where to store it. The intrepid Booth, who had also helped burn the navy yard before the British could capture it, escorted the president to a spot near Wiley's Tavern, where Madison spent some hours with his wife. Intent on joining General Winder and as much of the army as remained, Madison rode off for Maryland at midnight.[15]

Arriving at Montgomery Court House only after the army had left, Madison traveled on in pursuit of it to Brookeville, where he spent the night of August 26 at the two-story brick home of Henrietta Bentley and her husband, Caleb, a silversmith and watchmaker who also served as Brookeville's postmaster. By now the president, who was given Mrs. Bentley's room, was traveling with a substantial entourage. "Beds were spread in the parlor," a late arrival to the scene reported: "The house was filled and guards placed around the house during the night. A large troop of horse likewise arrived and encamped for the night. . . . The tents were scattered along the riverlet and the fires . . . kindled on the ground." Villagers came out to catch a glimpse of the president, who was reported to be "tranquil as usual, and though much distressed by the dreadful event which had taken place, not dispirited."[16]

The president learned the next day that the British had left Washington. Knowing how important it was to reestablish the government as soon as possible, he sent messengers to tell cabinet members to return to the capital and wrote to Mrs. Madison that he was setting out immediately. "You will all of course take the same resolution," he wrote. "I know not where we are in the first instance to hide our heads, but shall look for a place on my arrival."[17]

The president hadn't been in Washington long when he heard a huge explosion coming from the direction of Fort Warburton. If the fort were lost, Washington would soon be subject to bombardment and invasion from the river. The citizens of Alexandria, farther down the Potomac, were already planning to capitulate, and that seemed a fine idea to some citizens of the capital as well. Madison wrote to his wife that she should stay where she was until she heard from him, but the very day he wrote, she appeared at the Cutts residence on F Street, where he was staying—the same house in which the Madisons had lived when he was secretary of state. When her friend Margaret Bayard Smith visited Mrs. Madison, she found her "much depressed. She could scarcely speak without tears."[18]

Madison, riding out with Monroe and Rush, inspected the devastated city. They started at Greenleaf's Point, where British soldiers in the process of laying waste to what was left of the navy yard had accidentally set off an explosion, leaving some thirty of their soldiers dead and a forty-foot-wide crater in the ground. Madison and his party passed alongside the Potomac, and while Monroe picked out positions from which artillery could defend the capital, Madison tried to lift the spirits of Washingtonians. "Our good president is out animating and encouraging the troops and citizens not to despair," wrote a local banker. Although he was trying to boost morale, the tour had to be a sad and solemn one for him. The president's house, which some had begun calling the White House, now consisted of "cracked and blackened walls." The Capitol was a scene of devastation, particularly the House of Representatives wing. The lovely domed roof had collapsed into the cellar, where it was still smoking. The Library of Congress, housed in the Capitol, was utterly destroyed. Dead horses lay around. Houses in the neighborhood had been burned.[19]

While the president was on Capitol Hill, William Thornton, who had designed the Capitol, brought the message that certain citizens of the city wanted to send a deputation to the British to capitulate. Madison forbade them to do so, and Monroe, who was riding with the president, added that anyone trying to approach the enemy with surrender in mind would "be repelled by the bayonet." Thornton returned home, got his sword, and went out into the town to rally citizens for its defense.[20]

The next day, near the Cutts residence, the president was approached by a two-man delegation bringing word from the Washington and Georgetown militias. They blamed Secretary of War Armstrong for the town's inadequate defenses and refused to take further orders from him. That evening the president visited Armstrong at his lodgings and relayed the message: "Every officer would tear off his epaulettes if General Armstrong was to have anything to do with them." While Armstrong had been absent from Washington, Monroe had been giving the orders. The militia found him acceptable, Madison said, but now that the secretary of war had returned, the secretary of state could not continue to issue commands. Armstrong immediately offered to resign, a move the president discouraged. A temporary retirement from the scene until things settled was best, he said.[21]

Armstrong then began to dwell upon how "groundless" were the charges of his having fallen short in defense of the capital, and the president agreed that some of them were. But he added that he "could not in candor say that all that ought to have been done had been done and in proper time." He noted that Armstrong "had never appeared to enter into a just view . . . of the danger to the city" and that he had not put forward "a single precaution or arrangement for its safety." He had not even carried out the preparations agreed upon in the July 1 cabinet meeting.

The president reported that despite their frank exchange, he and the secretary "parted as usual in a friendly manner." They had agreed that Armstrong would think about resigning while visiting his family in New York, but by the time he reached Baltimore, Armstrong had made up his mind. He sent his resignation to the president and would for years cast blame on others for it.[22] James Monroe, whom the president put in charge of the War Department as well as the State Department, spent the rest of his life trying to refute the notion that he had pushed Armstrong out.

A FEW WEEKS LATER the British decided to try to repeat their Washington success at Baltimore, but the city was prepared. Madison's Senate nemesis Samuel Smith of Maryland was in command of its defense, and he knew how to train and command militia. When some four thousand British regulars anchored at North Point, he sent out a militia brigade of about three thousand to meet them. Many of the men had broken ranks and fled at Bladensburg less than three weeks before, but now they successfully carried out their mission of delaying the British, and one of the American skirmishers dealt the enemy a severe blow. From his hiding place in a hollow, he shot and mortally wounded Major General Robert Ross, the British commander.[23]

On the morning of September 13, the British fleet began bombarding Fort McHenry, trying to silence the guns protecting Baltimore's harbor. All day and night they pounded the fort, firing cannon and Congreve rockets, but the next morning, the flag of the United States was still aloft. Francis Scott Key, a lawyer from Georgetown, had approached the British about freeing an American prisoner, Dr. William Beanes, and thus was aboard a British ship to witness "the rockets' red glare, the bombs bursting in air," and "by the dawn's early light," the American flag, "the star-spangled banner," waving in triumph "o'er the land of the free and the home of the brave." Key's inspired words would eventually become the lyrics of our national anthem.[24]

The British withdrawal from Baltimore was heartening news, as was a report from Lake Champlain, where an American squadron under the command of thirty-year-old Thomas Macdonough had seized control— and in most dramatic fashion. The battle was largely carried out by the flagships of the opposing forces, Macdonough's *Saratoga* and the British captain George Downie's *Confiance*. Punishing fire eventually took out all the guns on one side of the *Saratoga*, whereupon Macdonough, who had strategically deployed his kedge anchors before the battle, wound his ship around 180 degrees and brought new guns to bear on the *Confiance*, delivering so many broadsides that its crew refused to go on with the battle.[25]

Meanwhile, the British lieutenant general Sir George Prevost made a coordinated move into New York with what Henry Adams called the most "formidable" force ever sent by the British to America. Proceeding down the west side of Lake Champlain with ten thousand men, he intended to attack the only thing standing in his way: a force of some thirty-four hundred men under the command of Brigadier General

Alexander Macomb at Plattsburgh, New York. Prevost had barely begun his assault, however, when he learned of the American victory on Lake Champlain. Worried about his supply lines being cut, or, indeed, his whole army being cut off, he hastily—and to the consternation of nearly everyone on the British side—withdrew to Canada.[26]

Congress gathered in emergency session in the Patent Office, one of the few public buildings that remained in Washington. Addressing members on September 20, 1814, the president spoke of recent American victories and observed that the British invasion, which had occurred within the month, had "interrupted for a moment only the ordinary public business at the seat of government." He was putting a brave face on what was, in fact, a grim situation. It started with the nation's having only five million dollars in the Treasury, an amount that would fall far short of covering expenditures Congress had already authorized and meeting the expenses of an expanding war. Madison urged members "to take up without delay" the subject of the nation's financial needs, which there was only one way of meeting, and that was by imposing additional taxes. He also prepared the way for Monroe to approach Congress with plans for filling out the ranks of the regular army and reforming the militia.[27]

In the weeks ahead, Congress failed to address these pressing matters, and the nation's prospects grew increasingly dire. Madison learned that the peace negotiations taking place in Ghent were not going well. The British were making extravagant demands—that the United States cede part of Maine and give over military control of the great inland lakes, among other things—and Madison expected his negotiators to depart Ghent soon. He also learned that the British likely intended a massive attack on New Orleans. When attorney William Wirt visited in October, he wrote to his wife that the president "looks miserably shattered and woebegone. In short he looked heart-broken." Madison might not have been well. The month before, he and Mrs. Madison had moved into the Octagon House, a striking brick structure designed by William Thornton, but it was, unfortunately, dark and damp. Mrs. Madison believed that it was making the president ill.[28]

Bad as he might have felt, the president beat back an attempt, mostly by northern congressmen, to move the capital to Philadelphia permanently. It would be cheaper than rebuilding, they claimed. It would be safer for the people of Washington, because the British were unlikely to return if the government moved. Southerners argued that it would "exhibit a panic" to flee now "from that enemy who has so precipitously fled from us." In a Saturday session that Wirt attended ("I was crowded and suffocated for about three hours," he reported), members rejected the Philadelphia option by 83 to 74.[29]

Still, the president was worried. "New England sedition" weighed on him, Wirt wrote: "He introduced the subject and continued to press it, painful as it obviously was to him. I . . . diverted the conversation to another topic, but he took the first opportunity to return to it and convinced me that his heart and mind were painfully full of the subject." Within the week a call would go out from the Massachusetts legislature for a convention of New England states, the purpose being "to lay the foundation for a radical reform in the national compact." Connecticut and Rhode Island both agreed to attend. Counties in New Hampshire and Vermont chose delegates.[30]

To Republicans, the convention, to be held in Hartford, looked like a step on the road to secession. Vice President Elbridge Gerry urged Madison to issue a "spirited manifesto." Philadelphia publisher Mathew Carey castigated him for inaction. As "conspirators openly and fearlessly avowed their projects, . . . you regarded the whole with [a] calm and philosophical tranquility."[31]

Wilson Cary Nicholas, who was about to become governor of Virginia, wanted the president to send in troops. "I think it most likely there will be an explosion in the east," Nicholas wrote. "I take the liberty to recommend to you to take such measures as will prevent the rebels (if there is to be a rebellion) from gaining the start of the movement." In his response, the president sidestepped Nicholas's recommendation, writing that the outcome of New England's "profligate . . . experiment" remained to be seen, but "in the meantime the course to be taken by the government is full of delicacy and perplexity." What Madison couldn't tell Nicholas was that he was making plans to send two infantry divisions into Connecticut, ostensibly for recruiting purposes, but Lieutenant Colonel Thomas Jesup, commander of one of the divisions, would carry secret orders. His mission was to gather information, and should there be any threatening action, such as a British attack coinciding with the convention's gathering, Jesup was to coordinate a military response.[32]

As word began to come in from November congressional elections, it was clear that Federalist strength in New England was growing. When the results were final, New Englanders would have thirty-nine Federalists representing them and just two Republicans. On November 23, the cascade of bad news continued with the sudden death of Vice President Elbridge Gerry, whom Madison had known for nearly thirty years and genuinely liked. Federalists began plotting almost immediately to make Rufus King, a Federalist from New York, president pro tem of the Senate and thus next in line of succession, but the effort failed, which only made Federalists angrier. Newspaper publisher Alexander Hanson, a congressman from Maryland now, stood on the floor of the House to call the president the "cool, remorseless, perverse plotter of our afflictions and perils." He declared that only if Madison stepped aside could the country truly be saved. As if to make the sentiment appear widespread, Hanson's newspaper, the *Federal Republican,* reprinted an article from Virginia claiming that many of Madison's friends were calling on him to retire less than halfway through his term. Some even wished "he was quietly asleep with the late vice president."[33]

ON NOVEMBER 29, 1814, a congressional committee that had been investigating the burning of Washington issued a report that frustrated the president's enemies as much as it probably relieved him. The committee found that "the plan of force" that Madison had laid out in the cabinet meeting of July 1, 1814, authorized means that "were ample and sufficient as to the extent of the force and seasonable as to the time when the measures were authorized"; however, the force was not collected, and the committee cited three "unfortunate circumstances" that had produced "a great and manifest failure." The first was Maryland's not fulfilling its militia call; the second was the delay in calling up Pennsylvania militia caused by Secretary Armstrong's authorizing letter having taken three weeks to reach General Winder; and the third was the failure to provide arms to General Minor's militia in a timely manner.[34] Minor and his seven hundred men had, in fact, missed the main battle entirely.

DECEMBER WAS a month of waiting for news from the Gulf Coast, where thousands of British troops were gathering for an attack. Madison's enemies increasingly tied his fate to that of Major General Andrew Jackson, on whose shoulders the defense of New Orleans rested. Should there be a loss, they were ready to declare that the president had failed to provide Jackson with the necessities of victory. Through late summer and early fall, however, Madison and Monroe had been ordering militia to New Orleans from surrounding states. They also sent Treasury notes valued at some $200,000.[35]

As 1814 drew to an end, Congress had done nothing to shore up the nation's finances. Not even a notice going out from the Treasury in November declaring that the United States could no longer pay the interest on its loans motivated members to seek tax revenue. Nor had they provided for filling up the ranks of the army and reforming the militia. "Alass, alass," Dolley Madison wrote to her friend Hannah Gallatin, "we are not *making* ready as we *ought to do*. Congress trifle away the most precious of *their days,* days that ought to be devoted to the defense of their *divided* country."[36]

In early January the president learned the results of the Hartford Convention. There had been no insistence on immediate secession, as many had feared, but the demands that were made, as Patrick Henry might have said, "squinted" toward secession. The convention insisted that the U.S. government "consent to some arrangement whereby the [New England] states may separately or in concert be empowered to assume upon themselves the defense of their territory"—and allow the states to pay for this by withholding federal tax money. If the U.S. government resisted this demand, as it surely would, then, said the report of the Hartford Convention, "it will . . . be expedient for the legislatures of the several states to appoint delegates to another convention to meet at Boston . . . with such powers and instructions as the exigency of a crisis so momentous may require."[37]

On January 14, Mrs. Madison wrote to Hannah Gallatin that "the fate of New Orleans" would be known at any minute. But one week passed, then another, and it was not until Saturday, February 4, that the glorious news of a great victory arrived. Jackson and his brave men had dealt the British heavy losses while incurring few of their own. That night the citizens of Washington lit candles in their windows to celebrate, and, one imagines, the illumination at the Octagon House was as bright as any.[38]

On the following Monday, the *National Intelligencer* printed letters from Jackson to Monroe that provided details of the victory:

> Early on the morning of the 8th, the enemy, after throwing a
> heavy shower of bombs and Congreve rockets, advanced their
> columns. . . . I cannot speak sufficiently in praise of the firmness
> and deliberation with which my whole line received their
> approach—*more* could not have been expected from veterans
> inured to war. For an hour the fire of the small arms was as incessant
> and severe as can be imagined. The artillery, too, directed by
> officers who displayed equal skill and courage did great execution.
> Yet the columns of the enemy continued to advance.

Twice the British were repulsed, Jackson reported, "and twice they formed again and renewed the assault. At length, however, cut to pieces, they fled in confusion from the field, leaving it covered with their dead." Jackson estimated that some twenty-six hundred British troops had been killed, wounded, or captured. On the American side seven were killed and six wounded.[39]

On February 13, 1815, delegates from the Hartford Convention arrived in the capital to ensure that their dissatisfactions were known, but Jackson's victory overshadowed them, particularly since news of it was followed by word that a peace treaty had been signed in Ghent—two weeks before the Battle of New Orleans. On February 14, Secretary Monroe appeared at the Octagon House with an official copy, and on February 15, 1815, it was laid before the Senate. "Americans, Rejoice!" proclaimed the *National Intelligencer.* "Republicans, rejoice!" "Federalists, rejoice!" But it was hard for the Hartford delegates to feel much joy. They were condemned to wandering the celebrations of Washington largely unnoticed—which was not how they had thought things would be. They had expected the president to invite them to dine, and when they had to settle for attending a reception, they were mightily miffed. "What a mean and contemptible little blackguard," Harrison Gray Otis, the delegation leader, said of the president.[40]

The peace treaty was an agreement to restore matters to the state they had been in before the war, which for critics then and since has been the main point: the War of 1812 accomplished nothing. The Treaty of Ghent, the argument goes, failed to address the main reasons that Madison had cited for going to war, namely, impressment and onerous Orders in Council, thus rendering the struggle futile. But the world had changed since Madison had invited Congress to declare war. Napoleon was on Elba. Britain was no longer at war with France, which meant it was no longer desperate to impress men into the Royal Navy and seize American ships. In these changed circumstances, the importance of assurances about these matters had lessened considerably.

The War of 1812 had a most significant impact on the course of American expansion. The defeat of Tecumseh at the Battle of the Thames led to consolidated American control over the Northwest Territory, thus encouraging further settlement there. Treaties following the victory of Andrew Jackson over the Creeks at Horseshoe Bend would open up large swaths of the South. But good fortune for those eager to settle new lands was a tragedy for Indians, who from time untold had lived on those lands. At the end of 1818, John C. Calhoun, who had become secretary of war, reported to Congress that tribes east of the Mississippi "have in a great measure ceased to be an object of terror and have become that of commiseration."[41]

In waging the War of 1812, Americans had almost immediately shown that despite the small size of their navy, they had the potential to be a great sea power. And though it took some time, the United States ultimately demonstrated the strength it could field in a land force. In late 1814, a British writer offered this perspective in the prestigious *Edinburgh Review*:

> We have been worsted in most of our naval encounters and baffled in most of our enterprises by land. With a naval force on their coast exceeding that of the enemy in the proportion of ten to one we have lost two out of three of all the sea fights in which we have been engaged and at least three times as many men as our opponent while their privateers swarm unchecked round all our settlements and even on the coast of Europe and have already made prize of more than seventeen hundred of our merchant vessels.

The writer went on to note that British land forces, even when reinforced as they had been after Napoleon's defeat, "gained no substantial or permanent advantages." Meanwhile, the Americans were "increasing every hour in skill, confidence, and numbers." Witness the result: "A long campaign has just been closed with a series of disasters."[42]

The writer of the *Edinburgh Review* article admitted that his view was unpopular, but it was not so dissimilar from the one offered to the British government by the Duke of Wellington. He had advised that given the state of the war in November 1814, British negotiators had no right "to demand any concession of territory from America." He noted that the British had been unable to carry the war "into the enemy's territory" and had not cleared their "territory on the point of attack." Wellington's opinion was of great influence in persuading the British ministry to back off the stringent demands it had been making and settle for the American offer of returning to the status quo ante.[43] The

Battle of New Orleans had not yet occurred when the Edinburgh reviewer and the Duke of Wellington wrote. Had they known of it, Jackson's success would have underscored their opinions that the Americans had learned to fight quite well.

In the middle of the conflict with Great Britain, John Adams had declared that "a more necessary war was never undertaken," explaining that "it is necessary against England, necessary to convince France that we are something, and above all necessary to convince ourselves that we are not nothing."[44] Particularly after the dramatic Battle of New Orleans, Americans knew they were something.

THE SENATE RATIFIED the Treaty of Ghent, and on February 18, 1815, Madison laid it before Congress, noting that "peace, at all times a blessing," was particularly gratifying "when the nation can review its conduct without regret and without reproach." He closed his message by urging that members of the House and Senate "never cease to inculcate obedience to the laws and fidelity to the Union," which might have been a mild reproach to those who had encouraged talk of secession, but most Federalists were so bitter that they probably did not care.[45] Their party, tainted in the public mind for the ways in which some members of it had opposed the war, was about to go into the dustbin of history.

During the celebrations, Senator William Barry of Kentucky observed that the president was "much elated." Wrote Barry, "The glad tidings of peace procured by the glory of the American arms under his management has inspired him with new life and vigor." Dolley was radiant with joy, but on the third week of happy crowds flocking to the Octagon, even she became exhausted. "In truth, ever since the peace my brain has been turned with noise and bustle," she wrote to Hannah Gallatin. "Such overflowing rooms I never saw."[46] After arranging to move their Washington residence to a much sunnier place, Seven Buildings, the Madisons left for Montpelier, where they would stay for eleven weeks.

At the end of April, the president traveled from Montpelier to Monticello, where he found his friend Jefferson engaged in a task at once celebratory and sad: arranging and numbering some sixty-five hundred books from his library for transport to Washington. Needing money, Jefferson had sold his collection—the most extensive in the United States—to Congress to replace the library that the British had burned. The packing up was a sign of the nation moving forward, but the former president would miss his books and start ordering new ones almost before these were out the gate. "I cannot live without books," he wrote to John Adams.[47]

BACK HOME at Montpelier, President Madison received stunning news. Napoleon had escaped from Elba and returned to France, and the French army was rallying to him—which could mean another war between the British and the French. Should the American army continue its return to peacetime strength? Should the mission to the Mediterranean to deal with the dey of Algiers, who was holding American prisoners, be allowed to sail? The president decided both matters in the affirmative, and some three months later his judgment about the army was proved correct. Instead of a prolonged European conflict that might once more require the United States to defend its rights, there was a stunning—and final—defeat for Napoleon at Waterloo.

Payne Todd returned home in September, handsome as ever and a joy to his mother. He had acquired excellent French during his European sojourn, appeared knowledgeable on many topics in conversation, and seemed to have good judgment. "To these advantages," a French visitor, the baron de Montlezun, noted, "he joins those of a fine physique, distinguished manners, and urbanity. It is easy to see that he has frequented the good society of our European capitals." But there were reasons to worry. While in Europe, he had dropped out of Gallatin's party, apparently preferring Paris to Ghent, and hadn't bothered to tell his family what he was doing. And he had missed the ship on which he was originally to sail back to the United States, though somehow his baggage and paintings that he had bought for Montpelier had managed to make it on board. Behind his fine appearance and social graces, Payne Todd was fast becoming a ne'er-do-well who would eventually break his mother's heart.[48]

IN MADISON'S MESSAGE to the Fourteenth Congress, which convened in December 1815, he was able to announce a new victory: within weeks of Commodore Stephen Decatur's squadron appearing in the Mediterranean, the dey of Algiers had signed a treaty favorable to the United States. Madison also announced "the revival of the public credit" and tactfully urged Congress to take up consideration of a national bank. Having argued strenuously in 1791 that Congress did not have constitutional authority to charter a bank, Madison would, not surprisingly, find himself charged with inconsistency. He defended himself by citing "legislative precedents." Paying due heed to what legislative bodies had previously sanctioned was a way of protecting "the established course of practice in the business of the community." But having gone through such crises as the government default of November 1814, he had surely also concluded that a national bank was necessary.[49]

In April 1816, Madison not only signed legislation creating the Second Bank of the United States; he also signed a bill creating an army general staff and expanding the navy. John Randolph of Roanoke, who was back in Congress again, declared that the president "out-Hamiltons Alexander Hamilton," and as in many things Randolph said, there was a measure of truth.[50] Over the course of a long public life, Madison had learned to learn. Although he had long regarded an army, in particular, as dangerous in a republic, he now realized that military strength was essential to the nation's security. When experience proved that his opponents' ideas had merit, he incorporated them into his own thinking—though like any good politician he didn't go out of his way to advertise that he was doing so.

After the congressional caucus nominated James Monroe for president in 1816, Mr. and Mrs. Madison took a long break from the nation's capital. The Fourth of July 1816 brought cool and pleasant weather to Montpelier, making it the perfect day for a large gathering. "We had ninety persons to dine with us at one table, [which was] fixed on the lawn under a thick arbor," Dolley wrote to her sister. When Richard Rush heard of the event, he cited it as an example of Madison's "profuse hospitality," noting that "not a week, scarcely a day, passes that he is not doing hospitality in a large way." Rush had himself been a guest at Montpelier, and he noted that Madison appeared at "eminent advantage" in his Piedmont home: "He was never developed to me under so many interesting lights as during the very delightful week I spent under his roof. Perhaps I should add that French cookery and Madeira that he purchased in Philadelphia in '96 made a part of every day's fare!"[51]

The baron de Montlezun, the visitor who had been so impressed with Payne Todd, repaid the Madisons' hospitality at Montpelier with an idyllic portrait of their lives at that moment, when summer was coming to an end. Mrs. Madison was gracious in her bearing and gentle in her speech, and the president, according to the baron, was "hale and vigorous," enjoying "perfect health." Their house was unpretentious, as was the created landscape, with a green meadow interrupted by groves of trees here and there, leading the eye to the mountains, which "stood out boldly in a very blue tint against a pure sky." Montlezun, who had several opportunities to converse with the president, wrote, "Mr. Madison has a quick and accurate mind, profound wisdom, and an excellent tone in discussion, never sharp (he is not a young man), appearing to impute more ability and education to the one with whom he is talking than to himself." Like visitors before him, Montlezun noted the president's reserve on first meeting and his pleasure at being among friends: "When he goes among company, his brow loses its furrows and his face becomes expansive. He enjoys a witticism, he talks brightly—with a simplicity which does him honor and which is all the more noticeable on account of the high position in which his talents have placed him. No one could be more courteous or have more attention and respect than he has for those whom he has received beneath his hospitable roof." During these golden days, the president was still working hard.

Montlezun reported that "he reads and writes nearly all day and often a part of the night."[52]

As happens to those at the end of distinguished careers, Madison found that people wanted to know the details of his life. One was a Philadelphia publisher named Joseph Delaplaine, who wrote to him repeatedly for a biographical sketch—"birth, parentage, education, offices, profession . . . and other things." Madison dutifully set out the details and also wrote about his health, describing his "constitutional liability to sudden attacks, somewhat resembling epilepsy, and suspending the intellectual functions." Lest anyone think they had been simply an affliction of his youth, he specified, "These continued thro' his life, with prolonged intervals."[53]

Perhaps he thought his frankness would help others. He had long ago read that "great men are like looking glasses" in providing models that people look to. Those who suffered with epilepsy might take comfort in his experience—as he had long ago found comfort in knowing that John Locke had endured repeated illnesses. But in the end Madison excised the reference to his sudden attacks. In his youth he had also written, "Secrets that are discovered make a noise. but these that are kept are silent."[54] The public furor that writing about his sudden attacks would have caused was likely more than he wanted to deal with.

President and Mrs. Madison returned to Washington for the last time in October, and they basked in acclaim. The United States felt very good about itself, and its citizens celebrated the man who had led them through perilous times to peace and prosperity and the woman who had already created a legend all her own.

Despite the adulation, the president was modest when he spoke to Congress for the last time in December. He spoke of his pride "that the American people have reached in safety and success their fortieth year as an independent nation" and "that for nearly an entire generation they have had experience of their present Constitution." He did not mention his role in creating that Constitution, instead attributing it to the citizens of the United States. It was, he said, "the offspring of their undisturbed deliberations and of their free choice."[55]

Monroe had been elected to be the fifth president, and the attention of the country began to turn to him. But the day before he was to put his hand on the Bible to take the oath of office, the fourth president stepped back onstage. He had encouraged Congress to consider internal improvements, urging members to consider "the prescribed mode of enlarging" their powers "in order to effectuate a comprehensive system of roads and canals." The members of Congress had, however, passed a bill without heeding his words about amending the Constitution so they had the authority to do so. Thus, on his last full day in office, James Madison vetoed the improvements bill, arguing as he had since the days of *The Federalist* that the general government did not have general powers. It had specified powers, and recognizing its limits was essential to "the permanent success of the Constitution." It was a statesmanlike way of saying what he had once opined to Harry Lee, that if the limits the Constitution imposed on government were unrecognized, "the parchment had better be thrown into the fire at once."[56]

A few days after Monroe was sworn in, the mayor of Washington, Dr. James Blake, paid tribute to Madison for respecting liberty during war as well as peace:

> Power and national glory, sir, have often before been acquired by the sword; but rarely without the sacrifice of civil or political liberty. . . . When we reflect that this sword was drawn under your guidance, we cannot resist offering you our own as well as a nation's thanks for the vigilance with which you have restrained it within its proper limits, the energy with which you have directed it to its proper objects, and the safety with which you have wielded an armed force . . . without infringing a political, civil, or religious right.

Mayor Blake had not always been a favorite among Washingtonians. William Thornton's wife, Anna, claimed he had run away "in the hour of danger."[57] But he might well have improved his reputation with this nearly perfect acknowledgment of one of Madison's key achievements: he had proved that a republic could defend itself and remain a republic still.

When everything had been packed and sent to Montpelier, the Madisons set out themselves, boarding a steamboat for the first leg of their journey. Thirty years earlier a boat driven by steam had been tested in the Delaware River during the Constitutional Convention. Now it was revolutionizing transportation, carrying the Madisons south on the Potomac to Aquia Creek, where a carriage awaited that would take them the rest of the way. A passenger on the steamboat described the president as completely relieved of his cares: he "talked and jested with everybody on board, and reminded me of a schoolboy on a long vacation."[58]

Chapter 18

THE SAGE OF MONTPELIER

DURING HIS PUBLIC CAREER, Madison had watched the nation he helped found double in size and grow from thirteen states on or near the Eastern Seaboard to a continental power. There had been a change in the character of the United States as well, which a group called Republican Citizens of Baltimore attributed to the War of 1812: "That struggle has revived with added luster the renown which brightened the morning of our independence; it has called forth and organized the dormant resources of the empire; it has tried and vindicated our republican institutions; it has given us that moral strength which consists in the well-earned respect of the world and in a just respect for ourselves. It has raised up and consolidated a national character, dear to the hearts of the people, as an object of honest pride and a pledge of future union, tranquility, and greatness."[1] Madison had a legacy to be proud of, and he left it secure in the hands of a Republican president and Congress. Indeed, across the nation, the Republican Party that he had helped found was almost entirely dominant.

At age sixty-six, he could now turn his thoughts to Montpelier and practice what he had long preached: a scientific form of agriculture, one that looked at what had succeeded and what had failed to determine future decisions. Such an approach had worked for him in politics, and he believed it would work for him at Montpelier.

Madison happily accepted the presidency of the Agricultural Society of Albemarle and in an address to its members in 1818 put caring for the land in the larger perspective of man's place in nature. "The human part of the creation" had a clear responsibility to preserve nature's balance, to protect "that symmetry in the face of nature, which derives new beauty from every insight that can be gained into it." To that end he recommended principles heretofore "too generally neglected." Land should not be impoverished by cultivation as had so often happened in Virginia, where tobacco, known to exhaust the soil, was planted year after year. Horizontal rather than vertical plowing should be employed to keep soil from being carried off in the rain. Manures and other fertilizers should be used to enrich the soil, and irrigation applied. Madison made a special plea for preserving trees, which since the country's beginnings had been cleared for houses and farms: "Prudence will no longer delay to economize what remains of woodland; to foster the second growths where taking place in convenient spots; and to commence, when necessary, plantations of the trees recommended by their utility and quickness of growth."[2]

Madison had long—and often futilely—recommended such measures to his father and the overseers at Montpelier, and he was surely gratified to be able to implement them in his retirement. But they would not be enough to overcome drought, early frosts, or the Hessian fly, and soon the chinch bug was also ravaging his crops. "It attacks the Indian corn as well as wheat and the other small grains," he wrote, "hiding itself under the folds of the plants and feeding on the stems." Nor could he do anything about grain prices, which, with the end of the Napoleonic Wars, had begun a steep decline. "Without good prices and good crops, the people in some quarters of the Union cannot well be relieved from their pecuniary distresses," he told Richard Rush.[3]

He heard from his old friend Francis Corbin, who was much saddened by Virginia's situation and its prospects. At the root of the problem, as Corbin saw it, was that "slavery and farming" were "incompatible." The great plantations of Virginia supported communities of slaves, the young and the old as well as the laboring force, and these costs held steady even when crops failed and prices fell. "Our non-effectives consume all our effectives make," is how Corbin put it. "The profits of my estate will not do more this year than pay the expenses of it," he wrote. "I suppose yours will hardly do more."[4]

Corbin's supposition was almost certainly correct. The Madisons might not have yet felt the pinch that other Virginia farmers and planters were experiencing, because during his eight years in the White House he had earned a salary considered quite handsome at the time— twenty-five thousand dollars a year—and savings from it might have provided a cushion. The money would not last forever, though, which meant land would have to be sold, but given the current economy where would one find buyers? It was not Madison's way to despair, but he admitted to Corbin that "the times are hard indeed, the more so as an early change is so little within the reach of any fair calculation."[5]

Madison had concerns for his nation as well as his state, particularly after the Missouri Compromise divided the nation in two: north of parallel 36°30', with the exception of Missouri, slavery would be prohibited; south of that line it would be permitted. Setting section against section, though it might have provided a way out of the impasse over admitting Missouri to the Union, promised ever-escalating conflict. "A fire bell in the night," Jefferson called the compromise, "the knell of the Union."[6]

The stinging words hurled by the North at the South in the Missouri debate prompted Madison to take up a literary form that he had been familiar with since he had started reading the *Spectator* but that he had not turned his hand to before. He wrote an allegory, featuring Jonathan Bull, who represented the North, and Mary Bull, representing the South. The Bulls owned two large and neighboring estates and were happily married until a dispute arose over who could and who could not settle new farms on their vast tracts of land. Jonathan, intent on prohibiting Mary's people from removing "with their property to new farms," became fixated on a black stain on Mary's arm and began to taunt her for it, though he had known it was there before their marriage. He demanded that she get rid of the stain, even if that meant cutting off her arm. Mary was stunned and, although angry at first, resolved to defend herself "with the calmness and good feelings, which become the relation of wife and husband." He had once had black spots on his person, she reminded Jonathan:

> You ought surely when you have so slowly and imperfectly relieved yourself from the mortifying stain, although the task was comparatively so easy, to have some forbearance and sympathy with me who have a task so much more difficult to perform. Instead of that you abuse me as if I had brought the misfortune on myself and could remove it at will, or as if you had pointed out a ready way to do it and I had slighted your advice. Yet so far is this from being the case that you know as well as I do that I am not to be blamed for the origin of the sad mishap; that I am as anxious as you can be to get rid of it; that you are as unable as I am to find out a safe and feasible plan for the purpose; and moreover that I have done everything I could in the meantime to mitigate an evil that cannot as yet be removed.

As for tearing off her arm, she said, "I remind you of what you cannot be ignorant, that the most skillful surgeons have given their opinions that if so cruel an operation were to be tried, it could hardly fail to be followed by a mortification or a bleeding to death."[7] Madison used allegory to say what many southerners believed: that slavery was a great evil, which the current generation had not caused and saw no way of ending quickly without destroying the South.

Madison did hold out hope that slavery could be ended gradually. As he explained to Robert J. Evans, a Quaker who advocated gradual emancipation, masters would have to be compensated, and "to be consistent with existing and probably unalterable prejudices in the U.S., the freed blacks ought to be permanently removed beyond the region occupied by or allotted to a white population." After leaving the presidency, Madison had become a founding member of the American Colonization Society, an organization that settled on Liberia as the destination for manumitted slaves. The ACS had many luminaries in its ranks—including Henry Clay, Daniel Webster, Francis Scott Key, and John Marshall. It was nonetheless controversial, not so much because, as we might think today, it advocated expatriating former slaves, but because it was regarded as an antislavery organization.[8]

DURING HIS retirement years, Madison observed, he had less leisure than he had experienced as a public man. His correspondence consumed much time, in part because he graciously responded to requests such as one sent to him by Jacob Engelbrecht of Fredericktown, Maryland. Engelbrecht wanted a letter that he might display after Madison's death and even directed the former president to leave proper margins for framing. Madison answered that he wanted to be sure the letter was worthy of the purpose Engelbrecht intended, and to that end he copied out and enclosed a lovely poem that naturalist John Bartram had composed for Benjamin Franklin, a Horatian ode, filled with American images of mountains, plains, and mighty waters.[9]

Even a pamphlet elicited a thoughtful reply. When Frederick Beasley, provost of the University of Pennsylvania, sent him an a priori proof of "the being and attributes of God," Madison responded by noting that "the belief in a God all powerful, wise, and good is so essential to the moral order of the world and to the happiness of man that arguments which enforce it cannot be drawn from too many sources." But, he told Beasley, coming as close as he ever would to describing his own religious disposition, he thought that for most people the most convincing argument came not from an "abstract train of ideas" but from the world around: "Reasoning from the effect to the cause, 'from nature to nature's God,' will be of the more universal and more persuasive application." Madison recommended a work he had read by Samuel Clarke some fifty years before, perhaps remembering that Clarke, although constructing an a priori argument, also noted that the existence of an intelligent being "appears abundantly from the excellent *variety, order, beauty, and wonderful contrivance* and *fitness of all things in the world*."[10]

Madison often responded at length to requests for his commentary on constitutional matters. When Chief Justice John Marshall ruled in *McCulloch v. Maryland* that the necessary and proper clause of the Constitution allowed Congress to enact legislation merely "appropriate" to carry out its constitutional mandates, Madison offered his critique to Virginia Appeals Court judge Spencer Roane, writing, "What is of most importance is the high sanction given to a latitude in expounding the Constitution which seems to break down the landmarks intended by a specification of the powers of Congress." He added that "few if any of the friends of the Constitution" who were present at its birth antici-pated "that a rule of construction would be introduced as broad and as pliant as what has occurred." Moreover, he wrote, if such a rule had been set forth in the state conventions, it was hard to believe that the Con-stitution would have been ratified. When the Speaker of the House, Andrew Stevenson, asked him to expound on "the origin and innocence of the phrase 'common defense and general welfare,'" Madison set out a history of the phrase in the Articles of Confederation, the Constitu-tional Convention, and the ratifying conventions to show that the words were regarded "merely as general terms, explained and limited by the subjoined specifications."[11]

DESPITE POOR CROPS and poor prices, the Madisons entertained often and fulsomely. Hospitality was bred in the bone, a Virginia tradi-tion that had to be honored even if it meant going into debt to do so. Twenty at the table was not unusual, and the food was abundant: "good soups, flesh, fish, and vegetables, well cooked—dessert and excellent wines of various kinds," as one visitor described it. Some of those the Madisons entertained had been invited, but others, including those sim-ply curious to meet the former president, were also welcomed.[12]

One of the early visitors to Montpelier, James K. Paulding, described the personal attention Madison paid him during a visit that lasted "some weeks." After breakfast, they would converse on the portico: "He spoke without reserve . . . sometimes on literary and philosophical subjects and not infrequently—for he was a capital story teller—he would relate anecdotes highly amusing as well as interesting. He was a man of wit, relished wit in others, and his small, bright blue eyes would twinkle most wickedly when lighted up by some whimsical conception." Mid-morning there would be a tour on horseback to different parts of the five-thousand-acre estate, with Madison nimbly mounting his horse (as he would be able to for many years to come), talking as he rode, and dexterously opening gates "with a crooked stick without dismounting." The conversation was "sometimes didactic, sometimes scientific, and at others diverging to lighter topics." As Madison gave a behind-the-scenes view of momentous happenings, Paulding learned, he later wrote, "that many great events arise from little causes and that as relates to the real motives and moving causes of public measures, history knows about as much of the past as she does of the future."[13]

Guests arriving at Montpelier were shown into the red drawing room, where they found an abundance of paintings and statuary. The portraits that Gilbert Stuart had done of the president and Mrs. Madison were there, as well as Stuart's portrait of Jefferson and a copy he had made of his original Washington. The room had many large paintings, including one four feet high and seven feet long to the right of the fireplace. It showed Pan admiring a scantily clad nymph and was likely among the artworks that Payne Todd brought home from Europe. Busts were everywhere. One could contemplate Homer and Socrates or turn to more recent history and admire Franklin and Lafayette. In front of one of the room's floor-to-ceiling mirrors was a fine bronze figure of Napoleon at Elba, and the mantelpiece featured a bronze of Louis XVIII, who had been restored to the throne of France after Napoleon's defeat in 1814. When the top of the French king's statue was lifted off, visitors found a tiny figure of the former emperor inside.[14]

One of the drawing room's finest features was that it opened to a portico and lawn in back of the house. Beyond the lawn were woods and mountains, which the drawing room's large mirrors reflected. In summer, when the doors to the portico were opened, the sweet scent of the jasmine and roses that twined around the portico's pillars drifted into the room, adding, in the words of one visitor, "an air of indescribable charm to the whole scene, like a bit of fairyland in this prosaic world."[15]

Guests reported dining at about 4:00 p.m. and, after lingering over excellent wines, adjourning with the Madisons to the portico, where they could view the Blue Ridge Mountains and admire the classical temple that Madison had built to disguise the icehouse. There was also a telescope on the portico with which guests could amuse themselves by bringing distant fields into view and espying visitors as they wound their way up the road to Montpelier. One day, challenging a young guest to a footrace, Mrs. Madison told of another entertainment that the portico provided. "Madison and I often run races here when the weather does not allow us to walk," she said.[16]

MADISON SPENT untold hours writing and talking to Jefferson about the creation of the University of Virginia, a project in which Jefferson had involved Madison even before he had settled back into Montpelier. Madison's work on behalf of the university was more than dutiful service to a friend. As he explained to a correspondent in Kentucky, knowledge was essential to a free people: "A popular government without popular information or the means of acquiring it is but a prologue to a farce or a tragedy or perhaps both. Knowledge will forever govern ignorance, and a people who mean to be their own governors must arm themselves with the power which knowledge gives." By establishing institutions of learning, the United States showed the world that free governments "are as favorable to the intellectual and moral improvement of man as they are conformable to his individual and social rights." This thought led him to one of the most charming images in all of his writings. "What spectacle can be more edifying or more seasonable," he asked, "than that of liberty and learning, each leaning on the other for their mutual and surest support?"[17]

The great walls of the university's Rotunda, designed by Jefferson after the Pantheon in Rome, began to rise, and when the thrilling news came that Lafayette was to visit the United States, Jefferson invited him to dine in the magnificent building. In the early afternoon of November 4, 1824, the sixty-seven-year-old Lafayette arrived at Monticello, where he and the eighty-one-year-old Jefferson, who had been ill, had a tearful reunion. Madison, a spry seventy-three, joined them at sunset. "My old friend embraced me with great warmth," he reported to Mrs. Madison. "He is in fine health and spirits but so much increased in bulk and changed in aspect that I should not have known him."[18]

The next day the three men traveled from Monticello to the university in what a French visitor called an "elegant calash." Cavalry accompanied them, and a large crowd followed. Lafayette and the two presidents walked up the lawn to the Rotunda amid much waving of handkerchiefs, and although the building was not quite complete, four hundred people were seated for dinner on the top floor beneath the dome. As a French visitor described the scene, "The sight of the nation's guest seated at the patriotic banquet between Jefferson and Madison, excited in those present an enthusiasm which expressed itself in enlivening sallies of wit and humor. Mr. Madison . . . was especially remarkable for the originality of his expressions and the delicacy of his allusions." From Monticello, Lafayette went to Montpelier, where one of the French guests observed that Madison's "well preserved frame contained a youthful soul full of sensibility, which he did not hesitate to show when he expressed to General Lafayette the pleasure he felt at having him in his house." Mrs. Madison was praised for "the graces of her mind" and the way that "the amenity of her character" exalted "the excellence of that frank hospitality with which strangers are received at Montpelier."[19]

The university opened in March 1825. Jefferson, who had declared that it would "be based on the illimitable freedom of the human mind," shied away from prescribing "the principles which are to be taught"—except in the case of the law school. There he believed that the board of visitors ought to require certain texts: the Declaration of Independence, *The Federalist,* and the resolutions of Virginia against the Alien and

Sedition Laws. Madison, seeing subtleties where his friend did not, argued that if books and documents were to be required, the list should be lengthened to include George Washington's inaugural speech and Farewell Address. He also made the case that dictating the way these texts should be taught, which Jefferson clearly intended, would excite controversy and ultimately prove unworkable. "The most effectual safeguard against heretical intrusions into the school of politics," Madison wrote, "will be an able and orthodox professor."[20] While he was ahead of Jefferson in his notion of academic freedom, that principle did not in his mind require the trustees of the university to blind themselves to the views of candidates for the law professor's post—a feat that would have been impossible in any case.

FAMILY, BEGINNING WITH DOLLEY, was a great source of happiness for Madison in his later years. Mrs. Madison, according to her niece Mary Estelle Elizabeth Cutts, was the former president's "solace and comfort": "He could not bear her to leave his presence, and she gratified him by being absent only when duty required. No matter how agreeably employed [she was], he was her first thought, and instinct seemed to tell her when she was wanted. If engaged in conversation, she would quickly rise and say 'I must go to Madison.' On his return from riding round the plantation she would meet him at the door with refreshment in her own hands." One guest who observed them together noted that "they looked like Adam [and] Eve in their bower."[21]

Relatives from both sides of the family were among the frequent visitors to Montpelier. Madison particularly enjoyed the company of Nelly Madison Willis, the cheerful and good-hearted daughter of his late brother Ambrose. In the summer Dolley's sister Anna Cutts and her children made long visits. Anna's oldest son was a namesake, James Madison Cutts, and her youngest, Richard D. Cutts, was the apple of his uncle James's eye. Madison sent young Richard a copy of the *Spectator*, telling him that he had read it as a boy and recommending it for the "lively sense of the duties, the virtues, and the proprieties of life" it imparted. There were strains between Madison's brother William and other members of the family, particularly Frances Madison Rose, the youngest sister, arising from the settlement of James senior's estate. William seemed perpetually angry, perhaps because of the awful circumstances of his life. Tuberculosis decimated his family. By the time of James Madison's retirement, William had lost four children, and during James's retirement he would lose five more and his wife. James seems to have looked beyond his brother's bitterness to recognize the gifts of William's son Robert, whose way he paid at Dickinson College. Robert's wedding was celebrated at Montpelier.[22]

Other family members were also a source of worry. After Anna's husband, Richard Cutts, lost his inherited fortune during the War of 1812, he persuaded Madison to lend him $11,500 so that he could invest his way out of his financial troubles. Dolley Madison contributed another $4,000. But Cutts's ventures failed, and he was forced to declare himself insolvent. A bank to which he owed money seized the home he had built for his family on the square north of the White House, and Madison signed notes for another $6,000 to buy it so that Anna Cutts and her children would not be displaced. This arrangement infuriated other creditors of Cutts's (including architect William Thornton), who resented his living in fine style while he owed them money. It also led to Madison's being named and having to hire lawyers to defend him in two suits brought against Cutts.[23]

Payne Todd was angered by the initial loan to Cutts because, he wrote, the four thousand dollars his mother contributed was from his trust and he had not been consulted. It is hard to have confidence in many of Todd's statements, but this one has the ring of truth about it. Dolley Madison had raised Anna and regarded her as her daughter as well as a sister. She would have gone to almost any length to prop up the Cutts family's fortunes. Todd brooded over the Cutts loan, and although he already had a habit of disappearing for months at a time and running up bills that James Madison ended up being responsible for, Todd's resentment over his mother's spending a significant part of his patrimony might have made matters worse. In 1825, after one long period of not hearing from him, Madison wrote, "What shall I say to you? It is painful to utter reproaches; yet how can they be avoided?" Todd was not only beggaring him, he was bringing grief to Mrs. Madison, "the tenderest of mothers." She was "wound up to the highest pitch by this addition to your long and mysterious absence," Madison wrote, urging Todd to explain the reasons for it. "You owe it to yourself as well as to us to withhold them no longer."[24] Both Madisons were concerned that Todd had ended up in debtors' prison, as indeed he had.

Until 1825, Madison had managed to stay afloat with bank loans, but in April of that year, when he had tried to borrow six thousand dollars from the Bank of the United States, the bank's president, Nicholas Biddle, turned him down, explaining that the bank was no longer lending money secured by real estate. Madison managed to get Payne out of prison and, in an effort to keep him from going back, assumed responsibility for a number of his debts. Short of funds himself, however, he had to seek delays and make excuses. In 1826 he wrote to a Philadelphia boardinghouse owner, "Inconsiderable as the amount may be thought, such have been the failures of my crops and the prices for them for a series of years and such the utter failures of payments when I am the creditor, and I may add, such the pecuniary distress and prospects here at present, that in undertaking unforeseen payments the time must be left to my own conveniency." In 1827, when Philadelphia's postmaster, Richard Bache, covered a three-hundred-dollar draft of Todd's "to prevent his arrest and imprisonment," Madison had to ask for time in repaying him. He simply didn't have the money.[25]

Madison found buyers for Montpelier lands as well as some adjacent and in 1827 gratefully received a loan of two thousand dollars from Edward Coles, the young Virginian who had been his private secretary while he was president. Since his time with Madison, Coles, who was just six years older than Payne Todd, had accomplished many things, including freeing ten slaves he had inherited from his father. He had taken them out of state, as Virginia law required, and settled them in Illinois, giving each family 160 acres of land. Subsequently elected governor of Illinois, Coles had tried but failed to change the infamous "black code" of Illinois, which placed restrictions on free blacks. He did manage to turn back a serious effort to make slavery legal in the state.[26]

Coles had been fervently opposed to slavery since he was a young man and had not hesitated to let Madison know his views. When Madison continued as a slaveholder, Coles tried to understand how a good man could tolerate such a great moral wrong. He described Madison's principles as "sound, pure, and conscientious": "To give pain always gave him pain; and no man had a more instinctive repugnance to doing wrong to another than he had; yet from the force of early impressions, the influence of habit and association, and a certain train of reasoning which lulled in some degree his conscience, without convincing his judgment (for he never justified or approved of it), he continued to hold slaves." Madison congratulated Coles for his success in pursuing "the true course" but cautioned him that white prejudice would keep those whom he had freed from full liberty. Over the years the people Coles had emancipated worked hard and did well, but along the way they were also duped and cheated, as well as deprived of their rights by the Illinois black code. Coles, convinced that all free blacks would find better lives in Africa, became an outspoken member of the American Colonization Society.[27]

Madison had other young friends who wanted to leave Virginia. Nicholas Trist, grandson of Eliza, studied at West Point, read law, and tried unsuccessfully to make a career for himself as a planter in Louisiana. Trist returned home to marry his sweetheart, Virginia Jefferson Randolph, Thomas Jefferson's granddaughter, but like many of his generation couldn't find a way to make a living in the Old Dominion and spent most of his life outside it. His friend (and Thomas Jefferson's grandson) Francis Eppes expressed the frustration of a younger generation of Virginians as financial depression continued. He wrote to Trist, "*We* will never witness better times here."[28]

MADISON WAS NOT the only former president with financial woes. Jefferson's troubles made the newspapers when he sought permission from the Virginia legislature to organize a lottery to sell Monticello property. After the stories appeared, Madison received a letter from his friend mentioning the "mortification" he was going through and explaining how it had happened: poor crops, low crop prices, plummeting property values, and former governor Wilson Cary Nicholas's default on a twenty-thousand-dollar note that Jefferson had co-signed and for which he was now liable. That, Jefferson explained, was "the *coup de grace*."[29]

Madison wrote back that he, too, was struggling: "Since my return to private life (and the case was worse during my absence in public) such have been the unkind seasons and the ravages of insects that I have made but one tolerable crop of tobacco and but one of wheat, the proceeds of both of which were greatly curtailed by mishaps in the sale of them. And having no resources but in the earth I cultivate, I have been living very much throughout on borrowed means." Madison did not mention Payne Todd, though surely it must have occurred to him that Todd was a greater blight on Madison fortunes than Wilson Cary Nicholas was on those of Jefferson. Receipts that Madison saved from payments he made on Todd's behalf would eventually total some twenty thousand dollars—about half, Madison would estimate, of the amount he had actually paid.[30]

When Jefferson, nearly eighty-three, wrote the letter explaining his financial woes, he was weighed down not only by debt but by thoughts of dying, "as I soon must." He told Madison that "the friendship which has subsisted between us now half a century and the harmony of our political principles and pursuits have been sources of constant happiness to me through that long period." He took "great solace," he wrote, in knowing that Madison would live on to vindicate their efforts: "If ever the earth has beheld a system of administration conducted with a single and steadfast eye to the general interest and happiness of those committed to it . . . , it is that to which our lives have been devoted. To myself you have been a pillar of support through life. Take care of me when dead, and be assured that I shall leave with you my last affections."

Madison wrote back, "You cannot look back to the long period of our private friendship and political harmony with more affecting recollections than I do. If they are a source of pleasure to you, what ought they not to be to me? We cannot be deprived of the happy consciousness of the pure devotion to the public good with which we discharged the trusts committed to us. And I indulge a confidence that sufficient evidence will find its way to another generation to ensure, after we are gone, whatever of justice may be withheld whilst we are here." Madison could not bring himself to acknowledge that his friend would soon be "beyond the bourne of life," as Jefferson expressed it, but Jefferson died on July 4, 1826—the fiftieth anniversary of the Declaration of Independence and the same day that John Adams died. Jefferson's physician, Robley Dunglison, brought Madison a gift that Jefferson had bequeathed him as a token of their long friendship, a walking stick of animal horn, mounted in gold.[31] Madison accepted the staff—and the duty of taking care of his dead friend's reputation.

In the last months of his life, Jefferson had been particularly troubled by a message delivered to Congress by John Adams's son John Quincy Adams, who had become president in 1825. In his first formal message, the sixth president had set forth plans for the federal government to undertake a wide range of internal improvements, from a canal connecting the Chesapeake Bay and the Ohio River to the continuation of the Cumberland Road. Jefferson had nothing against such projects, but he was extraordinarily concerned that the federal government would undertake them without constitutional authority. It was the same point that Madison had made on his last full day as president when he vetoed the improvements bill, but Jefferson's reaction to Adams's message, no doubt heightened by sickness and financial distress, was extreme. He composed the "Declaration and Protest," which he planned to send to the Virginia legislature for its use. In it he returned to the ideas he had advanced in 1798: the Constitution was a compact that the states had entered into that granted certain powers to the federal government while retaining the rest; and when the federal government usurped state powers by "constructions, inferences, and indefinite deductions," it was the right of the state to "protest" those usurpations "as null and void."[32]

As he had done for decades when he knew he had written something likely to inflame opinion, Jefferson sent the protest to Madison for review.

With wisdom and patience, Madison discouraged him from sending it, and Jefferson listened, but he had already mailed a letter to the contentious William Branch Giles bemoaning "the rapid strides with which the federal branch of our government is advancing towards the usurpation of all the rights reserved to the states and the consolidation in itself of all powers, foreign and domestic." Although Jefferson counseled patience in his letter to Giles, he also wrote that "when the sole alternatives left are the dissolution of our Union . . . or submission to a government without limitation of powers . . . there can be no hesitation."[33]

Jefferson had written at the letter's beginning that it was "not intended for the public eye," but after his death Giles, who had run for and won the governorship of Virginia by attacking government encroachments, released the letter. Giles argued that not only were roads and canals "unauthorized oppressions of the general government" but so were tariffs that protected eastern manufacturers at the expense of southern agricultural interests, and his release of the letter made it seem as though Jefferson endorsed Giles's views on tariffs—and supported going so far as secession should the federal government become too domineering.[34]

In fact, Jefferson, like Madison, was on record in favor of tariffs that protected American manufactures, and Madison, while privately admitting that Jefferson had been careless in his language, nonetheless thought it "monstrous" that a private communication would be used to make the former president "avow opinions in the most pointed opposition to those maintained by him in his more deliberate correspondence with others and acted on through his whole official life." He took it as his mission to show the constitutionality of the Tariff of 1828 (known in the South as the Tariff of Abominations). The levying of tariffs was among the powers granted to Congress under the commerce clause, he wrote, and the practice had the weight of precedent behind it. For nearly forty years, tariffs had been sanctioned by every branch of federal and state government, and to overturn "so prolonged and universal a practice," Madison wrote, would mean "an end of that stability in government and in laws, which is essential."[35]

Because the issue of the tariff had become so hotly disputed, Madison held off publication of his pronouncements until after the presidential election of 1828. In that year, Andrew Jackson defeated John Quincy Adams, and John C. Calhoun, who as Adams's vice president had worked mightily to defeat him, was reelected and became Jackson's number two. Brilliant and ambitious, Calhoun sensed the power of the tariff issue, particularly when it was understood as he chose to understand it, as part of a larger effort to destroy "the peculiar domestic institution of the southern states and the consequent direction which that and her soil and climate have given to her industry." In seizing upon the tariff to defend the right of a state to declare a law unconstitutional and thus "null and void," he positioned himself as a defender of the southern way of life, and he pointed to two other southerners as having provided him precedent, Jefferson in the Kentucky Resolutions and Madison in the Virginia Resolutions and the *Report of 1800.*[36]

Thus Madison, who had tried to avoid the political storm, was drawn into the center of it. Far more was at stake now than a tariff. "Nullification," in his words, "has the effect of putting powder under the Constitution and Union and a match in the hand of every party to blow them up at pleasure." Madison did not say the words "civil war," but the violence of his image suggests that he, so good at discerning the course of events, understood well that the doctrine of nullification opened the possibility of bloody conflict between the North and the South.[37]

He argued that neither the Virginia Resolutions nor his report had ever contemplated a single state's overturning a federal law. The idea that such a thing was possible rested on an erroneous idea of how the Constitution had been created. State governments hadn't formed it but rather the people of each state, "acting in their highest sovereign capacity." Such a compact "constituting the people" of the states as "one people for certain purposes . . . cannot be altered or annulled at the will of the states individually."[38]

Madison's opposition to nullification brought out the worst in its supporters. They accused the former president of being senile and inconsistent. Governor Giles wrote that "what Mr. Madison's opinions at seventy-nine years of age may be," he could not guess. He would "rely upon his opinions of fifty and the incontestable arguments which support them."[39]

Madison made light of the charge that he was in his dotage: "A man whose years have but reached the canonical three score and ten (and mine are much beyond the number) . . . should never forget that his arguments whatever they be will be answered by allusions to the date of his birth." He took the accusations of inconsistency more seriously but found himself faced with a knotty problem when denying that he had contemplated anything like nullification in the days of the Alien and Sedition Acts. Jefferson had caused the words "null, void, and of no force or effect" to be inserted into the Virginia Resolutions after Madison had drafted them but before they were presented to the House of Delegates. Madison could not, while remaining faithful to his friend, point this out, nor could he take the credit that was likely his due for getting the words omitted. He was left with arguing that the fact they had been struck showed that Virginia was "precisely against the doctrine."[40] Madison's silence on Jefferson's role in the Virginia Resolutions was a gift to his friend, all the more generous because it robbed Madison of his own best defense.

Madison never quit trying, but defending Jefferson against the nullifiers' use of Jefferson's words was a nearly impossible task. The thing to do, Madison advised Nicholas Trist, was to call attention to what Jefferson had said and done in earlier epochs of the Republic. He advised that "allowances also ought to be made for a habit in Mr. Jefferson, as in others of great genius, of expressing in strong and round terms impressions of the moment."[41] Madison, a man of steadier and more patient genius, had been doing exactly this for fifty years.

As part of his battle against the idea that a state could nullify a federal law, Madison publicly affirmed the constitutional authority of the federal judiciary to do so. It was impossible to conceive, he wrote in a letter to the *North American Review*, that there could be "a supremacy in a law of the land," as provided for in article 6 of the Constitution, "without a supremacy in the exposition and execution of the law." He was also clear, however, that the power of the Supreme Court had "not always been rightly exercised." He and John Marshall had by now become personally reconciled. Regarded as great sages, they had both been called upon for their wisdom when Virginia rewrote its constitution in 1829, and during the months of the convention they were often seen walking together on Shockoe Hill, the site of the Virginia capitol. But Madison had not reconciled himself to Marshall's latitudinarian constructions of the Constitution, nor to the idea that the federal judiciary's was the only opinion that counted. There were "proper measures" that citizens and state legislatures could take—as Virginia had in 1798—that could bring about a change in public opinion sufficient to alter judicial opinion.[42] The Supreme Court might have the last word—but not for all time.

Madison did not cease his struggles against nullification even as he entered his ninth decade. He continued to send expository letters to Nicholas Trist, now an aide to Andrew Jackson, that Trist turned into newspaper essays opposing nullification. It was also to Trist that Madison lamented as South Carolina rushed headlong toward enacting a nullification ordinance: "The idea that a constitution which has been so fruitful of blessings and a union admitted to be the only guardian of the peace, liberty, and happiness of the people of the states comprising it should be broken up and scattered to the winds without greater than any existing causes is more painful than words can express."[43]

Henry Clay devised a compromise tariff that calmed both nullifiers and President Jackson, who was intent on forcing compliance with federal law. Madison congratulated Clay for the "anodyne" he had provided for "the feverish excitement under which the public mind was laboring," and he optimistically predicted that the South's surplus of agricultural workers, both free and slave, would be partly absorbed into manufacturing in the North and that the South would increasingly turn to the North for manufactured goods. He even predicted that his beloved Virginia "must soon become manufacturing as well as agriculture," and if he was troubled by this dimming of the agrarian vision, he did not say so. At stake was something much greater—healing the potentially calamitous rift between the North and the South. His hope was that the intermixing of manufacturing with agriculture would alleviate the sharp divide and provide "a new cement of the Union."[44]

Still, he was worried by "the torch of discord" that had been lit by the nullification crisis, "by the insidious exhibitions of a permanent incompatibility and even hostility of interests between the South and the North, and by the contagious zeal in vindicating and varnishing the doctrines of nullification and secession, the tendency of all of which, whatever be the intention, is to create a disgust with the Union and then to open the way out of it." He wrote a statement to be released only after his death:

> As this advice, if it ever see the light, will not do so till I am no more, it may be considered as issuing from the tomb, where truth alone can be respected and the happiness of man alone consulted. It will be entitled therefore to whatever weight can be derived from good intentions and from the experience of one who has served his country in various stations through a period of forty years, who espoused in his youth and adhered through his life to the cause of its liberty and who has borne a part in most of the great transactions which will constitute epochs of its destiny. The advice nearest my heart and deepest in my convictions is that the Union of the States be cherished and perpetuated. Let the open enemy to it be regarded as a Pandora with her box opened and the disguised one, as the serpent creeping with his deadly wiles into Paradise.[45]

He wanted his fellow citizens to contemplate the awful consequences of dissolving the Union, and a posthumous statement was the most powerful way he could think of to encourage that.

MADISON SPENT long hours at Montpelier collecting and editing his papers. He wrote to friends and their descendants to retrieve copies of letters he had written, separated official correspondence from private, and, to the everlasting regret of Madison scholars, destroyed or gave away documents that he considered personal. Mrs. Madison often worked with him, and both he and she struck out lines in letters that they thought might be hurtful. When Madison came across a letter he had written to Jefferson some fifty years before, he changed the description of Lafayette it contained from "I take him to be as amiable a man as his vanity will admit" to "I take him to be as amiable a man as can be imagined." The description had originally been in code, but Jefferson's decipherment of it was plain for all to see. Thus in order to change the passage, Madison had to imitate Jefferson's writing, which he did. Madison clearly thought that after a half century of friendship and all that Lafayette had endured, he deserved better.[46]

Scholar that he was, working on his notes of the Constitutional Convention must have brought him particular gratification. They were a gift for posterity, contributing, in his words, to "the history of a constitution on which would be staked the happiness of a people great even in its infancy and possibly the cause of liberty throughout the world." He also hoped that the sale of his papers would prove a financial benefit to family members and institutions that he valued. He no doubt particularly hoped to protect Mrs. Madison from the poverty that was beginning to encroach on Montpelier. A visitor noted that Madison's well-designed house was "decayed and in need of considerable repairs, which, at a trifling expense would make a great difference in favor in the first impression of his residence."[47]

Although Madison sold off land, he did not want to sell slaves, which meant that there were fewer and fewer resources to support an enslaved workforce that continued to grow. Finally, in 1834, he sold sixteen slaves to William Taylor, a relative in Louisiana. He told Edward Coles that the slaves had consented "to be transferred," and although slaves were generally—and rightfully—terrified of being sent to the sugar and cane fields of the Deep South, there is contemporary testimony to slaves as well as slaveholders wanting to leave an increasingly impoverished Virginia. It would have been obvious to those who were enslaved at Montpelier, as it was to its master, that the farmland that remained could not produce enough to feed and clothe all those who lived there.[48]

Madison had intended for the sale to take care of his most urgent debts, but one of the first creditors he paid was Edward Coles, who does not seem to have been pressing for payment. But Coles had become agitated by what he called the "revolting heresies" of Andrew Jackson and peremptorily demanded that the eighty-three-year-old Madison step forth and condemn the president. Madison answered that given "the debilitating effects of age and disease," he had "withdrawn from *party* agitations," which is what he believed the quarrels surrounding Jackson were about. He no doubt also had in mind Jackson's firm opposition to nullification. The president had been on the right side of that controversy. Coles responded furiously that Jackson was violating the Constitution and again demanded that Madison speak out. Coles was not the first person to think that being a creditor entitled him to more than money, but Madison, apparently finding his attitude intolerable, used proceeds from the slave sale to pay Coles. He also wrote him a stern letter that had apparent effect: Coles, though still not lacking in self-righteousness, henceforward was respectful.[49]

MADISON'S MOTHER died in 1829 at the age of ninety-eight, and he was also losing younger people whom he loved: Robert Madison, the nephew in whom he had placed such hopes, died in 1828. Anna Cutts, whom he had helped Dolley raise and seen through many troubles, died in 1832. As happens to those who attain great age, compatriots passed from his life, including James Monroe, who, having fallen into financial ruin, had been forced to sell his Albemarle property. Plagued by ill health, Monroe went to live with his daughter in New York City, and it was from there that he wrote to Madison, "I deeply regret that there is no prospect of our ever meeting again." Madison responded, "Closing the prospect of our ever meeting again afflicts me deeply. . . . The pain I feel at the idea, associated as it is with a recollection of the long, close, and uninterrupted friendship which united us, amounts to a pang which I cannot well express."[50] Monroe died a few months later—on July 4, 1831.

In a letter to historian Jared Sparks, Madison observed that since the death of Georgia's William Few, he was "the only living signer of the Constitution of the United States," and he joked, "Having outlived so many of my contemporaries, I ought not to forget that I may be thought to have outlived myself." In his last years, he suffered from what he called "the crippling effects of a tedious rheumatism" that made it very difficult for him to write and caused him to spend much of his time on a couch. When friends came to visit him, he excused his reclining posture by saying that "he could converse better lying."[51] Despite age, illness, and financial stress, signs of good humor remained.

His life became ever more narrowly circumscribed, until he was living in a single room where he had a bed and a chair, next to the Montpelier dining room, but even then visitors noted the vigor and relish of his spirit. They often gave Dolley credit for the loving care she provided him, and it was well deserved. During one eight-month period when he was ill, she did not venture farther than the black picket fence surrounding their Montpelier home. One particularly astute guest, English writer and feminist Harriet Martineau, noted how much Madison owed to his wife's "intellectual companionship." Martineau, who arrived to visit the Madisons on "a sweet day of early spring" in 1835, found Mrs. Madison "a strong-minded woman, fully capable of entering into her husband's occupations and cares." Dolley had been with the man whom she called her best beloved through presidential elections, war, and the burning of Washington, and during his long retirement she helped him edit his papers. One doubts that she any longer prefaced political questions as she once had by stressing her "want of talents."[52]

The Madisons had specifically invited Martineau, who was touring the United States, to visit Montpelier, perhaps because they had heard that she admired the former president's political philosophy, but the fact that she was an abolitionist probably played an important part. Madison did not want to die without making clear that he, too, abhorred slavery, that it was guilty of every evil with which it had ever been charged.

Perhaps it was the recent effort of working on his will that made him feel a need to explain himself. Certainly the task was a harsh reminder of the realities of trying to disentangle himself from an institution he despised. Friends were encouraging him to free his slaves in his will, but to do so immediately upon his death would leave Dolley Madison with an indebted estate and no way to run it. To free them upon her death would leave her in the same situation in which George Washington's will left his wife. Martha Washington became so afraid of being killed that she freed his slaves a year after his death. But she had 153 slaves of her own remaining, "dower slaves" they were called, with which to manage Mount Vernon.[53] There were no "dower slaves" at Montpelier.

And even if there were a way for Dolley to manage with the slaves at Montpelier freed, where were they to go? As Madison explained to Martineau, "The free states discourage the settlement of blacks; . . . Canada disagrees with them; . . . Haiti shuts them out." He told her that "Africa is their only refuge." The American Colonization Society, of which he had become president, was, he said, the only thing that kept him from utter despair about ending slavery.[54]

Martineau was deeply skeptical of the colonization scheme, and Madison admitted the difficulties, primary among them being that enslaved people did not want to go to Liberia. But it was all he had found to cling to and he held on hard, deluding himself, but refusing to die without some hope that the "dreadful calamity" of slavery would end.[55]

Slavery was the subject Madison talked most to Martineau about, but their conversation ranged widely, from the death of British scholar Thomas Malthus to the size of Roman farms. Observing Madison's keenness for conversation and the remarkable vigor of his mind, Martineau asked herself what uplifted him as he faced the yawning grave, and she concluded that it was his "inexhaustible faith; faith that a well-founded commonwealth may . . . be immortal; not only because the people, its constituency, never dies; but because the principles of justice in which such a commonwealth originates never die out of the people's heart and mind." He had used his remarkable gifts in one of the most important ways a man could, by playing a key role—the key role, one might say—in creating a framework for laws and establishing institutions that would secure liberty and happiness for generations to come.

"This political religion resembles personal piety," Martineau observed, "in its effect of sustaining the spirit through difficulty and change, and leaving no cause for repentance, or even solicitude, when, at the close of life, all things reveal their values to the meditative sage."[56]

ON THE MORNING OF June 28, 1836, Madison died at home, in his room. An enslaved woman named Sukey had brought his breakfast, but he had trouble swallowing. "What is the matter, Uncle James?" asked his favorite niece, Nelly Willis. "Nothing more than a change of *mind*, my dear," he answered. Paul Jennings, born a slave at Montpelier and now Madison's manservant, described what happened next: "His head instantly dropped, and he ceased breathing as quietly as the snuff of a candle goes out."[57]

He was buried in the family graveyard, where his grandfather Ambrose and his grandmother Frances lay and near where he had buried his mother and father. Modest to the end, he had not, as his friend Jefferson had, designed a tombstone, and for twenty years his grave remained unmarked.

Epilogue

MADISON LEFT MOST of his worldly goods to his wife, including the slaves at Montpelier. Friends clung to the idea that there was a secret codicil instructing Mrs. Madison to free them upon her death, but if Madison left such instructions, they have never been found. His will simply asked that Dolley Madison sell slaves only with their consent or if they misbehaved, a request that for several years she largely managed to fulfill.[1]

In the expectation that the sale of his papers would bring $100,000, Madison left bequests amounting to $5,500 to institutions such as the American Colonization Society, the University of Virginia, and Princeton. In addition to individual bequests of land and cash amounting to $7,000 to specified relatives, he made a general bequest of $9,000 to be divided among his nieces and nephews, or, if they should be deceased, their heirs. But when Congress purchased the first three volumes of his writings in 1837, it was for just $30,000. Even as Mrs. Madison was distributing funds according to his will, creditors were almost certainly dunning her for payment of debts incurred before his death, and meanwhile Payne Todd continued his wastrel ways. A friend, noting that Todd's friends were "blacklegs and gamblers," worried that "this money will in all likelihood be lost to Mrs. Madison if he has any power over it."[2]

In October 1837, Dolley returned to Washington for a long stay, occupying the house on Lafayette Square where her sister had once lived. Warm and gracious as ever, she soon found her days filled with visiting and her evenings with elegant events. At one dinner to which she was invited, twenty courses were served, each accompanied by wine. But even as she attended such festivities, she was falling into a genteel but very real poverty. No longer able to buy new clothes, she wore outfits she had had for years. Among her favorites was an old black velvet dress that she paired with a worn white satin turban.[3]

Back at Montpelier in the summer of 1839, Dolley found herself a caregiver again. Her sister Lucy, who had suffered a stroke, moved in, and Dolley became her devoted nurse. Dolley's son, Payne, constructed an eccentric home near Montpelier that he called Toddsberth, and that project ended as badly as the rest of his ventures, with the main structure burning to the ground in the spring of 1841. The economy persisted on its downward path, and Virginia continued its long agricultural decline. Making matters worse, the overseer neglected the fields, and Dolley lost an entire season's crop. In her early seventies now, she was often not well. A recurrent and painful eye inflammation made it difficult for her to write.[4]

She was also under pressure from William Madison, who still harbored resentment over the settlement of James senior's will. Determined to get his due, he sued Dolley for two thousand dollars that he claimed was owed him from his work on that will. When he died in 1843, his son continued the suit, and when the court ruled in his favor, Montpelier slaves were seized to pay off the debt. By countersuing, Dolley managed to stay the sale of the slaves, and she transferred ownership of some forty of them to Payne Todd.[5]

It was impossible to keep Montpelier any longer, and after a long negotiation she sold it and the rest of the estate's slaves to merchant Henry Moncure. She wrote to him, "No one, I think, can appreciate my feeling of grief and dismay at the necessity of transferring to another a beloved home."[6]

Living on Lafayette Square in Washington again, Dolley received more invitations than she could possibly accept and was even given her own seat on the floor of the House of Representatives. But the sale of Montpelier had not alleviated her financial distress. A journal she kept in 1845 and 1846 shows her dependent on a seventy-dollar loan on which she paid thirty-five cents a month in interest. In 1847, she wrote to her son, "I have borrowed as you *must* know to live since and before we parted last, but now I am at a stand until supplies come from you."[7] Recognizing that Payne was a financial threat to his mother rather than a resource for her, Congress, in purchasing an additional four volumes of James's papers in 1848, paid Dolley Madison five thousand dollars outright but put the remaining twenty thousand dollars of the purchase price in a trust from which she could draw the interest.

Word of the congressional purchase led creditors to demand payment, and Dolley was soon making plans to sell off paintings that had hung at Montpelier, which she had managed to keep out of Payne Todd's hands. In the years before Henry Moncure bought the estate, Payne had regularly removed valuable items from the mansion to sell—including some of his stepfather's papers—but Dolley had some items remaining, and she intended either to auction or to raffle them to raise cash to fend off creditors.[8]

Dolley found comfort for her trials at St. John's Episcopal Church near the White House, where she was confirmed as a member, and in loving friends and relatives who were with her in her dying days. Not long after her eighty-first birthday, she fell into a coma from which she woke occasionally to smile at those gathered around her. On the evening of July 12, 1849, she drew her last breath. Her funeral, held at St. John's four days later, was the largest that the capital city had ever seen. Afterward, a cortege of dignitaries, led by President Zachary Taylor, accompanied her body to the Congressional Cemetery, where her casket was placed in a vault. Her son, Payne, did not long outlive her, dying on a cold and stormy day in 1852.[9]

In 1858, one of her beloved sister Anna's sons traveled with her remains to Montpelier, where she was buried in the family graveyard next to James.[10] Once again she was with her darling—and he with the woman to whom he had pledged his unalterable love.

. . .

JAMES'S GRAVE was marked by an obelisk now, paid for by admirers who could not bear to let his final resting place go unacknowledged. Five years after Mrs. Madison's interment, his grave marker would be sketched by a soldier in the Confederate Army of Northern Virginia. Private Watkins Kearns drew the obelisk in August 1863 after he had retreated with General Robert E. Lee from Gettysburg, the bloodiest battle of the Civil War. Upward of fifty thousand men had been killed or wounded.[11]

The Constitution, without which there would have been no Union, could not prevent the war that threatened the Union's destruction, but when peace finally came, the Constitution remained. It was amended to end slavery according to the process Madison had drafted in Philadelphia three-quarters of a century before, the same process he had used to achieve the Bill of Rights, the same process that would be used to extend the vote to women, the same process that would achieve— by way of the Fourteenth Amendment and later rulings—one of his longest-sought goals: the protection of individual rights in the states.[12]

The founding framework endured and pays tribute to Madison's genius still today, as does the great nation that the Constitution has made possible. The United States of America is testimony to the strength of the well-founded commonwealth—and proof of the righteousness of James Madison's unbounded faith in liberty.

ACKNOWLEDGMENTS

THE DEBTS I HAVE ACCUMULATED in writing *James Madison* go back more than a quarter century to my service on the Commission on the Bicentennial of the United States Constitution. Former chief justice Warren E. Burger, the chairman of the commission, impressed on us all what a wondrous document the Constitution is, and I will never forget his wise disquisitions on it. As my interest in James Madison, the father of the Constitution, deepened, I was increasingly puzzled by the disjunction between the grandeur of his accomplishments and the portrayal of him as weak and shy. In 2007, I began extensive research to try to understand this seeming contradiction and soon found myself embarked on a book about Madison's life.

I am extraordinarily grateful to Clare Ferraro, president of Viking, for having faith in my project. Wendy Wolf at Viking is a paragon among editors, knowledgeable, insightful, and direct. Thank you, Wendy, and my thanks as well to associate editor Maggie Riggs and to Bruce Giffords, who oversaw the editorial production process with precision and patience. I was also fortunate to have an outstanding copyeditor, Ingrid Sterner. My gratitude to Brianna Harden, who designed the striking jacket for *James Madison*, and to Amy Hill, designer of the lovely interior of the book. I am also grateful to marketing director Nancy Sheppard, publicity director Carolyn Coleburn, senior publicist Meredith Burks, and publicist Kristen Matzen.

Let me also acknowledge attorney Bob Barnett, my adviser for many years. He encouraged me to write this book and brought to the project, as he has to all the others with which he has helped me, an amazing knowledge of the publishing industry and lively good cheer.

THE INTERNET HAS REVOLUTIONIZED research in recent years, but physical libraries and archives remain indispensable. I cannot imagine writing this book without the amazing resources of the Library of Congress, where I received invaluable assistance from Mary Yarnall in the Collections Access, Loan, and Management Division. I am indebted to Eric Frazier in the Rare Book and Special Collections Division, where I was able to read health manuals to which people in the eighteenth century turned, and to Patrick Kerwin and Lewis Wyman in the Manuscript Division, where among other original documents, I was able to study Madison's letter describing the end of his romance with Kitty Floyd and decipher some of the words he tried to obliterate. Our great national repositories, which are rapidly digitizing their holdings, are also a source of expert guidance through the electronic world. Digital research specialist Jennifer Harbster at the Library of Congress provided help with weather records, directing me to a periodical that reported rain and thunder on May 5, 1787, the day Madison arrived in Philadelphia for the federal convention.

At the National Archives, another of the nation's great treasures, I was aided immeasurably by Jacqueline Budell, who helped me find my way to documents on the archives' Web site, such as letters written by high officials, and to items as yet undigitized, such as an account written by a clerk, Mordecai Booth, who in 1814 helped burn the Washington Navy Yard before the British could seize it. I thank her and also David Langbart for his help. My gratitude as well to Nancy Smith, who was kind enough to arrange for me to bring my grandchildren to the archives so that we could all marvel over the Constitution of the United States, the world-changing document on display there.

In the Firestone Library of Princeton University, I first saw the draft autobiography that Madison wrote in 1816 in which he described his "constitutional liability to sudden attacks, somewhat resembling epilepsy, and suspending the intellectual functions." These attacks, he wrote, speaking of himself in the third person, "continued thro' his life." In private hands until 1953 and unpublished still as I write, this manuscript persuaded me that it was time to take Madison at his word and explore what he meant by his "sudden attacks." I want to thank Ben Primer of Rare Books and Special Collections in the Firestone Library for assisting me in locating the draft autobiography. I would also like to thank reference librarian Gabriel Swift for his assistance, and AnnaLee Pauls as well. Andrew Kilberg was an excellent guide to the Princeton campus, where Madison attended college.

As I tried to understand Madison's disorder, I had the best advice possible. Dr. Orrin Devinsky, director of the Comprehensive Epilepsy Center of New York University's Langone Medical Center, met with me, responded to e-mails, and actually believed that I would finish this book someday. I am most grateful to have had Dr. Devinsky's help—and I hereby absolve him of any errors in my interpretation. I would also like to thank Dr. Brian Litt, director of the Penn Epilepsy Center, who offered an excellent reading suggestion. Stephen J. Greenberg in the History of Medicine Division at the National Library of Medicine of the National Institutes of Health was helpful as well.

At the University of Virginia, I would like to thank Karin Wittenborg for her assistance at the Alderman Library and express my gratitude to Robert Perkins of the Mary and David Harrison Institute for American History, Literature, and Culture. I would like to thank Clay Davis as well. The Albert and Shirley Small Special Collections Library at the university is a magnificent resource, and it was there that I read the account book that shows James Madison Sr. paying for a cradle for his firstborn. I would like to thank Nicole Bouché, Michael Plunkett, and Margaret Hrabe for their assistance.

At the University of Pennsylvania, where I saw the second orrery built by David Rittenhouse (I viewed the first at Princeton), I was welcomed by director of libraries H. Carton Rogers III and David McKnight, who directs the Rare Book and Manuscript Library. I was ably assisted in that library by Daniel Traister and John Pollack. At the University of Michigan's William L. Clements Library, research specialist Janet Bloom provided valuable assistance. William diGiacomantonio of the First Federal Congress project was kind enough to advise about which member of Washington's administration wrote under the penname Scourge. I am also grateful to Frederick Madison Smith, president of the National Society of Madison Family Descendants, who was helpful with Madison genealogy.

At the Presbyterian Historical Society in Philadelphia, I viewed the unpublished Madison family papers in the Shane Collection. They include the pocket-sized piece of paper listing medicines "for an epilepsy" that James Madison's grandmother Frances ordered. When my time in Philadelphia was unexpectedly cut short, I was graciously assisted by Elaine E. Hasleton of the Family History Library in Salt Lake, which microfilmed the Shane Collection.

At the Virginia Historical Society, Frances S. Pollard, director of library services, was most helpful, as were Katherine Wilkins, Matthew Chaney, and Jamison Davis. My gratitude for their assistance at the Historical Society of Pennsylvania to Lee Arnold, senior director of the library and collections; Jack Gumbrecht, director of research services; Hillary S. Kativa; and Christopher Damiani. At Independence National Historical Park, I am indebted to chief curator Karie Diethorn and historian Coxey Toogood, as well as to Andrea Ashby. I would also like to acknowledge the assistance of librarian James N. Green at the Library Company of Philadelphia, as well as Cornelia S. King, Linda August, Sarah Weatherwax, and Erika Piola.

At the Massachusetts Historical Society, a number of people have been of great help, including Elaine Grublin, head of reader services, and Tracy Potter, reference librarian. I would also like to thank Anna J. Cook, Andrea Cronin, Betsy Boyle, and Rakashi Chand.

I would like to acknowledge the assistance of Robin Kipps, who supervises the Pasteur and Galt Apothecary in Colonial Williamsburg, and Del Moore, reference librarian at the John D. Rockefeller Jr. Library.

The homes of the early presidents are sources of enlightenment and inspiration for anyone working in the founding period. I would particularly like to acknowledge the excellent leadership of Kat Imhoff, president and executive director of the Montpelier Foundation, and her predecessor, Michael C. Quinn, as well as the outstanding work of Sean O'Brien, executive director of the Center for the Constitution. They lead a wonderful team that during the time of my research included Lee Langston-Harrison, Christian Cotz, Lynne Dakin Hastings, Meg Kennedy, Matthew B. Reeves, C. Thomas Chapman, Ellen Wessel, Grant S. Quertermous, Tiffany W. Cole, Allison Deeds, and Lisa Timmerman. I also want to recognize Ann L. Miller's meticulous and valuable work. The energy and inspiration of the Montpelier team has made it possible to see James Madison's home as he and Mrs. Madison knew it and to better understand the greatness of Madison's accomplishments. Their ongoing efforts are daily bringing forth more information, not just about James and Dolley, but also about James's ancestors and Mount Pleasant, the small home to which his grandfather brought his grandmother Frances and their children. The lives of those who were enslaved at Montpelier are becoming part of the historical record thanks to the ongoing work of the Montpelier team.

At Monticello, Daniel P. Jordan, then president of the Thomas Jefferson Foundation, was a gracious host, and Susan R. Stein, the Richard Gilder curator and vice president for museum programs, a marvelous guide. I was also the beneficiary of time spent with Andrew Jackson O'Shaughnessy, who directs the Robert H. Smith International Center for Jefferson Studies, and J. Jefferson Looney, editor of *The Papers of Thomas Jefferson: Retirement Series*. My thanks as well to Jack Robertson, Endrina Tay, and Anna Berkes.

At Mount Vernon, Gay Hart Gaines, former regent of the Mount Vernon Ladies' Association, provided many opportunities for me to visit Washington's lovely home. We spent one early summer evening on the piazza at Mount Vernon with a full moon overhead. It was a reminder that although much separates us from the eighteenth century, there are timeless aspects of life on this earth that connect us.

At James Monroe's home, Dorothy Brown was my informative guide, and I would like to thank her as well as Jarod Kearney, the curator of the James Monroe Museum and Memorial Library in Fredericksburg, Virginia. I would also like to acknowledge the generous assistance of Michele R. Lee, the librarian and archivist at Gunston Hall, George Mason's home, and Judith S. Hynson, director of research and library collections at Stratford Hall, fabled home of the Lees. Thanks as well to archivist Elise Allison at the Greensboro Historical Museum in Greensboro, North Carolina. Gratitude also to Clive and Susan Duval for having graciously welcomed me into their home, Salona, where Madison is said to have spent the night of August 24, 1814.

J. C. A. Stagg, David B. Mattern, Ralph Ketcham, Catherine Allgor, and Holly C. Shulman, whose staggering contributions to Madison scholarship are acknowledged in the prologue to this book, were kind enough to read the manuscript, as were Celeste Colgan and Janet Rogers. This outstanding group was wise in its guidance, saved me from mistakes—and any that remain are entirely my own.

As I described in this book, John Payne Todd, Madison's stepson, regularly pilfered things from Montpelier and sold them, which is one of the reasons that uncataloged Madison documents remain in private hands. If someone tells you that he or she has a Madison letter, you should listen carefully, as I did to Robert Shannahan, a friend from the Eastern Shore of Maryland. Bob, in fact, has two important letters, which he generously shared.

I want to thank the American Enterprise Institute for supporting my work on James Madison. I would particularly like to acknowledge Arthur C. Brooks, AEI's dynamic president, and Karlyn Bowman, who in addition to writing insightful articles on public opinion keeps those of us who work in the humanities from disappearing into our libraries. AEI attracts amazing young people to work as research assistants, and two of the best aided me in writing this book. I would like to thank the smart, creative, and meticulous Hannah Gray, who knows what questions to ask, finds the right answers with astonishing speed, and brings a cheerful, can-do attitude to every task. Indeed, I have yet to find an assignment she cannot fulfill. Here is a prediction: we will all be hearing about Hannah in the future. Her predecessor, Cristina Allegretti, my right-hand person in the first years of writing this book, is sharp, efficient, and organized, with a great eye for detail that will serve her well in the years ahead. I want to thank her for her tireless efforts on this project and congratulate her as she finishes Columbia Business School and launches what I am certain will be a very successful career. I also want to thank the bright and hardworking interns who undertook various tasks: Gabriella Angeloni, Sarah Balakrishnan, Karen Brentano, Rachel Elias, Jeffrey Gerlomes, Elizabeth Gunnell, Julia Harvey, Lauren Hewitt, Margaret Inomata, Christina Johannsen, Steven Lindsay, Annelise Madison, Meredith Manning, Marissa Miller, Cars Paulan, Camille Santrach, and Lindsay Schare.

I end these acknowledgments by expressing gratitude to my husband, Dick Cheney, first and foremost for his love and support. I also thank him for the longtime front-row seat I have had on congressional and presidential politics. That experience has been invaluable in helping me understand—and I hope convey—what a master of the political arts James Madison was.

Notes

Abbreviations

Repositories and Collections

LC Library of Congress.

LC-GW Library of Congress, George Washington Papers.

LC-JM Library of Congress, James Madison Papers, series 1, unless otherwise indicated.

LC-TJ Library of Congress, Thomas Jefferson Papers, series 1, unless otherwise indicated.

UVA University of Virginia.

Abbreviated Titles

ASP-FR *American State Papers, Foreign Relations.* Edited by Walter Lowrie, Matthew St. Claire Clarke, Walter S. Franklin, Asbury Dickins, and James C. Allen. 6 vols. Washington, D.C.: Gales and Seaton, 1833–1858.

ASP-MA *American State Papers, Military Affairs.* Edited by Walter Lowrie, Matthew St. Claire Clarke, Walter S. Franklin, Asbury Dickins, and John W. Forney. 7 vols. Washington, D.C.: Gales and Seaton, 1832–1861.

PMHB *Pennsylvania Magazine of History and Biography.*

VMHB *Virginia Magazine of History and Biography.*

Published Papers from the Founding Period

DHRC   *Documentary History of the Ratification of the Constitution.*

 PDM   *Papers of Dolley Madison Digital Edition.*

  PH   *Papers of Alexander Hamilton.*

  PJ   *Papers of Thomas Jefferson.*

 PMC   *Papers of James Madison, Congressional Series.*

 PMP   *Papers of James Madison, Presidential Series.*

 PMR   *Papers of James Madison, Retirement Series.*

 PMS   *Papers of James Madison, Secretary of State Series.*

PWCE   *Papers of George Washington, Confederation Series.*

 PWD   *Papers of George Washington, Diaries.*

 PWP   *Papers of George Washington, Presidential Series.*

 PWR   *Papers of George Washington, Revolutionary War Series.*

PWRT   *Papers of George Washington, Retirement Series.*

PROLOGUE

1. Grigsby, *Virginia Convention of 1776,* 36n; Billy G. Smith, *"Lower Sort,"* 33–36; Lippincott, *Early Philadelphia,* 51–54; Cutler and Cutler, *Life, Journals, and Correspondence of Rev. Manasseh Cutler,* 1:271–72; "Meteorological Observations." In quotations throughout this book, spelling and punctuation have, with a few exceptions, been modernized, and abbreviations have been written out. Although writers of the period covered in the book underscored words more often than twenty-first-century writers do, their underscorings have been reproduced by italicizing them because they provide useful hints about what the writers wanted their readers to pay attention to. When dates for documents were uncertain, the best estimates of documentary editors have been accepted.

2. Watson, *Annals of Philadelphia,* 1:362–63; Terrio, *Philadelphia 1787;* Grigsby, *History of the Virginia Federal Convention,* 1:96.

3. Dunbar, *History of Travel in America,* 1:174; Annette Kolodny, ed., "The Travel Diary of Elizabeth House Trist: Philadelphia to Natchez, 1783–84," in *Journeys in New Worlds,* 185–95. In *PMC,* 9:409, to William Irvine, May 5, 1787, Madison wrote that he left New York "on Thursday last," which was May 3, 1787. He probably crossed the river to Paulus Hook that evening in order to catch the Flying Machine, a stage that left for Philadelphia on Friday mornings and arrived there Saturday afternoon.

4. Rives Papers, Coles to Grigsby, Dec. 23, 1854; Grigsby, *History of the Virginia Federal Convention,* 1:95; Jefferson, *Autobiography,* 55.

5. Joseph Addison, "No. 231," *Spectator,* 2:92, Nov. 24, 1711.

6. Rives, *Life and Times of James Madison,* 2:612n.

7. Jefferson, *Autobiography,* 55; *PMC* 1:194, from Samuel Stanhope Smith, Nov. 1777–Aug. 1778; Farrand, *Records,* 3:94–95, William Pierce, "Character Sketches of Delegates to the Federal Convention."

8. *PJ,* 7:97, from Eliza Trist, April 13, 1784; De Coppet Collection, Madison to Delaplaine, memo, Sept. 1816; Brant, *Madison,* 1:106–7.

9. Rives Papers, Coles to Grigsby, Dec. 23, 1854.

10. *PMC,* 10:269, *Federalist* 10, Nov. 22, 1787.

11. Gordon Wood described this transformation as "the end of classical politics" in *Creation of the American Republic,* 606–7.

12. Howe, *Genius Explained,* 14–15; Levitin, *This Is Your Brain on Music,* 199; Gladwell, *Outliers,* 40–41; Isaacson, *Einstein,* 36.

13. *PMC,* 1:101, to William Bradford, Dec. 1, 1773.

14. *PMC,* 8:474, 501, to Jefferson, Jan. 22 and March 18, 1786.

15. Howe, *Genius Explained,* 3; Isaacson, *Einstein,* 36, 90–140; Howard Gardner describes the "acid test" of large-scale creativity as being whether the creative person changes the domain in which he or she works in *Intelligence Reframed,* 116.

16. *PJ,* 14:650, to Francis Hopkinson, March 13, 1789; *PMC,* 14:371, "A Candid State of Parties," *National Gazette,* Sept. 22, 1792.

17. *Adams-Jefferson Letters,* 508, Adams to Jefferson, Feb. 2, 1817.

18. Ingersoll, *Historical Sketch,* 1:260; McCoy, *Last of the Fathers,* 25–26.

19. Another two volumes of Madison's papers are planned for the presidential series and an estimated eleven additional volumes for the years he was secretary of state and in retirement.

Chapter 1: Sunlight and Shadows

1. Nugent, *Cavaliers and Pioneers,* 1:280.

2. Ibid., 280, 350, 369, 389, 466, 469, 565–66.

3. [Old] Rappahannock County Deed Book 7, 26–27; Jones, *Present State of Virginia,* 34; Miller, *Short Life and Strange Death of Ambrose Madison,* 7, 36n7; Nugent, *Cavaliers and Pioneers,* 2:255; *Executive Journals of the Council of Colonial Virginia,* 3:147, 371; Boorstin, *Americans,* 111; Kulikoff, *Tobacco and Slaves,* 267; Horn, *Adapting to a New World,* 188–89.

4. Miller, *Short Life and Strange Death of Ambrose Madison,* 51–52.

5. *Executive Journals of the Council of Colonial Virginia,* 4:172; Miller, *Short Life and Strange Death of Ambrose Madison,* 23–25, 81; Taylor, *American Colonies,* 153; Boorstin, *Americans,* 100–101; Kulikoff, *Tobacco and Slaves,* 320; Baylor Family Papers, Baylor Ledger no. 1, 155.

6. Miller, *Short Life and Strange Death of Ambrose Madison,* 25–28.

7. Chambers, *Murder at Montpelier,* 68; Miller, *Short Life and Strange Death of Ambrose Madison,* 67.

8. Meade, *Old Churches,* 2:96; *PMC,* 1:190, 191n2, to Madison Sr., March 29, 1777.

9. "Will of Ambrose Madison, 1732," in "Notes and Queries," 434–35; Orange County Deed Book 2, 11.

10. Orange County Deed Book 2, 11–12; Horn, *Adapting to a New World,* 316–21; Dorman, *Orange County, Virginia: Deed Books 1 and 2, 1735–1738; Judgments, 1735,* 33–37.

11. Jones, *Present State of Virginia,* 39; Middleton, *Tobacco Coast,* 111–13; Breen, *Tobacco Culture,* 46–53.

12. Madison Sr. Account Book, 1744–1755; Shane Collection, Presbyterian Historical Society, Madison Family Papers, invoice from John Maynard & Son, Feb. 21, 1742, and invoice from Hunt & Waterman, March 16, 1749.

13. Kulikoff, *Tobacco and Slaves,* 79; Madison Sr. Account Book, 1744–1755; Shane Collection, Presbyterian Historical Society, Madison Family Papers, Madison Sr. Account Book, 1755–1763; W. W. Scott, *History of Orange County, Virginia,* 73.

14. Hayden, *Virginia Genealogies,* 244.

15. Hunt, *Life of James Madison,* 22; LC-JM, Chew to Madison Sr., Sept. 6, 1749, and May 21, 1750.

16. Madison Sr. Account Book, 1744–1755.

17. Reeves and Fogle, "Excavations at the Madisons' First Home, Mount Pleasant," 17.

18. Morgan, *American Slavery, American Freedom,* 158–61.

19. Aristotle, *Problems II,* 155.

20. Madison Sr. Account Book, 1744–1755; Shane Collection, Presbyterian Historical Society, Madison Family Papers, "List of Drugs for Mrs. F. Madison," Oct. 11, 1753; Quincy, *Complete English Dispensatory,* 73, 82, 84, 112–13, 169–70, 172–74, 178–79, 290–94, 495; Hill, *History of the Materia Medica,* 125.

21. "Febrile Seizures Fact Sheet," National Institute of Neurological Disorders and Stroke, http://www.ninds.nih.gov/disorders/febrile_seizures/detail_febrile_seizures.htm; *Family Letters of Thomas Jefferson,* 252, Martha Randolph to Jefferson, Jan. 14, 1804.

22. Interview with Dr. Orrin Devinsky, director, Comprehensive Epilepsy Center, Langone Medical Center, New York University, May 10, 2009; Devinsky to author, e-mail, Sept. 22, 2013; De Coppet Collection, Madison to Delaplaine, memo, Sept. 1816.

23. Richard Steele, "No. 20," "No. 340," and "No. 154," *Spectator,* March 23, 1711, 1:80; March 31, 1712, 2:484; Aug. 27, 1711, 1:529; "James Madison's Autobiography," 197.

24. Kulikoff, *Tobacco and Slaves,* 104–7; Burnaby, *Travels Through the Middle Settlements in North-America,* 25.

25. Shane Collection, Presbyterian Historical Society, Madison Family Papers, Madison Sr. Account Book, 1755–1763; Fithian, *Journal and Letters,* 63–64.

26. W. W. Scott, *History of Orange County, Virginia,* 43; Meade, *Old Churches,* 2:86, 98; Bernard Bailyn, "Politics and Social Structure in Virginia," in *Seventeenth-Century America,* 111.

27. Meade, *Old Churches,* 2:89; "James Madison's Autobiography," 197; Brant, *Madison,* 1:64.

28. LC-JM, ser. 6, "A Brief System of Logick"; *PMC,* 1:32–37, "Notes on a Brief System of Logick," 1766–1772. The name James A. Garlick, written on the cover of this book, connects it to Madison's time at Robertson's school, when at least two students named Garlick attended. The initials "hB" doodled twice on one of the book's first pages might also connect it to Robertson's, where Horace Bruckner was Madison's fellow student in the Latin curriculum for several years.

29. LC-JM, ser. 6, "A Brief System of Logick"; *PMC,* 1:36, "Notes on a Brief System of Logick," 1766–1772.

30. Miller, "Historic Structure Report," 41; Reeves and Fogle, "Excavations at the Madisons' First Home, Mount Pleasant," 10.

31. W. W. Scott, *History of Orange County, Virginia,* 208.

32. *Proceedings and Addresses at the Celebration of the One Hundredth Anniversary of the Founding of the Cliosophic Society of the College of New Jersey,* 9.

33. Richard A. Harrison, *Princetonians,* xix; Malone, *Jefferson,* 1:52; "James Madison's Autobiography," 197.

34. Brant, *Madison,* 1:411n1; Jefferson, *Memorandum Books,* 1:397–98, reports this route; Burnaby, *Travels Through the Middle Settlements in North-America,* 82; Fithian, *Journal and Letters,* 152–54, 168–69, also describes crossing the Chesapeake.

35. Burnaby, *Travels Through the Middle Settlements in North-America,* 93–94.

36. De Chastellux, *Travels in North-America,* 160; *PMC,* 1:43, to Martin, Aug. 10, 1769.

37. Fithian, *Journal and Letters,* 7–8.

38. *PMC,* 1:78, from Freneau, Nov. 22, 1772; 1:83, to Bradford, April 28, 1773.

39. Fithian, *Journal and Letters,* 256–57; Looney, *Nurseries of Letters and Republicanism,* 4–8; *PMC,* 1:65, "Collegiate Doggerel," June 1771–April 1772.

40. Collins, *Princeton,* 75–76; *PMC,* 1:50, to Madison Sr., July 23, 1770.

41. Woods, *John Witherspoon,* 40; Witherspoon, "Lectures on Moral Philosophy," in *Works,* 3:407, 419; Morrison, *John Witherspoon,* 4.

42. Morrison, *John Witherspoon,* 72, 130.

43. Collins, *Princeton,* 63; Wertenbaker, *Princeton,* 72.

44. Rice, *Rittenhouse Orrery,* 33; Bruff, "The Federalist Papers: The Framers Construct an Orrery," 7.

45. Rice, *Rittenhouse Orrery,* 73.

46. Witherspoon, "Introductory Lecture on Divinity," in *Works*, 4:46; Green, *Witherspoon*, 122, 132; Edwards, *Works*, 26:93.

47. Witherspoon, "Lectures on Moral Philosophy," in *Works*, 3:367–68.

48. *PMC*, 1:46, to Madison Sr., Sept. 30, 1769.

49. "James Madison's Autobiography," 197; *PMC*, 1:68, 69n1, to Madison Sr., Oct. 9, 1771; De Coppet Collection, Madison to Delaplaine, memo, Sept. 1816; Devinsky, *Epilepsy*, 61.

50. *PMC*, 1:194, from Samuel Stanhope Smith, Nov. 1777–Aug. 1778; Witherspoon, "Introductory Lecture on Divinity," in *Works*, 4:43, 47.

51. Aristotle, *Problems II*, 155; Hippocrates, *Medical Works*, 179.

52. Temkin, *Falling Sickness*, 92, 221–23; Churchwell, "Epilepsy and Holy Orders in the Canonical Practice of the Western Church," 67; Harle, *Historical Essay on the State of Physick*, 22. The canon law of the Catholic Church, promulgated in 1918, maintained that those "who either are or have been epileptics, madmen, or possessed by a demon" could not be ordained. Churchwell, "Epilepsy and Holy Orders in the Canonical Practice of the Western Church," 172. References to people with epilepsy and demoniacs were removed in 1983.

53. De Coppet Collection, Madison to Delaplaine, memo, Sept. 1816; Vickers, *Coleridge and the Doctors*, 134–43.

54. Witherspoon Collection, "Titles of Volumes Once Belonging to President Witherspoon and Bought by the College from President Smith"; Tait, *Piety of John Witherspoon*, 197; Clarke, *Paraphrase on the Four Evangelists*, 1:115; *Catalogue of Books in the Library of the College of New Jersey*, 26; Eadie and Bladin, *Disease Once Sacred*, 85, 171.

55. *PMC*, 1:4–7, "Commonplace Book: Editorial Note"; 1:7, 13–14, "Commonplace Book," 1759–1772; de Retz, *Memoirs*, 2:307.

56. Locke, *Some Familiar Letters*, 280, from Dr. Molyneux, Dec. 20, 1692; *PMC*, 1:21, "Commonplace Book," 1759–1772.

Chapter 2: SEASON OF DISCONTENT

1. *PMC*, 1:74–75, to Bradford, Nov. 9, 1772.

2. Shane Collection, Presbyterian Historical Society, Madison Family Papers, Madison Sr. to Clay and Midgley, Aug. 4, 1770; Orange County Will Book 4, 56, "Inventory of the Estate of James Madison Deceased," Sept. 1, 1801; Burkitt, *Expository Notes with Practical Observations*, 37–38.

3. *PMC*, 1:52, "Notes on Commentary on the Bible," 1770–1773; Burkitt, *Expository Notes with Practical Observations*, 284.

4. *PMC*, 1:52–57, 59n18, "Notes on Commentary on the Bible," 1770–1773.

5. *PMC*, 1:76, to Bradford, Nov. 9, 1772; "James Madison's Autobiography," 198; Orange County Will Book 4, 56–57, "Inventory of the Estate of James Madison Deceased." Some of the books in the inventory were likely acquired after 1772; the ones discussed were all published long before.

6. Todd, *Imagining Monsters*, 1–7; Blondel, *Power of the Mother's Imagination over the Foetus Examin'd*, xi, 40–42, 53–54.

7. Temkin, *Falling Sickness*, 229.

8. *PMC*, 1:80, from Bradford, March 1, 1773.

9. *PMC*, 1:84, to Bradford, April 28, 1773; Orange County Will Book 4, 56, "Inventory of the Estate of James Madison Deceased"; Wesley, *Primitive Physic*, iv, vii, ix.

10. Wesley, *Primitive Physic*, x; Blondel, *Power of the Mother's Imagination over the Foetus Examin'd*, 95–96; *PMC*, 1:84, to Bradford, April 28, 1773. See also Cheyne, *Essay of Health and Long Life*, 159.

11. *PMC*, 1:89, to Bradford, June 10, 1773; 1:86, from Bradford, May 27, 1773.

12. *PMC*, 1:96, to Bradford, Sept. 25, 1773.

13. Little, *Imprisoned Preachers and Religious Liberty in Virginia*, 163.

14. *PMC*, 1:106, 101, 112–13, to Bradford, Jan. 24, 1774, Dec. 1, 1773, and April 1, 1774; "James Madison's Autobiography," 198.

15. *PMC*, 1:105, to Bradford, Jan. 24, 1774.

16. Walter Berns, "Religion and the Founding Principle," in *Moral Foundations of the American Republic*, 219–20; Jefferson, *Notes on the State of Virginia*, 170; Meade, *Old Churches*, 2:99–100.

17. Witherspoon, "Lectures on Moral Philosophy," in *Works*, 3:395; *PMC*, 14:427, for the *National Gazette*, Dec. 20, 1792; Hume, *Essays and Treatises on Several Subjects*, 2:452.

18. Hume, *Treatise of Human Nature*, 269, 353; Ferling, *Leap in the Dark*, 94–107.

19. *PMC*, 1:105, to Bradford, Jan. 24, 1774; Brant, *Madison*, 1:137; *PMC*, 1:101, to Bradford, Dec. 1, 1773.

20. Force, *American Archives*, ser. 4, 1:350–51.

21. *PMC*, 1:121, to Bradford, Aug. 23, 1774; 1:126, from Bradford, Oct. 17, 1774.

22. *PMC*, 1:126, from Bradford, Oct. 17, 1774; 1:145 and n8, to Bradford, May 9, 1775; 1:131, 133n1, from Bradford, Jan. 4, 1775; 1:160, to Bradford, July 28, 1775.

23. *PMC*, 1:131, from Bradford, Jan. 4, 1775; 1:129, 135, to Bradford, Nov. 26, 1774, and Jan. 20, 1775.

24. *PMC*, 1:135, to Bradford, Jan. 20, 1775; *Naval Documents of the American Revolution*, 1:204; *PMC*, 1:144, to Bradford, May 9, 1775; Wirt, *Sketches of the Life and Character of Patrick Henry*, 141–42.

25. Wirt, *Sketches of the Life and Character of Patrick Henry*, 149–61.

26. Brant, *Madison*, 1:180; *PMC*, 1:147 and n1, "Address to Captain Patrick Henry and the Gentlemen Independents of Hanover," May 9, 1775; *PMC*, 1:145, to Bradford, May 9, 1775. Strengthening the case that Madison wrote the address is the fact that he referred readers of his autobiography to it: "James Madison's Autobiography," 199.

27. *PMC*, 1:152, 162n11, to Bradford, June 19 and July 28, 1775.

28. *PWR*, 1:3, to Martha Washington, June 18, 1775.

29. Ferling, *Leap in the Dark*, 146.

30. Brant, *Madison,* 1:162–63; Crary, "Tory and the Spy."

31. *PMC,* 1:161, to Bradford, July 28, 1775.

32. Eckenrode, *Revolution in Virginia,* 50–54; "Williamsburg—the Old Colonial Capital," 49; Theobald, "Monstrous Absurdity"; "Magazine," Colonial Williamsburg, http://www.history.org/almanack/places/hb /hbmag.cfm; *PMC,* 1:153, to Bradford, June 19, 1775.

33. *PMC,* 1:153, to Bradford, June 19, 1775; Alexander Purdie, *Virginia Gazette,* Nov. 24, 1775; Olmert, *Official Guide to Colonial Williamsburg,* 92; Selby, *Revolution in Virginia,* 57–58; *PWR,* 2:611, to Richard Henry Lee, Dec. 26, 1775.

34. Pybus, *Epic Journeys of Freedom,* 18–20.

35. *PMC,* 1:153, to Bradford, June 19, 1775.

36. John Hughlings Jackson, *Selected Writings,* 1:390, 399; Devinsky, *Epilepsy,* 19, 31.

37. *PMS,* 1:394, to Wilson Cary Nicholas, July 10, 1801; *PMC,* 3:10, from the Reverend James Madison, March 9, 1781; Devinsky, *Epilepsy,* 19–20; De Coppet Collection, Madison to Delaplaine, memo, Sept. 1816; Devinsky to author, e-mail, Sept. 22, 2013.

38. "James Madison's Autobiography," 199; Rives Papers, George Tucker, untitled memoir of James Madison.

39. Paine, *Common Sense,* 36–37.

40. Ibid., 24.

41. Ibid., 19–20.

Chapter 3: GREAT MEN

1. Ketcham, *Madison,* 63.

2. Grigsby, *Virginia Convention of 1776,* 19n, 15; "Edmund Randolph's Essay on the Revolutionary History of Virginia," *VMHB,* April 1935, 126–27; Charles D. Lowery, "Edmund Pendleton," in *James Madison and the American Nation,* 335.

3. Grigsby, *Virginia Convention of 1776,* 76–78; McCullough, *1776,* 40–41; "Edmund Randolph's Essay on the Revolutionary History of Virginia," *VMHB,* Oct. 1935, 308.

4. Wirt, *Sketches of the Life and Character of Patrick Henry,* 23–33; "Edmund Randolph's Essay on the Revolutionary History of Virginia," *VMHB,* April 1935, 120, and Oct. 1935, 308.

5. Selby, *Revolution in Virginia,* 95–97; Grigsby, *Virginia Convention of 1776,* 17–18.

6. "Edmund Randolph's Essay on the Revolutionary History of Virginia," *VMHB,* Jan. 1936, 42–43.

7. Selby, *Revolution in Virginia,* 97; Alexander Purdie, *Virginia Gazette,* May 17, 1776.

8. Rowland, *Life of George Mason,* 1:226, 204–5.

9. Ibid., 226.

10. *PMC*, 1:173, "Committee's Proposed Article on Religion," May 27–28, 1776; Locke, *Works*, 5:5–58.

11. Brant, *Madison*, 1:247–48; Ketcham, *Madison*, 72–73; *PMC*, 1:173, "Committee's Proposed Article on Religion"; *PMC*, 1:174–75, "Article on Religion Adopted by Convention," June 12, 1776.

12. *PJ*, 1:133, "Draft of Instructions to the Virginia Delegates in the Continental Congress," July 1774.

13. "Edmund Randolph's Essay on the Revolutionary History of Virginia," *VMHB*, Jan. 1936, 43–44.

14. LC-TJ, to Augustus B. Woodward, April 3, 1825; in notes, *PJ*, 1:384–85, "The Constitution as Adopted by the Convention," the editors make the case that Jefferson underestimated how much his draft influenced the constitution of Virginia.

15. *PMC*, 8:77, "Notes for a Speech Favoring Revision of the Virginia Constitution of 1776," June 14 or 21, 1784.

16. *PJ*, 1:354, "Second Draft by Jefferson," before June 13, 1776; *PMC*, 10:17, "The Virginia Plan," May 29, 1787.

17. Alexander Purdie, *Virginia Gazette*, Oct. 11, 1776.

18. Alexander Purdie, *Virginia Gazette*, Oct. 18, 1776; Brant, *Madison*, 1:298; Ketcham, *Madison*, 75.

19. Jefferson, *Autobiography*, 50–53; LC-JM, to Samuel H. Smith, Nov. 4, 1826.

20. Alexander Purdie, *Virginia Gazette*, Dec. 20, 1776, supp., and Dec. 27, 1776; Tyler, *Patrick Henry*, 203–4.

21. Thomas, "Politics in Colonial Orange County," 5, 8–9; Rives, *Life and Times of James Madison*, 1:180–81.

22. Brant, *Madison*, 1:316.

23. *PMC*, 1:216, "Session of Virginia Council of State," Jan. 14, 1778; 1:219–21, "Patrick Henry in Council to Virginia Delegates in Congress," Jan. 20, 1778.

24. *PMC*, 1:216–17, "Session of Virginia Council of State," Jan. 14, 1778; *Official Letters of the Governors of the State of Virginia*, 1:227–29, Henry to Gálvez, Jan. 14, 1778.

25. Lowell H. Harrison, *George Rogers Clark and the War in the West*, 5–17; Selby, *Revolution in Virginia*, 189–203.

26. Brant, *Madison*, 1:343–44, 348; *PMC*, 1:285, 287nn2–3, from Mazzei, June 13, 1779.

27. Brant, *Madison*, 1:349; *PMC*, 7:421, to Jefferson, Feb. 17, 1784; 8:15, from Jefferson, March 16, 1784.

28. Rives, *Life and Times of James Madison*, 1:190; Brant, *Madison*, 1:326–27; *PMC*, 8:9, to Jefferson, March 16, 1784.

29. Jefferson, *Autobiography*, 55.

30. Selby, *Revolution in Virginia*, 197; *Republic of Letters*, 1:74–76, "Order Placing Lieutenant Governor Henry Hamilton of Detroit and Others in Irons," June 16, 1779; 1:79, 89–90, to Washington, June 19 and July 17, 1779.

31. *PJ*, 3:61, from Washington, Aug. 6, 1779.

32. *PMC*, 1:222–23, to Madison Sr., Jan. 23, 1778; Randall, *Life of Thomas Jefferson*, 2:326n; John Clarkson and Augustine Davis, *Virginia Gazette*, Oct. 30, 1779; *PMC*, 1:298, to Madison Sr., June 25, 1779.

33. *Republic of Letters*, 1:52; Randall, *Life of Thomas Jefferson*, 1:68.

34. Rives Papers, Edward Coles to Hugh Grigsby, Dec. 23, 1854; Randall, *Life of Thomas Jefferson*, 2:326n.

35. Coolidge Correspondence, letters from Ellen Coolidge to Henry S. Randall, 37; *PMC*, 1:105–6, to Bradford, Jan. 24, 1774; Peterson, *Thomas Jefferson and the New Nation*, 266.

36. Malone, *Jefferson*, 1:216; Jefferson, *Autobiography*, 25; *PMC*, 12:466, to Washington, Jan. 4, 1790.

37. *PJ*, 1:241–42, to Randolph, Aug. 25, 1775.

38. *PJ*, 1:482, to John Page, July 30, 1776 (italics added); Edward S. Evans, *Seals of Virginia*, 37.

39. Burnaby, *Travels Through the Middle Settlements in North-America*, 42–43; Malone, *Jefferson*, 1:101.

40. *Republic of Letters*, 1:60, 61n17; LC-JM, to Samuel H. Smith, Nov. 4, 1826.

Chapter 4: A ROPE OF SAND

1. *PWR*, 18:448–49, to Harrison, Dec. 18–30, 1778.

2. Conway, *Omitted Chapters of History Disclosed in the Life and Papers of Edmund Randolph*, 41–47.

3. *PMC*, 1:319, to Harrison, Dec. 16, 1779.

4. *PMC*, 1:304, "Money," Sept. 1779–March 1780; Francis Bowen, *Principles of Political Economy*, 374–75.

5. Selby, *Revolution in Virginia*, 227.

6. *PMC*, 2:6, to Jefferson, March 27, 1780.

7. *PMC*, 2:37, to Jefferson, June 2, 1780; Brant, *Madison*, 2:29–30; *Journals of the Continental Congress*, 17:477, 492, 571–72, June 1, 6, and 29, 1780; Papers of the Continental Congress, State Papers, 1777–1788, 2:392–93, June 6, 1780; *Letters of Delegates to Congress*, 15:268, Samuel Huntington to Washington, June 6, 1780; LC-GW, ser. 4, to Continental Congress War Board, June 21, 1780.

8. *PMC*, 2:21, to Page, May 8, 1780; 2:20, to Jefferson, May 6, 1780.

9. *PMC*, 2:20, to Jefferson, May 6, 1780; Golway, *Washington's General*, 1–3, 165–66, 124.

10. Papers of the Continental Congress, "Letters from General Nathanael Greene," 1:303–14, to Huntington, June 19, 1780; *PMC*, 2:45, "Committee Report on Letter from Nathanael Greene," July 22, 1780; Flexner, *George Washington in the American Revolution*, 368–69.

11. Chernow, *Washington*, 379–82; *PMC*, 2:111, to Jefferson, ca. Oct. 5, 1780.

12. Brant, *Madison,* 2:17; Ketcham, *Madison,* 88, 107; *PMC,* 2:123, 124n6, to Jones, Oct. 10, 1780.

13. *PMC,* 2:97, "Expense Account as Delegate in Congress," Sept. 25, 1780; Maxwell, *Portrait of William Floyd,* 30; Brant, *Madison,* 2:27; *PMC,* 3:206, 4:64, 126, to Madison Sr., Aug. 1, 1781, ca. Feb. 12, 1782, and March 30, 1782; 5:87, 170, to Randolph, Aug. 27 and Sept. 30, 1782.

14. "Randolph and Tucker Letters," 41–43, Martha Bland to Frances Tucker, March 30, 1781.

15. Flexner, *George Washington in the American Revolution,* 360; *PMC,* 2:81, to Edmund Pendleton, Sept. 12, 1780; 2:89, to Jones, Sept. 19, 1780.

16. *PMC,* 2:120, from Jones, Oct. 9, 1780; 2:145, to Jones, Oct. 24, 1780.

17. *PMC,* 2:144, from Pendleton, Oct. 23, 1780; 2:157, to Pendleton, Oct. 31, 1780.

18. *Revolutionary Diplomatic Correspondence of the United States,* 4:184, Arthur Lee to the President of Congress, Dec. 7, 1780; Bland, *Papers,* 1:xxvii.

19. Brant, *Madison,* 2:65–69, 192–200.

20. Ibid., 70–78; *PMC,* 2:92n4, from Jones, Sept. 19, 1780; 2:132–34, "Draft of Letter to Jay, Explaining His Instructions," Oct. 17, 1780.

21. *PMC,* 2:224, to Jones, Dec. 5, 1780; 2:195–96, Bland to Jefferson, Nov. 22, 1780.

22. Bemis, *Diplomacy of the American Revolution,* 107–8; *Revolutionary Diplomatic Correspondence of the United States,* 4:738–65, Jay to the President of Congress, Oct. 3, 1781.

23. *PMC,* 2:191, 136–37, to Jones, Nov. 21 and Oct. 17, 1780.

24. Brant, *Madison,* 2:99–101.

25. *PMC,* 2:279, to Jefferson, Jan. 9, 1781; Freeman, *Washington,* 453–55; Neimeyer, *America Goes to War,* 148–51.

26. *PMC,* 2:297, to Pendleton, Jan. 23, 1781.

27. *PMC,* 3:10, 13n12, from the Reverend James Madison, March 9, 1781.

28. *PMC,* 3:172, from Pendleton, July 6, 1781; 3:207, 209n11, to Madison Sr., Aug. 1, 1781; Thomson, *Account of the Life, Lectures, and Writings of William Cullen, M.D.,* 2:104–5.

29. Cullen, *First Lines of the Practice of Physic,* 2:iii, 86–108; De Coppet Collection, Madison to Delaplaine, memo, Sept. 1816. In a description approved by Madison, Edward Coles described Madison's sudden attacks as "an affection of the breast and nerves." Grigsby, *Virginia Convention of 1776,* 84n.

30. Cullen, *First Lines of the Practice of Physic,* 2:104, 106, 108; *PJ,* 4:567–68, from Bland, Feb. 9, 1781.

31. LC-JM, Washington to Jones, March 24, 1781; Brant, *Madison,* 2:55.

32. *Letters of Delegates to Congress,* 17:38, Thomas Rodney's notes, post–March 8, 1781; William Baskerville Hamilton, *Thomas Rodney,* 4, 25.

33. *PMC*, 3:71, 73n4, to Jefferson, April 16, 1781; 3:17–18, "Proposed Amendment of Articles of Confederation," March 12, 1781.

34. Selby, *Revolution in Virginia*, 274–75, 281–82; Malone, *Jefferson*, 1:357.

35. *PMC*, 3:178, to Philip Mazzei, July 7, 1781; Brant, *Madison*, 2:162; *PMC*, 3:247, to Pendleton, Sept. 3, 1781.

36. Brant, *Madison*, 2:165; *PMC*, 3:296, to Pendleton, Oct. 30, 1781.

37. Brissot de Warville, *New Travels in the United States of America*, 102.

38. *Journals of the Continental Congress*, 24:291, "The Address and Petition of the Officers of the Army of the United States," April 29, 1783; *PMC*, 6:55–56, to Randolph, Jan. 22, 1783.

39. *PMC*, 6:142, "Notes on Debates," Jan. 28, 1783.

40. Ibid., 143–47.

41. *PMC*, 6:273–74, "Notes on Debates," Feb. 21, 1783.

42. *PMC*, 6:292, "Notes on Debates," Feb. 26, 1783; 6:406, "Amendment to Report on Restoring Public Credit: Editorial Note"; 6:407–8, "Notes on Debates," March 28, 1783.

43. *PMC*, 2:209, to Jones, Nov. 28, 1780; *PMC*, 7:304, 305n4, to Madison Sr., Sept. 8, 1783.

44. LC-GW, ser. 3h, to Hamilton, April 4, 1783; *Journals of the Continental Congress*, 24:295–97, to the Officers of the Army, April 29, 1783.

45. *PMC*, 6:481, to Jefferson, April 22, 1783.

46. *PMC*, 6:493–94, "Report on Address to the States by Congress," April 25, 1783.

47. Monroe, *Papers*, 2:55–56, to John Francis Mercer, March 14, 1783; Brant, *Madison*, 2:14.

48. LC-JM and *PMC*, 6:221, to Jefferson, Feb. 11, 1783; 6:235–36, from Jefferson, Feb. 14, 1783.

Chapter 5: LOVE AND OTHER RESOURCES OF HAPPINESS

1. South Carolina delegate Francis Kinloch, who entered Congress about a week after Madison, had married his fifteen-year-old sweetheart, Mildred Walker, in 1781. Kinloch was just ten years older than his bride, while Madison was sixteen years older than Kitty, or twice her age during their courtship, but examples of much greater age disparities are easy to find. John Witherspoon, famed president of Princeton, was almost three times the age of his second wife when they married.

2. Maxwell, *Portrait of William Floyd*, 20.

3. Ibid., 31.

4. *PMC*, 6:459, from Jefferson, April 14, 1783.

5. *PMC*, 6:481, 7:18, to Jefferson, April 22 and May 6, 1783.

6. *PMC*, 7:177, "Notes on Debates," June 21, 1783.

7. Brant, *Madison*, 2:294–95; *PMC*, 7:177–78, "Notes on Debates," June 21, 1783; 7:196, "Proclamation by Elias Boudinot," June 24, 1783.

8. *PMC*, 7:216, 217n2, to Randolph, July 8, 1783; 7:230, to Jefferson, July 17, 1783.

9. LC-JM, to Jefferson, Aug. 11, 1783; Brant, *Madison*, 2:283–87; *PMC*, 7:268, to Jefferson, Aug. 11, 1783. Brant was the first to decipher crossed-out portions of the letter; further decipherments can be found in *Letters of Delegates to Congress*, 20:539; and this author added a few phrases.

10. *PMC*, 7:298–99, from Jefferson, Aug. 31, 1783.

11. Gay, *James Madison*, 42–44; Maxwell, *Portrait of William Floyd*, 13; Torres-Reyes, "William Floyd Estate," 34–35.

12. *PMC*, 7:401, to Jefferson, Dec. 10, 1783 (many words encoded).

13. *PMC*, 7:401, 404nn15–16, 418–19, to Jefferson, Dec. 10, 1783, and Feb. 11, 1784; 8:3, to Randolph, March 10, 1784; 7:411–12, from Jefferson, Jan. 1, 1784.

14. *PMC*, 7:298, from Jefferson, Aug. 31, 1783; 9:51–53, 78–81, to Jefferson, May 12 and June 19, 1786; 8:514–44, Appendix B: "Meteorological Journal for Orange County, Virginia, in Madison's Hand"; 9:77, 8:266, 9:49, to Jefferson, June 19, 1786, April 27, 1785, and May 12, 1786.

15. *PMC*, 8:11, to Jefferson, March 16, 1784.

16. Brant, *Madison*, 2:313; *PMC*, 8:3, to Randolph, March 10, 1784; Madison, *Writings*, 2:396, "Origin of Constitutional Convention," 1835.

17. *PMC*, 8:37, "The General Assembly Session of May 1784: Editorial Note"; Conway, *Omitted Chapters of History Disclosed in the Life and Papers of Edmund Randolph*, 56, to Jefferson, May 15, 1784.

18. Jean Edward Smith, *John Marshall*, 88–89; Schoepf, *Travels in the Confederation*, 2:64.

19. Tyler, *Patrick Henry*, 267; *PJ*, 7:257, from Short, May 15, 1784.

20. *PMC*, 8:34, to Jefferson, May 15, 1784.

21. *PMC*, 8:80, to Madison Sr., June 15, 1784.

22. *PMC*, 8:93, to Jefferson, July 3, 1784; 8:178, from Jefferson, Dec. 8, 1784; 8:227, to Jefferson, Jan. 9, 1785.

23. Breckinridge Family Papers, Archibald Stuart to John Breckinridge, Dec. 7, 1785.

24. Malone, *Jefferson*, 1:270–72; *PMC*, 9:211–12, from Jefferson, Dec. 16, 1786; 9:267, to Jefferson, Feb. 15, 1787; Brant, *Madison*, 2:357.

25. Jefferson, *Autobiography*, 58; *PMC*, 9:244, to Edmund Pendleton, Jan. 9, 1787; 8:230–31, to Jefferson, Jan. 9, 1785.

26. Lance Banning, "James Madison, the Statute for Religious Freedom, and the Crisis of Republican Convictions," in *Virginia Statute for Religious Freedom*, 133n23.

27. *PMC*, 8:198, "Madison's Notes for Debates on the General Assessment Bill," Dec. 23–24, 1784; 8:157–58, to James Monroe, Nov. 27, 1784.

28. *PMC*, 8:264, from George Nicholas, April 22, 1785; 8:298–304, "Memorial and Remonstrance Against Religious Assessments," June 20, 1785.

29. *PMR*, 1:612, "Detatched Memoranda," ca. Jan. 31, 1820.

30. Hening, *Statutes at Large,* 12:84–86, "An Act for Establishing Religious Freedom"; *PMC,* 8:474, to Jefferson, Jan. 22, 1786.

31. Martin Marty, "Virginia Statute Two Hundred Years Later," in *Virginia Statute for Religious Freedom,* 1–3.

32. Taylor Diary, March 2, 1786; *PMC,* 8:542, Appendix B: "Meteorological Journal for Orange County, in Madison's Hand."

33. *PMC,* 8:113, to Jefferson, Sept. 7, 1784.

34. Bernier, *Lafayette,* 18; *PMC,* 8:121, to Jefferson, Oct. 17, 1784; Franklin, *Writings,* 7:62, to George Washington, Aug. 1777.

35. *PMC,* 8:114, to Jefferson, Sept. 7, 1784.

36. *PMC,* 8:115, to Jefferson, Sept. 15, 1784; Evans Journal, Sept. 15–22, 1784; Brant, *Madison,* 2:328–29.

37. Barbé-Marbois, *Our Revolutionary Forefathers,* 178–85.

38. *PMC,* 8:120–21, 121n2, to Jefferson, Oct. 17, 1784; 8:245, 186, from Lafayette, March 16, 1785, and Dec. 15, 1784; 8:345, to Jefferson, Aug. 20, 1785 (many words encoded).

39. LC-TJ, from Madison, May 15, 1808.

40. Buchan, *Domestic Medicine,* 434; *PMC,* 8:270, to Jefferson, April 27, 1785.

41. *PMC,* 8:178, from Jefferson, Dec. 8, 1784.

42. *PMC,* 8:270, to Jefferson, April 27, 1785; Brant, *Madison,* 2:306.

43. *PMC,* 8:328, to Randolph, July 26, 1785.

44. *PMC,* 9:97, to Jefferson, Aug. 12, 1786.

45. Ammon, *James Monroe,* xi; Wirt, *Letters of the British Spy,* 174; *PMC,* 8:32, from Jefferson, May 8, 1784.

46. Brant, *Madison,* 2:340–42; *PMC,* 9:97–98, to Jefferson, Aug. 12, 1786; 9:212–13, from Jefferson, Dec. 16, 1786.

47. Kaminski, *George Clinton,* 92.

48. *PMC,* 9:94–95, to Jefferson, Aug. 12, 1786; Madison, *Writings,* 2:395, "Origin of the Constitutional Convention," 1835.

49. *PMC,* 8:501, to Jefferson, March 18, 1786; 9:4–22, "Notes on Ancient and Modern Confederacies," April–June 1786; 10:210, to Jefferson, Oct. 24, 1787.

50. *PMC,* 6:425, "Notes on Debates," April 1, 1783.

51. *PMC,* 8:471, "Resolution Authorizing a Commission to Examine Trade Regulations," Jan. 21, 1786; 9:118, "The Annapolis Convention, Sept. 1786: Editorial Note"; 8:483, to Monroe, Jan. 22, 1786; 9:119, "Lodging Account from George Mann," Sept. 4–15, 1786.

52. "The Mount Vernon Compact and the Annapolis Convention," Maryland State House, http://msa.maryland.gov/msa/mdstatehouse/html/compact _convention.html.

53. *PH*, 2:402, 407, to James Duane, Sept. 3, 1780; Morse, *Life of Alexander Hamilton*, 1:167; *PH*, 3:689, "Address of the Annapolis Convention," Sept. 14, 1786.

54. *PMC*, 9:163–64, "Bill Providing for Delegates to the Convention of 1787," Nov. 6, 1786.

55. *PMC*, 9:166, to Washington, Nov. 8, 1786; 9:161–62, from Washington, Nov. 5, 1786.

56. Flexner, *George Washington in the American Revolution*, 514n; *PMC*, 9:170–71, from Washington, Nov. 18, 1786.

57. *PMC*, 9:199, to Washington, Dec. 7, 1786; Freeman, *Washington*, 537; *PMC*, 9:315, to Washington, March 18, 1787.

58. *Journals of the Continental Congress*, 31:606–7, Aug. 30, 1786; *PMC*, 9:200, to Washington, Dec. 7, 1786.

59. *PMC*, 9:259, to Eliza Trist, Feb. 10, 1787; "James Madison's Autobiography," 202; *PMC*, 9:285, to Washington, Feb. 21, 1787; 9:291, "Notes on Debates," Feb. 21, 1797; *Journals of the Continental Congress*, 32:72–74, Feb. 21, 1787; Brant, *Madison*, 2:401–2; *PMC*, 9:294–95, to Pendleton, Feb. 24, 1787.

60. *PMC*, 9:309–11, "Notes on Debates," March 13, 1787; 9:401, to Jefferson, April 23, 1787 (many words encoded).

61. *PMC*, 10:159, from William Grayson, Aug. 31, 1787.

62. *PMC*, 9:259, to Eliza Trist, Feb. 10, 1787; 11:43n2, 42, from John Brown, May 12, 1788; 9:383, to Washington, April 16, 1787; 9:348–49, "Vices of the Political System of the United States," April 1787.

63. *PMC*, 9:353–56, "Vices of the Political System of the United States."

64. *PMC*, 9:141, to Monroe, Oct. 5, 1786.

65. *PMC*, 9:356–57, "Vices of the Political System of the United States."

66. Adair, "That Politics May Be Reduced to a Science," 348–49; *PMC*, 9:409, to William Irvine, May 5, 1787.

Chapter 6: THE GREAT WORK BEGINS

1. Catherine Drinker Bowen, *Miracle at Philadelphia*, 16; *PMC*, 9:415, to Jefferson, May 15, 1787; *PWD*, 5:237, May 13–14, 1787.

2. Farrand, *Records*, 3:23, Mason to George Mason Jr., May 20, 1787; 3:24, Mason to Arthur Lee, May 21, 1787; *PMC*, 9:318–19, to Jefferson, March 19, 1787; 9:369–70, to Edmund Randolph, April 8, 1787; 9:383–85, to Washington, April 16, 1787.

3. Karie Diethorn, chief curator, Independence National Historical Park, e-mail, July 6, 2007; *DHRC*, 1:226, General Assembly to the President of Congress, Sept. 1787; *PMC*, 9:359, to Madison Sr., April 1, 1787.

4. Farrand, *Records*, 1:423, Madison's notes, June 26, 1787; 3:550, James Madison, "Preface to Debates in the Convention of 1787"; Grigsby, *History of the Virginia Federal Convention*, 1:95n107.

5. Farrand, *Records*, 3:91, William Pierce, "Character Sketches of Delegates to the Federal Convention"; Cutler and Cutler, *Life, Journals, and Correspondence of Rev. Manasseh Cutler*, 1:267; Catherine Drinker Bowen, *Miracle at Philadelphia*, 34–35, Isaacson, *Benjamin Franklin*, 431–32.

6. *PJ*, 12:69, to John Adams, Aug. 30, 1787; Farrand, *Records*, 3:479, Jared Sparks: Journal, April 19, 1830.

7. Farrand, *Records*, 3:95, William Pierce, "Character Sketches of Delegates to the Federal Convention"; 1:20, Madison's notes, May 29, 1787.

8. *PMC*, 9:335, from Randolph, March 27, 1787; 9:369, to Randolph, April 8, 1787.

9. Farrand, *Records*, 1:38, Yates's notes, May 30, 1787; Jay, *John Jay*, 1:821, to Robert Morris, Sept. 16, 1780; Farrand, *Records*, 1:41, McHenry's notes, May 30, 1787.

10. Farrand, *Records*, 1:41–43, McHenry's notes, May 30, 1787; 1:34–35, Madison's notes, May 30, 1787.

11. Farrand, *Records*, 1:37–38, Madison's notes, May 30, 1787.

12. Farrand, *Records*, 1:48–50, Madison's notes, May 31, 1787; Mays, *Edmund Pendleton*, 2:229.

13. Farrand, *Records*, 1:134–36, Madison's notes, June 6, 1787.

14. *PMC*, 10:16, "Resolutions Proposed by Mr. Randolph in Convention," May 29, 1787; 9:318, to Jefferson, March 19, 1787; 9:370, to Randolph, April 8, 1787; 9:383, to Washington, April 16, 1787. Farrand, *Records*, 1:54, Madison's notes, May 31, 1787. "In all cases whatsoever" is underscored in letters to Jefferson and Washington.

15. Farrand, *Records*, 1:159, King's notes, June 7, 1787.

16. Farrand, *Records*, 1:164–65, Madison's notes, June 8, 1787.

17. Farrand, *Records*, 3:92, William Pierce, "Character Sketches of Delegates to the Federal Convention"; 1:167, Madison's notes, June 8, 1787.

18. Farrand, *Records*, 1:168, Madison's notes, June 8, 1787.

19. Farrand, *Records*, 3:90, William Pierce, "Character Sketches of Delegates to the Federal Convention"; *Journals of the Continental Congress*, 32:74, Feb. 21, 1787; Farrand, *Records*, 1:177–79, Madison's notes, June 9, 1787. Descriptions of the weather here and elsewhere in this chapter are from Farrand, *Records*, 3:552, William Samuel Johnson: Diary, 1787, and *Supplement to Max Farrand's The Records of the Federal Convention of 1787*, 325–37, "The Weather during the Convention."

20. Farrand, *Records*, 1:242–45, Madison's notes, June 15, 1787.

21. John Quincy Adams, *Eulogy on the Life and Character of James Madison*, 37; Farrand, *Records*, 1:242n, Madison's notes, June 15, 1787.

22. Farrand, *Records*, 1:253, 255, Madison's notes, June 16, 1787.

23. Farrand, *Records*, 1:296–301, Yates's notes, June 18, 1787.

24. Farrand, *Records*, 1:292, Madison's notes, June 18, 1787; 1:432–33, Yates's notes, June 26, 1787; John Quincy Adams, *Memoirs*, 4:383, May 31, 1819.

25. Farrand, *Records*, 1:317–18, 320, Madison's notes, June 19, 1787.

26. Ibid., 322.

27. Farrand, *Records,* 1:437, Madison's notes, June 27, 1787. Martin would successfully defend Supreme Court justice Samuel Chase and former vice president Aaron Burr.

28. Farrand, *Records,* 1:445, Madison's notes, June 28, 1787. New Jersey, which required that three of its delegates be present in order to vote, might have had only two present on June 27; on June 28 it definitely had only two present. See Lloyd, "Quorum Requirements and Elected Delegates by State" and "Constitutional Convention Attendance Record," in *Constitutional Convention.*

29. Farrand, *Records,* 1:450, Madison's notes, June 28, 1787; 1:457, Yates's notes, June 28, 1787.

30. Farrand, *Records,* 1:450–51, 464, Madison's notes, June 28–29, 1787.

31. Farrand, *Records,* 1:485–87, Madison's notes, June 30, 1787.

32. Ibid., 488; Farrand, *Records,* 1:498–502, Yates's notes, June 30, 1787.

33. Sparks, *Life of Gouverneur Morris,* 1:283.

34. Beeman, *Plain, Honest Men,* 185–87; Farrand, *Records,* 3:188, Luther Martin, "Genuine Information." Maryland's quorum requirements allowed a vote to be cast even if only a single delegate was present. See Lloyd, "Quorum Requirements and Elected Delegates by State," in *Constitutional Convention.*

35. Beeman, *Plain, Honest Men,* 186–87.

36. *Pennsylvania Packet,* July 6, 1787.

37. Farrand, *Records,* 1:526–28, Madison's notes, July 5, 1787.

38. Ibid., 529–30; Farrand, *Records,* 3:56, Washington to Hamilton, July 10, 1787.

39. Cutler and Cutler, *Life, Journals, and Correspondence of Rev. Manasseh Cutler,* 1:270–77.

40. Farrand, *Records,* 2:18, Madison's notes, July 16, 1787.

41. Ibid.

42. Ibid., 20.

43. Farrand, *Records,* 2:27–29, Madison's notes, July 17, 1787.

44. Ibid., 33–35.

45. Ibid., 34–35.

46. Brant, *Madison,* 3:101–2.

47. Farrand, *Records,* 1:68–69, 80, 2:99, Madison's notes, June 1 and 2 and July 24, 1787.

48. Farrand, *Records,* 2:109–11, Madison's notes, July 25, 1787.

49. Ibid., 111, 114.

50. Farrand, *Records,* 2:73–74, 298, Madison's notes, July 21 and Aug. 15, 1787.

51. Farrand, *Records,* 2:318, Madison's notes, Aug. 17, 1787.

52. *Supplement to Max Farrand's The Records of the Federal Convention of 1787,* 300–301, Dickinson to George Logan, Jan. 16, 1802; Farrand, *Records,* 2:114, 497–98, Madison's notes, July 25 and Sept. 4, 1787. Bennett, "Problem of the Faithless Elector," 129, notes that "with very few exceptions popular election of electors has been used in every state since the 1830s."

53. Farrand, *Records,* 2:513, 527, Madison's notes, Sept. 5 and 6, 1787.

54. Farrand, *Records,* 2:536–37, Madison's notes, Sept. 7, 1787.

55. Farrand, *Records,* 2:498–99, 539–40, Madison's notes, Sept. 4 and 7, 1787.

56. Farrand, *Records,* 2:221, Madison's notes, Aug. 8, 1787.

57. Farrand, *Records,* 2:415, Madison's notes, Aug. 25, 1787.

58. Ibid., 415–17; Goldwin, *Why Blacks, Women, and Jews Are Not Mentioned in the Constitution,* 15.

59. Farrand, *Records,* 2:35, 1:66, Madison's notes, July 17 and June 1, 1787; 3:127, Randolph to the Speaker of the Virginia House of Delegates, Oct. 10, 1787.

60. Farrand, *Records,* 2:633, Madison's notes, Sept. 15, 1787; 2:635–36, Gerry's Objections, Sept. 15, 1787; *PMC,* 10:215, to Jefferson, Oct. 24, 1787; Farrand, *Records,* 2:639, "Mason's Objections to This Constitution of Government," Sept. 15, 1787.

61. Farrand, *Records,* 3:499, Madison to Jared Sparks, April 8, 1831.

62. Farrand, *Records,* 2:643, Madison's notes, Sept. 17, 1787.

63. Ibid., 648; *PMC,* 10:163–64, to Jefferson, Sept. 6, 1787 (some words encoded).

Chapter 7: IF MEN WERE ANGELS

1. John Quincy Adams, *Eulogy on the Life and Character of James Madison,* 84.

2. *PMC,* 10:10, to Madison Sr., May 27, 1787.

3. *Journals of the Continental Congress,* 5:425 and n2, June 7, 1776; Richard H. Lee, *Memoir,* 1:251.

4. Farrand, *Records,* 2:641–43, Madison's notes, Sept. 17, 1787; *PMC,* 10:208, to Jefferson, Oct. 24, 1787; 10:232, 325, to Archibald Stuart, Oct. 30 and Dec. 14, 1787.

5. *DHRC,* 1:337, Melancton Smith's notes, Sept. 27, 1787; 1:337–39, "Richard Henry Lee's Proposed Amendments," Sept. 27, 1787.

6. *DHRC,* 1:335, Melancton Smith's notes, Sept. 27, 1787; *PMC,* 10:215, to Jefferson, Oct. 24, 1787; Farrand, *Records,* 2:637, "Mason's Objections to This Constitution of Government."

7. *DHRC,* 1:345, Lee to George Mason, Oct. 1, 1787; *PMC,* 10:189, from Washington, Oct. 10, 1787.

8. *PMC,* 10:192, to Ambrose Madison, Oct. 11, 1787; 10:197, to Washington, Oct. 18, 1787; *PH,* 4:301, *Federalist* 1, Oct. 27, 1787.

9. *PMC,* 10:253, to Washington, Nov. 18, 1787.

10. *PMR,* 1:618, "Detatched Memoranda," ca. Jan. 31, 1820.

11. *PMC,* 10:182, 230–31, from Randolph, Sept. 30 and ca. Oct. 29, 1787; 10:252, 290, to Randolph, Nov. 18 and Dec. 2, 1787 (most words encoded).

12. *PMC,* 10:310–14, to Jefferson, Dec. 9, 1787.

13. *PMC,* 9:248, from Jefferson, Jan. 30, 1787; 9:318, to Jefferson, March 19, 1787; 10:64, from Jefferson, June 20, 1787 (italics added).

14. *PMC,* 10:337, from Jefferson, Dec. 20, 1787.

15. *PMC,* 10:208, to Jefferson, Oct. 24, 1787; 10:337, from Jefferson, Dec. 20, 1787.

16. *PMC,* 10:264–69, *Federalist* 10, Nov. 22, 1787.

17. *PMC,* 10:288, *Federalist* 14, Nov. 30, 1787.

18. *PMC,* 10:264, *Federalist* 10, Nov. 22, 1787.

19. *PMC,* 10:476–77, *Federalist* 51, Feb. 6, 1788.

20. *PMC,* 10:431, *Federalist* 45, Jan. 26, 1788; 10:396–97, *Federalist* 41, Jan. 19, 1788.

21. *PMC,* 10:424, *Federalist* 44, Jan. 25, 1788.

22. Chernow, *Hamilton,* 261; Kesler, *Federalist Papers,* xi.

23. *PMR,* 1:618, "Detatched Memoranda," ca. Jan. 21, 1820.

24. Rossiter, *Federalist Papers,* vii.

25. *PMC,* 10:360, 363–64, *Federalist* 37, Jan. 11, 1788; 10:461–62, *Federalist* 49, Feb. 2, 1788.

26. *PMC,* 10:261–63, "Madison's Authorship of *The Federalist:* Editorial Note"; Adair, "Authorship of the Disputed Federalist Papers," 102.

27. *PMR,* 1:619, "Detatched Memoranda," ca. Jan. 31, 1820.

28. *PMC,* 10:446, from Madison Sr., Jan. 30, 1788; 10:350, from Randolph, Jan. 3, 1788; 10:419, to Washington, Jan. 25, 1788.

29. *PMC,* 10:469, from Washington, Feb. 5, 1788; 10:526–27, to Washington, Feb. 20, 1788.

30. *PWD,* 5:284–87, March 15–19, 1788; *PMC,* 10:516, from James Gordon Jr., Feb. 17, 1788.

31. *PMC,* 10:541, from Spencer, Feb. 28, 1788; Leland and Greene, *Writings of the Late Elder John Leland,* 223–24.

32. Butterfield, "Elder John Leland, Jeffersonian Itinerant," 190; Leland and Greene, *Writings of the Late Elder John Leland,* 53.

33. *PMC,* 11:5, to Trist, March 25, 1788; Scarberry, "John Leland and James Madison," 769.

34. *PMC,* 11:10, 40–41, from Nicholas, April 5 and May 9, 1788; 11:44–51, to Nicholas, May 17, 1788; *DHRC,* 10:1250–52, speech of George Nicholas, June 13, 1788.

35. *PMC,* 11:19, to Randolph, April 10, 1788; 11:25–26, from Randolph, April 17, 1788.

36. *PMC,* 11:9, from Nicholas, April 5, 1788.

37. *PMC,* 11:64–65, from Carroll, May 28, 1788; 11:36, from Jefferson, May 3, 1788.

38. Gish, *Virginia Taverns, Ordinaries, and Coffee Houses,* 199; Christian, *Richmond, Her Past and Present,* 32–33; Grigsby, *History of the Virginia Federal Convention,* 1:99; *DHRC,* 9:785, Richard Henry Lee to Mason, May 7, 1788; *PMC,* 11:77, to Washington, June 4, 1788.

39. *DHRC*, 9:917, 929–30, speeches of Patrick Henry and Edmund Pendleton, June 4, 1788.

40. *DHRC*, 9:931–36, speech of Edmund Randolph, June 4, 1788.

41. *DHRC*, 10:1573, William Grayson to Nathan Dane, June 4, 1788; *PMC*, 11:77, to Washington, June 4, 1788.

42. *DHRC*, 9:951–64, speech of Patrick Henry, June 5, 1788.

43. *PWCE*, 6:316, from Bushrod Washington, June 7, 1788. *DHRC*, 9:989–91, speech of James Madison, June 6, 1788. Madison only temporarily forgot Rhode Island, which did not send representatives to the Constitutional Convention. He was soon talking about the way "the smallest state in the Union has obstructed every attempt to reform the government."

44. *DHRC*, 9:1035, speech of James Madison, June 7, 1788; *PMC*, 11:101–2, to Hamilton and King, June 9, 1788; De Coppet Collection, Madison to Delaplaine, memo, Sept. 1816; LC-JM, to Jonathan Elliott, Nov. 1827. Migraines, thought by Hippocrates to result from too much yellow bile, were called "bilious headaches" or "bilious attacks" well into the twentieth century, and the distinction between migraines and epilepsy was not sharply drawn—which may also help explain Madison's terminology. See Daniel, *Migraine*, 105; Vining, "Bilious Attacks and Epilepsy," 122; Gowers, *Borderland of Epilepsy*, 76–93.

45. *DHRC*, 9:1143–44, 10:1206, speeches of James Madison, June 11 and 12, 1788.

46. *DHRC*, 9:1052, speech of Patrick Henry, June 9, 1788; *PJ*, 12:571, to Donald, Feb. 7, 1788; *DHRC*, 10:1223, speech of James Madison, June 12, 1788.

47. *DHRC*, 10:1229, 1242, 1248, speeches of Patrick Henry and James Madison, June 13, 1788.

48. Brant, *Madison*, 3:227; *PMC*, 11:144, to Hamilton, June 16, 1788; 11:153, to Washington, June 18, 1788; *DHRC*, 10:1687–88, extract of a letter from Richmond dated June 18, 1788, *Pennsylvania Mercury*, June 26, 1788; 10:1651, Stuart to John Breckinridge, June 19, 1778.

49. *DHRC*, 10:1474, 1477, speech of Patrick Henry, June 24, 1788.

50. *DHRC*, 10:1499–1504, speech of James Madison, June 24, 1788.

51. *DHRC*, 10:1506, speech of Patrick Henry, June 24, 1788; Grigsby, *History of the Virginia Federal Convention*, 1:316–17; *DHRC*, 10:1512, Roane memorandum, post-1817.

52. *DHRC*, 10:1507, speech of James Madison, June 24, 1788.

53. *DHRC*, 10:1538, June 25, 1788.

54. *DHRC*, 10:1704, Monroe to Jefferson, July 12, 1788 (most words encoded); 10:1690, Oster to Luzerne, June 28, 1788; Brant, *Madison*, 3:227.

55. *PMC*, 11:170, from Washington, June 23, 1788.

56. *PWD*, 5:357, July 4–6, 1788; *PMC*, 14:300–301, "Memorandum on a Discussion of the President's Retirement," May 5, 1792.

57. *PMC*, 14:301, "Memorandum on a Discussion of the President's Retirement," May 5, 1792; *PWP*, 1:32–33, to Hamilton, Oct. 3, 1788.

58. Koch, *Jefferson and Madison*, 44–54; *PMC*, 11:197, 227, to Jefferson, July 24 (most words encoded) and Aug. 10, 1788.

59. *PMC*, 11:353, from Jefferson, Nov. 18, 1788.

Chapter 8: SETTING THE MACHINE IN MOTION

1. Brissot de Warville, *New Travels in the United States*, 101.

2. Ibid., 102; Ketcham, *Madison*, 273; *PMC*, 11:230, to Washington, Aug. 11, 1788.

3. *PMC*, 11:311, from Francis Corbin, Oct. 21, 1788.

4. *PMC*, 11:267, to John Brown, Sept. 26, 1788; 11:275, from Pendleton, Oct. 6, 1788.

5. *PMC*, 11:296, to Jefferson, Oct. 17, 1788.

6. Ibid., 297; *DHRC*, 10:1507, speech of James Madison, June 24, 1788.

7. *PMC*, 11:297–99, to Jefferson, Oct. 17, 1788.

8. *PMC*, 11:356, from Henry Lee, Nov. 19, 1788.

9. *PMC*, 11:388, from Henry Lee, Dec. 8, 1788; 11:352, from Carrington, Nov. 18, 1788; 11:386, from Burgess Ball, Dec. 8, 1788.

10. *PMC*, 11:351, from Washington, Nov. 17, 1788; 11:329, to Randolph, Nov. 2, 1788.

11. *PMC*, 11:418, to Washington, Jan. 14, 1789; Brant, *Madison*, 3:240; *PMC*, 11:404–5, to Eve, Jan. 2, 1789; 11:428–29, to a Resident of Spotsylvania County, *Virginia Herald*, Jan. 27, 1789.

12. Hunt, *Life of James Madison*, 165.

13. *PMC*, 11:442, from Leland, ca. Feb. 15, 1789.

14. *PMC*, 11:446, 447n1, from Washington, Feb. 16, 1789; 12:120–21, "Address of the President to Congress: Editorial Note."

15. Brant, *Madison*, 3:243; *PMC*, 12:3, to Washington, March 5, 1789.

16. McCullough, *John Adams*, 402; Baker, *Washington After the Revolution*, 131; Freeman, *Washington*, 564–65; Gordon S. Wood, *Empire of Liberty*, 64n35.

17. "Farewell to New York," Aug. 12, 1790, U.S. Senate, 1787–1800, http://www .senate.gov/artandhistory/history/minute/Farewell_NY.htm; *PMC*, 12:123, "Address of the President to Congress," April 30, 1789; Madison, *Writings*, 2:410, "Origin of the Constitutional Convention."

18. *PMC*, 12:120–23, "Address of the President to Congress," April 30, 1789; 12:131–32, from Washington, May 5, 1789; 12:166, from Washington, May 17, 1789.

19. Gordon S. Wood, *Empire of Liberty*, 55; *Documentary History of the First Federal Congress*, 12:xiii–xiv; Ames, *Works*, 1:36, to George Richards Minot, May 3, 1789.

20. *Annals*, 1st Cong., 1st sess., 107, April 9, 1789.

21. Ibid., 233–36, April 28, 1789.

22. Ames, *Works,* 1:35, 48–49, to Minot, May 3 and 29, 1789; *PMC,* 12:54, "Madison at the First Session of the First Federal Congress: Editorial Note."

23. Remini, *House,* 25.

24. *Annals,* 1st Cong., 1st sess., 385, 387, May 19, 1789.

25. *PMC,* 12:268–69, to Jefferson, June 30, 1789; Bemis, *Jay's Treaty,* 31–32; *Annals,* 1st Cong., 1st sess., 247, May 4, 1789.

26. *PMC,* 12:269–70, to Jefferson, June 30, 1789; Bemis, *Jay's Treaty,* 54.

27. Maclay, *Journal,* 248, April 26, 1790.

28. Ibid., 24–26, May 8–9, 1789; *PMC,* 12:182, to Jefferson, May 23, 1789 (most words encoded); 12:315, from Jefferson, July 29, 1789 (all words encoded).

29. Farrand, *Framing of the Constitution,* 163; Sullivan, *Public Men of the Revolution,* 120; "After-Dinner Anecdotes of James Madison," 257–58.

30. *Annals,* 1st Cong., 1st sess., 257, May 4, 1789.

31. *PMC,* 11:404, to Eve, Jan. 2, 1789.

32. *PMC,* 12:175–76, to Trist, May 21, 1789. Bland would die a little over a year later.

33. *Annals,* 1st Cong., 1st sess., 441, 444–45, June 8, 1789.

34. Ibid., 448–49.

35. Ibid., 450.

36. Ibid., 453–55.

37. Ibid., 451–52.

38. Ibid., 452–53.

39. *PMC,* 12:283, from Peters, July 5, 1789; 12:347, to Peters, Aug. 19, 1789.

40. *Annals,* 1st Cong., 1st sess., 731, Aug. 13, 1789.

41. Ibid., 741.

42. Ibid., 747–57, Aug. 14, 1789.

43. Ibid., 759, Aug. 15, 1789.

44. Ibid., 759–61.

45. Ibid., 774; Goldwin, *From Parchment to Power,* 124.

46. *Creating the Bill of Rights,* xv, 278–79n1, 279, Elbridge Gerry to Samuel Gerry, June 30, 1790, and Leonard to Sylvanus Bourne, Aug. 16, 1789.

47. *Annals,* 1st Cong., 1st sess., 784, Aug. 17, 1789.

48. Goldwin, *From Parchment to Power,* 130–39; *Annals,* 1st Cong., 1st sess., 790–92, Aug. 18, 1789.

49. *PMC,* 12:301–2, from Peters, July 20, 1789; 12:346–47, to Peters, Aug. 19, 1789; 12:348, to Pendleton, Aug. 21, 1789.

50. The amendment concerning congressional pay was finally ratified in 1992.

51. Elkins and McKitrick, *Age of Federalism,* 62.

52. *Annals,* 1st Cong., 1st sess., 816, 868, Aug. 27 and Sept. 3, 1789.

53. Ibid., 876, 890, Sept. 3, 1789.

54. Ibid., 912, Sept. 5, 1789; Ames, *Works,* 1:69, to Minot, Sept. 3, 1789; *PMC,* 12:402, to Pendleton, Sept. 14, 1789; Bowling, *Creation of Washington, D.C.,* 138–39.

55. Maclay, *Journal,* 166, Sept. 25, 1789.

56. Brant, *Madison,* 3:281.

57. *PMC,* 12:402–3, to Pendleton, Sept. 14, 1789; 12:433, to Jefferson, Oct. 8, 1789.

58. *PMC,* 12:452, to Washington, Nov. 20, 1789; Bowling, *Creation of Washington, D.C.,* 168.

59. Taylor Diary, Nov. 15 and Dec. 3 and 24, 1789; Meteorological Journals, Nov. and Dec. 1789.

Chapter 9: THE EARTH BELONGS TO THE LIVING

1. "First Monticello" and "House Transition," Monticello, http://www
.monticello.org/site/house-and-gardens/first-monticello and http://www
.monticello.org/site/house-and-gardens/house-transition.

2. *PJ,* 15:305, to Cosway, July 25, 1789; *PMC,* 12:304, from Jefferson, July 22, 1789.

3. *PMC,* 12:382–87, from Jefferson, Sept. 6, 1789.

4. *PMC,* 13:18–21, to Jefferson, Feb. 4, 1790; 12:386, from Jefferson, Sept. 6, 1789.

5. Rush, *Autobiography,* 181; Koch, *Jefferson and Madison,* 95–96; Jefferson, *Writings,* 15:470–71, to Thomas Earle, Sept. 24, 1823.

6. John Quincy Adams, *Jubilee of the Constitution,* 111.

7. *PMC,* 13:4, to Jefferson, Jan. 24, 1790.

8. John C. Hamilton, *History of the Republic of the United States,* 4:29n; Maclay, *Journal,* 194–95, Feb. 11, 1790; *Annals,* 1st Cong., 2nd sess., 1235–36, Feb. 11, 1790.

9. *Annals,* 1st Cong., 2nd sess., 1250, 1265, Feb. 15, 1790, 1308–14, Feb. 18, 1790; Leibiger, *Founding Friendship,* 22; *PMC,* 3:124, "Motion on Impressment of Supplies," May 18, 1781.

10. *Annals,* 1st Cong., 2nd sess., 1314, Feb. 18, 1790.

11. Maclay, *Journal,* 201–2, Feb. 22, 1790; Cutler and Cutler, *Life, Journals, and Correspondence of Rev. Manasseh Cutler,* 1:458.

12. Maclay, *Journal,* 178, 332, Jan. 15 and July 17, 1790; "James Madison's Autobiography," 203–4.

13. Jefferson, *Notes on the State of Virginia,* 176.

14. McCoy, *Elusive Republic,* 121–32.

15. *Annals,* 1st Cong., 2nd sess., 1225, 1240, Feb. 11–12, 1790.

16. Ibid., 1246, 1241, Feb. 12, 1790.

17. Ohline, "Slavery, Economics, and Congressional Politics, 1790," 337, 346–51; *Documentary History of the First Federal Congress,* 12:727–28, *Daily Advertiser,* March 18, 1790; *Annals,* 1st Cong., 2nd sess., 1505, March 17, 1790; *PMC,* 13:110, to Edmund Randolph, March 21, 1790.

18. Pennsylvania Abolition Society Collection, John Pemberton to James Pemberton, March 8 and 17, 1790; *PMC,* 13:109, to Rush, March 20, 1790.

19. Pennsylvania Abolition Society Collection, John Pemberton to James Pemberton, March 9, 1790; Ohline, "Slavery, Economics, and Congressional Politics, 1790," 346–51; *Annals,* 1st Cong., 2nd sess., 1525, March 23, 1790; Pennsylvania Abolition Society Collection, John Pemberton to James Pemberton, March 20, 1790.

20. *Annals,* 1st Cong., 2nd sess., 1524, March 23, 1790; Ellis, *Founding Brothers,* 118; Wiecek, *Sources of Antislavery Constitutionalism,* 16.

21. Ellis, *Founding Brothers,* 115; Farrand, *Records,* 1:135, Madison's notes, June 6, 1787; *Annals,* 1st Cong., 2nd sess., 1505, March 17, 1790; *PMC,* 12:437–38, "Memorandum on an African Colony for Freed Slaves," ca. Oct. 20, 1789.

22. Ohline, "Slavery, Economics, and Congressional Politics, 1790," 354; Pennsylvania Abolition Society Collection, John Pemberton to James Pemberton, March 16 and Feb. 23, 1790; Sedgwick Family Papers, Sedgwick to Ephraim Williams, March 17, 1790; microfilm edition of Adams Papers, Adams to Colonel Ward, Jan. 8, 1810; Maclay, *Journal,* 196, Feb. 15, 1790; microfilm edition of Adams Papers, Adams to Thomas Crafts, May 25, 1790; Ames, *Works,* 1:76, to George Richards Minot, March 23, 1790.

23. *PMC,* 13:175, "Motion on the Death of Franklin," April 22, 1790; Maclay, *Journal,* 246–47, April 23, 1790; Franklin, *Writings,* 10:87–91, to the editor, *Federal Gazette,* March 23, 1790.

24. *PH,* 6:106, "Report Relative to a Provision for the Support of Public Credit," Jan. 9, 1970; *PMC,* 13:148, to Lee, April 13, 1790.

25. Maclay, *Journal,* 209, March 9, 1790; Huger had suffered a fracture: "Letters of William Loughton Smith to Edward Rutledge," *South Carolina Historical Magazine,* Jan. 1968, 11.

26. Maclay, *Journal,* 237, April 12, 1790; *PMC,* 13:151, to Monroe, April 17, 1790; 13:89, 137, from Lee, March 4 and April 3, 1790.

27. *PMC,* 13:222, to Randolph, May 19, 1790; Abigail Adams, *New Letters,* 49, to Mary Cranch, May 30, 1790.

28. Jefferson, *Works,* 7:224–27, "The Assumption," Feb. 1793; Jefferson, *Complete Anas,* 33–34; Maclay, *Journal,* 292–93, June 14, 1790; Virginia's allowance was increased by $500,000 in the bill that finally passed; Ferguson, *Power of the Purse,* 321.

29. Maclay, *Journal,* 311, June 30, 1790; Bowling, *Creation of Washington, D.C.,* 185–86, 196; "Letters of William Loughton Smith to Edward Rutledge," *South Carolina Historical Magazine,* April 1968, 125.

30. Shippen Family Papers, Thomas Shippen to William Shippen, Sept. 15, 1790.

31. Peirce, *Meteorological Account,* 212; *PMC,* 13:404–5, from Jefferson, March 13, 1791; 13:405, to Jefferson, March 13, 1791.

32. *PMC,* 13:336, "Excise," Dec. 27, 1790.

33. *PMC,* 13:374–76, "The Bank Bill," Feb. 2, 1791.

34. *PMC*, 10:424, *Federalist* 44, Jan. 25, 1788.

35. *Annals*, 1st Cong., 3rd sess., 2008, Feb. 8, 1791; *PMC*, 10:41, "Power of the Legislature to Negative State Laws," June 8, 1787; Farrand, *Records*, 3:534, N. P. Trist Memoranda, Sept. 27, 1834.

36. *PMR*, 1:603, "Detatched Memoranda," ca. Jan. 31, 1820.

37. *PMC*, 13:93, to Rush, March 7, 1790; *PJ*, 19:351, to Freneau, Feb. 28, 1791.

38. *PMC*, 14:23, to Jefferson, May 12, 1791; *PH*, 8:478, from Troup, June 15, 1791 (italics added); John C. Hamilton, *History of the Republic of the United States*, 4:506.

39. *Vermont Historical Gazetteer*, 1:170–71; Maxwell, *Portrait of William Floyd*, 35; *Annals*, 1st Cong., 2nd sess., 1755, July 26, 1790.

40. *PMC*, 10:264, *Federalist* 10, Nov. 22, 1787; 10:477, *Federalist* 51, Feb. 6, 1788; Hofstadter, *Idea of a Party System*, 54–55.

41. *PJ*, 20:463–64, to Martha Randolph, May 31, 1791; *PMC*, 14:27, "Notes on the Lake Country Tour," June 1, 1791; 13:303, "Instructions for the Montpelier Overseer and Laborers," ca. Nov. 8, 1790; Brant, *Madison*, 3:380.

42. *PJ*, 20:568, to Martha Randolph, June 23, 1791; 20:297, to James Monroe, July 10, 1791; *PMC*, 14:39, 46, to Jefferson, July 1 and 13, 1791; 14:51, from Edmund Randolph, July 21, 1791; Tucker, "Autobiography," in *Life and Philosophy of George Tucker*, 1:70.

43. *PMC*, 14:43, to Jefferson, July 10, 1791.

44. *PMC*, 14:73–74, from Lee, Aug. 24, 1791.

Chapter 10: THE SPIRIT OF PARTY

1. *PWP*, 9:111, to the U.S. Senate and House of Representatives, Oct. 25, 1791.

2. *PMC*, 14:86, "Address of the House of Representatives to the President," Oct. 27, 1791; 14:183, from Lee, Jan. 8, 1792.

3. Irwin and Sylla, *Founding Choices*, 14–15; Haggard, MacIntyre, and Tiede, "Rule of Law and Economic Development," 206–9, 213.

4. *PMC*, 14:193–94, to Lee, Jan. 21, 1792.

5. *PMC*, 14:245–46, "Republican Distribution of Citizens," *National Gazette*, March 3, 1792; 14:258, "Fashion," *National Gazette*, March 20, 1792.

6. *PH*, 10:267, 253, "Final Version of the Report on the Subject of Manufactures," Dec. 5, 1791.

7. *Annals*, 2nd Cong., 1st sess., 388, Feb. 6, 1792; *PMC*, 14:180, to Henry Lee, Jan. 1, 1792.

8. *PMC*, 14:263, to Pendleton, March 25, 1792; Elkins and McKitrick, *Age of Federalism*, 278–79.

9. *PMC*, 14:274, "The Union: Who Are Its Real Friends?," *National Gazette*, March 31, 1792.

10. *PMC*, 14:208, "Universal Peace," *National Gazette*, Jan. 31, 1792; *Annals*, 2nd Cong., 1st sess., 504, March 30, 1792; *PMC*, 4:154n14, from Pendleton, April 15, 1782.

11. *PH*, 11:426–39, to Carrington, May 26, 1792.

12. *PMC*, 14:197, "Parties," *National Gazette*, ca. Jan. 23, 1792.

13. *PMC*, 14:301–4, "Memorandum on a Discussion of the President's Retirement," May 5 and 9, 1792.

14. *PH*, 12:107, "T. L. No. 1," *Gazette of the United States*, July 25, 1792; 12:124, 124–25n3, "T. L. No. 2," *Gazette of the United States*, July 28, 1792; 12:159, "An American No. 1," *Gazette of the United States*, Aug. 4, 1792.

15. *PH*, 12:191, "An American No. 2," *Gazette of the United States*, Aug. 11, 1792; 12:394, "Catullus No. 2," *Gazette of the United States*, Sept. 19, 1792; 12:160, "An American No. 1," *Gazette of the United States*, Aug. 4, 1792.

16. Brant, *Madison*, 3:362; *PMC*, 14:368–70, 387–92, for *Dunlap's American Daily Advertiser*, Sept. 22 and Oct. 20, 1792.

17. Marsh, "Freneau and Jefferson," 187; Jefferson, *Complete Anas*, 159.

18. *PMC*, 14:370–72, "A Candid State of Parties," *National Gazette*, Sept. 22, 1792.

19. Kaminski, *George Clinton*, 230–31; *PMC*, 14:383–85, from Beckley, Oct. 17, 1792.

20. *PMC*, 14:421, to Pendleton, Dec. 6, 1792.

21. *PMC*, 14:384, from Beckley, Oct. 17, 1792.

22. *PH*, 21:258, "Printed Version of the Reynolds Pamphlet," 1797; *Annals*, 2nd Cong., 2nd sess., 836, Jan. 23, 1793; *PH*, 14:34, "Report Relative to the Loans Negotiated Under the Acts of the Fourth and Twelfth of Aug. 1790," Feb. 13–14, 1793; *PJ*, 25:280–86, "Jefferson and the Giles Resolutions: Editorial Note."

23. *PJ*, 25:284–88, "Jefferson and the Giles Resolutions: Editorial Note."

24. Jefferson, *Complete Anas*, 113–14; *PMC*, 14:472, to George Nicholas, March 15, 1793.

25. Elkins and McKitrick, *Age of Federalism*, 265–66.

26. *PMC*, 15:4, to the Minister of the Interior of the French Republic, April 1793.

27. Schama, *Citizens*, 782–89; *PMC*, 15:7, to Jefferson, April 12, 1793; Brackenridge, *Incidents of the Insurrection*, 52.

28. Elkins and McKitrick, *Age of Federalism*, 335; Washington Irving, *Life of George Washington*, 5:197–98; *PMC*, 15:12, to Jefferson, May 8, 1793.

29. *PWP*, 12:472, "Neutrality Proclamation," April 22, 1793; *PMC*, 15:12, to Jefferson, May 8, 1793; 15:37, from Jefferson, June 23, 1793.

30. *National Gazette*, June 1 and 5, 1793; *PMC*, 15:33, to Jefferson, June 19, 1793; Leibiger, *Founding Friendship*, 172; *PJ*, 26:522–23, "Notes on James Cole Mountflorence and on Federalist Intrigues," July 18, 1793.

31. Elkins and McKitrick, *Age of Federalism*, 360; *PH*, 15:33, "Pacificus No. 1," June 29, 1793.

32. *PMC*, 15:43, from Jefferson, July 7, 1793; 15:51, to Jefferson, Aug. 5, 1793.

33. *PMC*, 15:44, 48, to Jefferson, July 18 and 30, 1793; 15:56, from Jefferson, Aug. 11, 1793; 15:65, "Madison's 'Helvidius' Essays: Editorial Note"; 15:94–95, to Jefferson, Sept. 2, 1793. Thanks to J. C. A. Stagg for pointing out the possibility that Madison's pen name was a comment on the Washington administration.

34. *PMC*, 14:111, "Madison's *National Gazette* Essays: Editorial Note"; Cunningham, *Jeffersonian Republicans*, 69.

35. Malone, *Jefferson*, 3:150, 156–57.

36. Drinker, *Extracts from the Journal*, 194–207; *PMC*, 15:90, from Jefferson, Sept. 1, 1793.

37. Drinker, *Extracts from the Journal*, 209–10.

Chapter 11: DOLLEY

1. Murphy, *American Plague*, 99; *PMC*, 15:xxviii, Madison Chronology; 15:167, "Commercial Discrimination," Jan. 3, 1794.

2. Bemis, *Jay's Treaty*, 210–68; Varg, *Foreign Policies of the Founding Fathers*, 101; *ASP-FR*, 1:428–29, letters communicated to Congress, March 25, 1794.

3. *Annals*, 3rd Cong., 1st sess., 433, Feb. 6, 1794.

4. Elkins and McKitrick, *Age of Federalism*, 392; *PMC*, 15:288, 294–95, to Jefferson, March 24 and 26, 1794.

5. "After-Dinner Anecdotes of James Madison," 257.

6. *PMC*, 15:57, from Jefferson, Aug. 11, 1793; 15:338, to Jefferson, May 25, 1794.

7. Cutts, *Queen of America*, 94–95.

8. Holly Shulman, "History, Memory, and Dolley Madison," in Cutts, *Queen of America*, 46; UVA, Papers of James Madison Project, Anonymous, Essay Prepared for Mrs. George Hammond, June 1809.

9. Allgor, *Perfect Union*, 21–23; Cutts, *Queen of America*, 91–92.

10. Cutts, *Queen of America*, 95; *PDM*, from Coles, June 1, 1794.

11. *PDM*, from Wilkins, 1794.

12. *PDM*, to Elizabeth Lee, Sept. 16, 1794.

13. *PDM*, from James Madison, Aug. 18, 1794; Cutts, *Queen of America*, 97.

14. *PDM*, to Lee, Sept. 16, 1794; Brant, *Madison*, 3:410, 501n15; De Coppet Collection, Madison to Delaplaine, memo, Sept. 1816.

15. Brant, *Madison*, 3:411.

16. Elkins and McKitrick, *Age of Federalism*, 462–63.

17. Malone, *Jefferson*, 3:121; *ASP-FR*, 1:24–25, "Speech of President Washington," Nov. 19, 1794.

18. *PMC*, 15:153, "Madison in the Third Congress: Editorial Note"; 15:396, to Jefferson, Nov. 30, 1794; 15:406, to Monroe, Dec. 4, 1794.

19. *Annals*, 3rd Cong., 2nd sess., 899, Nov. 24, 1794; *PMC*, 15:391, 388n1, Addresses of the House of Representatives to the President, Nov. 27 and 21, 1794; 15:397, to Jefferson, Nov. 30, 1794; *ASP-FR*, 1:27, president's reply.

20. *PMC*, 15:397, to Jefferson, Nov. 30, 1794.

21. *PMC*, 15:428, from Jefferson, Dec. 28, 1794; 15:479, to Madison Sr., Feb. 23, 1795; 15:473, to Jefferson, Feb. 15, 1795; Ketcham, *Madison*, 384; *Aurora General Advertiser*, Feb. 25, 1795.

22. *PMC*, 15:479, 415, 16:228, 434, to Madison Sr., Feb. 23, 1795, Dec. 14, 1794, Feb. 21 and Dec. 19, 1796.

23. *PMC*, 15:153, "Madison in the Third Congress: Editorial Note"; 15:432, "Naturalization," Jan. 1, 1795.

24. *PMC*, 15:488, to Monroe, March 11, 1795; 16:15, from Butler, June 12, 1795.

25. *PMC*, 16:94, to Henry Tazewell, Sept. 25, 1795.

26. *PMC*, 16:168, to Monroe, Dec. 20, 1795; Elkins and McKitrick, *Age of Federalism*, 420; Stahr, *John Jay*, 336; Adams and Cunningham, *Correspondence*, 36; Malone, *Jefferson*, 3:248; Gordon S. Wood, *Empire of Liberty*, 198; Chernow, *Hamilton*, 487, 490.

27. *PMC*, 16:168, to Monroe, Dec. 20, 1795; 11:311, from Francis Corbin, Oct. 21, 1788; Elkins and McKitrick, *Age of Federalism*, 420–21; Randolph, *Vindication*, 49–75.

28. Bowers, *Jefferson and Hamilton*, 326–28; Brant, "Edmund Randolph, Not Guilty!," 185–86; Elkins and McKitrick, *Age of Federalism*, 425–29.

29. *PMC*, 16:169, to Monroe, Dec. 20, 1795; Combs, *Jay Treaty*, 165–70; Elkins and McKitrick, *Age of Federalism*, 429.

30. Brant, "Edmund Randolph, Not Guilty!," 187–88; *PMC*, 16:204, to Monroe, Jan. 26, 1796.

31. *PMC*, 16:88, from Jefferson, Sept. 21, 1795; Bemis, *Jay's Treaty*, 265–91; Varg, *Foreign Policies of the Founding Fathers*, 103–4.

32. *PMC*, 16:88–89, from Jefferson, Sept. 21, 1795; 16:62–69, "Draft of the Petition to the General Assembly of the Commonwealth of Virginia: Editorial Note."

33. *PMC*, 16:163, to Jefferson, Dec. 13, 1795.

34. *Annals*, 4th Cong., 1st sess., 400, March 2, 1796; *PMC*, 16:259, "Jay's Treaty," March 10, 1796.

35. *PMC*, 16:256–62, "Jay's Treaty," March 10, 1796.

36. *PMR*, 1:604, "Detatched Memoranda," ca. Jan. 31, 1820; *Annals*, 4th Cong., 1st sess., 771, April 6, 1796; Remini, *House*, 57–58.

37. *PMC*, 16:313–25, "Jay's Treaty," April 15, 1796.

38. *PMC*, 16:333, to Monroe, April 18, 1796 (most words encoded); 16:343, to Jefferson, May 1, 1796; Kurtz, *Presidency of John Adams*, 63.

39. Kurtz, *Presidency of John Adams*, 67–69; *PMC*, 16:335, to Jefferson, April 23, 1796.

40. *Annals*, 4th Cong., 1st sess., 1259–60, April 28, 1796.

41. Ibid., 1263; Adams Family Papers: An Electronic Archive, John Adams to Abigail Adams, April 30, 1796. Ames lived another twelve years, ill most of that time.

42. Hess, *America's Political Dynasties,* 156; *Annals,* 4th Cong., 1st sess., 1280, April 29, 1796; Kurtz, *Presidency of John Adams,* 71.

43. Kurtz, *Presidency of John Adams,* 71; Maier, *Ratification,* 472.

44. Morison and Commager, *Growth of the American Republic,* 1:308; Beschloss, *Presidential Courage,* 31; *PMC,* 16:325, "Jay's Treaty," April 15, 1796; Cross, *History of England and Greater Britain,* 834.

45. *PMC,* 16:343, 364, to Jefferson, May 1 and 22, 1796.

46. *PMC,* 15:493, to Jefferson, March 23, 1795.

47. *PMC,* 15:428, from Jefferson, Dec. 28, 1794; 15:493, to Jefferson, March 23, 1795; 16:232–33, to Monroe, Feb. 26, 1796 (most words encoded); Malone, *Jefferson,* 3:273–74.

48. *PJ,* 29:187, to William Booker, Oct. 4, 1796; "Monticello (House) FAQ," Monticello, http://www.monticello.org/site/house-and-gardens/monticello-house-faq#when; *PMC,* 16:404, to Monroe, Sept. 29, 1796 (most words encoded); Malone, *Jefferson,* 3:278.

49. Chernow, *Hamilton,* 510.

50. Pasley, "Journeyman, Either in Law or Politics," 532–34, 553; Elkins and McKitrick, *Age of Federalism,* 520.

51. *PMC,* 16:422, to Jefferson, Dec. 5, 1796; Kurtz, *Presidency of John Adams,* 177–91; Elkins and McKitrick, *Age of Federalism,* 520–21. Elkins and McKitrick note that delayed returns accounted for the loss of the one vote, 860n81.

52. *PMC,* 16:424, to Jefferson, Dec. 10, 1796.

53. *PJ,* 29:235, to Adams, Dec. 28, 1796; *PMC,* 16:455–56, to Jefferson, Jan. 15, 1797.

54. "James Madison's Autobiography," 203; Kennedy, *Memoirs of the Life of William Wirt,* 1:246.

55. Malone, *Jefferson,* 3:296; Brant, *Madison,* 3:451.

56. Adams Family Papers: An Electronic Archive, John Adams to Abigail Adams, Jan. 14, 1797.

Chapter 12: Reign of Witches

1. *ASP-FR,* 2:64, from Rufus King, April 19, 1797.

2. Ketcham, *Madison,* 373.

3. Green and Miller, *Building a President's House,* 5–6, 14–15, 21.

4. Hunt-Jones, *Dolley and the "Great Little Madison,"* 61–62, 67–68; Green and Miller, *Building a President's House,* 6, 14–15.

5. *PMC,* 17:63, 123, to Jefferson, Dec. 25, 1797, and April 29, 1798; 17:128, from Jefferson, May 10, 1798.

6. *PMC,* 17:74, to Monroe, Feb. 5, 1798; *PDM,* to Lee, Oct. 1794–97.

7. Monroe Papers, from Burr, March 10, 1796; Tissot, *Traité de l'épilepsie,* 29; Ketcham, *Madison,* 370–71, 477. Jefferson purchased Tissot's *Oeuvres* in seventeen volumes in 1783 and purchased another seventeen-volume set in

1788. Jefferson Papers: An Electronic Archive, "1783 Catalog of Books," 65; Coolidge Collection of Jefferson Manuscripts, Froulle account statement for Jefferson, 1788.

8. *PMC,* 8:328, to Randolph, July 26, 1785; Ketcham, *Madison,* 372–74, 389; *PMC,* 16:174, 17:147, to Madison Sr., Dec. 27, 1795, and June 9, 1798; Kat Imhoff, "Slave Quarter Excavation at James Madison's Montpelier," video, National Endowment for the Humanities, www.neh.gov.

9. Chernow, *Hamilton,* 537–41; Marsh, "Hamilton and Monroe," 467; *PMC,* 17:50, from Monroe, Oct. 15, 1797; 17:53, to Monroe, Oct. 19, 1797.

10. *PMC,* 17:145, 146n1, from Monroe, June 8, 1798; 17:148–49, to Monroe, June 9, 1798; 17:60, from Monroe, Dec. 10, 1797; 17:61–62, to Monroe, Dec. 17, 1797.

11. *ASP-FR,* 2:157–63, dispatches from the envoys to Timothy Pickering, April 3, 1798; Elkins and McKitrick, *Age of Federalism,* 561; *PMC,* 17:113, to Jefferson, April 15, 1798.

12. Toll, *Six Frigates,* 99; Abigail Adams, *New Letters,* 171, to Mary Cranch, May 10, 1798.

13. Toll, *Six Frigates,* 101.

14. *PMC,* 17:133–34, to Jefferson, May 20, 1798.

15. James Morton Smith, *Freedom's Fetters,* 200; *PMC,* 17:162n2, from John Dawson, July 5, 1798.

16. Taylor Diary, July 2, 1798.

17. *PMC,* 17:134, to Jefferson, May 20, 1798; *PJ,* 30:389, to John Taylor, June 4, 1798; Koch and Ammon, "Virginia and Kentucky Resolutions," 152.

18. James Morton Smith, *Freedom's Fetters,* 442.

19. Elkins and McKitrick, *Age of Federalism,* 710; James Morton Smith, *Freedom's Fetters,* 226, 258–60, 270–71; Gordon S. Wood, *Empire of Liberty,* 260–61; Banning, *Sacred Fire of Liberty,* 385–86; Ames, *Works,* 1:247, to Christopher Gore, Dec. 18, 1798.

20. Koch and Ammon, "Virginia and Kentucky Resolutions," 157–58; Malone, *Jefferson,* 3:401–4; *PJ,* 30:550–55, "Resolutions Adopted by the Kentucky General Assembly," Nov. 10, 1798.

21. Koch and Ammon, "Virginia and Kentucky Resolutions," 159; *PMC,* 17:175, from Jefferson, Nov. 17, 1798; 17:188–90, "Virginia Resolutions," Dec. 21, 1798.

22. *PMC,* 17:187–88, "Virginia Resolutions: Editorial Note"; 17:191n2, "Virginia Resolutions," Dec. 21, 1798; Ketcham, *Madison,* 397; Elkins and McKitrick, *Age of Federalism,* 720–24.

23. Gordon S. Wood, *Empire of Liberty,* 271; DeConde, *Quasi-war,* 161; *PMC,* 17:184; to Jefferson, Dec. 11, 1798; 17:193, 195n3, 209, 223, 225, from Jefferson, Jan. 3, 16, and 30 and Feb. 5, 1799.

24. Kurtz, *Presidency of John Adams,* 307; John Adams, *Works,* 8:613, to McHenry, Oct. 22, 1798; Chernow, *Hamilton,* 555–58.

25. *PH,* 22:452–53, to Sedgwick, Feb. 2, 1799.

26. Elkins and McKitrick, *Age of Federalism*, 615–16; Billias, *Elbridge Gerry*, 297; microfilm edition of Adams Papers, Adams to Harrison Gray Otis, May 9, 1823.

27. McCullough, *John Adams*, 523; *PMC*, 17:234, from Jefferson, Feb. 19, 1799; *PWRT*, 3:389, from Pickering, Feb. 21, 1799; Elkins and McKitrick, *Age of Federalism*, 618; Kurtz, *Presidency of John Adams*, 282.

28. *PMC*, 17:245–46, from Taylor, March 4, 1799; 17:227–28, from Walter Jones and others, Feb. 7, 1799; Taylor Diary, April 24, 1799.

29. *PMC*, 17:287, "Election of James Monroe," Dec. 6, 1799.

30. Lear, *Letters and Recollections of George Washington*, 130–35.

31. Malone, *Jefferson*, 3:444; *PMC*, 17:295, "Death of George Washington," Dec. 18, 1799; Royster, *Light-Horse Harry Lee*, 202.

32. *PMR*, 1:603, "Detatched Memoranda," ca. Jan. 31, 1820.

33. *PDM*, from James Madison, Dec. 2, 1799; Gish, *Virginia Taverns, Ordinaries, and Coffee Houses*, 231, 245; Creighton, *History of Epidemics in Britain*, 2:788.

34. *PMC*, 17:297, to Jefferson, Dec. 29, 1799; 17:308–11, *Report of 1800*, Jan. 7, 1800.

35. Elliot, *Debates*, 4:539; *PMC*, 17:336–44, *Report of 1800*.

36. *PMC*, 17:312–16, *Report of 1800*.

37. *PMC*, 17:306, "*Report of 1800*: Editorial Note."

38. *PMC*, 17:415–16, "The Election of 1800: Editorial Note"; 17:357, to Jefferson, Jan. 18, 1800; *Calendar of Virginia State Papers*, 9:74–87.

39. Rives Papers, George Tucker, untitled memoir of James Madison.

40. *PMC*, 17:377, to Jefferson, April 4, 1800.

41. *PMC*, 17:371–72, from Mason, March 7, 1800.

42. *PMC*, 17:377, to Jefferson, April 4, 1800.

43. *PMC*, 17:386, from Dawson, May 4, 1800; 17:387, from Jefferson, May 12, 1800.

44. *PJ*, 31:562–63n, to Thomas Mann Randolph, May 7, 1800; Larson, *Magnificent Catastrophe*, 121, 125–26.

45. James Morton Smith, *Freedom's Fetters*, 337–55; Smith and Lloyd, *Trial of Samuel Chase*, 1:372–80; *PMC*, 17:390, to Monroe, May 23, 1800.

46. *PMC*, 17:393, from Jefferson, June 13, 1800; Meteorological Journals, July 1800.

47. Chernow, *Hamilton*, 616–18; *PH*, 25:186–234, "Letter from Alexander Hamilton Concerning the Public Conduct and Character of John Adams," Oct. 24, 1800.

48. Chernow, *Hamilton*, 622; *PMC*, 17:454, to Jefferson, Jan. 10, 1801.

49. *Republic of Letters*, 2:1139–40; Larson, *Magnificent Catastrophe*, 62, 236–38; *PJ*, 32:215, 257, from Pinckney, Oct. 12 and Dec. 2, 1800.

50. *PMC*, 17:418–19, 438, from David Gelston, Oct. 8 and Nov. 21, 1800.

51. "James Madison's Autobiography," 206.

52. Malone, *Jefferson*, 3:499; *PH*, 25:311, from Sedgwick, Jan. 10, 1801; *PMC*, 17:444, 448, from Jefferson, Dec. 19 and 26, 1800.

53. *PMC*, 17:453, to Jefferson, Jan. 10, 1801; Brant, *Madison*, 4:27; *PH*, 25:303, from James Gunn, Jan. 9, 1801; King, *Life and Correspondence*, 3:391, from Robert Troup, Feb. 12, 1801; Larson, *Magnificent Catastrophe*, 246; *PJ*, 32:594, to Monroe, Feb. 15, 1801.

54. Larson, *Magnificent Catastrophe*, 262–65; *Annals*, 6th Cong., 2nd sess., 1024–28, Feb. 11–17, 1801.

55. Bayard, *Documents Relating to the Presidential Election in the Year 1801*, 11–12; *PJ*, 32:594, to Monroe, Feb. 15, 1801; *PH*, 25:257, to Oliver Wolcott Jr., Dec. 16, 1800; 25:276–77, to Bayard, Dec. 27, 1800.

56. *PMC*, 17:447, 455–56, to Jefferson, Dec. 20, 1800, and Jan. 10, 1801.

57. *PMC*, 17:475, to Jefferson, Feb. 28, 1801; Miller, "Madison Family's Land in the Region of 'Montpelier,'" 1–2, 16–24; Ketcham, *Madison*, 390.

58. *PMS*, 1:7, 110, to Jefferson, March 7 and April 22, 1801; *PJ*, 33:203, to Randolph, March 6, 1801; Shulman, "Madison v. Madison," 363–64; *PMS*, 8:58, from Robert Taylor, Sept. 16, 1804.

59. *PMS*, 1:127, from Jefferson, April 30, 1801.

Chapter 13: THE REVOLUTION OF 1800

1. Margaret Bayard Smith, *First Forty Years*, 25.

2. Tinkcom, "Caviar Along the Potomac," 74; Henry Adams, *Jefferson*, 23–24.

3. Tinkcom, "Caviar Along the Potomac," 70–71, 85; Young, *Washington Community*, 42.

4. Tinkcom, "Caviar Along the Potomac," 73–74; Seale, *President's House*, 1:90–91; Margaret Bayard Smith, *Winter in Washington*, 2:261.

5. Seale, *President's House*, 1:94; Tinkcom, "Caviar Along the Potomac," 71.

6. *PMS*, 1:393, to Wilson Cary Nicholas, July 10, 1801.

7. DeConde, *Quasi-war*, 294–95; *PMS*, 1:59, from David Howell, March 30, 1801; 1:37–38, from William Irvine, March 23, 1801; 1:66, from Polk, April 2, 1801.

8. *PMS*, 1:119, from Callender, April 27, 1801; 1:244, to James Monroe, June 1, 1801; *PJ*, 34:205, to Monroe, May 29, 1801.

9. *PJ*, 30:557, to Nicholas, Oct. 5, 1798; Gordon-Reed, *Hemingses of Monticello*, 12, 541.

10. Seale, *President's House*, 1:94–95; Margaret Bayard Smith, *First Forty Years*, 385; *PMS*, 1:79, from William Eaton, April 10, 1801; 1:188, from James Leander Cathcart, May 16, 1801; *PJ*, 34:114–15, "Notes on a Cabinet Meeting," May 15, 1801; Brant, *Madison*, 4:60; Farrand, *Records*, 2:318, Madison's notes, Aug. 17, 1787.

11. *PMS*, 1:200, to Eaton, May 20, 1801; Toll, *Six Frigates*, 224, 257–62; *PMS*, 3:xxxi.

12. Toll, *Six Frigates*, 261.

13. *PMS*, 1:394, to Nicholas, July 10, 1801; 1:476, to Levi Lincoln, July 25, 1801; De Coppet Collection, Madison to Delaplaine, memo, Sept. 1816.

14. *PMS*, 2:60, from Jefferson, Aug. 22, 1801; Brant, *Madison*, 4:61.

15. Brant, *Madison*, 4:64.

16. Gordon S. Wood, *Empire of Liberty*, 534–36; Egerton, *Gabriel's Rebellion*, 186.

17. Henry Adams, *Life of Albert Gallatin*, 99, 109, 115–19.

18. Henry Adams, *Jefferson*, 137, 161–64; Malone, *Jefferson*, 4:101–6.

19. Malone, *Jefferson*, 4:126, 131–32; *PH*, 25:544, to Gouverneur Morris, Feb. 29, 1802; Ames, *Works*, 1:298, to Thomas Dwight, April 16, 1802; 1:310, to Christopher Gore, Dec. 13, 1802.

20. Malone, *Jefferson*, 4:73–79.

21. Henry Adams, *Jefferson*, 279–82, 316.

22. Brant, *Madison*, 4:90–91; Henry Adams, *Jefferson*, 276–77, Kukla, *Wilderness So Immense*, 230.

23. *PMS*, 4:146–47, to Pinckney, Nov. 27, 1802; 4:xxvi; 4:198, to Livingston, Dec. 17, 1802.

24. Ammon, *James Monroe*, 38–39; Malone, *Jefferson*, 4:269–70.

25. Kukla, *Wilderness So Immense*, 261–62; Ammon, *James Monroe*, 203; *PJ*, 7:512, to Monroe, Nov. 11, 1784; Brant, *Madison*, 4:111; *PMS*, 4:397n1, from Monroe, March 7, 1803; Hunt-Jones, *Dolley and the "Great Little Madison,"* 22–25; Tinkcom, "Caviar Along the Potomac," 97.

26. Hunt-Jones, *Dolley and the "Great Little Madison,"* 26; Margaret Bayard Smith, *First Forty Years*, 29; Allgor, *Perfect Union*, 70–73; Ellis, *American Sphinx*, 227; *Diaries of John Quincy Adams: A Digital Collection*, Feb. 13, 1806.

27. Cutler and Cutler, *Life, Journals, and Correspondence of Rev. Manasseh Cutler*, 2:154; Allgor, *Perfect Union*, 74–75; Tinkcom, "Caviar Along the Potomac," 84.

28. Kukla, *Wilderness So Immense*, 267–68; Henry Adams, *Jefferson*, 320; *PMS*, 4:500–501, from Livingston, April 11, 1803.

29. *PMS*, 5:248, to Monroe, July 30, 1803; Margaret Bayard Smith, *First Forty Years*, 38–39; Ambrose, *Undaunted Courage*, 102.

30. Brodie, *Thomas Jefferson*, 349, 354, 361–63.

31. Ibid., 365–68; *PMS*, 4:541, to Monroe, April 20, 1803.

32. Brodie, *Thomas Jefferson*, 374.

33. "Reminiscences of Madison Hemings," in Brodie, *Thomas Jefferson*, 473. Gordon-Reed, *Hemingses of Monticello*, 517–18. Gordon-Reed points out that the naming incident almost certainly occurred when Hemings was carrying Madison Hemings rather than after he was born, 589.

34. *PMS*, 5:248–49, to Monroe, July 30, 1803; Jefferson, *Complete Anas*, 222; Henry Adams, *Jefferson*, 348–49.

35. Gallatin, *Writings*, 1:111–14, to Jefferson, Jan. 13, 1803; Malone, *Jefferson*, 4:318; *PMS*, 5:156, "Proposed Constitutional Amendment," ca. July 9, 1803.

36. *PMS*, 5:323, from Jefferson, Aug. 18, 1803; 5:328, to Jefferson, Aug. 20, 1803; *Republic of Letters*, 2:1290; Ketcham, *Madison*, 421.

37. *Annals*, 8th Cong., 1st sess., 14, Oct. 17, 1803; Hermann, *Louisiana Purchase*, 37; Malone, *Jefferson*, 4:403.

38. Henry Adams, *Jefferson*, 334–35.

39. Forte, "Marbury's Travail," 351–55, 397–99. Both Jefferson's and Marshall's mothers were Randolphs.

40. *Marbury v. Madison*, 5 U.S. 137 (1803); *PMR*, 1:191, to Monroe, Dec. 27, 1817; *PMC*, 11:293, "Observations on Jefferson's Draft of a Constitution for Virginia," ca. Oct. 15, 1788.

41. *PMC*, 17:311, *Report of 1800*.

42. Tinkcom, "Caviar Along the Potomac," 72; Henry Adams, *Jefferson*, 547–50.

43. Tinkcom, "Caviar Along the Potomac," 72.

44. *PMS*, 6:361, to Monroe, Jan. 19, 1804; Rives Papers, Edward Coles to Hugh Grigsby, Dec. 23, 1854; Henry Adams, *Jefferson*, 552–57.

45. *PMS*, 6:186–87, to King, Dec. 18, 1803; 6:197–99, from King, Dec. 22, 1803; 6:362, to Monroe, Jan. 19, 1804; Jefferson, *Works*, 10:47–48, "Rules of Etiquette," 1803; Malone, *Jefferson*, 4:384–85.

46. *PMS*, 6:362–63, to Monroe, Jan. 19, 1804.

47. Ibid., 361–66; Malone, *Jefferson*, 4:383–84; Margaret Bayard Smith, *First Forty Years*, 46–47.

48. *PMS*, 6:361, to Monroe, Jan. 19, 1804; Plumer, *Memorandum*, 212.

49. Henry Adams, *Life of Albert Gallatin*, 287–88.

50. Isenberg, *Fallen Founder*, 235–49, 252; Jefferson, *Complete Anas*, 224; Malone, *Jefferson*, 4:398.

51. LC-TJ, from Clinton, Jan. 20, 1804.

52. *PMS*, 2:485, to John Francis Mercer, Feb. 24, 1802. *PMC*, 15:493, to Jefferson, March 23, 1795. Madison also suffered a contagious illness the month following: *PMS*, 3:9, to Andrew Ellicott, March 8, 1802.

53. *PMS*, 7:498, to Monroe, July 21, 1804; Plumer, *Memorandum*, 64.

54. Henry Adams, *Life of Albert Gallatin*, 266; *PH*, 25:544, to Morris, Feb. 29, 1802; Isenberg, *Fallen Founder*, 256–61; Chernow, *Hamilton*, 700.

55. Bickham, *Weight of Vengeance*, 32; Harrison Papers, "Private Notes of Conversation with Mr. Madison," Nov. 27–30, 1827.

56. Risjord, *Old Republicans*, 38–39.

Chapter 14: PORTRAITS

1. Cutts, *Queen of America*, 142; Barratt and Miles, *Gilbert Stuart*, 239–42; Few, "Diary," 351; *PDM*, to Anna Cutts, ca. May 8, 1804.

2. Jefferson, *Autobiography*, 55; Brissot de Warville, *New Travels in the United States*, 101; Rives Papers, George Tucker, untitled memoir of James

Madison; Dorinda Evans, *Genius of Gilbert Stuart*, 42; Hunt, "First Inauguration Ball," 756.

3. Cutts, *Queen of America*, 94.

4. Barratt and Miles, *Gilbert Stuart*, 239, 262–63.

5. *PDM*, to Cutts, May 25, 1804; Barratt and Miles, *Gilbert Stuart*, 272.

6. Malone, *Jefferson*, 4:381–82; Brant, *Madison*, 4:194, 205; Barratt and Miles, *Gilbert Stuart*, 243.

7. Dawidoff, *Education of John Randolph*, 25; Bruce, *John Randolph of Roanoke*, 2:320–21.

8. Gordon S. Wood, *Empire of Liberty*, 128, 456; Malone, *Jefferson*, 4:246–47, 448–49; Brant, *Madison*, 4:234–36; Bruce, *John Randolph of Roanoke*, 1:180–200.

9. *Annals*, 8th Cong., 2nd sess., 1026, 1103, Jan. 29 and 31, 1805.

10. Plumer, *Memorandum*, 269; Brant, *Madison*, 4:237, 240; Malone, *Jefferson*, 4:450, 456.

11. Henry Adams, *John Randolph*, 202; Henry Adams, *Jefferson*, 402–8, 455–56; Malone, *Jefferson*, 4:476; *Liberty and Order*, 292–93, "Articles of Impeachment," Nov. 30, 1804.

12. John Quincy Adams, *Memoirs*, 1:359, Feb. 27, 1805.

13. Henry Adams, *Jefferson*, 463; John Quincy Adams, *Memoirs*, 1:365, March 1, 1805; *PMS*, 9:416, to an unidentified correspondent, May 29, 1805.

14. Malone, *Jefferson*, 4:481–82; Risjord, *Old Republicans*, 42.

15. Ketcham, *Madison*, 436.

16. *PDM*, to Cutts, June 4 and July 8, 1805.

17. *PDM*, to Cutts, July 29, 1805; De Coppet Collection, Madison to Delaplaine, memo, Sept. 1816; *PMC*, 11:101–2, to Alexander Hamilton and Rufus King, June 9, 1788; 11:102, to Tench Coxe, June 11, 1788; 13:292, to Madison Sr., Aug. 14, 1790; 14:39, to Jefferson, July 1, 1791; *PMS*, 1:394, to Wilson Cary Nicholas, July 10, 1801.

18. *PDM*, to Mary Morris, Aug. 20, 1805.

19. *PDM*, to Cutts, Aug. 19, 1805.

20. *PMS*, 9:356, from Monroe, May 16, 1805; Brant, *Madison*, 4:266; Malone, *Jefferson*, 5:57; *PMS*, 8:191–92, from John Armstrong, Oct. 20, 1804; Plumer, *Memorandum*, 208, 383; *PDM*, to Cutts, June 4, 1805.

21. *Republic of Letters*, 3:1375, 1376, 1378, Jefferson to Madison, Aug. 4, 7, and 17, 1805; 3:1380, Madison to Jefferson, Aug. 20, 1805; 3:1382, 1391, Jefferson to Madison, Aug. 27 and Oct. 11, 1805; Malone, *Jefferson*, 5:58.

22. Ketcham, *Madison*, 443; Malone, *Jefferson*, 5:99; Jefferson, *Writings*, 8:419, to the comte de Volney, Feb. 11, 1806.

23. Henry Adams, *Jefferson*, 696.

24. *PDM*, to James Madison, Oct. 23, 1805.

25. *PDM*, from James Madison, Oct. 31, 1805; to James Madison, Oct. 30, 1805.

26. *PDM,* to James Madison, Nov. 1, 1805.

27. *PDM,* from James Madison, Nov. 6, 1805; to James Madison, Nov. 12, 1805.

28. LC-TJ, to Thomas Lomax, Jan. 11, 1806; Monroe, *Writings,* 4:358–63, to Madison, Oct. 18, 1805.

29. Malone, *Jefferson,* 5:104; *Annals,* 9th Cong., 1st sess., 561, March 5, 1806.

30. Smith Family Papers, Letter 13, March 5, 1806; *Annals,* 9th Cong., 1st sess., 600, March 6, 1806; Plumer, *Memorandum,* 444.

31. *Annals,* 9th Cong., 1st sess., 563, 571, March 5, 1806; Breckinridge Family Papers, John Breckinridge to Mary Breckinridge, Jan. 26, 1806.

32. *Annals,* 9th Cong., 1st sess., 851, March 26, 1806.

33. Smith Family Papers, Letter 13, March 5, 1806; Malone, *Jefferson,* 5:112, 149n8; LC-TJ, to Monroe, March 16 and 18, 1806.

34. Beckley Papers, to James Monroe, July 13, 1806; Malone, *Jefferson,* 5:153.

35. Malone, *Jefferson,* 5:199; Isenberg, *Fallen Founder,* 292, 312; Plumer, *Memorandum,* 515.

36. Jean Edward Smith, *John Marshall,* 353; Thomas Jefferson, "Special Message to Congress on the Burr Conspiracy," Jan. 22, 1807, Miller Center, http://millercenter.org/president/speeches/detail/3497; Newmyer, *Treason Trial of Aaron Burr,* 30–31; Plumer, *Memorandum,* 584; Isenberg, *Fallen Founder,* 289–90; Henry Adams, *Jefferson,* 576, 757–69.

37. Beveridge, *Life of John Marshall,* 3:376; LC-JM, from Harry Toulmin, April 14, 1807; *Republic of Letters,* 3:1466–67, 1471, Jefferson to Madison, April 14 and 25, 1807.

38. Henry Adams, *Jefferson,* 908, 923; Robertson, *Reports of the Trials of Colonel Aaron Burr,* 2:64.

39. Malone, *Jefferson,* 5:337; Robertson, *Reports of the Trials of Colonel Aaron Burr,* 2:445–46.

40. Malone, *Jefferson,* 5:339; Robertson, *Reports of the Trials of Colonel Aaron Burr,* 1:128; Henry Adams, *Jefferson,* 912–15.

41. UVA, Papers of James Madison Project, Armstrong to Madison, Oct. 10, 1806.

42. *Republic of Letters,* 2:1343, Madison to Jefferson, Aug. 28, 1804; Foreign Copying Project, Great Britain, vol. 52, Erskine to Lord Howick, March 6, 1807; Brant, *Madison,* 4:374–75.

43. *PDM,* to Cutts, March 27, 1807; *Republic of Letters,* 3:1464, Jefferson to Madison, Feb. 1, 1807; John Quincy Adams, *Memoirs,* 1:465–66.

44. Ammon, *James Monroe,* 265–67; Jefferson, *Writings,* 10:374–76, to Monroe, March 21, 1807; LC-JM, to Monroe, March 20, 1807.

45. Toll, *Six Frigates,* 289.

46. Henry Adams, *Jefferson,* 934–37; Toll, *Six Frigates,* 294–96.

47. Henry Adams, *Jefferson,* 939–42; Toll, *Six Frigates,* 296–98.

48. Gordon S. Wood, *Empire of Liberty,* 629–30; Jefferson, *Works,* 10:454, to James Bowdoin, July 10, 1807; Brant, *Madison,* 4:381–82; Jefferson, *Works,* 10:447–48n1, "*Chesapeake* Proclamation," July 2, 1807.

49. Henry Adams, *Jefferson*, 948; Brant, *Madison*, 4:382–83.

50. Brant, *Madison*, 4:388.

51. Henry Adams, *Jefferson*, 1040–41.

52. Malone, *Jefferson*, 5:483; Brant, *Madison*, 4:402–3; *National Intelligencer*, Dec. 23, 1807.

53. *National Intelligencer*, Dec. 25 and 28, 1807.

54. Henry Adams, *Jefferson*, 1028; Plumer, *Memorandum*, 527.

55. Tinkcom, "Caviar Along the Potomac," 71–72.

56. Mitchill, "Dr. Mitchill's Letters from Washington," 752, to Mrs. Mitchill, Nov. 23, 1807; Brant, *Madison*, 4:420; LC-JM, from Nicholas Voss, March 20, 1806; John Quincy Adams, *Memoirs*, 1:420, March 13, 1806.

57. Plumer Papers, from Jeremiah Smith, Jan. 28, 1804; to Smith, Feb. 10, 1804; to Jeremiah Mason, Feb. 15, 1804.

58. Pickering Papers, from Richard Peters, Jan. 9, 1804.

59. Mitchill, "Dr. Mitchill's Letters from Washington," 753, to Mrs. Mitchill, April 1, 1808; Bruce, *John Randolph of Roanoke*, 1:337; Pickering Papers, from Peters, Jan. 9, 1804; Allgor, *Perfect Union*, 116–17.

60. Ammon, *James Monroe*, 273; Brant, *Madison*, 4:428–29; Kennedy, *Memoirs of the Life of William Wirt*, 1:238.

61. Kennedy, *Memoirs of the Life of William Wirt*, 241–47; *Richmond Enquirer*, March 29, 1808.

62. Brant, *Madison*, 4:443–45; Rives Papers, George Tucker, untitled memoir of James Madison.

63. Brant, *Madison*, 4:427.

64. Ibid., 426, 430–31; Plumer, *Memorandum*, 635; Madison, *Writings*, 8:5, "Negotiations with Mr. Rose," Feb. 14, 1808; 8:18, to William Pinkney, Feb. 19, 1808; Brant, *Madison*, 4:440; *Farmers' Register*, reprinted in *American Citizen*, Aug. 15, 1808; George B. Wood, *Treatise on Therapeutics and Pharmacology*, 1:551.

65. Toll, *Six Frigates*, 310–11; Malone, *Jefferson*, 5:609; *Republic of Letters*, 3:1542, Madison to Jefferson, Sept. 14, 1808.

66. Gallatin, *Writings*, 1:368, to Jefferson, Dec. 18, 1807; Malone, *Jefferson*, 5:583–86; Gordon S. Wood, *Empire of Liberty*, 655.

67. LC-JM, from Pinckney, Jan. 2, 1809; from the Reverend James Madison, Feb. 8, 1809.

68. Malone, *Jefferson*, 5:622; Jefferson, *Writings*, 11:195, to Levi Lincoln, Nov. 13, 1808; *Republic of Letters*, 3:1557–58, Madison and Gallatin to Jefferson, Nov. 15, 1808.

69. Buel, *America on the Brink*, 74–75, 82–84; LC-TJ, to Joseph C. Cabell, Feb. 2, 1816.

70. LC-JM, to Nicholas, Feb. 6, 1809; Nicholas Papers, from Madison, n.d.

Chapter 15: MR. PRESIDENT

1. Margaret Bayard Smith, *First Forty Years*, 59; *PMP*, 1:16–18, "First Inaugural Address," March 4, 1809.

2. Brant, *Madison*, 5:13; LC-JM, from Robert R. Livingston, Jan. 24, 1809; Margaret Bayard Smith, *First Forty Years*, 58; Hunt, "First Inauguration Ball," 757.

3. Hunt, "First Inauguration Ball," 756.

4. Ibid.; Margaret Bayard Smith, *First Forty Years*, 61–62; Few, "Diary," 352.

5. Hunt, "First Inauguration Ball," 757; Margaret Bayard Smith, *First Forty Years*, 61–63.

6. Margaret Bayard Smith, *First Forty Years*, 61; Hunt, "First Inauguration Ball," 758; Brant, *Madison*, 5:23–25.

7. Brant, *Madison*, 5:40–41, 48–49; *PMP*, 1:125–26, "Presidential Proclamation," April 19, 1809.

8. *National Intelligencer—Extra*, April 19, 1809; Carey, *Olive Branch*, 176.

9. Brant, *Madison*, 5:31; Seale, *President's House*, 1:123–27.

10. Seale, *President's House*, 1:128–30.

11. Dick Journal, June 1809.

12. Henry Adams, *Madison*, 59; *PMP*, 1:262, to Jefferson, June 20, 1809.

13. Green and Miller, *Building a President's House*, 20–22.

14. Margaret Bayard Smith, *First Forty Years*, 81–82.

15. *PMP*, 1:262, to Jefferson, June 20, 1809; Henry Adams, *Madison*, 81–82; *ASP-FR*, 3:300, Canning to Erskine, Jan. 23, 1809; *PMP*, 1:317, to Jefferson, Aug. 3, 1809.

16. *PMP*, 1:316, from Robert Smith, July 31, 1809; Brant, *Madison*, 5:76.

17. *PMP*, 1:358, from Rodney, Sept. 6, 1809.

18. George Jackson, *Bath Archives*, 1:20–21, to Mrs. Jackson, Oct. 7, 1809.

19. Henry Adams, *Madison*, 89–91; *ASP-FR*, 3:309, Jackson to Smith, Oct. 11, 1809.

20. George Jackson, *Bath Archives*, 1:26, to George Jackson, Oct. 24, 1809; *ASP-FR*, 3:311–12, Smith to Jackson, Oct. 19, 1809.

21. *ASP-FR*, 3:315, Jackson to Smith, Oct. 23, 1809; 3:317, Smith to Jackson, Nov. 1, 1809; 3:317–18, Jackson to Smith, Nov. 4, 1809; 3:319, Smith to Jackson, Nov. 8, 1809.

22. *National Intelligencer*, Nov. 13 and 22, 1809; George Jackson, *Bath Archives*, 1:44–45, to G. Jackson, Nov. 14 and 15, 1809; Henry Adams, *Madison*, 95.

23. Henry Adams, *Madison*, 153, 112–13; Brant, *Madison*, 5:108; Story Correspondence, from Bacon, Nov. 27, 1809.

24. *PMP*, 2:150–51 and nn1–3, from Isaac A. Coles, Dec. 29, 1809; *Annals*, 11th Cong., 2nd sess., 685, Nov. 30, 1809.

25. *PMP*, 2:151n1, 539, from John G. Jackson, Sept. 13, 1810; Brown, *Voice of the New West*, 86–87, 90–92.

26. *PMP*, 2:158, to Congress, Jan. 3, 1810; *Annals*, 11th Cong., 2nd sess., 1158, Jan. 6, 1810.

27. *Annals*, 11th Cong., 2nd sess., 1611–12, 1863, March 22 and April 16, 1810 (italics added).

28. Ibid., 1864, April 16, 1810; *PMP*, 2:321, to Jefferson, April 23, 1810.

29. *PMP*, 2:348, to Pinkney, May 23, 1810.

30. Risjord, *Old Republicans*, 106; Henry Adams, *Madison*, 387; *ASP-FR*, 3:387, duc de Cadore to Armstrong, Aug. 5, 1810; Stagg, *Mr. Madison's War*, 55.

31. *PMP*, 2:565, to Rodney, Sept. 30, 1810; 2:585, 388, to Jefferson, Oct. 19 and June 22, 1810; Ketcham, *Madison*, 508.

32. *PMC*, 15:518, "Political Observations," April 20, 1795.

33. Henry Adams, *Madison*, 244–45; Brant, *Madison*, 5:263; Malone, *Jefferson*, 6:90.

34. *PMP*, 2:595–96, "Presidential Proclamation," Oct. 27, 1810.

35. *PMP*, 2:585, to Jefferson, Oct. 19, 1810.

36. Stagg, *Borderlines in Borderlands*, 76–79; "The Censure Case of Timothy Pickering of Massachusetts," U.S. Senate, http://www.senate.gov/artand history/history/common/censure_cases/010_TimothyPickering.htm.

37. Henry Adams, *Madison*, 234.

38. Brant, *Madison*, 5:273; *PMP*, 3:255–63, "Memorandum on Robert Smith," ca. April 11, 1811.

39. Gilmer Correspondence, Eliza Trist to Mary Gilmer, Sept. 1, 1808; *PMP*, 3:250, 2:95–96, from Jefferson, April 7, 1811, and Nov. 30, 1809; Brant, *Madison*, 5:283–85.

40. Brant, *Madison*, 5:304–5.

41. Ketcham, *Madison*, 514; Henry Adams, *Madison*, 325–26, 338–39.

42. Henry Adams, *Madison*, 313–17; Hickey, *War of 1812*, 22; Brant, *Madison*, 5:331.

43. Henry Adams, *Madison*, 321; Brant, *Madison*, 5:332, 479; *PMP*, 3:390, to Henry Dearborn, ca. July 23, 1811; Coles, "Letters" 163, to William Rives, Jan. 21, 1856.

44. Pierre M. Irving, *Life and Letters*, 1:263; *PMP*, 2:419, to Jefferson, July 17, 1810; 2:439, to Paul Hamilton, July 26, 1810; 3:392, "Presidential Proclamation," July 24, 1811; *PDM*, to Ruth Barlow, Nov. 15, 1811.

45. Clay, *Papers*, 1:498, to Monroe, Nov. 13, 1810; 1:449, "Speech on Proposed Repeal of Non-intercourse Act," Feb. 22, 1810.

46. Wiltse, *John C. Calhoun*, 16; William Henry Smith, *Speakers of the House of Representatives*, 70–71; Heller, *Democracy's Lawyer*, 21.

47. *PMP*, 3:535–38, from Gallatin, memorandum, ca. Nov. 1, 1811; 4:1–5, "Annual Message to Congress," Nov. 5, 1811; Stagg, *Mr. Madison's War*, 4, 31; Coles, *War of 1812*, 34.

48. Stagg, "Between Black Rock and a Hard Place," 388, 392; *Annals,* 12th Cong., 1st sess., 414, Dec. 6, 1811; Ravenel, *Life and Times of William Lowndes,* 90.

49. *Annals,* 12th Cong., 1st sess., 425, Dec. 9, 1811; Glenn Tucker, *Tecumseh,* 26, 42, 123; Perkins, *Prologue to War,* 283; Hickey, *War of 1812,* 23–24.

50. *Annals,* 12th Cong., 1st sess., 425–26, Dec. 9, 1811.

51. Murrin et al., *Liberty, Equality, Power,* 1:220; *Annals,* 12th Cong., 1st sess., 450, 533, Dec. 10 and 16, 1811.

52. Stagg, *Mr. Madison's War,* 86–87; *PMP,* 4:168, to Jefferson, Feb. 7, 1812; 4:195, from Jefferson, Feb. 19, 1812.

53. *Annals,* 12th Cong., 1st sess., 416, Dec. 6, 1811.

54. *PMP,* 4:228, to Jefferson, March 6, 1812.

55. *Annals,* 12th Cong., 1st sess., 1165, 1192, March 9, 1812.

56. Ibid., 1174, 166, March 9 and 10, 1812; *Facts Relative to John Henry and His Negotiation,* 1–3; Morison, "Henry-Crillon Affair of 1812," 222; Stagg, *Mr. Madison's War,* 98–99; Buel, *America on the Brink,* 141.

57. Henry Adams, *Madison,* 427–28; Stagg, *Mr. Madison's War,* 99–102; Clay, *Papers,* 1:637, to Monroe, March 15, 1812; *PMP,* 4:287, to Jefferson, April 3, 1812.

58. Billias, *Elbridge Gerry,* 316–18; Brant, *Madison,* 5:457–59.

59. Stagg, *Mr. Madison's War,* 153–54, 161; *PMP,* 6:175, to John Nicholas, April 2, 1813.

60. Henry Adams, *Life of Albert Gallatin,* 461n, George Bancroft to Henry Adams, memorandum, April 11, 1878; *Annals,* 12th Cong., 1st sess., 1407, May 6, 1812.

61. Stagg, *Mr. Madison's War,* 109; *PMP,* 4:432–38, to Congress, June 1, 1812.

Chapter 16: A FRIEND OF TRUE LIBERTY

1. *PMP,* 5:8–9, from the Inhabitants of Charlemont, Massachusetts, July 10, 1812; 5:18, from the Inhabitants of Lyman, District of Maine, July 13, 1812.

2. Carey, *Olive Branch,* 321.

3. Royster, *Light-Horse Harry Lee,* 144–45.

4. Scharf, *Chronicles of Baltimore,* 309–31, 339; Royster, *Light-Horse Harry Lee,* 157–64, 232–47.

5. Morison, *Life and Letters of Harrison Gray Otis,* 2:49–51; *PMP,* 5:150, to John Montgomery, Aug. 13, 1812.

6. Coles, *War of 1812,* 36; Hickey, *War of 1812,* 80–83; Stagg, *Mr. Madison's War,* 201–5.

7. Hickey, *War of 1812,* 83, 85; Stagg, *Mr. Madison's War,* 225.

8. Hickey, *War of 1812,* 85–86.

9. Stagg, *Mr. Madison's War,* 258–68.

10. *PMP,* 5:165, to Jefferson, Aug. 17, 1812; 4:519, from Jefferson, June 29, 1812; Story, *Life and Letters,* 1:244, to Nathaniel Williams, May 27, 1813; *PMP,* 4:561, Story to Pinkney, June 26, 1812; 4:560–61, from Pinkney, July 5, 1812; 5:149, from Carey, Aug. 12, 1812; 5:335, to Carey, Sept. 19, 1812.

11. Toll, *Six Frigates,* 346–48; "Biographies in Naval History: Captain Isaac Hull," Naval History and Heritage Command, http://www.history.navy.mil /bios/hull_isaac.htm.

12. Henry Adams, *Madison,* 556–58; Toll, *Six Frigates,* 349–54; Black, "British View of the Naval War of 1812."

13. Hickey, *War of 1812,* 101; *PMP,* 5:392, to Jefferson, Oct. 14, 1812; Ketcham, *Madison,* 544–45; Henry Adams, *Madison,* 581.

14. *PMP,* 5:429–33, 434n9, 435n13, "Annual Message to Congress," Nov. 4, 1812; Hickey, *War of 1812,* 96; *ASP-FR,* 3:587–88, extract—Secretary of State to Mr. Russell, Aug. 21, 1812; 3:589, Russell to Lord Castlereagh, Aug. 24, 1812.

15. *National Intelligencer,* Nov. 28, 1812.

16. *PMP,* 5:488, from George Luckey, Dec. 8, 1812; 5:494, from Charles Pinckney, ca. Dec. 10, 1812; Cutts, *Queen of America,* 119–20; Mitchill, "Dr. Mitchill's Letters from Washington," 753, to Mrs. Mitchill, Dec. 10, 1812.

17. Hickey, *War of 1812,* 80, 88; *PMP,* 3:53–54, "Annual Message to Congress," Dec. 5, 1810.

18. Brant, *Madison,* 6:125–26.

19. Ibid., 127; Skeen, *John Armstrong Jr.,* x, 20.

20. Brant, *Madison,* 6:125; Clay, *Papers,* 1:750, to Caesar Rodney, Dec. 29, 1812; *Annals,* 12th Cong., 2nd sess., 562, 600n, 664, Jan. 5, 6, and 8, 1813.

21. *PMP,* 6:340–41, to Congress, May 25, 1813; Hickey, *War of 1812,* 95–96; Henry Adams, *Madison,* 726–27.

22. Pickering and Upham, *Life of Timothy Pickering,* 4:230–31; Carey, *Olive Branch,* 302.

23. Ingersoll, *Historical Sketch,* 1:120.

24. Henry Adams, *Madison,* 640–42; Ruegsegger, "Finally, 1813 Battle Gets Some Respect"; Lossing, *Pictorial Field-Book,* 944; *PDM,* to Edward Coles, May 13, 1813. Tradition has it that the defense of St. Michaels was helped by citizens darkening their homes and hanging lanterns in tall trees, thus misdirecting British fire.

25. Monroe, *Writings,* 5:271, to Jefferson, June 28, 1813; *Oxford English Dictionary,* s.v. "malaria"; Cullen, *First Lines,* 1:6–84, 2:105; *PJ,* 16:436, to Thomas Mann Randolph Jr., May 23, 1790.

26. Brant, *Madison,* 6:187; *PDM,* to Coles, July 2, 1813; Monkman, "Reminders of 1814," 33–34, recounts how the family of the British sailor Thomas Kains, who obtained the medicine chest from the White House during the British invasion of 1814, returned it to President Franklin D. Roosevelt in 1939.

27. *Federal Republican,* Aug. 13, 1813.

28. Webster, *Letters,* 44, to Chas. March, June 24, 1813.

29. *PDM,* to Coles, July 2, 1813; *PMP,* 6:xxv; 6:503, to Dearborn, Aug. 8, 1813; 6:442, 443n1, from William Jones, July 15, 1813; 6:443, from Armstrong and enclosure, July 16, 1813; 6:445, from Monroe, July 18, 1813; 6:448, to Monroe, July 19, 1813; Brant, *Madison,* 6:206–7; Coles, *War of 1812,* 92–93.

30. Ketcham, *Madison,* 563.

31. Powell, "Some Unpublished Correspondence of John Adams and Richard Rush," *PMHB,* Oct. 1936, 442, 449; Ingersoll, *Historical Sketch,* 1:47.

32. *PMP,* 6:525, to Jones, Aug. 14, 1813; 5:372, to Dearborn, Oct. 7, 1812; Hickey, *War of 1812,* 128–30.

33. Hickey, *War of 1812,* 131–32.

34. Powell, "Some Unpublished Correspondence of John Adams and Richard Rush," *PMHB,* Oct. 1936, 454.

35. Hickey, *War of 1812,* 141–44; Stagg, *Mr. Madison's War,* 344–45.

36. John Quincy Adams, *Memoirs,* 6:5; Monroe, *Writings,* 5:276, to Madison, Dec. 1813.

37. Richardson, *Compilation,* 1:525, "Special Messages," Dec. 9, 1913; LC-JM, from Tompkins, Jan. 3, 1814.

38. Paul Johnson, *Napoleon,* 134–35, 142–43.

39. Ingersoll, *Historical Sketch,* 2:21, 53–54; Slosberg, "Site Lines."

40. Ingersoll, *Historical Sketch,* 2:26–27.

41. Stagg, *Mr. Madison's War,* 380–85; Henry Adams, *Madison,* 878–80; *Annals,* 13th Cong., 2nd sess., 1965, April 6, 1814.

42. Brant, *Madison,* 6:255; Madison, *Letters and Other Writings,* 3:401, to Armstrong, May 24, 1814, postscript May 25, 1814.

43. Skeen, *John Armstrong Jr.,* 140; Madison, *Letters and Other Writings,* 3:373–85, "Review of a Statement Attributed to General John Armstrong"; Stagg, *Mr. Madison's War,* 398–99.

44. Gallatin, *Writings,* 1:602, to William Crawford, April 21, 1814; 1:612, Gallatin and Bayard to Monroe, May 6, 1814; Madison, *Writings,* 8:281, Cabinet Memorandum, June 27, 1814; Brant, *Madison,* 6:268.

45. Hickey, *War of 1812,* 187–90, 193; Pitch, *Burning of Washington,* 29, 180; Powell, "Some Unpublished Correspondence of John Adams and Richard Rush, 1811–1816, II," *PMHB,* Jan. 1937, 52; *ASP-MA,* 1:540, from Jones, Oct. 31, 1814; 1:541, from Richard Rush, Oct. 15, 1814; 1:538, letter of Armstrong, Oct. 17, 1814.

46. *ASP-MA,* 1:541, from Rush, Oct. 15, 1814; 1:524, proceedings of the cabinet, July 1, 1814.

47. Henry Adams, *Madison,* 996; *ASP-MA,* 1:554, narrative of General Winder, Sept. 26, 1814.

48. Winder, *Remarks on a Pamphlet,* 12–13; National Archives, Records of the Office of the Secretary of War, RG 107, 7:253–54, Armstrong to Moses Porter, July 16, 1814; *ASP-MA,* 1:531, recapitulation.

49. Skeen, *John Armstrong Jr.,* 20; Madison, *Writings,* 8:287–90, to Armstrong, Aug. 13, 1814.

50. LC-JM, to Armstrong, Aug. 16, 1814; *PDM*, to Gallatin, July 28, 1814; *ASP-MA*, 1:581, General Van Ness's statement, Nov. 23, 1814.

51. *ASP-MA*, 1:536, letter of Monroe, Nov. 13, 1814; 1:537, Monroe to Madison, Aug. 21, 1814; Madison, *Writings*, 8:291, to Monroe, Aug. 21, 1814.

52. *ASP-MA*, 1:527, correspondence of Monroe with the governors; 1:563, General W. Smith's statement, Oct. 6, 1814; 1:555, narrative of General Winder, Sept. 26, 1814.

53. *ASP-MA*, 1:527, correspondence of Monroe with the governors; 1:555, narrative of General Winder, Sept. 26, 1814.

54. *PDM*, to Lucy Todd, Aug. 23, 1814; Hildt, "Letters Relating to the Capture of Washington," 65.

55. *PDM*, from Madison, Aug. 23, 1814; *ASP-MA*, 1:555, narrative of General Winder, Sept. 26, 1814; McKenney, *Reply to Kosciusko Armstrong's Assault*, 25–26; *ASP-MA*, 1:563, General W. Smith's statement, Oct. 6, 1814.

56. *PDM*, from James Madison, Aug. 23, 1814; *ASP-MA*, 1:571, Lieutenant Colonel J. Lavall's statement, Oct. 31, 1814.

57. Armstrong, *Review of T. L. McKenney's Narrative*, 5; *ASP-MA*, 1:556, narrative of General Winder, Sept. 26, 1814.

58. Pitch, *Burning of Washington*, 21, 56; James Scott, *Recollections of a Naval Life*, 3:283–84.

59. McKenney, *Reply to Kosciusko Armstrong's Assault*, 23; Madison, *Writings*, 8:290, to Armstrong, Aug. 13, 1814.

60. *PDM*, to Lucy Todd, Aug. 23, 1814.

Chapter 17: Trial by Fire

1. *ASP-MA*, 1:568–69, Colonel George Minor's statement.

2. *ASP-MA*, 1:556–57, narrative of General Winder, Sept. 26, 1814; 1:529, correspondence of James Monroe with the governors; 1:560, General Stansbury's report, Nov. 15, 1814.

3. *ASP-MA*, 1:539, Monroe to Madison, Aug. 23, 1814.

4. Madison, *Writings*, 8:294–95, memorandum, Aug. 24, 1814; *ASP-MA*, 1:570, Lieutenant Colonel J. Lavall's statement, Oct. 31, 1814.

5. Madison, *Writings*, 8:295, memorandum, Aug. 24, 1814.

6. Ibid., 295–96.

7. *ASP-MA*, 1:596, William Simmons's letter, Nov. 28, 1814; Madison, *Writings*, 8:296–97, memorandum, Aug. 24, 1814.

8. *ASP-MA*, 1:584, Dr. Catlett's statement; Madison, *Writings*, 8:297, memorandum, Aug. 24, 1814; *ASP-MA*, 1:565, General W. Smith's statement, Oct. 6, 1814; 1:537, letter of Colonel Monroe, Nov. 13, 1814.

9. *ASP-MA*, 1:565, General W. Smith's statement, Oct. 6, 1814; Madison, *Writings*, 8:297 and n1, memorandum, Aug. 24, 1814.

10. *ASP-MA*, 1:548, Wm. H. Winder to John Armstrong, Aug. 27, 1814; 1:579–80, Barney to W. Jones, Aug. 29, 1814.

11. *PDM*, to Lucy Todd, Aug. 23, 1814.

12. Jennings, *Colored Man's Reminiscences of James Madison*, 10–11; *PDM*, to Lucy Todd, Aug. 23, 1814; to Mary Latrobe, Dec. 3, 1814.

13. Madison, *Writings*, 8:297n1, memorandum, Aug. 24, 1814; *PDM*, to Lucy Todd, Aug. 23, 1814; Foreign Affairs, Political Correspondence, Paris–United States, Louis Sérurier to Talleyrand, Aug. 27, 1814.

14. Williams, *History of the Invasion and Capture of Washington*, 274–75.

15. Cutts, *Queen of America*, 125; Cazenove Gardner Lee, *Lee Chronicle*, 291, 297. The president's stay at Salona, largely based on tradition, gains some support from Matilda Lee Love's memory that Madison "had gone farther up the country." See *Lee Chronicle*, 291, and Herrick, *August 24, 1814*, 107–8; Pitch, *Burning of Washington*, 42–43, 101–3, 127–28.

16. Dietsch, "Brookeville's James Madison House"; Margaret Bayard Smith, *First Forty Years*, 107.

17. Pitch, *Burning of Washington*, 162; *PDM*, from James Madison, Aug. 27, 1814.

18. Hickey, *War of 1812*, 209; Thornton, "Diary," 177–78; *PDM*, from James Madison, Aug. 28, 1814; Margaret Bayard Smith, *First Forty Years*, 110. Fort Warburton, it would turn out, had been blown up by its commander, who was subsequently discharged from the army.

19. LC-JM, "James Monroe's Notes Regarding the Burning of the Capitol," Aug. 1814; Brant, *Madison*, 6:312; Margaret Bayard Smith, *First Forty Years*, 109.

20. LC-JM, "James Monroe's Notes Regarding the Burning of the Capitol"; Thornton, "Diary," 177–78.

21. McKenney, *Reply to Kosciusko Armstrong's Assault*, 6; Madison, *Writings*, 8:300–302, memorandum, Aug. 29, 1814.

22. Madison, *Writings*, 8:302–4, memorandum, Aug. 29, 1814.

23. Henry Adams, *Madison*, 1027–30; Hickey, *War of 1812*, 210–11; Lossing, *Pictorial Field-Book*, 951.

24. Hickey, *War of 1812*, 211–13.

25. Ibid. 197–98; Henry Adams, *Madison*, 985–86.

26. Henry Adams, *Madison*, 978; Hickey, *War of 1812*, 196–99.

27. Madison, *Writings*, 8:306–12, "Sixth Annual Message," Sept. 20, 1814.

28. Madison, *Writings*, 8:315–16, to Jefferson, Oct. 10, 1814; Gallatin, *Writings*, 1:637–38, to Monroe, Aug. 20, 1814; Kennedy, *Memoirs of the Life of William Wirt*, 1:381, to Mrs. Wirt, Oct. 14, 1814; *PDM*, to Hannah Gallatin, Dec. 29, 1814.

29. Pitch, *Burning of Washington*, 223–25; *Annals*, 13th Cong., 3rd sess., 320, 396, Sept. 26 and Oct. 15, 1814; Kennedy, *Memoirs of the Life of William Wirt*, 1:381, to Mrs. Wirt, Oct. 14, 1814.

30. Kennedy, *Memoirs of the Life of William Wirt*, 1:381, to Mrs. Wirt, Oct. 14, 1814; Henry Adams, *Madison*, 1066–67; Hickey, *War of 1812*, 275–77.

31. "Elbridge Gerry, 5th Vice President (1813–1814)," U.S. Senate, http://www
.senate.gov/artandhistory/history/common/generic/VP_Elbridge_Gerry
.htm; LC-JM, from Carey, Oct. 30, 1814.

32. LC-JM, ser. 2, from Nicholas, Nov. 11, 1814; Madison, *Writings*, 8:319, to
Nicholas, Nov. 26, 1814; Stagg, *War of 1812*, 148–49; Ingersoll, *Historical
Sketch*, 2:234–35.

33. Henry Adams, *Madison*, 1068; *Annals*, 13th Cong., 3rd sess., 664, Nov. 28,
1814; *Federal Republican*, Dec. 9, 1814.

34. *ASP-MA*, 1:524, 531, "Proceedings of the Cabinet the 1st of July" and
"Recapitulation."

35. Henry Adams, *Madison*, 1123; Stagg, *Mr. Madison's War*, 489.

36. *PDM*, to Gallatin, Dec. 29, 1814.

37. *DHRC*, 9:963, Debates, June 5, 1788; "Report and Resolutions of the
Hartford Convention," in *Liberty and Order*, 343.

38. *PDM*, to Gallatin, Jan. 14, 1815; "Events of the War," 356; *Daily National
Intelligencer*, Feb. 6, 1815.

39. *Daily National Intelligencer*, Feb. 6, 1815.

40. *Daily National Intelligencer*, Feb. 16, 1815; Morison, *Life and Letters of
Harrison Gray Otis*, 2:168.

41. Stagg, *War of 1812*, 155; Hickey, *War of 1812*, 308–9; *American State
Papers, Indian Affairs*, 2:183, "Alteration of the System for Trading with the
Indians," Dec. 5, 1818.

42. Hugh Gray, "Necessity and Expediency of Peace with America," in
Selections from the "Edinburgh Review,*"* 4:242, 246–47.

43. Henry Adams, *Madison*, 1211–12.

44. Powell, "Some Unpublished Correspondence of John Adams and Richard
Rush," *PMHB*, Oct. 1936, 454.

45. Madison, *Writings*, 8:324–26, "Special Message to Congress," Feb. 18, 1815.

46. Barry, "Letters," 237; *PDM*, to Gallatin, March 5, 1815.

47. "Jefferson's Library," Library of Congress, http://www.loc.gov/exhibits
/jefferson/jefflib.html; *Adams-Jefferson Letters*, 443, Jefferson to Adams,
June 10, 1815.

48. Moffatt and Carrière, "Frenchman Visits Norfolk, Fredericksburg, and
Orange County, 1816," 199, 212; *PDM*, to Hannah Gallatin, May 22, 1814; to
John Payne Todd, Aug. 6, 1814; Gallatin, *Writings*, 1:651, to Madison, Sept.
4, 1815; *PDM*, to Hannah Gallatin, Aug. 7, 1815.

49. Madison, *Writings*, 8:335, 338–39, "Seventh Annual Message," Dec. 5, 1815;
Madison, *Letters and Other Writings*, 4:183–87, to Ingersoll, June 25, 1831.

50. Randolph Papers, John Randolph–J. M. Garnett Letterbook, Randolph to
Garnett, Feb. 2, 1816.

51. *PDM*, to Anna Cutts, July 5, 1816; Ingersoll Papers, from Rush, Oct. 9, 1816.

52. Moffatt and Carrière, "Frenchman Visits Norfolk, Fredericksburg, and
Orange County, 1816," 198–202, 211–12.

53. LC-JM, from Delaplaine, Jan. 31 and Feb. 26, 1816; De Coppet Collection, Madison to Delaplaine, memo, Sept. 1816.

54. *PMC*, 1:52, "Notes on Commentary on the Bible," 1770–1773; 1:7, "Commonplace Book," 1759–1772.

55. Madison, *Writings*, 8:383–84, "Eighth Annual Message," Dec. 3, 1816.

56. Ibid., 379; *Annals*, 14th Cong., 2nd sess., 212, March 3, 1817; *PMC*, 14:180, to Lee, Jan. 1, 1792.

57. Brant, *Madison*, 6:419; *Daily National Intelligencer*, March 10, 1817; Thornton, "Diary," 177 and n9.

58. Vile, *Constitutional Convention of 1787*, 1:lxxii; Ketcham, "Unpublished Sketch of James Madison by James K. Paulding," 435.

Chapter 18: THE SAGE OF MONTPELIER

1. Watts, *Republic Reborn*, 317.

2. *PMR*, 1:263, 270, 283, "Address to the Agricultural Society of Albemarle," May 12, 1818.

3. LC-JM, to Rush, July 22, 1823.

4. *PMR*, 2:145, from Corbin, Nov. 13, 1820.

5. Ketcham, *Madisons at Montpelier*, 37; *PMR*, 2:161, to Corbin, Nov. 26, 1820.

6. LC-TJ, to John Holmes, April 22, 1820.

7. *PMR*, 2:446–49, "Jonathan Bull and Mary Bull," 1821.

8. *PMR*, 1:468–69, to Robert J. Evans, June 15, 1819; Shulman, "'Constant Attention,'" 60.

9. LC-JM, to Robert Walsh Jr., Dec. 22, 1827; from Engelbrecht, Sept. 5, 1825; to Engelbrecht, Oct. 20, 1825.

10. LC-JM, to Beasley, Nov. 20, 1825; Clarke, *Demonstration of the Being and Attributes of God*, 118.

11. *McCulloch v. Maryland*, 17 U.S. 316 (1819); LC-JM, to Roane, Sept. 2, 1819; to Stevenson, Nov. 27, 1830.

12. Mattern and Shulman, *Selected Letters of Dolley Payne Madison*, 218; *Washington Globe*, Aug. 12, 1836.

13. Ketcham, "Unpublished Sketch of James Madison by James K. Paulding," 435–36; Levasseur, *Lafayette in America*, 1:225.

14. Semmes, *John H. B. Latrobe and His Times*, 240; Moffatt and Carrière, "Frenchman Visits Norfolk, Fredericksburg, and Orange County, 1816," 202–3; "Mr. Livingston, I Presume?" and "Pan in the Drawing Room," Montpelier Foundation, http://www.montpelier.org/blog/mr-livingston-i-presume and http://www.montpelier.org/blog/pan-drawing-room.

15. Slaughter, "Anne Mercer Slaughter," 35.

16. Cutts, *Queen of America*, 154; Ketcham, *Madisons at Montpelier*, 25–26; Margaret Bayard Smith, *First Forty Years*, 237.

17. LC-JM, to W. T. Barry, Aug. 4, 1822.

18. *PDM*, from James Madison, Nov. 5, 1824.

19. Levasseur, *Lafayette in America*, 1:220–22.

20. Jefferson, *Writings*, 15:303, to William Roscoe, Dec. 27, 1820; *Republic of Letters*, 3:1923, Jefferson to Madison, Feb. 1, 1825; 3:1924–26, Madison to Jefferson, Feb. 8, 1825.

21. Cutts, *Queen of America*, 163; Lee Family Papers, B. Miller to Betsey Lee, March 16, 1819.

22. Ketcham, *Madisons at Montpelier*, 15–17, 19–20; LC-JM, to Richard Cutts, Jan. 4, 1829; Holly Cowan Shulman, "History, Memory, and Dolley Madison," in Cutts, *Queen of America*, 58.

23. Todd Memorandum Book; *PMR*, 1:25, "Promissory Note from Richard Cutts," April 4 and 1, 1817; LC-JM, from Thornton, Sept. 2, 1823; to Walter Jones, Sept. 9, 1828; 2:19–21, "Madison and Richard Cutts's Financial Difficulties: Editorial Note."

24. *PMR*, 1:25 and n, "Promissory Note from Richard Cutts," April 4 and 1, 1817; *PDM*, James Madison to Todd, Nov. 13, 1825.

25. LC-JM, to Biddle, April 16, 1825; from Biddle, April 26, 1825; to Chester Bailey, 1826; UVA, Papers of the Madison Family, Bache to Madison, June 4, 1827; Madison to Bache, June 8, 1827, letter owned by Robert Shannahan.

26. Shulman, "'Constant Attention,'" 47; Coles Papers, Coles to Madison, July 12, 1827; McCoy, *Last of the Fathers*, 313, 316; Washburne, *Sketch of Edward Coles*, 238–39.

27. Ketcham, "Dictates of Conscience," 52; *PMR*, 1:505, to Coles, Sept. 3, 1819; Ketcham, *Madison*, 626; McCoy, *Last of the Fathers*, 316.

28. McCoy, *Last of the Fathers*, 208–12, 217–20.

29. *Republic of Letters*, 3:1965–66, Jefferson to Madison, Feb. 17, 1826; Malone, *Jefferson*, 6:473–75.

30. *Republic of Letters*, 3:1967, Madison to Jefferson, Feb. 24, 1826; Ketcham, *Madison*, 616.

31. *Republic of Letters*, 3:1966–68, Jefferson to Madison, Feb. 17, 1826, and Madison to Jefferson, Feb. 24, 1826; LC-JM, from Thomas Jefferson Randolph, July 8, 1826; Jefferson, *Works*, 12:481, Jefferson's Will, March 1826.

32. John Quincy Adams, "First Annual Message," Dec. 6, 1825, Miller Center, http://millercenter.org/president/speeches/detail/3514; *Republic of Letters*, 3:1944–46, "Declaration and Protest."

33. *Republic of Letters*, 3:1947–48, Madison to Jefferson, Dec. 28, 1825; Malone, *Jefferson*, 6:439n48; Jefferson, *Works*, 12:424, 426, to Giles, Dec. 26, 1825.

34. Jefferson, *Works*, 12:424, to Giles, Dec. 26, 1825; Anderson, *William Branch Giles*, 222–26.

35. LC-JM, to Joseph C. Cabell, Dec. 5, 1828; to William C. Rives, Jan. 23, 1829; to Cabell, Sept. 18 and Oct. 5, 1828.

36. Hunt, *John C. Calhoun*, 73; Calhoun, "Rough Draft of What Is Called the South Carolina Exposition," in *Union and Liberty*, 349–51.

37. LC-JM, to Coles, Aug. 29, 1834.

38. Madison, "Speeches Made in the Senate of the United States," 538.

39. *Richmond Enquirer,* Sept. 8, 1829.

40. LC-JM, to Nicholas P. Trist, Feb. 15, 1830; *PMC,* 17:187–88, "Virginia Resolutions: Editorial Note"; LC-JM, to Trist, Dec. 1831.

41. LC-JM, to Trist, May 1832.

42. Madison, "Speeches Made in the Senate of the United States," 541–45; Jean Edward Smith, *John Marshall,* 504–5; *PMC,* 17:190, "Virginia Resolutions," Dec. 21, 1798.

43. See, for example, LC-JM, to Trist, Dec. 1831, and Trist Papers, to Madison, Dec. 14, 1831; LC-JM, to Trist, May 1832.

44. Clay Papers, from Madison, April 2, 1833; Madison, *Writings,* 9:525–27, to unknown, 1833.

45. Clay Papers, from Madison, April 2, 1833; *Republic of Letters,* 3:2002 and n112, "Advice to My Country," 1834; Brant, *Madison,* 6:530–31, 580n12.

46. *PJ,* 7:446, 451–52n5, from Madison, Oct. 17, 1784.

47. Madison, *Writings,* 2:410, "A Sketch Never Finished nor Applied"; *PDM,* "James Madison's Will," April 15, 1835; *Washington Globe,* Aug. 12, 1836.

48. LC-JM, to Coles, Oct. 3, 1834; McCoy, *Last of the Fathers,* 256–58.

49. *PDM,* to Mary Cutts, Oct. 1834; Coles Papers, to Madison, Aug. 17, Sept. 15, and Oct. 31, 1834; LC-JM, to Coles, Aug. 29 and Oct. 3, 1834.

50. James Monroe Museum and Memorial Library, Monroe to Madison, April 11, 1831; LC-JM, to Monroe, April 21, 1831.

51. LC-JM, to Sparks, June 1, 1831; to Le Ray de Chaumont, June 9, 1832; Cutts, *Queen of America,* 176.

52. *PDM,* to Frances Lear, March 1832; Martineau, *Retrospect of Western Travel,* 2:2, 8; *PDM,* to James Madison, Nov. 1, 1805.

53. Chernow, *Washington,* 815, 800.

54. Martineau, *Retrospect of Western Travel,* 2:4–5.

55. LC-JM, to R. R. Gurley, Dec. 28, 1831.

56. Martineau, *Retrospect of Western Travel,* 2:4, 17.

57. Jennings, *Colored Man's Reminiscences of James Madison,* 20–21.

EPILOGUE

1. McCoy, *Last of the Fathers,* 318–22; *PDM,* editorial note by Amy Larrabee Cotz, "Dolley Madison and the Montpelier Enslaved Community, 1836–1843."

2. *PDM,* "James Madison's Will," April 15, 1835; Rives Papers, from George Featherstonhaugh, April 6, 1837.

3. Mattern and Shulman, *Selected Letters of Dolley Payne Madison,* 320; Allgor, *Perfect Union,* 380.

4. *PDM*, Holly Shulman, "Widowhood: The Final Years at Montpelier"; to Lucy Todd, Nov. 13, 1842.

5. Mattern and Shulman, *Selected Letters of Dolley Payne Madison*, 324.

6. *PDM*, to Moncure, Aug. 12, 1844.

7. Dolley Madison Papers, "Items Extracted from Accounts of Payments and Expenses," 1845–1848; Mattern and Shulman, *Selected Letters of Dolley Payne Madison*, 385, to Todd, Sept. 24, 1847.

8. Mattern and Shulman, *Selected Letters of Dolley Payne Madison*, 324, 390, to Todd, July 10, 1848.

9. Ibid., 324–25; Allgor, *Perfect Union*, 397–99.

10. "Madison Family Cemetery," Montpelier Foundation, http://www .montpelier.org/mansion-and-grounds/landscape/madison-family-cemetery.

11. Kearns Diary, July 1–Aug. 3, 1863.

12. Farrand, *Records*, 2:27–28, Madison's notes, July 17, 1787; *PMC*, 10:212, to Jefferson, Oct. 24, 1787.

BIBLIOGRAPHY

Books

Adams, Abigail. *New Letters of Abigail Adams, 1788–1801.* Edited by Stewart Mitchill. Boston: Houghton Mifflin, 1947.

Adams, Henry. *History of the United States of America During the Administrations of James Madison.* New York: Literary Classics of the United States, 1986.

——. *History of the United States of America During the Administrations of Thomas Jefferson.* New York: Literary Classics of the United States, 1986.

——. *John Randolph.* Boston: Houghton Mifflin, 1889.

——. *The Life of Albert Gallatin.* Philadelphia: J. B. Lippincott, 1880.

Adams, John. *The Works of John Adams, Second President of the United States: With a Life of the Author, Notes, and Illustrations by His Grandson Charles Francis Adams.* 10 vols. Boston: Little, Brown, 1850–1856.

Adams, John, and William Cunningham. *Correspondence Between the Hon. John Adams, Late President of the United States, and the Late Wm. Cunningham, Esq., Beginning in 1803, and Ending in 1812.* Boston: E. M. Cunningham, 1823.

Adams, John Quincy. *An Eulogy on the Life and Character of James Madison, Fourth President of the United States.* Boston: American Stationers' Company, 1836.

——. *The Jubilee of the Constitution: A Discourse Delivered at the Bequest of the New York Historical Society in the City of New York, on Tuesday, the 30th of April 1839; Being the Fiftieth Anniversary of the Inauguration of George Washington as President of the United States, on Thursday, the 30th of April, 1789.* New York: Samuel Colman, 1839.

——. *Memoirs of John Quincy Adams, Comprising Portions of His Diary from 1795 to 1848.* Edited by Charles Francis Adams. 12 vols. Philadelphia: J. B. Lippincott, 1874–1877.

The Adams-Jefferson Letters: The Complete Correspondence Between Thomas Jefferson and Abigail and John Adams. Edited by Lester J. Cappon. Chapel Hill: University of North Carolina Press, 1988.

Allgor, Catherine. *A Perfect Union: Dolley Madison and the Creation of the American Nation.* New York: Henry Holt, 2006.

Ambrose, Stephen E. *Undaunted Courage: Meriwether Lewis, Thomas Jefferson, and the Opening of the American West.* New York: Simon & Schuster, 1996.

American State Papers: Documents, Legislative and Executive, of the Congress of the United States. 38 vols. Washington, D.C.: Gales and Seaton, 1832–1861.

Ames, Fisher. *Works of Fisher Ames.* Edited by Seth Ames. 2 vols. Boston: Little, Brown, 1854.

Ammon, Harry. *James Monroe: The Quest for National Identity.* Newton, Conn.: American Political Biography Press, 2008.

Anderson, Dice Robins. *William Branch Giles: A Study in the Politics of Virginia and the Nation from 1790 to 1830.* Menasha, Wis.: George Banta, 1914.

Annals of Congress. 42 vols. (1st Cong.–18th Cong., 1st sess.). Washington, D.C.: Gales and Seaton, 1834–1856.

Aristotle. *Problems II.* Translated by W. S. Hett. London: William Heinemann, 1957.

Armstrong, Kosciuszko. *Review of T. L. McKenney's Narrative of the Causes Which, in 1814, Led to General Armstrong's Resignation of the War Office.* New York: R. Craighead, 1846.

Baker, William Spohn. *Washington After the Revolution.* Philadelphia: J. B. Lippincott, 1898.

Banning, Lance. *The Sacred Fire of Liberty: James Madison and the Founding of the Federal Republic.* Ithaca, N.Y.: Cornell University Press, 1995.

Barbé-Marbois, François, Marquis de. *Our Revolutionary Forefathers: The Letters of François, Marquis de Barbé-Marbois.* Edited by Eugene Parker Chase. 1929. Freeport, N.Y.: Books for Libraries Press, 1969.

Barratt, Carrie Rebora, and Ellen G. Miles. *Gilbert Stuart.* New York: Metropolitan Museum of Art, 2004.

Bayard, Richard Henry. *Documents Relating to the Presidential Election in the Year 1801: Containing a Refutation of Two Passages in the Writings of Thomas Jefferson, Aspersing the Character of the Late James A. Bayard of Delaware.* Philadelphia: Mifflin and Parry, 1831.

Beeman, Richard. *Plain, Honest Men: The Making of the American Constitution.* New York: Random House, 2009.

Bemis, Samuel Flagg. *The Diplomacy of the American Revolution.* Bloomington: Indiana University Press, 1957.

——. *Jay's Treaty: A Study in Commerce and Diplomacy.* New Haven, Conn.: Yale University Press, 1962.

Bernier, Oliver. *Lafayette, Hero of Two Worlds.* New York: E. P. Dutton, 1983.

Beschloss, Michael. *Presidential Courage: Brave Leaders and How They Changed America, 1789–1989.* New York: Simon & Schuster, 2008.

Beveridge, Albert J. *The Life of John Marshall.* 4 vols. Boston: Houghton Mifflin, 1916–1919.

Bickham, Troy. *The Weight of Vengeance: The United States, the British Empire, and the War of 1812.* New York: Oxford University Press, 2012.

Billias, George Athan. *Elbridge Gerry: Founding Father and Republican Statesman.* New York: McGraw-Hill, 1976.

Bland, Theodorick, Jr. *The Bland Papers: Being a Selection from the Manuscripts of Colonel Theodorick Bland Jr.* Edited by Charles Campbell. 2 vols. Petersburg, Va.: Edmund & Julian C. Ruffin, 1840–1843.

Blondel, James Augustus. *The Power of the Mother's Imagination over the Foetus Examin'd.* London: John Brotherton, 1729.

Boorstin, Daniel J. *The Americans: The Colonial Experience.* New York: Random House, 1958.

Bowen, Catherine Drinker. *Miracle at Philadelphia: The Story of the Constitutional Convention, May to September 1787.* 1966. Boston: Little, Brown, 1986.

Bowen, Francis. *The Principles of Political Economy Applied to the Condition, the Resources, and the Institutions of the American People.* Boston: Little, Brown, 1868.

Bowers, Claude G. *Jefferson and Hamilton: The Struggle for Democracy in America.* 1925. Boston: Houghton Mifflin, 1972.

Bowling, Kenneth R. *The Creation of Washington, D.C.: The Idea and Location of the American Capital.* Fairfax, Va.: George Mason University Press, 1991.

Brackenridge, Hugh. *Incidents of the Insurrection.* Edited by Daniel Marder. New Haven, Conn.: College and University Press Services, 1972.

Brant, Irving. *James Madison.* 6 vols. Indianapolis: Bobbs-Merrill, 1941–1961.

Breen, T. H. *Tobacco Culture: The Mentality of the Great Tidewater Planters on the Eve of Revolution.* 1985. Princeton, N.J.: Princeton University Press, 2001.

Brissot de Warville, Jacques-Pierre. *New Travels in the United States of America.* Bowling Green, Ohio: Historical Publications, 1919.

Brodie, Fawn M. *Thomas Jefferson: An Intimate History.* 1974. New York: W. W. Norton, 2010.

Brown, Stephen W. *Voice of the New West: John G. Jackson, His Life and Times.* Macon, Ga.: Mercer University Press, 1985.

Bruce, William Cabell. *John Randolph of Roanoke, 1773–1833: A Biography Based Largely on New Material.* 2 vols. New York: G. P. Putnam's Sons, 1922.

Buchan, William. *Domestic Medicine; or, A Treatise on the Prevention and Cure of Diseases by Regimen and Simple Medicines.* London: Printed for A. Strahan, 1785.

Buel, Richard, Jr. *America on the Brink: How the Political Struggle over the War of 1812 Almost Destroyed the Young Republic.* New York: Palgrave Macmillan, 2005.

Burkitt, William. *Expository Notes with Practical Observations on the New Testament of Our Lord and Saviour Jesus Christ.* London: Richard Evans, 1818.

Burnaby, Andrew. *Travels Through the Middle Settlements in North-America: In the Years 1759 and 1760, with Observations upon the State of the Colonies.* Dublin: Printed for R. Marchbank, 1775.

Calendar of Virginia State Papers and Other Manuscripts. Edited by H. W. Flournoy. 11 vols. Richmond, Va.: Superintendent of Public Printings, 1875–1893.

Calhoun, John C. *Union and Liberty: The Political Philosophy of John C. Calhoun.* Edited by Ross M. Lence. Indianapolis: Liberty Fund, 1992.

Carey, Mathew. *The Olive Branch; or, Faults on Both Sides, Federal and Democratic: A Serious Appeal on the Necessity of Mutual Forgiveness and Harmony.* Winchester, Va.: J. Foster, 1817.

A Catalogue of Books in the Library of the College of New Jersey, January 29, 1760. 1760. Princeton, N.J.: Princeton University Library, 1949.

Chambers, Douglas B. *Murder at Montpelier: Igbo Africans in Virginia.* Jackson: University Press of Mississippi, 2005.

Chernow, Ron. *Alexander Hamilton.* New York: Penguin Press, 2004.

——. *Washington: A Life.* New York: Penguin Press, 2010.

Cheyne, George. *An Essay of Health and Long Life.* London: George Strahan, 1745.

Christian, W. Asbury. *Richmond: Her Past and Present.* Richmond: L. H. Jenkins, 1912.

Clarke, Samuel. *A Demonstration of the Being and Attributes of God: More Particularly in Answer to Mr. Hobbs, Spinoza, and Their Followers.* London: Will Botham, 1705.

——. *A Paraphrase on the Four Evangelists.* 2 vols. London: W. B., 1736.

Clay, Henry. *The Papers of Henry Clay.* Edited by James F. Hopkins. 11 vols. Lexington: University of Kentucky Press, 1959–1992.

Coles, Harry L. *The War of 1812.* Chicago: University of Chicago Press, 1965.

Collins, Varnum Lansing. *Princeton.* New York: Oxford University Press, 1914.

Combs, Jerald A. *The Jay Treaty: Political Battleground of the Founding Fathers.* Berkeley: University of California Press, 1970.

Conway, Moncure Daniel. *Omitted Chapters of History Disclosed in the Life and Papers of Edmund Randolph, Governor of Virginia; First Attorney-General United States, Secretary of State.* New York: G. P. Putnam's Sons, 1889.

Creating the Bill of Rights: The Documentary Record from the First Federal Congress. Edited by Helen E. Viet, Kenneth R. Bowling, and Charlene Bangs Bickford. Baltimore: Johns Hopkins University Press, 1991.

Creighton, Charles. *A History of Epidemics in Britain.* 2 vols. Cambridge, U.K.: Cambridge University Press, 1891–1894.

Cross, Arthur Lyon. *A History of England and Greater Britain.* New York: Macmillan, 1914.

Cullen, William. *First Lines of the Practice of Physic, for the Use of Students in the University of Edinburgh.* 2 vols. Philadelphia: Steiner and Cist/Charles Cist, 1781–1783.

Cunningham, Noble E., Jr. *The Jeffersonian Republicans: The Formation of Party Organization, 1789–1801.* Chapel Hill: University of North Carolina Press, 1957.

Cutler, William Parker, and Julia Perkins Cutler. *Life, Journals, and Correspondence of Rev. Manasseh Cutler, LL.D.* 2 vols. Cincinnati: Robert Clarke, 1888.

Cutts, Mary. *The Queen of America: Mary Cutts's Life of Dolley Madison.* Edited by Catherine Allgor. Charlottesville: University of Virginia Press, 2012.

Daniel, Britt Talley. *Migraine.* Bloomington: AuthorHouse, 2010.

Dawidoff, Robert. *The Education of John Randolph.* New York: W. W. Norton, 1979.

De Chastellux, Marquis. *Travels in North-America, in the Years 1780, 1781, and 1782.* 2 vols. London: Printed for G. G. J. and J. Robinson, 1787.

DeConde, Alexander. *The Quasi-war: The Politics and Diplomacy of the Undeclared War with France, 1797–1801.* New York: Charles Scribner's Sons, 1966.

de Retz, Cardinal. *Memoirs of Cardinal de Retz.* Introduction by David Ogg. 2 vols. London: J. M. Dent, 1917.

Devinsky, Orrin. *Epilepsy: Patient & Family Guide.* New York: Demos Medical Publishing, 2008.

Documentary History of the First Federal Congress of the United States of America. Edited by Linda Grant DePauw, Helen E. Veit, Charlene Bangs Bickford, Kenneth R. Bowling, LaVonne Siegel Hauptman, and William Charles DiGiacomantonio. 20 vols. Baltimore: Johns Hopkins University Press, 1972–2012.

The Documentary History of the Ratification of the Constitution. Edited by Merrill Jensen, John P. Kaminski, Gaspare J. Saladino, Richard Leffler, Charles H. Schoenleber, Margaret A. Hogan, et al. 26 vols. Madison: Wisconsin Historical Society, 1981–2013.

The Documentary History of the Ratification of the Constitution Digital Edition. Edited by John P. Kaminski, Gaspare J. Saladino, Richard Leffler, Charles H. Schoenleber, and Margaret A. Hogan. 20 vols. Charlottesville: University of Virginia Press, 2009. http://rotunda.upress.virginia.edu/founders/RNCN .html.

Dorman, John Frederick. *Orange County, Virginia: Deed Books 1 and 2, 1735–1738; Judgments, 1735.* Washington, D.C., 1961.

Drinker, Elizabeth. *Extracts from the Journal of Elizabeth Drinker.* Edited by Henry D. Biddle. Philadelphia: J. B. Lippincott, 1889.

Dunbar, Seymour. *A History of Travel in America.* 4 vols. Indianapolis: Bobbs-Merrill, 1915.

Eadie, Mervyn J., and Peter F. Bladin. *A Disease Once Sacred: A History of the Medical Understanding of Epilepsy.* Eastleigh, U.K.: John Libbey, 2001.

Eckenrode, Hamilton James. *The Revolution in Virginia*. Boston: Houghton Mifflin, 1916.

Edwards, Jonathan. *The Works of Jonathan Edwards*. Edited by Paul Ramsey et al. 26 vols. New Haven, Conn.: Yale University Press, 1957–2008.

Egerton, Douglas R. *Gabriel's Rebellion: The Virginia Slave Conspiracies of 1800 and 1802*. Chapel Hill: University of North Carolina Press, 1993.

Elkins, Stanley, and Eric McKitrick. *The Age of Federalism*. New York: Oxford University Press, 1993.

Elliot, Jonathan. *The Debates in the Several State Conventions, on the Adoption of the Federal Constitution, as Recommended by the General Convention at Philadelphia in 1787*. Collected and revised by Jonathan Elliot. 5 vols. Washington, D.C.: Printed for the editor, 1836.

Ellis, Joseph J. *American Sphinx: The Character of Thomas Jefferson*. 1996. New York: Vintage Books, 1998.

——. *Founding Brothers: The Revolutionary Generation*. New York: Alfred A. Knopf, 2000.

Evans, Dorinda. *The Genius of Gilbert Stuart*. Princeton, N.J.: Princeton University Press, 1999.

Evans, Edward S. *The Seals of Virginia*. Richmond: Davis Bottom, 1911.

Executive Journals of the Council of Colonial Virginia. Edited by Henry Read McIlwaine. 4 vols. Richmond: Virginia State Library, 1925–1930.

Facts Relative to John Henry and His Negotiation. Washington, D.C., 1812.

Farrand, Max. *The Framing of the Constitution of the United States*. New Haven, Conn.: Yale University Press, 1913.

——, ed. *The Records of the Federal Convention of 1787*. 3 vols. New Haven, Conn.: Yale University Press, 1911.

Ferguson, E. James. *The Power of the Purse: A History of American Public Finance, 1776–1790*. Chapel Hill: University of North Carolina Press, 1961.

Ferling, John. *A Leap in the Dark: The Struggle to Create the American Republic*. New York: Oxford University Press, 2003.

Fithian, Philip Vickers. *Philip Vickers Fithian: Journal and Letters, 1767–1774*. Edited by John Rogers Williams. 1900. Freeport, N.Y.: Books for Libraries Press, 1969.

Flexner, James Thomas. *George Washington in the American Revolution, 1775–1783*. Boston: Little, Brown, 1968.

Force, Peter. *American Archives*. 9 vols. Washington, D.C., 1837–1853. http://dig.lib.niu.edu/amarch/index.html.

Franklin, Benjamin. *The Writings of Benjamin Franklin*. Edited by Albert Henry Smyth. 10 vols. New York: Macmillan, 1905–1907.

Freeman, Douglas Southall. *Washington*. Abridgement by Richard Harwell. 1968. New York: Collier Books, 1992.

Gallatin, Albert. *The Writings of Albert Gallatin.* Edited by Henry Adams. 3 vols. Philadelphia: J. B. Lippincott, 1879.

Gardner, Howard. *Intelligence Reframed: Multiple Intelligences for the 21st Century.* New York: Basic Books, 1999.

Gay, Sydney H. *James Madison.* 1884. Boston: Houghton Mifflin, 1912.

Gish, Agnes Evans. *Virginia Taverns, Ordinaries, and Coffee Houses: 18th–Early 19th Century Entertainment Along the Buckingham Road.* Westminster, Md.: Willow Bend Books, 2005.

Gladwell, Malcolm. *Outliers: The Story of Success.* New York: Little, Brown, 2008.

Goldwin, Robert A. *From Parchment to Power: How James Madison Used the Bill of Rights to Save the Constitution.* Washington, D.C.: AEI Press, 1997.

———. *Why Blacks, Women, and Jews Are Not Mentioned in the Constitution, and Other Unorthodox Views.* Washington, D.C.: AEI Press, 1990.

Golway, Terry. *Washington's General.* New York: Henry Holt, 2005.

Gordon-Reed, Annette. *The Hemingses of Monticello: An American Family.* New York: W. W. Norton, 2008.

Gowers, William R. *The Borderland of Epilepsy: Faints, Vagal Attacks, Vertigo, Migraine, Sleep Symptoms, and Their Treatment.* Philadelphia: P. Blakiston's Son, 1907.

Green, Ashbel. *The Life of the Revd. John Witherspoon, D.D., L.L.D.: With a Brief Review of His Writings, and a Summary Estimate of His Character and Talents.* Princeton, N.J.: Princeton University Press, 1973.

Green, Bryan Clark, and Ann L. Miller. *Building a President's House: The Construction of James Madison's Montpelier.* With Conover Hunt. Orange, Va.: Montpelier Foundation, 2007.

Grigsby, Hugh Blair. *The History of the Virginia Federal Convention of 1788, with Some Account of the Eminent Virginians of That Era Who Were Members of the Body.* 2 vols. Richmond: Society, 1890–1891.

———. *The Virginia Convention of 1776: A Discourse Delivered Before the Virginia Alpha of the Phi Beta Kappa Society in the Chapel of William and Mary College, in the City of Williamsburg, on the Afternoon of July the 3rd, 1855.* Richmond: J. W. Randolph, 1855.

Hamilton, Alexander. *The Papers of Alexander Hamilton.* Edited by Harold C. Syrett and Jacob E. Cooke. 27 vols. New York: Columbia University Press, 1961–1987.

———. *The Papers of Alexander Hamilton Digital Edition.* Edited by Harold C. Syrett. Charlottesville: University of Virginia Press, Rotunda, 2011. http://rotunda.upress.virginia.edu/founders/ARHN.html.

Hamilton, John C. *History of the Republic of the United States of America, as Traced in the Writings of Alexander Hamilton and of His Contemporaries.* 7 vols. New York: D. Appleton; Philadelphia: J. B. Lippincott, 1857–1864.

Hamilton, William Baskerville. *Thomas Rodney: Revolutionary & Builder of the West*. Durham, N.C.: Duke University Press, 1953.

Harle, Jonathan. *An Historical Essay on the State of Physick in the Old and New Testament, and the Apocryphal Interval: With a Particular Account of the Cases Mentioned in Scripture, and Observations upon Them*. London: Printed for Richard Ford, 1729.

Harrison, Lowell H. *George Rogers Clark and the War in the West*. Lexington: University Press of Kentucky, 1976.

Harrison, Richard A. *Princetonians, 1769–1775: A Biographical Dictionary*. Princeton, N.J.: Princeton University Press, 1980.

Hayden, Horace E. *Virginia Genealogies*. 1891. Baltimore: Genealogical Publishing, 2004.

Heller, J. Roderick, III. *Democracy's Lawyer: Felix Grundy of the Old Southwest*. Baton Rouge: Louisiana State University Press, 2010.

Hening, William Waller. *The Statutes at Large: Being a Collection of All the Laws of Virginia from the First Session of the Legislature, in the Year 1619*. 13 vols. Richmond: Printed for the editor, 1823.

Hermann, Binger. *The Louisiana Purchase and Our Title West of the Rocky Mountains, with a Review of Annexation by the United States*. Washington, D.C.: Government Printing Office, 1900.

Herrick, Carole L. *August 24, 1814: Washington in Flames*. Falls Church, Va.: Higher Education Publications, 2005.

Hess, Stephen. *America's Political Dynasties*. New Brunswick, N.J.: Transaction, 1997.

Hickey, Donald R. *The War of 1812: A Forgotten Conflict*. Urbana: University of Illinois Press, 2012.

Hill, John. *A History of the Materia Medica*. London: Printed for T. Longman, C. Hitch, and L. Hawes; A. Millar; and J. and J. Rivington, 1751.

Hippocrates. *The Medical Works of Hippocrates*. Translated by John Chadwick and W. N. Mann. Springfield, Ill.: Charles C. Thomas, 1950.

Hofstadter, Richard. *The Idea of a Party System: The Rise of Legitimate Opposition in the United States, 1780–1840*. Berkeley: University of California Press, 1969.

Horn, James. *Adapting to a New World: English Society in the Seventeenth-Century Chesapeake*. Chapel Hill: University of North Carolina Press, 1994.

Howe, Michael J. A. *Genius Explained*. Cambridge, U.K.: Cambridge University Press, 1999.

Hume, David. *Essays and Treatises on Several Subjects*. 2 vols. Edinburgh: Printed for Bell & Bradfute, 1825.

———. *A Treatise of Human Nature*. Edited by L. A. Selby-Bigge. 1739. Oxford: Clarendon Press, 1888.

Hunt, Gaillard. *John C. Calhoun*. 1907. Philadelphia: George W. Jacobs, 1908.

——. *The Life of James Madison.* 1902. New York: Russell & Russell, 1968.

Hunt-Jones, Conover. *Dolley and the "Great Little Madison."* Washington, D.C.: American Institute of Architects Foundation, 1977.

Ingersoll, Charles J. *Historical Sketch of the Second War Between the United States of America and Great Britain.* 2 vols. Philadelphia: Lea and Blanchard, 1845–1849.

Irving, Pierre M. *The Life and Letters of Washington Irving.* 3 vols. 1863. Honolulu: University Press of the Pacific, 2001.

Irving, Washington. *Life of George Washington.* 5 vols. New York: G. P. Putnam's Sons, 1857.

Irwin, Douglas A., and Richard Sylla, eds. *Founding Choices: American Economic Policy in the 1790s.* Chicago: University of Chicago Press, 2011.

Isaacson, Walter. *Benjamin Franklin: An American Life.* New York: Simon & Schuster, 2003.

——. *Einstein: His Life and Universe.* New York: Simon & Schuster, 2007.

Isenberg, Nancy. *Fallen Founder: The Life of Aaron Burr.* New York: Viking, 2007.

Jackson, George. *The Bath Archives: A Further Selection from the Diaries and Letters of Sir George Jackson, K. C. H., from 1809 to 1816.* Edited by Lady Jackson. 2 vols. London: Richard Bentley and Son, 1873.

Jackson, John Hughlings. *Selected Writings of John Hughlings Jackson.* Edited by James Taylor. 2 vols. London: Hodder and Stoughton, 1932; New York: Basic Books, 1958.

James Madison and the American Nation, 1751–1836: An Encyclopedia. Edited by Robert A. Rutland. New York: Simon & Schuster, 1994.

Jay, John. *John Jay: The Making of a Revolutionary.* Edited by Richard B. Morris. New York: Harper & Row, 1975.

Jefferson, Thomas. *Autobiography of Thomas Jefferson.* Introduction by Dumas Malone. New York: Capricorn Books, 1959.

——. *The Complete Anas of Thomas Jefferson.* Edited by Franklin B. Sawvel. New York: Round Table Press, 1903.

——. *The Family Letters of Thomas Jefferson.* Edited by Edwin Morris Betts and James Adam Bear Jr. 1966. Charlottesville: University Press of Virginia, 1986.

——. *Jefferson's Memorandum Books: Accounts, with Legal Records and Miscellany, 1767–1826.* Edited by James A. Bear Jr. and Lucia C. Stanton. 2 vols. Princeton, N.J.: Princeton University Press, 1997.

——. *Notes on the State of Virginia.* Richmond: J. W. Randolph, 1853.

——. *The Papers of Thomas Jefferson.* Edited by Julian P. Boyd, Charles T. Cullen, John Catanzariti, and Barbara B. Oberg. 39 vols. Princeton, N.J.: Princeton University Press, 1950–2012.

——. *The Papers of Thomas Jefferson Digital Edition.* Edited by Barbara B. Oberg and J. Jefferson Looney. Charlottesville: University of Virginia Press, Rotunda, 2008. http://rotunda.upress.virginia.edu/founders/TSJN.

——. *The Papers of Thomas Jefferson: Retirement Series*. Edited by J. Jefferson Looney. 10 vols. Princeton, N.J.: Princeton University Press, 2005–2014.

——. *The Works of Thomas Jefferson*. Edited by Paul Leicester Ford. 12 vols. New York: G. P. Putnam's Sons, 1904–1905.

——. *The Writings of Thomas Jefferson*. Edited by Andrew A. Lipscomb and Albert Ellery Bergh. 20 vols. Washington, D.C.: Thomas Jefferson Memorial Association, 1903–1904.

Jennings, Paul. *A Colored Man's Reminiscences of James Madison*. Brooklyn: George C. Beadle, 1865.

Johnson, Calvin H. *Righteous Anger at the Wicked States: The Meaning of the Founders' Constitution*. 2005. Cambridge, U.K.: Cambridge University Press, 2009.

Johnson, Paul. *Napoleon*. New York: Viking, 2002.

Jones, Hugh. *The Present State of Virginia*. New York: Reprinted for Joseph Sabin, 1865.

Journals of the Continental Congress, 1774–1789. Edited by Worthington C. Ford et al. 34 vols. Washington, D.C.: Government Printing Office, 1904–1937.

Journeys in New Worlds: Early American Women's Narratives. Edited by William L. Andrews. Madison: University of Wisconsin Press, 1990.

Kaminski, John P. *George Clinton: Yeoman Politician of the New Republic*. Madison, Wis.: Madison House, 1993.

Kennedy, John P. *Memoirs of the Life of William Wirt, Attorney General of the United States*. 2 vols. Philadelphia: Lea and Blanchard, 1849.

Kesler, Charles, ed. *The Federalist Papers*. Edited by Clinton Rossiter. Introduction and notes by Charles Kesler. New York: New American Library, 2003.

Ketcham, Ralph. *James Madison: A Biography*. 1971. Charlottesville: University of Virginia Press, 1990.

——. *The Madisons at Montpelier: Reflections on the Founding Couple*. Charlottesville: University of Virginia Press, 2009.

King, Rufus. *The Life and Correspondence of Rufus King*. Edited by Charles R. King. 6 vols. New York: G. P. Putnam's Sons, 1894–1900.

Koch, Adrienne. *Jefferson and Madison: The Great Collaboration*. New York: Alfred A. Knopf, 1950.

Kukla, Jon. *A Wilderness So Immense: The Louisiana Purchase and the Destiny of America*. New York: Alfred A. Knopf, 2003.

Kulikoff, Allan. *Tobacco and Slaves: The Development of Southern Cultures in the Chesapeake, 1680–1800*. Chapel Hill: University of North Carolina Press, 1986.

Kurtz, Stephen G. *The Presidency of John Adams: The Collapse of Federalism, 1795–1800*. Philadelphia: University of Pennsylvania Press, 1957.

Larson, Edward. *A Magnificent Catastrophe: The Tumultuous Election of 1800, America's First Presidential Campaign*. New York: Free Press, 2007.

Lear, Tobias. *Letters and Recollections of George Washington: Being Letters to Tobias Lear and Others Between 1790 and 1799, Showing the First American in the Management of His Estate and Domestic Affairs; with a Diary of Washington's Last Days, Kept by Tobias Lear.* New York: Doubleday, Page, 1906.

Lee, Cazenove Gardner, Jr. *Lee Chronicle: Studies of the Early Generations of the Lees of Virginia.* Compiled and edited by Dorothy Mills Parker. New York: New York University Press, 1957.

Lee, Richard H. *Memoir of the Life of Richard Henry Lee, and His Correspondence with the Most Distinguished Men in America and Europe, Illustrative of Their Characters, and of the Events of the American Revolution.* 2 vols. Philadelphia: William Brown, 1825.

Leibiger, Stuart. *Founding Friendship: George Washington, James Madison, and the Creation of the American Republic.* Charlottesville: University Press of Virginia, 1999.

Leland, John, and L. F. Greene. *The Writings of the Late Elder John Leland Including Some Events in His Life, Written by Himself, with Additional Sketches.* New York: G. W. Wood, 1845.

Letters of Delegates to Congress, 1774–1789. 25 vols. Edited by Paul H. Smith et al. Washington, D.C.: Library of Congress, 1976–2000.

Levasseur, Auguste. *Lafayette in America in 1824 and 1825; or, Journal of a Voyage to the United States.* Translated by John D. Godman. 2 vols. Philadelphia: Carey and Lea, 1829.

Levitin, Daniel J. *This Is Your Brain on Music: The Science of a Human Obsession.* New York: Plume, 2007.

Liberty and Order: The First American Party Struggle. Edited by Lance Banning. Indianapolis: Liberty Fund, 2004.

Lippincott, Horace Mather. *Early Philadelphia: Its People, Life, and Progress.* Philadelphia: J. B. Lippincott, 1917.

Little, Lewis Peyton. *Imprisoned Preachers and Religious Liberty in Virginia: A Narrative Drawn Largely from the Official Records of Virginia Counties, Unpublished Manuscripts, Letters, and Other Original Sources.* Lynchburg, Va.: J. P. Bell, 1938.

Lloyd, Gordon. *The Constitutional Convention.* http://www.teachingamerican history.org/convention/.

Locke, John. *Some Familiar Letters Between Mr. Locke, and Several of His Friends.* London: Printed for A. and J. Churchill, 1708.

——. *The Works of John Locke in Nine Volumes.* 9 vols. London: Printed for C. and J. Rivington, 1824.

Looney, J. Jefferson. *Nurseries of Letters and Republicanism: A Brief History of the American Whig-Cliosophic Society and Its Predecessors, 1765–1941.* Princeton, N.J.: Trustees of the American Whig-Cliosophic Society, 1996.

Lossing, Benson J. *The Pictorial Field-Book of the War of 1812.* New York: Harper & Brothers, 1868.

McCoy, Drew R. *The Elusive Republic: Political Economy in Jeffersonian America.* Chapel Hill: University of North Carolina Press, 1980.

——. *The Last of the Fathers: James Madison & the Republican Legacy.* Cambridge, U.K.: Cambridge University Press, 1989.

McCullough, David. *John Adams.* New York: Simon & Schuster, 2001.

——. *1776.* New York: Simon & Schuster, 2005.

McKenney, Thomas L. *Reply to Kosciusko Armstrong's Assault upon Col. McKenney's Narrative of the Causes That Led to General Armstrong's Resignation of the Office of Secretary of War in 1814.* New York: William H. Graham, 1847.

Maclay, William. *Journal of William Maclay: United States Senator from Pennsylvania, 1789–1791.* Edited by Edgar S. Maclay. New York: D. Appleton, 1890.

Madison, Dolley. *The Papers of Dolley Madison Digital Edition.* Edited by Holly C. Shulman. Charlottesville: University of Virginia Press, Rotunda, 2008. http://rotunda.upress.virginia.edu/dmde/.

Madison, James. *Letters and Other Writings of James Madison.* 4 vols. Philadelphia: J. B. Lippincott, 1865.

——. *The Papers of James Madison, Congressional Series.* Edited by J. C. A. Stagg, David B. Mattern, William T. Hutchinson, William M. Rachal, Robert A. Rutland et al. 17 vols. Chicago: University of Chicago Press; Charlottesville: University Press of Virginia, 1962–1991.

——. *The Papers of James Madison Digital Edition.* Edited by J. C. A. Stagg. Charlottesville: University of Virginia Press, Rotunda, 2010. http://rotunda.upress.virginia.edu/founders/JSMN.html.

——. *The Papers of James Madison, Presidential Series.* Edited by Robert A. Rutland, J. C. A. Stagg, Angela Kreider et al. 7 vols. Charlottesville: University Press of Virginia, 1984–2012.

——. *The Papers of James Madison, Retirement Series.* Edited by David B. Mattern and J. C. A. Stagg. 2 vols. Charlottesville: University of Virginia Press, 2009–2013.

——. *The Papers of James Madison, Secretary of State Series.* Edited by Robert R. Brugger, Robert A. Rutland, David B. Mattern, J. C. A. Stagg, Mary A. Hackett et al. 9 vols. Charlottesville: University Press of Virginia, 1986–2011.

——. *The Writings of James Madison.* Edited by Gaillard Hunt. 9 vols. New York: G. P. Putnam's Sons, 1900–1910.

Maier, Pauline. *Ratification: The People Debate the Constitution, 1787–1788.* New York: Simon & Schuster, 2010.

Malone, Dumas. *Jefferson and His Time.* 6 vols. 1948–1981. Charlottesville: University of Virginia Press, 2005.

Martineau, Harriet. *Retrospect of Western Travel.* 3 vols. London: Saunders and Otley, 1838.

Mattern, David B., and Holly C. Shulman. *The Selected Letters of Dolley Payne Madison.* Charlottesville: University of Virginia Press, 2003.

Maxwell, William Q. *A Portrait of William Floyd: Long Islander.* Long Island, N.Y.: Society for the Preservation of Long Island Antiquities, 1956.

Mays, David John. *Edmund Pendleton, 1721–1803: A Biography.* 2 vols. Richmond: Virginia State Library, 1984.

Meade, William. *Old Churches, Ministers, and Families of Virginia.* 2 vols. Philadelphia: J. B. Lippincott, 1910.

Middleton, Arthur Pierce. *Tobacco Coast: A Maritime History of Chesapeake Bay in the Colonial Era.* 1953. Baltimore: Johns Hopkins University Press, 1984.

Miller, Ann L. *The Short Life and Strange Death of Ambrose Madison.* 1995. Orange, Va.: Orange County Historical Society, 2001.

Monroe, James. *The Papers of James Monroe.* Edited by Daniel Preston and Marlena C. Delong. 4 vols. Westport, Conn.: Greenwood Press, 2003–2011.

——. *The Writings of James Monroe.* Edited by Stanislaus Murray Hamilton. 7 vols. New York: G. P. Putnam's Sons, 1898–1903.

The Moral Foundations of the American Republic. Edited by Robert H. Horwitz. Charlottesville: University Press of Virginia, 1986.

Morgan, Edmund S. *American Slavery, American Freedom: The Ordeal of Colonial Virginia.* 1975. New York: W. W. Norton, 2003.

Morison, Samuel Eliot. *The Life and Letters of Harrison Gray Otis, Federalist, 1765–1848.* 2 vols. Boston: Houghton Mifflin, 1913.

Morison, Samuel Eliot, and Henry Steele Commager. *The Growth of the American Republic.* 2 vols. New York: Oxford University Press, 1968.

Morrison, Jeffry H. *John Witherspoon and the Founding of the American Republic.* Notre Dame, Ind.: University of Notre Dame Press, 2005.

Morse, John T., Jr. *The Life of Alexander Hamilton.* 2 vols. Boston: Little, Brown, 1876.

Murphy, Jim. *An American Plague: The True and Terrifying Story of the Yellow Fever Epidemic of 1793.* New York: Clarion Books, 2003.

Murrin, John M., Paul E. Johnson, James M. McPherson, Alice Fahs, Gary Gerstle, Emily S. Rosenburg, and Norman L. Rosenberg. *Liberty, Equality, Power: A History of the American People.* 2 vols. Boston: Cengage Learning, 2010–2011.

Naval Documents of the American Revolution. Edited by William Bell Clark. 11 vols. Washington, D.C.: U.S. Navy Department, 1964.

Neimeyer, Charles Patrick. *America Goes to War: A Social History of the Continental Army.* New York: New York University Press, 1996.

Newmyer, R. Kent. *The Treason Trial of Aaron Burr: Law, Politics, and the Character Wars of the New Nation.* Cambridge, U.K.: Cambridge University Press, 2012.

Nugent, Nell Marion. *Cavaliers and Pioneers: Abstracts of Virginia Land Patents and Grants.* 2 vols. 1934. Richmond: Virginia State Library, 1977; Baltimore: Genealogical Publishing, 1983.

Official Letters of the Governors of the State of Virginia. Edited by H. R. McIlwaine. 3 vols. Richmond: Virginia State Library, 1926–1929.

Olmert, Michael. *Official Guide to Colonial Williamsburg.* 1985. Williamsburg, Va.: Colonial Williamsburg Foundation, 2007.

Paine, Thomas. *Common Sense: Addressed to the Inhabitants of America.* New York: Peter Eckler, 1918.

Peirce, Charles. *A Meteorological Account of the Weather in Philadelphia from January 1, 1790, to January 1, 1847, Including Fifty-Seven Years.* Philadelphia: Lindsay & Blakiston, 1847.

Perkins, Bradford. *Prologue to War: England and the United States, 1805–1812.* Berkeley: University of California Press, 1961.

Peterson, Merrill D. *Thomas Jefferson and the New Nation.* New York: Oxford University Press, 1970.

Pickering, Octavius, and Charles W. Upham. *The Life of Timothy Pickering.* 4 vols. Boston: Little, Brown, 1867–1873.

Pitch, Anthony S. *The Burning of Washington: The British Invasion of 1814.* 1998. Annapolis, Md.: National Institute Press, 2000.

Plumer, William. *William Plumer's Memorandum of Proceedings in the United States Senate, 1803–1807.* New York: Macmillan, 1923.

Proceedings and Addresses at the Celebration of the One Hundredth Anniversary of the Founding of the Cliosophic Society of the College of New Jersey, Princeton, N.J., June 27, 1865. Philadelphia: Sherman & Co., Printers, 1865.

Pybus, Cassandra. *Epic Journeys of Freedom: Runaway Slaves of the American Revolution and Their Global Quest for Liberty.* Boston: Beacon Press, 2006.

Quincy, John. *A Complete English Dispensatory.* London: Printed for Thomas Longman, 1739.

Randall, Henry S. *The Life of Thomas Jefferson.* 3 vols. New York: Derby & Jackson, 1858.

Randolph, Edmund. *A Vindication of Edmund Randolph.* Richmond: Charles H. Wynne, Printer, 1855.

Ravenel, Mrs. St. Julien. *The Life and Times of William Lowndes of South Carolina, 1782–1822.* Boston: Houghton Mifflin, 1901.

Remini, Robert V. *The House: The History of the House of Representatives.* New York: HarperCollins, 2006.

The Republic of Letters: The Correspondence Between Thomas Jefferson and James Madison, 1776–1826. Edited by James Morton Smith. 3 vols. New York: W. W. Norton, 1995.

The Revolutionary Diplomatic Correspondence of the United States. Edited by Francis Wharton. 6 vols. Washington, D.C.: Government Printing Office, 1889.

Rice, Howard C., Jr. *The Rittenhouse Orrery: Princeton's Eighteenth-Century Planetarium, 1767–1954.* Princeton, N.J.: Princeton University Library, 1954.

Richardson, James D. *A Compilation of the Messages and Papers of the President.* 11 vols. New York: Bureau of National Literature and Art, 1911.

Risjord, Norman K. *The Old Republicans: Southern Conservatism in the Age of Jefferson.* New York: Columbia University Press, 1965.

Rives, William C. *History of the Life and Times of James Madison.* 3 vols. 1859–1868. Freeport, N.Y.: Books for Libraries Press, 1970.

Robertson, David. *Reports of the Trials of Colonel Aaron Burr (Late Vice President of the United States), for Treason, and for a Misdemeanor.* 2 vols. Philadelphia: Hopkins and Earle, 1808.

Rossiter, Clinton, ed. *The Federalist Papers.* New York: New American Library, 1961.

Rowland, Kate Mason. *The Life of George Mason, 1725–1792.* 2 vols. New York: G. P. Putnam's Sons, 1892.

Royster, Charles. *Light-Horse Harry Lee and the Legacy of the American Revolution.* 1981. Baton Rouge: Louisiana State University Press, 1994.

Rush, Benjamin. *The Autobiography of Benjamin Rush: His "Travels Through Life" Together with His "Common place Book" for 1789–1813.* Edited by George W. Corner. Westport, Conn.: Greenwood Press, 1970.

Schama, Simon. *Citizens: A Chronicle of the French Revolution.* 1989. New York: Random House, 1990.

Scharf, J. Thomas. *The Chronicles of Baltimore; Being a Complete History of "Baltimore Town" and Baltimore City from the Earliest Period to the Present Time.* Baltimore: Turnbull Brothers, 1874.

Schoepf, Johann David. *Travels in the Confederation, 1783–1784: From the German of Johann David Schoepf.* Translated and edited by Alfred J. Morrison. 2 vols. Philadelphia: William J. Campbell, 1968.

Scott, James. *Recollections of a Naval Life.* 3 vols. London: Richard Bentley, 1834.

Scott, W. W. *A History of Orange County, Virginia.* Richmond: Everett Waddey, 1907.

Seale, William. *The President's House: A History.* 2 vols. Washington, D.C.: White House Historical Association, 1986.

Selby, John E. *The Revolution in Virginia, 1775–1783.* 1988. Williamsburg, Va.: Colonial Williamsburg Foundation, 2007.

Selections from the "Edinburgh Review," Comprising the Best Articles in That Journal, from Its Commencement to the Present Time. Edited by Maurice Cross. 6 vols. Paris: Baudry's European Library, 1835–1836.

Semmes, John E. *John H. B. Latrobe and His Times, 1803–1891.* Baltimore: Norman, Remington, 1917.

Seventeenth-Century America: Essays in Colonial History. Edited by James Morton Smith. Chapel Hill: University of North Carolina Press, 1959.

Skeen, C. Edward. *John Armstrong Jr., 1758–1843: A Biography.* Syracuse, N.Y.: Syracuse University Press, 1981.

Smith, Billy G. *The "Lower Sort": Philadelphia's Laboring People, 1750–1800*. Ithaca, N.Y.: Cornell University Press, 1994.

Smith, James Morton. *Freedom's Fetters: The Alien and Sedition Laws and American Civil Liberties*. Ithaca, N.Y.: Cornell University Press, 1956.

Smith, Jean Edward. *John Marshall: Definer of a Nation*. New York: Henry Holt, 1996.

Smith, Margaret Bayard. *The First Forty Years of Washington Society*. Edited by Gaillard Hunt. New York: Charles Scribner's Sons, 1906.

——. *A Winter in Washington; or, Memoirs of the Seymour Family*. 2 vols. New York: E. Bliss & E. White, 1824.

Smith, Samuel H., and Thomas Lloyd. *Trial of Samuel Chase*. 2 vols. Washington, D.C.: Samuel H. Smith, 1805.

Smith, William Henry. *Speakers of the House of Representatives of the United States*. Baltimore: Simon J. Gaeng, 1928.

Sparks, Jared. *The Life of Gouverneur Morris: With Selections from His Correspondence and Miscellaneous Papers; Detailing Events in the American Revolution, the French Revolution, and in the Political History of the United States*. 3 vols. Boston: Gray & Bowen, 1832.

The Spectator. Edited by Henry Morley. 3 vols. London: George Routledge and Sons, 1891.

Stagg, J. C. A. *Borderlines in Borderlands: James Madison and the Spanish-American Frontier, 1776–1821*. New Haven, Conn.: Yale University Press, 2009.

——. *Mr. Madison's War: Politics, Diplomacy, and Warfare in the Early American Republic, 1783–1830*. Princeton, N.J.: Princeton University Press, 1983.

——. *The War of 1812: Conflict for a Continent*. Cambridge, U.K.: Cambridge University Press, 2012.

Stahr, Walter. *John Jay: Founding Father*. New York: Hambledon & Continuum, 2005.

Story, Joseph. *Life and Letters of Joseph Story, Associate Justice of the Supreme Court of the United States, and Dane Professor of Law at Harvard University*. Edited by William W. Story. 2 vols. Boston: Charles C. Little and James Brown, 1851.

Sullivan, William. *The Public Men of the Revolution*. Philadelphia: Carey and Hart, 1847.

Supplement to Max Farrand's The Records of the Federal Convention of 1787. Edited by James H. Hutson. New Haven, Conn.: Yale University Press, 1987.

Tait, L. Gordon. *The Piety of John Witherspoon: Pew, Pulpit, and Public Forum*. Louisville, Ky.: Geneva Press, 2001.

Taylor, Alan. *American Colonies*. New York: Viking, 2001.

Temkin, Owsei. *The Falling Sickness: A History of Epilepsy from the Greeks to the Beginnings of Modern Neurology*. 1945. Baltimore: Johns Hopkins Press, 1971.

Terrio, Bob. *Philadelphia 1787: The Heart of the City for the Constitutional Convention, May 25th to September 17th, 1787* [map]. Philadelphia: Friends of Independence National Historical Park, 1986.

Thomson, John. *An Account of the Life, Lectures, and Writings of William Cullen, M.D.* 2 vols. Edinburgh: William Blackwood and Sons, 1859.

Tissot, Samuel Auguste. *Traité de l'épilepsie: Faisant le tome troisième du "Traité des nerfs & de leurs maladies."* Paris: P. F. Didot, 1770.

Todd, Dennis. *Imagining Monsters: Miscreations of the Self in Eighteenth-Century England.* Chicago: University of Chicago Press, 1995.

Toll, Ian W. *Six Frigates: The Epic History of the Founding of the U.S. Navy.* New York: W. W. Norton, 2006.

Tucker, George. *The Life and Philosophy of George Tucker.* Edited by James Fieser. Bristol, U.K.: Thoemmes Continuum, 2004.

Tucker, Glenn. *Tecumseh: Vision of Glory.* Indianapolis: Bobbs-Merrill, 1956.

Tyler, Moses Coit. *Patrick Henry.* 1887. Boston: Houghton Mifflin, 1897.

Varg, Paul A. *Foreign Policies of the Founding Fathers.* East Lansing: Michigan State University Press, 1963.

The Vermont Historical Gazetteer. Edited by Abby Maria Hemenway. 5 vols. Burlington, Vt.: A. M. Hemenway, 1867–1891.

Vickers, Neil. *Coleridge and the Doctors, 1795–1806.* Oxford, U.K.: Clarendon Press, 2004.

Vile, John R. *The Constitutional Convention of 1787: A Comprehensive Encyclopedia of America's Founding.* 2 vols. Santa Barbara, Calif.: ABC-CLIO, 2005.

The Virginia Statute for Religious Freedom: Its Evolution and Consequences in American History. Edited by Merrill D. Peterson and Robert C. Vaughan. Cambridge, U.K.: Cambridge University Press, 1988.

Washburne, E. B. *Sketch of Edward Coles, Second Governor of Illinois, and of the Slavery Struggle of 1823–4.* Chicago: Jansen, McClurg, 1882.

Washington, George. *The Papers of George Washington, Colonial Series.* Edited by W. W. Abbot and Dorothy Twohig. 10 vols. Charlottesville: University Press of Virginia, 1983–1995.

——. *The Papers of George Washington, Confederation Series.* Edited by W. W. Abbot. 6 vols. Charlottesville: University Press of Virginia, 1992–1997.

——. *The Papers of George Washington, Diaries.* Edited by Donald Jackson and Dorothy Twohig. 6 vols. Charlottesville: University Press of Virginia, 1976–1979.

——. *The Papers of George Washington Digital Edition.* Edited by Theodore Crackel. Charlottesville: University of Virginia Press, 2008. http://rotunda.upress.virginia.edu/founders/GEWN.html.

——. *The Papers of George Washington, Presidential Series.* Edited by Dorothy Twohig, Mark A. Mastromarino, Jack D. Warren, Robert F. Haggard, Christine S. Patrick, John C. Pinheiro, David R. Hoth, and Carol S. Ebel. 16 vols. Charlottesville: University Press of Virginia, 1987–2011.

——. *The Papers of George Washington, Retirement Series.* Edited by W. W. Abbot and Edward G. Lengel. 4 vols. Charlottesville: University Press of Virginia, 1998–1999.

——. *The Papers of George Washington, Revolutionary War Series.* Edited by Philander D. Chase, Frank E. Grizzard Jr., Edward G. Lengel, David R. Hoth, and William M. Ferraro. 21 vols. Charlottesville: University Press of Virginia, 1985–2012.

Watson, John F. *Annals of Philadelphia, and Pennsylvania, in the Olden Time; Being a Collection of Memoirs, Anecdotes, and Incidents of the City and Its Inhabitants, and of the Earliest Settlements of the Inland Part of Pennsylvania.* 3 vols. Philadelphia: J. J. Stoddart, 1881.

Watts, Steven. *The Republic Reborn: War and the Making of Liberal America, 1790–1820.* Baltimore: Johns Hopkins University Press, 1987.

Webster, Daniel. *The Letters of Daniel Webster, from Documents Owned Principally by the New Hampshire Historical Society.* Edited by C. H. Van Tyne. New York: McClure, Phillips, 1902.

Wertenbaker, Thomas Jefferson. *Princeton, 1746–1896.* 1946. Princeton, N.J.: Princeton University Press, 1996.

Wesley, John. *Primitive Physic; or, An Easy and Natural Method of Curing Most Diseases.* Boston: Cyrus Stone, 1858.

Wiecek, William M. *The Sources of Antislavery Constitutionalism in America, 1760–1848.* Ithaca, N.Y.: Cornell University Press, 1977.

Williams, John S. *History of the Invasion and Capture of Washington, and of the Events Which Preceded and Followed.* New York: Harper & Brothers, 1857.

Wiltse, Charles M. *John C. Calhoun, Nationalist, 1782–1828.* Indianapolis: Bobbs-Merrill, 1944.

Winder, R. H. *Remarks on a Pamphlet, Entitled "An Enquiry Respecting the Capture of Washington by the British on the 24th of August, 1814."* Baltimore: J. Robinson, 1816.

Wirt, William. *The Letters of the British Spy.* New York: J. & J. Harper, 1832.

——. *Sketches of the Life and Character of Patrick Henry.* Hartford: S. Andrus & Son, 1849.

Witherspoon, John. *The Works of the Rev. John Witherspoon, D.D. L.L.D., Late President of the College at Princeton, New Jersey.* 4 vols. Philadelphia: William W. Woodward, 1802.

Wood, George B. *A Treatise on Therapeutics and Pharmacology or Materia Medica.* 2 vols. Philadelphia: J. B. Lippincott, 1856.

Wood, Gordon S. *The Creation of the American Republic, 1776–1787.* 1969. Chapel Hill: University of North Carolina Press, 1998.

——. *Empire of Liberty: A History of the Early Republic, 1789–1815.* New York: Oxford University Press, 2009.

Woods, David Walker. *John Witherspoon*. New York: Fleming H. Revell, 1906.

Young, James Sterling. *The Washington Community, 1800–1828*. New York: Columbia University Press, 1966.

Selected Articles

Adair, Douglass. "The Authorship of the Disputed Federalist Papers." *William and Mary Quarterly*, 3rd ser., 1, no. 2 (April 1944): 97–122.

——. "'That Politics May Be Reduced to a Science': David Hume, James Madison, and the Tenth Federalist." *Huntington Library Quarterly* 20, no. 4 (Aug. 1957): 343–60.

"After-Dinner Anecdotes of James Madison: Excerpt from Jared Sparks' Journal for 1829–31." Edited by "CC" Proctor. *Virginia Magazine of History and Biography* 60, no. 2 (April 1952): 255–65.

Barry, William T. "Letters of William T. Barry." *William and Mary Quarterly* 13, no. 4 (April 1905): 236–44.

Bennett, Robert W. "The Problem of the Faithless Elector: Trouble Aplenty Brewing Just Below the Surface in Choosing the President." *Northwestern University Law Review* 100, no. 1 (2006): 121–30.

Black, Jeremy. "A British View of the Naval War of 1812." *Naval History Magazine* 22, no. 4 (Aug. 2008). http://www.usni.org/magazines/navalhistory/2008-08/british-view-naval-war-1812.

Brant, Irving. "Edmund Randolph, Not Guilty!" *William and Mary Quarterly*, 3rd ser., 7, no. 2 (April 1950): 179–98.

Bruff, Harold H. "The Federalist Papers: The Framers Construct an Orrery." *Harvard Journal of Law and Public Policy* 16, no. 1 (Winter 1993): 7–12.

Butterfield, Lyman H. "Elder John Leland, Jeffersonian Itinerant." *Proceedings of the American Antiquarian Society* 62, pt. 2 (Oct. 1952): 155–242.

Coles, Edward. "Letters of Edward Coles." *William and Mary Quarterly*, 2nd ser., 7, no. 3 (July 1927): 158–73.

Crary, Catherine Snell. "The Tory and the Spy: The Double Life of James Rivington." *William and Mary Quarterly*, 3rd ser., 16, no. 1 (Jan. 1959): 61–72.

Cunningham, Noble E., Jr. "John Beckley: An Early American Party Manager." *William and Mary Quarterly*, 3rd ser., 13, no. 1 (Jan. 1956): 40–52.

Dietsch, Deborah K. "Brookeville's James Madison House Is Historic Home Contest Winner." *Washington Post*, Oct. 19, 2012. http://articles.washingtonpost.com/2012-10-19/news/35500457_1_madison-house-white-house-original-features.

"Edmund Randolph's Essay on the Revolutionary History of Virginia (1774–1782)." *Virginia Magazine of History and Biography* 43, no. 2 (April 1935): 113, 115–38; 43, no. 4 (Oct. 1935): 294–315; 44, no. 1 (Jan. 1936): 35–50.

"Events of the War." *Niles' Weekly Register*, Feb. 4, 1815, 356–66.

Few, Frances. "The Diary of Frances Few, 1808–1809." Edited by Noble E. Cunningham Jr. *Journal of Southern History* 29, no. 3 (Aug. 1963): 345–61.

Forte, David F. "Marbury's Travail: Federalist Politics and William Marbury's Appointment as Justice of the Peace." *Catholic University Law Review* 45, no. 2 (1996): 349–402.

Haggard, Stephen, Andrew MacIntyre, and Lydia Tiede. "The Rule of Law and Economic Development." *Annual Review of Political Science*, no. 11 (2008): 205–43.

Hildt, John C. "Letters Relating to the Capture of Washington." *South Atlantic Quarterly* 6 (Jan.–Oct. 1907): 58–66.

Hunt, Gaillard. "The First Inauguration Ball." *Century Magazine*, March 1905, 754–59. http://www.unz.org/Pub/Century-1905mar-00754.

"James Madison's Autobiography." Edited by Douglass Adair. *William and Mary Quarterly*, 3rd ser., 2, no. 2 (April 1945): 191–209.

Ketcham, Ralph L. "The Dictates of Conscience: Edward Coles and Slavery." *Virginia Quarterly Review* 36, no. 1 (Winter 1960): 46–62.

——, ed. "An Unpublished Sketch of James Madison by James K. Paulding." *Virginia Magazine of History and Biography* 67, no. 4 (Oct. 1959): 432–37.

Koch, Adrienne, and Harry Ammon. "The Virginia and Kentucky Resolutions: An Episode in Jefferson's and Madison's Defense of Civil Liberties." *William and Mary Quarterly*, 3rd ser., 5, no. 2 (April 1948): 145–76.

Madison, James. "Speeches Made in the Senate of the United States, on Occasion of the Resolution Offered by Mr. Foot, on the Subject of the Public Lands, During the First Session of the Twenty-first Congress." *North American Review* 31, no. 69 (Oct. 1830): 462–546.

Marsh, Philip. "Freneau and Jefferson: The Poet-Editor Speaks for Himself About the *National Gazette* Episode." *American Literature* 8, no. 2 (May 1936): 180–89.

——. "Hamilton and Monroe." *Mississippi Valley Historical Review* 34, no. 3 (Dec. 1947): 459–68.

"Meteorological Observations." *Columbian Magazine*, June 1787, 2.

Mitchill, Samuel Latham. "Dr. Mitchill's Letters from Washington: 1801–1813." *Harper's New Monthly Magazine*, April 1879, 740–55.

Moffatt, L. G., and J. M. Carrière. "A Frenchman Visits Norfolk, Fredericksburg, and Orange County, 1816." *Virginia Magazine of History and Biography* 53, no. 3 (July 1945): 197–214.

Monkman, Betty C. "The White House Collection: Reminders of 1814." *White House History*, no. 4 (Fall 1998): 33–37.

Morison, Samuel Eliot. "The Henry-Crillon Affair of 1812." *Proceedings of the Massachusetts Historical Society*, 3rd ser., 69 (Oct. 1947–May 1950): 207–31.

"Notes and Queries." *Virginia Magazine of History and Biography* 6, no. 4 (April 1899): 429–36.

Ohline, Howard A. "Slavery, Economics, and Congressional Politics, 1790." *Journal of Southern History* 46, no. 3 (Aug. 1980): 335–60.

Pasley, Jefferson L. "'A Journeyman, Either in Law or Politics': John Beckley and the Social Origins of Political Campaigning." *Journal of the Early Republic* 16, no. 4 (Winter 1996): 531–69.

Powell, J. H. "Some Unpublished Correspondence of John Adams and Richard Rush, 1811–1816." *Pennsylvania Magazine of History and Biography* 60, no. 4 (Oct. 1936): 419–54.

———. "Some Unpublished Correspondence of John Adams and Richard Rush, 1811–1816, II." *Pennsylvania Magazine of History and Biography* 61, no. 1 (Jan. 1937): 26–53.

"Randolph and Tucker Letters." Contributed by Mrs. George P. Coleman. *Virginia Magazine of History and Biography* 43, no. 1 (Jan. 1935): 41–46.

Ruegsegger, Gary. "Finally, 1813 Battle Gets Some Respect." *Virginian-Pilot*, June 24, 2008. http://hamptonroads.com/2008/06/finally-1813-battle-gets-some-respect.

Scarberry, Mark S. "John Leland and James Madison: Religious Influence on the Ratification of the Constitution and on the Proposal of the Bill of Rights." *Penn State Law Review* 113, no. 3 (April 2009): 733–800.

Shulman, Holly C. "'A Constant Attention': Dolley Madison and the Publication of the Papers of James Madison, 1836–1837." *Virginia Magazine of History and Biography* 118, no. 1 (2010): 41–70.

———. "Madison v. Madison." *Virginia Magazine of History and Biography* 119, no. 4 (Sept. 2011): 350–93.

Slaughter, Jane C. "Anne Mercer Slaughter: A Sketch." *Tyler's Quarterly Historical and Genealogical Magazine* 19 (July 1937): 30–44.

Slosberg, Steven. "Site Lines: The Mysterious Blue Lights." Connecticuthistory.org. http://connecticuthistory.org/site-lines-the-mysterious-blue-lights/.

Smith, William Loughton. "The Letters of William Loughton Smith to Edward Rutledge: June 8, 1789, to April 28, 1794." Edited by George C. Rogers Jr. *South Carolina Historical Magazine* 69, no. 2 (Jan. 1968): 1–25; (April 1968): 101–38.

Stagg, J. C. A. "Between Black Rock and a Hard Place: Peter B. Porter's Plan for an American Invasion of Canada in 1812." *Journal of the Early Republic* 19, no. 3 (Autumn 1999): 385–422.

Theobald, Mary Miley. "The Monstrous Absurdity: The Gunpowder Theft Examined." *Colonial Williamsburg Journal* (Summer 2006). http://www.history.org/foundation/journal/Summer06/plots.cfm.

Thomas, William H. B. "Politics in Colonial Orange County." *Bicentennial Series*, no. 6 (April 1976).

Thornton, Anna. "Diary of Mrs. William Thornton: Capture of Washington by the British." Edited by Wilhemus B. Bryan. *Records of the Columbia Historical Society, Washington, D.C.* 19 (1916): 172–82.

Tinkcom, Margaret Bailey. "Caviar Along the Potomac: Sir Augustus John Foster's 'Notes on the United States,' 1804–1812." *William and Mary Quarterly*, 3rd ser., 8, no. 1 (Jan. 1951): 68–107.

Vining, C. Wilfred. "Bilious Attacks and Epilepsy: The Relationship of the Bilious Attack and Certain Other Morbid Phenomena to the Epileptic State." *Lancet* 199, no. 5134 (1922): 122–23.

"Williamsburg—the Old Colonial Capitol." *William and Mary Quarterly* 16, no. 1 (July 1907): 1–65.

Unpublished Manuscripts

Churchwell, Stephen T. "Epilepsy and Holy Orders in the Canonical Practice of the Western Church." Ph.D. diss., Catholic University of America, 1982.

Miller, Ann L. "Historic Structure Report: Montpelier, Orange County, Virginia." 1990. Prepared for James Madison's Montpelier, a National Trust Historic Site, 2007–2008.

——. "The Madison Family's Land in the Region of 'Montpelier.'" Master's thesis, University of Virginia, 1985.

Reeves, Matthew, and Kevin Fogle. "Excavations at the Madisons' First Home, Mount Pleasant (1723–1800): Summary of Archaeological Investigations, 1997–2004." Montpelier Archaeology Department, 2007.

Torres-Reyes, Ricardo. "Historic Resource Study: The William Floyd Estate, Fire Island National Seashore, New York." Denver Service Center, Historic Preservation Team, June 1974.

Special Collections

Adams Family Papers: An Electronic Archive. Massachusetts Historical Society, Boston. https://www.masshist.org/digitaladams/aea/index.html.

Adams Papers, 1639–1899. Microfilms. Massachusetts Historical Society, Boston.

The Diaries of John Quincy Adams: A Digital Collection. Massachusetts Historical Society, Boston. http://www.masshist.org/jqadiaries.

Baylor Family Papers, 1653–1915. Albert and Shirley Small Special Collections Library, University of Virginia.

John James Beckley Papers, 1773–1807. Transcription. Virginia Historical Society, Richmond.

Breckinridge Family Papers, 1752–1965. Manuscript Division, Library of Congress.

Henry Clay Papers. Manuscript Division, Library of Congress.

Edward Coles Papers. Manuscripts Division, Department of Rare Books and Special Collections, Princeton University Library.

Coolidge Collection of Thomas Jefferson Manuscripts. Massachusetts Historical Society, Boston.

Ellen Wayles Randolph Coolidge Correspondence. Albert and Shirley Small Special Collections Library, University of Virginia.

Andre De Coppet Collection. Manuscripts Division, Department of Rare Books and Special Collections, Princeton University Library.

Alexander Dick Journal, 1806–1809. Albert and Shirley Small Special Collections Library, University of Virginia.

Griffith Evans Journal, Aug. 30, 1784–Nov. 13, 1785. Huntington Library, San Marino, Calif.

Foreign Affairs, Political Correspondence, Paris–United States. Manuscript Division, Library of Congress.

Foreign Copying Project, Great Britain, Foreign Office. Manuscript Division, Library of Congress.

Francis Walker Gilmer Correspondence, 1784–1826. Albert and Shirley Small Special Collections Library, University of Virginia.

Burton Norvell Harrison Papers. Manuscript Division, Library of Congress.

Charles Jared Ingersoll Papers, 1801–1891. The Historical Society of Pennsylvania, Philadelphia.

Thomas Jefferson Papers. Manuscript Division, Library of Congress. http://memory.loc.gov/ammem/collections/jefferson_papers/.

Jefferson Papers: An Electronic Archive. Massachusetts Historical Society, Boston. http://www.masshist.org/thomasjeffersonpapers.

Watkins Kearns Diary. Virginia Historical Society, Richmond.

Lee Family Papers. Albert and Shirley Small Special Collections Library, University of Virginia.

Papers of the Madison Family, 1786–1866. Tracy W. McGregor Library, Special Collections, University of Virginia.

Madison Family Papers. Shane Collection. Presbyterian Historical Society, Philadelphia.

Dolley Madison Papers. Manuscript Division, Library of Congress.

James Madison Papers. Manuscript Division, Library of Congress. http://memory.loc.gov/ammem/collections/madison_papers/.

James Madison Sr. Account Book, 1744–1755, Journal of James Madison, 1744–1757. Albert and Shirley Small Special Collections Library, University of Virginia.

Meteorological Journals, 1784–1788, 1789–1793. American Philosophical Society, Philadelphia.

James Monroe Museum and Memorial Library, Fredericksburg, Va.

James Monroe Papers. Manuscript Division, Library of Congress.

Wilson Cary Nicholas Papers. Manuscript Division, Library of Congress.

[Old] Rappahannock County Deed Books. Microfilm. Library of Virginia, Richmond. http://www.lva.virginia.gov/.

Orange County Deed Books. Microfilm. Library of Virginia, Richmond. http://www.lva.virginia.gov/.

Orange County Will Books. Microfilm. Library of Virginia, Richmond. http://www.lva.virginia.gov/.

Papers of the Continental Congress, 1774–1789. National Archives.

Pennsylvania Abolition Society Collection. The Historical Society of Pennsylvania, Philadelphia.

Timothy Pickering Papers, 1731–1927. Massachusetts Historical Society, Boston.

William Plumer Papers. Manuscript Division, Library of Congress.

John Randolph Papers, 1806–1832. Manuscript Division, Library of Congress.

William C. Rives Papers. Manuscript Division, Library of Congress.

Sedgwick Family Papers, 1717–1946. Massachusetts Historical Society, Boston.

Shippen Family Papers, 1671–1936. Manuscript Division, Library of Congress.

Samuel Smith Family Papers. Manuscript Division, Library of Congress.

Joseph Story Correspondence, 1807–1943. Manuscript Division, Library of Congress.

Colonel Francis Taylor Diary, 1786–1792, 1794–1799. Homer Babbidge Library, University of Connecticut, Storrs.

John Payne Todd Memorandum Book, 1844–1848. Peter Force Collection. Manuscript Division, Library of Congress.

Nicholas Trist Papers, 1791–1836. Virginia Historical Society, Richmond.

George Washington Papers. Manuscript Division, Library of Congress. http://memory.loc.gov/ammem/gwhtml/gwhome.html.

John Witherspoon Collection. Manuscripts Division, Department of Rare Books and Special Collections, Princeton University Library.

Index

Image Credits

Frontispiece: Courtesy of the Library of Congress, LC-USZ62-16960
Insert Page 1 (top): Courtesy of the Library of Congress, LC-USZC4-4098
Page 1 (bottom): Courtesy of the Library of Congress, LC-USZC4-4099
Page 2: Louis S. Glanzman
Page 3 (left): Excerpt courtesy of the Newspaper and Periodicals Division of the Library of Congress
Page 3 (right): Photograph © 2014 Museum of Fine Arts, Boston
Page 4 (top): *George Washington* (oil on canvas), Stuart, Gilbert (1755–1828) / Sterling & Francine Clark Art Institute, Williamstown, Massachusetts, USA / The Bridgeman Art Library
Page 4 (bottom): Charles Willson Peale, *James Madison,* from the collection of Gilcrease Museum, Tulsa, Oklahoma
Page 5 (left): The Colonial Williamsburg Foundation. Gift of Mrs. George S. Robbins
Page 5 (right), 10 (top left), 13 (top), 14 (bottom): White House Historical Association (White House Collection)
Page 6: Courtesy of The Montpelier Foundation, James Madison's Montpelier, and Partsense, Inc.
Page 7 (top left): © National Portrait Gallery, Smithsonian Institution, and the Thomas Jefferson Foundation at Monticello
Page 7 (top right): Collection of The New-York Historical Society, negative #6227
Page 7 (bottom): Courtesy of the Library of Congress, LC-USZ62-4702
Page 8 (top): Courtesy of the Library of Congress, LC-USZ62-1804
Page 8 (bottom): © Fundación Lázaro Galdiano, Madrid
Page 9 (top left): Gilbert Charles Stuart, *Marquis de Casa Yrujo,* 1804. Collection of Thomas R. and Susan McKean; photograph courtesy of the Philadelphia Museum of Art
Page 9 (top right): Gilbert Charles Stuart, *Marchioness de Casa Yrujo,* 1804. Collection of Thomas R. and Susan McKean; photograph courtesy of the Philadelphia Museum of Art
Page 9 (bottom): Courtesy National Gallery of Art, Washington
Page 10 (top right): Gilbert Stuart, 1944.15. Virginia Historical Society
Page 10 (bottom): Wood, Joseph (1778–1830), (attributed to). *John Payne Todd.* ca. 1817. Watercolor on ivory, 2 ⅝ x 2 ¹⁄₁₆ in. (6.7 x 5.26 cm). Gift of Miss Mary Madison McGuire, 1936 (36.73). The Metropolitan Museum of Art, New York, NY, U.S.A. Image copyright © The Metropolitan Museum of Art. Image source: Art Resource, NY
Page 11 (top): Naval History & Heritage Command, Washington, DC
Page 11 (bottom): Naval War College Museum Collection
Page 12 (top): *John Armstrong* by Rembrandt Peale, from life, c. 1808. Courtesy of Independence National Historical Park
Page 12 (bottom): © Bettmann/Corbis
Page 13 (bottom): Armed Forces History Division, National Museum of American History, Smithsonian Institution
Page 14 (top): Library of Congress, Prints & Photographs Division, photograph by Carol M. Highsmith, LC-HS503-5367
Page 15 (left): Joseph Wood, 1967.14. Virginia Historical Society
Page 15 (right): Joseph Wood, 1967.13. Virginia Historical Society
Page 16 (top): Photograph by Kenneth Wyner. Courtesy of The Montpelier Foundation, James Madison's Montpelier
Page 16 (middle): Photograph by Philip Beaurline. Courtesy of The Montpelier Foundation, James Madison's Montpelier
Page 16 (bottom): Courtesy of The Montpelier Foundation, James Madison's Montpelier